Grace VanDuzen

THE
VIBRATIONAL
ARK

THE VIBRATIONAL ARK

Grace Van Duzen

Eden Valley Press

Publisher: Eden Valley Press
5569 North County Road 29
Loveland, CO 80538

Editors: Shareen Ewing
Doreen Thompson
Book and Jacket Design: Georgene Higerd
Jacket Photo: Michael Paige
Printer: Johnson Printing
Loveland, Colorado

Printed in the United States of America

First Edition
June 1996

ISBN 0-932869-05-X

For Uranda and Martin,
great leaders whose lives were dedicated to
fulfilling their purpose on earth and who opened the door
whereby countless others came and shared
in the place prepared for them.

CONTENTS

1   DAWN OF A NEW DAY   1
FEBRUARY 1907 ~ MAY 1939

2   THE MEETING   22
AUGUST 1939 ~ APRIL 1940

3   THE HARVEST   41
SEPTEMBER 1940 ~ FEBRUARY 1942

4   SEARCH FOR HEADQUARTERS   53
APRIL 1942 ~ NOVEMBER 1944

5   HEADQUARTERS!   70
JANUARY 1945 ~ JULY 1946

6   AN EXTENDED VISIT!   88
JULY 1946 ~ JANUARY 1947

7   MORNING STAR   101
FEBRUARY ~ DECEMBER 1947

8   HOME TO EDEN VALLEY   112
DECEMBER 1947 ~ MARCH 1949

9   UNEXPECTED JOURNEY   124
MARCH 1949 ~ MAY 1950

10 PEAKS OF FULFILMENT 140
MAY ~ SEPTEMBER 1950

11 A NEW ERA 154
SEPTEMBER 1950 ~ MAY 1951

12 SERVERS TRAINING SCHOOL 165
MAY 1951 ~ APRIL 1952

13 ALL THE TITHES 177
APRIL ~ SEPTEMBER 1952

14 OUR PURPOSE—AND THE SERVER'S CODE 190
OCTOBER 1952 ~ MARCH 1953

15 WONDERS UNFOLDING 202
APRIL ~ NOVEMBER 1953

16 EXPANSION IN THE FIELD, AND AT HOME 217
NOVEMBER 1953 ~ APRIL 1954

17 PORTALS OF HEAVEN—MAGIC 234
APRIL ~ JUNE 1954

18 THE THRILLING THRESHOLD 245
JULY ~ AUGUST 1954

19 WITHOUT A BREAK 256
AUGUST 1954 ~ FEBRUARY 1955

20 A YEAR OF CHALLENGE 270
FEBRUARY 1955 ~ MARCH 1956

21 PRIVILEGES AND RESPONSIBILITIES 286
MARCH 1956 ~ JANUARY 1958

22 OVERSEAS 305
APRIL 1958 ~ DECEMBER 1960

23 CLEARING THE AIR 326
JANUARY 1961 ~ JANUARY 1963

24 FLYING NEWS 348
FEBRUARY 1963 ~ JULY 1965

25 COORDINATED ACTION 363
AUGUST 1965 ~ OCTOBER 1968

26 THE WORLD ENCOMPASSED 384
OCTOBER 1968 ~ JUNE 1970

27 EXCITING DEVELOPMENTS 406
JUNE 1970 ~ SEPTEMBER 1973

28 THE DOME CHAPEL 427
SEPTEMBER 1973 ~ MAY 1975

29 THE SETTING FOR THE JEWEL 446
MAY 1975 ~ DECEMBER 1976

30 INTO AFRICA! 463
JANUARY 1977 ~ MARCH 1979

31 CONQUEST! 483
JULY 1979 ~ DECEMBER 1980

32 BALANCE AMIDST CHANGE 501
JANUARY ~ DECEMBER 1981

33 CIRCLING THE EARTH—AND 520
EMISSARY INTERNATIONAL CONGRESS
JANUARY ~ DECEMBER 1982

34   THE FIRE INTENSIFIED   539
JANUARY ~ DECEMBER 1983

35   THE RISING TIDE OF CHANGE   556
JANUARY 1984 ~ MAY 1985

36   CLIMATE FOR THE GARDEN   574
JUNE 1985 ~ JULY 1986

37   THE BURGEONING WHOLE   592
JULY ~ DECEMBER 1986

38   CHEESTAYE NYEBA   609
DECEMBER 1986 ~ MAY 1987

39   THE VIBRATIONAL ARK   626
JUNE ~ SEPTEMBER 1987

40   "LET YOUR LIGHT SO SHINE"   635
SEPTEMBER 1987 ~ JANUARY 1988

PREFACE

All things, seen and unseen, are contained in the vibrational world. We hear of viruses, invisible yet with very potent effects. The distortions in our world of seeing, hearing and feeling have their (seemingly monstrous) counterparts in the vibratory levels which are beyond the comprehension of our narrow range of outer perception. And, while they are causative factors in the health and well-being of earth's inhabitants, they were not planted by a God whose creations reveal a love for, and knowledge of, beauty and vigor of design. Man (male and female) is the author of those self-destructive denizens of the deeps of his world. They do not represent a power in and of themselves, but are a reversal of the use of the one power.

"With God all things are possible." Identified *with* the creative power which irradiates and enlivens all substance, visible and invisible, that same power which seems to have peopled an eerie world of shadows can easily restore the design to its original state of well-being, peace and fulfilment. In that bright realm, subconscious creations have been pictured by artists through the ages as angels, with wings—radiant beings (in white), moving freely through realms not limited to the one which mankind has made into a prison.

Of Noah's ark it was said that "it was lift up above the earth." In the daily functions at hand for each one, it transcends the manipulations of mind and emotion separate from the guidance and inspiration of a God who is ever ready to work *with* His image and likeness on this planet to accomplish His cosmic wonders.

It is happening. The vibrational ark is a reality in men and women whose consciousness is lifted up above the earth—so that in the season of the Lord (no man's) the design of the new heaven becomes a visible reality, the new earth.

ACKNOWLEDGMENTS

There are many, too numerous to mention, who were, themselves, the substance in the building of the Emissaries of Divine Light. Nothing truly given—the fruits of many lives—can ever be lost: treasures laid up where neither moth nor rust corrupt, and where thieves do not break through nor steal.

Shareen Ewing's assistance has been an essential part in the production of this book: her research of myriad services and publications, her expertise in editing and countless other areas, and, crowning it all, her loving support. In the face of challenges that masqueraded as obstacles, especially in the final days, her word was, always, "We're almost there."

Georgene Higerd's contribution of her talents was invaluable. One of the best in her field of layout and related areas, her artistic spirit imbues each page.

Doreen Thompson repeatedly offered, before I accepted, to contribute in some way to my work. Her training and experience in the field of editing were a treasured part of the unfoldment of my story, her strong spirit a beacon.

Jude Repar was a great help in the early phases of this book. Her eagerness to participate in this creation with me was a delight.

For these dear friends I cannot express enough gratitude and profound appreciation, and I trust that in reading my story you will share the joy I experienced in writing it.

INTRODUCTION

The Vibrational Ark is my story of the lives of two great men and of that which was built as a result of their devotion to the Lord and His work on earth. I was blest beyond measure to work closely as secretary with each of them. I knew the vastness of their spirits, their joys and disappointments, and above all their victories, which are as available now as they were then to be shared by all who are willing.

This book presents a chronological account of the beginning and subsequent movement of a group that acquired the name "Emissaries of Divine Light." Some entries may lend a journalistic aspect to my story; for instance, reports of Board meetings and other related gatherings. Nevertheless these contribute to a balanced view. It might be of interest to observe the incredible gaps between the costs of items and services in days long gone by compared with those of the present.

Also included are portions of addresses by the founder, Lloyd Arthur Meeker, and his fellow worker, Martin Cecil. These appear in the settings and times in which they were given, and reveal the spiritual dimension of what was happening at the more familiar levels of function in this world. There are expressions by others also which provide further color and clarity to the picture.

I tell my story, first because I love it and know deeply its value and significance; second, to fill a great need in many to know what actually occurred during those eventful and wonderful years. For you who may read and who actively participated in it, I share your joy in reviewing this history, a continuation of the greatest story ever told, the story of love and truth and life.

1

DAWN OF A NEW DAY

February 1907 ~ May 1939

*A*s I gaze out my window I see a vast carpet of green encircling a field crowded with stuffed bales of yellow hay. On the horizon the rimrock forms a crown that spreads north and south the length of the valley, red-gold above bushes so closely covering the graceful sweep from top to bottom that they form a flowing robe of wondrous green. To the south nestles a lovely little lake. Above it all, the bluest of blue skies contrasts and completes the richly colorful panorama.

This was not always so. My first view of this same scene was of a brown and arid, thirsty land. There was no green anywhere, and no water. Even the sky seemed to reflect a rusty hue.

The events that occurred between then and now, resulting in the unimaginable transformation of this place, compose the story I am about to tell.

It began with the birth of a babe, in a small town in Iowa on February 25, 1907, which signaled a new day for many people. When true perspective is restored to this part of the universe, with the final chapter finished to the story mankind has written, that advent will shine as a beacon. At the time the event was entirely unnoticed, except of course by the parents, Francis and Nancy Meeker, who welcomed their firstborn and named him Lloyd Arthur.

Francis was a stern man, imbued with a spirit of service that became obsessive. His delicate wife Nancy, with a temperament completely unlike that of her husband, nevertheless shared the same indomitable compulsion to aid their fellow beings.

A circuit minister, Francis tried at the same time to fulfil the endless and, for the most part, frustrating demands of farming, in an area completely unsuited to such occupation. His family was of English-Welsh descent and came to the "land of promise" several generations before the time of our story. Nancy Throckmorton was of Dutch descent. Francis and Nancy had met when they were taking a course in practical nursing, which provided a vehicle to accommodate their urge to serve selflessly. On the part of Francis, heavily influenced by a strict father dedicated to the Adventist faith, this compulsion developed into religious fanaticism.

It was to a rugged and challenging surround that the infant Lloyd was brought, his parents moving from his birthplace in Ferguson, Iowa, to North Dakota. Home was a tiny sod house on the prairies, with primitive conditions. His father was away much of the time, which placed a great burden of the chores on his mother, who had never been strong physically. Water had to be hauled on a sled drawn by a cow.

Parenthetically, just two years after the birth of this child, on April 27, 1909, another being of immense spiritual stature found his way into the world. The lives of these two were destined, some thirty years later, to be inextricably entwined in the same clearly recognized purpose for their being on this planet. One could not imagine two outer circumstances more completely opposed than those of their births—or more diverse parents. William Martin Alleyne Cecil was the third child born to the Fifth Marquess of Exeter and his wife the Marchioness, in their ancestral palace, Burghley House, in Stamford, England. The fascinating story of Lord Martin Cecil will be resumed later.

In that little house on the prairies a second son, Marvin, was born in 1908. Francis received title for their homesteaded land, but because of the poor state of his health a higher altitude was recommended. A member of his church offered to trade his property in Colorado for the Meeker homestead. Lloyd's father traded the land sight-unseen for what was described to him as a peach orchard of several acres located near Palisade in western Colorado.

The growing family arrived at Palisade, with their meager worldly goods, and found their expectations of finding a home shattered. They were shocked. A peach orchard! It may have been, in some day long passed, but now all that remained was a miserable patch of alkali-covered ground, with skeletons of peach trees protruding grotesquely from the whitish earth. What a far cry from the picture of a home, that had sustained them on their journey to the majestic Rockies!

A few months after they arrived, with the family living in a tent in extreme poverty, Nancy gave birth to their third child, a girl, to be named Ioma. Nancy had suffered from heart trouble all her life, and the primitive conditions, the trials of moving, the change in climate and altitude were detrimental to the health of this delicate woman. But the strength of her loyalty precluded any questioning of her dedication to the highest that she knew.

One day in desperation Francis set out, pushing a bicycle in the hope of finding a road that would lead to a possible location for a new home for his family. Southwest of Grand Junction, back up into the mountains about twenty-five miles he toiled, to rim-rock country called Glade Park. He filed a claim on a quarter-section of wilderness, ribbed with sandstone rimrocks, with canyons covered with pinion trees, junipers, scrub oak, and thick with sagebrush that grows to a height of four to eight feet. What could one do with a place like that?

Grubbing sagebrush under the burning sun all day for endless weeks is a grueling task. Winter presents another equally merciless challenge. The land had to be cleared for dry-land farming. It had been open range for cattle since the arrival of the white man, and the cattlemen did everything to drive out the squatters. They tore down fences, turned cattle in to destroy crops, and threatened murder.

By the time he was seven, Lloyd was working in the fields from daylight till dark. His father got a job on a ranch farther back in the mountains, and spent most of his time away from home herding goats. Lloyd's mother spent that winter nursing in the Grand Valley district. Of necessity she kept her baby daughter with her. Francis had placed Lloyd, with his younger brother Marvin, in the care of an Indian squaw, who had married a white man. Of prodigious size and strength, she was the source of some further rugged training for the two boys.

The years that followed on the dry-land farm were filled with unending work, in conditions of dreadful poverty, punctuated by one dreary disappointment after another. Five bushels of corn per acre was counted a good yield. Milk from cows was the main source of income, which was small at best. The cream from the separator had to be shipped to Grand Junction, over twenty miles away. A tiny shack now was home, and a dug-out much like an old-fashioned cellar.

Strict discipline, which included beatings, was the working creed of Francis. He was filled with a passion to impose his religious fanaticism on his family. The unreasonable severity was applied to Lloyd in particular, and in retrospect it can perhaps be understood why an element of antagonism developed. There was, always, inherent in this boy a spirit that would not, could not, accept his father's narrow views. Subconsciously through his very early years, Lloyd knew there was something utterly wrong about his father's beliefs and actions, a reaction which evidently was sensed by his father. His gentle mother's atmosphere provided a haven in which he could begin to be consciously aware of what was emerging from within himself.

The children could go two or three months without seeing anyone outside the family. Once a year, sometimes twice, the growing boys had the treat of going to town, an all-day journey by lumber wagon one way. They would stay overnight with friends, members of their church. Then back to the mountains.

Lloyd often sought release in a realm inside himself, away from the superficiality of strict rules and regulations. He would weave wonderful stories that were far removed from his circumstance and those who peopled it. Marvin listened hungrily as they worked in the fields. When their father became aware of them, the "fantasies" were strictly forbidden on religious grounds. Lloyd often suffered severe treatment for indulging in "foolish imagination."

It was here that the fourth child was born in 1915, a boy named Merl Freedom. There were still no neighbors in the immediate vicinity, so the children had no opportunity to play with others, except at the noon hour in the little schoolhouse. They had to return as soon as school was out to work on the farm. Lloyd attended school for four and one-half terms, in which time he went through the first eight grades. There were usually ten or twelve children, divided into the eight grades. The boys walked several miles each way to school through the wilderness, in any kind of weather, which often meant bitter winter storms.

Half a century later a fortunate connection was made with a sister of Francis, Olive McIntyre, then eighty-three years old and living in Edmonton, Alberta, Canada. She recalled:

> I was one of seven children (Francis among them), and my upbringing was strict Seventh Day Adventist—something I could not accept, but which made a deep and lasting mark on Francis. We were taught subservience, fear, and little or nothing of love. When Francis married Nancy he was admonished by his father not to worship or show too much love for this "pretty little woman." Nannie was a true beauty, and Lloyd inherited her loving nature. They were very close.

Nancy wrote often to her mother, Elizabeth Munden, in Marshalltown, Iowa. The contact provided an outlet, in an atmosphere of severity and physical hardship, for her gentle spirit. These precious letters were preserved by Olive and provide a poignant insight into the hearts of the members of that little family. Here is one, dated August 24, 1918, from Glade Park. Lloyd was eleven years old at the time.

> *We are not having a bit of time for school work, and I am really afraid we*

won't until about November. It is too bad, but I don't know how to help it. We do study one Bible lesson every morning at worship.

*Of course there are **lots** of things we need and you would probably think it awful to do without them. But I think, unless changes should come very soon, that it will grow easier each year to buy the necessaries.*

*I have sewing I want to do as soon as possible but I can't get to it for a while. As usual bedding is one of my fall and winter problems. I think we **must** have blankets but then I'll find we can get along without them. It hasn't frosted here yet. Lloyd and I want to plow whenever Francis isn't using the horses. Francis has so many jobs that he can't get to the plowing.*

Lloyd recalled, later, the fact that his father refused to let his mother do "fancy work" with her needle, which she enjoyed, because it was "too hard on her eyes." Yet she did a man's work in the fields, and elsewhere, that demanded more than her frail body could long endure. It is painfully obvious that Francis felt trapped in a situation where he could not possibly do all the work. It also reveals an attitude in Lloyd's mother of trust and a deep religious loyalty—not of the fanatical variety but an abiding love for the Lord. It carried her through many an otherwise unbearable situation.

She finished her letter:

I must close now. I took my shoes off earlier and I believe I am taking a cold. Goodnight, my mother, with much love to you. (Kisses)

As ever, Nannie

Another heart-tugging missive begins:

I am glad you are well and I hope you will stay at home until this epidemic is over [a reference to the flu epidemic which was rampant after World War I. It was reported that many more people died as a result of that "plague" than from the war itself.]

*I am afraid it would go hard with you because you have had pneumonia a number of times. I have little time to write. It seems as if I must not manage right or I would sometimes have time I could call my own, but even Sabbaths seem full what with reading or keeping the children amused in some way that will be profitable to them. O well, I only go this way **once**. The children are growing up fast.*

I am glad, Mama, that I have smaller feet than any of the rest of the family. I think my real size is 3 1/2, but my feet seem to fit most everything you send. I would be especially glad to get the fleece-lined shoes, for my feet are always so cold. You folks are very good to me to keep me so well supplied with shoes. I have good underwear, but I wonder if Lloyd could wear what you mentioned you have. He is out of underwear and is almost as large as I am.

*I am trying hard to keep cheerful today but it has frozen hard the last two nights. It will make me feel bad to pick up **big** frozen potatoes. It is said, "All things work together for good for those who love the Lord" and of course we shouldn't worry. I try not to but every once in a while my thoughts **will** wonder, for it is **cold** today and will freeze harder tonight and I feel—sort of sick all over. Bye bye for now. Will let you know how things turn out before I mail this.*

*It is now Monday night and the weather is still rather stormy. Yesterday morning we went out to dig potatoes and found all of them frozen, so we stopped when one row was partly dug out. It is a **big** disappointment, for the best three acres of potatoes are all frozen. They will make lots of cow feed. This loss makes a big problem in how to make both ends meet, but of course we will come out some way. [Was there ever a more enduring spirit in a frail body?]*

*I guess we will have to disappoint the boys again, for it doesn't seem best to let them go to town now. Lloyd has no potato money to spend anyway. I felt **so** bad **his** potatoes were frozen. The missionary potatoes too—we expected about $30 to $40 for the "Investment Fund."*

I don't feel like writing any more now. Do be careful not to get sick.

Your loving Nannie

Approaching Christmas, on December 11, 1918, she wrote:

Dear Mama,

*We got the two Christmas packages yesterday. The children think it is **awful** hard to wait two whole weeks to open them. But we will wait.*

*I am very sorry Carrie [her sister] has the flu. I do hope she stays in bed long enough. If I had stayed in bed a day or two longer in the beginning I don't suppose I would be here now. I am so impatient! I feel as if I had been in bed a month and it is only 10 days since I took sick. If I was **real** sick it would seem different too, but I haven't been real sick at any time. Now I am just weak and haven't got up enough nerve to fight it off yet.*

*Poor Lloyd has to stay in and get dinner while the others coast on their sleds. He said he didn't care if only he could knit something for Ioma. I haven't anything but big needles but I'll have to let him do **something**.*

I won't mail this until Tuesday and by that time I hope I can tell you I can wash all the dishes. I was just watching Lloyd clear the table. He is getting so big—and wise.

Those simple words convey the perception of this remarkable woman regarding her son, with whom she was very close, quietly observing his process of self-realization which she interpreted as wisdom—as indeed it was.

In the light of these letters I have pondered the mystery of why certain individuals find themselves with their particular parents. In this instance, perhaps an invincible strength of will (however it found expression through his father) combined with a depth and profundity of love and incredible patience regardless of circumstances in his mother contributed essential ingredients in the creation of a human vehicle for a great spirit. How vast are the implications contained in design.

Letter written by Lloyd Meeker to his Grandma Munden:

Dear Grandma,

> *I love you too, even though I am not sending you a present. I am making Ioma a "Needle Book" for a present. It is just like Marvin's only mine has green thread. I made Ioma a pair of crocheted wristlets with Mama's help. She made most of them.*

> *I wish I had some thing for you but I have not. I have been very busy since Mama has been sick or I would have made you something. I wish you a Merry Christmas and a happy New Year. Good-bye with a kiss from your loving grandson.*

> *Lloyd A. Meeker, age 11 years, 9 months, 21 days*

Nancy wrote again on January 5, 1919:

My Dear Mama,

> *The cistern is dry now. [What misery a few words can convey.] That means the boys must take all the stock to the creek to water every day. It seems impossible to give them as much study time as they should have. I haven't been able to touch Merl's shirt since the day I started it. The next day I had a splitting headache, spent most of the day in bed, since then it seems the housework and lessons are about all I can do. There are so many sewing jobs to do that should be done.*

> *Lloyd and Marvin rode horseback up to Elder Curtis's yesterday to spend the Sabbath. They seemed to enjoy going together horseback.*

> *We are having a very cold spell of weather. The nights are **awful** cold, although the days are warm. Everything is freezing up. We always have kept our fruit down-stairs without fire. This winter we have a hot fire two or three hours every morning and evening and still the tomatoes have frozen hard, broke three cans and **lots** are raising the covers and leaking a little. I'll have to re-can them, won't I? Isn't that a shame? We use them mostly in the spring when we are so busy.*

> *I just remembered I promised to make some new linings for Francis' mittens*

before he went to town. I must get busy.

["Town" was the grocery store high on a plateau—Glade Park —along with a sprinkling of homes.]

I got another present from Mother Meeker yesterday. Olive had given her a pair of skating shoes and they were a little small for her so she sent them to me. They fit me **exactly.** *I never saw any like them, they lace to the toe and are very heavy fleece lined. Yes, I'll be glad when Mother M. comes, though it is only natural I would be even more pleased if it was you.*

Francis has taken a spell tonight to plan our house. If only he stays well he will get the logs down in June. It will be lots of work, but O! how nice to have a house! If Mother Meeker can help pay for the windows, doors, plastering and so on I think we will get it. Won't you be glad? I am almost afraid to allow myself to think of it yet. Francis plans it about 30 x 36 feet.

Francis has taken a bad cold. It is our first real cold this winter. He has felt pretty tough today but he and Lloyd got up three big loads of wood.

I can't get Francis to go to bed. He is trying to figure the lumber we would need. I am so afraid Mother Meeker can't put so much in it, and we can't this year on account of those old debts. We haven't any idea of what Mother M. has, but I don't see how it could be a great deal. Well, I'll close.

Goodnight. Much love.

There were times when the family experienced simple joys, though with meager provisions, and the influence of Nancy's characteristic optimistic attitude can be felt throughout. One time, in a letter to her mother she said:

We had a simple Sabbath dinner. It was a fruit dinner of fresh apples, pears, oranges and a few plums. Lemonade to drink along with barley bread (my first barley bread and we like it) with peanut butter, pear butter and cream pie.

I can't write straight. Francis and the pup make so much noise! Francis sings and the pup accompanies him. He is such a cute, lively little fellow. Right now we have him tied up, for though he **knows** *eggs are not good to eat, for didn't he have a couple that just bit and smarted his mouth something terrible, he also knows that if a puppy is careful not to crack them they are fun to play with and afterward they may be buried on the hillside. [Tiny holes were punched in the end of eggs once in a while and hot pepper inserted, to teach dogs not to eat eggs.]*
January 15, 1919

Night time—after Sabbath. Elder Curtis has been here today. My! He is such a fine old man. He made arrangements for all of them to come here next Sabbath for a quarterly service. [E. A. Curtis was a retired minister, and the Curtis family were friends of the Meekers.]

*Francis' cold has gone through the family. Merl had a little fever last night, and Lloyd has a **bad** cold today. They will be gone in a few days. I love you dearly, my mother, and you are the best mother in the world.*

Finally, on February 11, 1919, Nancy Meeker passed from this sphere, from a life filled with many years of hardships, while maintaining a constant spirit of love and selfless service.

Following are a few excerpts from letters written by Francis to his wife's mother and sister after Nancy's death.

When my own dear wife was sick, I was too sick myself to take care of her or to even know how sick she was. I was delirious with a high fever and she took care of me twenty-four hours after she should have been in bed. That same day she baked a big baking of bread, and I don't know what else she did. I don't know much about what was going on that day.

That was February 4th. I was taken sick the 3rd. The morning of the 5th she gave up and went to bed. She had Lloyd look after things in the house and take care of us the best he could, and she had the other children stay downstairs. About 8 o'clock that morning Lloyd gave up and went to bed.

At times, in the years when I was secretary to Lloyd Meeker, he would recall those early days, and one memory deep in his heart was the time when the whole family was very ill, and he was trying to take care of his mother, besides the house and the other children—all the while being very sick himself. He said, "There, in a cot at the foot of her bed, I heard my mother draw her last breath."

Not once in Nancy's letters is there found a word of blame of her husband, or impatience, and if one had not heard some things from their oldest son later one might get an entirely different picture from that of a domineering figure intent on producing a family fit for a world to come, by enduring hardships and suffering in this one. There are a few portions in her letters where a feeling of desolation could not help but get through, but one always senses Nancy's love for her husband and children, for all who came into her world, and the sustaining warmth it provided for that crowded little household. And when she was gone there was a dearth indeed. Francis continued:

Tuesday morning we all thought Nannie was a little better. I could not think that we would lose her. I was so dazed with grief and anguish that I could not think clearly. I had to leave the planning and preparation for the funeral mostly to others. We were twenty miles from town and telephones and I was too weak to do anything much myself, and too grief-stricken to think straight.

My brother made a coffin out of lumber I had. He is a carpenter, and did a very neat job. They sent to Grand Junction by the stage for material to trim it, and when it was finished it looked very neat. The trimmings cost about $15. Sister Curtis prepared the body and dressed it. The funeral was at 2:30 p.m. February 13. They were afraid I was not able to attend the funeral, but though I could hardly sit up to ride that far I could not let them take her away without me. They placed the coffin in my spring wagon, and Elder Curtis and I rode in the seat. There were about six rigs, and fifteen people followed her to the grave. They requested us not to take the body into the church for fear someone might get the "flu," so the service was held at the cemetery with Elder Curtis officiating.

The children do not realize what a loss they have sustained, and it is better so. They confidently look forward to meeting their dear mother again when Jesus comes. Lloyd realizes the most, and he has been having a deep religious experience. I think he can be baptized this summer. [It seems that Francis had detected something of the spiritual nature of his son, which he could only interpret as his becoming a pillar in the church.]

It came to my mind the other day that I have prayed many times in the last few months that God would draw me to Him and help me to see my shortcomings by whatever means He saw fit; that if He thought it necessary to send us trouble and trial, His will be done. But little did I think He would answer that prayer in the way He did. When the trouble came it nearly overwhelmed me. But I praise God that His grace is sufficient even for this trial.

Francis's mother came to help out with the family, with the possible intention of staying indefinitely. Francis wrote:

My mother's health is quite good and she is not so nervous as she used to be. She says the noise of the children playing does not annoy her like it used to. I believe that we shall get along quite nicely with her help, and she will be someone to love us and for us to love.

Again, words from Lloyd down through the years revealed the fact that this did not work for very long. In fact I sensed a rebellion in him against the strict discipline imposed, akin to that in which his father was brought up. One week after his mother's death, when he was twelve years old, he wrote:

I tell you what, it's awful lonely now since Mama died. Merl is the only one who cried that I know of, but it was pretty hard. I do the chief cooking and I don't seem to be able to get things up as nice as Mama did. I am doing my best to keep things going right. Mama died the 11th of February, Tuesday evening. She was buried the 13th. I haven't anything more to write now, so good-night.

The following letter was written by Mrs. Curtis to Nancy's mother, in answer to a request from her:

*This is a **great** sorrow to Brother Meeker and I think he realizes it **more** and **more** as the lonely days go by.*

We live about seven or eight miles from Brother Meeker's over a mountain road, so that to go there and stop a little while and get back home before night keeps one busy.

Sunday morning we got ready and went over there and when we saw their condition we did not return home until the evening before she was to be buried the next day... Sister Meeker talked very little after I saw her. Of course you knew she had a weak heart and it gave her so much trouble and she breathed so hard, she could not talk with any comfort.

*I don't think that the children **fully** realize their loss—they can't.*

*I feel so thankful that Brother Meeker did not have a relapse. He was up much sooner than he ought to have been and then all that care and **awful loss**— O! It's awful.*

In another letter by Francis to Nancy's mother, he said:

God has made my own heart more tender, and especially the last few months. He has helped me not to speak harshly. Nannie's last request to me about the future was, "Stay on the place and keep the chidren together." This I shall try to do, for the present at least, but I feel so alone, so lost, so helpless without my precious darling wife. The future looks black, but I am trusting God and trying to do my best.

In the days that followed, in the atmosphere of the terrible loss emphasized in the letters, the harsh treatment by Francis became worse, with emphasis on his deteriorating relationship with Lloyd.

Not long after his mother's passing Lloyd had a vivid spiritual experience of contact with her, a vision that was to sustain him often in the troubled years ahead. Filled with its wonder, he perhaps unwisely spoke of it. Francis could not accept this, and the gulf between them widened, with little promise of healing.

Lloyd found comfort in the conviction that his mother was free from suffering and in his compulsion to help his brothers and sister.

He was fifteen years old when a severe case of typhoid fever presented the next hurdle in what seemed to be a hostile world to this young man. He was in bed forty days, and was not expected to survive. But he did—and was barely out of bed when he had to nurse other family members who had succumbed to the dread disease. They all recovered.

A year later, after a bloody beating from his father which left his body bruised and his eyes swollen shut, sixteen-year-old Lloyd left home. He rejected the religion he had been taught, equating its value with his father's actions, in which he saw only a hypocritical fanaticism.

His first "job" was working on a dairy ranch in western Colorado. That was the summer of 1925. His day began at 4:30 in the morning and went on until 10 or 11 at night. The only respite was a few hours in the middle of the day every Sunday. He stayed with that until fall and then quit. With fifteen dollars in his pocket and the rough clothes he was wearing, he set out to find he knew not what, or where, or with whom. He rode the freight trains and while crossing the mountains in bitter cold nearly froze to death.

There were narrow escapes, like almost being discovered by the authorities while huddling in the corner of a drafty freight car, covered by some filthy rags left there. He got off at Pueblo, Colorado, and then walked for miles outside of town to avoid the railroad yards. He managed, finally, to catch an eastbound freight, and spent the night on the end of a loaded coal car, jumping up and down on the brake platform to keep from freezing.

When the train stopped he found himself in Fort Scott, Kansas. He had to find a means of support, and his fifteen dollars barely sustained him while he hunted for work. It seemed a hopeless task until, finally, he landed a job as a laborer on a building construction gang. For five years he was with that company, during which he did many different kinds of work. He shoveled sand and gravel. He unloaded and handled reinforcing steel and structural steel. He unloaded carloads of cement and plaster on hot, stifling August days. He worked with steel when it was so cold that hands and gloves stuck to the metal. He became intimately familiar with all aspects of labor required to build concrete forms—in all kinds of weather.

In his mature years Lloyd often spoke tenderly of the superintendent of that job, a man called Cort by the men who worked for him. He began to see the wonder in the way things work when one follows the direction of an indwelling compulsion, regardless of obstacles and hardships that seem to defy all resolution. Cort brought to Lloyd's world the experience of a man who was a friend. Known on the job as a hardboiled "boss," to Lloyd he was remembered only as fair, considerate and encouraging. He expected, and got, a real day's work from each one, but he was always just.

In company with other men, Lloyd had an opportunity to observe them and the way they worked. He watched with delight the way Cort's mind never overlooked the slightest detail and knew in advance how he would deal with some problem that arose. There were both college graduates and men of little education in the gang, factors which had no weight in Cort's evaluation of a man. This began to make Lloyd ask questions within himself that had been dormant for many years.

Cort saw into the heart of this young man, who was swiftly promoted from one job to another. In those five years he worked his way up from laborer to timekeeper to bookkeeper, and finally became office manager in the home office of this large construction company. With a wide range of responsibilities, he frequently worked till midnight in addition to his regular duties. And he loved it.

Some of his childhood dreams began to take renewed though nebulous form and he was inspired to look into other areas of thought, with Cort always emphasizing good old "common sense." He read a few books on psychology, but some important factor was missing. He began to give attention to natural means of increasing his health, which had suffered over the years. He considered diet and exercise, but, always, an unknown element evaded him.

He began to search for this tantalizingly elusive factor, and frequented libraries but found no answer in the endless books that sit on those dusty shelves. He opened the Bible again, having rejected it in the disillusionment of his early training. Seeing it anew, without the crystallized concepts forced upon him as a child, he experienced a thrill. A tiny crack in a door was beginning to let in a ray of light.

Then, it was all gone!—everything, in the stock-market crash of 1929 and 1930. Without warning he lost his job, his bank went broke, and soon he lost the house he had purchased, more than half paid for. He was, once more, penniless. Meanwhile he had married a young woman, Paulene Foster, and on Valentine's Day in 1930 a beautiful baby girl was born to them. They named her Marjorie Lee.

In July of 1931 Lloyd heard that Ioma, the little sister of his childhood days, was living in Tennessee and needed help. Compelled by a strong sense of responsibility, he went, with his family, to Nashville. Upon arrival he found that his sister had departed for Iowa, obviously the need no longer urgent. A stranger in a strange city, without enough money to buy his family a meal, he had never felt more alone.

He was able to secure a few odd jobs, and for the next three months they existed on less than two dollars a week. The first week they ate nothing but unsalted, boiled potatoes, the next tomatoes, and thus they survived.

He attended a few lectures, seeking to find answers to some burning questions—so many "Why's?"—and met several people who shared the longings in his heart. All the while the search within himself for that elusive Something was persisting. The factors were coming together in his passionate hungering and thirsting for—what? He did not know the answer to that question, but moved with an irresistible compulsion in a direction that would not be denied.

And so he came, blindly through a maze of confused concepts and tuggings of the world of material needs, to September of 1932. In his heart he rejected, in a clean break, all the ideas he had contacted in his searching. None of it mattered anymore. It all fell away—all except that ever-deepening insistence of one thing. What?

In this state of consciousness—or the lack of it—he went to bed on the night of the 12th. He awakened around four o'clock on the 13th, with the first signs of dawn beginning to color the sky. He tried to go back to sleep but was overcome by a feeling of restlessness that would not go away. He arose, walked about the room, considered dressing and taking a walk out on the streets. He got something to read, but the page was a mass of meaningless words. He tried the Bible, a source of help many times, when he would open it at random and find words that brought light into a disturbing situation. Not this time. Nothing helped.

In his own words:

> A tablet of paper and a pencil on the table caught my eye and I had an urge to sit down and write. But what? I had no outer awareness of anything I might write, but the compulsion was greater than the questioning. I picked up the pencil and sat down at the table in the tiny room. My wife and baby were asleep. I found myself letting go into a deeper relaxation than I had ever known. Gradually the room filled with a silvery cloud of light, in which all objects were blotted from my view. Enfolded in that cloud I became aware of a Presence, and an indescribable peace penetrated my entire being.
>
> I began to write, a word at a time. As fast as one came, the next appeared, as if by magic. Without any desire to question, or seek to understand, or rebel, I wrote for about an hour. And then, as suddenly as it had begun, it stopped. There was nothing more to write. The cloud disappeared. I read what had been written under my hand and found, amazingly, the answers to questions that had been in my mind and heart for many years, seeking solution.
>
> I felt that my whole being glowed, from some inner light, and thought it must be that an angel from heaven had visited me. "But this," I whispered, awestricken, "was not something outside of myself. These words came from somewhere inside of *Me*."

With astonished eyes he read and reread what he had written, and moved through the day in an aura of wonderment. That night he retired as usual.

The morning of the 14th found him awake, again at dawn. Without hesitation this time he took pencil and paper and sat down to write. Again the white cloud enveloped him. On that occasion he wrote for about three hours. Then the inspiration ceased, as did his writing.

At dawn on the 15th it happened the third time. When the writing was finished on that day he knew it would not need to happen again—and it never did.

This transcendent experience signaled the birth of life, in its dynamic sense, for Lloyd Meeker. The 16th of September would be the anniversary date of what was to take form as his "ministry," dedicated to revealing to humanity the age-old truths which had emanated from his being in those three intense days.

Continuing to dwell in the Presence, so that any feeling of separation dissolved, Lloyd came to the realization that he had another name. That name was *Uranda,* and he later spoke about its meaning as it had come to him. He said:

> My name *Uranda* is of the language of the Motherland or the original Lemuria [a point of focus but not limited to one area on the face of the planet], synonymous with the biblical Garden of Eden, the original state of consciousness in which man was created. The literal meaning of the name *Uranda* is: "One who lets the light of Christ shine forth."

A few of his friends became aware of a remarkable change in this twenty-four-year-old man and were drawn to be with him. In his little room, over a store in the poorest section of the city, a handful of students gathered once a week to drink thirstily of the cup which he so gladly offered. Increasingly, the Bible became alive with hidden treasures, and together they mined for its gold. Unexplored vistas opened up; nature beckoned with new meaning; it was becoming a different world.

From that little study group he drew his first patients; for he was, always, passionately absorbed in the work of healing —traits and talents emphasized in both his parents. Gradually the word spread by those who had been blest in body, mind and heart, and his practice grew. Some of the wealthiest and most prominent members of society heard, and came to see for themselves. Lives were saved, lives were transformed, problems solved. And some people found, behind it all, the Light, which was the one thing Lloyd was interested in. It was during this early period that he wrote a series of lessons, titled "Steps to Mastership."

He used the name "L. Meeker" as health editor of a magazine, *Metaphysical Star,* in Nashville; "L. A. Meeker" for his writing on numerology; and his pen name "Uranda" in other material.

It was about this time that he sent for his youngest brother, Merl Freedom, then living in Jacksonville, Florida. Lloyd arranged for him to take business training in night school, while seeking to share with him the wonder which he himself had found. He had envisioned the two of them developing a strong foundation for what he sensed was being built. It was not to be quite that easy! Merl continued for a while with his brother, and then left to pursue his own interests.

Lloyd's whole being underwent some basic changes during this experience and he was consumed by a feeling of urgency to get "out there" and share it with the many he knew must be waiting for what he had found. A gap began to be apparent between him and his wife and they were divorced after seven years of marriage. They had weathered much in the "depression" years and she had filled a great need in his early life. He had to obey an impulse which came from the core of his being, and that cycle of his life came to a close.

Lloyd left patients, students and friends in Nashville on December 21, 1934, and went by train (not riding in a boxcar this time!) to New Orleans, across Texas, New Mexico and Arizona to Los Angeles, then north to Atascadero. There he was met by Wilm Kullgren, editor of *Beacon Light* magazine, and stayed at the Golden Way Hotel. That was on Christmas Day, and his worldly goods all fit into his pocket, a total of thirty dollars.

As early as May 23, 1935, a paper entitled "Uranda's Personal Message" was being released to a mailing list from "Central Council" in Atascadero (P.O. Box 253). He signed himself "Your fellow wayfarer" and spoke of being blest with a "small but very good printing press." "The Secrets of Our Master's Prayer" was one of the early releases. His Personal Messages dealt with clarifying the initiating principles that were burgeoning in his consciousness. He often referred to "your many letters" and of the steady increase in response to the lesson material, a substantial amount of which dealt with interpreting the wonders in the Bible, though he did not limit himself to any one source of subject matter. The seven seals received as much attention as, for example, the Great Pyramid of Gizeh and the Sphinx; and the thread which bound it all together was soul-satisfying.

His Message of August 3 referred to the 52nd lesson of the course *Steps to Mastership*, which he said had been "going forth each week for one year." He said that the past year had seen marvelous growth and development and he had just returned from San Francisco where they held classes for eleven days, with a lecture in the Rosicrucian Hall. There was reference also to moving into larger quarters in Atascadero, where classes were regularly held.

In Uranda's Personal Message (UPM) of August 8 he revealed that

> the name selected for the School here is of the Motherland tongue—*Sa-Sor-Ra*—and means "The Sacred School of God, which fills the whole earth," and all are in the sacred school of God. Thrice blessed are they who know this truth, that they may be fully aware of their being in Sa-Sor-Ra.

In UPM of September 9 he expressed his gratitude for the provision by students in

Paso Robles and Atascadero for furnishings for the School, which he said was open to all who seek the Way. His Message of October 10 spoke of a "Mountain Sanctuary" where some could find spiritual relaxation.

It was in the beginning of 1936 that Uranda's masterpiece, *The Triune Ray*, was sent out.

In April the way opened for services to be held in Oakland, and in early June in San Jose and Santa Cruz.

In August he was contacted by Joe Benner, inviting him to come to the Sun Center in Akron, Ohio, which he did and addressed the Summer School there for a few days. It looked as though some printing of Uranda's work might be done there, but it did not materialize.

UPM of August 22 announced that headquarters was moved from Atascadero to P.O. Box 1106, Oakland. Uranda's first radio broadcast was on September 13. A Message in April of 1937 made reference to his secretary, Lydia, whose name had appeared a number of times previously.

During this period, in the audience of one of Uranda's lectures in San Francisco was Fern, a student of comparative religions and philosophies, and lecturer on metaphysical subjects. She was immediately drawn to the focus of truth finding expression through him. He found something refreshingly satisfying in this new kind of association, experiencing an interchange with its emphasis on a spiritual level.

Uranda and Fern were married on May 12, 1937, in Reno, Nevada. She chose to assume the name Wanu, taken from a character in a story told at one time by Uranda. Together they provided a magnet to which people were drawn, traveling extensively in the United States and Canada during the Thirties, visiting groups that were forming from coast to coast, with Uranda lecturing and teaching.

The connection with Brother Benner of the Sun Center in Akron was nearing its close. Uranda wrote him an open letter on December 6, pointing out that in using portions of Uranda's writings in conjunction with his own views in his editorial, the result was distorted.

The year 1938 was ushered in with Uranda addressing his flock in UPM thus:

> In the past it has been necessary to so write in my Personal Messages, and in the Lessons, that the entire range of response was provided for in every expression; therefore many have felt that my expression was too complicated and deep, and they have been inclined to judge. However, with the formation of "The New Naacal Norm" this necessity has been removed, so that those who require the expression in the deeper range are provided for therein. The Earnest Ones who choose to harmonize in the outer cycles of the Third Sa-

cred School will be provided for through the general, weekly mailings. [Those in the NNN would receive all the mailings.]

On February 2 there was a clarifying portion regarding Jesus:

> Many think they are to be swallowed up, so to speak, in Jesus, so that they are to "be Jesus Christ." Such an idea is false. You are to be yourself in your own reality. Jesus is the only one who can be Jesus Christ. You can let your Father within you clothe you with His radiance of the Christ light, love and life, and then you as an individual will be harmonious with and under the direction of your individual Lord who in turn is harmonious with the one who is the LORD of Lords, or Jesus the Christ...
>
> The three outer planes of the world revolted against our rightful ruler... In the outer planes all things are very ethereal, and they quickly decay and vanish away. Not so with the inner planes. There all things are solid, and made of everlasting substance... Human beings have been inclined to think of the outer world as having the true material phase of being. This is not so. There are material things in the inner world. If you try to understand those things now, you will only be confused. Anyone who attempts to describe them to you is only giving voice to fictions and fancies of his own human mind. "Verily, verily, I say unto thee, We speak that we do know, and testify that we have seen; and ye receive not our witness. If I have told you earthly things, and ye believe not, how shall ye believe, if I tell you of heavenly things?" [John 3:11,12].

Uranda referred to a so-called "modern bible" popular at that time but short-lived, as being "for those who like to study the remarkable wanderings of the human mind through the endless maze of human concepts that must contain some degree of truth in order to manifest but which are absolutely meaningless and of no value."

In his Message of March 24 he spoke of the inevitable "dividing of the sheep from the goats":

> Stand steadfast in the fire of the Christ Love. If you fight not, murmur not, and be not afraid, but stand upon the Rock, rendering "unto Caesar the things that are Caesar's, and to God the things that are God's," you shall find that you function not in your own strength alone. "Vengeance is mine, I will repay, saith the Lord." It is for the responding one to stand unmoved and calm in rejoicing, unmoved by unreality but moving by and in reality.

His word in the April 4th Message included this:

> Anyone who places his own needs or ideas before the right function of the whole is not worthy of a place in this service. Those who permit others to

impose upon them are thereby guilty in company with the wrong-doer. There is a popular expression, "Whatever is, is best." The sense in which these words are generally used makes them absolutely false. They are used to excuse wrong action and wrong choice, used to make people be satisfied with failure and defeat, to justify subjugation to evil and limited conditions... We have no quarrel with any, but irrespective of men and the concepts of men, we move serenely in that expression and function which we recognize to be of reality.

A series of instruction papers entitled "The Central Way" was initiated.

Uranda and Wanu began a tour which encompassed Councils from coast to coast. Leaving the Bay area on June 12, they stopped first in Reno, Nevada. From there they drove the 540 miles to Salt Lake City, Utah, in one day and visited the Mormon church. Uranda commented about the trip:

> Following Salt Lake City, the next stop was the 290 miles through majestic mountains to find abode that evening in Grand Junction, Colorado. As nine years of my boyhood were spent in the rimrock country of Glade Park, about 23 miles back in the mountains southwest of Grand Junction, we drove up the Serpent's Trail Road to acquaint Wanu with the rugged and majestic silences that enfold that barren wilderness that is everywhere overshadowed with the awe-inspiring formations of the rimrock to which I was taken as a seven-year-old boy. It was there that the Lord my God revealed to me the secrets of life which prepared the way for my present ministry.

> Leaving Glade Park, we drove the 45 miles which I walked years ago to the desert wastes of the Whitewater country where I had lived for about three years as a young man. There the volcanic ash soil, filled with lava boulders, will yield fruitage only by dint of the hardest toil and would be a barren waste except for the waters of Kannah Creek which are diverted to moisten the thirsty earth. We drove to the foot of Grand Mesa, the highest flat-top mountain in the world, whose majesty inspired my youth and upon whose summit I breathed deeply of the rarefied atmosphere long years ago. There where desert and mountain meet, beside the rushing waters, I find a peculiar fragrance which is like unto that of the Motherland.

> After leaving Montrose, Colorado, we drove through the awe-inspiring mountains and across the Great Divide at Monarch Pass at a height of over 11,000 feet above sea level. At the high point of the Pass we walked a little way on the mountainside to the melting snow banks, from which little streams were flowing—and a question of only a few feet east or west determined

whether the water should flow down into the Arkansas River, and so to the Gulf of Mexico through the Mississippi, or flowing westward be taken by the Silver Colorado to the Pacific Ocean. We considered the ways of man. Some turn right, and some turn left; and one may go to the right as easily as to the left—if we will only let it be so.

On the 19th Uranda spoke for about eight hours to a group in Pueblo, driving the following day to Denver where he spoke at the home of friends in Littleton. From there the journey took them through Nebraska and Iowa, then on to Wisconsin. From the 26th to the 29th he held nine services in Milwaukee and Cedarburg, speaking to a large audience in a public hall on the 28th. Several attended from Minneapolis.

The connection with Cedarburg and Milwaukee was through Marie and Roy Johnson. In 1936 a piece of Uranda's literature came to the hand of Marie via Bill Martens. Marie travelled in 1937 to California because of the death of her brother, at which time she and her mother Jennie Olsson met Uranda. Roy and Marie's daughter Lillian met him when he was in Milwaukee, and she recalls later playing the piano at one of his public lectures in the Republican Hotel.

There was another woman from Milwaukee, Dorothea Rasmussin, a close friend of Marie Johnson, who was immediately drawn to Uranda and his work. It was through a booklet left in her beauty parlor by Marie that she was introduced to Uranda and his work. She married Mike McCann, and their daughter Pam shared that same love for the truth and has allowed it to be paramount in her living. An interesting parallel in the pattern of the two women, Marie and Dorothea, is the fact that their mothers, Jennie Olsson and Nina Rasmussin, along with them were faithful pillars of Uranda's ministry throughout their lives. And their daughters, Lillian Johnson and Pam McCann, carried that same dedication through the next generation.

Bill and Frieda Martens provided vital points of leadership in the Milwaukee area, with Bill focusing services in group meetings.

Continuing their tour, on July 4, 1938, Uranda and Wanu drove from Lansing on a route north of Detroit into Canada for over 200 miles, to Niagara Falls, then into Buffalo, New York, where Uranda was delighted with the Council. After a few days they went to New York City, where the Council secretary was Lily McCann. They visited Philadelphia, where a group was forming, followed by a visit to Washington, D.C., and four days spent in Pittsburgh.

Back in California on schedule they met with a group in San Diego on August 10 and 11, on the 12th at Long Beach, with their first class at Los Angeles on the 14th, with public services through the 17th and a closed Norm service the 18th. On August 21 they drove into Oakland, having been gone ten weeks and driven 9,111 miles. It was an intensive trip, with many people contacted and much achieved.

A triumphant announcement was made in August that a new headquarters was established, in Burbank, California, where weekly services would replace those conducted previously in the chapel at Oakland. The mailing list then included twenty-three names.

In December of 1938 in a message entitled "1939—The Time of Testing," Uranda said that from a cosmic standpoint the new year would be a time of testing, wherein the choices of all would begin to be tested and proven, whether of the real or the unreal, true or false. "This testing," he said, "of national choices, and group choices within nations, will bring about an increase in war and turmoil in the world."

"A Report of Your Service," in May of 1939, offers a study in contrast with the current financial situation in the world, though probably with percentages not unrelated to the present state of affairs:

> Of the 414 on our mailing list, which includes all groups except Explorers (young people), who were receiving the lessons in May, there were 72 who failed to write their required monthly letter. However, these 72 are included in the figures which follow. Of the 414, there were 246 who did not send in anything toward the support of the Lord's Service.
>
> Of those 246, there are about 40 who actually are not in position to send in a monetary gift, but who are responding splendidly. That leaves more than 200 who could have given and did not. Consider for a moment what we could have accomplished if those 200 had done their part. This state of affairs is unfair to those who do give, and who have long waited for material that we could have printed if those in position to do so were faithful in stewardship.
>
> Some have undertaken to tell us something about being liberal and of giving of the Truth without mentioning money, but they have been those who themselves failed to give. You yourselves know of the abundance we have sent to you, and you have seen how the Lord has multiplied your gifts in our hands, in blessing to all who will receive.

2

The Meeting

August 1939 ~ April 1940

*D*elightedly observing the presence of young people of teen age in the forming groups, Uranda wrote a series of papers especially for them entitled "The Young Explorers." Cosmic in nature, the subject matter would be as captivating today, for young and old, as any modern TV show. After introducing the series with a beautiful explanation of the truth contained in the story of the seven "days" of creation in Genesis, he continued: "Now it is possible to tell you the story of creation that you will not find in any source outside of the Third Sacred School. Each one will have to look within him- or herself in order to relax into this new vision of reality."

Following are some excerpts from "The Young Explorer's Club" papers of 1939:

Beloved Explorers: Come and let me enfold you in the silent melodies of the spheres, and as you relax into the spirit of my presence with you, you will see my Magic Word. In it there is a door, and now it opens wide for you. As you find your places I close and seal the door. As you relax you begin to feel a soft warm glow inside your body and all around you. You will notice a soft radiance of light that seems to change in color as the vibrations and your realizations change. Sometimes the light is almost white, then it takes on a golden hue, changing to a lovely blue, and then rich purple as a surge of power flows through you. Do not "try" to see this light, and if you see it not, be content to feel its gentle radiance.

Time no longer holds us, and the things of this present world fade from view as our Magic Word moves swiftly out into space. Distance is no obstacle to the Magic Word, and we draw close to Siomra, the sun of our solar system. But what of those huge flames of fire leaping out toward us? Almost fearful, yet not afraid, you watch them leap out into space for tens of thousands of miles. As the ascending substance that is drawn from the various worlds comes within the active orbit of the sun, the flames reach out to receive it, and there is a chemical change that releases what we may call gaseous substance, which immediately appears to burn.

The rays from the sun do not appear as light, nor give heat, in "outer space." Light and heat, as man knows them, do not appear until they are re-flected by the earth's surface...

Our Magic Word has been moving, more slowly now, through the flames of the sun, and you see them moving in many directions as they envelop us, and a constant play of colors more vivid and gorgeous than any known in the human world. You have the deep assurance that your Master-Self is at home here and can read the meaning revealed by every changing hue, detecting a wonderful order and rhythm. You see why you have to be *inside* the Magic Word to understand it. Every cell of your body is becoming more alive, and you realize that you are enfolded in a sea of soft music, hearing the lovely colors. The flames are no longer moving, only the colors move now. The deeper layers of the sun are permanently fixed, created out of sun-substance which endures for all eternity; and it never grows old, eternally new. We are moving through the outer boundaries of Siomra.

Your human identity is not lost, and you enfold that part of you inside yourself. When we are ready to return to man's world the human part will come forth again and you will be as you were before in many ways—yet there will be a difference, which I shall leave for you to find and know. But now we are to give our full attention to Siomra, and I see the joy that surges through you as you arrive for a visit in the Home where you have lived and worked.

And now you have your own Magic Word, which you will use while we stay in Siomra. I open the door to my Magic Word, and as you step out of it you draw your own Garment about you and you are dressed in the Robe you wore in other days and which you see worn on every hand here in this glorious City of Light.

Uranda went on to speak of the One who welcomed them, and then referred to other great beings, each with a name. It was a series which delighted the hearts of the young (and older) ones, affording a glimpse into a world of new, and yet the oldest, perspective in the cosmos.

Uranda found rich reward in the eager response of these young adults and said, in a message in August 1939:

> Whether you choose to consider the story of the visit to Siomra as fact or fiction is unimportant for the moment. I leave each one to determine within himself whether or not there is a realization of actuality in the story—but the important thing is that you should let go in the spirit of it and find the multitude of lessons of practical fact and principle revealed thereby—and there is a great deal of symbolism in it.

Later that same year a pattern which was to prove invaluable in the ensuing days in the form of Summer Sessions was introduced at Glendale, California, with representatives from thirteen states and Canada. This one was entitled the Council of the Golden Veil and lasted over two weeks, with two or three services daily, Uranda speaking for seven hours a day! "The Council of the Golden Veil" indicated a certain level of function in realization of the truths of being, rather than a prescribed number of individuals in a group.

He considered a wide range of topics, and some of his points of clarification are of special interest. Concerning "prophecies" he said:

> Repeatedly I have pointed out that in all cases where I suggest dates in a prophetic sense they are stated from a cosmic, not an outer, standpoint. Under present conditions it takes considerable time for a cosmic fact to come into full manifestation in the earth. In the perfect state that which is done from a cosmic standpoint outmanifests immediately—but until the change into the new state is completed there will be periods of lapse between the cosmic finality and the outer fruition.

In answer to questions from a few concerning which Bible he would recommend, Uranda said,

> We do not endorse any of the special, or "modern" translations. I would recommend *The Scofield Reference Bible*, which is the King James Authorized Version of the Holy Bible with a special arrangement of subheadings in the text. Not all of Scofield's comments are accurate but his system of references can be helpful.

In December of 1939 he dealt with cycles of outworking and their cosmic relatedness, with the reminder that the self-active human mind is what has been called the serpent.

> Ascension takes place during the period of your physical lifespan to the degree of your response to reality. If your primary concern is to ascend, it shows that you are afraid of death, and therefore subject to death. In the present state of the world it is of very little importance whether you completely ascend or not, and you cannot be truly polarized in life until you recognize this fact and function accordingly.
>
> The promise of God for the New Earth shall be fulfilled, as given in Rev. 21:4: "And God shall wipe away all tears from their eyes; and there shall be no more death, neither sorrow, nor crying, neither shall there be any more pain: for the former things are passed away." In that day the inhabitants of the earth, which shall then be the New Earth in the Edenic State, shall experience birth and ascension, rather than birth and death.

The location of Headquarters was moved from Burbank to 1771 E. 2nd Street, Long Beach, California. Headquarters was increasingly a busy place and was blest with some very capable and devoted workers, essential to the development of the ministry in those early days. Anna Latourelle, a middle-aged lady, provided a consistent atmosphere of calm strength. Two young women, Louise Vetterle and Mercedes Betancourt, offered their skills in office procedure, with the passion to serve the Lord so characteristic of those who found themselves in Uranda's orbit. Mercedes, a beautiful Negro girl, brought to her surroundings the unique essence of her race in a loving nature which allowed cracks to appear in some age-old ceilings of consciousness.

An unusual, vibrant member of the fast-growing group in California was Elsa Fischel, a seasoned actress familiar in Hollywood at that time, with substantial parts in some top movies. And there were many more, as the borders of the tent enlarged rapidly and other groups appeared throughout the world.

Attending one of Uranda's public talks was a man, sitting in the second row, who had a persistent cough. Uranda usually had a few Sucrets in his pocket for emergencies. These very effective little cough drops are each encased in a silver wrapper. One was passed to the man, and afterward Uranda was informed that, assuming it to be an amulet with magic properties, he had held it in his hand for the remainder of the talk. But he stopped coughing!

Incidents along the way come to mind which may not have been earth-shaking but contributed to the particular atmosphere of those days, a special aura. Anna Latourelle, for instance, lived alone in an apartment downtown and was taken completely by surprise one night, while preparing for bed, to see a huge figure of a man climbing into her room through a window. Without hesitation, she stood, figure erect and commanding, her finger pointed at him, radiance emanating from every pore, and said, in positive and penetrating tone, "In the Name of Jesus Christ, *Begone!*" I had the impression he never got both feet on the floor! He was out of there in a hurry. It worked, that's all, regardless of method, belief or anything else. She knew—and so did he!

In a completely different place and circumstance but in the same assurance of the working of the power of God in any circumstance, there was a little lady, middle-aged, a member of the group in Vancouver, who was accosted on a busy street of that city by a burly stranger. He tried, and almost succeeded, to snatch her purse. Her first flush of feeling was devoid of negative reaction as she drew herself up as far as her little birdlike self would permit, and in stentorious voice said, "I am covered with feathers!" The man did not wait to see—but made a swift exit. The text that came to her in the moment was from the Psalms, "He shall cover thee with his feathers, and under his wings shalt thou trust: his truth shall be thy shield and buckler." However it came out, it worked! The spirit of God is all-powerful when it can *actually* use the facility at hand. The tool may not seem to have cosmic significance, but the complete faith, or love, or whatever name may be in vogue for the power, is the one essential ingredient, the results absolute.

In Uranda's first Message since his induction into the office of Bishop of the Church of the Emissaries of Divine Light, February 7, 1940, he joyously proclaimed that the process of Incorporation of the Church had been completed in January, and as a Charter Church Body was recognized under the laws of the land, with a legal right to conduct the Spiritual Education program through the Third Sacred School, and to ordain ministers of the Church. The activities of the Third Sacred School would continue as before, with no change in the basic functions in any manner, the matter of legal organization a simple necessity to operate in the world the way it is. When asked about such matters two millennia ago, Jesus replied, "Render therefore unto Caesar the things which are Caesar's; and unto God the things that are God's." Uranda said:

> I have served and ministered for over seven years without any outer form of manifestation to reward such function—but as surely as the creative cycles were set up and maintained in the spiritual vibrations of my ministry, just so was it inevitable that the spiritual formation should bring forth a living outer formation. All now enrolled in the Third Sacred School are given an opportunity to become charter members of the Church. No one can "join" the Emissaries by any declaration of belief, but one becomes

a true Emissary of Divine Light to the degree that he becomes one with and
in his own Lord within himself.

In February of 1940 Uranda completed a book, *Revelation Revealed,* and referred to
it as "one of my most profound expressions of reality." Its message is as compelling today
as it was the day of its inspiration, the radiance undiminished.

The Church and School were separate entities. A member of the Church was asked
to sign a Declaration of Response; students of the School were not so required. One
could resign from the Church and continue in the School. By March of that year 416
were receiving regular mailings and 253 of those had Certificates of Harmonization.

At this time Uranda warned against distorted theories that have been built around
numerology, astrology and reincarnation, "twisted fancies around partial truths," and
added that the true design is present, behind appearances, in all things; otherwise they
could not exist.

The rapidly growing Church had no income outside of love gifts (donations), and
owned nothing but the equipment at headquarters. Nor did Uranda have any property
other than clothes and personal effects. The organization of the Church was in dynamic
process, with a Central Council and Branch Councils, each having a leader, or "focal
point." The membership of the Central Council was composed of those who were members of the Church and of the Norm (the group of more advanced students who had
passed a specific examination and were dedicated to selfless service). A number of those
were given the opportunity to serve as Tutors to assist others, with the assurance that
their work would be kept under Uranda's close personal supervision.

He used the term *Third Sacred School* to identify this time of the movement of the
inhabitants of this planet, under leadership consciously aware of the need, to return the
earth with mankind to its Creator. He spoke of two such previous endeavors, one initiated by Abraham in the Old Testament of the Bible, the First Sacred School, and after
that one failed, the Second Sacred School which, with the advent of Jesus, furthered the
great work of restoring men and women to their right relationship with God. The cycle
of the Third Sacred School began with Uranda's initiation.

Brother or *Sister* referred to a "responding one" in that initial period. The *Holy Norm*
was composed of those who were closest, in a spiritual sense, to Uranda, as was true also
of the Council of the Golden Veil. The term *Anomon* was used to describe one devoted to
a search for the Truth. The word *Priests* was applied to individuals who had proved a
certain dedication and ability to serve, in a variety of capacities. Also a group was selected who were by nature and training especially fitted to work in the field of healing.

There were two types of leaders: those appointed by Uranda to focalize Council activities but not ordained as focal points; and ordained focal points, who had received First Ordination. Harmonization in both Church and Holy Norm were requisite for First Ordination. There was a Second and a Third Ordination, and the Third bestowed the status of Ordained Minister.

A tour of the "Harvest Field" by Uranda and Fern began April 1, 1940, in the "Rolling Embassy" (by car, and a trailer which contained office equipment) near Salinas, California. It was in that month that Uranda went to Vancouver, B.C., where arrangements had been made through Martin Cecil, then residing in Canada.

Earlier I referred to Martin, an English Lord, who was to provide a vital point of focus in close conjunction with Uranda and his ministry. This connection surfaced, in an outer sense, in 1939 when Martin contacted Uranda's word and drank immediately and deeply of the water that quenches all thirst. The upcoming meeting in Vancouver afforded the first meeting between them, nervously anticipated by Martin awaiting the event.

Lord Martin Cecil's home was in the interior of British Columbia, Canada, some three hundred miles from Vancouver in a picturesque valley nestled between magnificent ranges of mountains. His father was the Fifth Marquess of Exeter, who resided with the Marchioness and their family at Burghley House, built by Martin's famous ancestor in the sixteenth century.

The founder of the Cecil family was William Cecil, Lord High Treasurer and chief adviser and counsellor to Queen Elizabeth I. His influence was vital in bringing about England's ruling place as a world power at that time. One of his great achievements was the furthering of Protestantism. Then in its precarious infancy, it had been initiated by Henry VIII in the sixteenth century as the Church of England, threatening the strangling control of the Roman Catholic Church. Outstanding qualities in that first William were dominant in Martin's expression, four centuries later. Each had an absolute dedication to his purpose in life, with a golden aura of loving kindness.

The family tree finds a root in Robert Sitsilt (from which the name Cecil emerged) who participated in the conquest of Glamorganshire in 1091 and acquired estates in Herefordshire and Monmouthshire. A generation later David Cecil, who fought under Henry VIII and possessed a considerable fortune, settled in Stamford, a small town in Lincolnshire. He was the grandfather of William Cecil.

Bitter fighting between Catholics and Protestants characterized the England of 1558, upon whose throne Elizabeth sat. Mary I's marriage had rendered the nation a satellite of Phillip's Spain, its wealth greatly depleted since Henry VIII. Yet, before long, Queen Elizabeth and William Cecil brought the country out of a most precarious situation into an orderly and prosperous state, at which time the Spanish Armada was defeated by the

Royal Navy. Eventually made a peer, William Cecil became the 1st Lord Burghley.

When, on August 4, 1598, Queen Elizabeth was informed of the death of her friend the Lord High Treasurer, she deeply mourned her (and her country's) loss. Following an elaborate funeral at Westminster Abbey his body was buried in St. Martin's Church in Stamford. There his life-size effigy in stone reclines on a marble tomb, his wand of office in his hand. That occupies a place of honor in the church's interior and has been, and is, viewed and revered by worshippers Sunday after Sunday.

William's motto, "Cor Unum Via Una—One Heart, One Way," has graced the coat-of-arms of the family through the centuries. The Exeter branch of the Cecil family was initiated when William's elder son Thomas became the 1st Earl of Exeter. A younger son, Robert, became Earl of Salisbury, thus creating another dynasty of the family at Hatfield House, in Hertfordshire. Henry, the 10th Earl of Exeter, received the title of 1st Marquess of Exeter in 1801. Members of that illustrious family have continued to play a vital part in the development of their country.

It was on April 27, 1909, that Martin was born at Burghley House to William, who had become the Fifth Marquess of Exeter in 1898 at age twenty-two, and his wife Myra. Two children had preceded him, Winifred and David. Martin's father was very civic-minded, occupying such positions as Mayor of Stamford, Lord Lieutenant of Northamptonshire, and aide-de-camp to King George V. He was made a Knight of the Garter, the highest order of knighthood, in recognition by the King of his invaluable contributions and spirit of service.

At the outbreak of war in August of 1914 Myra, a lady of the nobility and raised in a castle, proved her great moral strength in running Burghley House and raising the children. Relationships in that setting and level of society were very formal. The children, dressed for the occasion, would be presented at teatime in the drawing room to share time with their parents. Martin referred to his mother as "Queen Mummy" after seeing the painting of her that graces a wall in the Great Hall at Burghley House, dressed in coronation robes with a coronet on her beautiful head.

Of necessity a nanny provided the closer physical presence with the children on a daily basis, and through the years we enjoyed hearing Martin's reminiscences of Mrs. Needs, a cheerful and kindly woman with lots of love, from Devonshire.

A younger daughter, Romayne, joined the family three years after Martin's arrival. She was "Baby" to him, and he found the new little one a source of joy which continued throughout his life. As small children, the two elder were stronger than Martin (as in pounding each other) and Martin resorted to other means of retaliation. At one such time Winifred was heard to shriek, "He bited a *Lady!*" (her title).

It was a delight to hear Martin recount his childhood experiences, some of which were in company with a cousin, Gervase Falkiner, who contributed an element of mischief. One incident had to do with a pair of boots, property of Oliver Cromwell when he was at Burghley during the English Civil War where he shot some cannonballs. Returning for dinner at a later time, he left his boots behind. So, in their play, Martin donned the boots and Gervase, in possession of a sword which he was flourishing, accidentally cut one of the boots. Instantly sobered, the boys tried to conceal the disaster by rubbing dirt into the cut to make it appear of ancient vintage. Later Gervase overheard Myra say, as she displayed the boots, "Look, you can see the mark of a sword!"

Winifred, the eldest, and David were alike in many ways, extroverted and positive in expression. Martin, with his quiet, contemplative nature, felt inferior to his older brother, who bore the title Lord Burghley (heir to the family "throne") and was very gifted, for the most part in areas that differed from Martin's abilities. Outstanding was David's physical prowess, which eventually won him a gold medal in the Olympic 400-meter hurdles in Amsterdam in 1928.

There were times when, with innocent enough motivation, events conspired to emphasize his feelings toward his brother. The Burghley Estate, noted for its horse racing and famous for "fox-and-hound" spectaculars, was holding an event in which Martin was to participate. He had worked diligently to prepare a high-strung horse of fine quality for a point-to-point race and was sure that together they could win it. Before the great day, however, his father, realizing the danger in the obstacles and jumps involved, asked the more experienced David to ride the horse—which he did, coming home the victor!

As they matured, of course all the children found their relationships changing, and it was not many years before Martin became very close to his brother and Winifred.

I always felt that Martin's special talent in art was one evidence of the fine nature of his character. Each line in his sketches was meticulously drawn, no detail too small to receive his complete attention. That was his attitude toward his world—people, circumstances, each worthy of the specialized care and wisdom inherent in his great spirit. His reminiscences of days at Burghley were often accompanied by a twinkle in his eye as, for instance, when he spoke of the landscape artist Capability Brown or the dairy farmer Mr. Rowebottom—wonderful names!

Though he was born in a palace, Martin was raised in an atmosphere where the right use of money played an important role. The country was experiencing one traumatic experience after another, and uncertainty regarding the future was prevalent. He had a strong sense of responsibility, to which both his parents substantially contributed. His mother, for instance, would save unused half-sheets of her stationery for

Martin to use for his drawing.

She was very faithful in keeping a close correspondence with him when he was away at school. One of his letters in her prized collection was in answer to what he would like for Christmas that year: "One medium-sized bird" (alive of course).

During much of his childhood Martin did not see a great deal of his father, who was participating in the War as an artillery officer. At the close of that time Martin was in boarding school. An opportunity for closer communion between them only appeared in later years.

At a very early age he had to decide his next step, and he chose the Navy over the Army or the Church. At the tender age of thirteen on January 17, 1923, he departed for Dartmouth Royal Naval College. Enrolling with him was a lifelong friend and close companion, his senior by one day, Michael Culme-Seymour of Rockingham Castle, near Burghley. The fact that a childhood friendship continued in their shared experience at Dartmouth was an inestimable blessing to both.

After his school experience in Lockers Park, the Royal Naval College was indeed an imposing edifice. It opened in 1905 in the little town of Dartmouth in Devonshire on the River Dart, which enjoyed the distinction that Richard the Lionheart had set sail for the Crusades from there in 1190, and in 1620 the Mayflower and Speedwell spent time there before sailing to America. He enjoyed visiting some fascinating places, such as the French Riviera, Greece and Egypt.

He learned practical skills, among them engineering and mechanical drawing. He also learned, in no uncertain terms, to obey, to accept discipline, at the same time practicing the art of discerning and carrying out what awaited the doing—and seeing the job finished.

Having transferred to the new flagship of the Fleet, the battleship *Queen Elizabeth*, while visiting the French port of Villefranche, Martin and some fellow midshipmen accepted an invitation to a dance. On April 23, 1929, he wrote of the event to his mother: "We have left Villefranche at last after, as far as I was concerned, a wonderful time, with much dancing. I fell in love last Thursday night with a sweet little Hungarian called Edith whom I met at Baroness Orczy's dance. She is the niece of Mrs. Grant Richards (also Hungarian), the publisher's wife." Martin wrote to Edith at Monte Carlo where she was staying with her aunt, and opened up a continuing friendship via correspondence.

There was an incident when, as junior midshipman, one of his duties was to serve as the captain's "doggie," or dogsbody, which included running errands of whatever nature. This particular one occurred when the *Queen Elizabeth* was berthed at Malta. Martin was asked by the captain if he would get his new car, which had just arrived from

England, from the Customs office and drive it to his house, five or six miles on the other side of the harbor. Martin had never driven a car in his life. To refuse was not an option, regardless of the turmoil going on inside. He saluted and departed.

There was no problem at Customs, but here was a shiny new wonder to be transported—by him! It was housed in a customhouse shed, a stone building with a narrow exit. He got in, and studied the controls. He had observed how cars were driven when riding in them many times—all theory! Gingerly he turned on the ignition and very carefully inched his way out of the building. So far all right, he traveled the narrow roads, crowded with pedestrians, animals, bicycles and carts. He crept along, determined to deliver the vehicle without a mark on it, ignoring impatient motorists honking their horns and people who stopped to stare. His assignment completed, with the car safely in its new home, he returned to his ship and with relief reported to the captain his mission accomplished.

The spring of that year found Martin considering the path of his future, which he did not feel would be continuing in the regular Navy. He wrote to his mother that he was applying for the Fleet Air Arm: "This will not be absolutely binding, but allowing that I remain in, it is the only thing worthwhile as far as I am concerned—the air is the coming thing. In fact it has already come, but still is only in its youth. Each year, since I have been here, the aircraft and their carriers have played an increasingly important part in the fleet exercises." Definitely "in its youth," with all the attendant uncertainties, that news did not elicit a feeling of joy in the heart of his mother.

And there was another possibility. The Marquess had purchased a cattle ranch in 1912 at 100 Mile House in British Columbia, Canada. As was happening with others at that time, this was undertaken as an investment for the future. Having visited the property several times and continuing in touch with his agent, he was vividly cognizant of the improbability of operating the ranch as an absentee landlord. With the question mark around Martin's future becoming more pronounced, the possibility of his going to Canada to develop the potential of this investment began to emerge.

Contemplating his decision many years later, Martin said:

> Everything was beautifully set for what should unfold in the days to come, if I continued on in the usual, traditional way. But this was the thing that troubled me, because while there was everything there apparently, I knew it wasn't what I am. The easy way, in a sense, in such case is to accept the status quo and stay with that, but there was a compulsion in me which said, in effect, "You need to find yourself, and you can't find yourself if you're wrapped in all these swaddling clothes."

So, after his last few months in the Royal Navy studying at the Greenwich Royal

Naval College, he retired as an acting sub-lieutenant and before long found himself on the Canadian Pacific liner, *Duchess of Richmond,* in the Liverpool harbor, setting sail with his father for Canada. It was on a dreary April day in 1930, and he was very young. As he waved farewell to his mother and family, in his handsome face with its strong yet delicately refined features and striking blue eyes could be read the indomitable yet pliable will that would carry him through the rugged route he had chosen.

It is difficult to relate to the abrupt and total contrast between that primitive place which was his destination in the wilds of a huge continent, and the palatial home in which he had been born. Those were pioneering days in the interior of British Columbia in western Canada. But he was obeying a compulsion that defied any rationalizing of the mind, on his way to the place he would call home for the rest of his life.

It was an eight-day journey, on a rough and bitterly cold Atlantic, which afforded Martin and his father opportunity for a more intimate interchange than they had known. After a brief stop in Quebec city, they went on to Montreal, where they continued their travel by train. Martin's twenty-first birthday was celebrated on the Canadian Pacific on April 27th as they crossed the empty prairies of Manitoba and Saskatchewan. His first glimpse of this vast country kept changing as the miles sped by, through the Rocky Mountains to their destination at Kamloops in British Columbia.

There they were met and welcomed by C. G. Cowan, Lord Exeter's agent, through whom the Bridge Creek Ranch at 100 Mile House had been purchased. From Londonderry, Ireland, Cowan had a colorful past, as did most who settled in that rugged area. A big-game hunter, he had been in the Boer War and the Northwest Mounted Police.

The final leg of the journey was by car, through Cache Creek into the Cariboo, a four-thousand-feet-high plateau between the Coast Range and the Rockies. Martin viewed the majestic scenery he would love for the rest of his life, climaxed by arriving at 100 Mile House, set in a valley surrounded in the distance on all sides by hills thickly covered with fir and pine.

The highway was begun at the time of the Cariboo gold rush in 1860 (the same as the renowned one in San Francisco, then known as Stanleyville), with its destination the tiny town of Barkerville, a day's journey north of 100 Mile House. The name of the latter stemmed from its location one hundred miles from the beginning of the gold trail at Lillooet. Before that it was known as Bridge Creek.

The "stopping house" which greeted Martin at his new home was a sorry sight, built in 1862 to accommodate miners headed north in their search for gold, fur traders, and whoever else would be in that area for whatever reason!

If ever a man was confronted with a challenge, it was Martin. His background experience exclusively in the Navy, he found himself manager of the fifteen-thousand-acre Bridge Creek Cattle Ranch which contained eight hundred cattle. There was every kind of hard physical labor to be done (and he came to be very familiar with each one) in the blistering heat of summer and bitter cold of winter, with 50 below zero not uncommon. Workers were scarce, and the timing incredible, with the Great Depression in full swing.

His diminutive (eight by nine feet) room in the old stopping house accommodated a tiny cot which was, of necessity, very close to the small cook stove used for heating; so in the cold night when the fire went out he would stuff the kindling (which he had at arm's length) into the firebox and duck back under the covers.

The stopping house was a busy place, with great pack trains and freight wagons stopping on the way to the goldfields, for a meal or for the night. There were also the Concord stagecoaches, brightly decorated with canvas tops. Later ranchers settled in the area, cowboys eventually replacing miners and prospectors.

With such activity, there were of course other facilities appearing as time passed. A large barn still stands and is in use today, a noble relic of the past. There was a general store and post office, and across the road on the property behind the stopping house a beautiful log building which was used as a carpentry and blacksmithing shop, built by Syd Stephenson. He and his brother Frank owned the property before Lord Exeter and were responsible for its brand, a quarter circle over a reversed "S," a bridge over a running creek. Ten to twelve people comprised the population: ranchhands, the storekeeper and his wife, a government telegraphist and his housekeeper.

Martin's father left for England after a month's stay, during which time they had made some vital decisions, such as building a hotel or lodge; the old one *was* impossible! A novice in that field, Martin came prepared with a book, *Every Man His Own Builder*. From its preface:

> In the following pages I have endeavoured to show how any man of normal bodily strength can at need build his own house without the aid of skilled labour. To the ordinary Englishman the idea of building houses without skilled artisans no doubt appears strange, but to our colonists, who in out of the way places and for various reasons—often financial ones—are frequently compelled to do so, it will appear far less strange. It is my hope that when he has read this book the idea of the impossibility or incongruity of building a house with other than skilled labour will also have disappeared from the most stay at home and old-fashioned Englishman's mind.

That was one very "new-fashioned" Englishman who promptly set about to build. His first project stands today, a solid and beautiful testimony to the practical nature of the spirit of God when allowed to operate in accordance with the laws that govern the universe—as well as the atom. Martin took a correspondence course in architecture, plumbing, wiring, etc. He loved drawing plans and his expert training in that field in the Navy was invaluable.

Lumber was hauled from a small sawmill a mile away from the Ranch. There were times when Martin ran it himself. Often there were catastrophes, for which there were no answers in the book. That was when Martin's innate ingenuity came into play, and it found many avenues for practice. That ability to create, at any level, would be a powerful asset in working with people in years to come.

There are wonderful tales of how water was brought in, and eventually electricity. They cannot all be told here, but after two years the 100 Mile House Lodge was built, an amazing achievement considering the short season available for that sort of work.

It would be ridiculous to undertake to manage a cattle ranch without being a cowboy! Martin, who always had a love for horses, learned new ways of relating to them, and it was a privilege to observe man and beast as they worked in oneness and the joy and satisfaction so obvious in each.

Charles Cowan kept in touch with Lord Exeter and on July 10, 1930, wrote: "It does not take long to find out that Martin is OK for us out here. We are right glad to have him and I am so very pleased to find everyone as well as myself looking upon him as quite settled and one of ourselves. He is working very hard." With his health failing, it was not long before Cowan asked Martin if he would assume the management of the Highland Ranch, with its headquarters at the 105 Mile House. The combined acreage of the two ranches was fifty-thousand, a heavy responsibility, especially for someone learning the business, but Martin accepted and operated the two as one. Alex Morrison, a shepherd from the Isle of Skye, was foreman of the Highland until its sale and later became foreman of the Bridge Creek Ranch, a tried and true friend to Martin. (He later married Harriet, a faithful waitress in The Lodge for many years.)

The Canim Lake Indian reserve, twenty miles east of 100 Mile House, was a source of some of Martin's recruits for haying, cowboying and branding. Stampedes and rodeos, also the renowned bull sales, were, and still are, events held at Williams Lake.

A game of polo afforded some familiar relaxation in the early days for Martin, who had brought his equipment from England. The cowboys learned the game, after a fashion, and there was the occasional welcome visit of Constable Green from Clinton, an excellent player who had served in the cavalry in India. The large area west of 100 Mile House was the (not very smooth) playing field.

A winter sport was skiing. Lacking equipment, Martin resorted to sawing a birch board in half, to which he attached thongs to hold his boots.

The opening of the "100 Mile Lodge" took place in April 1932. Nine rooms on the second floor afforded excellent accommodation for travelers, with an inviting living room and dining rooms downstairs, also an apartment for Martin. The beautiful fireplaces seemed to warm the whole Cariboo!

Martin's parents were present on the great day, the first guests to sign the register. The entire population of 100 Mile House was proud to be in attendance. It was a fulfilling time for Martin, and indeed for his family. His parents stayed several months, enjoying the fast-changing Cariboo, and returned to England in July.

People began to appear from many places, and the register for that first summer at The Lodge makes interesting reading. From Shanghai was a Mr. Campbell, Victor Cazalet from the British House of Commons, Lord Brassey and son Peter from England. Peter later married Martin's sister Romayne. It was a rewarding time when Michael Culme-Seymour, Martin's lifelong friend, visited while serving in Ottawa as aide-de-camp to the Governor-General.

The Lodge very quickly became a haven in the "wilderness," the finest facility on that long road from the coast into the north country. Today the "Alaska Highway," greatly widened and improved, with its constant flow of traffic day and night, is the same as that first road that saw the old stagecoaches bumping their way over tortuous terrain. The Depression was still an inhibiting factor in the lives of people, and Martin made a rule that he would feed anyone who needed it, if they did some work—of which there was plenty.

It was in that year that Uranda, in Nashville, Tennessee, was moving to the climactic experience of illumination which would change the course of his, and Martin's, life.

In an article for publication Martin described the abundance of available food thus:

There are plenty of good trout in the lakes and creeks asking to be caught if there is a moment to spare; not to mention duck, geese, different kinds of grouse and, in some parts, even pheasants for the shotgun; or moose, caribou, mule deer, bear, mountain sheep, and goat for the rifle.

Certainly there were times of loneliness and homesickness, which he kept to himself, and the occasional suggestion from his brother David overseas that he return to Burghley and assist in running the estate. But the conviction persisted that he was in the place where he belonged.

What about the little lady with whom Martin had fallen in love? From an aristocratic background, her father was a senior civil servant, and Edith and her brother Aurel spent many happy days of their childhood in sunny Hungary, Budapest, near the Tisza River. Martin had continued correspondence with Edith since their first meeting in Monaco, and events moved to the point where on January 18, 1934, in a small church in England, Martin married Miss Edith Lillian Csanady de Telegd.

After a honeymoon in Portugal, Martin brought his bride to 100 Mile House. It was spring in the Cariboo. The couple shared a love for horseback riding, and also sailing, which they enjoyed in a small boat which Martin kept at a lake at the "108." He never lost his love for sailing; the Navy did have an impact. In the winter they would ski on the hills.

A son was born to Martin and Edith on September 1, 1935, in the Royal Inland Hospital at Kamloops, B.C., and named William Michael Anthony Cecil. Martin's parents and sister Romayne attended the christening at 100 Mile House.

This was a difficult time, still in the Depression. The fact that Martin was born in a palace to an auspicious and ancient family caused some to think he had unlimited resources. Nothing could have been further from the fact. The allowance from his father was slight, and it would be years before he could receive remuneration from the ranch, though he had to pay his workers. I am caused to recall the beginnings of Uranda, and later Sunrise Ranch. Regardless of the conditions surrounding his birth, Martin too found himself in the position of beginning the creation of something great, the significance of which he was unaware, from a seeming void. It was pregnant with the embryonic substance of the spirit of God, awaiting rich substantial form in its seasons through His faithful servant.

In those days of privation for the entire country, cattle ranching was a challenge, and the cattlemen in the Cariboo area were centralizing their operations in order to survive. In that situation, Martin found himself an increasingly important part of the industry. It was never his desire to be in the public eye, content to play his vital part in a comfortable background. But that was not to be, then or in the days to come, and he soon found himself vice-president of the Cariboo Stockmen's Association in 1934. By 1937 the co-operative marketing method initiated by that body was adopted throughout British Columbia and beyond as the means of survival for the industry.

Martin's managerial responsibilities included just about everything then in evidence at 100 Mile House: overseeing the operation of the Lodge and General Store and keeping the books. He was Postmaster for many years, responsible for the mail reaching its destination at Exeter station via the Pacific Great Eastern railway (well-earned nicknames for PGE being "Please Go Easy" and "Past God's Endurance"). When the water and power systems refused to work, he was the one to be roused at any hour of day or night. Under his direction the first school was built in the area, and of necessity he filled the position of agent for the Imperial Oil station for twenty years.

There was as yet no doctor or hospital at 100 Mile House, and in the spring of 1937

Martin had an emergency operation for acute appendicitis at Kamloops, arriving just in time after a fast and fearfully bumpy ride on Cariboo roads.

The old stopping place had finally seen its day. It burned to the ground, the value then purely historical in view of the functional facility of The Lodge which was becoming very popular.

It was observed that there were more California license plates on the Cariboo Road than those of B.C. One visitor was ex-United States President Herbert Hoover.

By 1938, with war an inescapable reality, the Depression was over, with employment in munition plants, factories, on farms, and of course the armed services.

In the summer of 1939 Martin made the acquaintance of Conrad O'Brien-ffrench (known then by his nickname "Tim"), from Vancouver Island, originally Ireland, England, Italy—and other places! He came to visit Lady Romayne, Martin's sister, who was staying at the "100." As with most occurrences in our lives, that was the obvious reason, the deeper, more vital ones to be revealed in season. An immediate life-long bond was formed between the two men. His visit was brief; and with the announcement in September that war had begun, Lady Romayne left immediately for England.

Though Lady Martin had always shared Martin's interest in the spiritual life, she was experiencing difficulty in adjusting to the dramatic changes which living in the Cariboo demanded of her. While none of that ever altered the beautiful expression of her sweet spirit, she was increasingly enveloped in an atmosphere of depression. In an effort to assist his wife, at some point Martin arranged for a residence in Vancouver, where she could spend some time and in which he joined her whenever possible. They studied Rosicrucianism and read other books of that nature, as well as together taking a course which Martin hoped would be helpful to Edith.

Then it happened. A friend of Edith's in Vancouver, Sylvia Little, was on the Emissary mailing list and suggested that Martin write to Lloyd Arthur Meeker and request to receive the Emissary mailings. Martin acted immediately and on December 23rd received a letter and parcel of literature. As he sat down and read his treasure he knew the meaning of the words in the ancient Psalm: "He prepareth a table before me in the presence of mine enemies"—in the presence of all the things in his own consciousness which had been threatening the harmony of his world. And he began to know that the peace that passes human understanding comes not by seeking to be free from the "enemies," but in partaking of the feast available in any moment, already prepared by the One of whose presence he was fast becoming aware. This was expressed in his first letter to Uranda:

> It was indeed a great joy to receive and peruse your correspondence and literature, adding to my conviction of the presence within of One who surely knows.

I recognize how necessary it is to cut a channel so that reality may flow out into expression through every activity of my life. I am thankful to have been led to you, and I give thanks for the many truths you have sent forth that have already found a response in me.

And so on that April day in 1940 he was to meet Uranda, who had informed him of his desire to give a series of talks in Vancouver and asked if he would help with arrangements. The answer of course was affirmative and Martin had the setting prepared in the Georgia Street Medical Dental Building. In their house on Blenheim Street, with Edith and Michael, then four years old, he nervously awaited the arrival of this man. Commenting later, he said, "In his unassuming charm he revealed reality in a manner which appealed to me as genuine and fulfilled my expectations to the greatest possible degree. After that first meeting all my doubts and fears vanished." He said he had expected an older man, associating his wisdom with many years of seasoned experience, surprised that he was of his own age. He experienced an overwhelming sensation that he had known him before.

These two men epitomize to me the essences of masculine charm, yet it would be difficult to find such complete opposites in appearance and nature as were evident in Uranda and Martin. About the same height of six feet, strongly built and lean, they were both very active. The softness of Uranda's features did not conceal their strength. His nose had a slight curve which could be the despair of a portrait artist. Martin's was aquiline, curving in the other direction, contributing to what could have been a haughty mien, heritage of many generations. In him it proclaimed an unwavering dedication to purpose. There was a dimple in the strong chin, and his wide and generous smile was instant and irresistible. Eyes of clearest blue conveyed the profound blessing of still waters or, when needed, flashed as with the steel of a sword. Again, though different in appearance, Uranda's eyes carried the same message in their magnificent depths.

The inviolate dedication to the Truth which they came to bring into the world characterized both, yet their modes of expression differed greatly. Uranda loved to talk, and his words flowed freely and eloquently. Martin preferred to be in the background and had to learn to speak to groups, which he certainly did. An element of shyness never completely disappeared, to the delight of all who truly knew him. There was a resonant and penetrating quality to their voices, again of a different nature, and dominant in each was a sense of humor. Their laughter was infectious and when combined (which happened often) I'm sure could be heard in the far reaches of the cosmos.

Among those who attended Uranda's talks in Vancouver were Edith's brother, Aurel, and Conrad O'Brien-ffrench. Martin wrote, afterward:

You have given me a picture of true greatness, a picture that has been hover-ing in my consciousness but had never until now become fully revealed to my outer vision. It is a picture that is joyously familiar now that it is more fully perceived.

Martin began to feel old ties loosening, and shared it with Uranda in a letter:

Being born a member of an aristocratic English family, a certain friction has developed between them and myself. I know that some important and necessary changes are taking place through this, because probably what troubles me most is the feeling that I am losing something. This "something" I must willingly let go. Though my immediate course is clear to me and I cannot falter, yet the dropping away of these ties causes a certain uneasiness within. May the spirit of God, to which I can alone be loyal, guide me in the way.

An integral part of the core of this world's pattern of royalty and nobility, this young man was called to relinquish an identity with his hereditary past, and he felt as though his very roots were being dissolved.

He also recognized "a field of service just coming within the range of my vision which as it were runs parallel with my material 'job.'" All that he had accomplished, and was taking shape out of the misty future, was viewed in a new perspective, wherein externals were tools by which the great purpose for which he was on earth could be achieved.

In 1940 Martin became president of the Cariboo Stockmen's Association. In 1943 he was a key figure in forming the Cariboo Cattlemen's Association and was its first presi-dent. This all played an essential part in unifying the cattle industry in British Columbia and eventually producing a Canadian Cattlemen's Association.

3

THE HARVEST

September 1940 ~ February 1942

T he year 1940 was marked with momentous milestones along an ever-widening highway. Uranda traveled extensively, giving public talks in Seattle, Washington; Butte, Montana; Milwaukee, Wisconsin; Chicago, Illinois; and Pontiac, Michigan.

In September Uranda appointed Richard and Dorothy Thompson to coordinate the activities of the Church in Ontario. Born in Cheshire, England, Richard attended King William's College on the Isle of Man, and later became head of the school. After a time in Cambridge in 1921, he was in business in Liverpool when he met Dorothy Ada Yeadon whom he married in 1927. They had a daughter, Mary. He taught at St. Lawrence College, Ramsgate, then went to Dulwich College in London, also Victoria College in Jersey, Channel Islands. Intensely interested in the Social Credit government in Alberta, he moved to Canada with Dorothy and Mary in 1936.

Later they settled for a time in Winnipeg where they came in contact with a chiropractor, Dr. John Oshanek, and formed a group for the study of philosophies and religions, in the course of which they received a copy of Uranda's *Seven Steps to the Temple of Light* from John. That was the open door to their association with the Emissaries of

Divine Light and Uranda. In Toronto Richard taught at Upper Canada College, then moved to Trinity College in Port Hope, designated the finest boys' school in Canada. It was then, in 1940, that Richard and Dorothy accepted Uranda's invitation to provide a focus for the Emissaries in Ontario.

Dr. George Shears and his work first came to Uranda's attention that year through Dr. Hall, a chiropractor in Palo Alto, California, who had attended a number of Uranda's services. A great man, George was destined to play a role of immeasurable value with Uranda, though a decade would pass before they made personal contact.

At that time the military draft was reinstated, and Uranda, being of draft age himself, admonished all who were eligible not to seek to evade registration.

The tour of the "Rolling Embassy" progressed. In a message of September 16 it was announced: "Tomorrow evening we begin our series of public services in Pittsburgh, Pennsylvania. What will the harvest be?" It so happened that I was part of that harvest.

That date proved to be as important for me as the day I was born. It was on a memorable night in Pittsburgh, a suburb of which was my birthplace and home until that time, that I met him. My life was changed, forever, from that moment.

How did I meet him? The answer to that question will always fill me with awe at the wonder-working power of the spirit to move human flesh. It was like this:

One busy day at the office (I was married but still working for a while), when I would have liked nothing better than to go home and relax, I had a strong urge to call a friend, Kate Moyer, my husband's cousin, who worked in a different part of that large city. She had often invited me to stay in town after work to hear speakers on esoteric subjects, in which she was avidly interested. My hungry heart would thrill at first, but I soon became disenchanted as the flaws inevitably appeared, in speaker and teaching.

On this occasion I asked her if she was going to stay in town and she said yes—but volunteered nothing further. It went completely against my nature to impose myself on anyone, and I was appalled at what I was doing; but I seemed to have no choice, and persisted. I asked her if she would mind if I joined her and she said she would love it. So I did. During dinner I relentlessly pursued the course I was on, and asked her why she was staying in town. She said, "It's another one of 'those' speakers, and I didn't think you would be interested; I didn't want to bother you." I asked his name, and when she answered "Uranda," every fiber in my being resonated to the music of the spheres. I said I would like to go, and she said, "I'd be delighted; you know I would." And I did know. Kate was a beloved friend, simply being considerate.

It was in a large hall in Pittsburgh that I saw him for the first time—in a glow of radiance. And I heard him. I knew I would never be the same again. My presence there was the result of my own action, because I refused to let the "reasoning" of my mind deny the seemingly irrational impulse of the spirit.

His talk was entitled "Revelation Revealed," part of a series of public talks in the area, beginning on September 17. I took immediate steps to be on the mailing list, and found, with each paper released, a door opening into new worlds. A group had begun to form in Pittsburgh, under the leadership of John and Maud Martin, an elderly couple. I regularly attended meetings in their home—in the East End, as far away from my home as possible!—and soon became the secretary, sending in weekly reports to Uranda at Headquarters.

Uranda's tour continued. It took seven months, from April to November, and covered 18,000 miles. The first of its kind in the ministry, presaging what would prove to be the way of life from then on, it included cities in California; Chicago, Illinois; Pittsburgh, Ardmore and Reading, Pennsylvania; and Bridgeport, Connecticut; culminating in Florida. On November 8 the ministry was notified of Uranda's address: P.O. Box 9045, Sulpher Springs Station, Tampa, Florida.

It may be of interest to note an analysis of the monetary income during September, October and November of 1940, those months being considered as representative. This was based on the enrollment of 400 persons in good standing, excluding a few in distant lands.

Of those 400, 148 did not contribute anything during the three-month period. The average monthly contribution of the remaining 252 for the three-month period was as follows:

15 who gave an average of from 3 cents to 29 cents a month,

52	"	"	33	"		
25	"	"	34	"	83	"
25	"	"	$1.00			
37	"	"	$1.01	1.99		
61	"	"	2.00	4.99		
37	"	"	5.00 or over per month			

Uranda commented, "On the basis of the above figures you can see that 98 persons, or the last two groups listed, gave the financial support that made this Service possible during those three months—and have, in fact, provided the necessary funds all through the year."

Copies of Volume One of *Talks Beside the Sun-Dial* were sent out as Christmas gifts to all in the ministry by Uranda and Wanu. The innate generosity of this man's spirit sought, always, to inspire that in others.

In January of 1941 Uranda spoke on the question in some minds, of individual function being opposed to collective:

> Let us briefly examine the principles involved in the action of some who have chosen to turn away. To illustrate, some have said, because William Oshanek pointed out in one of his recent papers that all would have to learn to stand on their own feet in this new cycle, that they chose to be "on their own" outside of the School and continue to function more fully in reality than if they were to remain. Here we see how the human mind twists to its own ends a perfectly true statement, using it as an excuse for wrong action. It is true that each must, for himself, learn to stand alone in the outer on the sure foundation. World conditions make it necessary for each unit in the whole to be ready to function as a true representative of the whole—but that cannot be achieved through segregation from the whole.

> We are arranging to begin immediately, in this new year, to hold special periods of radiation to all of you twice weekly, on Saturday and Wednesday evenings, for one-half hour beginning at nine o'clock.

Uranda was ever diligent in carefully watching over his people, a good shepherd. Accepting the responsibility of leading those who heard the Word, he gave all his strength to his great task.

In order to answer as much correspondence as possible, he utilized some rubber stamps containing messages such as "An excellent realization," "Keep on keeping on," etc., and others of a more corrective nature, inserting them in the appropriate places in letters. Also, a paper entitled "The Councillor" was initiated, the purpose of which was to publish some expressions by individuals, under the subheading "Gems of Realization." These were extracts from letters to him containing realizations of increased understanding of the truth. This proved invaluable in encouraging others to find ways of expressing their expansion of consciousness. Also, it was a revelation to read, in print, not only another's but one's own "gem"!

At this time Uranda's "Letters to You" and "A View from the Mountaintop" were released.

As is always true when one's service begins to expand, past events in personal life seem to become public property, subjects for discussion and dissection; and sentence is passed, in ignorance of all the factors involved. To answer questions in this regard, Fern wrote a special message in March of 1941.

> Although this paper will go out to the whole School, I should like it to be understood that it is written to the few who have been troubled about the points we shall consider, dealing with Uranda's early life. Yes, it is true that Uranda has been married before and has a fine daughter, eleven years of age.

It might be well to remember that his first marriage took place when he was a very young man. Also, that was before he was teaching.

Remember that although I was a Truth student, and my first recollections of life were of hearing the Bible read, listening to prayer, spending a great deal of time in church as a child, and later becoming an ardent student of philosophy, etc., not once since I first heard the truth as presented by Uranda have I had the slightest inclination to doubt.

The ministry was notified in April that Uranda and Fern were leaving Florida, destination Buffalo, New York. In that notice were comments referring to the general reaction to Wanu's message. Uranda said:

Many have taken the attitude that my first marriage was a "mistake," about which no one in the School should be concerned. It is true that it should not cause concern to any, but I could not agree that it was a mistake. Far from it. It was the only means by which I could lead the way to victory through a multitude of conditions, vibrations and experiences—not, as some have supposed, as needed training for my temple but as an example of correct function in meeting such problems as those involved.

Before dismissing the matter, I would emphasize another fact, for some have falsely accused Wanu of having something to do with the causing of that separation; but the fact is that the final choice had been established, and the separation completed, before I ever thought of Wanu other than as a very fine student in the School, or she thought of me in any way other than as her teacher whom she reverenced and respected. As these points and facts have been made clear we now leave the matter.

In "A Word to the Wise" several popular and controversial subjects were approached. Uranda said,

It is only as the ill conditions are brought to the surface, and dealt with frankly and squarely, that they can actually be eliminated. Some people have expressed the idea that there must be more things wrong with the people in the Third Sacred School than with any other group. I would state emphatically that such is not the case. The difference is that we bring the ill things out in the open, and deal with them, refusing to be ashamed of them; while in other activities they do everything possible to cover up anything that might not appear to be pleasing. Our Master said "Woe unto you, scribes and Pharisees, hypocrites! for ye are like unto whited sepulchres, which indeed appear beautiful outward, but are within full of dead men's bones, and of all uncleanness."

New vistas beckoned, and were opened up, in 1941. In June it was announced that three Sessions would be held that year. A Canadian Session was scheduled for July 9 through 20, in Winnipeg, Manitoba; the Eastern Division Session August 17 through 31, in Pittsburgh, Pennsylvania; and the Western Division Session would probably consist of one week of services in each of three cities: Seattle, Washington; San Francisco and Long Beach, California. The primary Session was to be held in Pittsburgh, and there would be no attempt to duplicate that Session in full at any of the other points.

The Canadian Summer Session was held, as announced, and in Uranda's words "carried through gloriously," with several brief services in Strathroy and Toronto. Following that, Uranda and Fern returned to Buffalo, New York.

So one year after Uranda had made his first appearance in Pittsburgh, people from all over the United States and Canada gathered for a Summer Session there in a beautiful old church on the North Side. His daughter Marjorie was there from California with her guardians, Buzz and Betty Armacost. Her mother was ill with tuberculosis in a sanatorium, and died a few years later.

Kathleen and Billie Groves, two sisters from Ravenden, a small town in Arkansas, were present. Their parents, David and Rosa Groves, were on the mailing list and there was another, older daughter, Rosalind. Kathleen was sixteen years old at this time, Billie a few years older. The Pittsburgh group had raised the funds to make their visit possible, having been alerted to the opportunity by Uranda.

Also attending was Dorothy Cameron, having come from the recent Session in Winnipeg, her place of residence. Her response at that time was of particular value to Uranda, and she was to play an important part in his life and that of the ministry shortly. It was obvious at the time that the Session produced much fruit, and hindsight reveals an interesting setting which included Fern, Dorothy and Kathleen all in the same place.

A few of the others attending were Richard and Dorothy Thompson with daughter Mary from Toronto; William Oshanek, Winnipeg; Joseph Wilson, New York; Sally Bainbridge, California; John and Maude Martin, Frank and Betty Protzman, Dr. Frank Hudson, all of Pittsburgh.

As for me, that intervening year had filled me with an all-consuming passion for the truth, for what I had always felt in my heart and hungered to hear expressed. Rather naively I sought to share this with my husband, Ezra William Van Duzen, who tried but simply could not relate. This caused a division to surface, which had always been there but was becoming painfully evident. However, a quality of unswerving loyalty is inbred in my nature, and I felt that our relationship required my complete devotion. This posed a challenge, as outworking events would prove.

Those were glorious days, with the Pittsburgh Sessions every morning, afternoon and evening. In the afternoon Uranda would often open it for interrogation, and his young and lovely daughter Marjorie was right there, freely asking one question after another. On one occasion Uranda commented, "I have to answer them; they're good questions." The rest of us were delighted; she opened up areas which most of us were hesitant to articulate, regarding the Motherland and the Earth and its peoples before the fall, and the room was filled with the magic of Uranda's reminiscent words.

Later Uranda spoke of his joy in the successful outworking of that Summer Session. All the services were recorded and were to be released in "as complete an expression as may be feasible, according to the response." There was enough material from those sessions to make several large books. He spoke on an average of at least five hours a day for fifteen days. Each service was taken down on dictaphone records, and a team of five expert transcribers, headed by Betty Armacost, Uranda's secretary, worked every morning to get the services into typewritten form. There were still over a hundred records yet to be transcribed after the Session. I took down in shorthand and then transcribed everything expressed during the intervals in which records were changed on the dictaphone, eliminating any gaps that would otherwise have appeared.

Also, under the instigation of Marjorie O'Connor of St. Louis, Missouri (our blind friend who participated in the Session), a Braille department was formed, a project to which many there contributed.

There was a delightful group of young people, from eight-year-old Mary Thompson through teen ages, and they enjoyed functioning together as a Young Explorers Club, under the effective chairmanship of Marjorie Lee Meeker.

Uranda gave the Second Ordination to Richard and Dorothy Thompson, with commendation for outstanding service.

The organization of the expanding body was discussed during these sessions, the incorporation of the Church having been completed in Buffalo, New York.

Uranda and Fern had no home at that time but lived in the trailer in which they had traveled on this extensive tour. Now the time of their togetherness was drawing to a close. An essential ingredient for Uranda's ministry during that period had been provided by Fern, who had a background of esoteric research and awareness. Emerging out of traumatic events in his childhood, followed by a marriage to Paulene Foster, a fine young woman who was a comfort and help in very limited physical circumstances and mother of his daughter, and leading into a healing ministry, he had met Fern. Together they moved through a cycle which arrived at a climactic point during that Session in Pittsburgh.

Returning from Winnipeg in October, Uranda spoke in a Personal Message of the publication of "The Dawning Day" as evidence of a new cycle of service into which we had entered. He also announced that he had shaved his beard, "the first time in three years." At about this time Headquarters was moved from Buffalo to Grand Forks, Iowa.

There followed an announcement which was to affect a number in the School in different ways. However, there would be many incidents in the history of this ministry whereby individuals would find their devotion to the Truth tested, and those who remained, without exception, would experience greatly increased strength and understanding.

I feel I owe you who are harmonizing faithfully in the Third Sacred School an explanation of some of the changes that have worked out during the past year, and of the policy which has been in effect during the past four years. From the time of my marriage with Fern she insisted on maintaining her concept of privacy, and as a result did not at any time wish me to let the School know our exact location. During our tours my refusal of dinner invitations was at her insistence. This hampered my ministry, but in that I received her with the expectation that she would work out into the fulness of the ideal, just as I have received all of the rest of you without expecting perfection to begin with, I allowed her to have her way.

When we left California in April of 1940 Fern stated positively that she did not wish to return to that state. I wished to be there in order to work from the Headquarters in Long Beach, but she refused, and at her insistence I finally agreed to take her to Florida. As a result I was under the handicap of attempting to carry on the work from a point about three thousand miles from Headquarters. Nevertheless, both the office workers in Long Beach and I made the best of this disadvantage, and served you to the fullest possible extent.

This Spring I again wished to return to California for a period before holding further services in the East, and again she objected, with the result that I found it necessary to establish a headquarters in the East. The headquarters in Buffalo was established in an effort to please Fern. The equipment was just arriving in Buffalo when I left for Canada to hold the Winnipeg Summer Session, and during that time she decided she would like to break up the Buffalo headquarters and move back to Long Beach. This is a sample of the erratic attitude and uncertain vibration which had developed and with which I have had to work.

I would here advise you that as a result of such attitudes, Fern and I have come to the parting of the ways. Those restrictions will no longer impose limits upon the School. As a result of this move to Grand Forks there will be a reduction in expenses at Headquarters. Also, being released from the necessity of spending a great deal of time attempting to help Fern find herself, my time will be more available in essential service to all of you.

In this new cycle it is my intention that your Headquarters will be a home where the workers may enjoy the natural home comforts, and where the students of the School will be free to come at all reasonable times. We will have an "open house" policy designed to place the entire School on a closer basis of fellowship and association whereby all may come to better know and understand each other. I am naturally a very sociable person, and I love to give instruction to the students in a sociable home atmosphere, around the dinner table or during a pleasant social evening. For over four years I have not been privileged to have a single student in my home as a guest, and no one ever sat down at our table with us to share a meal.

There will be no more withholding of my address, and no more secrecy about the place where I may stay. In the future wherever I go I will be happy to accept dinner invitations, to the degree that my time and work will allow. My own home, as well as Headquarters, will be a place where the workers and the students may enjoy happy evenings together. When I speak of social periods of fellowship I am not talking about empty hours of gossip and parties, but about that which is a true expression of the joys of living in a natural way.

The Lord is working all things out gloriously in the opening of this new cycle, and I look forward to your letters of response to this announcement, and to the greater opportunities now at hand to serve you and all responding ones everywhere. I am happy to say that Fern intends to continue as a student in the School.

Predictably, with the ingrained emotional patterns regarding the sanctity of marriage as established in the world in its present state, there were those who left the School at that time. However, it is remarkable to observe that through the years when a crisis arose, of whatever nature, the resultant process of "staying with the stuff," or moving out, unerringly brought about a clarification of the body which allowed a fresh breath of air to blow away the cobwebs. Uranda repeatedly found himself in the position of proving his absolute devotion to the Lord, that nothing else came first. "Thou shalt have no other gods before me," and it mattered not whether that "god" was a person or one of the crystallized concepts that have characterized fallen man.

His next step involved a visit to Winnipeg, where Dorothy Cameron lived with her family, which consisted of a married daughter who lived in Calgary, three other daughters and a son, the youngest, at home.

In November, in his first message from the new Headquarters in Grand Forks, a town of about twenty thousand, he spoke glowingly of the welcome he found from the people and business firms there. He added,

> I know that all of you will rejoice with me that my daughter, Marjorie Lee, will shortly be with us and that she will be privileged to share in the new home which I am establishing. Those of you who are parents will understand how very much this means to me, in that I have been separated from her most of the time for about five years.

In a Message of December 2, Uranda said:

> During the changes of the transition period from the second cycle, which has now closed, into the third cycle of my ministry, you have been tested, and being weighed in the balance you have not, as a whole, been found wanting. I am very happy to be able to tell you that even those of you, who were few in number, who did waver somewhat during the testing time have almost all allowed themselves to be drawn back upon the rock of reality. As soon as the Lord has provided me with the necessary freedom to let it be so, Dorothy Cameron will become my wife.

He answered those who said he must have made a mistake in marrying Wanu, assuring all that there was no mistake on his part and that all things were being caused to work out in perfection. An overview reveals a transcendent design at work in the affairs of men—in this as in all instances. Fern provided an essential element in the life and movement of Uranda and his ministry at that time, but there came a point when the unfoldment necessary for the body was impossible within the limitations imposed, not only upon him but the entire ministry.

At the close of that year the title "Uranda's Personal Message" was changed to "Bishop Uranda's Personal Message," which lasted only a few months, the final one being "Your Bishop's Personal Message."

In January of 1942, with World War Two in full swing, some people questioned participation in war-related activities. Uranda addressed this, giving assurance that it was right to participate in anything such as Red Cross, or civilian air raid protective work. He also pointed out that we are in position to offer special assistance if we are alert to opportunities to render spiritual aid in cases of responsive needs. He added that the Church certainly advocates full cooperation with all constructive government programs. He said:

> Remember that it is not by much talking of spiritual things that you can render the greatest aid, but by much living of spiritual truths in a practical, everyday manner. Avoid giving the impression that you are visionary or impractical. False impressions have been given of the work of the Church and School through much talking without first having true understanding. To those who are not acquainted with the Church and School you are a representative of the whole Church. If you are not certain of the correctness of what you are talking about, learn to keep still and say nothing. Let those who wish to know of our work write or come to Headquarters, for our work is open to the inspection of all.

Shortly after this, Dorothy sent out a message entitled "My Word to You." It was a homey, newsy letter, beginning with the information that Uranda had started to grow his beard again.

This was followed soon by a Message from Uranda in which he stated that the recent outworking of events should not be taken as a reflection against Fern.

> It should be recognized that to the degree that she continues to carry on in harmonization and reality she shall surely be drawn into the fulness of that which is right for her, just as surely as that is true for the rest of you.

> There have been many ideas expressed in the School about cosmic mates which I have not endorsed and I have discouraged that general consideration, pointing out that whether or not people were cosmic mates was of little importance in the present outworking. The important thing is for each one to let the reality of his own being come forth here and now under the circumstances in which he finds himself in accomplishing the work which is at hand. If there was less talking about things that are not understood, and more *doing* in the realm of that which is seen and recognized, that which is not understood would shortly be clarified. If more consideration was given to the necessities of the outer planes, so that there was understanding of that, it would be much easier to understand the inner reality.

> There have been a few instances where individuals have read their own meanings into my words and jumped to the conclusion that I was advocating so-called "free love." Such ideas are utterly false and I have never said anything that would provide a basis for such wrong conclusions.

It was announced that the headquarters and office in Winnipeg were closed, and no more lessons would be published or distributed in Canada, this in view of the uncertainty of Uranda's location in the immediate future.

He and Dorothy Cameron were married in Salt Lake City, Utah, on February 12, 1942, with Sonya, Dorothy's daughter, in attendance. On the way home to Grand Forks (where the headquarters would be located for an indeterminate period), they held a service in Helena, Montana.

Uranda had looked forward over the years to having his daughter Marjorie be a part of his family, and in a message released in March he outlined the reasons why it would not happen at that time. Marjorie had many challenges in her childhood, and it would be a while yet before she would find a home with her father.

4

SEARCH FOR HEADQUARTERS

April 1942 ~ November 1944

*I*n response to some questions regarding the buying of bonds, Uranda said that it is lending money to the government and there need be no hesitation in doing so, pointing out that when you have lent this money you are not responsible for the government's use of it.

In the ensuing period, with the establishing of Uranda's residence not yet settled, the headquarters in Grand Forks was being closed, and members of the Church advised that mail should be sent to the legal headquarters in Williamsville, New York, where Joseph T. Wilson, Vice President of the Church Board, would forward it to Uranda.

William Oshanek and Muriel Lambert were married on April 16 and were residing in Winnipeg, rendering valuable service there.

A new series of Instruction Papers entitled "The Open Bible" was ready for release.

In April Uranda and Dorothy were located at Excelsior, Minnesota, near Minneapolis. Uranda spoke of his dream of many years of finding a setting such as this that would be ideal for a permanent headquarters of the Church, a beautiful place in the country where those who wished might come for a vacation, or if in position to do so could remain as long as they chose.

He described the thirty-acre spot, by a beautiful lake, where they could grow any-thing they desired in the rich soil, and raise cows, goats and chickens. Swimming, boat-ing and fishing possibilities were abundant. An old hotel held great promise for accom-modations, plus a large number of fine cabins ready for almost immediate use. There were over thirty buildings on the property.

The owners had reached the point in their declining years when it was necessary to dispose of the property, though they had in the past refused to sell for $85,000. Uranda was offered the property at a price of $30,000 (a monstrous sum in those days), one half down and terms on the balance. "We know that this sum cannot be raised in the School," he said, "so my only reason for telling you of it is, first, that you may join with us in prayer that the way may open in some manner for us to secure this place for a home for the Church, and, second, that those of you who feel that you might take advantage of such an opportunity if we do secure it may write and tell us so."

One can feel the poignant longing in his heart, and though the fulfilment of that dream was not possible at that time his limitless vision was never caused to shrink nor its sparkling clarity tarnish. This applied to all aspects of his living and mission, and through the years it has been proven that the vitality of his dream was not lost but found the form and substance possible as the years unfolded.

Later he reported that since he had described the property in Excelsior the income of the Church had fallen off to a very marked degree. "Where there is no vision the people perish" was his comment. He also acknowledged the vision of those faithful in steward-ship. He continued with some interesting observations.

It appears that some among you have jumped to the conclusion that if we could talk about purchasing a $30,000 place we must have ample funds at our command.

Because we were thinking of you and the welfare of the entire Church we took you as a whole into our confidence, but some do not have the ability to envision future possibilities without allowing a sense of futility in relation to greater things of a potential nature to become a sense of futility in relation to present things of a smaller nature. Because some of you could not see how a $30,000 place could be secured in the future you have apparently felt that the comparatively small amounts that you could give now were of no importance.

I presented the matter to you that through your unified response and prayers the way might be opened for us to secure such a place in due season. Instead of whole-hearted response, some questioned the wisdom of having such a place. Some thought it was too cold in this vicinity, some wished it could be in California, and some wished it could be in the eastern states. All in all, while a goodly number of you responded on an excellent vibration, the lack of sufficient vision and response to cooperate fully has prevented us from doing anything effective in this direction, and has also worked a decided hardship on the Service.

Their next location, that summer, was in Hot Springs, South Dakota, with a General Delivery address. In his message Uranda warned the Church about the consequences of a lack of vision and made a remarkable proposal, with the preparatory words:

Coordination of futuristic vision and present action is most essential to the accomplishment of the mighty task to which we are called. So-called spiritual people have been inclined to hold themselves aloof from material activities with the idea that they were above such things, which proves they do not know what true spirituality is. Recently when I portrayed the possibility of a place for a permanent headquarters there were those who were surprised that I would consider such a thing, because they felt that events were working out too rapidly to make such a place practical, and also that I should be more or less above a consideration of things at that level.

For many years I have had a vision of a possibility. This does not mean that the outline which I am about to present will necessarily be fulfilled either in detail or in the manner presented.

Let us now consider the outline of a possibility which could be very easily acccomplished, and which would greatly facilitate the outworking of cosmic events in relation to the world. If some of you were somewhat staggered at the thought of securing a thirty thousand dollar place for a permanent headquarters I would suggest that you find an easy chair and take a deep breath before proceeding. I trust that no one will be foolish enough to suppose that I give the following outline just to be talking, or just to amuse you. I have a number of deep and fundamental reasons for this presentation, and it will be of value in the service of the Lord and in the outworking of the cosmic plan to the degree of your response and to the degree that you let your consciousness expand on the vibrations of the outline which I present. Actually, while some of you may think the thing that I am about to present is a "big order," it is an insignificant matter as compared with the complete outworking of that toward which we are moving.

If you are great enough to comprehend this presentation, and if your response is deep enough to allow you to conceive of the possibility of its fulfilment, you may be assured that you will, in due season, be great enough to take part in the greater things to be accomplished in the more distant future. If the magnitude of any given task is greater than the magnitude of your own manifest consciousness and being, you thereby automatically classify yourself as being more insignificant than the material things which you consider. Man was created to have dominion over the world. Every true Emissary recognizes that the purpose of this Service is to restore that dominion. "A word to the wise is sufficient."

The program which I have mentioned would require the small sum of thirty million dollars to start it. That may sound like a great deal of money to some of you, but actually it is not so very much when compared to the wealth there is in the world and when compared to the amount of money being spent daily, and almost hourly, on activities that are generally of a destructive nature. We may then change the method of presentation for the moment to a basis of a consideration of what I would do if I had thirty million dollars at my command now. You should realize from a consideration of the above that it is not at all impossible that such a sum might be provided for the Lord's Service in the near future. By this I do not say that it will, nor do I know how such a possibility might outmanifest. If, then, the world response to reality were to provide this Service with thirty million dollars, the following is an outline of the possible use to which I might put it.

The first step in Uranda's dream would involve the purchase of a thousand acres of land "in the proper location, upon which would be erected buildings, a central settlement of Emissaries who had proven worthy of such a responsibility." One section would be devoted to farming and gardening "on a comparatively large scale." A model dairy would be included, milk goats, chickens and other types of fowl, an apiary. All food products and supplies essential would be grown on the place, making it as self-sustaining as possible.

There was to be a church building for services; a school for children and young people, initially for the first twelve grades, with accredited teachers; a school for the training of ministers; a large sanatorium with capable and licensed practitioners in all fields; music would be given a special place. A printing plant would be provided, and there would be provision for translating, making our literature available for all nations. In season broadcasts to other countries, particularly South America, would be anticipated. Our work in Braille translation would be greatly augmented. As rapidly as ministers could be ordained, branch activities all over the world would be undertaken.

Another message followed swiftly with the report that "we are now engaged in a very important undertaking by which we are proving the effectiveness of the principles of reality in practical application in the realm of the business world. The Lord is blessing us in most wonderful ways, and when success crowns our activities, there will be additional funds available for our work."

Not long after this Uranda announced that he and Dorothy wished to visit the eastern portion of the United States and Canada, and that with gasoline rationing they would go in easy stages by car, and by train as much as possible, depending on the funds available.

On September 16, 1942, the tenth anniversary of his ministry, Uranda said:

> As the world has forgotten God and turned from Him who is the source of life, it must pay the price of its own folly. However, let each one remember that there are hundreds of thousands of fine men and women in all walks of life, and in all parts of the world, whose lives are honestly dedicated to the high ideals for which we stand—and that which all of these sincere ones are doing is of vital importance in the fulfilment of the plan of God. It is needful that you always remember this great fact—for we are not alone in our determination to do the will of God. The noble qualities of divine nature are to be found in people all around us, and you will contact them in the most unexpected ways and places. They are filling their places, doing that which they are supposed to do, to a very high degree. It is not needful that you should try to judge them, or tell them what they should or should not do or believe. It is for you to fill your place by doing that for which you are responsible, thereby letting your Light shine.
>
> The world is being shaken, as by a mighty wind, and that shaking is causing the real ones to go up and the unreal ones to come down. When you are under pressure you reveal what you are. Sometimes it seems that the pressure lasts a very long time—and with the world as it now is that can be expected.
>
> Discouragement, a feeling of "what's the use," opens the way for failure. We have to keep at it, day in and day out, without let-up, to endure to the end. Evil is so entrenched in the world, and its proponents can dodge the real issue for a time in so many different ways, that it sometimes seems hopeless. As we move forward our problems do not lessen; they increase. Only in the strength of God can any endure unto the end—in meeting your problems day by day.

In "A Special Message to the Church" in November Uranda dealt with a delicate subject, introducing it with extreme care. It related to one's attitude toward war. He cautioned that every true Emissary is always willing to learn and to let his consciousness expand. He admonished each one to read prayerfully to avoid jumping to false conclusions, emphasizing the need to understand both the letter and the spirit of the words.

He said:

> Grave responsibility rests upon your Bishop, and in piloting the Church body through the troubled waters of the present world turmoil I am called upon to set a course that is consistent with the needs in the world and harmonious with divine principles. You may abide in the assurance that full understanding will appear in due season.
>
> As we consider the cosmic forces which are possible of release in the earth, we know that if we were of a sufficient number, and all were fully trained in the way of the Lord, and properly placed in the world, it would be possible to release a current of divine power so strong and all-inclusive that those who do wickedly and have chosen the way of evil would be almost instantly annihilated from the face of the earth.
>
> The commandment, "Thou shalt not kill," cannot be violated by the destruction of that which is already dead. In Ecclesiastes 3:1-8 we find an outline of facts which is in harmony with reality. In the third verse it will be noted that there is a "time to kill." Also, in the eighth verse, we note that there is "a time of war and a time of peace." We all look forward with confident expectation to the time of true and lasting peace, but we are living now in a time of war.
>
> We did not cause the war. We desired to avoid the necessity of war. Before the final choices were made it was necessary for us to place our choice on record, and this we did as a Church with the issuance of the paper entitled "Our Attitude Toward War." However, since the issuance of that paper our country has become involved in war, and also the definite choices of those responsible for the war have been established. These facts free us from the limitations which were originally essential, that we may act in harmony with reality on the basis of the choices which have been manifest. We cannot endorse all phases of the activities of many participating in the war activities of our nation, but under present world conditions certain limitations and ill conditions must be anticipated. We cannot endorse activities, for instance, of those who are utilizing the war to make money out of the life blood of human beings. We cannot endorse those who lend themselves to dishonorable and unjust activities. We cannot endorse that which is less than the truth and freedom and high morality which is established as the standard of life symbolized by our flag.

We realize that some in our nation and in our allied nations are inclined to lose sight of true spiritual values and consequently are more or less subject to the same evils of attitude and nature as those portrayed in the nations against which our country has been called to fight. This is not remaining true to that for which our flag stands.

Our President, and certain Army leaders, have gone on record to the effect that we should not, individually and as a nation, be motivated by hatred or a desire for revenge. We cannot endorse any attitude based upon a desire for revenge against a people as a whole which has become subject to evil leaders. If we recognize the presence of injustice, we ourselves must remain just, and be merciful to those who are not individually responsible for atrocities. We ourselves must remain true to that for which we claim, as a nation, to fight.

It is to be remembered that the Church still endorses non-combatant activity for its members but there is, at the same time, a provision for more flexible function according to recent needs and developments.

In "Your Bishop's Personal Message" of January 14, 1943, Uranda emphasized a vital point:

There are those who are inclined to either disregard or resent the expression of ministry from anyone but myself—not that there have not been plenty who objected to me! Rev. William Oshanek had to meet this sort of thing, and now Robert Patton is beginning to. Here are men who are giving themselves willingly and selflessly to the Lord's service. How *should* they be received? How *are* they received? They are not trying to be an imitation of me; if they were I would not deem them ready to serve you. Their ministry is as individual as mine, and they are filling necessary places in the scheme of things. Who among you is worthy to set yourselves up in judgment of those whom I commend unto you in ministry? The outer mind is a sly thing, even among Emissaries! Students of the Third Sacred School should, by this time, be well trained in the art of *looking* for that which is fine and helpful and lovely.

At this time Joseph T. Wilson, a former attorney from New York City, was making his home at the headquarters with Uranda, Dorothy and her family. In January in a paper entitled "The Meekers at Home," at Uranda's invitation he undertook to share his experience of living in that home, and conveyed a spirit of lightness that was contagious simply in the reading. One can sense that Uranda was experiencing a freedom and joy unknown heretofore in his home life. Certainly in his childhood there were times of wonderful family closeness, but this present situation provided an opportunity to experience a happy, though unmistakably crowded, family pattern.

Joseph described the members of the family:

> In order of seniority, Sonya, Natausha, Diana and Glenn; sad-eyed Sally, the one hundred-fifty-pound St. Bernard puppy; three cats; and a sweet little Cocker Spaniel. To the foregoing I should like to add the name of Robert Patton, with apologies for introducing him after the livestock, his place on the list not indicating his relative importance. Finally, I am privileged to count myself as one of this interesting assembly, for before I left Hot Springs, South Dakota, I was affectionately assured by all of them that I had been adopted.

> When I arrived the Meeker family was living in a trailer camp about a mile and a half out of Excelsior, on Lake Minnetonka. There Robert and I occupied one room of a two-room cabin, the other being used as an office for conducting the business of the Service. The rest of the Meeker family occupied the one trailer which, together with the Lincoln car and the truck, comprised the full inventory of rolling stock owned by the Church at that time. The other trailer was added just before we left for the West.

> Robert enjoys the double distinction of having been the youngest focal point in the Service and the author of some outstanding articles. I had expected someone much older than this slender young man with the friendly, boyish smile. Robert and I had two sleeping companions in the cabin: Glenn, who occupied a cot on the porch and became active at about six a.m. every day, and sad-eyed Sally, who lay on a blanket at the foot of our bed and snored until the rafters rattled.

> The Meeker family is thoroughly unified. When the harmonization is broadly inclusive enough so that children of mature years, as well as little tads, immediately accept and respond to the stepfather as if he were their natural parent, that is a bit extraordinary. From seven-year-old Glenn and nine-year-old Diana to and including the young ladies of regal bearing, in the sweet-sixteen age bracket, he is affectionately called "Daddy," hugged, kissed, teased for nickels and dimes, criticized, questioned, forced to hold his own in argument upon adverse parental rulings, with as much freedom and abandon as if he had indulged their childish whims and fancies from earliest infancy.

> Occasionally we went swimming in beautiful Lake Minnetonka; a favorite sport was archery; and once in a while we went to town and took in a movie. Often there were lengthy discussions about outworkings in the Church and in the world, the needs of the Service and plans for fulfilling them.

The trip to California involved frequent interruptions for tire repairs or replacements. From there the group traveled back through the Midwest and down to Arkansas.

Robert Patton married Natausha, Dorothy's daughter, and departed soon after to Texas for training in the Army Medical Corps. Back home, Natausha helped Uranda with his work.

In "My Word to You" Dorothy spoke of the possibility of Uranda going into the Army, and assured everyone that he would continue to write the lessons, which would be released through Headquarters no matter where he might be located. She emphasized the need to have a permanent Headquarters and admonished: "Even Uranda depends on the response given to him, and he must accept the limitations established thereby."

In an "Official Notice to the Church" Uranda said he was setting his house in order, that he might render the service with the Armed Forces to which he might be called. In such case he delegated his authority as Bishop of the Church to his wife, and appointed William Oshanek and Joseph Wilson as Church officials.

The "Bishop's Personal Message" of June 30 conveyed a profound depth of appreciation for the wholehearted acceptance of the essential changes taking place, with the reminder that regardless of the outer circumstance:

> The Plan of God will be fulfilled, either through those of us who have heard the call and seen the vision, or through others who shall be raised up in great tribulation should we fail in the easy way which the Lord has provided in the extraordinary privileges granted unto us. Let us let that which now is established come unto fruition, that still greater tribulation need not be than now shall be.
>
> Through your response in filling current Church needs we were able to make a substantial payment on a lovely little place in Loveland, Colorado, with the balance handled by the local Building and Loan Company on reasonable monthly payments. Just outside of town we have a one-acre tract, a small, white, five-room house, with space to park the trailers for extra sleeping quarters. A lovely front lawn gives the house a nice setting among the trees—apples, plums and cottonwoods. Back of the house we have a chicken house and yard, a barn and yard for our milk goats, our dogs, a fine garden with a large patch of blackberries, and a half acre of alfalfa for hay, with water rights for irrigating the whole. As rapidly as possible we shall send for the things in storage in California, Denver and North Dakota, so that eventually the house and office will be fairly well equipped.

We have rented an office in the First National Bank Building in Loveland, and secured a Post Office address, P.O. Box 238, which you will please use at once. [That box became as familiar to a great many people as their own names, for a long time.]

Dorothy followed this with a Message in which she spoke of a beautiful place, Sylvan Dale Ranch, twelve miles out of Loveland that would be ideal for holding summer sessions and a training center for workers and ministers.

In July, after expressing appreciation for the faithful service of many, Uranda again had to emphasize finances. The first of the month was looming, without any reserve fund on hand to meet obligations, with the possibility of not only the Church credit being endangered but the possession of part of our equipment.

You might be interested to know that when the Church was incorporated a stipulated salary was authorized for me, but in order to keep things going for the Church I have drawn only what I actually had to have, with the result that the Church now owes me over three thousand dollars in back salary. I am not concerned about that, except to indicate that I have contributed to the well-being of the Church.

With his meticulous concern that all things should be taken care of, Uranda spoke in a Message in August of a viewpoint regarding himself:

Regardless of the fact that we all seek a unity of function in moving toward the goal in which we have an unquestioned unity of purpose, and that I have sought through every right means at my command to secure that unity, there has been a basic division within the Church body for many years, which has caused most of the trouble and uncertainty that has been experienced.

This relates to myself, and you will recall that I have never, at any time, told you that you *had* to have any certain belief about me. Individually you have built up your concepts about me as an individual, but they all fall naturally into two groupings. Briefly, the two groups are: (1) those who conceive me to be filling a specific place of leadership in the cosmic plan, and so have complete faith in my action in any matter, and (2) those who consider me to be a 'fine minister' with a great deal of spiritual insight, but still quite an ordinary man whose statements should be weighed and judged, rejecting that which does not appear to be correct to the individual.

The adherents to the basic concepts of each group feel strongly that those of the other group must, sooner or later, come to the same viewpoint, and that then the Service will progress much more rapidly. Let it be understood that it is no longer necessary that this be given consideration on any basis of friction, for regardless of what the truth of the matter may be, and regardless of what I may write or say or do, and regardless of what any other may feel or realize through his own experience, it remains for each one to function under the concepts, ideas (good or bad), and realizations which make up the sum total of the individual's mental conditioning; and beyond a certain point wherein we may present such light as the Lord may have given us we are unable to prevent such suffering as may come as the result of inadequate understanding. We must let things work out in due season in others as well as in ourselves. May the Lord draw you into a full realization of that which is of Him, that you may be lifted up to stand upon the Rock that is present in the valley of the shadow.

I praise God for those who are real enough, man or woman enough, and have courage enough, to write to us frankly of any point that troubles them or they cannot understand. There are those who are fair to us and to themselves in all matters wherein there may be questioning.

Uranda was alluding in a general sense to an attitude which had emerged, not far afield but very close at home, in Joseph Wilson, and he was working in every way possible to let it clear. He continued:

Usually you are not in position to judge as to your own progress. As you let things work out in your own life you must be patient with yourself, with those around you, and with the world. Remember that in due season this shaking of the world will be over, and those who have been faithful will be found in their appointed places.

In November William and Muriel Oshanek arrived in Loveland and immediately went to work in the office at Headquarters. These two, with many years of training and experience—William in the field of law and Muriel as court stenographer—proved invaluable in the oftimes trying years to follow. With his irrepressible spirit Uranda reveled in the prospect that with William and Muriel, also Joseph Wilson, on the Headquarters staff, they were in better position than ever before to undertake further expansion.

Joseph accepted the position of Treasurer of the Church. He had come to Loveland on December 2nd for a brief visit to Headquarters, when there was a possibility that Uranda might be called to military service. Dorothy had been acting as Secretary and Treasurer and with all her domestic duties it was more than she could handle. Joseph found that excellent records had been kept and the business of the Church conducted economically and with painstaking care. It seemed almost impossible to him that there could have been an adequate, businesslike administration under the conditions of that time, moving around, working in cramped quarters, etc., but it had been accomplished. He commented, "We are deeply indebted to our Bishop and his lovely wife on that score for many hours of conscientious toil."

Not long after Joseph's arrival Uranda learned that his voluntary offer to serve in the Army had been turned down. Joseph nevertheless decided to continue indefinitely as a member of the Headquarters Staff.

Expansion continued. Uranda conducted a half-hour radio service broadcast from KFKA, Greeley, Colorado, to be followed by a series of fifteen-minute talks early in January 1944. He observed that the periods of most rapid growth and development in the ministry had been when he was holding public services and expressed a desire to resume that function. Those present agreed that the Church must enter upon an era of unprecedented expansion in order to fulfil its destiny and lead the way in the performance of the "greater works" in the not distant future. It seemed obvious that the best means at this time to bring about the necessary expansion was by appeal to the masses of humanity, and that this would require Uranda's personal appearance in many places.

It was planned that a beginning be made in February, in Southern California where the climate was favorable, Church membership strong and public response reasonably certain to be good. From this starting point, if conditions in the world permitted, tours would be initiated. The question was put to the members of the Church: "What do you think of it? Can you and will you give it the needed support?"

The property on Taft Street in Loveland, purchased in the summer as a parsonage, was soon acknowledged as being inadequate, so in November a property on Jefferson Street was purchased. The profit from the sale of the Taft Street place and the remaining trailer rendered available substantial equities. These sales, combined with the increased income from offerings in January, released the Church from pressing debt. Essential office equipment and furniture had been acquired, and there was assurance of sufficient cash to enable Uranda and Dorothy to begin their travels in the field at the proper time.

A note of caution was introduced by the Treasurer at this point, stating that on the basis of past experience an extra expense of $500 or $600 monthly was to be anticipated when the program of public services started. There would be traveling expense, hotel bills, printing, advertising, rental of public halls, etc. He pointed out that there would be a partial return of expense by contributions of the public and the support of local groups which sponsor them; but group contributions to Headquarters would in turn be reduced.

He drew attention to the fact that the hundreds and thousands who attend the services do not generally contribute liberally to the expense of bringing the Word of Truth to them.

> They never have done so and we cannot anticipate that they will do so now. It is only through the gradual process of expansion which takes place by increase of the numbers on our mailing list that Church income will increase. In the meantime expenses at Headquarters will continue unabated and will probably increase as the number of students increases. We are in a good starting position, but that is all.

He said that much had been accomplished by way of reorganization in the office in anticipation of a substantial increase in their work and to facilitate a smooth-running, efficient operation under increased pressure. He elaborated:

> If we were required to pay for the labor required to grind out the lessons by mimeograph we probably could not afford to continue the use of it. If a way could be found to enable us to print most of the material we mail out, there would be a great saving of labor and our field of service expanded. There is much demand for many of the older lessons, such as the *Steps to Mastership* series, and no available supply. These could easily be printed for further distribution, whereas under the present system it is impossible to reproduce them and carry on the preparation of current lessons.

Along the way, a son was born to Dorothy's daughter Sonya, who had married Vernon Fahey, then in Cheyenne, Wyoming, in Army training.

Uranda gave a radio series, "The Hour of Challenge," in thirteen broadcasts over the Greeley station, and wistfully commented on the lack of written response to them, outside of Church members.

Uranda announced in March that a new series of instruction papers, "All Things Made New," would be used in connection with distribution of "The Hour of Challenge." In closing that announcement he said:

> The whole world is enfolded in the flaming fire of the Christ Love of the Lord our God, and we rejoice that we may watch the refining process that now takes place in the furnace. It is ordained that in this present point of eternity the fire of the furnace is being heated "seven times hotter than it is wont to be heated." In the whole earth the gold and the dross are so mixed that they can be separated only through the fire of the furnace. The gold-bearing quartz, which humanity is, responds not to the processes of refining which man has designed and attempted to use, and so man has thought that our great Master's claim would never prove to be rich in the gold of being. However, His method of

refining in the fire of love has proven to bring a rich reward, and though the gold and the dross have been so mixed together in the quartz as to appear to be blended, the gold that is drawn forth in the furnace is pure and perfect.

In his Treasurer's Report Joseph Wilson announced that there was a little over $180 in the printing fund and if it continued to accumulate at that rate it would not be long before we could do some printing. It was suggested that a plan of special offerings could be set in motion, so that the amount of existing literature might be moved. He said it would not be a pricing of the literature but intended to assist those who might wish the magazines and booklets for distribution among their friends and acquaintances, by giving them our idea of a fair money value from the standpoint of printing cost.

There followed this list:

NAME OF PUBLICATION	SUGGESTED OFFERING
Letters to You	25 cents
Talks Beside the Sun-Dial, No. 1	15 "
Talks Beside the Sun-Dial, No. 2	25 "
Dawning Day Magazine, Nos. 1, 2 & 3	10 "
The Christ Attitude	05 "
Lighting the Way in You	10 "
Introducing the Third Sacred School	10 "
The Way Revealed	10 "

Joseph said that putting a price on the material was not the goal; however his function in this regard proved to be an area where he disagreed with Uranda.

Enclosed with this guideline were three copies of a leaflet, and people were invited to have a part in scattering them far and wide as rapidly as possible, remembering the parable of the sower. Distribution will be made without regard to whether the seed falls on fertile ground. They can be left generously, although not deliberately wasted, with the assurance that someone, somewhere, will be touched by the spirit of the message and respond.

Over 25,000 copies of the leaflet had been printed, with the thought that each one might distribute at least a hundred each week.

Joseph reported in August that Uranda, William Oshanek and he had had a week of intensive training at Camp George West in Golden, Colorado, with Troop B Cavalry of Colorado State Guard, of which they were all members. He revealed a proposal suggested by Dorothy to have a Summer Session in Loveland in September. It had received some consideration by Uranda and the Board of Trustees, and all at Headquarters recognized how valuable this could be in that time of world crisis.

The plan was to accommodate people in Loveland, which had two hotels and a population of about seven thousand. The dates would be September 10-17, with morning and afternoon services for members of the Church, and evening services open to the local public. The estimated cost of attendance (transportation not included) was about $45 for the eight days, based on a calculation of a $2 per day hotel rate.

In his Message of August 22 Uranda announced the upcoming session:

> In a former instruction paper you were told that the climax of the present world conflict should come on or about August 17. That day has come and gone, and as I listened to the newscasts and commentators on the evening of August 18 I heard repeatedly that in the "last day or two" the whole picture had changed on the European battleground. The developments since the 17th reveal that the climax has indeed been reached, and it is now simply a matter of finishing the job as quickly as possible. Let us remember that it takes much more than the cessation of firing and bombing to bring peace.

Through the cooperation of Rev. and Mrs. West of the First Christian Church of Loveland, facilities for the Session were secured at Sylvan Dale Ranch, about ten miles out of Loveland in the foothills. Sylvan Dale is a beautiful spot with very comfortable quarters, fine meals, and the use of a lovely rustic chapel in which to hold services. The owners, Maurice and Tillie Jessup, shared a warm relationship with Uranda and the people at Sunrise through the years. Maurice has left this sphere, but Tillie and their daughter Susan still visit the Ranch from time to time, and the ever-beautiful Sylvan Dale is available and used by us to this day when there is further need for accommodation, classes, whatever.

About fifty people attended the Session, including John Martin, the focal point of the Pittsburgh group; Richard Thompson from Ontario, Canada; and a number of others in places of leadership at that time. Most important, Lord Martin Cecil was there, with his wife Edith. His vital place in the ministry was continuing to unfold. Also of note is the fact that Kathleen and Rosalind Groves were in attendance. Muriel Oshanek and Dorothy Levoy recorded all the services in shorthand.

In a wedding service for Earl Lonsbury and May Hume conducted by the Bishop during that Session, he spoke of the Biblical story in which Adam was to have a helpmeet, and Eve was taken from a rib in Adam's side. He used the analogy to point out that the bone was not taken from his foot, with the surmise that a woman was supposed to be walked upon, or from the head so that it might be presumed she should be the head.

The ribs house the vital organs of the body. They are close to the heart, neither of the head nor of the foot. Woman was brought forth on the negative vibration of that which produced man, that she might stand by his side, that she might be close to his heart, an helpmeet unto him, walking in the way with him.

In the Session five ministers received the Third Ordination and were fully authorized to represent the Church in an official capacity; five others received the First Ordination, moving toward that field of ministry. Uranda observed that these ordinations stemmed from a completely unified recognition of the need for practical function in everyday life, individually and collectively. He said, "Mighty currents of divine power were released by means of which many wonderful things are in the making. We here at Headquarters are doing our utmost under the conditions which exist and with the means at our command to keep these currents focalized and moving toward fulfilment."

Shortly after that Summer Session a message dated October 28 was released to the School with the heart-tugging title, "My Final Word to You, by Dorothy Meeker," in which she said that she could no longer

fully harmonize with the Bishop's ministry and continue in the Church or as his wife. Therefore I have filed suit for divorce and hereby advise you that I have resigned from the Church.

I appreciate deeply all the love and consideration you have given me, and I hope that I have been of some service to you. I feel that, if you have confidence in the Bishop, you should not feel it necessary to discuss this situation among yourselves or require any explanation from him. As we come to this parting of the ways I would assure you of my love and earnest prayers for your continued welfare.

Less than a month later Uranda shared some "Notes From My Book of Life," No. Two:

As the earth and the sky have meaning by reason of each other, so is it with man and woman—and as the sky circumscribes the sphere of the earth's function, so does woman set the scope and the limits of man's function in the earth. All too often the woman bewails the limited scope of man's function within the limits she herself set, and few are the men who have the strength and the courage to ignore and transcend the unreasonable limits established. Blessed is the man who has the inspiration of a woman whose vision is so far-reaching that the world becomes his sphere of service, and yet is content to live with him in such temporary limits as circumstance may inscribe.

Soon afterward Joseph Wilson reported that the Bishop was taking a much needed rest and was not in Loveland, that those who remained at Headquarters were charged with the administrative responsibility of keeping the service running smoothly and were also undertaking a work of indexing all known writings of Bishop Meeker. Details were set forth, establishing guidelines for the easy handling of such matters as responses and contributions.

Before long Uranda informed the School:

> I am back at work, in good health, and a tremendous amount of work has already been done, but there is so very much yet to do. An able secretary has been provided who is assisting in getting out many letters and important papers, as well as making it possible to continue the "Fireside Talks" series, of which there are now twelve ready to go out. Let us work together as one to serve the Lord our God.

5

HEADQUARTERS!

January 1945 ~ July 1946

*T*oward the close of 1944 Uranda received a letter from John Oshanek, of The Oshanek Chiropractic Health Service in Winnipeg, stating the need for a worldwide educational organization

that would not look too religious, because the average person is "fed up" with the old religious fads that have been crowding in everywhere. On the other hand the word *science* has lost its savory meaning, the many pseudosciences giving a bad taste in the mouth to a growing number of people who realize that a materialistic approach cannot solve the world problems. So we must find the middle of the road policy, which we call the Central Way in the Third Sacred School.

In another letter of January 9, 1945, John said, "For years I personally have been the target for the medical profession. I seem to have focalized all their Chiropractic problems since I came to Winnipeg." This "persecution" of the Chiropractic profession by the Medical Association seemed to be standard practice in those turbulent times for the healing professions, in Canada and the United States. With some of our chiropractors spending time in prison, an increasing number of practitioners in the ministry were up against a stumbling block—with some not quite making the hurdle.

In his Message of April 26 Uranda said:

> With world events unfolding in a mighty drama that is so full of tragedy, I remind you once again that only those who stand on the rock foundation and walk in the central way can hope to be secure against the onslaughts of destructive vibrations that are present in world currents. As Emissaries you know and understand, to a degree at least, the significance of those things which are taking place in the world. To the degree that you have let yourselves become oriented to reality in harmony with the truths of being which have been offered to you in the Third Sacred School, you are able to stand un-moved in the storms of world reaction which cause such houses as are builded upon sand to fall with a mighty crash.
>
> The work of the Lord is moving forward definitely and strongly. You have passed through a very important period of preparation. Only a very few have failed to pass recent tests thus far. The door of the School stands open. All who will may enter in and participate in its activities and training, and all who so choose may depart. I praise God that the "mixed company" of those who are with us is very small. Our Service is expanding and going forward and the Church as a whole is participating.

Later, Uranda said:

> If you do not have absolute faith and confidence in the function of your Bishop in his work of piloting the ship through the troubled waters, you should recognize that he is the only one who can answer questions relating to this Service. Therefore they should be brought directly and frankly to him. Should you find the answers that await you to be fully satisfying, you will be free to make continued and effective progress in the sphere of service to which you have been called—and if not, then you can turn away with the assurance that you were at least fair to the degree of presenting your questions before mak-ing your decision to walk in some other path. It does not pay to jump to conclusions—you might be wrong.

The admonition that questions regarding recent events should be addressed to him rather than anyone else referred to the continuing and intensifying situation with Joseph Wilson, to whom he extended his unfailing friendship. One of the "reasons" put forth by the Treasurer was that "Uranda was not a businessman." When confronted with efforts to put a price on his publications, though he listened, Uranda was firm in his stand that the Word had to be freely given, with voluntary donations the sole means of financial return. As it proved through the years, it worked, indeed far surpassing the seeming success in the world man has made, characterized as it is by greed and lust for power. It was just one of the vital areas of man's function in which Uranda was seeking to establish a design and operation long forgotten, and restore sanity to a mad, mad world. Finance was by no means the only one—and the others came in for their share of criticism at this crucial time.

Further word from Uranda stated that current issues of "Notes From My Book of Life" and "Fireside Talks" dealt with the principles underlying all those situations which had developed during the last few months, and that careful reading between the lines would greatly assist in an understanding of the significance of many occurrences which had been obscured.

> You already have the answers to many of your questions, and more answers will be given in season. An open mind makes for clarity of vision; preconceived ideas and prejudices are to one's sense of spiritual discernment as cataracts are to the sight of the physical eye.
>
> The world Peace Conference is now in session. [That was fifty years ago; one might have heard it on this evening's news!] Tonight I heard a radio commentator make the statement that everyone is for peace until it begins to cost something. That is very true. Nations will spend billions of dollars and undergo all kinds of hardships, to say nothing of the sacrifice of human life, to carry on war, because that is the price of war. How many are willing to pay the price for peace?
>
> The same principle is true in the service of the Lord. It is one thing to say that we wish to serve the Lord and another to dedicate all that we have and are to that service. To fulfil the commission which has been given to us we must give ourselves, all of our potentialities and our resources toward the fulfilment of that commission.

In June, Uranda announced that the Church, which included the Board of Trustees and every member individually, had accepted increased responsibility in the function and welfare of the Church, and that consequently he was left free to lead the way into new spheres of service. He said he had plenty to do and could keep several more stenographers busy, concluding:

> Our Church, and ourselves individually as members of it, represents an Organization 20,000 years old. All the great spiritual leaders, and the great spiritual movements, of the past ages were manifestations of that activity of which we are a part. We enjoy the greatest heritage which can be bestowed upon any person. I pray that we may prove worthy of it.

After the dissolution of Uranda's marriage to Dorothy, Kathleen Groves, who had attended the 1944 Conference at Sylvan Dale, was drawn into closer proximity with him. During that period Uranda visited Ravenden, Arkansas, the home of David and Rosa Groves and their three daughters, Rosalind, Billie and Kathleen, the youngest. Back in 1937 a lady who had just moved to the small town stopped at the Groves home and inquired of Rosa where she could get some fresh eggs and milk. Then on a later visit she brought some literature which she gave to Rosa, sensing that she too was looking for something more. The written material was from Uranda, and while the lady did not continue on the mailing list, Rosa wrote in at once and before long she and David and the girls were reading the words which would be a part of them for the rest of their lives.

On June 5th, in a small town in Illinois, Uranda and Kathy were united in marriage in a quiet civil ceremony. Accompanying them was Uranda's daughter, Marjorie Lee.

In "A Personal Message" on June 30 Uranda spoke of a Foundational Norm, the body composed of those Emissaries of Divine Light who functioned with him in a sphere of activity which extended above and beyond the outer manifestation of the Church as it existed at the present time.

> You will understand that which I would now convey to the degree that you have learned to read and comprehend the Word within the word, such understanding resulting from the natural processes of growth and development along the path of your life. What may not now be fully clear will become clear in due season as you continue on in harmony with reality.

> The Church is the net result of the cumulative processes of creative generation down through the ages as made manifest since the time of the fall of man. Tens and hundreds of thousands of individuals have lived and worked and died that this present manifestation of the Church might exist, but there is a realm of vibrational activity between the manifest formation of the Church and the inner reality of that which we call the kingdom of heaven. The positive inner reality provides the correct point of polarization for the sum total of the negative triune world. Various levels of life as manifest in the negative triune world respond to the eternal positive of the inner reality to various degrees in various ways according to the nature of the manifestation involved as found in the vegetable and animal kingdoms and in the realm of human existence.

> The present outer manifestation of the Church provides a nucleus of responding vibrations in the world, and this nucleus is moving toward increasing degrees of coordination with the inner reality and an ultimate fusion therewith. I am concerned with that intermediate realm of vibratory activity through

which the manifest form of the Church and all responding formations and manifestations of the whole world must pass in order to reach a point where fusion with and in the inner reality becomes possible. Activity in this realm could not be undertaken on any suitable scale until the outer manifestation of the form of the Church had reached a point where it could function as a unified body without requiring my full and constant attention. That point has now been reached.

This which I have been sharing with you is an outline of the understanding necessary to a basic approach to coordination in the Foundational Norm.

Joseph Wilson, in his report in July, expressed relief and gratitude for the "advent of Rose Forker, about the middle of May, and the return of William and Muriel early in June." He noted that in spite of increased unemployment and stresses in the ministry, the monetary support had not been shaken, also that the indexing project had completed its primary phase, sponsored and performed by a little group of enthusiastic Emissaries in Helena, Montana, primary contacts being Byrdie Jane Dahl and Agnes Batten.

He then referred to Uranda's announcement in "A Step in Church Expansion," and his Personal Message of June 15, stating that "at some point the Bishop had been made a member of the Board, and a change was being indicated whereby he would no longer serve in that capacity," following which he quoted from a letter he had written to Uranda:

From your viewpoint and in the light of your greater understanding of inner reality it may be clearly evident that my limitations and false concepts are the cause of many difficulties. I am quite prepared, ready and willing, to concede that it may be so. Nevertheless I am irrevocably committed to the conviction that in my place I can render no real service to the advancement of your ministry except as I function in unwavering loyalty to my highest realizations of truth— my realizations, not yours.

Upon that concept of my true place of service hangs the explanation of my letters to different ones in which I sought to minimize the importance of your personality and leadership, emphasizing the truth of the teachings as the bedrock upon which we must stand or fall. You have told me that some of my expression in these letters was unfair to you and incorrect in presentation of fact. Maybe it was.

In July of 1945 Bishop Meeker suggested to the Board that an Advisory Board should be formed to represent the Church body as a whole and work with the Board of Trustees "in all matters wherein the latter might properly seek advice and assistance in solving difficult problems that might arise."

He recalled that the delegation of authority to the Board was designed to open the way for increased activity and responsibility in the membership of the Church, and that in accordance with a message of June 2nd his position and function as Spiritual Director must be effective "in order to permit the active and unified support of the Church as a whole in conjunction with the activities of the Board."

He drew attention to the fact that legal organizations and technicalities may be properly utilized in the furtherance of the Lord's Service, that the essence and spirit of the activity of the Emissaries transcends man-made organizations and legal technicalities, and that the Church had an opportunity to unify and coordinate outer activities with inner reality.

Uranda then suggested that the Elders of the Church should be ordained as members of the Church Advisory Board, and nominated the following:

> Marvin J. Allen, Denver, Colorado
> Lord Martin Cecil, 100 Mile House, British Columbia
> Irving Harwood, Grand Lake, Colorado
> Paul Keenan, Military Liason Officer, Red Cross, Boston, Massachusetts
> Rev. John B. Martin, Pittsburgh, Pennsylvania
> M. Gordon Marks, Toronto, Ontario
> William Martens, Milwaukee, Wisconsin
> Frank Protzman, Pittsburgh, Pennsylvania
> Charles Olsson, Milwaukee, Wisconsin
> Dr. J. P. Oshanek, Winnipeg, Manitoba
> Charles Strikwerda, Dallas, Oregon
> Richard H. Thompson, Trinity College School, Port Hope, Ontario

Uranda further stated:

> I suggest that these twelve Elders should be consulted and their viewpoints carefully considered in relation to all matters wherein questions arise as to proper policies and activities, whether action or expression should be endorsed as being beneficial to the Church and School as a whole. I deem this step to be necessary to the fulfilment of the spirit, purpose and intent of the changes which have already been made.

On August 14 a message to the Board entitled "Proclamation by the Board of Trustees" was released to the entire Church and was signed by William Oshanek, President, and Joseph Wilson, Treasurer. This development rang a warning note that some questionable elements were appearing in the control area of the Board of Trustees.

In Arkansas, where he was having a much-needed rest, Uranda conducted a service on August 26 entitled "God's Atomic Bomb," in which he outlined progression of events which seemed to be rendering the development of the atomic bomb inevitable. He said:

Some years ago we had what was called a world war and yet the whole world was not involved. Finally, after many had perished, it came to a close. Efforts were made to establish a peace that would last. The League of Nations was set up, many earnest men and women labored long and hard, and prayed, for a time at least. But there were other forces at work.

Selfishness and greed began to overthrow the efforts of many who were working for peace. Prosperity began to claim people's attention and we moved toward a boom period; people began to forget again. That boom period was produced as an artificial measure to remove more money from the masses of the people. Then came a depression, and people's primary concern was to find something to eat and a place to sleep. They forgot their responsibilities in the family of nations and were inclined to ignore what was happening across the oceans, both "shining seas." Then, on a fateful December 7th after terrible things had been perpetrated in Europe, the American nation was shocked into an awareness that another war was in progress.

The family of nations in the Allied Cause gave all their scientific resources to finding a means of utilizing atomic energy. Under the stress of war, scientists were brought together from many parts of the world, facilities were made available. Millions of dollars were spent in construction—money did not matter. One purpose was in focus, and to that degree was achieved; what was called the atomic bomb was produced.

The atom has a positive center, a nucleus called a proton, and when by bombardment of the neutrons that positive center is split, two positives repel each other. That principle is recognized in the use of electricity and operates throughout the universe. In the atomic bomb, man has not used a hundredth part of its potential energies. All he has done is split it in two.

Atoms are constructed like solar systems. The positive center is surrounded by one or more electrons. That secret operates through all the elements. In uranium, the ninety-second element, we have what may be called the outer fringe classification. This process of breaking down has been going on all the time. Man did not cause it to be; he simply discovered it.

The atomic bomb is a divine warning to the world that it had better repent, turn to God and live according to His Law, that what happened in Japan will not happen again.

Uranda continued to work with national and world themes, and conducted a service at Ravenden on September 9th subsequently entitled "A Nation God Used." This referred to the United States, and he used as an analogy the story of Joseph in Egypt, who said:

"God hath caused me to be fruitful in the land of my affliction." We in America have been blessed. Of all the great powers, the great nations in the world, we alone have not been subjected to the bombings and plagues of battle around our own shores. We have been touched deeply because our loved ones have gone over there and some are not coming back; nevertheless the victory in the conflict of arms has come to us. I heard a commentator say yesterday that the next war would be fought in forty minutes. We do not have privileges without responsibilities, and we who are citizens of America must lead the way in letting the healing from the Great Physician be provided for the world body.

Jim Allen became aware of a property located on the Western Slope about twelve miles from Delta, Colorado, and Uranda and Kathy hastened back from Arkansas, directly to Delta. Jim was already there, with William Oshanek, Joseph Wilson, Irving Harwood, and Charles Strikwerda from Oregon. They viewed the twelve-hundred-acre ranch, set in an exquisite little valley with a background of Grand Mesa—in Uranda's words, "one of the most majestic sights to be found anywhere." This was in the area of Uranda's boyhood haunts, which always held a magic for him.

The owner was most cooperative and desired very much for us to have this property, having caught the spirit of our envisioned purpose for it. He quoted a price $10,000 below what he was asking. The ranch was priced at $50,000, to which would need to be added $10,000 for essential equipment for plowing, etc. The appraised value of the water itself was $60,000.

Uranda set forth a plan which he said would not involve contributions from the Church membership but investment, separate from contributions vital to the Church. When it became obvious that the acquisition of this property was beyond the material substance available at the time, Joseph Wilson reported that if agreeable to those concerned, any paid subscriptions toward the Delta property would be used to establish a trust fund, so that cash would be immediately available if and when the opportunity to make a desirable purchase arose, with the expectation that it would naturally grow.

A perspective view of the ministry is highlighted by a series of disappointments, when increasingly seductive but elusive plums seemed there just for the picking. These are all factors which played a part in establishing a wealth of vibratory substance in future outworkings, in spite of the turns in the road which lured some from the Way which they themselves had helped prepare.

At the helm of a ship moving in uncharted waters, Uranda took advantage of every possibility, however remote, that appeared on his horizon, without becoming discouraged or losing a vision unrestricted by that horizon. Over the years these beginnings were not lost, but were nourished, in his boundless imaginative spirit and by those who steadfastly watched with him as the waves moved the little seaworthy vessel on its way. There were times when turbulence threatened to overwhelm it but always carried in its wake was the message, "Peace, be still."

In a Report from the Treasurer the students were informed that the title index had been finished and things were running smoothly, the Bishop had returned to Loveland and was working closely with the Board, anticipating that he and Kathy would make a trip to California when it was feasible.

In a "Report on Developments," September 18, Uranda said that a permanent headquarters which would include a program for training ministers and general expansion of the Church was a vital necessity, "as cosmic pressure gradually increases."

One day, in the fall of 1945, Rosalind (Roz) Hooper was riding her horse through the countryside and happened to pass a run-down old ranch in what was then known as the Missouri Valley, about twelve miles west of downtown Loveland. A "For Sale" sign attracted her immediate attention, the need for a permanent home-headquarters uppermost in her consciousness. Her horse sensed the urgency which had suddenly come over Rozzie, and in record time they had returned to Uranda and she was breathlessly telling him of her "find."

The stark difference, even sight unseen, between this and the recently considered property did not deter Uranda from immediate investigation. That was a typical attitude: whatever was offered, regardless of its nature, rich or poor, received his complete attention, in the realization that it was a gift from the Lord and not to be judged. Uranda went at once to see the 123-acre property, and found the antithesis of the luxurious places that had been beckoning for the past few years.

An outworking of this nature never detracted one iota from the vision Uranda had of a place for headquarters. It just wasn't time yet—and he no doubt knew it all along—but it was every bit as real in ethereal substance as if he drove through the gates of palatial grounds instead of a dirt road that led to a run-down house; as surely heaven, a gift from God.

He conferred with the Board, and with their agreement sent word to those on the mailing list, outlining the wisdom of establishing a headquarters in a setting that would allow for expansion and development in every way. The response was enthusiastic, and with a feeling of joyous fulfilment the property which would henceforth be known as Sunrise Ranch was purchased early in December of 1945.

In a Treasurer's Report, Joseph Wilson said:

As I sit down to prepare this report for you I have a feeling that many corners have been safely turned, that old cycles of long standing are coming to a close and that the Church is now entering a period of expansion which will witness the outworking of the things of which we have dreamed and for which we have hoped. We have been told that they would come to pass and I have believed it, but now I feel it.

The 123-acre farm is only a mile or two from Sylvan Dale, where the Summer Session of 1944 was held. There is a large barn on the premises, two ramshackle old residences and other out buildings. Much labor and some expense will be necessary in order to make the property suitable for a Headquarters and it is too small to be serviceable for the Community Project which we presented for your consideration in connection with the large acreage at Delta; but it can, in the course of time, be made a means of housing the Service and the Headquarters Staff at cost greatly reduced in comparison with our present operating expenses.

Cost of the property was $6,000. Almost all who participated in the Delta project offered their subscriptions to the development of this new endeavor. Enough subscriptions were paid to enable the Church to pay about half the purchase price, the rest to be financed by a mortgage at a Loveland bank. Money was also required to purchase tools and equipment to operate the farm, put down a well, install enough conveniences for comfortable living and construct additional buildings. This, as with the other proposed ventures, presented its challenges.

In the near vicinity, just over the rimrock, excellent building stone in abundance was available at little or no cost except the labor involved. The rimrock is one of the results of a cataclysmic event which involved the entire planet, with very particular phenomena in this area. It extends from one end of the Valley to the other, an outcropping of red stone that shines like a golden crown in the brilliant Colorado sun.

Volunteers were coming forward to help. Among major expenses were farming tools and equipment, household furniture, linens, dishes, and so forth. The stock of household goods was meager, and it was suggested that some might have surplus stores of these things or be aware of sources from which the needs could be supplied at low enough cost to warrant paying shipping expenses.

Originally the idea was that this property should be sold as soon as the Church was in position to support the Community Project, with the proceeds of the sale applied to the purchase of a large acreage somewhere on the Western Slope, probably near Delta.

Another possibility that emerged was that the Community Project envisioned could be gradually developed by the process of expanding the present holdings and without acquiring a new location. Uranda said,

> This place we have purchased is located in a very beautiful valley and we find that there are other properties which it is reasonable to suppose could be acquired in season to expand into the Community Project. Such an outworking is well within range of possibility. We are moving open-mindedly toward the ultimate objective of the Community Project and our feeling is that this beginning will prove to be a stepping stone.

The "ultimate objective" proved to be that place, Sunrise Ranch. In later years all but one of the adjacent homes were acquired, one by one, so that most of the beautiful valley became the International Headquarters of the Emissaries of Divine Light, home in a spiritual sense to people all over the world.

On this unassuming piece of land in a lonely, arid valley, the extent of its assets consisted of a very old ranch house, a smoke house, a large barn, a granary, a dilapidated shed used as a shop, and another small and well-worn house just down the road to the south, which had been used as quarters for the few ranch-hands. Outhouses provided bathroom facilities, and would continue to for some time to come.

It was Kathy who suggested that a fitting name for the place would be Sunrise Ranch. That has continued to this day. Uranda changed the name of the surround, Missouri Valley, to Eden Valley; that too remains unchanged.

Thus was born the International Headquarters of the Emissaries of Divine Light. It proved to be the origin, and focal point, of the uninterrupted expanding and beautifying action of the Spirit of the living God through this small beginning of His body which now covers the face of the earth. I have emphasized the state of disrepair into which the place had fallen, yet the setting was, and is, one of the most beautiful to be found anywhere, with the rimrock on the east and Green Ridge on the west, Horsetooth Mountain on the north and a clear stretch to the south.

The Bishop and his wife came onto the property, just as it was, before Christmas and were ensconced in the old ranch house, actually taking residence later, in March of 1946. The kitchen walls and ceiling were covered with coal dust and smoke accumulated over the years from two giant coal wood ranges that stood like sentinels at opposite ends of the room. Uranda and Kathy, with the few who were with them at the time, were to have Christmas dinner together. The house was soon cleaned and made ready, with excited anticipation, not just for Christmas but for a wealth of living waiting to find form in years that lay ahead. Kathy happily set the table with a white cloth and arranged a centerpiece of evergreen boughs and bayberry candles. Meanwhile the food was prepared in primitive conditions, under the loving and capable hands of her sister Billie.

Afterward they gathered in the living room to share a service with Uranda. The joy and solemnity of that hour established a sacred atmosphere of home, with the agreement and lasting support of those few faithful ones in that beginning cycle. An added cause for rejoicing was that Uranda and Kathy were expecting their first child in June.

About two miles down the road to the south of Sunrise Ranch is a dam, where the Big Thompson River, having tumbled its way through the canyon, spills over with gusto into the depths below. Gigantic rocks, each unique in its arrogant ruggedness, contrast with the peaceful atmosphere in the valley. A house perches seemingly on the very top of this spectacular waterfall, a building that had once been used as a restaurant by one of Loveland's pioneering inhabitants.

Bob Palmer, the owner at that time, was a friend of Uranda and offered it to him to use as he wished. It was a timely and welcome provision during the following months needed to repair the buildings on Sunrise Ranch. As Uranda and Kathy were lulled to sleep each night by the "sound of many waters," the music of the falls formed a symphony that sang of a New Day for mankind.

Of necessity the Headquarters office continued in Loveland for a period, as there were no facilities for anything but bare essentials on the Ranch; so there was much commuting for a while.

Water was hauled in a tank truck, filled from a pipe just across from Big Thompson School two miles to the south. Oil and gas lamps were used in those pre-electricity days. Improvements were undertaken as rapidly as possible, one of the first being the installation of a new gas range in the kitchen. A cistern was dug to contain water for the recently installed sinks that replaced two large pans. Laundry was boiled and scrubbed by hand on a washboard.

The ready-made "paradise" settings were not to be, and Uranda readily accepted the design as it presented itself. Obviously it was to be built, step by step, as had been the creation of the world, and he found himself and his company happily "in the beginning."

In a service on January 31, 1946, entitled "Mountainside Meditations," he spoke, as always from the depths of his heart:

> As we gather here on the mountainside where the stillness of nature is felt and brings peace, the afternoon sun is moving toward its place of setting beyond Green Ridge Mountain which is behind us, and as we look out across the valley below we know we stand on holy ground; for this is the place that has been dedicated to our Master's service in the earth.
>
> As pioneers we live a rather rugged form of life, devoid of many conve-

niences deemed to be essential to city dwellers. Here in the wilderness we are building an altar unto our God, that all who will may come to worship Him in spirit and in truth. Here is a place of training, where each one works with his hands, that he may fulfil the age-old obligation placed upon man when he first sinned—and in so doing we find that once again we are privileged to hear the Master's voice as He comes walking in the garden in the cool of the day.

Back through the ages the Lord has wrought wonders in human beings who have served Him in the wilderness. Shall there be murmurings and wanderings because of shortness of vision? Or shall we see the promise fulfilled that the wilderness shall blossom as the rose? Shall the dry ground yield watersprings for the faithful ones? As we have come into the wilderness to serve our King, so also have we come to that place of testing which shall in season prove as to "who shall be able to stand" and share in the victory of our Lord.

In February Uranda said:

We are not here on an ordinary ranch. The Lord drew us to this place. There are seven veins of water coming off the hill behind us and they come together at one point and one point only—seven veins of water. To me it is like the brand of the Lord upon this ground. It is His name written there.

After moving onto the property in March, Uranda attended farm auctions and purchased a tractor and other farm equipment. The first crop, sown in the spring of 1946, was wheat.

He had acquired a beautiful old organ of ancient vintage while still in Loveland (the kind where you got your exercise by pumping) which was used on the Ranch in the early days in services. Today it graces the living room in the present Executive House, its beautiful, delicately carved wood having undergone refinishing along the way by expert and loving hands.

It was not long before services, which originated in the old barn, were held in the living room of the ranch house. Uranda bought a second-hand piano for Kathy who had an exquisite singing voice and enjoyed accompanying herself. I loved hearing her strong, clear soprano tones fill the house.

People took turns offering meditations mornings and evenings. Uranda gave four services a week, and was often up until two or three in the morning sharing discussions with the group. He was delighted with any response, which drew forth the sparkling waters from the well of his amazing understanding. And while these talks often moved into depths which disturbed untouched areas, they were always filled with light, and the walls of the old house became imbued with the sound of his hearty laughter, joined by a chorus of relieved and happy voices.

In an April 10 Message he said:

> Kathy and I have just returned from California, my first trip there since 1942, and in each place we visited we were given a royal welcome and treated to the hospitality that is characteristic of Emissaries. We held wonderful services in many places.
>
> The enclosed paper, "Mountainside Meditations, Number Two," focalizes for you the intensified work of the last six weeks which climaxes and focalizes the work of the past year and a half. This in turn was brought to a climax through a four-day Special Session here on Sunrise Ranch involving all Headquarters personnel. Services began about one o'clock each day and, with time out for short recesses and the evening meal, continued until nearly midnight for each of the four days.

He said that the work at Sunrise Ranch had been proceeding effectively, and "the outer manifestation of our work is well coordinated with the spiritual activities in which we are engaged." He voiced appreciation for the expressed desire on the part of many to be of more active service and to do more in a financial sense, and acknowledged that as faithful stewards they were doing their parts as effectively as possible in the circumstance.

> The Lord has truly blest in most wonderful ways, and the substance available to His Service has been multiplied in our hands, permitting the accomplishment of much that might well be thought of as miraculous.
>
> We are preparing a special altar upon which will be placed, for appointed seasons, your special letters of realization, that in the focalized light of illumination and radiation, especially during our services, they may provide vibrational connections whereby you may more fully share in the outpouring of the holy spirit. This shall be a special altar dedicated to those who are present with us in spirit, though absent in person.

Later in the spring Martin Cecil arrived from 100 Mile House for a visit and, as always when those two met, the atmosphere was charged with the intensity of their interaction. Shortly after this, on April 26, Uranda informed the Church that he and the Board of Trustees had worked out a program for holding a Summer Session on Sunrise Ranch from July 15 to about September 15. The planned accommodation consisted of five tents, available on a reservation basis. Uranda hoped to secure army cots for sleeping facilities, although participants were to provide their own bedding. The number of people attending was to be limited to those who could be properly accommodated in the five tents. Three or four members of a family group were to use one tent. Individuals coming alone were assigned to a cot in a tent to be shared with three or four others of the same sex. The tents would be equipped with electric lights and have flat sandstone floors.

The facilities for preparing meals and providing other requirements would not permit more than about fifteen to actually stay on the Ranch at any one time. Participants were expected to share in the general work program, in the preparation of meals, etc., and the canning of foods. The work program would start in the morning and continue until two o'clock, with time out for lunch, after which there would be a service. The time from four until eight o'clock would be devoted to preparing meals, eating, taking care of chores, etc., with some time for relaxation. Meals would be served buffet style on army mess kits. Another service would begin each evening at eight o'clock and last "as long as may be found pleasing and wise."

Uranda suggested that for any who did not wish to participate in the rather rugged form of life on Sunrise Ranch reservations could be had at the Omaha Auto Court, at the Dam Store, or perhaps at Sylvan Dale, for those who came by car.

Uranda proudly announced that "the Lord sent a new Emissary into the world on Sunday morning, June 9th, at 10:10 o'clock. As the church bells were ringing, Nancy Rose Meeker was born to my darling wife and myself." They welcomed their first child and bestowed upon her the names of the beautiful and beloved mothers of both her parents.

Meanwhile Martin was returning home from Toronto where he had to leave his wife in a hospital after an operation intended to correct her state of deep depression. Facing the fact that her function would be limited for the rest of her life, in the depths of despair he wrote a poem. It embodies the anguish that can be experienced in this world, and the victory possible when one so entrapped lets his true Self find expression through the capacities of body, mind and heart.

The Abyss of Nothingness

There are times in life when the human heart
Is thrust through, it seems, by the fiery dart
Of remorse and pain and a wordless grief,
So that pity of self steals in like a thief.

Then what shall we do when we reach the place
Where courage is gone and it's hard to face
The years ahead. Shall we quit?

Or cry? Shall we weakly submit
To the voice of discouragement whispering low:
"Why should I, of all people, be treated so?"

And then perhaps sad conscience brings
Its burden, and there rings
Through troubled mind a tragic air
Of endless discord and despair.

O God, where art Thou in my desolation?
I feel Thee not, nor hope for Thy salvation.
But Thou art near at hand, my Lord, I know,
Because there have been times I knew it so.
Brought low am I; my strength is gone;
What is there left to lean upon?

In the silence of exhaustion the fevered mind is
*   still,*
And there comes a relaxation of distraught human will.
So through the darkness of the night the first faint
*   flush of dawn*
Comes gently, giving promise of a new day to be born.

"O Man, why fear? Why doubt ye me?
Who am the Source of Life in thee.
Dost live and breathe? Canst see and feel and hear?
How else these things except your Lord be near?"

So sweetly as the summer breeze
Stirs soft response in grass and trees,
The silent sounding of Thy Word,
Like distant music faintly heard,
Awakes an echo in my heart
To bring assurance that Thou art
The One whose Presence now in me
To life gives meaning, sets me free

From doubt and fear and bleak despair!
For in Thy strength I surely dare
To let all burdens roll away
And give to Thee the fullest sway
In me. For I am not mine own
Nor any man's, but Thine alone.

This earthly form which I have thought as mine,
With all its weakness and its woe, is Thine.
It take, O Lord, and train me in Thy Way,
*To **let** Thy Life be lived in me today*
And always.

— Martin Cecil
Toronto/Vancouver
6-22-46

As soon as possible Martin brought Edith to a facility in Vancouver where she could be cared for, and his frequent visits allowed her to share the light and comfort of his love for her remaining eight years.

Uranda delightedly reported on June 26 that with the approaching harvest more of the food supply for Headquarters would come from the Ranch itself, and that in the fall the office and most of the staff would be moved from town to the Ranch, thereby eliminating rent payments. He emphasized the necessity, however, to meet current expenses and have sufficient funds in addition to complete necessary remodeling of the large and substantial barn, which was being converted into office space and apartments. He added that the treasury was empty!

Uranda experienced a serious heart attack about the time of the beginning of the Summer Session. There was a period of several weeks during which he could not even walk the two or three hundred feet from the house to the Chapel. At no time, however, did he allow his condition to interfere with his conducting of services and participation in other necessary activities.

The Summer Session began on July 14th. All but five people were housed, or "tented," on the Ranch. The sessions took place in the barn and continued for two months with about fifty people present at any given time. That event witnessed the birth of a collective body consciously aware of its unified purpose, which would expand into the far corners of the earth.

One can sense Uranda's deep, fulfilling joy in the words, "Today, for the first time, I have the privilege of welcoming you to our new chapel. This is our first service here." He spoke of the significance, in the birth of what he termed the Christ Body, of the fact that the setting was in a stable and likened it to the birth of our Master, noting that the place where they were sitting had, a few weeks earlier, been a manger.

Later, reporting on the Summer Session, Joseph Wilson spoke of the barn, which had been remodeled for use as the Headquarters office and residential quarters for staff members. When the Session opened, the work had progressed to a point which made it possible to use the spacious ground floor as a chapel. The building was lit by electricity from the Ranch's own generator, and life seemed relatively comfortable. The "spacious ground floor" was, however, still literally "ground," and little creatures were often drawn to attend services. They were welcome.

6

AN EXTENDED VISIT!

July 1946 ~ January 1947

*D*uring this special time three-month-old Nancy Rose was baptised. Uranda's sixteen-year-old daughter, Marjorie Lee, was attending High School in Loveland and living with Rose Forker, who had moved from California to work in our Headquarters office. Before long they both moved to the Ranch.

Shortly after the conclusion of the Session, on September 10th I arrived on Sunrise Ranch. I had been on the Emissary mailing list since 1940, faithfully sending letters of response to Uranda and, as secretary of the Pittsburgh group after its formation in 1941, submitting weekly reports. I had continued somehow to attend the meetings at the home of John and Maud Martin, leaders of the group, after the birth of my son in 1943 and to perform my secretarial duties. My baby accompanied me, to be passed around to willing arms (mostly Betty Protzman's) while I recorded the meeting in shorthand.

Frank and Betty Protzman traveled with me on that journey to Loveland. Frank was a detective, employed by one of the largest department stores in the country. Unsurpassed in his field, his services were coveted by all the other large establishments in Pittsburgh.

To Frank, however, his job had become a source of guilt and he was haunted by thoughts of young children whom he had apprehended for stealing. Most of them were from the slum district of Pittsburgh, manipulated by the greed of their elders. Both Frank and Betty found the answers to the dilemmas in their lives when they heard Uranda, and eagerly offered themselves to assist in his work.

These two were planning a one-week visit to Sunrise Ranch, whereupon Uranda wrote to John Martin, suggesting that if possible it would be wise for me to accompany them. Frank and Betty were delighted at the prospect. The group, numbering between twelve and fifteen, decided they would like to share in my last-minute venture by raising funds to contribute to my train trip to Colorado. This sudden outworking had an impact on my husband, who had kindly tolerated my intense interest in Uranda and my Emissary friends. All I knew was that I had to go on this journey. It was a crucial point on the spiral of my life, like jumping into a sea without a horizon.

The Protzmans had left several days earlier, stopping to visit relatives in Ohio, and Billy and I were to join them in Chicago, where we would board the train for Denver. The train from Pittsburgh was very late, introducing at the start an element of apprehension which intensified throughout the trip.

Utterly exhausted when we detrained at Chicago, I ran as fast as was possible with my heavy luggage and pulling a small, sleepy boy for a seemingly interminable distance. When I reached the train it was on the verge of pulling away. The brakemen were leaning out on the steps, ready to give the signal for departure, having waited until the last minute, at the urgent request of Frank and Betty. *But* we made it!

Uranda had made arrangements for Joseph Wilson to meet us in Denver the next day and drive us the sixty miles to Loveland, but somehow Joe managed to miss us. So we located the bus and finally, after a sleepless night on the train, I collapsed into a seat. In spite of the hectic trip, I sensed an inexplicable thrill of coming home at the sight of snow-tipped mountains in the distance against a clear blue sky as the bus sped us to a place of which I knew nothing. Upon arrival in Loveland we phoned Uranda, who was unhappy that his careful preparations for an easy arrival had been aborted, and we waited for someone to come and drive us the eleven miles to our final destination.

When we arrived on Sunrise Ranch Uranda was waiting to greet us with wide-open arms and a smile like the sun itself. The state of the Ranch was not inviting, the ground sparse of vegetation, brown and infested that year with a plague of grasshoppers. And yet I was filled with a wonder that I could not explain.

A small group resided on Sunrise Ranch at that time in primitive conditions. The housing consisted of the old "Ranch House," the residence of the original builders, still used, with some alterations; the barn, later completely remodeled and presently providing beautiful accommodation, with its charming name "Stable Gables" surviving over the years—but then a barn; and a little house situated just down the road, later to become the residence of Uranda and his family. Over the years it was remodeled, then completely rebuilt, today a beautiful residence.

When I arrived the old Ranch House was the main inhabitable accommodation, consisting of a kitchen, living room and two small rooms, one of which Uranda and Kathy, with baby Nancy, used as a bedroom. My small son and I occupied the other. All of these buildings were very run-down, lacking any modern conveniences. Little Billy despised the outhouse, its seat enormous for his small body, a challenging monster with the weather turning cold.

My ticket was valid for one week. Before it expired, at Uranda's suggestion I exchanged it to extend my stay a further week. At the end of that time I knew I was destined to live and serve with this man and all that he represented, though there were giants looming large in my heart. How could I ever expect those closest to me to understand the reasons for the decision I was making? But I cashed that ticket in—and stayed.

My "office" was in a small, primitive tent adjacent to the Ranch House. On the loose dirt floor I sat on a chair, the legs of which tended to gradually sink as I worked at a little typewriter on a rickety table, with my feet in the dust and my head in the clouds of heaven as I transcribed the services Uranda gave. I had thought I was through using my secretarial skills as a profession, but I have been at it ever since, loving every minute working with the Word. In the corner of the tent would often sit my small son with a book upside-down in his lap as he extemporaneously "gave a service," and the sound of his voice was music to my ears.

A cistern adjoined the Ranch House, supplied with water from our tank truck, which made regular trips for refills several miles down the road. A new experience for me was using a community dipper to drink water from a pail. It was a time of togetherness! Before long a shower was installed, in a tiny room on the west side of the house.

To this arid, seemingly isolated valley in the foothills of the Rocky Mountains would be drawn, over many years, those who would provide the substance for the seed of a body dedicated to letting the ways of God find manifest expression in their day-to-day living. That tiny body of people sharing a mutual purpose in their work and play together flourished over the years and eventually expanded to the far corners of the earth.

After those who had come to the Summer Session had departed, there were left a precious few. Marjorie Lee and Rose Forker had moved to the Ranch from Loveland. Kathy's sisters, Billie Groves and Rosalind Hooper, were indispensable in those pioneering days, the continuity of their dedicated service unbroken through the years. Ralph Hooper,

Rosalind's husband, joined his wife and the group after completing his service in the Armed Forces and provided a vital function for a number of years as the Ranch Manager. William and Muriel Oshanek moved to the Ranch when the Headquarters office was transferred from Loveland. Richard and Dorothy Thompson, with their young daughter Mary, were a vital part of the Sunrise Ranch family from its infancy, coming from Canada, as did the Oshaneks. There were Charles Strikwerda and his small son Chuck from Oregon. Charlie was the first farmer on the place, using mules to pull the plow. Rose Forker, in addition to her invaluable assistance in the office, brought a special gift in the field of healing. And there were others who came with their valuable substance to nurture and expand that very fertile seed. Irving Horowitz (later Harwood), Frank Humphries, Albert and Gordon Christiansen were near the top of the long list taking form.

Uranda informed the School in November that a printing plant, tentatively named "The Eden Valley Press," was emerging, fulfilling a dream of many years. John Oshanek, of Winnipeg, William's brother, was generously giving his equipment to Sunrise Ranch. "In making this and other new departments possible," Uranda commented, "we have acted on faith, using all of our available material resources in the assurance that the way would open to allow us to keep going and *keep growing* without being forced to encumber our debt-free equipment." He and others hoped to print that year's Christmas Message, provided that a stock of suitable paper could be obtained.

Also under consideration was the possibility of publishing a sort of Church newspaper once or twice a month, under a name such as *The Eden Valley News*. Intended to deal with the personal experiences of those living at Headquarters, it would provide a means "for dealing with subject matter that does not properly find a place in the lesson material." This developed into a beautiful magazine over the years, distributed worldwide.

By this time leaflets and other materials were waiting to be printed. Curtis Bunce of Illinois had already had 3,000 copies of Uranda's interpretation of the 91st Psalm printed in leaflet form as a contribution to the Service. In season Curtis, an experienced printer of many years, moved to the Ranch and established a printshop on the ground (literally) floor of the big barn. He later married Faith Langworthy from California, who was already living on the Ranch.

The condition of Uranda's health had not improved satisfactorily after his heart attack and was complicated by the cumulative effects of poor nutrition in his early years. From the beginning of his ministry in Nashville, with its dominant emphasis on the healing aspect, he had practiced what might be referred to as the laying on of hands. Now there were those who provided this vital care for Uranda, and certainly he for others. But there was a critical need in his own body, and the necessity for a time away from the Ranch with its growing pains was becoming daily more obvious.

Another factor beginning to surface was, as he confided to a few of us, that the little group in Eden Valley was at a point where it would have to prove it had the substance, the seed strength, to function on its own for a while. At the same time he was imbued with such a love for this embryonic body and for Sunrise Ranch, the core of all he had worked for, that the thought of leaving presented serious questions. He would be in close touch, caring for and guiding those at Headquarters as much as was rightly possible. Keenly aware that everything was at stake, depending on a few faithful ones to play their parts during this vital phase of the Lord's work, Uranda addressed the Board of Trustees on Sunrise Ranch on January 9, 1947, in which he said:

> I felt it was impossible to consider any definite moves or undertake action of any kind until we were assured that, in case it seemed wise for us to be away for a while, we knew we had some place to go. I have written to Sally Bainbridge, giving a brief outline, and this evening I received an answer from Helene Bender. It was a very beautiful letter and indicated her oneness with you in her concern that all things should work out to perfection.

He read the letter from Karl and Helene, dated January 7th.

This couple, originally from Germany, had become a part of the Emissary movement. Inspired by Uranda's literature, they had expressed a desire to share their substance with the Lord. This consisted, in part at least, of an orange grove and avocado orchard in Riverside, California. The letter contained an invitation to Uranda to visit them, offering a setting in which he could experience a time of relaxation and healing. Uranda' words concerning this:

> My central interest and concern is for the entire program. The welfare of the Unit is the central point in question. For you to continue here effectively with the Project will require a degree of harmony and coordination over that period that would be outstanding in its excellence if we are to accomplish that which is necessary. All things being equal, it would be nice for a little visit, but to have any particular value it should be for at least two or three months, and possibly longer.

He went on to say that, outside of the cost of getting there, he thought he could work it out so that the stay in California would be virtually without expense to the Church. He was thankful for the careful management of many up to that point and felt confident it would continue. He emphasized that "the primary responsibilities with respect to direction and management" would rest upon those at Sunrise Ranch.

> I take the attitude that every individual is going to prove himself, one way

or another, and anyone who decides that he or she has excuse for turning into the wrong path would find such excuse sooner or later anyway. Those who will carry through will carry through, and those who will not, will not in any case, and you cannot drag people through in spite of themselves. It has to come from within.

I would rather come back and find a group really working together, even if it was half the size it was when I went away, than to find everyone here but with frictions and bickerings and discords. I can do more with a handful who are truly harmonized and coordinated than with any number of individuals who are not.

Uranda then gave some suggestions to consider in his absence, saying that where there were discords the individuals involved should naturally seek to find harmony between each other. That failing, the matter would then come to the attention of one or more of those in charge, perhaps all, who would assist them in finding the right way. Uranda mentioned his own attitude, that he had already offered in his teachings all that is essential to any situation. He invited those in responsible positions to bring the matter by mail to him if they wished.

William Oshanek, President of the Board, agreed that if the trip was needed for the Bishop's health it was the logical and sensible thing to do. Richard Thompson expressed complete agreement with what William had said, and added that "not only is the means of material communication open but the spiritual will be opened, and I think we have all experienced the wonderful spiritual communication with you when we could not hear the sound of your voice. I can hardly visualize Sunrise Ranch without you being here, but that is something which is personal, and I know that as we let the Lord direct us, everything is provided, and the step should be taken."

Uranda spoke, with deep feeling:

I am firmly convinced that the progress and development of the Unit is such that there is no reasonable danger of any serious setback and I certainly see no reason why there should be a break. I know that, basically and vibrationally, if I were to stay away a year I would still be having a very direct share in what was going on here, because there is something of myself in every one of your hearts, every one of your lives.

It is also true that from a practical standpoint there are some things, vibrationally, that I will be able to work out perhaps more easily being away than I could being here in person, provided the focalization here remains steady and the currents remain open. It has within it the potentiality of a great blessing, both for yourselves and myself, and for each one who is, or ever will be, connected with our Service.

If I were seeking to find some means to compliment you or give evidence of my faith in you, I could not conceive of a way that would do it more than to leave the care of this in your hands; I have worked since 1932 toward it. This period of rest would be of no value unless I could be content and in position to do my work. That would require, of course, the presence of my wife, our baby Nancy Rose, and my secretary Grace. I trust Marjorie may also be with us. Provided it can be worked out, the most logical proposition would be for me to take our bus and have a driver because I would not want to have to drive and meet all the emergencies myself.

On the following day Uranda dictated a message, entitled "Your Ministry—Retreat or Move Forward," in which he shared this crucial development with the Church members, stressing the fact that the ministry, if it was to continue, would need to be one in which Uranda himself did not need to shoulder all the main responsibilities himself, as he had over the past eleven years.

Also, during and since the Summer Session a nucleus has been formed here, with special training and perspective vision in relation to the needs of the Service and the necessities of carrying it forward effectively. For the first time we have a permanent location for our Headquarters, providing opportunity for expansion.

In the economy of the cosmos a specific provision which the Lord makes available at a given time and sends on the main line is that which is essential at the time it should arrive. When there is hindrance the timing is spoiled, so that the empty vessels are not filled when they should be, and a whole series of reactionary circumstances are thereby engendered. My responsibility has been with respect to the timing of the manifestation of the spiritual provision of that which the Lord would express through His ministry, and only indirectly with respect to the material substance, because only as I could inspire individuals to cease self-activity could the Lord cause that provision to manifest according to His timing.

To give an indication of the tremendous lag between the manifestation of the spiritual provision and the substance whereby that may be given form, I would mention that through lesson material which is already either in shorthand notes or typed form, we could send out a new lesson of from five to ten pages every week for the next three years, without my having to write or speak another word. If the responsive coordination through the membership of the School, and extending on out into the world, had allowed equally accurate timing in the manifestation of the essential material substance the effectiveness of this ministry would have been multiplied more than a hundredfold.

I have given myself in service without hesitation throughout the period of my ministry, often doing strenuous work which others should have done. Because no one else appeared to do what had to be done, I did it, in addition to carrying out the responsibilities of my primary sphere of service. As a result, the strain on my physical body has had its effect. For the past two years I have been gradually regaining my health but there have been setbacks.

Uranda referred, at this point, to the heart attack experienced at the beginning of the Summer Session:

For several weeks I could not walk the two or three hundred feet from the house to the Chapel. Nevertheless I conducted every service according to its proper timing, and my physical insufficiencies were not allowed to interfere. I have continued here holding regular services and doing everything possible toward that fulfilment to which we are all dedicated.

However, the group here is unanimously agreed that my physical welfare is a matter of concern and importance to everyone connected with this Service, and it appears to be wise and proper that I should have the opportunity of going apart for a little time, for relaxation, rest and recuperation. Let it be clearly understood that this does not mean that I would be cut off in any sense from Headquarters or from you. It does not mean that you should not write personal letters to me or feel that I have in any sense withdrawn.

Uranda stressed the vital importance of continued and increased financial support of those who lived at Headquarters, and stated that the alternative—reducing Sunrise Ranch personnel to match the current level of support—would amount to a strategic retreat "wherein all departments would come to a standstill for the time being, with the exception of the routine work of mailing out lesson material and the minimum of simple farming operations."

He pointed out that those working at Headquarters were doing so without being paid.

The critical time is the next six months, especially, because we anticipate that within a year many departments of the Project will become self-supporting. The greatest difficulty and expense is always incurred in getting under way. If we are forced to retreat to a point where we can operate within the range of a regular Church income, at least half of our present personnel will be forced to go back out into the world and secure employment of some sort. The problem is—which shall it be?

If you are not in agreement with me it would only be fair for you to so advise the headquarters staff, that they may know, before they decide whether to undertake to move forward on the present basis or to make the strategic retreat. It will have to go one way or the other, and I feel perfectly justified in leaving the whole responsibility of this matter in the hands of headquarters personnel and you who are in the field, that you may function according to your perception of the direction of the spirit.

So preparations were made for a journey to an unfamiliar place, to people whom Uranda had never met, with the full assurance in his heart of the rightness of the undertaking, yet with no hint of what would unfold in the days to come—a much longer period than he had dreamed of at the outset, leaving behind his beloved headquarters in the hands of a faithful few.

It was a strange caravan that pulled out of Sunrise Ranch in January of 1947. Uranda had acquired an ancient bus which seated fifteen people and had an ample trunk. This vehicle had seen its day, but was patched up sufficiently so that we could set out on our journey. The passengers consisted of Uranda, Kathy and Nancy; Billy and I; Marjorie Lee; Mabel Gulliver, visiting from Canada; and Gordon Christianson. Gordon was to drive us there and then return to Sunrise. Besides the passengers, of course, there was luggage—inside the bus and in a carrier on top, bulging!

Six-month old Nancy subsisted on goat's milk, so we had another passenger in the form of Mossy, who took up residence in the partially open trunk, the lid tied securely. Mossy shared her space with enough hay bales to get her to her destination. Whenever necessary Uranda would stop by the side of the road, reasonably close to water, remove the goat from her domicile and milk her, so that Nancy would have her needed bottle. Along with that came the feeding of Mossy, finding water for her, and walking this vital member of our entourage. After that we rolled along, often leaving behind in open-mouthed amazement an audience that just couldn't miss the performance.

Countless adventures added various hues of color to the trip. There was barely enough money to get the bus and its passengers to California, due in large measure to the fact that such funds as were meant to pay for food and lodging were gobbled up by unexpected repairs to the old bus, which was constantly breaking down. We would be delayed for hours in some isolated spot while Gordon found someone who could come to the rescue. So, after the food which we had brought with us disappeared, some real hunger pangs were experienced by all before we reached our destination—with the exception of Nancy and Mossy!

I have observed, in retrospect, that details of such experiences, of discomfort or deprivation, fade from memory. The ones I recall vividly are of a different nature, imbued deeply with heart substance as for instance a walk with Uranda at sunset in the golden-brown of New Mexico, bathed in the reflection of a breathtaking panorama in the sky, splashed seemingly at random by a heavenly paintbrush. Illusions of hunger, lack or discomfort paled in the radiant light of promise.

Finally—Riverside! I had my first view of palm trees—stately, fan-topped wonders that lined the highway leading us to the place we would call home for the next seven months. Our residence was not the home of our hosts but rather their small cottage in the middle of a hayfield, with the address 3812 Pyrite Street where they had a cow and kept some beehives. Although one could come upon avenues of palm trees or avocado orchards and orange groves within a few minutes, there were areas, such as ours, that were desert-like. Except for several large, beautiful trees close to the house, their thick, green branches bestowing heavenly shade, there was little protection from the searing Southern California sun. There was a big hay field and an abundance of sand. Among the very welcome trees was a fragrant eucalyptus. To pick a leaf and press it between the fingers would release a pungent aromatic healing essence. Mossy loved to graze nearby and nibble the leaves, and only baby Nancy could have described the taste of eucalyptus-flavored goat milk!

We were welcomed by our hosts, a middle-aged couple with a pronounced German accent. They had no children and had made a comfortable existence in that sunny land. We settled into the one-bedroom cottage. The problem of accommodation was handled by using a couch in the living room as a sofa by day and a bed by night. There was also space adjoining the living room which when necessary doubled as another bedroom.

A tiny bathroom had the luxury of a shower, with hot water available only during certain daylight hours when the desert sun beat unmercifully upon the little house. They had what I suspect was the original solar-heating system! Pipes were coiled on the outside of one wall of the house, and it worked well for part of the day. The supper dishes were washed as quickly as possible, while some heated water remained in the pipes as the evening hours advanced. Of course timing had everything to do with the possibility of taking a shower in other than cold water!

The only other building on the property was a garage, made of corrugated tin and without a door. It housed a tractor and whatever other vehicles needed accommodation at the moment.

The Benders' permanent residence was situated a few miles from this little farm, in a lovely home they called Winterwarm, two miles from Fallbrook. On our one visit there

I experienced for the first time the thrill of eating an orange I picked from the tree, and the comforting sensation of standing in the embrace of the huge green cool umbrella of an enormous avocado tree.

Our fare consisted mainly of fruit salads; of oranges fresh from the tree, always the ripest, which are not as saleable as the greener fruit; cottage cheese for protein; plus an endless supply of avocadoes, again the ripest. The provision of the Lord was awesomely fitting and timely, as is always proven when His bounty is accepted for what it is—manna from heaven. It was ideal for the needs of Uranda's health, and of course monetary expenditure for food was minimal—that also timely!

During this crucial period when so much came to focus in the ministry, Uranda used those days, relaxing under the sun in a hammock slung between two beautiful big old trees in the yard, letting substance be drawn together that would be caused to expand in the days and years to come.

One of the things which began to unfold was in conjunction with what Sally Bainbridge (an early Emissary from California, later residing on Sunrise Ranch) brought regarding her vast knowledge and perception of astronomy/astrology—a striking example of how all aspects of man's knowledge could be used when under the control of the spirit of God. In this instance it was a matter of sitting down with Sally and letting her draw on her prolific fund of knowledge. It was amazing to witness the process as facts were brought into the light of truth and distorted patterns were caused to rearrange into a new and exciting design. I recorded this in shorthand, and thus was begun what could have developed into a magical series entitled "The Science of Mazzaroth." However, Sally was not able to continue this for long, and so there was another sad abortion of the endless flow of the Lord's bounty.

This instance affords an opportunity to see how every aspect of man's world of knowledge could be cleared of the distortions implanted through the millennia. The Truth is present behind all that is manifest and can easily be changed from the destructive current into the life-giving one of upliftment into the exciting level of the ceaseless unfolding wisdom of the creator.

It is clear in this example that it can happen only as there is present one who is attuned to the reality of the truth—and also obvious is the difficulty for the human ego to relinquish the ingrained conviction of its own impeccable "wisdom."

Far, far in the past, but not lost to memory, there was a man named Job, and in his mind was the wonder of the wisdom and understanding of the cosmos. He spoke of places like Orion, and Pleiades, and Arcturus—and Earth. A word also appears in that amazing record, preserved through the millennia: *Mazzaroth,* the truth of the science behind the intriguing areas of astronomy and astrology. Nor is that limited to vast bodies in "space," for Job revealed his meticulous knowledge of the workings of the inhabitants of the earth. Nothing was excluded in his awe-inspiring references to the habits of animals and other creatures of this planet—all the kingdoms of this world—even the weather! It is all Mazzaroth.

On one still, especially peaceful warm day while Uranda was relaxing in the hammock and dictating one of many letters, he suddenly ceased talking, and I looked up from my notebook. He gestured to me to be still, without taking his eyes off the tree branch directly above us. In the same instant I heard the frantic cries of a frightened bird. There, almost imperceptibly gliding along the thick branch right above our heads was a large snake, its goal obviously the nest of the bird that would not move from its place of vigil close by.

Uranda whispered to me to silently go in and get his gun, which I did. Returning, I slipped it to him, and with his expert aim he shot the snake. Its heavy, writhing body made a sickening thump when it hit the ground. Then Uranda shot it again. Through all of this, that little bird never moved from its position of guarding its nest, even when the blast from the gun shattered the stillness. Then the air was quiet again, with the bird still in its place. While we watched it we shared something of indescribable beauty as that tiny creature poured out its heart in a thrilling song of thanksgiving.

Billy played outside most of the time. He found it was not easy to ride a tricycle in sand! One day he came running into the house, eyes starred with wonder. "Come and see. Come and see." We ran with him, and beheld a miracle that had just occurred, at least in the eyes of a three-year-old boy. He had just witnessed the birth of twins to Mossy and we shared in the final stages of that ever new and wondrous process.

While we were at Riverside, Edna Henderson came to join us from Sarnia, Canada, her husband having recently passed away. She was coming to spend her later life near Uranda and his ministry. The finances which she provided were a blessing, at a time when there was very little in the Lord's coffers. Among other things, it made possible the purchase of some farm machinery, bought later in California and transported to Sunrise Ranch when we returned. When money, or substance of whatever nature, was given to Uranda it was used, without exception, for the needs of the ministry—and with joy.

An event of unsurpassed importance occurred during this time in Riverside. Lord Martin Cecil came from 100 Mile House to spend some time with Uranda, his unique expression perfectly complementing that of Uranda's.

I recall a day, before our trip to California and having recently arrived on Sunrise Ranch, when Uranda, who was experiencing a particularly low point in his physical health, was reading his mail in the living room of the old Ranch House. I was in the next room and heard his voice suddenly ring out with a note of triumph, "*This* is what I've been waiting for!" In his hand he held a letter from Martin Cecil and in his heart the absolute assurance that he had, finally, that steady point of agreement in form on earth so necessary if his work was to continue, and that it would never waver. It never did.

We had been in Riverside almost two months when Martin arrived, accompanied by Capt. Conrad O'Brien-ffrench and an elderly English lady, Lucy Twining, a member of the Vancouver group. Martin and Conrad slept in the garage, their cots tucked in between machinery of various sorts. Of course the absence of doors presented no problem; the weather was *hot!* One very early morning Martin awoke with the strange sensation of having his face rubbed with sandpaper. Opening his eyes, he looked into the big brown eyes of the resident cow, that was soberly, lovingly and thoroughly licking his face.

Those were wonderful days, and on into the nights, of listening to the interchange between Uranda and Martin, that must have made the stars in the heavens shine with a special luster. Much that was finding focus at that time dealt with particular points in divine hierarchy, such as Lords, or focalizations, of particular essences of being. One day Lucy Twining, tall and slender, with a delightful English accent and sense of humor, regally sailed into the kitchen en route to the bathroom, towel over her arm and a gleam of anticipation in her eye, and announced that she was going to take a shower. We informed her that Uranda, and then Martin, had just finished showers and the solar-heated water would be cold by now. She did an about-face, marched into the living room and declared, to anyone who would listen: "The *Lords* of creation got there before me!"

On another intensely hot day, Nancy, one year old, and Billy, three and a half, were playing in the sandy yard near the house. Taking dictation in the house, I stepped to the door to check on them and saw, oblivious to them and very close, a large rattlesnake. Slowly I backed up and breathlessly told Uranda. In no time he had his gun, and the rattlesnake was dead in a matter of seconds. The children were startled by the sudden shot but, like the little bird in the tree when Uranda shot another snake, made no outcry. With upturned faces devoid of fear, and without moving from their places, they smiled their innocent thankfulness.

7

MORNING STAR

February ~ December 1947

*I*t was not long after Uranda left his beloved Sunrise Ranch in Eden Valley that the hidden factors which were troubling the waters surfaced. The implications of this were contained in his message before leaving. Then, from Riverside, on February 10th, he outlined some of those factors as follows:

> Some months ago Joseph T. Wilson left Headquarters, with his official positions in connection with the Church completely severed. I understand he is unhappy that his leaving was not announced. The reactionary attitudes which led to his severance from the headquarters staff had been very prominent for over a year, and for his sake I was not inclined to make public the difficulties which he engendered in the outworking of our Project, so I simply said nothing. The high personal regard which Joe and I have always held for each other has not been changed by the differences of viewpoint which led to his removal, and this personal friendship has made me wish to keep silent. However, he has not kept silent, so I can no longer do so.
>
> Prior to his leaving, Joe wrote me a letter in which he predicted the failure of the Service, on the basis of his judgment as to the manner in which it should

be operated. I could not agree with the methods he suggested, though I repeatedly emphasized that I was in hearty agreement with the end to be attained: that is, a practical function on a sound basis at headquarters by reason of which spiritual realities and material functions might be unified.

Joe Wilson and Paul Keenan are working together in an endeavor to promote what I would classify as an insurrection. Their primary point of contention is that I have failed, and they are advancing the idea that very soon someone will be appointed to take my place. They claim to accept the Teachings of the Third Sacred School and are advocating response to the LORD of Lords, and individually to the Father within, but are rejecting the instrument through which that Teaching was made available to all of you. They take the attitude that *they* will have to act in order to save the Service from some great catastrophe.

Over a period of several years I have sought to assist both of these men into a true understanding of reality. I can point to writings released over ten years ago which clearly reveal the error of their attitude and contention. However, there is now in the fringe of the Service, among those with no responsible positions, the start of a movement designed to attract any who feel that my Teachings should be accepted but that I, as the instrument, should be rejected.

Ever since 1934 there has been a reaction, on the part of one or more people at intervals of from one to three years, to try to separate me from my Teaching, so it is not something new in my experience. It has always been my policy to make public to the entire Church any situation wherein there has been a considerable rebellion against the authority of my leadership on the part of those who have been closely connected with headquarters.

The group on Sunrise Ranch is working effectively and harmoniously with me, so this is merely on the fringe of the Service. Nevertheless, it has reached out to touch quite a number who have walked in the Way with me for a long time. There are only five or six who have acted definitely on the basis of the insurrection. Whether any of these will find it in their hearts to return to the fold is a matter which only time can determine.

The temporal authority of the Church is vested in the Board of Trustees. I am the Bishop and carry full authority with respect to spiritual matters. The Board and I are in perfect harmony and stand together. The Teachings of the Third Sacred School belong to the Board of Trustees and to myself. No one who rejects me has any right to the use of these Teachings, and only those who remain harmonious to the Church as presently constituted will receive papers not yet released.

Should any of you feel inclined to reject my authority and leadership, so that you should wish to try to accept my Teaching without accepting me, you may write to Headquarters asking for Joseph T. Wilson's address and it will be sent to you, but at the same time your name will be removed from our mailing list.

You will be happy to know that my health has already shown considerable improvement. I bless you in the fire of the Christ Love, that you may let the Spirit of God direct you in the Way wherein you may truly serve as a member of the One Christ Body.

A few weeks after the above message to the School, he wrote from Riverside to "all my assistants at Headquarters":

Since our arrival here I have frequently had a sensation of being a focalization of consciousness in spirit hovering over Sunrise Ranch and able to look down, as if from a height of five or six hundred feet, upon the trees and buildings, and the comings and goings of individuals. The varying degrees of attunement which I could feel from the vibrational currents connected with each individual have been interesting to watch. I heartily commend your faithful endeavors, for you are learning the art of maintaining equilibrium in reality.

Accompanying this letter was a special message of February 16th entitled "A Morning Star," to be sent to those who expressed agreement in reply to his message of February 10th. Uranda had previously revealed that he brought a representation of the Spirit of Truth to focus at this time. Referring to Martin, he said:

The representation of the Spirit of Life, coming into manifest expression through the body, established according to the pattern of the Spirit of Truth, moving under the power of the Spirit of Love, provides the means for the intensified function of the creative triangle on earth, by which resurrection from darkness into the light may cause the restoration to become a reality.

After referring to the passage in Job 38, where it speaks of the morning stars singing together at the time of the laying of the foundations of the earth, Uranda eloquently shared his experience "in the early dawn" at the time of Martin's realization of his divine commission. He beheld in the sky the morning star with a special brilliance, like a beacon "sending earthward a message that the Sons of God still reign supreme and shall once again shout for joy when the earth shall have been cleansed from all sin, suffering, sorrow and death."

Martin Cecil then responded:

> Our great Master said, "I am the way, the truth and the life." In Him all that was necessary to the salvation of the human race was, and is, focalized. The Way is the way of the Christ Love and we recognize that He in His place is the Lord of Love. When He was on earth He was the supreme focalization of the divine on earth, and therefore focalized the Spirit of Truth and the Spirit of Life within Himself. The accomplishment then was possible only under His personal direction.
>
> After His ascension into the inner planes He remained of course the focalization of the Spirit of Love and resumed His responsibilities as the supreme Being at the apex of the seventh plane, but the responsibilities of the Spirit of Truth were returned to that particular focalization. We have then remaining the Spirit of Life, which relates primarily to the Christ Body made manifest on earth. As the body begins to take form, the focalization of that Spirit of Life automatically begins to become aware of the currents of life focalized in himself and flowing through the body. There is no separation in this. It is One.

Uranda then noted that

> seven years ago an important step in the outworking of the plan of God on earth was fulfilled, when the Lord opened the way by which Martin Cecil harmonized with us in this ministry. The initial fruitage of that seven years of faithful function now begins to appear, making possible the next great step in the fulfilment of the cosmic plan, by reason of which the Service of the Lord shall be caused to increase; for that Rock cut out without hands shall grow, and fill the whole earth.

In a "Special Message" of March 4 Uranda dealt specifically with the removal of Joseph T. Wilson as Treasurer. The excerpts that follow reveal some of the factors with which Uranda was working.

> When I delegated to others the responsibility of taking care of the church funds, those who were looking at the matter from the standpoint of "good business" were surprised to find that my conveyance of that responsibility did not include the power of control in the activities of the church. It was incomprehensible from any human standpoint, or upon any supposedly sound business basis of the world, that the holder of the purse could not and did not control church policy or function, and especially that, though the Bishop of the Church had been as completely segregated from any money matters as it was possible technically to achieve, so that he had no funds and could not

write a check on the church account, etc., he could not be controlled.

Up until this time I have never, even when the finances were under my own personal control, been in position to establish what I consider to be an absolutely clear vibration with respect to church income and church expenditure. In my estimation this fact has, through the years, cost this Service literally hundreds of thousands of dollars that might otherwise have been available to our use. But those associated with me could never get me to conform to the principles of the world or to compromise with the things of this world in order to increase either our membership or our financial resources.

Uranda went on to speak of his trust in the current Board's devotion to the same ideals which motivated his actions.

I detect no crosscurrents in the consciousness of the Board members. Every gift that comes to the church, whether small or large, should be received in His Name with equal thankfulness, and those who give in the right attitude and on the right vibration give most, regardless of amount.

We trust the Lord, but we are cautioned not to tempt the Lord. We are not under the necessity of any penurious attitude or action, but we are under the necessity of avoiding waste. The Lord provides for the effective function in service, but not for waste. That is true, whether of money or of any other form of material substance.

This is the beginning of a new creative period, and as we all function correctly and hold steady, that which limits and binds must fall away. I have always had more faith in the methods of God than in the methods of men.

A service at Riverside on March 23rd entitled "Martin's Ordination" culminated a five-hour session during which Martin was ordained the second Bishop of the Church and acknowledged as the focalized representation of the Spirit of Life.

Upon receipt of several letters from Albert Christiansen, one of the points of focus on Sunrise Ranch, Uranda addressed the group there via Albert on April 16. He emphasized that at this time there was need for discipline in specific areas; namely: the use of alcohol, profane or foul language, gambling, and uppermost "the essential respect with which women and girls should be treated."

In his Message of June 20 Uranda announced that the Expansion Program would be under the authority of "The Eden Valley Proctorage," which was composed of the Board of Trustees, with related correspondence focalized by Richard Thompson.

During our stay at Riverside the Benders made regular visits to their property. There was the cow that needed tending by Karl, bees to keep; and they maintained a vigilant eye on what was going on, with growing unease about a number of their observations. It is one thing to read the mailings and agree from afar; it is quite another to let those principles be applied in daily living, with emphasis on the primary law, "Judge not." Indications were that this was not going to happen with Karl and Helene.

Looking back upon those days in Riverside, at the doors that were opened in the seemingly impenetrable walls of mankind's deeply entrenched consciousness, one must admit the wonder of the working of the Law. Some thirty years later a manifestation in very substantial form came into the hands of the Lord in that same area of His garden on earth. In 1977 a beautiful place called Glen Ivy, with a public Spa, very close to Riverside, was purchased and has become a vital center for the ministry. Three decades after its inception that seed bore rich fruit, on a scale undreamed of in those pioneering days. Avocado trees grow in abundance there, with a variety of oranges, grapefruit, lemons, and much, much more, to say nothing of tropical flora everywhere, wooded hills and in the distance oftimes snow-covered mountains.

We have searched for that old cottage in Riverside and the lane that led off the highway into the field, which would have been close to our present California center, but it is long gone. The contrast of that with our Glen Ivy paradise taxes the credulity of the most imaginative. For these many years those who have attended a variety of councils and classes there have reveled in its exotic yet very practical atmosphere.

Never to be forgotten, in all of this, is the primary provision that appeared at the precise time when Uranda's health was in sore need, with a time of rest and healing in a sunny clime, and the ideal setting for the outworking of Martin's ordination and vital exchange between them, establishing the foundation for the years to come. Coincident with this, and essential to the outworking, was the presence of a few stalwart angels on a primitive ranch in Colorado, moving through a period of crisis and proving in their living that a body had been born and would grow in grace and stature, fulfilling the prophecies of the ages.

Martin and his friends returned to Canada, and it was approaching the time when we would be moving on. Karl and Helene Bender were, by this time, anxious to have us depart. They could not reconcile Uranda's (and our) function in close proximity with their ideas of what divine action would be. As with all human beings, concepts ingrained from childhood and hereditary influences produce barriers that must be allowed to dissolve if the age-old, death-dealing way of existence is to come to an end. Some of these can seem to be ridiculously unimportant in the light of the greater issues—such as using the bed in the living room as a couch during the day, or a dent in a piece of equipment—but all such, of whatever nature, are excuses for the deeper reasons for rejecting the divine design which brings true order out of chaos.

The next step was beginning to take form in Uranda's consciousness, and the setting proved to be Salinas, near San Francisco. Our journey took us to the home of Patty Uhl, whose expressed desire was to make the substance over which she had stewardship available to further the work of the Lord which focused in Uranda and his ministry. So we said good-bye to Riverside and headed north, arriving in Salinas on August 6th.

Gabilan Ranch, our new home for a season, had a beauty completely different from the one we had left behind. It consisted of a rambling ranch-style house where Patty and her husband lived, along with Bob Smith who was in charge of the operation of the ranch. A large barn and accommodations for guests who attended this variation of a dude ranch stood not far from the main house. We were housed in the guest facility, a one-story row of connected motel-like apartments, simple but adequate. On the same property, barely visible from the residence, was a track for sulky-racing, stables for the horses, and housing for the hired hands.

Patty was expert at the sport, a source of great enjoyment to herself—and anyone in the vicinity. She presented an elegant picture, small body erect, black hat perched jauntily on her head—a remarkable woman whom I liked instantly. We shared a closeness, the common denominator being a profound love for the Lord and a recognition of Uranda in his place. Patty was born into the strata of society in San Francisco known as "Nob Hill." Her natural mien of calm but assured authority never obscured but rather enhanced the light of tender love in her warm brown eyes.

Her husband was appreciably older than she. They had no children, and he barely tolerated our arrival and continued presence at Gabilan. His disapproval of Uranda and all that pertained to him increased daily. I am not aware of the extent to which he knew of Patty's desire to share her prosperity with the church, but there were definitely some obstacles in the path of that fulfilment.

Gabilan Ranch was surrounded by gently rolling hills, serene and inviting. It was a definite change from the heat of Riverside, with the moist air from the nearby West Coast often forming a mist that covered the valley, bringing chilly days and chillier nights. As it happened, we were to be there for over a year, staying until the early fall of 1948—not exactly the "possible four months or more" that seemed to be indicated when we left Sunrise Ranch.

Bob Smith was an outstanding man in many ways, well built, handsome, intelligent, with an extensive and varied education. He had been a writer for *The New Yorker* magazine and it was a delight on rare occasions in the "big house," such as a holiday when we were invited to share a much appreciated festive meal, to hear him recite some of his witty poems and short pieces published in that magazine. He managed the Gabilan business and the property well, and provided a friendship for Patty in her difficult situation. His friendship with Uranda and the rest of us was warm and welcoming, and in his own "worldly" way offered an understanding that had a comforting, healing quality.

In San Francisco, Uranda purchased some farm equipment and a small trailer home with finances provided by Edna Henderson, the elderly lady recently widowed, from Sarnia, Ontario, who had joined our party in Riverside. The trailer provided living quarters for me and my son and doubled as Uranda's office, with my typewriter in a corner. It had no bathroom, and the little sink was nonfunctional without a connection with water. This was no problem, situated as it was in close proximity with the accommodation of the rest of our party. The sorely needed farm vehicles were to go to Sunrise Ranch when we returned, also the trailer, which would continue there temporarily in its multiple capacity.

At Salinas we did not have the provision of beautiful fruit ripe from the trees of Southern California. With almost no financial resources there were days when our food supply was practically nil, but, paralleling the state of our journey to Riverside, we got through each day somehow, trusting the Lord. I recall putting adhesive tape on the soles of Billy's shoes, when there was nothing left to them but the tops! And then, just at that time, I received a letter from an angel, my mother, who would only know there was a need because of her closeness in spirit and her enfolding love. In it was tucked a $50 bill. So, shoes for Billy and the same for Nancy, and in those days it would even go further. That was a time for breaking ceilings, and I cannot think of any that were left intact!

There were incidents to be recalled later with tenderness, one of which included an elderly ranch-hand, Dave, who would take Billy by the hand and go down to the race-track. One day my son came to me, and with wonder in his eyes asked, "Mommy, what's a friend?" With tears in mine, I faced the stark reality of just where my little boy was, and how occupied I was—of necessity, I felt—with business other than his. Yes, that sweet man was a friend to a lonely little boy, and I loved him for it. One day he took him to a rodeo in the big city, and Billy came home with cowboy boots and a cowboy hat. Oh, joy!

I experienced my first earthquake at Salinas. I was busily typing when suddenly the contents of my desk were flung to the floor, and my typewriter and I found ourselves in a close embrace. There were other lesser tremors, often at night when in bed.

Uranda made sure there were special times when we packed up and went for a day on the beach, not far away, or enjoyed a jaunt into downtown Salinas. Occasional trips to San Francisco were a great treat to me, and I found my first visit to Chinatown with its different culture an exciting and rewarding experience, heralding much that would appear in years to come.

During our sojourn in Salinas, Fern Meeker accepted the invitation of Uranda and Kathy to come and be with them. What a remarkable outworking, to see this woman, who had recognized the great one that Uranda was and had provided something for him at a crucial period of his ministry, follow through unwaveringly in that devotion. In spite of involvement with her own personal shortcomings in the past, she could not deny the reality of the spirit expressing through him. She had found employment in the interval, overtaxing her capacities, and after this visit with Uranda she soon quit her job and moved to Sunrise Ranch where she happily spent the rest of her days. She coordinated the mailing department before its inevitable expansion, and lived contentedly in a tiny cottage, the first of its kind to be built on the Ranch, later moving to a larger accommodation.

Many things came to focus while we were at Salinas, as was true of our time in Riverside—days of unsurpassed importance as the foundation for the ministry was established. One such occurrence was a session held at Gabilan Ranch, including people from many places. Martin Cecil attended; Ralph and Roz Hooper, who continued on with us there for a while; John Oshanek from Winnipeg; Bill and Frieda Martens from Milwaukee, and others. Much was accomplished, and it was absorbing to watch Uranda at work, passionately using every conceivable opportunity to let such substance be drawn together, including people, as could be mustered, to further the purpose for which we had all come on earth—days filled with him speaking of "things pertaining to the kingdom."

Another landmark during those eventful days was Uranda's first trip to 100 Mile House in the fall of 1947, Martin's home in British Columbia, Canada. The car was loaded to capacity, and then some! But that was the norm in those days. All those things were accepted, not grudgingly but in the spirit of adventure and a certain innocence. It just did not occur to us to complain!

It was my first trip to Canada. We arrived, finally, at 100 Mile House late at night and drove up to Martin's home. Uranda knocked on the door and we were greeted by Martin's incomparable smile and hearty "Welcome!" which engraved on my heart the message that this was another true home, which it has ever been. We were billetted in Martin's modest home, his office being used as extra sleeping quarters for the visit. He had built the house some time after coming to the Cariboo.

A Special Session took place then. I recorded all their words in shorthand, which I had been doing since my arrival on Sunrise Ranch in 1946 and would continue until we had our first tape recorder in 1953, after which, of course, it all still had to find its way on paper—this, to say nothing of endless correspondence. It has always been a joy and privilege for me to work thus with the Word.

Then, back to Salinas. Shortly after this Uranda instructed Albert Christiansen, the new Treasurer (Gordon and he were brothers) to ask William Oshanek to call a special Board meeting to consider a letter, addressed to the Board and entitled "The Atmosphere of Heaven," dated October 31st, to be read later to the Unit. In it Uranda spoke of his concern that there be a clarity of consciousness with regard to something that had been working out through their president, William Oshanek. He said:

> Any limitation of function in the vibratory field which may have been evident in your president in the past came about because of his extreme earnestness and sincerity and the zealousness with which he sought to discharge his duties and responsibilities of ministry.... Those things which tend to appear as contentions among you never cause me to take sides with anyone on a basis of one being against another.

Uranda asked the Board to assume wise control of its resources:

> Devise a method of function which will keep your expenditures within the range of income, so that you are not constantly spending money that you do not have. Such a program will allow an increase of income, but there must first come a decrease in expenditure so that a balance is obtained in the vibrational field. There has been a tendency to feel that if your expenditures were beyond income, the fact could be reported to me and I would in some manner clear the matter. This type of function is not in harmony with reality.
>
> You have been overly concerned about the manifestation of things to fill the voids which you see. I see them also and am not unmindful of them, but you need to let your coordinated function as a unit manifest in the field now within the range of your control. That includes the Church income, but in relation thereto we have all the things present on the Ranch. When you use that which you have as effectively as possible, and at the same time have clearly established a vibrational pattern according to reality in the creative field harmonious to that ultimate fulfilment to which we are called, what rests between these two extremes, as they might be called, will naturally begin to appear.
>
> If you fail to properly utilize and control that which is within your range of control, you have no means of controlling that which is as yet unmanifest or invisible. What you do in miniature sets up the vibration that reaches out to that which is not yet visible. I have always caused those things which were within the range of my control to do more than they were ever intended to do. I have made quarters that were supposed to take care of two or three people be sufficient for a dozen. I keep that which is made manifest so filled, so "pressed down, shaken together and running over," that it has got to grow. That is the

pressure from above in which you are called to cooperate and participate.

You have done this to some degree, but what has been achieved is a step along the way. When any of you act or think or speak as if the Lord is weak today, as if the supply of His provision had come sadly to an end, you are shutting off the currents and denying those things which He would abundantly provide. The Lord is strong. The Lord's wisdom and knowledge is sufficient to every need and problem. His supply is sufficient to the filling of every void. The things of heaven cannot manifest except in the atmosphere of heaven. Your first responsibility is to establish and make manifest the atmosphere of heaven in your immediate environment. Then the Lord will take care of causing the things of heaven to appear in that atmosphere.

I recall a Christmas dinner at the Uhl house with a range of feeling memories. One is of being under a heavy cloud, in spite of the magnificent Christmas tree extravagantly decorated, and the delicious turkey dinner with all the holiday trimmings. The oversized body of Mr. Uhl ensconced in sullen disapproval seemed to challenge the spirit of Christmas. However, Patty had so wished to provide us with something special, and we let nothing spoil our enjoyment of the feast prepared in love by our dear friend.

8

HOME TO EDEN VALLEY

December 1947 ~ March 1949

*U*randa sent a letter to Sunrise from Gabilan Ranch on December 12 entitled "Reorganization for Sunrise Unit," in which he outlined some basic organizational guidelines for the community. He began by acknowledging the Unit members' willingness to cooperate and said that the guidelines were the result of "agreements reached during the Special Session ending October 19 at 100 Mile House, through Martin and myself":

 1. Beginning January 1, 1948, each one shall be employed by the church at a fixed, uniform wage, regardless of ability or type of work, which I suggest should be, to start at least, 45 cents an hour for a 36-hour week, that is six hours a day for six days. At a later time I will make suggestion regarding essential overtime which may be required, for instance at seed time and harvest. Further I suggest that each one will be charged $1.25 a day for meals and a certain amount for lodging, so that after the individual has paid for meals and lodging and has paid tithe to the church from his weekly wage he will have remaining to himself approximately $2 in cash, which shall be for his personal necessities. For thirty people this will amount to $240 a month paid by

the church for their personal incidentals.

2. In addition, the church shall offer to advance $50 each to the young folks who will begin an authorized project as members of a 4-H Club; and for adults who develop a plan for projects approved by the Church Board which may provide individual income, the church will advance $100 per person—to be taken care of during time when the individual is not working as an employee of the church.

Many details will need to be worked out, and certain regulations established, as for instance regarding tools belonging to the church. Also, for those who need a certain amount of land for their projects, I propose that lots 50 x 150 be allocated at a rental rate of $1 per month.

3. The church would purchase a truck, say a 1 1/2-ton Ford and equip it with a dump body, also a new tractor, to be equipped with a sand and gravel loader, which could be used for many things such as excavating work and the making of Cemadobe blocks; and, further, an air compressor, possibly a Hobart, which shall be powered with the engine purchased with the sawmill outfit, making it possible to have a complete and satisfactory air compressor unit for about $500, items essential to construction projects, as well as farming and general operations.

4. There should be a uniform method of construction of dwellings and other buildings, the main wall construction to be of Cemadobe blocks.

5. Four large cisterns are to be dug and prepared, each capable of holding 24,000 gallons of water, one to be filled from the run-off water from the barn roof, for laundry and hair-washing purposes, and the other three to be filled at the time of the Spring thaws and whenever sufficient rainfall makes it possible, to be used for showers, stock, dishwashing, etc., and that one well be developed for provision of water necessary to specially designed toilets.

For those who do not drill wells on approved sites I propose cisterns of a uniform 1,500 gallon capacity, which should supply a family of two or three for at least a month, in view of the provision of central laundry facilities, and that such cistern water will be utilized for lawns, etc. This will be hauled by the church at $1.25 a load ($3.75 a month for water) or the individual may haul his own water, utilizing a small trailer tank which we anticipate making available at a nominal rental fee. There will of course be a drinking water cistern provided for the main Project and piped to the community kitchen for drinking and cooking purposes.

The outer form of regulation is important but the individual spirit of function and cooperation will be even more important.

Uranda repeatedly emphasized the importance of cohesion within the Unit, and warned of the danger of letting anything come between each other.

These insignificant reactions may be transparent mica-thin sheets of insulation, so that to some they may not even appear to be, but they are slippery, they do not permit true cohesion and, if allowed to continue indefinitely, when the pressures come the fault will appear, the damage done.

From Isaiah, he quoted:

"Wherefore the Lord said, Forasmuch as this people draw near me with their mouth, and with their lips do honor me, but have removed their heart far from me, and their fear toward me is taught by the precept of men: Therefore, behold, I will proceed to do a marvelous work among this people, even a marvelous work and a wonder: for the wisdom of their wise men shall perish, and the understanding of their prudent men shall be hid. Woe unto them that seek deep to hide their counsel from the Lord, and their works are in the dark, and they say, Who seeth us? and who knoweth us? Surely your turning of things upside down shall be esteemed as the potter's clay: for shall the work say of him that made it, He made me not? or shall the thing framed say of him that framed it, He had no understanding?" Let it not be so with us!

Back along the way Uranda had suggested there might be a publication that would carry the atmosphere and news of Sunrise Ranch and bear the name, *Eden Valley News*. This took form, with Richard Thompson as Editor. An insight into the lives of Richard and Dorothy Thompson and their introduction to the ministry is contained in a letter written by Richard on November 2, 1949, to K. N. Ogier, Lloyds Bank, London:

It was in the early months of 1939 that I came to the conclusion that there was no hope of making a valid contribution to the wellbeing of mankind through political action or economic reform. As far as the first was concerned I had bitter personal experience that politics was a morass of putrefaction, and that those who held the substantive power would not allow any change to come about that would free their slaves from economic bondage. As to the second, the use that men made of their lives when they were economically independent did not show any firm basis for the idea that economic freedom for all would bring about any basic change in human nature in the direction of peace and goodwill.

We were in Winnipeg in 1937-40. Dorothy had had a number of major op-

erations and she was very ill indeed, becoming paralyzed on her right side. Through it all she knew she could be healed, and the first steps in this long process, which only now is reaching completion, were taken when we made the acquaintance of a wonderful doctor, a chiropractor in Winnipeg. Besides helping Dorothy, John Oshanek asked us to join a study group.

I wrote to Bishop Meeker and received a large quantity of literature. Since then I have been reading what he has written, hearing him speak and observing him live his teaching. I am absolutely convinced that he offers the way of life that is truly practical, not only for myself but the way whereby the order of the universe may find expression on earth.

My work, since coming here in 1945, has been much occupied with doing. Until then it was almost exclusively teaching, lecturing, reading, writing. In Winnipeg, besides organizing a political party, I published a monthly review and gave a series of forty radio broadcasts. In 1940 we moved to Toronto and I took a job at Upper Canada College. Then we moved to Port Hope, where I taught Spanish, French and English at Trinity College School, to which numbers of the progeny of industrial magnates, etc. came to be fitted for the struggle for existence. These were very interesting years. The teaching of Bishop Meeker provided keys to the understanding of so many things that had before seemed inexplicable.

I have been laying concrete blocks in a hen house. In the summer my work has been mainly in the garden which reached an area of five acres last year; I have the use of a Rototiller. Dorothy is in charge of the kitchen. She also bakes the bread for the four dozen members of the group. It is the most wonderful bread made from the wheat grown on our own land, ground by me. Mary is taller than her mother, and goes to the High School in Loveland.

We have had plenty of opportunity to prove our faith. Some weeks we have had as little as five dollars with which to buy groceries for the group which then numbered about forty. Time and again it was necessary to know that all things necessary are provided if we have absolute trust in God. This does not mean sitting back and doing nothing; on the contrary it means vigorous action to do all that can be done.

My experience is that there is in this Teaching a satisfactory answer to every question necessary to one's development according to the law spiritually, mentally and physically.

In May of 1948 the first issue of *Eden Valley News* was released. This simple three-page publication of happenings on Sunrise Ranch was the forerunner of a beautiful magazine which acquainted people in the ministry with everyday life in Eden Valley. Filled with excellent photographs, artwork, and imaginative and informative articles by those who live and work there, it was produced annually and has proved to be a most effective and welcome emissary around the world.

Richard evoked, in that first issue, the magical atmosphere of Sunrise Ranch:

Come and walk with me in the valley. The rain clouds have passed, and the warm sun is pouring down on the teeming earth. The air, rain-washed, is exhilarating, charged with the perfume of wild plum blossom which lies like deep drifted snow in the hollows of the hills. We cross the road and climb a knoll, the highest point in the valley, which stretches north and south; enclosed to the east by a line of red sandstone rimrock, laid in strata in the days when the earth's crust was bent and cracked by cataclysmic forces; and to the west by the heights of Green Ridge, pine clad, where the trees grow between great outcroppings of granite. To the north, majestic against the blue sky stands the landmark of Horsetooth Mountain; to the south the wide valley bed stretches, turning westward between low hills.

We have a fine view of the ranch buildings. Most striking is the barn, a magnificent wooden structure, with a turret-like ventilator rising from the roof. The ranch house, a five-room wooden building, stands below to the northeast. To the west of the barn is the rabbitry, housing some two hundred angora rabbits, at present attended by Stanley Grindstaff and Faith Langworthy. Chris, Norma and Gordon Christiansen have worked to establish this important undertaking. Many pounds of wool have been collected, and later this will be spun and made into garments. Nearby is the large implement shed, recently completed, to shelter trucks and farm machinery, and next to it an excellent greenhouse built by Lee Forker and Curtis Bunce. We expect to have green salads the year around.

To the south of this group of buildings is the cow barn housing three fine pedigree Jersey cows which, under the care of Charles Strikwerda, supply an abundance of rich, fresh milk. We have three calves and a number of goats. Across the green pasture southward is the "Lower House," where William and Muriel Oshanek, Richard, Dorothy and Mary Thompson live.

Now let's meet the rest of the family. Chris directs the activities in a most effective and understanding way, and Norma mimeographs and sends out the mailings. [Norma Allison, a gifted pianist, visited several years earlier with her parents and sister, Byrdie Jane Dahl. When her family left she remained and in season married Albert Christiansen.] Maud, Charles' wife, cooks the breakfast. Frank Humphrey drives the truck and participates in many activities. Vivian Grindstaff is here with her baby, Larry, and Stanley Jr. full of vitality and just beginning to talk. Then there are the young people back from school, Lee Forker (Rose's son), Mary Thompson and Chucky Strikwerda. Dorothy cooks the lunch with Rose's help, and Richard looks after the garden.

Looking northward from our vantage point, we can see the neighboring ranch owned by Bill and Frieda Martens. Bill and Jim, their sons, help to look after their cows and poultry.

Uranda's daughter Marjorie had married Chuck Horne and they were living, with their baby daughter Diane, in California.

In 1948 the Canadian Headquarters of the ministry was established at 100 Mile House, with a few dedicated pioneers. Many from other places participated in the Unit for varying periods of time. Sally Bainbridge and Irving Harwood from Sunrise contributed substantially to that developing body. Allen Graham arrived shortly after, and worked for many years in the town as well as the Unit.

In a Message of July 21 Uranda dealt with a condition prevalent in any gathering of people, one of the most insidious barriers to a state of genuine oneness—gossip. He said:

Suppose so-and-so did say such-and-such a few weeks or a few months back. When you repeat that, do you know that it is true in this instant? Do you know the heart of that one, understand his or her problems? Do you know that forgiveness has not been accepted?

If repeating the unreal expression of another is to have any meaning or value, it must be in the hands of someone who is responsible for directing the course of the one involved. Otherwise such repetition is simply maintaining the expression of the unreal. If you do have a tale that you simply must tell— tell it to me.

If we are true branches of the One Vine we are friends one of another, and friendship suggests loyalty. I have been amazed sometimes how members of the Unit can be disloyal to those about whom tales are told while showing a most peculiar loyalty to the tellers of the tales. In repeating the tale, the individual may mention the name of someone who did the unreal thing, but would the teller of the tale repeat the name of the one from whom he first learned his juicy gossip? Oh, no—*that* would be disloyal!

Your unrealities, your peculiarities, do not govern my attitude toward you.

My attitude is governed by your expressions of reality, and as far as I am allowed I ignore the unreal that may be in you. However, if I ignore the unreal
in you and you do not ignore the unreal in each other, crosscurrents develop.
If you are looking for things to criticize you can find them in any individual;
but the way of the true Emissary is to rejoice in the realities that are present
and ignore the unreality, knowing that as we go along each one is making
progress, learning lessons. And as we, being with one accord in one place, let
the spirit of the Lord work, each one will be purified.

In July Bertha Meyer arrived on Sunrise Ranch from New York City. An elderly lady
of German birth, she had made twenty crossings of the Atlantic by ship during her many
years of employment as governess for the child of the director of a famous orchestra in
the top strata of New York society. She reveled in the opportunity to sit in the magnificent theater and share some of the finest performances in the country, directed by her
dear and talented friend, also from Germany. She adored Uranda, and identified immediately with the truth which he brought. She and a friend, Lily McCann, also from New
York and an employee of Bob Ripley, of "Believe It or Not" fame, had a small house built
on Sunrise Ranch, which they meant to share. However, along the way Lily felt she could
not leave her job and life in the big city. So Bertha spent her remaining years in her
comfortable little home. She was a great blessing to all and a particular comfort, with her
seasoned wisdom, to Uranda in those oftimes turbulent days.

In the third issue of *Eden Valley News,* in August, the editor invited the readers:

Come again to the knoll across the road, and let us see how the promise is
being fulfilled.

At our feet in the hollow to the eastward the barley is white, awaiting the
reaper. This barley was not seeded, but has grown from the grain which fell
from the ripe ears of last year's sowing. On the far slope of the hollow the
great field below the rimrock is dotted with shocks of hay which, added to the
huge stack of alfalfa standing to the south of the cowbarn, will be more than
ample for the winter's needs for stock feeding. Thirty acres of rye offer a lovely
sight; the stalks are fully five feet high. We have just finished hoeing the field
corn. Add to this the sunflowers and soybeans and one of the most beautiful
stands of winter wheat you could hope to see.

Directly to the east lies the garden. We can see the orderly rows of potatoes, sweet corn, beans and carrots. In the open garden the new Rototiller
has been used. The table has been supplied with spinach, beets, carrots,
peas, lettuce, radishes, endive, green beans and onions and strawberries,

and in addition more than two hundred pounds of produce has been stored in the cold locker in Loveland.

Faith Langworthy reported on "Our Rabbitry," proudly proclaiming that the rabbit population had grown to 150 angoras, some of which gave as much as a pound of wool a year. A gift of a spinning wheel was on its way, with the exciting prospect of making yarn.

Under "News Items" it was reported that on Sunday, July 4, Richard Thompson conducted a service in Greeley at the home of Lily May Barton. On the following Sunday her daughters, Della Bever and Hazel McKenney, drove over from Greeley and spent the day with us here at the Ranch.

This introduces the McKenneys, a family that has contributed greatly to Sunrise Ranch from that first visit in 1948, each bringing a unique spirit of home. Their constant supply of garden produce to Sunrise, which they themselves grew or would just "happen" to come their way at little or no cost (like a truckload of potatoes!) was an inestimable gift straight from heaven—via Greeley. Nadine Selwood (McKenney), Hazel's daughter, moved onto the Ranch shortly after that, and is there still, serving over the years in countless capacities. Hazel lived many years on the Ranch until her death, having reached her 90s.

Della, with her husband Roy and their family, had lived on the Western Slope of Colorado, and came to live at Sunrise in 1958. Roy visited his old haunts often, enjoying fishing escapades. He was a colorful character, much loved, his talents in the mechanical shop a vital factor in the smooth-running operation on the Ranch. He and Frank Protzman developed a friendship over the years which delighted everyone. They built a "liar's bench," for special relaxation and entertainment, which anyone could use if they so desired.

At one point Richard Thompson wrote to Martin of his concern that there was "not a single name in Europe on the mailing list," that he and Dorothy had some money in England which they could not get out and would like to establish a center there. This dream was destined to find fulfilment through others many years later—again, evidence of rich fruit from seeds sown in good soil and tended in the warm atmosphere of love, with the assurance that what may seem to be made of dream-stuff is often very solid.

Throughout all these developments Uranda was able to stay in close touch with Sunrise activities through many reports and letters. Then, in August of 1948, he felt it was time to return. So, with more than a year and a half of what seemed a lifetime of experience since leaving, we came home to Sunrise Ranch. This trip was by car, one of the purchases consequent upon Edna Henderson's financial gift. The bus, and other equipment acquired in California, were transported later. With the addition of Edna our party consisted of Uranda, Kathy, Nancy, Billy and me. Kathy was expecting her second child in a few months.

Our overnight stays in motels involved the washing of diapers. Usually the laundry was not dry by departure time next morning, and our car could be seen flying along with what seemed to be white flags streaming from rolled-up windows. It was a very efficient method.

Finally, after this sojourn in which no day went by without new ceilings being forever shattered, I found myself again driving into Eden Valley. Uranda's glorious smile revealed the victory apparent in this reunion with the ones who had remained faithful, true to the spirit of Sunrise Ranch, in oneness with him, wherever he was. There was a body established, it was a reality on Sunrise Ranch, and Uranda's health was greatly improved.

At that time Uranda and Kathy, Nancy Rose, Billy and I made our abode in the house just down the road from the main ranch house, called in those early days "the lower house." Prior to our purchase of the place it had housed ranch-hands. Edna Henderson was a part of Uranda's household at that time.

Uranda wasted no time sharing his thoughts in a paper entitled "Sunrise Ranch," August 11.

> It is good to be home again. We journeyed out into the field to do certain things. Some of those things we accomplished; and it might appear that, with respect to some of them there was failure, but we do not know yet what will develop from the seeds that were sown. In the meanwhile I praise God that you who have "stayed by the stuff" have kept the home-fires burning.
>
> I am not going to review what we might call the development of the battle lines back along the centuries that have passed, up to this present day, but you do know that there has been too much go into the development of that which is in accordance with God's plan for it to ever fail. As long as there are even a few who are willing to give that which they are to that Plan, as long as it means something in the heart and life of any individual, it has not failed.

In August, just prior to our return, Lillian Call arrived for a visit on Sunrise Ranch, with her three-year-old daughter Sharon and grandmother Jennie Olsson, from Pewaukee, Wisconsin. Uranda had expected to be on the Ranch when they arrived, and although Lillian was disappointed, she joined freely in the activities. They were scheduled to leave the day after our arrival. Jennie left but Lillian and Sharon stayed, Lillian obeying an inner compulsion that could not be denied. That time marked the beginning of her participation in Uranda's core pattern, which included the focus for music, first on Sunrise Ranch and then extending into the ministry worldwide. She had been divorced from her husband some time before, and there was considerable pressure from her family to return, finish her education and get the degree in music not quite completed during the war. She made the decision to stay, however, and found no difficulty with the farm atmosphere, outhouses, etc., having lived on a farm as a child.

Billie Groves, who had been married briefly to Irving Harwood and divorced, was presently the wife of Vernon Fahey, and the couple was coming to join the Unit. Ralph and Roz Hooper with infant son Groves were already there, and Fern Meeker was en route. Bob Patton, who had married a lovely girl Mildred, was looking forward to bringing her, her small daughter Jody and Bob's baby son Bobby to join the Sunrise family in the Spring.

Bob Palmer, prominent in Loveland affairs, found a mutual friendship with Bishop Meeker and was instrumental in solving some of the problems which had accrued—mortgage for instance. Bob remained a faithful friend through the years, and he and his wife Dixie were frequent visitors on the Ranch.

With the resolving of past debts, Uranda remarked:

> If we had not had faith enough so that we could move forward and accept indebtedness we would not be here with what we have—and the Lord has blessed us wonderfully—but having attained to this degree I would like to see us now function with sufficient faith so that we could move forward without incurring indebtedness as a practice, or policy. There may be times when it is practicable; I have in mind a few projects which would require something of a miracle if there were no indebtedness. But what I am talking about is that order of faith which will let us, as a Unit, clear to a higher order of manifestation, so that we can move forward more steadfastly and a greater increase in the Lord's substance appear.

Soon after our arrival on the Ranch the trailer, which had provided me with living quarters at Salinas, arrived and Billy and I moved into it again. Accommodation was at a premium, with the numbers of Emissaries increasing and a constant stream of visitors—a situation that has not altered through the years, even with vastly improved and expanded facilities.

Lloyd Arthur Meeker, Jr., was born, on November 15, 1948, in the Bishop's house on Sunrise Ranch. A few of us, including Kathy's mother, were in an adjoining room. Rosa sighed her great relief as her precious Kathy relaxed after the athletic event of delivering a being into this world. Uranda welcomed his son with profound joy.

In "Your Bishop's Personal Message" (YBPM) of December 29 Uranda spoke of a request for permission to build a cabin on Sunrise Ranch and said that after considering it with the Board and the Unit it was decided that a single room cabin, eight by twelve feet, inside measurements, would be adequate with the existing provision of communal meals, etc. It would involve leasing a plot of ground 25' by 30', for five years, at thirty dollars a year, "anticipating that at least two years shall be paid in advance as part of the arrangement for its construction, so that the individual can maintain the lease for life. The cabin will become the property of the Church if the lease expires or the individual so desires for some reason." The cabin was to be constructed of a mixture of sawdust and cement, and would cost $285. One such cabin was built, at the end of the road leading into the Ranch, and provided space in various capacities through the years: first for the builder, Rose Forker; then an office; and today accommodates the audio-video department.

William Oshanek announced, in 1948, that he had written a book, anticipating that it could fill what he felt to be a need for a textbook for students, and entitled it *The Cosmic Destiny of Man.* It was printed, but did not fill the requirement. The Classes proved to be the most effective means of conveying the principles of being in the practical living of life.

Conditions on Sunrise Ranch were at a low point financially and remained that way for some time to come. During those first years food was scarce, and for a number of months we subsisted on the whole grains of wheat, usually served with a little thin milk poured over them, and some peaches on the side.

Once in a while I would receive a box from my mother filled with edibles which she knew were favorites of mine. She sent cans of salmon, cans of mixed nuts, and other delectables, which were used to great advantage—not as snacks for me and my son, but salmon patties and other goodies constituted a meal for the group.

Uranda often spoke of his vision of a place on Sunrise Ranch set apart for special purposes, perhaps a small building which would provide space for a private, or protected, experience. On March 15, 1949, this dream found fulfilment when he laid the cornerstone of the building he named The Little Chapel. His words on this occasion were recorded in the May 1949 edition of *Eden Valley News:*

> We are gathered here this afternoon to share in an undertaking we have looked forward to for a long time—the laying of the cornerstone of our Little Chapel. This symbolizes for us many things: first, the outer form of the centering of the spirit made manifest in this Unit, the spirit and nature of our unified dedication to the Service of our Lord and King.

> Here we look forward to the building of a Chapel large enough not only to accommodate our own numbers but all who will find it pleasing to share in our worship before God. We look forward to that development in building by which all necessary accommodations shall be provided, but in that vision we have recognized that first place should properly be given to our God. [Uranda had reference to his expectation of a large chapel being built in the future, to

welcome the many who would come. That too was fulfilled, but not in Uranda's time. The Dome Chapel now stands closely beside the Little Chapel, and people from all over the world have found their way through its doors.]

> We have not heretofore had a place dedicated solely to the spirit of worship. This Little Chapel is a place where a few of us at a time can gather for special prayer and ministry.

Uranda then laid the cornerstone of the Little Chapel, and closed with a devotion:

> And, behold, as this cornerstone is laid, in the Name of our Lord and King, so let us let the cornerstone of His Love sustain us in the living of our lives, that the power of His Love working through the patterns of His Truth may accomplish all things needful to His glory and to the blessing of the children of men, in the Christ. Aum-en.

The words *in the Christ* at the closing of a prayer were used by Uranda for many years. They indicated that the words were being spoken in the same spirit as was made manifest by the one called Jesus the Christ. The word *Christ* (*Jehovah* in the Old Testament) designates the expression through man as he was originally created; hence the use of it in the context of this ministry conveys the state of man restored. Also, *Aum-en* indicates the state of being in the *Aum,* or the *all-that-is. Om,* with the same sound, portrays the same truth, in certain cultures, such as that of India.

9

UNEXPECTED JOURNEY

March 1949 ~ May 1950

Martin was visiting Sunrise Ranch that spring, and another dramatic event, blest by his presence, was also related in *Eden Valley News:*

On the Friday before Easter, darkness engulfed the world of men, as it had done on that day nineteen centuries ago, but that darkness was powerless against the light that filled the servants of the Lord. In the early morning services from Monday onward Uranda had been asking again and again the question, "Are you ready to drink of His cup?" We knew in the depths of our being that in His strength we were able to drink deeply of it. He had been waiting these thousands of years to pour forth His blessings. The time was come.

On Saturday the final preparations for the Easter Pageant had been made. The choir, under the director, Lillian Call, was ready after many weeks of practicing.

At six o'clock on Easter morning the sun was rising above the last ridge to the east looking out over the Great Plains; the rimrock lay yet in shadow as the first gentle notes of the *Shepherd's Psalm* set the cool morning air vibrating.

The group of mourners sleeping below awakened as the music became louder, and gazed upward in wonder. Three angels came down to the tomb (Kathy with her sisters Roz and Billie), and as the last notes of *Lamb of God* roused echoes from Green Ridge to the west the valley thrilled to the triumphant note of the Angel's trumpet. The stone was rolled away from the mouth of the tomb. In a pulsating silence the Lord, played by Uranda, came forth. As he disappeared from view, the three angels rejoined the choir and the stirring notes of the *Song of Victory* rang out.

As the angel choir withdrew, the attention was drawn to the figure of a woman, Mary Magdalene (Grace), moving sadly through the garden toward the tomb. She looked inside, and finding it empty she wept. At first failing to recognize the risen Lord, when he spoke her name "Mary!" she stood trans-fixed in wonder and joy. He bade her carry the good news to the others.

Mary wakened Peter and John (Richard and William) who ran to the tomb, looked in, and knew that the Lord was risen. Other mourners joined them, and together they walked toward Jerusalem. Suddenly they paused, and every eye was drawn upward toward a majestic figure clothed in white, standing upon the height of the rimrock above them. He began to speak in tones that had stirred the depths of their hearts so many times and which they thought they would never hear again. "I am risen, even as I told thee."

Silence filled the valley, a silence vibrant with love. Those who had come to mourn went away rejoicing. The voices of the choir sang *Christ the Lord Is Risen Today, Hail Bright Easter Morn,* and finally *The Song of Praise.* In shin-ing majesty upon the height above stood the Lord, hand outstretched in bene-diction, and as the last Aumen drew an echo from the surrounding hills, the voices of birds took up the song.

Rosalind Hooper, reporting visitors to Sunrise in her "News" column, mentioned Mike and Dorothea McCann and their two-year-old daughter, Pam, of Iowa. They had accompanied Charles and Jennie Olsson of Milwaukee, all of these a special joy to Lillian, Jennie's granddaughter, the McCanns being family friends from the Milwaukee group. Years later Pam married John Gray and today they focus the group at the Glen Ivy Spa. Also visiting were Sally Bainbridge, Allen Graham, Irving Harwood and Mary Mackenzie from 100 Mile House, valuable members of Martin's staff at the "100" for the past year.

The concrete block-making machine was ready for production, and through a for-tunate development we often obtained, merely for the hauling, gravel and sand that was left by the construction crew of the Government Irrigation Project behind the Ranch.

The frequent unexpected blessing of last-minute, end-of-the day, left-over cement marked a substantial step forward in our building program. This project has provided a source of much needed irrigation for our property through the years, and bears the distinction of being the longest overland canal at this altitude in the world. Situated at the base of Green Ridge, one of the tunnels is only a quarter of a mile south of our property, the others a few miles distant.

Before Martin's departure he and Uranda each planted a tree, Uranda's on the south side of the entrance to the Chapel and Martin's to the north. That spring there was the planting of 1800 trees in strategic settings, some fruit trees, some nuts, others shade and windbreaks, some ornamental.

Quoting further from *Eden Valley News:*

> On the 9th of May, Grace Van Duzen and Billy left for what we hope will be a short stay away from Sunrise Ranch. Her mother is seriously ill and our prayers are with her and her family.

Those few words reported an event that wrought unimagined changes in my life, coincidental with some vital outworkings in the entire ministry.

Approximately a year before that time I had received word from my father, in Pittsburgh, that my mother was afflicted with cancer and probably had no more than a year to live. In that ensuing year there was not a day without an ache deep in my heart, and I kept in close touch with them throughout. Finally, my son and I were on our way to be with her, having been informed by my father that the time was short. We were there for two weeks before she passed away, and it was a most fulfilling experience shared by both my mother and me.

My father seemed to be in good health, but before long he began complaining about pain in his lungs, and other symptoms led me to call the doctor, who was puzzled and said he wished to have him hospitalized for diagnosis. His spirit was bright, with a characteristic cheerful outlook. He told me, one night when I was visiting him in the hospital, that he was to have a test the next morning. He looked up at the doctor and asked him, "What will that do, Doc, half kill me?" As it turned out, it did more than half; it finished the job. Before he went for the bronchoscope test he was his normal self; when they brought him back he was never removed from the oxygen tent, never again rational, and died shortly afterward. That was on Father's Day. Our family doctor said he would like to have an autopsy, that it never should have happened. My sister objected, however, and it was not performed.

Some months later, when Uranda felt he could tell me, he said that my father's lung had been punctured in the test, and added, "But he committed suicide as surely as if he had used a gun." Though he had maintained his usual cheerful exterior, life without his beloved wife was more than he could face. Only then did I recall a question my father asked me shortly after Mom passed away: "Do you think they [the departed] wait for you [meaning her waiting for him]?" It had been decided that he would move in with my sister and her family, and he asked if Billy and I would stay and live with him in his home. Might it have been a different story if I had? Oh, there were heartaches, many pressures, in those days of pioneering. But there was only one way; and feelings, no matter how deep, presented the means by which the necessary maturing could occur.

So the passing of each of my parents was less than a month apart. My father's experience moved so quickly that I could not contact Uranda to let him know that he was not well, as he was already on his way to Pittsburgh. When I had called him at the time of my mother's death I told him there was a houseful of furniture, etc., that could be moved to the Ranch, where there was great need, whereupon he and Kathy, Nancy and baby Lloyd; Lillian and Sharon Call; and Edna Henderson packed up a car and were on their way. En route also was a truck, driven by Albert Christiansen, to transport the furniture.

It was the night of the day that my father died. The doorbell rang and I answered it. There stood Uranda, the others still in the car, and I just looked at him. I was in a daze, unbeknownst to me then, and I said, "Hello." Puzzled, he asked, "Aren't you going to ask me in?" And then, "Where is your father?" I answered, "He's gone." "Where did he go?" was the logical next question. "He's dead," I said. Then of course it all began to come out.

An event of great significance occurred during our stay in Pittsburgh. A letter was forwarded to Uranda from John Oshanek, of Winnipeg, who was excited about a letter he enclosed, received from a fellow chiropractor in Toronto.

I sensed a mounting tension as Uranda read the letter from Albert Ackerley and was not surprised when he jumped up and exclaimed, "This is it!" Albert was relating an incident preparatory to adjusting a patient. At that time the method of ascertaining the need for an adjustment was to check the leg-lengths. After a successful adjustment the discrepancy would be corrected, the legs even. In this instance Albert was at the point of taking the ankles in his hands for the check. Before he touched the patient he was amazed to watch the short leg move visibly to join the other in perfect alignment. "I didn't do that!" he exclaimed, "Spirit did that." This marked the beginning of what later would be called attunements, or no-touch technique.

From the beginning of Uranda's ministry he practiced what has been called the "laying on of hands," including radiation without touch. But he knew there would at some point need to be the experience emerging from the body itself, and it was a solemn joy to behold that moment of rewarding fulfilment, pregnant with rich promise.

After my father's funeral and settling of affairs there, we took our leave of Pittsburgh, the loaded truck returning to Sunrise Ranch while Uranda and Kathy, Lillian and I and the children drove on to Toronto. We crossed the Canadian border on the 4th of July and were deposited, the lot of us, at the home of Gordon and Emily Marks, who were in the process of packing to move to 100 Mile House. So some of the sleeping accommodation during our stay consisted of mats on the floor. These two, with their family, were deeply loved among the company of pioneers who helped to establish the Unit at 100 Mile House. Their son Ross was a graduate of Guelph Agricultural College, and daughter Carolyn of high school. Ross had joined the group at the Hundred in 1948 and would prove to be Martin's right-hand man, the bond between them knitting ever more closely through the years. He had returned to Toronto at this time to assist his family in the most important venture of their lives. Martin was present also, having recently returned to Canada from a visit to his family in England.

One of the first things to be done upon arrival was to contact Dr. Albert Ackerley, who had a chiropractic office on Bayview Street. Recently his son Alan, in a conversation with me while visiting Sunrise Ranch, recalled his father's remark when he returned home from work that day in 1949. Alan was twelve years old at the time. Albert said, with his roguish smile, "Guess what?! Today in my office I met an American Bishop and an English Lord!"

Dr. Ackerley came to the Marks' home that evening, accompanied by his partner, Dr. Lorne French. Then came attunements—not yet carrying that label—performed by these two, under the guidance of Uranda, in any spot available, mostly on the floor. It was an awesome and rewarding time of discovery. As a very young man, alone in the acceptance of his divine commission, Uranda had always found the healing power flowing through him to be a vital point of contact with people. And now the conscious awareness of it had surfaced from the body itself, through a man who was already serving the public in the health field.

There were "miracles" manifest in many individuals at that time, always with emphasis on the fact that healing comes from within, possible only through the action of the power of God, and that the nature of the spirits expressing through the one being served determines the extent of healing. It was "spirit," we heard over and over again, that moved that leg to correct the difference in length, to adjust the spine, to do whatever was necessary.

While in Toronto we met another couple, Mac and Jane Duff, with their two young sons, Hugh and Ross. We visited their farm and enjoyed a hospitality that has weathered the years.

From Toronto our party drove to Pewaukee, Wisconsin, where Lillian Call's parents resided and where she had been born and spent her early life. We filled their home to the brim and overflowed to some friendly neighbors, where Billy and I stayed. Roy and Marie Johnson were loving friends of Uranda and loyal supporters of his ministry from the beginning. They later moved to Sunrise Ranch and provided a constant atmosphere of welcome in their home there. In the interim, on many occasions through the years when our travels took us to their vicinity we were always warmly welcomed and accommodated in their home.

Back in Canada, the next stop was Winnipeg, home of Dr. John and Ann Oshanek, who later took her original name, Hanya. They had two teen-age children, a son David and daughter Yvonne. Here was another family in the throes of packing for a move—yes, to the same destination, 100 Mile House, to join that expanding family. John's secretary, Vera Parsons, shared his family's dedication to Uranda and his ministry and also made the move.

There were great days of working with attunements, I being one who experienced a crucial healing involving my spine, under the hand of Uranda. A method which he called "retracing" emerged, whereby old distorted patterns, of body, mind and heart, could be experienced in an atmosphere of thanksgiving and forgiveness and restored into the correct design. The healing, in such case, was complete; there was no recurrence of the problem.

Also, the phenomenon of long-distance healing found specific focus then. There was an outstanding instance of this when Uranda took into his own body the condition present in a man who was many miles distant. For hours he paced the floor in what seemed to be a crippled and painful condition, all of which was breaking ceilings, dissolving long-established barriers in the consciousness of the man who was receiving the radiation. We learned, afterward, that the recipient had allowed the miracle to happen, resulting in a spinal realigning correction.

Healing, we were to learn, is not limited to the instrument through which it is achieved, the radiant current moving to whoever is open to receive it. This is absolute, as long as there is a clear channel. We say it goes to the ends of the earth—but why limit it to that? Perhaps there is no barrier in all the cosmos except in the consciousness of fallen man. The word of the Lord through Job was: "Canst thou bind the sweet influences of Pleiades or loose the bands of Orion?" These were references to bodies far beyond our solar system.

During our stay with the Oshaneks their son David had a severe accident while riding his motorcycle and was in the hospital in a coma, with a concussion and badly injured leg. Uranda spent hours at his side and in a few days David returned to consciousness with his faculties intact and the bright prospect that his leg would be saved.

Those early years were characterized by rapid changes, with scarcely a break between them, conveying the conviction that there was no time to waste in the "spiritual regeneration of the human race." That year, 1949, witnessed the dissolving and moving out of old patterns in a remarkable way, with first the unexpected experience with my parents and old home, and then movement of two outstanding families from their long established living conditions in large cities to an isolated spot in the interior of British Columbia. True pioneers in every sense, they provided substance of inestimable value through the years, represented today by children and grandchildren.

Up to this point in our journey we had been driving. Now, with the next destination Banff, Alberta, we left the car in Winnipeg and traveled by train through the breathtaking scenery of the Canadian Rocky Mountains. Our next hosts were Conrad O'Brien-ffrench and his wife Rosalie.

"Fairholme" was the name of their beautiful estate, an ideal setting for this exceptional artist. His specific training in visual art was later in life, after he had served many years in Secret Service for his homeland, Great Britain. His beautiful works hang in many places, at Sunrise Ranch, 100 Mile House, and all over the world in homes and centers of those who loved him.

The story of his life could fill a book—and has! He titled his autobiography *Delicate Mission*. Many of us knew him by his nickname "Tim." Marquis of Castel Thomond, K.M. was his title and he was born in London on November 19, 1893. Taken to Italy shortly afterward, Conrad lived there until 1902 at the ducal palace of Villa Torlonia in Frascati, near Rome. (In 1944 Villa Torlonia, one of the showplaces of Italy, was used by General Kesselring as German Army headquarters—and destroyed by the RAF.) He had what he called "an idyllic childhood under Italian skies" and left at the age of eight with his brother Rollo to be educated in England. At that time he spoke only Italian and French and a little broken English.

After the personal trauma of his brother's death in a rugby match, Conrad left for Canada. He said:

Adventurous and romantic at heart, I went to Canada at the age of seventeen to join the "Mounties" [Royal Canadian Mounted Police] where I served in the field and as the assistant riding instructor at Regina. I returned to England and by 1912 found myself cramming for my army examination. Hardly had I been commissioned to a regular Battalion in the British Expeditionary Force when the 1914-18 war broke out and I landed in France on August 13, 1914. My regiment was meeting the full impact of the German army spearhead of attack at the battle of Mons. This ended in a walkover for the Germans and a "victorious" tactical retreat by the British.

Conrad won the Mons Star at that battle when, as he says:

> The flower of the British army was almost liquidated by Von Kluk's army corps. A large portion of our army was decimated or captured, including myself. An attempt to escape from a Belgian hospital ended in my being sent to a prison camp in Germany. In 1916 the Germans, objecting to their U-boat crewmen being treated as pirates by their British captors, chose thirty-nine of us as a reprisal and threw us into a common gaol where we languished for nine weeks in so-called solitary confinement.
>
> The contrast between a crowded prisoner-of-war camp, where I was unable to avoid my fellow prisoners, and a cell by myself was not altogether unpleasant, and after the vicissitude of the past two years life behind an iron door gave me a certain sense of security. There were drawbacks of course, such as bedbugs; but Judge Gerrard, the American Ambassador to Berlin, on learning of the conditions, had me changed to another cell. In the years I was there I learned two more languages, Russian and German, and also devised a unique means of communicating with the War Office in London, sending them reconnaissance reports of captured Royal Flying Corps pilots. [His fluency in six languages and ingenuity in supplying information while in prison caused him to be recommended later as a secret agent, which he fulfilled admirably—and upon which Ian Fleming later based his character James Bond.]
>
> I made various attempts to escape, all of which were frustrated.

In 1919 he was appointed assistant military attache with the British Legation in Stockholm, where his work involved surveillance of the Russian Revolution, then in its early stages. In 1920 he was in Helsinki, Finland, and negotiated an armistice between Finland and Russia, as well as effecting the passage of the first Soviet diplomatic representative from Petrograd [Leningrad] to London for talks with the Prime Minister, Lloyd George.

The following year he was in India with his regiment, the 16th Lancers, and Sir Harcourt Butler, Governor of the United Provinces, asked for his services as an extra A.D.C. This was during the time of Gandhi's civil disobedience campaign and, with the Prince of Wales staying at Government House in Lucknow, Tim had his hands full. He later returned to his duties as a captain with the 16th Lancers, participating in regimental training on the plains at temperatures that sometimes reached 120 degrees. He spent his leave in the high Himalayas, and his successful mission to climb Mt. Skorola was rewarded by a membership in the British Alpine Club. He commented:

> The impact of these experiences had a delayed action, the effects of which were not apparent until 1922, four years after the end of the war. During the hot

weather training on the plains of India I fell ill and was invalided out of the army.

Retiring from the army, he took up art, studying at the Slade School in London and at Andre L'hote's in Paris. He gave several one-man exhibitions in Paris and London. I find it interesting that the unique talent of this man was dormant until his middle years when it blossomed and consistently increased for the rest of his life. His skill was equally superb whether it was the area of animals or human portraiture. A sly humor and depth of understanding peeked out of everything, even his magnificent landscapes.

Tim never lost a "fellow-feeling for those in prison" and became an official visitor to Wormwood Scrubbs Prison, listening and sharing their experiences.

In 1930, in his travels he met Maud, a Swedish girl who became his wife. The marriage dissolved before long, but the result of that union was a beautiful daughter, Christina, with whom Conrad had contact in later years.

In 1933 he was in Lapland when he learned that almost the entire output of a famous Swedish iron mine was being shipped to Krupps. His report on this was apparently the first firm indication in Britain of Hitler's rearmament program. The impact of his news, he said, was "spectacular," and he was immediately summoned to a conference in London, following which he proceeded upon various assignments which involved intelligence work and surveillance of the southern German sector. With Hitler's invasion of Austria in 1938, the organization of which he was a part was dispersed. He later learned that his name, Castel Thomond, was included in the Gestapo's list of British war criminals under the "C's," along with that of Winston Churchill!

During the Second World War he was inspecting officer for censorship in Scotland and also served with the British Ministry of Information in Trinidad. After the war he returned to Canada and in season visited Riverside with Martin, with whom he had maintained a close connection. Shortly afterward Conrad married Rosalie, a girl he had known in England, and built Fairholme Ranch in the picturesque mountains of Banff. Incidentally it was occupied by Princess Margaret for a period during her 1958 tour of Canada. In season two sons, Rollo and John, were born to Tim and Rosalie. Not quite a year old at the time of our visit, Rollo was the same age as Lloyd.

Conrad was a Professor in the Banff School of Fine Arts, and in 1965 taught art to the inmates of the B.C. Penitentiary in New Westminster. He found the visual arts to be a very effective medium for creatively connecting with others. He commented:

Often prisoner art students will attempt to escape from their deprivations by drawing a woman or a field and distant landscapes, seeking to satisfy desires or a sense of freedom; but I point out that in so doing they identify themselves with a lack rather than coming into the recognition of a cosmic focal point, a presence within themselves which neither bars nor walls can inhibit. They can then release the need to sublimate freedom but actually know it within themselves. I have found that those deprived of their accustomed way of life are more open to a different approach to living than many who are free to pursue an often mistaken path.

We spent a few days in Fairholme, an enchanting place with Alpine-like views from every window. For diversion one day we attended the Calgary Stampede, Lillian and I in the back of a pickup truck with the children, being pelted with tar as we sped along a newly paved road. We couldn't make ourselves heard up front—and we never got it out of our clothes!

After a few days we left, traveling by train to Winnipeg where we packed the car we had left there, for the final lap of our eventful journey. Its humble beginning had seemed to be a trip for me and my son to be with my dying mother. As it turned out I was present at the funerals of both my parents, followed by a history-making journey to Toronto, Winnipeg and Banff with Uranda and the others. Now it was time for us to return home.

Meanwhile that faithful little group on Sunrise Ranch had been occupied with the Father's business in Uranda's absence, so that when he returned he could move without interruption in the way that opened vigorously before him. The International Headquarters of the Emissaries of Divine Light was a reality, taking responsibility for maintaining a home and freeing Uranda to accommodate the rapidly changing nature of his ministry which would include travel to far places. It was wonderful to be home again, and Eden Valley was wearing the magical smile of a neglected child that is being lovingly cared for, the land giving abundantly in return of its rich substance.

After a longer interval than usual, a Personal Message from Uranda was released dated October 23, in which he said:

> If you cannot give of material substance and do not do so, we will trust you and conclude that you are honest in your attitude, but that will not prevent you from responding properly to the lesson material itself, if you are honest. The Lord is blessing wonderfully, and great things are being accomplished, in which all of you have the privilege of sharing; but you cannot have privilege without responsibility.

> I am happy to be able to report, in a deep spirit of thanksgiving to God, that by reason of special gifts above and beyond regular contributions, we have been able to virtually clear the Church indebtedness, so that we are moving into this winter season free of debt. In addition to this, we have been able to make a large number of improvements and

purchase some much needed equipment.

In actual cash it costs us well over five dollars a month to send you the lesson material, to say nothing of all the work and selfless service that is back of every word you receive. The point is that we are so busy ministering to those who are letting our ministry have meaning, that we have no time to waste ministering to those who do not let it have meaning. Yes, I know all your excuses by heart; I have been hearing them for years. They mean nothing to me. The simple fact is: *You can if you will.*

My reason for emphasizing these things forcibly is that we wish to give more to you than we have been giving. I would like to send the record of four services to you every week. If you are going to receive this increased giving, you are going to have to prove by your letters that you are really studying all the material sent to you.

You are letting the Unit here get too far ahead of you, and there is no reason why it should be so. Those here make it possible for you to move effectively along the way. If you are not doing so, it is your own fault. Let us be, one and all, about our Father's business.

Preparing for the Christmas season that year, each person drew a name and made a gift for that one. A dollar was provided for materials needed. Yes, you could actually purchase, just (for instance) the material for a blouse, which is what I made for Lillian. A special intimate joy was experienced in the exchange of gifts that Christmas morning.

In a Message of December 12 Uranda said that the Sunrise Unit wished they could send some special symbol of the season to each one and that in the next mailing they would receive a copy of our latest song, *The Angel's Song of Praise,* words from the Bible and music by Lillian Call. He was enclosing a Christmas Greeting and Message, from him and each one at Headquarters. He expressed thanks for the "splendid response" to his recent Personal Message, and said, "The mailing sent out a few days ago was waiting for money enough to buy postage. I do not like delays in the release of the mailings, and we have prided ourselves on always getting them out even if we had to cut down on our purchase of essential groceries."

The year 1950 was packed with one remarkable outworking after another, the first announced by Uranda in his Personal Message of January 25:

Some time ago we arranged for a drill rig to come out to start operations for the drilling of a water well. I had carefully checked and re-checked the location for this well, which is directly north of the ranch house, just across the run-off waterway.

About 10:30 on the morning of January 17 we hit a wonderful supply of water at a depth of 96 feet, and the water overflowed in the casing at ground level. By 3 o'clock that afternoon the pocket had been drilled out as much as possible, and sand removed, so that drilling operations were completed and we began immediately the work of installing the pump—a half-horse power electric jet pump capable of pumping to a depth of 70 feet. On January 18 we had the pump installed and at high noon I threw the switch which pumped the first water from the well. That afternoon we pumped about 1,000 gallons and the water lowered only a few feet in the casing. The water returned to about 6 inches below ground level, and has continued to stand there when the pump is not in operation. On January 19 we pumped 2,500 gallons of water and only lowered the water in the casing about 27 feet, at which point the recovery appears to be equal with the pumping capacity of our pump.

On January 17 we hauled our last load of water. [Hurray!]

I took a sample of our water to the College Laboratory at Fort Collins to be tested. The chemist closed his report with the words, "You are indeed fortunate to have a flowing well of such excellent water."

A familiar sight on Sunrise Ranch was Uranda with his wand of willow, "witching" for water. The following is from Stan Grindstaff's book, *The Boy*. Uranda, in his wisdom, granted "The Boy" the privilege of calling him "Grandpa":

The Stick

Everybody on Sunrise Ranch was thirsty. Water was rationed. The tractor that pulled the water tank from town some twelve miles away had broken down. So, what was going on now? the Boy wondered. What was Grandpa doing walking around with a stick and looking down at the ground?

The young boy always watched Grandpa. Even when he was playing with the other kids, the Boy would stop and gaze at the bearded man, watching the way he moved with easy authority. But now he left the others to play by themselves, and silently followed Grandpa at a little distance. What was he doing with the stick? (Sometimes the Boy played with an old stick, but never with such concentration.) As he got closer, he noticed the branch was shaped like the letter "Y." Stooped over, Grandpa was holding the top part of the "Y" with both hands, keeping the end of the branch away from himself and out over the cracked, dry ground.

The Boy saw a couple of the Ranch residents talking together.

As grasshoppers jumped out of his way, the Boy sneaked closer and hid behind a propane gas tank. "He's looking for water!" he heard someone say. "He thinks he's already found some because that stick of his wiggled in his hands a couple times." They laughed. Grandpa looked their way, his customary smile gone. The laughter stopped abruptly. Then Grandpa returned to studying the baked earth, slowly pacing back and forth.

One of the Ranch residents saw the Boy hiding, and came over and quietly told him, "A lot of people think finding water in the earth with a stick is crazy."

At dinnertime, the Boy saw Grandpa. "Is it crazy?" he asked him about the stick-and-water question.

"If it works," Grandpa said, "it doesn't matter what anybody thinks!"

Then, a man from New York, who was supposed to be an expert with these "Y" sticks, came to Loveland. Grandpa invited him out to confirm his findings. The water expert arrived in a run-down pickup. He hobbled about, also with a Y-shaped stick but much bigger than Grandpa's. Over by the dry creek and next to the laundry room, Grandpa spend a lot of time with this man. Soon the visitor was jumping around, pointing at the ground, and smiling from ear to ear. Grandpa seemed quite pleased, too, and waved to everyone. It was the same place where Grandpa's stick had moved up and down in his hands ninety-three times.

It was later reported in *Eden Valley News* that four more wells had been drilled on the property, ranging from 75 to 125 feet deep, needing jet pumps with 1/4 to 3/4 h.p. motors. Augmenting this, arrangements had been made to secure water from the government water conservation project canal immediately west of us, thus affording ample supply for irrigation. Truly, the dry ground had turned into water springs, and the desert was to blossom as the rose.

A report from Dorothy Thompson in that same Message could pique the interest of those in charge of our kitchens in present-day units: "Ten days ago we had virtually no grocery supplies on hand necessary to our program. In this period our financial supply allowed us to spend only $19 for groceries. We are feeding 48 people. We served 1,435 meals in that ten-day period at a cash cost of less than 1 1/3 cents per meal."

Uranda commented:

We had good healthful meals. No one suffered, although some did not have some of the things they might have liked, and we could not continue indefinitely on such a basis. Of course we had canned foods, foods from our locker which had been frozen, and our wheat. Also we had eggs from our own chickens and our own milk supply, which helped tremendously. We have had good healthful meals. Nevertheless I ask that you join us in the prayer that the monetary supply will allow us to spend more than $19 for groceries in the coming ten days.

Uranda proceeded to tell of plans for building modern sanitation facilities, some of which required more years than envisaged. He also spoke of work being done on a dam, designed to produce a small lake "down by the willow trees," which would in season be planted with fish. This did materialize and, before it was inhabited by creatures, was a marvelous swimming hole.

Speaking of creatures, when the pond was built I experienced a real feel for the process of creation as recorded in the first chapters of the Bible. "And God said, Let the waters bring forth abundantly the moving creature that hath life." Suddenly there were strange aquatic "beasties" in what had been a valley utterly arid. Where did they come from? Not up the road, after a long and thirsty journey! Their "seed" had to be inherent in the water itself. There were salamanders, water dogs, all sorts of things—a miracle indeed to me.

Canadian by birth, William and Muriel Oshanek became citizens of the United States in February and officially changed their name to Oshane.

Meanwhile at 100 Mile House on February 15 of this fruitful year, a new paper was released, similar to *Eden Valley News* in purpose, as yet without a name. John Oshanek, its initiator and editor, requested suggestions, and the second issue, on April 1st, bore the (temporary) title *The Century Milestone.*

Uranda's message entitled "Need for Changes" sought to revitalize the awareness of the membership to existing conditions. He gave some facts and figures for the month of March, and continued:

If it were not for 23% of our membership who sent $5 or more it would be impossible to carry on this ministry. These facts should cause some serious heart searching in the remaining 78%. It costs us at least $5 a month to keep any individual on the mailing list. Until a person gives more than $5 he is not contributing toward growth and expansion.

We do not wish to make any financial regulation, but our generosity is being imposed upon in a manner that is not fair to anyone involved. Our personnel here have given their all—their lives, everything—to God's service, and those who receive without contributing are giving nothing. This situation is not fair, and this gives you the opportunity to do the changing.

Uranda and a party of nine accompanied Martin and his group to 100 Mile House, arriving April 29. He gave a service that evening, in which he spoke about Martin's health. He said:

For a perfect healing to manifest he is going to need your cooperation to an extent that he has not had. I am not finding fault with you, but you will have the responsibility of doing all you can to avoid producing unnecessary strain. This is one of the reasons I am here, to see that this is worked out right. He will be restricted for a time with respect to any heavy physical activities. It is your responsibility to see that this is done.

The strain I am speaking of is vibrational strain, and one of the most difficult things that either he or I have to contend with is vibrational discord. Any self-centeredness or selfishness on the part of anyone that brings a discord or spirit of the old world, a spirit of gettingness instead of givingness into the vibrational pattern is working for the adversary instead of for our King. The spirit of the new world is a spirit of givingness. Let us not have speculation, a lot of talk or even thinking in fields that are not constructive.

Martin followed with his word of assurance:

The cycle is working out because of that degree of faithfulness, of steadfast function, serving in your places, that has manifested through you. The cycle has worked out thus far and we are here gathered in the fulfilment of the initial phases of that for which we have longed and for which we are here.

Uranda gave many services during our stay at 100 Mile House. At one point he cautiously shared a situation with the Unit relating to a matter involving Albert Ackerley and a few others in Toronto regarding the integration of some members of the chiropractic profession with the Emissaries. It was vital to avoid tangent patterns and partial truths, with resulting confusion on the part of those seeking to serve with us.

The advisability of a trip to Toronto by Uranda and Martin was brought before the Unit for consideration, with wholehearted support and immediate action resulting in their flight to Toronto. For those who remained behind, the days of waiting were filled with loving and concerned enfoldment of the outworking; for we had been informed that much was at stake, and a failure in proper response by all concerned would cause untold loss. But the factors were allowed to be brought into a remarkable degree of harmony, with rich rewards to manifest in the years to come. Misunderstandings were resolved at the outset of what could have ballooned into a serious blockage in the unfolding connection between the Chiropractic organization and the Emissaries.

Uranda and Martin returned on May 8 and refocalized the service that was given to the group in Toronto, which clarified many false concepts prevalent in world consciousness that had come to specific focus in that gathering. It was an hour that made a profound impression on everyone.

A week later Uranda, Kathy, Martin and a few others traveled to Vancouver for a short stay, where Uranda spoke on May 17. He entitled his talk "Let Not Your Heart Be Troubled" and said he had been with a group there two and a half years before, in October of 1947, and that his first visit was in April 1940, ten years previous, observing that a great deal had been achieved since then.

Back at the Hundred, he spoke on "Vision," May 23:

> "Where there is no vision, the people perish." All through my ministry there has been a functional problem with which I have been confronted in relation to vision. (The greatest crisis in that regard in my whole ministry probably could be correctly stated as having appeared in 1943 and 1944.) This has to do with the necessity of remaining open to the vibrational patterns and creative currents from above, while dealing with manifest patterns and formations of the unreal, on a basis that will prevent colorations of what is seen and felt in the outer sense from impinging on that which is being projected from the unseen. We are under the necessity of dealing with the seen, acknowledging the forms and vibrational currents of the unreal as being a fact, no matter how temporary, while maintaining a true openness to the patterns and currents of that which is above and, from the outer standpoint, unseen.

"The Laws of God Always Work" titled a service on May 24, in which Uranda said:

> Back in the first years of my ministry there was no Unit, no group, no means of functioning from the standpoint of the kingdom except my own individual vibration. The beginning of the various formations back along the way were an appearance of what we could say belonged to me in reality, but because there was response in the wrong direction in certain points they were drawn away from me.
>
> We can go back to the group at Atascadero or down around the Bay region or any of those other places, and it might seem as though, when individuals left, if I had been thinking of them simply as individuals it would have appeared that the Law was not working, but because I continued to function on the right vibration, although some who could have been a part of that body fell away, the manifestation of you here and of those at Sunrise proves that no matter what anybody did, no matter who left, that which was mine could not be taken away from me—and here it is. You may say the particular individuals, or atoms in the body, are not the same. That is beside the point. It is that body which some thought they could take away from me.

10

Peaks of Fulfilment

May ~ September 1950

*I*n a service on May 27, "The Recreative Power That Brings Changes," Uranda spoke of one of his "greatest problems."

It appears in various ways, and seldom manifests when I am around. Almost always it is after I am gone—gone five minutes, five hours, five days or five weeks; it varies. In some who have come along the path and are well polarized the problem does not remain. In others it shows up as beginning to settle down, accept a lower standard of life expression for oneself.

To what truth can I point that will cause individuals to so let go that these little things that are not necessarily bad can be brought into the recreative power that brings changes? Perhaps some day some experience will knock off the appendages, break off the sharp points. When it comes to the actual application in practical, everyday life the individual is not much stronger than his weak point, than the level of limitation accepted for himself. I know we should not try to get anyone to function beyond his own true level of being, but these things that keep one so far below that true level of being—what about them? I am not talking about bad people; I am talking about good people. Some can go into virtually any situation, fill in with almost any job, discharge their duties well, and others—well, there are others!

Must we pattern the shape of the kingdom that is coming into manifestation to fit these appendages, the arbitrarily established levels of limitation? We know that is impossible. But we have seen evidences that human nature *can* be changed. It has been changed through the wonder-working power of God's love.

Still at 100 Mile House, Uranda asked the group the question,

What is our Purpose as Emissaries?

We are called by the name "Emissaries of Divine Light," remembering our Master's word, "Let your Light so shine *before men,* that they may see your good works, and glorify your Father which is in heaven." Being called an Emissary does not make us one. Our lives must prove it. Having become Emissaries in spirit and in truth, so that these things are fulfilled in us, then what is our purpose?

You have had to have faith, and others likewise will have to have faith. Working by faith is not working blindfolded, and working by faith does not take away one's God-given intelligence. The true Emissary has a perspective vision, a long range vision, not because he is trying to live in the past or in the future. He is living in this present moment, but he sees things as they are. Trust is a living, vibrant thing that fulfils its responsibilities. Did you ever stop to think that God cannot trust you one whit more than you trust God?

These things which are essential to an Emissary must somehow be caused to appear in their fulness in others. These qualities, characteristics, are already working to some degree in various ways in tens of thousands. Do our lives reveal in our expression and attitude toward others, not particularly with respect to spiritual things but with respect to all things, that there is something different in us? And does our expression in life make that difference to be desirable?

The Lord spoke of those who should function according to this plan and purpose as "a peculiar people." There are a great many peculiar people in the world and there are certain religious groups that pride themselves on their peculiar characteristics. We know the necessity of being natural, but the pride of our calling, the joy of our function, should be so deep, abiding, that the spirit of it all is vibrant in every contact we make in the world—not giving the appearance of self-righteousness, of condemnation of others, but that carries zeal and enthusiasm. A good salesman must be, himself, thoroughly sold on what he is selling.

Human beings are afraid of change because they are afraid of pain, because of movement from the known to the unknown. When we move forward according to God's plan in the current of His power, if we hold steady and do not resist the change and whatever it entails, the pain always changes to glory.

In a service on May 30 entitled "The Processes of Rebirth," Uranda said:

Martin and I have given some thought and attention to our future outworking. I have an outline of factors as they relate to one phase of our expansion program, and in some respects to all phases. The first part has to do with that which is of reality and the second has to do with the state of consciousness in the world with which we have to deal. So there are the two sets of factors. I have pointed out that we should function from the level of the kingdom as far as we are concerned, but our release into the world should be on the level of the individual with whom we are working.

Following is the first part of the outline:

1. "The earth is the Lord's, and the fulness thereof."

2. Those who are learning to let God's will be done are His servants, that they may learn to be His friends.

3. "Before they call I will answer." The reality of God's provision is always absolute, although that provision is not received into manifestation beyond the degree of correct function in reality under the Law, on the part of all those involved in a given outworking.

4. All function in the kingdom is polarized in the LORD of Lords and all function in the world beyond the Gate is constructive to the degree of response to the pattern of polarity that is established in the Kingdom.

5. All movement in the world is either toward life or toward death. To the degree that man shares in the old world spirit of gettingness he moves toward death, but to the degree that man shares in the spirit of God's givingness he moves toward life. In order to receive the wholeness of Truth it requires the giving of the wholeness of life.

Then we have an outline of factors as they relate to the world:

1. Generally speaking, human beings do not value that which they do not pay for, and the sense of value is generally proportionate to the price paid.

2. The willingness of the individual to pay a price depends largely upon two factors: (a) the individual concept of value to be obtained in relation to himself, and (b) the individual's own concept of his ability to pay the required price.

3. Due to lack of vision the natural urge of self-preservation, which correctly stimulates self-interest, has become so distorted through self-centeredness that individual action meant to be in the nature of self-interest is almost always self-destructive.

4. In most people there is little or no sense of the direct relationship between spiritual things and the practical necessities of daily living. Consequently the value of monetary expenditure in relation to that which is deemed to be religious or spiritual is not realized as a practical necessity in the individual's own fulfilment.

There we have a brief outline of some principles and factors that Martin and I were considering in recognition of the working of God's Law.

In a service on June 13 at 100 Mile House, "No Man Can Fight Against God and Live," Uranda spoke of the fruitful time this season at the Hundred proved to be, and that recent outworkings through the Unit at Sunrise Ranch were correlated with those at the Hundred during this period, emphasizing their agreement. He said:

I have pointed out many times that we are not playing children's games. We are involved in the climax of a great drama that has been unfolding these twenty thousand years. When I talk to you about these things I am not looking at it from the standpoint of man's life span on earth or of what, in that small span, can be learned about the things that have come and gone in ages past. The passage of a few years in the ordinary human concept is a small thing when viewed from the standpoint of the whole cycle of time as it relates to the entire human family. God has yearned for the restoration with a yearning that is greater than the combined longing in all the hearts of human beings in any age.

Virtually any good thing can be used to a bad end by the devil. Evil as such would vanish from the earth in a very short time if evil was not maintained by good people—no more taking up with it, supporting it or paying any attention to it; just leaving those who are already involved to do what they could. That evil would quickly destroy itself and be gone.

Those who come out in violent opposition must be met in the current of divine power. There must be no acquiescence. We love, but if we love humanity we do not yield to the manifestations of evil in any human being.

If individuals think they have the right to destroy themselves we have no course but to accept that choice.

"No man can fight against God and live." For twenty thousand years human beings have been trying to disprove that. The outworking of the cycles, the times and the seasons is not for our minds to determine. It is not by animosity, not by violating the Law ourselves, that anything is gained; but love for God and love for humanity means that the fire of divine love is released in radiation into each situation.

An event of profound importance to me occurred at this time. Martin, a member of the "Book of the Month" club, received the best-seller of the year. It was *Worlds in Collision* by Dr. Immanuel Velikovsky. After a cursory examination, he sensed a new and powerful element and called it to Uranda's attention. Here was another milestone, and it was exhilarating to hear the exclamations of delighted discovery from our two Bishops.

There followed days when, for an hour or two, they would take turns reading aloud from this book, with occasional comments. A few of us were privileged to be present. I was enthralled. On one of those days Uranda told me I would need to miss the reading to take my turn with the children. My heart sank and the expression on my face no doubt accompanied it. Always alert, he said nothing but returned shortly with the news that he had found somebody else. Joy, joy!

Dr. Velikovsky's ten years of research uncovered some amazing facts which shone new light on many stories recorded in the Bible, removing them from the category of fairy tales to factual occurrences. He brought a vital ingredient to a deeper understanding of the state in which fallen man finds himself. I found a new world opening in my awareness of the Bible, which would bear visible fruit in my "Story of Man" classes a few years later.

Uranda referred to the book in a service on June 17:

Dr. Velikovsky has gathered a vast amount of information from records dated into the far past. I remarked to Martin that if this man had been in the Third Sacred School and dedicated his life to the furthering of our work he could not have rendered a more worthy service. It is a monumental work which allows a deeper understanding regarding the outworking of events in the past, the present and the future. It portrays some awe-inspiring world cataclysms—which were not the first, nor are they the last. His portrayal of these events dovetails perfectly with the presentation in the Third Sacred School.

If spiritual force is to have meaning in a physical world it must have a means which will allow it to act in the physical realm to produce a physical result. Human beings have imagined that they could have spiritual power come out of the atmosphere by some magical means and accomplish something in the physical world. In the past there have been cataclysmic changes, and from the standpoint of the people in general there have not been sufficient points of control in relation to those outworkings.

Another very valuable aspect of such deliberations is the fact that there are many passages in the Bible which you have heard and read countless times with a woefully inadequate comprehension of their meaning. The tendency has been to attribute it to poetic licence, thus avoiding the possibility of a revelation that has vital meaning in relation to our function in this present day. He points out that there has been a subconscious rejection on the part of mankind of the truth behind the story of the Exodus, for example, because of the terror experienced at that time, which, being a master in psychiatry, he analyzed as "mankind in amnesia."

On July 1st the third issue of the paper that had carried the name *The Century Milestone* bore a note by the Editor which explained that a suggested name had come from Sunrise Ranch, *"Northern Light,* fitting and altogether pleasing, which we have adopted." Over the years this has proved to be one of our most effective publications, bringing news of our 100 Mile home, clothed with the individual expressions of love, dedication, fun and humor which characterize a true family.

Emily Marks wrote an article entitled "A Day in the 100 Mile Lodge Kitchen," and a few words from it portray the working conditions of the time:

It is 6 a.m. and time to arise. No extra few minutes this morning—this is your early "morning on." Having donned robe and slippers, you quickly slip out to the kitchen and kindle Leo, the big range, with the nicely arranged sticks which Gordon, or Allen, has thoughtfully split and placed in the woodbox along with newspaper. You fill the kettles in preparation for tea and coffee—and hurry back to dress, leaving Leo to do the job.

Back in the kitchen, there are many things to do before the cowboys appear for breakfast [these were not members of the Unit, but hired men who worked on Bridge Creek ranch]. If there are several cowboys expected, it is well to make a supply of toast and fry a quantity of bacon, to speed up breakfast. If there are a few minutes to spare, a fire can be laid in the fireplace in the lounge, for the Lodge is noted for its cheery atmosphere, and in the early mornings a fire does wonders. Here come our boys now, bringing the milk fresh from the cows, ready to partake of a hearty breakfast.

Now the guests begin to appear in the guest dining room. [These would include the itinerant occupants of the Lodge.] Soon the family, one by one, sleepily or otherwise, come to stand a moment before Leo and incidentally give their orders. Some prefer to cook their own breakfast, but this is not always appreciated by the cook, especially when three or four find themselves in "cook's alley" simultaneously.

Breakfast over, a study of the chart, tucked prominently by the staff dining room door, informs one of his or her duties for the day. Three do the dishes, Lina Lucyk takes her place before Leo to prepare lunch, Ann Broddy inquires, "What is there to bake?" Mary Mackenzie busies herself with milk, cottage cheese and butter. Annie starts the laundry, Yvonne Oshanek and Carolyn Marks tidy up the dining rooms, re-set the tables, and help with dishes. Frances Acheson goes upstairs to do the guest rooms, bathrooms, etc., and Jessie Stuckey proceeds to her sewing machine. All this with laughter, fun and quiet joy.

Speedily the morning passes. We move through lunch—for family, guests, ranch boys. John and Vera come from the Log House where they have been busily engaged in dictation, also Pat who has been helping John work on our Coach.

[This was an original stage coach from the early days of the Cariboo which was being renovated, preparatory to being put on display in front of The Lodge, a rare specimen which carried countless pioneers for many years along the seemingly endless rocky miles through the Interior of British Columbia. Miniatures were also being made for sale. This beautiful old coach still stands on display outside the Red Coach Inn.]

Then comes Ross from the Light Plant, followed by Gordon, Allen and the others. Now we are all gathered, and what a picture we make around the long table, eighteen of us, our beloved Martin at the head. If it is true that laughter aids digestion there should be no such problems here. After the evening meal, there is time for rest or preparing for the next day. Services are held three evenings, choir practice two, and often we gather in the Marks' apartment reading, discussing, listening to music, or just meditating together.

This is just one of many wonderful days in the Hundred Mile Lodge.

Having returned to Sunrise Ranch, in a service entitled "The Need to Abide in Love Response to God," given on July 19, Uranda spoke of having had a checkup in Denver the previous day and was informed of the need to slow down and give his body a chance for rest and recuperation.

> In this period of relaxation I anticipate doing something which will be of great value in our ministry in the days to come. In undertaking training which will allow me to secure a pilot's license I am looking forward to a closer unification between the two groups—100 Mile House and here—and a contact with others in the field who have been rather outside the range of personal contact.

> It is important that as nearly as possible we work on a basis that does not require any increase in our indebtedness, although to some degree we have to use our credit, and that is right. We have some very fine friends in Loveland and other places who have cooperated with us in a remarkable fashion and we have been moving forward on a basis to prove that their faith is more than justified, with no stress or strain in the range of our credit.

In a service on July 23, entitled "With God All Things Are Possible," Uranda said:

> Some may be inclined to think, seeing a condition that needs correcting, that a little doing could take care of it, but they go on and on, never getting around to doing something about it. How many things there are right here! Just before we left for Canada last April Martin and I took some steps toward putting a roof on our Little Chapel. We left it in a certain condition, and when I got back two months later it was still the same. Not one thing had been done on it. Are you going to tell me you did not have any time, that you did not have the ability—or did not have what? I was away two months and I have been back almost a month. In three months there was spare time that could have been used.

> I suspect there could be excuses by the bushel, but those supposed reasons do not rest upon one or two persons. They rest upon the Unit as a whole, men and women. I have heard it said, "I see what ought to be done but I cannot do anything about it. So-and-so will not let it work out." I do not believe that. It comes from the adversary, because you *can* do something about it. If you are true, if you carry the vibrational pattern, it will make a difference.

> There have not been very many days in my life when I did not face some useless nullifications, but it does not make any difference. What someone else does or does not do is beside the point. What did *we* do? What did *you* do? If we let the necessary changes work out voluntarily it will be so much better than to have them forced upon us under pressure. Let us do our part.

Stan Grindstaff wrote the following account of that summer at Sunrise Ranch in his book *The Boy:*

The Seagulls

The five-year-old Boy stood watching, dumbfounded, blinking at the first white bird he had ever seen in Colorado. It came flying over the northeastern rimrocks, from the direction of Horsetooth Mountain. It was sizable. He followed it as it swooped down Eden Valley, over the Sunrise Ranch crops everyone said would be ruined by the worst grasshopper infestation in memory. The bird flew back up the valley and left, only to bring back a couple other white birds who flew with it over the fields that buzzed with the insects.

Then the three birds vanished from the valley.

The Boy ran around telling about the huge white birds. Many people laughed; the Boy was known for his keen imagination. Someone said the birds sounded like seagulls. That made everyone laugh even louder: Right—seagulls all the way from the ocean. That was a good one!

The Boy returned to his favorite scouting place by the creek, with its great view of the garden and the mountains all around. He could see way down past the garden where he and his brother used to play Indian scout, crouching under a big tree by a dry creek bank, eating butter mixed with brown sugar. He stood apart from the adults, who continued to poke gentle fun at him and shake their heads about grasshoppers.

But then the Boy started shouting. He waved his arms wildly at the sky, jumping and running in circles and squares.

The adults stood dumb, watching the sky over their heads turn white.

The Boy ran around calling for everyone to come outside, knowing he'd been the first one to spot them.

Someone else said they really *were* seagulls—they'd probably come all the way from Salt Lake City to Loveland. Making a considerable racket, the birds flew down and covered the valley near the rimrocks like a snowy blanket. Walking up close to one of the fields, the Boy watched the birds eat grasshopper after grasshopper. They remained all afternoon and evening and the next day, noisily feasting away—it didn't look like any of them even bothered to chew.

The crops were saved. The Boy knew a deep sense of awe and thankfulness for how everything had worked out.

The next morning he was amazed at the stillness of the valley. Leisurely walking by himself through the fields in the gentle sunshine, he couldn't find even one grasshopper—but there sure was a lot of bird droppings!

Concurrently, at the head of the Chiropractic movement in the United States, with its focus in the Palmer School of Chiropractic in Davenport, Iowa, was one Dr. George Shears. Physically a giant of a man, with a heart of matching proportions, George would later prove to be an immovable rock in the body that was rapidly taking form. His love for Uranda and his work was immediate and boundless, and through him many with aching hearts and bodies found their way to the source of love and truth within themselves, from which all healing comes. Uranda referred to the fact that he had heard about George and his work a decade earlier, adding, "The G.P.C. organization was not aware of me, but I was very much aware of it."

A Chiropractic Convention was held during August in Davenport, Iowa, during which the G.P.C. section had a day. "God, Patient, Chiropractor" was depicted as a triangle, with "God" at the apex, "Patient" at the left point and "Chiropractor" at the right of the line drawn upon the earth. This movement which emerged out of the Chiropractic profession was the result of George Shears' insight and resultant action, in which he was joined by men and women who were seeking for a depth of healing and service which they had not yet found.

The obstacles which had been present regarding our movement with the G.P.C. organization had been resolved to the point where a Conference was held at Huntingburg, Indiana, beginning August 31. The fulfilment in Uranda's heart could be felt as he spoke there, in a talk later entitled "Creative Principles":

> It has been a joy to hear the speakers who have already commanded your attention. The program toward which we have all been looking is well under way, and I am interested in establishing a clear awareness that spiritual considerations, if real, are the most practical and scientific subjects to which we can give our attention.
>
> Two thousand years ago God sent the focus of deity for the earth, the divine essence brought to a point and revealed on earth. The greatest thing He did was to reveal God in action. Whatever else He did stems from that one fact, whether it be the victory in Gethsemane, on the cross, at the tomb. He said, "Follow me." He has waited for someone to dare to accept the challenge of His promise, dare to follow Him, dare to move forward in letting the will of God be done on earth as it is done in heaven. Can we afford to wait? Perhaps God can—but we cannot afford to waste a single moment, to live listless and uninspired lives, to drift through life. We need to become so inspired, so completely on fire with the Christ Love that we are *alive.*
>
> As servers, that which distinguishes you from the masses of people in the

world is the fact that you have, to some degree, given your hearts and minds to the spirit of givingness, while the majority of people cling to the spirit of gettingness. There is a text we should remember: "Eye hath not seen, nor ear heard, neither have entered into the heart of man, the things which God hath prepared for them that love (and serve) him." If we try to use our human vision to shape and mold our lives thus and so, failure is absolutely certain. Thousands and millions before us have proven that.

At the conclusion of that Conference in Huntingburg an invitation was extended to those interested in taking a further step, to come to Sunrise Ranch for a G.P.C. Convention which would be held there September 2 through 8. About twenty-five attended, with Albert Ackerley and John Oshanek from Canada, and the others from the United States. Before long the word Chiropractor in the G.P.C. symbol was changed to Christ.

Following a word from George at that Convention, Uranda said:

> We are not interested in trying to change anyone's religion. We are not interested in proselyting. You would not be engaged in your work if you did not recognize something of a higher power, which I think most of you at least think of as God. There is a great deal of fear in the world. Most people are afraid of what they think God to be, imagining that if they give heed to His Will, the joys and pleasures of life will be taken away and they will be unable to be effective individuals. If you are not convinced that that idea is utterly false I trust you will be, thoroughly, before these days are past.
>
> We cannot work with the things of God and deny God at the same time. I am not concerned about anyone's opinion, regardless of who it may be, but I am concerned about a recognition of the spiritual facts of life, with the truth. Truth is something that can be discovered, not modified on the basis of human opinion or likes or dislikes. I am not going to undertake to make you believe anything. Believing something that is false will not make it true, or disbelieving something that is true will not change the fact. Truth is so boundless, so far reaching, so beautiful in all its various phases, that it will take eternity to explore it adequately.
>
> Health is something that cannot be thought of in relation to the physical body alone. There is the necessity of health of mind and of the emotional or feeling realm, which involves the subconscious or unconscious part of the mind. The feeling realm is to some degree physical, some degree mental, and some degree spiritual. Most people have not allowed themselves to develop effectively in relation to true feeling, mentally and spiritually.

The manner in which this gathering worked out is remarkable. The fact that we are gathered here is a miracle. When I say miracle I do not mean something that disregards law. Nothing happens by chance. Always there is the working of a law.

I noted that there was a legal opinion that we could not properly call what we do attunements without being subject to some legal limitations. When I speak of attunements I am not talking about something that is done physically. I am talking about a process by which we assist the individual to become attuned to God, a process by which the individual is re-attuned with the natural life forces which come from the higher Source. If any of you can suggest a better name for what we do I am willing that it should be so, but until something more satisfactory than what I have heard is presented I can see no reason for not using the word attunement. It is not a physical act; it is a process of helping the individual to find his centering in the Source of health physically, mentally and spiritually.

I have been watching the development in G.P.C service for nearly ten years and I do not need to make a review of the work George Shears has done in this regard and the great influence exerted by him.

A session on September 3 concluded with the following words by Hippocrates (460-357 B.C.):

The affections suffered by the body, the soul sees quite well with shut eyes. Wise physicians, even among the ancients, were aware how beneficial to the blood is to make slight frictions with the hands over the body. It is believed by many experienced doctors that the heat which oozes out of the hand, on being applied to the sick, is highly salutary and suaging. The remedy has been found to be applicable to sudden as well as habitual pains, and various species of debility, being both renovating and strengthening in its effects. It has often appeared, while I have thus been soothing my patients, as if there were a singular property in my hands to pull and draw away from the affected parts aches and diverse impurities, by laying my hand upon the place, and by extending my fingers toward it. Thus it is known to some of the learned that health may be implanted in the sick by certain gestures, and by contact, as some diseases may be communicated from one to another.

One day during that Convention the participants traveled to Hidden Valley, one of many idyllic spots in scenic Colorado. Practically at the backyard of Sunrise Ranch a road winds its breathtaking way up the mountain to Estes Park and the "High Country."

In that company of seeking ones came also the inevitable element of challenge and doubt, bringing to focus what is present in world consciousness, to find resolution and bring order out of chaos. As the work of the Lord progressed, only those who let their perspective vision change with the ascent up His mountain would become acclimated to and delight in the rarefied atmosphere. Uranda reported to the School that he regarded that Convention as a peak in the graph of the history of the Emissary ministry.

A substantial number of chiropractors were attracted to Uranda and his program in those early days. Drs. Edward and Gladys Miller were pioneers and moved immediately from chiropractic adjustments to attunements in their very successful practice in Berwick, Pennsylvania. Gladys had, for a number of years, been Secretary of the Chiropractic Association in the United States. These two contributed beyond measure to the welfare and expansion of the work initiated by Uranda and were unequaled instruments for the healing power of the Lord, with a spiritual perception that worked miracles. Before long they joined the Sunrise Ranch family where they were indispensable contributors to the well-being of Uranda and later Martin, ready and willing to serve anyone anywhere with a need.

Albert and Edna Ackerley and their sons Alan and David moved to Sunrise Ranch. John and Hanya Oshanek, with son David and daughter Yvonne were already members of the Unit at 100 Mile House. Albert and John were very successful chiropractors with well established practices, who knew from their initial contact with Uranda that their purpose in life far exceeded what they had yet known, and left it all to live in seemingly limited conditions in places far removed from their homes.

George, with his wife Naomi, continued in his chiropractic office in Huntingburg for nineteen years before it worked out for him to join his beloved "family" on Sunrise Ranch. During that time he was a potent instrument for healing of body, mind and heart for many people. Inevitably there were those who left him because of the change from chiropractic to attunement service, reducing his practice considerably. However, those who remained soon found the answers to their questions and were greatly blessed. And of course there was always a constant flow of new ones anxious to share the magic of this great man.

Naomi's son, James Wellemeyer, was, and has continued to be, a vital leader at the core of our ministry. He returned to Sunrise Ranch a few months after Class, where he focalized the activities for over thirty years.

Betty Wellemeyer, the youngest of Naomi's three children, was also devoted to the furtherance of Uranda's work, and soon to be married to Lorne French, originally Albert Ackerley's partner in Toronto.

Alice Wellemeyer, a relative to Naomi by marriage, was a blessing of many years in

George's home, relieving Naomi of some household duties so she could be of more assistance to George.

At about this time a unique building, originally intended as a music room, was erected on Sunrise Ranch by Otis ("Ode") Bainbridge and his mother Sally, both residents on the Ranch. Its purpose, however, proved to be a Sanctuary, its subsequent name, a quiet and sacred haven for the practice of healing arts, primarily attunements. To the east, on the other side of the rimrock, is an area abounding in rock of varying shades of red, with several quarries close by. It was of these colorful rocks, transported over the hill into the valley, that Ode, with the help of others, built this exquisite structure, which stands today, with several additions but no basic changes, a true sanctuary in the foothills of the Rockies.

Beautiful stained glass windows imbue the interior with a rich, warm glow. Ode had become aware that all the buildings on a city block in Denver, at 9th and Federal, were being demolished in preparation for a highway and, in company with Nadine McKenney, took a truck and delivered the stained glass windows to Sunrise Ranch from what once was a Presbyterian church.

Later, artist Conrad O'Brien-ffrench painted a mural in the reception area of the Sanctuary, a beautiful depiction of the "purple mountain majesty" of this part of God's world replete with a few small creatures, an addition which Conrad simply could not resist in much of his work.

Meanwhile, at 100 Mile House in August of 1950, Martin had announced that he would be leaving for Vancouver for a few days and that Michael would be with him when he returned.

Fifteen years old, Michael had finished his first year at Eton College in England, living at Burghley House with his grandparents, the Marquess and Marchioness of Exeter. It was a joyous reunion of father and son. Then on September 10, Martin spoke poignantly of Michael's departure again for England. "Michael looks forward to coming again. Three years—it seems like a long time when you are that age. He feels in one sense that he is wasting his time for the next three years. I would not quite agree with him but there is a point there."

Martin's father visited from England occasionally in those early years. There was a depth of mutual appreciation and love between him and the members of the group.

11

A NEW ERA

September 1950 ~ May 1951

The purchase of our first airplane on August 23, 1950, dramatically punctuated this year of historical milestones. A four-place Bellanca Cruisair ushered in a new era of expansion and reemphasized the constant alertness of its founder to the swiftly growing needs of the ministry. His was not an imaginary vision but a practical view that demanded practical measures, utilizing to the full all that was available. We were often reminded that the spiritual body established in the earth had better be ahead of, and not just keeping pace with, the rapidly expanding movement in the world.

In his September 28 Message Uranda announced:

I am in the process of obtaining a private pilot's license, which will make it possible for us to maintain much more effective personal contact with you who are serving in the field; also much more effective cooperation between Sunrise Headquarters and the Canadian Headquarters at 100 Mile House. It is possible that we will be in position to make some trips the latter part of November and in December, but in any case, world conditions permitting, we trust that the new year will find me in position to be with you in person wherever needed.

He was licensed to fly after two months of intensive training under Marvin Lamb, instructor at the Loveland Municipal Airport.

Minutes of a September Board meeting reported that a new propeller had been installed on the airplane at a cost of $150.

The paper cutter was repaired for several hundred dollars. A new one would cost $2,600, a secondhand one $1,650. So—rejoicing! Uranda suggested we trade in our small press for a new one plus feeder, costing around $1,250—this in view of our contract for printing the *G.P.C. Server* and probability of the Sorority printing for Bob Palmer, Loveland, a large regular monthly account.

It was decided that the G.P.C. Servers Training School would open on Sunrise Ranch January 1, 1952.

Dr. Glenn Clark, head of a community called Camps Farthest Out, referred to Uranda as one of the major prophets. Incidentally, Dorothy Thompson, upon hearing the name of this community, for some time thought it was "Camps for the Stout"!

In a service on Sunrise Ranch on September 24 entitled "God's Power," Uranda spoke of the fact that turmoil, conflict, war, etc., are evidences that human beings, claiming to believe in God, are failing to let His will be done.

> It is God's will that there should be peace and harmony, the joy of life, free from the bondage of those things which prevent the fulfilment of life.
>
> Jesus Christ Himself came into the world to grant all this to the children of men. He said, "The works that I do shall ye do also; and greater works than these shall ye do; because I go unto my Father." It was not supernatural in the sense of being beyond the reach of our experience. If we think of the natural state of being as that which is in the world, of all this sin, suffering, sorrow and death, it might perhaps be called supernatural; but this miserable state of existence is not natural. It is subnormal, subnatural. The natural outworking of God's power in our lives is not a supernatural thing; it is what God intended should be the normal, everyday experience of every man, woman and child.
>
> Here, in this little valley, we are sharing in an experiment to prove that spiritual things are the most practical things on earth and that it is possible to let the power of God, the current of His spirit, have practical meaning in relation to everyday living. The idea that the things of God are impractical is ridiculous. Look at the human body. Who designed it? Is it impractically made?

On a golden Sunday afternoon in October the Unit gathered in beautiful Buckhorn country, not far from the Ranch to the north, where Uranda gave a service, "Builders of the Peace":

> We have made wonderful progress toward peace in our own hearts and in

our little community, but I think if we were to make an honest examination we would find that while we may all claim to want peace, there is some tendency as yet to fall into the same error that has threatened the peace of the world. We have here a lovely peaceful spot. If an environment of peace was all that was necessary to produce peace, then nature would eliminate war from the hearts and lives of the children of men. Because we have a peaceful place on Sunrise Ranch does not mean that all that is contrary to peace will automatically disappear. We have to do something about it; we have to take action. Peace is the gift of God's love.

Uranda announced, in "A Message of Thanksgiving" on November 21:

Recently Kathy and I completed our first trip by plane conveying the ministry to the field. We travelled approximately 2,180 air miles, going to Ponca City, Oklahoma; Fort Smith, Arkansas; Davenport, Iowa, and returning. We were away from Headquarters for six days and the total expense of operating the airplane for the entire trip was $66.50 plus depreciation which amounts to about $1.50 for each hour of flying time. Our personal expense for the trip was only about $20 because of the fine hospitality extended to us at each point.

He noted that the Church was free from debt, with thanksgiving for the "special gifts that made it possible, enabling us to maintain the pace of our expansion program." Also, twelve people were attending the special classes in ministerial training, giving rich promise of sorely needed workers in the harvest field.

It was about that time that Lloyd Jr. became seriously ill, having contracted a particularly menacing virus of some nature. It was a time of great concern for his parents and all of us. Eventually taken to a hospital in Denver, the two-year-old was successfully treated for a condition that included dehydration and returned home to be completely healed.

Minutes of a Board meeting reported that a one-room house next to the Bishop's residence was completed, to be home for me and my son, also providing office space for Uranda and me. Since our return from California in 1948, the small trailer that served in those capacities in Salinas had continued to be so used on Sunrise Ranch. So our new abode was instantly filled and overflowing, plus, a little later, with a mimeograph machine that couldn't find a home anywhere else. One of Uranda's familiar comments was that expansion did not occur until the present walls (of any circumstance) were pushed out. I can testify to that!

The little house was constructed of our home-made cinder blocks, and I recall once, when putting Billy to bed, he looked around and wistfully said, "I wish our house had walls." The inside walls were the same as outside! It had not occurred to me that memories of a different kind of house still lingered in the memory of this five-year-old. But victory was a way of life on Sunrise Ranch, and he loved it, learning that things were okay just the way they were.

With vital additions from time to time this little house has continued to this day to be my home and office while on Sunrise Ranch.

Kathy's parents, David and Rosa Groves, had moved to the Ranch, where they provided a special family atmosphere.

Mary Close, who reached the age of ninety while living on Sunrise, was a remarkable lady with a background of some amazing experiences. In the very early days, as a young and beautiful woman she crossed the untamed vastness of this country in a covered wagon and on more than one occasion defended herself, and the wagon, single-handed. She carried a gun. A touching scene for me one day was seeing my son run after her stooped figure as she climbed the hill to her cabin, and took the bucket of water she was laboriously carrying. It was heavier for him than he managed to make it appear!

Another item in the Board minutes revealed that a verbal transaction was worked out with our neighbors, the Olin brothers, wherein we exchanged a strip of land at the southwest end of our property for a small piece of their land just behind our fruit cellar. This gave them a passageway at the foot of the hill for their cows and preserved for us a backyard and some tillable soil at the Bishop's residence.

It was noted that Bishop and Mrs. Meeker attended the Annual Dinner of the Loveland Chamber of Commerce, welcome participants in the town's activities.

"Eden Valley Enterprises" was a name introduced at that time, enabling us to embark on endeavors new to the ministry. The officers were: Bishop Meeker, Director; Dick Cable, Assistant Director; Stanley Grindstaff, Secretary.

A vital step in Church expansion was taken when Sunrise Ranch was selected as the location for the new G.P.C. Servers Training School. Bishop Meeker read to the Board an outline of the proposed program and curriculum, to be sent to their Board of Directors for approval. Also, he had been presented with the G.P.C. Emblem.

In a Message on February 12, 1951, Uranda spoke of a Ministerial Training Class just held, and quoted from a previous paper of his on Prayer, used in that Class:

> In the Bible we are admonished, "Pray without ceasing." Unceasing prayer depends upon constant attunement with God through all the activities of every day. When the expression of the spirit of God is appearing through every thought and word and deed, our lives become a prayer. Prayer is that actualized obedience to the Law which lets the spirit of God find expression on earth. Any function that deepens attunement with God is prayer. The pur-

pose of prayer is not to cause God to do something, but rather to cause man to enter into an attitude which will let God do something.

Most so-called prayer disclaims individual responsibility and attempts to direct God with respect to His action. When human beings let themselves be directed by God and accept their own responsibilities in letting God's action appear, the power of God can truly work in the affairs of men. Our Master said, "Verily, verily, I say unto you, Whatsoever ye shall ask the Father in my name, he will give it you. Hitherto have ye asked nothing in my name: ask, and ye shall receive, that your joy may be full."

On March 13 in a service at 100 Mile House, "Examine Into Our Hearts," Martin shared his innermost feelings. Frances Acheson had filled a vital place as companion to him in the recent difficult period of his life, sharing his travels and contributing whole-heartedly in the activities of the Unit. He said:

This evening I have perhaps the most difficult and unhappy task to perform since this Unit came into being.

I received confirmation in the mail today that Frances will not be returning. It is something I have observed moving in that direction for some considerable time. That this precedent of failure should be one that has served closely with me makes for greater difficulties. Whenever there is failure, always it behooves us to examine into our own hearts.

Frances worked closely with me, necessitating that she had great responsibilities, and the failure in those responsibilities has far-reaching effects. In her place, and she served in it faithfully for some period of time, she was subject to pressures which none of you experienced, and I think that often her service and responsibilities were taken for granted, so that at times the pressures became almost unbearable. Perhaps I have some responsibility in this too.

You recognize that there is a personal element involved. Under the circumstances there must be those things; they are the points of contact. They are personal in one sense, and impersonal in another, things that are not limited to the individual who provides the focalization in the negative field but reach through her to all. I wrote to Frances today, accepting her choice, although I pointed out that the door is always open.

Minutes of a Board Meeting on Sunrise Ranch a month later revealed that Martin, and also Frances, were present, indication that she had reconsidered and returned. I include the foregoing expression about her departure, however, because that became the fact later and speaks eloquently of his feelings.

It was reported that a new engine had been installed in the Bellanca airplane, at cost of $596, which increased the value of the plane to $8,000. A loan was secured from the Home State Bank for $750, with the Kaiser automobile as security, payments on which were $50 over 10 months, balance to be paid in a lump sum at expiration date. The amount of $150 of this was put in the Church account as payment for the first half of our taxes on the Ranch. There were a few other expenses on the airplane—new tire, radio repairs, etc.— and a balance due Clinton Aviation Co. in Denver of $100. The plane had only 296 hours on it and this represented a big saving, since a new engine cost around $2,000.

William and Frieda Martens with son Bill Jr. had moved to the Ranch (adjacent house and property having been purchased by them), with the rest of the family to follow. William Martens was appointed Secretary of the Board of Trustees and Muriel Oshane Assistant Secretary.

It was reported that our G.P.C. Training School program was being temporarily delayed because of certain ones who opposed our Service and "sought through slanderous gossip to bring it into disrepute." A statement was formulated by the Board members and sent to the three officials of G.P.C. Servers, Inc.: George P. Shears, Director; Virgil Given, President; and Albert Ackerley. The situation was satisfactorily resolved and preparations continued for the opening of the School.

Uranda wrote a letter of clarification to those involved in the situation within the G.P.C. organization:

> Since 1940 this ministry, officially established in 1932, has watched with deep interest the growth and development of the G.P.C Program. Inasmuch as our Program has been conducted on a strictly giving basis with no charge for our literature, etc. we felt a special admiration for George Shears and all those who dared to share with him in developing the G.P.C Program.
>
> This ministry is completely nonsectarian, devoted to serving responding ones of all races, colors and creeds. Under the name "Emissaries of Divine Light" the Church was established in order to provide a spiritual centering for those who had not found satisfactory Church affiliation elsewhere. We make no effort to persuade anyone to change any such connection.
>
> Our fundamental concern is with healing—physically, mentally, emotionally and spiritually. Each phase requires particularized consideration, but each must be seen in its proper relation to the whole. Years of specialized study in all of these phases preceded the official inauguration of our Program in 1932. In 1929 I began using the approach to healing problems which we now refer to as attunements.

We gladly recognize and acknowledge the important contribution to the health and welfare of humanity that has been made through chiropractic methods. Likewise we gladly recognize and acknowledge the great benefits to humanity which have appeared through the medical profession. We have no quarrel with either professional group—or with any other.

However, we are convinced that there is a vast field yet to be explored with respect to the secrets of life and health, but also that we have an understanding of the laws and principles sufficient to warrant widespread use of the attunement method of dealing with the problems of suffering humanity, as rapidly as competent Servers can be trained and developed.

At the invitation of George Shears, Director of G.P.C. Servers, Bishop Meeker attended a Convention on February 24 and 25 at the Shears home in Huntingburg, Indiana. Accompanying him were Kathy and I, and Dick Cable. At that time the Board of Directors voted to cooperate in establishing a special G.P.C. Servers Training School at the International Headquarters of Emissaries of Divine Light on Sunrise Ranch, to be open to students wishing to become qualified G.P.C. Servers. Included in their training would be living and working side by side with Sunrise personnel to receive practical experience in getting along with their fellows—in the field, machine shop, office, kitchen, wherever.

The Board of Trustees and the Sunrise family joyfully welcomed this new project. An unfinished cement block house at the northern end of the property was completed to provide classrooms and living quarters for students. This became fondly known as the little red schoolhouse and its first residents were William and Muriel Oshane.

Uranda noted:

Most G.P.C. Servers tend to have financial difficulties. We are not suggesting that by some magic means this problem can be solved. In all things we must be practical, avoiding visionary extremes. That which the Server receives in the returning cycle depends upon the quality and quantity of his giving in true service. As we all work together we can easily solve all the problems which confront us.

The formulating of policies and preparation of courses has been delegated to me and that the fundamental principles of G.P.C. and E.D.L. are the same. The vast amount of literature available is proving to be of tremendous value to those G.P.C. Servers already practicing.

Technique should not be immediately considered, and the Sunrise Service series of 212 lessons is ideal for initiating the Course. As G.P.C. Servers our approach is from a spiritual standpoint and we do not desire or intend to encroach upon the field which properly belongs to the medical profession.

The force that is at work through attunements is not mysterious or diffi-cult to understand. It is not a figment of fancy, because it can definitely be felt by those who have trained perception and by those with a natural perception of the working of the life force. But the *results* of the working of the force can be seen and recognized in *any* individual who allows himself to respond thereto. It is not necessary that the individual be able to feel physically the working of this force in order for it to be effective in relation to himself. The Server does not at any time, under any circumstance, attempt to treat, or heal, the servee. All healing comes from God.

During the past twenty years I have shared in hundreds of specific in-stances where it was evident that the spirit of God can work through one individual to and through another without regard to space or distance. Where there is harmonization with the essential laws and principles the essential as-sistance in removing the obstacle and reestablishing the perfect pattern can be achieved without any physical contact between Server and servee. This introduces the No-Touch Technique of giving attunements.

At a Convention I held in Pittsburgh in 1941, I lectured on these subjects and gave an attunement on the platform before an audience of about a hun-dred people. I demonstrated in front of a blackboard the visible reality of the release of the radiation of spirit of God through the hands. [That incident was very impressive, the emanation of white light from his fingers clearly visible.]

When Albert Ackerley, through his study of *The Triune Ray,* came to a point of polarity in the giving of attunements, a basic triangle was established. The G.P.C. movement came into manifestation through George Shears about 1939 or 1940. I became aware of his function in this regard in 1940, through a Dr. Hall, since deceased, who was practicing in Palo Alto, California, at the time. There are many more creative triangles involved in all of this than here outlined, but these few serve the purpose for the moment.

On April 7, Uranda announced that he had joined the Civil Air Patrol, an auxiliary of the United States Air Force, and was commissioned as a Chaplain. He shared in the first National Convention of Chaplains in Washington, D.C., on March 28 and 29, and was enthusiastic in his appreciation of meeting representatives of many faiths from all forty-eight states, also Hawaii and Puerto Rico. He noted that in that organization religious boundaries meant little, and was inspired by the grouping of one hundred and fifty men serving together for a common purpose. He was required to wear the official uniform and to shave his beard.

In a dedication of the Little Chapel by Uranda on April 29, entitled "The Secret Place," he said:

> We have looked forward to this hour for a long time. This building is an outer form of something that must be in the heart of each one, and I feel that our Unit progress is such that this symbol may now be dedicated in that realization, in a spirit of devotion before our Lord and King, and looking forward to the day when we may have the privilege of dedicating a Church building where we may gather for worship.

Martin gave a devotion:

> Our gracious and loving heavenly Father, we rejoice to gather here upon this hill, bowing humbly before Thee in recognition of this symbol of the secret place in the heart of each one, that we may abide in what is symbolized. We rejoice in that vision which allows us to behold the Church building that shall be, in which we, and all who will, may come to worship Thee in spirit and in truth. [The location of that envisioned building, which took form as the Dome Chapel many years later under the inspired planning and direction of Martin, was adjacent to the spot where the Little Chapel stood.]

Uranda continued:

> "Lift up thine eyes unto the hills, from whence cometh thy help." "Let your light so shine before men, that they may see your good works, and glorify your Father which is in heaven." A true current of the spirit of God's blessing has been, and is, flowing forth from this Valley, from these hills, and we have the sacred privilege of giving meaning to those words for the people of the world, that as they lift up their eyes unto the hills they may find a place from whence comes help. There must be that secret place within the heart of each one which is never penetrated by the emotional storms of the outer world, thus maintaining a place from whence His spirit may flow in dealing with those problems and situations which arise.
>
> It has been a long time since the first stone was placed upon the foundation here. There were long periods when, in the outer sense, there was no building of this form, but in those intervals something was being done with respect to the building of that sanctuary within each heart by which, in season, this form might have true meaning on earth. And now we have built a Little Chapel to stand as a symbol of the secret place of the Most High.

This Prayer Chapel is dedicated to prayer, a secret place of communion with God, representing a labor of love. Each one has had some part therein. Likewise, each one has had a part in building that spirit of divine expression in our Unit function which gives meaning to the Chapel. We would not have a Chapel standing here upon this little hill and have it remain an empty form; even as we, wherever we go, whatever we do, are that for which this Chapel stands.

And now I open this door, aware that there must be an open door in our hearts through which the Master may pass when He comes to commune with us, and through which the spirit of God's blessing may flow forth into the world. This Little Chapel, though we now dedicate it, is not yet finished. It does not yet contain its altar. There is a little prayer rug, there is a candlestick, and that is all. It seems to me that this is much like our ministry at this time, not fully finished. The means of its manifestation are not yet apparent, but there is a secret place where each one is learning to abide and from which the light shines forth as we abide under the shadow of the Almighty.

Uranda stood in the doorway, facing into the Chapel, and said:

And now, in the Name of the Father, the Son and the Holy Spirit, I sanctify this Chapel, I dedicate this building, that it may be a symbol of the secret place of the Most High from whence the light of God's love shines forth, that it may stand here upon this little hill as the mustard seed planted in good ground which shall in season bring forth all those forms all over the world which are necessary to the full and complete ministry of our Lord Jesus Christ.

In a Board Meeting on Sunrise Ranch, May 11, it was reported that Mary Close had turned her cottage over to the Church to be used as necessary, not being in position to finance the balance of cost. However, she occupied the little house for the duration of her presence on the Ranch. This later became our first print shop and in season the Commissary, so functioning today.

A fire at the Bishop's residence was reported, caused by an overheated furnace. The response of the Loveland Fire Department at 3 a.m. was swift, courteous and effective. Before long the Ranch would have its own fire truck, adequate for any moderate emergency.

Twenty acres of barley had been seeded on Sunrise Ranch land, six acres of barley and six acres of oats on the Martens Ranch, and forty acres of winter wheat was up to about eight inches.

Dick Cable reported that 7,800 copies of the chiropractic issue of the *G.P.C. Server* had been printed and shipped. Work was proceeding on the attunement issue, a run of 6,500 copies. Dick's mother, Harriet Cable, visited, left shortly for Cleveland, and returned with her husband Wallace to take up permanent residence in Loveland, where they found a happy and profitable communion with the people in town.

Uranda and Kathy flew to 100 Mile House on May 2nd with Martin and Frances, to return immediately.

Eden Valley News of May 1951, reported some acquisitions: a new Kaiser, a deep freeze unit, and a 1949 Chevrolet pickup truck, to say nothing of a manure spreader, rotary scraper and subsoiler.

Albert Christiansen had completed a beautiful door made of oak and pine for the Little Chapel, also Bishop Meeker had drawn up designs for the altar. This found form in season, created by artist Egon Milinkovich, a simple but majestic stone structure carrying the sacred atmosphere that pervades that little sanctuary.

There was a crew of men averaging about eleven, two of whom were kept busy with the stock, another in the printshop, so that eight men were left to do the necessary work of farming, gardening, building, hauling, digging trenches, electrical wiring, carpentry, masonry, plumbing, and machine and motor repairs. An apiary was begun by Dad Groves.

It was noted that John Nordland of Pewaukee, Wisconsin, passed away. This fine man, born in Sweden some ninety years before, was the father of Marie Johnson, Lillian's grandfather. He had a great love for Uranda and was a dear friend to all who knew him.

The provision of irrigation from the Government water conservation project canal behind the Ranch was a blessing straight from heaven, further augmenting our water supply. "Just think!" Uranda was heard to exclaim, "they built the longest overland canal at this altitude in the world—just for us!" This sort of remark was characteristic. When traveling, for instance, on a newly improved highway, we would hear that there could be no other purpose for anything but to further the work of the Lord.

The soil was constantly being nourished and revived. Twenty tons of lime, for calcium, was received free for the hauling from the sugar beet factory nearby, and spread on the soil; also three tons of Soilife, a mineral product containing calcium, phosphorous and nitrogen were purchased, ingredients coming from deposits of sea life in Florida, from deposits of special minerals found on old ocean floors in Wyoming, and part from Colorado.

12

SERVERS TRAINING SCHOOL
May 1951 ~ April 1952

Martin visited Vancouver approximately every six weeks, at which time he conducted a service. In the interims, weekly meetings were held by Ernie Taylor, a chiropractor, with Lewis and Sylvia Little continuing their valuable contribution.

Art and Ruth Kirby, with children Jimmy and Melody, moved to Sunrise on May 28. This little family came as a result of a remarkable healing by attunement experienced by young Jimmy who had suffered third-degree burns on his leg in a severe accident.

One day Ruth, who had gone into the outhouse, experienced an outrageous sensation upon contact with the seat. It had a soft, spongy texture; and one look sent her screaming outside. It was our friend George, the large resident bull snake, curled up (in a most strategic position) for a nap. This beautiful creature (but not welcome in all situations!) led a charmed life on Sunrise Ranch. It knew its purpose, to dispose of rattlesnakes, which it did well, and by decree of Uranda was not to be harmed. Incidentally, the Kirby family stayed for a while, then moved on to other places.

In a Board Meeting on Sunrise Ranch of June 8 it was noted that a men's group had been organized, with weekly meetings.

And there was other news. Three thousand tomato plants were planted in land we rented from the Prays, not far from Sunrise, and about 3,500 celery plants in our Ranch garden. The walls of the basement of the apartment house were almost completed, with 300 blocks made to date.

Uranda expanded on "A View of our Goal" on June 24:

> Here in our little valley there is a danger of losing the perspective view of our true relationships with the rest of the human family. We are not here to encourage segregation or to please ourselves or satisfy some personal ends.
>
> Theory alone is not enough, even though that theory might be ever so true. We are working to prove that it is true. It is vital that we maintain the vision of what is at work in the world, that we see the relatedness between its parts and understand what motivates the people of the world. There must be no intolerance or prejudice directed toward human beings because of race or color or creed. At the same time we must maintain such a clear vision and understanding of the truths of life that we never allow ourselves to compromise with the realm of the unreal. This requires selflessness, it requires love for God and our fellow beings, fulfilling the two Great Commandments which the Master gave.

Meanwhile things were on the move overseas. In "A Review," August 4, Uranda spoke of receiving a letter from Africa, with pictures of the new church group established there. And in a service a few weeks later at 100 Mile House, "Those Who Dwell in Heaven," Martin referred to a brief letter received from an elderly lady in Budapest, Hungary, a country behind the Iron Curtain, subjected to the harsh dictatorship of the Communist regime.

> She says very little in her letter, but there is an underlying appeal, a crying out. Perhaps our service can be seen as the release of the current of the spirit, not only to this particular lady but to hundreds and thousands of other human beings in like, and worse, circumstances. Also I trust that by reason of our consideration you gain a more vivid appreciation, not only of the opportunities and blessings that are ours but of the responsibilities that go with them.

During the war Martin had written some special papers, specifically to fulfil a need in the young daughters of his brother in England. Later compiled and entitled *Child Light,* this beautiful booklet has been used extensively, filling needs in many youthful hearts.

At 100 Mile House on September 25, in his service "Life Is the Gift of God," Uranda spoke of his delight to be back in the log cabin in the Cariboo, and that oftimes there is not a sufficiently vivid realization that all life is God's gift to us.

> But life can take on special meaning under certain circumstances. I wonder

if I can share an illustration with you without making you fearful—perfect love casts out fear. It has to do with flying. And I intend to do a lot more flying.

We encountered a good deal of bad weather in our flight to and from Huntingburg. On the return journey, when we landed at Grand Island, Nebraska, for fuel and to check on the weather, they said there was a bad stretch of weather on the direct course, but that by turning up toward Scott's Bluff I could get down around it and fly over Cheyenne to Loveland. It would be impossible to fly the direct route.

So we started out and followed the Platte River and swung north and ran into a storm on course as we expected, then started back down the valley leading toward Cheyenne around what appeared to be the worst end of the storm, hoping to find a way through, but we searched in vain. We were under a ceiling of perhaps six or seven hundred feet. It looked like we might have sufficient ceiling above the mesa to circle around to Cheyenne, as there was no place in that vicinity to land. I knew the weather was open so we could get back north to Scotts Bluff.

I followed along this road, got over the rim, and the clouds were practically on the ground; it was not feasible to follow the road. I was probably not more than two or three hundred feet above the mesa level, and as I approached it the road began to grow so dim because of the interfering cloud that I could hardly see it. There was quite a large space where I could swing back up to return to Scotts Bluff.

I suppose I could be criticized in this. In any case in making this swing back in what I felt certain was adequate opening and space, we got closed in in a cloud. I was not climbing. There was extremely rough terrain below us, jagged, sharp peaks and when the cloud closed in we could not see anything, hardly the tips of the wings.

So I did some fast thinking. If we swung west toward the valley and I happened to miss the opening, I would be headed toward the mountains and higher clouds. If I tried to maintain that same level and fly back over the valley, there was no way of telling whether we were over it or not. I did not dare fly east because I knew there was turbulence, and to the north the cloud bank broke, and at the time I felt the only safe way was to set the ship on a course due north on a very gentle climb at about 75 feet per minute, which would carry us out of the edge of the cloud into the opening, probably one and a half or two miles, which should not take long in a plane.

I had the ship flying at a perfectly even keel. The turnbank was working and there was no possibility of stalling out at a speed of 120 miles an hour at a gentle climb, which from the standpoint of good calculations was perfect. Of course in these thunder clouds there are some very severe updrafts and downdrafts, what is called cumulus.

We were flying along—how long? How does one estimate time in such a situation? We were moving on a course calculated to bring us in the clear, and I knew that the terrain was such that at that gentle climb there was no possibility of hitting anything.

Then all at once my controls went crazy. Trying to fly the ship on a level keel was like trying to beat the air with hands, and instead of a gentle climb we were being carried straight up at a terrific speed. The controls would not control the ship. The indicator stood straight up and the ship was stalling out. I could not keep its nose down to keep enough speed to maintain the ship's position, it was slowing down, and it did not seem there was anything I could do to level it out.

I had to get the nose down or we would have stalled out. As the updraft stopped carrying us on the top of the cloud, I managed to get a little bit of control started. We were on the downdraft by that time and she nosed straight to the earth—how fast? I have no idea—with the power on. I did not dare take the power off moving toward the earth at a terrific speed, nose down. Something like that can seem like an eternity. I knew there was an air cushion at the bottom if the terrain was good to allow us to use it, but I also knew that it was pretty bad terrain, which made using the air cushion a ticklish business.

We had the two children with us. Nancy started to scream; she knew something was wrong. She asked us afterward what made the big wind that was screaming. If you ever heard the wind scream, this was terrific! Kathy looked back and smiled at the children and told them it would be all right. The ship was going down so fast it was a good thing the safety belts were holding. I had the wheels back working to the limit, undertaking to pull her out of the dive, but she was not taking. Straight down, and for a while it seemed the controls were made of melted butter. I knew it was the moment of crisis: either the controls would start working in the next instant and pull us out, or there would be nothing left. In this whole experience Kathy stayed calm; there was not a ripple in the vibratory pattern.

A few seconds later—maybe two or thirty—we broke through the bottom of the cloud, we began to see the earth, and under the cloud should be the air cushion. We were headed straight toward the ground with the power on at a terrific speed. It could not have been more than five or six hundred feet to the earth.

The little Bellanca is built with a 6-G safety factor. That means that they calculate the stresses of normal flying, normal landings, normal take-offs, normal still-air flying, whatever those stresses are, and whatever it takes to meet that requirement they multiply six times, so that the plane is built to stand six times more stress than would be ordinarily necessary. Well, my own private view is that the Lord must have been with us because I think the stress factors reached over that. The controls started to take hold as soon as we hit that air cushion, and we started pulling out of that dive, and I held her to it.

Perhaps you have heard stories or seen pictures of how it feels to come out of a very fast dive. All the blood rushes to your head, and you have to be careful to keep some center of consciousness to maintain control. It takes every bit of will and command you can force on your body. You cannot keep your mouth closed because the force of gravity opens it and stretches it out.

We circled around and the little ship took it. I checked the bearings and calculated the directions I felt Scotts Bluff would be and set the course. I did not alter that course one iota from the time I set it quite a few miles back. We flew dead-on over the Scotts Bluff airport and landed. We stayed overnight there. That night I wrote Martin a little note.

After such an experience one knows that one's life is a gift from God. There is nothing about it that is taken for granted. By the grace of God we were snatched, you might say, from a situation that perhaps in any other circumstance or perhaps any other ship, would have meant certain death. We flew afterward. We will fly again. It is not that there is danger in flying. How many times in driving one escapes from an accident by a split second. I do not want to make you fearful. If you become fearful when we are flying, it will not help us any. Kathy was there by my side, and she was not fearful. Our little ones were calm. Oh they were ready to get out of the ship!—but the next morning when we were getting ready to fly to Loveland they climbed in very sweetly.

I will be eternally grateful for the fact that in that moment of stress and crisis my wife was tranquil and serene, with faith and trust. Only where there is perfect trust can the things of God come forth in our lives. Rose Forker, with the children in the back, held the pattern too. When we were pulling out of that dive she had to use all her strength and will to keep her weight from crushing the little ones. She took care of them. No one was hurt.

It is when you stay steady consciously as a Unit, no cross currents, no spirit of judgment or condemnation or ill attitudes, with faith centered where it belongs, that you do your real part in allowing the things of God to come into manifestation. That is why you are granted this special privilege of sharing this ministry with your leader, Martin, why you have the privilege of his presence, and as you so function you will allow his service to have greater meaning.

Martin gave expression to the depths of feeling moving in his heart and of those present:

The plane plunging down was apparently going to destruction very rapidly. I suppose from a world-wide standpoint we can recognize a similar movement wherein the world body of human beings, of which we are members, is moving toward destruction. That rapid movement is something that tends to inspire fear in human hearts, and there appears to be no way out. The way out is made manifest by reason of trust when all appears to be lost. We may all share in the provision of the Lord for the salvation of mankind.

On September 29 at the Special Session at 100 Mile House, Uranda spoke of "The Power of God in Us":

In all the world there is just one 100 Mile House such as this, and Martin and those who serve here are doing their part toward making this a haven in the world, where there is the atmosphere essential to drawing near to the heart of God.

He also spoke of two men who came as atheists to the G.P.C. Conference and "left having found God."

It was on November 11, 1951, that Martin referred to the initiation of Sunday School at 100 Mile House as an important milestone. The first class was held under the leadership of Mary Mackenzie, Hanya Oshanek and Edith Brownlee. Through the years the group was enlarged on many occasions by some delighted little friends from the Village.

In November Martin announced the incorporation in Canada under the Societies Act of British Columbia, and that in conjunction with Uranda he had been working on the Constitution, a portion of which he read:

The Society accepts as the divinely ordained and supreme manifest head, leader and teacher in charge of the work to which the Society is dedicated, the Right Reverend Lloyd Arthur Meeker, Bishop of the superior body mentioned in Article I; and as sharing his authority with him, as the manifest head and Bishop of the Society in Canada, the Right Reverend William Martin Alleyne Cecil, of 100 Mile House, British Columbia.

I trust you will find it pleasing to sign it as the initial members of the
Society of Emissaries of Divine Light in Canada.

The Certificate of Incorporation was issued on December 6. In accordance with the
provisions of the Constitution, an interim Board of Directors was appointed to serve
until the first annual general meeting.

The membership of the Unit at 100 Mile House as of December 6 consisted of Gordon and Emily Marks with Ross and Carolyn, John and Hanya Oshanek with David and
Yvonne, Frances Acheson, Mary Mackenzie, Marion Murray, Jessie Stuckey, Vera Parsons, Edith Brownlee, Beverly Smith, Allen Graham, Lina Lucyk, Ronald Murray, Ann
and Ralph Pekary.

On December 8 on Sunrise Ranch the Little Chapel provided a beautiful setting for
the wedding of Richard Cable and Billie Groves. Uranda officiated, with attendants Ralph
and Roz Hooper, also William and Muriel Oshane. Parents of both participants were
present, as well as three children: Nancy as flower girl, Lloyd the ring-bearer, and Groves
(Ralph) Hooper as page boy. Add Kathy, Lillian and me, and it was a full chapel, brim-
ming over with the joyous spirit of love.

Martin left for Sunrise Ranch on December 26 for the opening of the G.P.C. Servers
Training School, accompanied by Frances Acheson, Jessie Stuckey, Carolyn Marks, David
Oshanek and Bud Murray. Martin would be staying at Sunrise for a few months after the
New Year to focalize activities there.

Uranda composed an "Initial Outline of Tentative Program for G.P.C. Servers Training School" and submitted it for the consideration of George Shears, Director; Virgil
Given, President; Albert Ackerley; and all other officers and Servers with a voice in relation to this program. Uranda welcomed suggestions and added:

> This program will of course be developed and carried forward in strict accor-
> dance with the G.P.C. principles. From present indications our cash costs involved
> in making this instruction available and providing housing and meals for stu-
> dents will be approximately $1 per day in summertime and $1.50 in wintertime
> per student. This figure does not include any remuneration or provision for living
> expenses for any of the instructors, who will not be on a salary basis.
>
> This program is nonsectarian and open to all students without regard to
> religious belief. However, regular attendance at Chapel services will be a re-
> quired part of the Training Program. Satisfactory completion of the training
> class would be recognized by a certificate or diploma.

Students were expected to work four or five hours a day: for women, in the kitchen,
gardens, sewing, general housekeeping; for men, work in the gardens, on buildings,

whatever was required. As much as possible, each would be allocated work harmonious to special abilities.

The suggested Program included four primary courses of instruction and training. Integrated with these four, as sidelight considerations, such things as organic gardening, dietetics, etc., could be included.

Uranda presented the faculty members as follows:

> William Oshane, B.A., D.C., Ph.D.—"The Divine Design of the Physical Body." This course is not intended as a study of disease but provides a new approach to a study of anatomy and the principles involved in the living organism.

> Richard Halliday Thompson, M.A., Cambridge—"Language and Cultural Influence." The purpose of this course is to help the student learn how to use language in influencing others on a constructive basis. It will also deal with human relationships.

> Lloyd A. Meeker—"Spiritual Realism in Practical Application." This course undertakes a consideration of divine law and examination of the principles of being. It is designed to assist the student to allow the pattern of his life to take form on the basis of his individual characteristics, qualities and abilities, expressing that potential peculiar to himself. Emphasis is on the practical nature of true spirituality in everyday living here and now.

> Lloyd A. Meeker, assisted by Richard Cable—"G.P.C. Server Technique and Professional Manner." This is designed to bring to focus in practical application all the other subject matter considered, in a manner that will allow the student to be effective in assisting his friends to find and experience healing in body, mind and spirit.

> In addition to assisting in the course just mentioned, Dick Cable will act as Student Counsellor, so that student problems may be dealt with effectively and any matter requiring attention may be brought promptly to the attention of the proper instructor.

January 1, 1952, marked a high point of fulfilment in Uranda's life and ministry, with the opening of the first Class of the G.P.C. Servers Training School on Sunrise Ranch. Those classes, in various formats, have continued through the years, held in countries all over the world. That initial one consisted of about twenty people, from many places.

Dealing with "The Problems of a Server," in a Class on January 8 Uranda said:

> Each problem holds the seed of tragedy, and only as you are equipped to hold forth the promise of life can that seed be removed and healing be known. When you are dealing constantly with those things that are tragic, or near

tragic, if you are not thoroughly centered in God yourself you are going to become subject to the tragic and incapable of serving.

At 100 Mile House John Oshanek had acquired some bees and initiated an apiary. He had also purchased some earthworms.

Regarding those earthworms! In later years, embarking on one of our return trips to Sunrise from the Hundred, Martin was loading the trunk of the car. He picked up a large, covered can from the pile of luggage and asked, puzzled, "What's this?" John and I exchanged guilty glances, and I answered, with eyes downcast, "Earthworms, in soil. They're scarce on Sunrise Ranch right now, and I need some for my rose garden. John gave them to me."

Martin, with a twitch at the corner of his mouth, said, "That's not a good idea. They don't approve of transporting dirt, with possible creatures, across the border." He set the can down and proceeded with the packing—until he looked up and saw two very long, sad faces. Hesitating only an instant, he turned around, picked up the can of worms and tucked it in between some pieces of luggage. On that trip it never occurred to the officials at Customs to look into the trunk, and Sunrise Ranch has been crawling with Canadian worms these many years.

Continuing the saga of finances in the early days on Sunrise Ranch, it was reported on January 30 that at the end of December 1951 our Accounts Payable amounted to $6,929.13. Of this, $2,027.55 was payable on our contract accounts. Some of our creditors had had faith in us for quite some time, and Martin suggested that instead of encumbering our assets by borrowing money locally he would undertake to borrow it in Canada. This was accepted with a sigh of relief by the Board members and followed by a letter to Martin from William Oshane:

> Your sharing of our financial difficulties in a material sense is significant in a spiritual sense. Since the beginning of our function here as a Unit, if we were to have conducted our expansion program on the basis of visible financial means and assets we would not have come very far. Uranda's spirit has not been bound by the visible financial means in inaugurating our program and its continuance. There was no logical basis for starting our activity here, for at the beginning we had debts of approximately three thousand dollars, not knowing where the money was coming from. In our emergency you came forth as a provision of the Lord to relieve our financial pressures and I wish again to express our heartfelt thanks.

Consideration was given to the purchase of some property by the Falls, described earlier, owned by Riggs and offered by Bob Palmer. The matter was tabled for the moment and acquired later, a gorgeous site at the edge of a mighty falls at the foot of the Big Thompson Canyon. This part of the country has a uniquely grand beauty, attracting tourists from around the world. Presently the building is used as an art gallery and studio for our resident artists, and has, in various capacities through the years, provided a setting and opportunity for public contact. Often Sunday tourists stop to look—and sometimes take home a choice piece of art.

Before leaving Sunrise, in a service on February 28, "The Evolving Process," Martin said:

> One of the limiting factors we have to deal with here has been with respect to a certain shortage of funds in the immediate sense; and it is difficult to find any projects that do not require the expenditure of some money. But there is a good deal of material of various kinds here, waiting to be used. You have all seen piles of lumber, for instance, in various places—and there are other things. And then there is the material we have in the way of man-power and woman-power. Before they undertake to do anything, people usually look in the bank account to see if they can proceed; but here we have another sort of bank account—a great deal of material, both human and inanimate. If we do not make right use of that, could we rightly expect the Lord to provide us with anything more?

Martin and Frances returned to 100 Mile House on March 8. David Oshanek, a member of the Class, remained and succeeded Martin as coordinator of physical activities on Sunrise Ranch.

Ross Marks reported in a Board meeting at 100 Mile House on March 24:

> We were not able to make the loan at the bank for $5,000 (suggested several months before), so we sent $2,000 to Sunrise Ranch from The Lodge. We succeeded in negotiating a loan of $2,400 to the Society, payable to Emissaries of Divine Light, Loveland. This, plus $600 from The Lodge, was sent, making a total of $5,000, the original amount suggested by Martin. Repayment to the bank is at the rate of $200 per month, plus interest, made up of $75 monthly from Sunrise, $50 from the Society at 100 Mile House, and $75 monthly from the Lodge, plus charges. After one year, when the bank loan will be paid off, the $2,600 forwarded from The Lodge will be repaid in the same manner.
>
> The purchase of an International pick-up truck, at cost of $2,302.03 in Vancouver, for part-time use in delivering gas, would involve some income.

On March 25, in a Class entitled "Vibrational Factors in an Attunement," Uranda said that response to doubt and fear in oneself can engender response by those who are doubtful and fearful, and conversely the expression of the things of God will engender response to God.

He went on to report that the president of the G.P.C. Servers Inc. had been arrested and charged with practicing falsely and was facing a trial:

> Some, thinking to destroy the things of God, have attempted to put the machinery of law in operation. It may be that you, as Servers, will have to face some kind of a contest. We know that President Virgil Given is going to hold steady. We do not worry about that; he will face the issue; but he needs our prayers, our vibrational support.
>
> I shall have the final word as to who shall receive a G.P.C. Certificate. You are going to prove that you value it, if you get it, by the way you face up to your responsibility. Some are carrying it already: George and Naomi Shears, Virgil Given, Albert Ackerley and the Millers. And there are others across the country who are facing up to their responsibilities, not just those in the G.P.C. Service but in the Third Sacred School, whose giving and faithful service over the years has made it possible for you to have this class.

In another Class, entitled "In Alignment," Uranda spoke of basic patterns of technique in the field of attunements, in which he said:

> Every human being is different. There are no two alike. Every situation is different. You cannot have a situation today that you could exactly reproduce tomorrow. It is impossible to have two identical conditions, either simultaneously in one place, or far apart, or successively, one one day and one the next. There may be many basic factors that seem identical, but as no two of those snowflakes out there are the same, so there are no two identical situations.
>
> It is necessary that we study the principles, that there may be in consciousness those elements essential to the working of the spirit of God through us; but in the field of application we must be constantly under the direction of the spirit, which is everlastingly original. God does not produce two identical things. Two identical things would have to both be in the same space, made of the same substance—an impossibility, and God does not do the impossible.

In season Curtis and Faith Bunce left the Ranch and lived for a number of years in the Midwest, with both their lives coming to a tragic end many years later, news of which reached us through a newspaper item.

On April 13 an early morning Easter Service was held on the knoll to the east beside the Little Chapel, later entitled "Holy Communion." These sunrise services became an annual event, eagerly welcomed by a group of sleepy but devoted people, unless there happened to be a snowstorm, in which case it would be transferred to the chapel. I would sit in the car nearby, with the window rolled down and wearing gloves as I recorded the words in shorthand. It could be quite cold at Eastertime!

At 100 Mile House on April 15 it was reported, in a meeting called especially to discuss the advisability of installing propane gas, that the hot water supply was very inadequate. They were quoted on 800 gallons of propane at $304 and that would last a year or more. The outlay would be about $1100.

13

ALL THE TITHES

April ~ September 1952

*I*n a service on April 26, "Ye Shall Know the Truth," Uranda spoke on the subject of marriage:

There have been many peculiar ideas with respect to the positive and negative aspects of being as they relate to men and women. It is the divine design that the male should carry the positive point of polarity and the female the negative point. But I have been repeatedly amazed at some of the distortion patterns which have appeared in this regard. There is the idea that in order to be negative the female had to be acquiescent and subservient, and that carrying the positive point of polarity gave the man leave to be dictatorial and arbitrarily impose his whims and desires without regard to the patterns in his wife.

Our meanings one to another are of many levels other than the mere fact of intimate physical relationship. A real foundation for marriage must also carry a pattern of blending in the mental plane with respect to the truth of life, and in the spiritual plane with respect to the reality of love. Sex has a part to play at every level of being. There is interplay between the positive and negative factors involved.

If there is a male through whom the pattern of truth is not functioning and he has a wife through whom there is the expression of truth, the positive manifestation in such a case would appear through the woman, because the truth at any level is positive to that which is below it, though negative to that which is above it. So we have the pattern of dominion through truth in woman just as surely as in man.

There can be no pattern of subservience spiritually, mentally or emotionally in a true companionship. Whether through male or female, a dictatorial attitude has no proper place.

The actuality of dominion is in truth, but the functioning of truth in relation to dominion is made possible only by love. Truth cannot make one free while one does not have love in the sense of the fulfilment of the First Great Commandment, to love God. So while certain expressions of truth have their primary manifestation through the female, and certain aspects through the male, it is not a question of maleness or femaleness but of "Is it the truth?"

The attempt to dominate on the part of the physical aspect of being, the desires of the body allowed to control, was the cause of the fall in the first place and has held mankind in bondage through the millennia. That is not to say that the physical part of us is not to share the experiences of life. That which is natural to the desires of the body in the true sense, without distortion, is natural also to the spiritual, and in its proper place and time has its expression.

Until you let go of the personal, graspy things, the greed of mind and heart, concern about what it is going to be as a man or woman, divine or something else, stop trying to get fulfilment for yourselves, stop trying to get to heaven, or position in heaven, dominion or power, you will not know true fulfilment. As long as you are trying to get something for yourself you are wrong, even if it is the things of God you seek. Until our primary concern is the fulfilment of truth for all humanity, without regard to personal desire or cost, what we have done or have not done, we are not worthy to be counted disciples of our Lord.

In May Martin received a letter from a place called Ado-Ekiti in Nigeria. It was written by a man who had somehow come upon a copy of *Northern Light* and was very anxious to find some connection with us and receive further issues. An interchange continued between him and Martin, and subsequently Sunrise Ranch. These points of light appearing in far places in those very early days were cherished as the vital seeds they were, fruits of which are seen in abundance today.

In a service on May 4 at 100 Mile House, "The Sword in Action," Martin said:

> I appreciate the faithful service in your several fields over the months and years. That we were in position, when the need arose, to provide a sum of money for Sunrise Ranch was one very important phase of ministry rendered thus far. If we had done nothing else but be in position to do that, it would have been well worthwhile.

On May 8 Uranda entitled a talk given on Sunrise Ranch "Money," a remarkable treatment of a sensitive subject. In it he asked:

> Why do human beings resist so stubbornly the process of putting a consciousness of spiritual riches and a consciousness of material riches into alignment? If we were to say that you have an unlimited spiritual credit rating, that should have meaningfulness in the material realm, so that spiritual riches may control on earth in the realm of form.

He emphasized the fact that people discount God's giving, and then are surprised to see the discount which is returned by the world:

> Until you stop discounting the things of God offered here, you have no control pattern by which you can influence the people of the world to stop discounting the service you render, because you set the patterns yourselves.
>
> "Bring me all the tithes into the store house, that there may be meat in mine house, and prove me now herewith, saith the Lord of hosts, if I will not open you the windows of heaven and pour you out a blessing, that there shall not be room enough to receive it." The tithes, the offerings, physical activity, the work you do, helps, but it includes the spirit within you, which includes everything, the wholeness of you in response to God—though it may be the widow's mite. And that will be but a tithe of what God gives to you.
>
> I am talking about value received and your acknowledgment of it with respect to every phase of your beings, so that there is a control pattern and you are no longer subject to a consciousness of being poor. Wastefulness, an abuse of physical things or material substance, is always a sign of a consciousness of being poor, a "don't care" attitude. We have available to us the wealth of the kingdom. The release of the wealth of heaven into the world will bring the wealth of the world under the control of heaven.

Minutes from a Board Meeting on May 9 on Sunrise Ranch reported that Albert Christiansen had attended the meeting on irrigation water on April 21 and arranged for

11 acre-feet at $30.25. Three new wells were dug at the south end of the property.

It was agreed that since Sunrise Ranch is a Church property supported by voluntary contributions we should not have to pay property taxes. A committee of Bishop Meeker, Albert Christiansen, Richard Thompson and William Oshane was appointed to go to Ft. Collins to clear this matter. Later, in a Board meeting on June 13, Bishop Meeker reported that the attorney consulted advised it was likely that the matter would need to be taken to a higher court. Bishop Meeker suggested that we should present the pertinent facts to Mr. Wright, the tax assessor at Ft. Collins, and invite him to come and look over the situation personally. (Over a period of time this matter was completed satisfactorily.)

In a service on Sunrise Ranch on May 18 Uranda spoke on "Accepting the Control of Truth":

> The human mind trying to use the truth just will not work. The truth makes you free.
>
> There are many evidences of a need to be made free right here in Eden Valley. We do not have to go to darkest Africa, we do not have to go to the slum districts of New York or Chicago. We find right here a need to be made free. Days go by and opportunities are passed up. Over and over again I have set the stage and opened the way before each one of you, and so often the invitation is ignored. Why put it off? While it is put off, there are tens of thousands of hungry ones out in the world seeking they know not what, looking for the truth they know not where.

Roy and Alice Kuykendall, prominent citizens of Loveland and proprietors of the shoe store, were frequent visitors to Sunrise Ranch. From her initial contact with Uranda, Alice found the answer to her quest for truth.

On May 25 in a service, "Oh, Give Thanks Unto the Lord for He Is Good," Uranda spoke of an experience of healing shared with Alice who, having suffered from polio from childhood, later had a leg amputated. She spent some months in Uranda's home, moving through an intense pattern of physical and emotional transformation. He used this as an example of how the spirit of God can reach many people through the experience of an individual who lets the consciousness transcend suffering and involvement with healing for oneself.

At 100 Mile House Martin gave a service on May 31 entitled "Integration of Heart and Mind," shortly after his return from a brief trip:

> I have been away from you for a few days. It has been six or eight years since I was down in that part of the country, except on one or two occasions

during the winter, and I had forgotten how beautiful it is between Kamloops and Merritt, a different sort of country from here. There is much more open land, and at this time of year the hills, that come down to touch the lakes that border the road, are a vivid green, colored by blue and yellow flowers. It would seem that anyone observing such beauty could not help function so as to keep from defiling it in any way.

In a Board Meeting held there on June 2 it was noted that on Martin's birthday the members of the Unit gave him a Marconi Mantel Model Radio. Ernie Taylor, from Vancouver, erected a prefabricated log cabin next to Mary Mackenzie's, for himself and family. Fifteen hundred dollars was credited to the Lodge on behalf of last year's activities. Twenty-three willows were planted between the lower garden and creek. The Amateur Radio station VE7-AIL was officially in operation by authority of the Department of Transport as of April 1. Successful contacts had been made by Ross Marks with amateurs throughout western Canada and the United States. Our men were helping construct the power plant building, install the machinery, work on the police building; and various members had been helping out in the store.

In a "President's Report, Society of Emissaries of Divine Light," Ross Marks shared some activities since the incorporation of the Society, among them the outstanding response to *Northern Light* and excellent attendance at Sunday School, including some children from the Village.

The First Annual General Meeting of the Society was held June 9. Bishop Martin Cecil presided at the request of the President, Ross Marks. The Board had not felt it necessary to appoint an Auditor, and a new system of keeping the Society books was inaugurated by the Bishop.

On Sunrise Ranch Uranda asked, in a service on June 12:

Who has heard? Who is doing? For nearly two thousand years human beings have been trying to translate the sayings of Jesus into the practical expression of life. In each generation there have been millions of earnest, sincere men and women of all denominations, colors and creeds seeking to let the sayings of our Lord have meaning. Untold numbers of lives have been devoted one-pointedly to that task; billions of dollars have been spent. Countless numbers of words have been spoken and pages written. And today we do not find the evidence that these sayings have been received into the hearts and lives of men and women in a manner that would allow them to be an effective part of their living. The whole structure of the world situation, buffeted by escalating storms of conflict, gives every sign of crumbling.

He added that in view of world happenings he was proud to be an American. "That includes the imaginary line just north of us, which means nothing to me. It is all one. We want to do everything we can to protect it."

It was reported on June 13 that the first cutting of alfalfa and sweet clover on Sunrise Ranch yielded approximately 40 tons of hay. The Chevrolet pickup had been overhauled at cost of $96, and a new Farmall Super C Tractor, including C-21 Mower, purchased for $1,873.33.

Martin was back on Sunrise Ranch in June, for the conclusion of the first Class, and said he found, after four months' absence, that much had been accomplished and he did not sense that there had been any break in the pattern. Uranda then expressed his joy at Martin's presence and acknowledged the splendid work being done by the members of the Canadian Headquarters.

The interesting theme in a service by Uranda on June 15, "Only Begotten Son of God," found focus in a few words:

> We recognize that the Spirit of God is One Spirit, but this One Spirit is made
> up of many phases of Spirit, seven focalizations, or seven primary aspects.

Virgil Given's time in prison was very short. He opened the 12th Annual G.P.C. Conference on Sunrise Ranch on June 21. Among other things, he said:

> We are indeed grateful for all that has been brought forth in these past
> years, in which these two groups of people with one desire have been brought
> together. In this movement that we are now so concerned about we realize
> that we are getting to the heart of things and I am sure that is the desire of
> each of us—not what we would do, but what the power of universal law could
> do through us.

Uranda expressed a hearty welcome to all, and continued:

> We must recognize that the biblical record of the creation of this world is
> a very brief statement covering an exceedingly great achievement. The ac-
> count is covered on two or three pages, hardly a column in one of today's
> newspapers. That great event is stated in principle. The details of the out-
> working are not particularly important to us here and now, but those prin-
> ciples by which creation was made manifest are the same by which re-cre-
> ation may be made known on earth, and are vitally important.

George Shears said:

> As I look back now I see it was inevitable that the G.P.C. movement and
> this little group of people in Eden Valley should come together, because the
> purpose is the same. The urge that gave birth to the G.P.C. movement was

born in the chiropractic profession, and I made a sincere attempt to try to convince the rest of our profession that their only salvation lay in trying our best to
carry out God's will through that blessed principle [God, Patient, Christ].

The G.P.C. movement was born because I had been so grossly out of line
with God's laws it wrecked my life physically and I had to find a solution. By
merely letting God show us the way, the G.P.C. principle was born. For years
before that I had been thoroughly convinced that man had been too long
packing Christian principles, that it was high time he began to practise them—
not only to save my own self but to try to save our profession.

Last January, Virgil, Don Buchan and I, of our Board of Trustees, were
fortunate to be here at the dedication of the G.P.C. School. Now we are at the
close of the first session, the first cycle of that school. We sent our son and our
daughter out here, as students in this school, because they were seeking the
same things to which the school was dedicated, and we wanted them to have
the honor of being members of that historic class.

The next speaker was James Wellemeyer, who was voted by the Class as its representative. James described the different classes and their instructors.

Following addresses by the faculty, President Virgil Given introduced the first speaker
of the class, Gladys Miller, Secretary of the Chiropractic Association. She said:

We have a beautiful practice established in Berwick, Pennsylvania. We began as Chiropractors and have changed to the Attunement practice for over a
year and a half. Our Service is made up of the same kind of people to be found
anywhere. We have the burgess, the wealthy, the poor, each one individual, a
wonderful group. Seldom a day goes by without new people coming to us. Many
people do not care what we are doing; the method does not interest them; they
are interested in receiving help. There are those who begin to question, and we
give them literature, etc. Of the few who stopped coming because of the change,
most have returned, except for a few of our immediate families.

On June 23 Uranda, expressing his appreciation that so many had remained after the
Conference, said:

Twenty years ago I began building to this end. I began using attunements
in 1929, and in 1932 when I became aware of a commission to establish a
focalization whereby God may act on earth, there was always the question of
where would be found those who would participate. Step-by-step we have
moved forward and you have been drawn from the north, the south, the east,
the west, to this time and place, to share this fulfilment.

To the degree that various ones in different places, including many who are not here today, learned to obey the impulse of the spirit without regard to results according to human concepts, we began to develop a control pattern. Many have come and many have gone, and by the grace of God we are here. Within our number are those who have worked through our first Class term. They have had their problems, and sometimes felt like they couldn't make it. Gradually this group learned about getting along with each other. Under the circumstances, a heavy class program and our work pattern, they learned about accepting responsibility. As each responded to the direction of the spirit, under the guidance of those who shared my responsibility in the faculty, we completed a six-months' term.

I had been searching for a man who would have the caliber, the basic honesty necessary to carry out the vibrational pattern, which finally connected up in George Shears. That did not just happen. He tried to shake it off, and searched carefully to see if there was an honest way out, and he could not find it. So he came on through.

George Shears spoke in response to this tribute:

I would be less than human if I did not experience pleasure and pride from the words Uranda so kindly said about me. But I assure you, friends, if there is any credit to be given it is not to me. I have often marvelled at what has taken place. If we let the spirit guide us, things way beyond our personal ability to accomplish can be done. We have passed through many trials and tribulations in the past few years, times of worry and discouragement, just as all of you will. The only advice I can give you is simply to trust God no matter what the difficulty may be—"Thank you, Father." Later, in season, you will understand the problem.

In a service on June 29, "Let Not Your Heart Be Troubled," Uranda shared an excerpt from a letter received from Marie Johnson. Marie was concerned because her husband Roy, who had been a superintendent at A.O. Smith Company, one of the biggest manufacturing plants in the United States for many years, was one of thousands who would soon be out of work, with the closing down of the company. This of course was just one of many companies in that situation, with the post-Korean war conditions. Ford Motor Company was laying off 90,000 men. She said:

At this writing the future looks very dark. Is this the beginning of the great struggle that you spoke of, such as man has never seen? I wonder, as I watch events unfold. But I feel no fear.

Uranda commented:

> This is a tremendously big subject. We need to be so centered, stabilized, that we are unmoved by what takes place round about, and understand that we are living in a time when men's hearts are failing them for fear and looking after those things which are coming to pass, in which there is every form of unreasonableness, of prejudice. Human beings who know not God and have been depending upon idols find under stress that their foundations are swept away. Then there is a need, as never before, for the light that shines through those who serve God.

On July 2 at 100 Mile House Martin spoke "Concerning Control Patterns":

> Human beings get everything backwards. They want to get the world in some sort of satisfactory pattern, and then they will have time to do something for people, getting them changed around. Of course it doesn't work that way. It is necessary to conform with the principles of being if the results are to appear, and there must be a pattern in miniature. In relation to our ministry, there had to be a starting point. We recognize that in relation to Uranda. That always involves one individual, which is something that human beings ignore, even though it was revealed by the Master himself. He was one individual. There is the idea that all we have to do is look to God somewhere and we will all come together in some miraculous fashion and produce something marvelous. But we have to begin at the starting point—one individual in whom a control pattern is established, which may be extended on out into the world as we share it—still in miniature in relation to the whole.
>
> Concerning our own group here, there could be no Unit until the pattern had been worked out in me, to provide a control pattern for you. As you let yourselves share in that, then the reality of the true vine may appear, and all together we let the control extend out into the world.

In July Stanley and Vivian Grindstaff, with their young sons Stanley Jr. and Larry, were welcomed to the 100 Mile House family to stay for an indeterminate period.

Martin spoke of "The Reality of Faith" on July 31, quoting the Master's words:

> "Verily I say unto you, If ye have faith as a grain of mustard seed, ye shall say unto this mountain, Remove hence to yonder place; and it shall remove; and nothing shall be impossible unto you."
>
> Since the conclusion of the Second World War, millions of human beings have had the opportunity of accepting their responsibility to God, particularly available to those who live on this North American continent. How many

have utilized these last seven years for that purpose? During this period there has been a great deal of expansion, called prosperity. And while always in the background there has been a devastating threat of another war, more terrible and destructive than anything yet known on earth, that fact has, generally speaking, been ignored as far as possible, so that selfish individuals might exploit the situation. Attention has been primarily placed upon getting—more money, shorter working hours, acquiring greater profits, maintaining and improving the standard of living. Of course such activity has been at least partially a subconscious endeavor to blot out the the awful underlying threat of worldwide devastation which might be let loose at any time.

Fred and Elsie Sierck, participants in the first Class, remained for a period to help with the work, returning later as permanent members of the Unit. They provided valuable assistance in many areas, including caring for Uranda and Kathy's children.

Don Clouston in Newfoundland requested the establishment of a service center there. It was agreed that Dick and Billie Cable could fill a position in that part of the world. So, with the "authority and blessing of the Board of Directors," they moved to a very different—and colder!—environment where they served effectively for several years in St. Johns.

As our sphere of influence in the world expanded there was a fast growing need for servers in the field, with calls coming in asking for help. There was a need in the Fort Collins area, also a request from a chiropractor in San Angelo, Texas, Dr. R. A. Cunningham, for someone to fill an opening there. William and Muriel Oshane were suggested, in which the Board concurred. Another opportunity appeared through a chiropractor in Georgia, Eddie Hoffman and his wife Helen, with their twenty-two acres near Columbus, ideal for a large center if they had proper assistance. The substance was being provided in abundance, the harvest field white, but the laborers few.

It was agreed to send a truck and several pickers to Palisade on Colorado's Western Slope, Uranda's boyhood country, to help to harvest the peach crop and obtain our winter's supply. This was a source of the best peaches in the world, and that great provision continued unbroken for many years.

A hearty welcome was extended to Albert and Edna Ackerley with their sons Alan and David, Oliver and Millie Latam, and Audrey Greenhough, as they joined the Sunrise family. Among visitors to the Ranch were Vida and Grace McMillan, Chip and Myrtle Smith with daughter Beverley and son Stanley, Marjorie Blythe and Doris Alexander. All of these were from Ontario, Canada.

It was at that time that Frank and Betty Protzman went to 100 Mile House to function as part of the Unit for a season. They managed the store in town and worked wherever there was a need, contributing greatly in the six months before moving to Sunrise Ranch.

There was an atmosphere of joyous anticipation at the Hundred in welcoming Michael's return from school in England to spend the holidays with his father.

In a service on August 25, "The Coming of the Ship," Martin said:

> I am going to read a portion of *The Prophet,* by Kahlil Gibran. The expression in this book is very beautiful. Human beings are inclined to think there must be something of true value in such expressions simply because they carry seeming beauty, but that is not always the case. In fact, in the literature of the world it very seldom is the case.

Martin was pointing to the fact that in that chapter, dealing with leaving the old and joining the true companions on the ship, the action is graphically imbued with wrenching agony. Identifying with that, the reader prolongs the suffering rather than letting it go and rejoicing in the wonder of the appearance of the ship and thanksgiving for the vision to behold it and join one's fellows on deck. Acknowledging the beauty in other sections of the book, Martin often used them in different ways to advantage.

He continued:

> Unless that which is being conveyed through beautiful words is true to the truth, it is not of much value. Human beings have produced so much ugliness in the world, so many ill conditions, that they seek to translate it in some way into something of beauty. And for the most part that is what poetry is in the world, an attempt to beautify ugliness. It is not God's design that there should be any ugliness in the world, any ill conditions. Therefore, just to attempt to beautify ugliness has no real value from the divine standpoint.

In a service on August 31, "Letting the Pattern of Movement Work Through Us," Uranda opened up some interesting fields of consideration:

> What of birth? It is something that carries the spirit of heaven, something divine, yes, but it is earthy, physical, and it is because of that physical something that the expression of the divine can appear on earth. The earthiness of the earth is not in any sense opposed to the spirituality of heaven, and when the waters are gathered into one place and the dry land begins to appear it is a fulfilment in creation. The form, the substance of the form, and that which springs forth through the form is the purpose of the earth.
>
> "And God saw that it was good," something divine, beautiful, acceptable to highest heaven, the earth bringing forth. So it is with us. In the crowning focalization of that creative process man was formed, in the image and likeness of God, for God said, "Let us make man in our image, after our likeness."

And He made man, male and female, out of the substance of the earth, to be
the form in manifestation of God Himself, for His purposes on earth. "And
God saw that it was good."

Human beings need to so realize this basic, fundamental truth, that they
stop trying to get away from the earth, stop separating heaven and earth as
if they were somehow disrelated, without meaning to each other; for heaven
and earth are really one. You cannot separate your body and mind, your
body and your feeling nature or heart; you cannot find the dividing line. It
is written: "Know ye not that ye are the temple of the living God, and the
spirit of God dwelleth in you?" Let us not try to get away from the earthiness of the earth in an effort to be spiritual, but let the earthiness of the
earth be the means by which the sweet essences of heaven are made manifest.

Speaking on "The Design and Control of the Kingdom" in a service on September 9,
Uranda said:

We have been giving consideration to the fundamentals involved in spiritual psychiatry as they relate particularly to mind and heart.

In the 23rd Psalm we have the true focalization of all sacred writings,
wherever they may be found, an epitome of the whole. It is what was taught
by our Lord and Master, Jesus Christ.

Friendly relations with neighbors of Sunrise Ranch was emphasized by a generous
gift of approximately 110 bushels of peaches by Fred Harbert and about 25 bushels of
pears by W. C. Strain. Over a ton of frozen peaches, plus some jam, was in storage.

James Wellemeyer arrived, from Huntingburg, Indiana, on September 12 to be a member of the Sunrise Headquarters staff. Jim endeared himself over many years to residents
and visitors in Eden Valley, and provides his unique service today in many places.

In response to Bob Palmer's recurring proposal that the Emissaries buy the property
by the dam, reducing the price of $12,000 by $1,000 as a donation to the Church, Bishop
Meeker was empowered by the Board to transact the purchase of this property of spectacular beauty. It was one of many blessings accruing from the friendship between Uranda
and Bob, a prominent businessman in the area.

In a service on September 17, "Learning to Lead," Uranda used the analogy of driving up the Big Thompson Canyon to Estes Park, not refusing to make necessary changes
at curves, emphasizing need for flexibility in living:

The strength of character essential to changing one's course, avoiding disaster, being wise, allows others to be inspired so that they too may know that
they do not need to stay in a crystallized pattern and bring destruction upon

themselves, but can yield to that control which will take them safely around the bend and out of the mountains of difficulty. Such function, nullifying the ill vibrational factors at work in others and inspiring a change in course, causes the old patterns to lose their power. That which would have happened will not happen when you change your course. The future is changed, the potentiality of disaster is nullified, and you can move forward, perhaps at first in a manner which requires many alterations but finally you begin to know how to balance, to calculate correctly all the factors, to be alert and see, so that you become a safe driver.

14

Our Purpose—
and The Server's Code

October 1952 ~ March 1953

*I*n a service on October 5, "I Must Be About My Father's Business," Uranda read from "Our Purpose at Sunrise Ranch" written by him on July 3, 1947. He emphasized the fact that it contained the basic pattern in our program regardless of time:

It has been all along. Some of you who have been here five years or so may feel that somehow you let some opportunities slip by or you would have made greater progress. I am keenly aware that you were participating in a pioneering program under difficult circumstances. As we prove the reality of that which is outlined here and open the doors and reach out into the world, individual abilities and material substance essential to the accomplishment of this purpose will be drawn.

"Our Purpose at Sunrise Ranch" was described in the first paragraph in four ways: First, "in all branches of our educational and training Program, to serve the Lord, which includes serving our brother man by serving the Lord." Second, "to promote the brotherhood of man for the whole human family in recognition of, and under, the Fatherhood of God." Third, "Our purpose is to so function in service to God and man that the Edenic state may be restored, thereby re-establishng the manifest expression of the things of God on earth, so that heaven and earth may be one." Fourth, "It might be said that our purpose is to fulfil the divine commission given by Jesus Christ to the end that His kingdom may manifest on earth forever, in blessing to all the children of men."

Uranda then referred to those who aspire to share in the program on Sunrise Ranch and the requirement of specific training:

The responding one must realize:

1) ...that while we are in the world we are not of it, and be ready to find that things work out differently for those who are coming under subjection to the laws of perfection than in the general world pattern, and not allow preconceived concepts to form a barrier to that outworking.

2) ...the basic significance of the Master's injunction, "Judge not," so that harmonizing with this principle he may function effectively in relation to the Unit program prior to the time when he may understand the reasons behind all those things with which he comes in contact...

3) ...that his overall choice to let the Father's will be done actually constitutes a choice to work harmoniously with those who are in a position of responsibility in directing the program...

4) ...that acceptance of the foregoing principle does not produce a regimentation in which individuality is lost but, rather, the means where the divine individuality may in season come into manifestion...

5) ...that he does not come into this program at Sunrise Ranch to impose his human personality on someone else, but is under training to learn how to get along well with his fellows who are moving with him on the same path...

6) ...that he who would learn to lead must first learn to obey. Jesus obeyed the divine commission of His Father, and He was the greatest leader the world has known in all recorded history. He who is not faithful in fulfilling his responsibilities in the little things can never be trusted with the greater things.

7) ...that genuine creative genius cannot be smothered by outer world circumstances. Regardless of circumstances, of limitations, genuine creative genius will always find a means of expression, and manifest regardless of so-called opportunities. He who drinks at the fount of inspiration by which genius is vitalized into reality cannot be bound by circumstances nor prevented from the expression of his genius.

8) ...that he needs to prove the power of love in his own individual expression of life, if he would be received as a true member of the one body. The

problems of harmonious fellowship are insurmountable without divine love. All concepts of, or about, love must be separated from lust, selfishness and human desire. He who cannot feel love toward another proves that he is still trying to function on the basis of human love and has not yet found true attunement in the current of divine love.

9) ...that no matter what one may have achieved in movement toward the goal of perfection, when direction, correction and instruction are given at any point along the way, there must be no human reactionary attitude by reason of which the individual assumes that the reality already made manifest is being ignored or rejected or denied, when the way is being opened for movement forward to a still higher level of consciousness.

10) ...having received consideration in his movement along the way, one is considerate of others, not arbitrarily expecting another to have full vision and understanding on any given point.

11) ...give careful consideration to the principle of coordination. All the former points relate to coordination. Those who coordinate effectively in the level of physical function are inclined to judge those who may be slow in attaining coordination at that level, even though such may have experienced coordination to a remarkable degree in the vibratory levels of realization intellectually or in the emotional realm. I have considered the service rendered by each individual at all levels. Effective function in service to the world requires that one reach a point of true coordination on all levels of function...

12) ...that the unreal has no weight, meaning or value when weighed in the balance against reality. You cannot add unlike things; therefore it should be easy to realize that you cannot add the real and the unreal. You can add the real to the real, but it is utterly impossible to add the real and the unreal. Let us make our calculations on the basis of the real. The reality in you was, and is, the starting point for you, and reality can be added to that. As that happens, the unreal is automatically pushed back and removed, because there is no place found for it... As you let the Lord add reality to the reality that is in you, you may be brought to the sum total of life in season.

13) ...that one must respond on the level on which he would receive assistance. Radiation is automatically released on the level on which response is made manifest. Response on the level in which the problem exists is essential to allow radiation to be effective in relation to the problem.

14) ...that the Unit includes all people on earth, of every race and creed,

who are responding to spiritual realities. You do not live to yourself alone. Nothing gives me greater joy and pleasure and satisfaction than to be able to do that which will be pleasing to others. This desire includes, as its primary point of focus, my desire to do that which is pleasing to the LORD of Lords and KING of Kings. It is His good pleasure to bestow upon us those things which are of the kingdom, and we know the laws and principles by reason of which the kingdom may manifest.

So we come to a focalized realization, intellectually and in the feeling realm, wherein we have a mutuality of agreement in recognition of the fact that humanly devised personal preferences must never be considered as factors in the equation of fulfilment. Functioning correctly, utilizing only the right factors, we find that it is the Father's good pleasure to give us those satisfactions which may be experienced through living in harmony with the laws of His kingdom, the only true satisfaction and pleasure there is. Thus is God glorified on earth and we are privileged to render true service to our brother man.

In a Board meeting at 100 Mile House on October 15, Martin spoke of the recently acquired property near Sunrise Ranch, renamed by us "Gateway Service Center," and suggested sending $1,000, in anticipation of more to follow. This was met with hearty agreement by all.

It was decided that all orders from mail order houses, C.O.Ds, etc., were to be centralized and go through a committee consisting of Ross, Edith and Emily. The matter of charging at the store in the town was also dealt with.

Outside the Chapel on Sunrise Ranch after a service on November 6, "God's Work Is Precision Work," we viewed the glory of the night sky. Uranda commented:

The fact that we are alive means that the things that God has made—there are the Pleiades, Orion, yonder—are doing their part or we could not be here. They have meaning to us. The human mind may not be able to comprehend it, but we have meaning to them, to all these parts; for every part of the whole has meaning to each other part. The mystery of God is simply that God knows the meaning of all the parts, and of the relatedness of each part to every other part.

At 100 Mile House in a service on November 6, "Toward Control," Martin spoke of having met Roger de Winton in July in Calgary through Conrad ffrench and a friend of Roger's, Frances Jennings, the occasion being the illness of Roger's wife Betty. Frances, the wife of a heart specialist in Calgary, also became a valued friend of Martin's for many years. Roger continued to move closely in the ministry, sharing attunements with his wife, whose time on earth came to a close soon afterward, leaving their two small daughters, Diana and Dallas.

In a Board meeting at Sunrise Ranch on November 14 Uranda expressed thanksgiving for the "marvelous response" to "A Statement of Circumstance," October 17, dealing with the Gateway property, and the many gifts received, amounting to approximately $4,200. Of that sum $500 was paid to Fred Woelfle on the Skelgas account, $500 toward the contract price of the Farmall Tractor and Corn Cultivator, and $325 for lumber and Bondex paint. Various improvements on the Ranch were reported, including a new Attunement room at the north end of the Chapel building.

The arrival of Oliver and Millie Latam from Richmond, Ontario, was of incalculable value on Sunrise Ranch, with Oliver's expertise in the field of accounting and Millie's in the office, to say nothing of their spiritual substance. Also joining our program on a permanent basis was Lorraine Cowan, formerly of Toronto. She worked in Uranda's home and was a valuable addition to the Class faculty, her contribution in the field of nutrition an essential element in the Class program.

On November 3 at 12:10 a.m. a third child was born to Uranda and Kathy. Helen Elaine made her appearance in the same house as did Lloyd four years before. There were a goodly number of us present to welcome her as Dr. Romans, a dear friend and able practitioner from Loveland, assisted in the natural birth.

In a service on November 16, "Trust God," Uranda likened his piloting of the airplane to his position of control in the ministry:

> The ship of the kingdom is more intricate in its control pattern than my little airplane. The adjustments are often so delicate that even an alert observer cannot readily see them. Those who would move with me must trust my work at the controls, just as surely as a passenger in my little ship must trust me. There are certain parts of the program in which you have the proper responsibility of exercising control, but that control must be coordinated with the whole pattern if it is to have meaning.

On November 22 in a service, "The Machinery of Reality," he said:

> I was rather startled not long ago to hear that someone here on Sunrise Ranch had expressed the attitude that it was expecting too much of a person here to remain centered in reality all the time without any break, without any letdown, without any violation of the agreement. That would be like saying that it is too much to expect anyone to serve God all the time, that each one should have a certain amount of time every day, or at least every week, to serve the devil; that it is too much to expect to have God's kingdom on earth,

that for happiness, or satisfaction, or relief, or something, one needs the king-dom of darkness part of the time, a bit of misery to contrast with such joys as God might give, a little sorrow and suffering to give real meaning and signifi-cance to happiness and health.

With respect to the vital importance of what I have so often called the ma-chinery of reality, if we are using a tractor in the field and it breaks down it stops running. Nothing is done until the tractor is repaired. There are those who think they can cause a breakdown in the equipment without delaying our progress; that vibrational breaks, distortions and disturbances should not be looked upon too seriously; that we should be able to go along and do our job anyway. There are many things not the way they should be, but emphasizing the problem is of no value. The tendency is to identify oneself with that, rather than with his or her own stable, centered response when taking it to the Lord.

After serving in Uranda's home at headquarters for the last five years of her life, Edna Henderson passed away on Sunrise Ranch on November 24, of a severe asthmatic condition of long standing. Her contribution had come at a time of great need, and was deeply appreciated.

Uranda held a baptismal service on November 30 for Mareda Christiansen, Mary Ann and Phyllis Miller, Sharon Call, Billy Van Duzen, Teddy and Tommy Mettlen. He spoke first to those assembled:

As you who are adults allow the baptism of the fire of God's love and the water of His truth to be constant in you, the baptism in the symbolical sense shall have meaning to these little ones, that they may grow into the maturity of that which God has ordained for them. And let no one offend one of the little ones with a baptism that is not of God. Let your expression in living be a baptism to all the children of God.

The ceremony of baptism followed, with each child kneeling before the altar in turn.

A service on December 6, "The Reality of Letting Go," dealt with the seven planes of being, in which Uranda said:

The prophets of ages past have looked with longing to this day which we share, the greatest opportunity and privilege for which any man or woman could ask, of letting the heavens of the Christ Body take form on earth. The form cannot go up into some far-off heaven, but the spirit can come down into the earth through men and women, the vibratory factors of heart, mind and body which constitute heaven.

We look out into the world and see the realm of form shifting back and

forth, rising and falling like molten metal in a furnace. It does not get anywhere. The chaotic vibratory pattern produces a chaotic outer realm of form.
We, or someones, somewhere, must provide the heavens on earth, the control
factors, where they are needed.

In a Board meeting on December 12 it was reported that the special contributions
continuing in response to "A Statement of Circumstance," dealing with the Gateway property, had reached the sum of $9,864. Part of this was used to pay some outstanding bills.
A gift from Vida and Grace McMillan of Toronto took the form of a Multigraph Dupli-
cator, Multilith Model 1250, and an IBM typewriter with 10-point printing type. This
equipment, with our presses, would enable us to handle our printing needs. (I must
insert a word about that IBM typewriter with its printing type. This was our pre-com-
puter means for releasing material with justified margins for our booklets and other
publications for a number of years—a friend indeed. I still have mine, perhaps a museum piece!)

It was reported that we now had a plot of ground designated as our Sunrise Cemetery.
Located on the southeast corner of the property at the foot of picturesque rimrock, this is
a beautiful spot, with the full sweep of the valley spread out below. One afternoon I walked
with Bertha Meyers to the cemetery and we stood together, sensing somehow that she was
nearing the end of her sojourn on this planet. She turned to me and said, "I wouldn't mind
being in this place; what a wonderful view!" At the last count there were seventy-three
markers in that little plot, each one bearing the name of a cherished friend or family member, precious pioneers who had chosen to serve the Lord together. A few of these had not
resided permanently on the Ranch but requested to have their remains in what to many is
hallowed ground—perhaps, with Bertha, to share the view.

Plans were under way for the 1953 irrigation water supply from the canal, and for
installing a sprinkling system. Water was beginning to reach every corner of Eden Valley.

In a service on Sunrise Ranch on December 21, "Opening the Seventh Seal—Rebirth," Uranda spoke poignantly of the greatest present, the greatest joy, that could come
to him that Christmas Season:

> It is that the angels of our King on earth should so yield to the working of His
> spirit, in a rebirth, that in this new year at hand each one should abide in polarity,
> no more yielding to the destructive impulses of self-centeredness, a living expres-
> sion of what our Master initiated through His birth and life on earth.
>
> It might seem to some human minds that this would be asking too much,
> but I do not believe it is. Not in human strength or self-determination, but by
> the working of that spirit which our Master brought into the world and made

available to us, we may share it.

In a service on December 28 at 100 Mile House, "In Spirit and in Truth," Martin asked:

> Why do you accept my leadership? Our Master spoke of His sheep hearing His voice and that they do not recognize the voice of a stranger. You hear His voice through my voice, and you recognize the authority, not because I try to impose anything on you but, because I worship God in spirit and in truth, you find me at a certain point in the divine pattern that makes leadership available to you. As we function together in that pattern, then I can say to you, "He that receiveth you receiveth me, and he that receiveth me receiveth Him who sent me."

Martin dealt with a crucial matter in a service on January 8, 1953 entitled "The Fear of Being Hurt," in which he said:

> There have been those who take the attitude that the spirit which finds focus in Uranda is a dominating thing which causes those in the Unit to be subservient to him. In several instances I know I was included in this, so that I was supposed to have lost all individuality and independence, just a rubber stamp, so to speak, for Uranda. Just how that works when, for most of the time, we are seventeen hundred miles apart, or more, would be difficult to comprehend, as would just how I would be able to meet and carry the responsibilities of leadership in relation to this Unit on such a basis.

> If I do what Uranda wants me to do, it is simply and solely because we are in agreement in the matter. Why? Because the same spirit that finds focus in him finds focus in me, and the same spirit that finds focus in us finds focus in you.

In a Board meeting on January 9 on Sunrise Ranch it was reported that Richard and Dorothy Thompson, with their daughter Mary, had established a center in Vancouver and were finding it to be a natural place for their effective service, with many people being drawn and showing interest in the program. Dick and Billie Cable were also making fine progress in their center in St. Johns, Newfoundland.

On February 9, after their six-month period of service at 100 Mile House, Frank and Betty Protzman arrived on Sunrise Ranch, their beloved home for the remainder of their long and very productive lives.

The special fund had exceeded $10,000. The $1,000 payment due on the Gateway property was paid at the end of 1952 and many other necessities taken care of.

A milestone in the effective movement of the ministry occurred with the purchase of a Revere Tape Recorder, and the first recording of a service of Uranda's on January 19 initiated a procedure that greatly enhanced the release of the ever-increasing number of services and classes. It was a major factor affecting my function, as one facet of this was that others could help in transcribing the wealth of material, without the medium of shorthand. There was enough to keep many more than were available busy every day, never really "catching up."

Uranda reported that his appointment to the faculty of the G.P.C. Servers Training School for the second term was confirmed, and that it would open on Sunrise Ranch on March 2, 1953. He announced that Albert Ackerley, for whom he expressed profound appreciation, would provide the primary focalization for the Training School in the forthcoming Class. Also, with the probability of Uranda's increased travel in the future, he saw Albert providing the primary point of focalization for the activities on Sunrise Ranch, a Trustee and Vice-President of the Board.

He continued:

> The pattern of attunements as it is being utilized in so many places, all over the United States and Canada, opened up in this present cycle through Albert after he had been studying *The Triune Ray*. I had used attunements in the early part of my ministry, the first one being in 1929, and for several years it was a primary aspect of our ministry. But the need for teaching, writing, lecturing, holding services, became so acute that I had no time to carry on that particular pattern for a number of years.
>
> Since Albert opened this pattern the influence of healing—physically, mentally, emotionally—through attunements has touched thousands of lives.

Albert's response to those words carried the passion of his vibrant spirit:

> This process of returning home, as a prodigal son, has taken nine years floating upon the sea of truth, not knowing where we were going or what was going to happen, only that something was taking place. And finally the flotsam and jetsam upon the sea lands upon this little island in the world. And what a wonderful feeling it is. Having been led by Uranda to see the greatness of what was being done here, the unselfishness of it, and the wonderful privilege of having a part in it, it was so easy and so wonderful to come. I am tempted to ask if you here realize the extent of what you are doing....

He mentioned George Shears, whose wife Naomi and her son and daughter, James and Betty Wellemeyer (raised by George as his own), had joined wholeheartedly with him in his work with Uranda from their initial contact. In season Jim married Anne Broddy, of Toronto, who had a young daughter Carol Anne. Later a daughter, Lana, was born to Jim and Anne. That little family was a familiar and beloved part of Sunrise Ranch for many years. Betty Wellemeyer had married Lorne French and they established a center in Calgary. With their family of seven children, they served a long time in that area. Their eldest daughter, Julie, with husband Peter Dalby and their two children, lived and worked in the Unit at 100 Mile House for many productive years. Betty presently lives in the village there.

The personnel on Sunrise Ranch was becoming a well-rounded entity composed of dedicated people who had been greatly valued and appreciated in their environs before moving to Eden Valley. Frank and Betty Protzman offered their finely trained and spiritually perceptive substance. One of Frank's many jobs was coordinating garden activities, later grinding our own flour in our mill, tucked in its own little house. In addition, he had the exclusive care of a flock of chickens. No hens ever enjoyed more loving attention and vocal exchange than Frank's "ladies," clucking excitedly at his approach. When one of them would be served at the table, providing a fine meal for the family, Frank made it known that he did not wish to know its name (which each one had, and recognized); otherwise all was well.

One of his most endearing characteristics was a keen and whimsical sense of humor. Also, his natural talent and extensive experience of "detecting" resurfaced on occasion. An example of this took place in Draper's Drug Store in downtown Loveland. After observing the scene one day, Frank approached Paul Draper, owner and friend, and directed his attention toward a woman looking over the merchandise.

"You would do well to watch her," Frank said, "I've observed her before and she's been helping herself."

Incredulous, and in fact incensed, Paul replied, "You must be mistaken. I know her well. She's a friend, and highly thought of in the community."

"Just watch," countered Frank, "maybe she'll do it again." And she did, expertly shifting a pair of gloves until it fell from the counter and landed on her shoe, whereupon she slowly walked toward the door, casually bent over, picked up her loot, and was quickly out the door. Open-mouthed, Paul nevertheless found his voice to thank him.

There were other instances, one of them on the Ranch some years later. A huge haystack was on fire, a hazardous situation, and it was fairly obvious the fire was of human origin. After some heroic effort it was put out, and some days later Jim Wellemeyer, coordinator of activities at the time, asked Frank if he could find out who might have been responsible. In calm tones the answer came, "I already know," and he revealed the name of the culprit, a child.

"Why didn't you tell me?"

"You didn't ask me," was the only satisfaction Jim ever got.

The name Eden Valley has continued and been adopted by others inhabiting the area. Often the strains of an old hymn could be heard filling the air: *Beautiful Valley of Eden.* My heart thrilled each time we gave lusty voice to the simple words in those initial sacred days of reestablishing in the earth a place where the spirit of Eden could be a reality.

Uranda commented in a service on February 8, "I Create," that forty-three years ago on that day the Boy Scout movement was initiated, and expressed his joy that there were three representatives of the Boy Scouts of America in the Chapel.

> We recognize that this movement has done much to promote the welfare of boys, that there may be a pattern of manhood, the strength of character necessary to face the issues of life. So we are particularly pleased to have these three Cub Scouts [Billy Van Duzen, Teddy Mettlen and another friend] with us this morning.

The Riggs house and lot adjacent to the Gateway property was purchased for $3,500. A payment of $1,300 was made, the Church assuming the $2,200 mortgage held by the bank.

The G.P.C. Servers Training School was accredited by the Department of Justice as an institution of learning. This simplified the process of obtaining visas for foreign students.

Uranda introduced the "Server's Code" in a service on February 14 with these words:

> This may be classified as the goal for all those who let their lives be dedicated to the selfless service of a G.P.C. Server. Also it is a code which may properly be accepted by all who would serve God in whatever capacity or sphere.

The Server's Code

> I pledge myself to remember:
> ~Whereas I was made in the image and likeness of God, so also every man, woman and child whose life I may touch was made in the image and likeness of God.
> ~Whereas the dignity of life, love and aspiration is precious to me, so also is it with those whom I serve.
> ~Whereas the all-wise Deity has been patient and merciful unto me in my processes of growing and maturing into the stature and nobility of a child of God, so also let me be patient and merciful in the expression of my life purpose to others.
> ~Whereas the centering of Almighty God is in love, so let it be with me.
> ~Whereas the nature of God is characterized by truth and life, so let it be with me.
> ~Whereas the divine qualities and characteristics which God has revealed from within Himself to me have inspired me to the highest and the best that I know, so must it be the expression of the highest and the best that I know, from within me, which shall inspire others to the attainment of a worthy goal.

~Whereas God has not imposed Himself upon me, but has freely given His bountiful blessings to me according to my response, so would I refrain from imposing myself or my concepts of service upon others, but rather give freely and selflessly of myself and my service to others according to their response to the noble ideals of God's love and truth and life.

~Whereas the evil spirits of shame, fear, hate and greed have caused divisions among men, turning men and nations in upon themselves and distorting their lives, let me never forget that only purity can remove shame, only love can cast out fear, only an understanding of truth can clear away hatred, and only the spirit of God's givingness can banish greed, that all man-made divisions may cease and that all may see that true self-interest requires the fulfilment of the whole, that the manifestation of the wholeness of God's design for all mankind may establish the condition wherein I myself may be truly whole.

The signed pledge constituted part of the certificate of authorization given to those recognized as Servers.

In "Attunements and Returning to God," a service on February 22, Uranda shared some instances of healing. One was focalized in an experience he had shared with Albert in which he recalled a time when he was six months old and fell about six feet through a trapdoor on a porch. This resulted in a broken bone below his right eye, involving related digestive problems ever since. Uranda delighted to let this process of letting old experiences be uncovered, and much healing appeared as a result under his hand. He cautioned that it would be constructive when it appeared under the action of the spirit but destructive if the mental and emotional apparatus was the mode of operation.

The building of a hangar and landing strip across the road from the Residence was considered as a possibility. This never materialized. At one point a strip was begun and used several times, but the location of telephone wires limited the available space. The decision to let it die an early death was greeted with a few sighs of relief.

15

WONDERS UNFOLDING

April ~ November 1953

*A*t 100 Mile House in a service on Easter Day, April 5, Martin commented about the new cycle that was opening with the advent of the tape recorder: I understand that some of you this morning suffered a little frustration in not being able to move or shuffle or sneeze, or whatever you felt necessary in the way of noise, for fear of getting on the recording. Of course I don't want you to explode or anything, so we will make available moments when you can move around a little. I will signal to Ross when you can make a noise if you wish, but as far as possible please do not do much shuffling while it is operating; it is a very sensitive microphone.

On Sunrise Ranch an old granary, located near Stable Gables, was moved down the road to a spot just west of the Bishop's residence, close to my little house. After extensive repairs and refurbishing, with some of Genie Pierce's stone magic around the base, it provided an attractive and adequate facility which served as an office for Uranda.

A thousand trees were planted along irrigation ditches and elsewhere on the Ranch. That beautiful valley was fast becoming a verdant haven, with nature reveling in the loving care for which it was starved.

In a Class on April 21 entitled "Joseph—Broad Outline," Uranda spoke of spring-time in the Rockies and the prospect of sharing some sessions with the Class up in the mountains. (The drive up the Big Thompson Canyon, just over Green Ridge behind Sunrise Ranch, is a beautiful adventure experienced by those who visit and a familiar but ever-new one for us who live here. A particular area at the foot of the canyon is formed of strata standing vertically, rather than horizontally, the result of some mighty cataclysmic events in ages past.)

> Though you begin to know basic realities it will take eternity for all the wonders of it to unfold. And do you think all those wonders are going to unfold through you? Some part of them, but some part you can see and know only because it manifests through someone else and you share it. In that way we begin to know the truth.

> Do you suppose that those of you who have never seen the Western Slope of Colorado, across the Divide, in this one State, could see it adequately in a journey of a week or ten days? No, even if I went along as a guide to introduce you to the highest flat-top mountain in the world, to behold the grandeur and majesty of scenes that unfold below you that cause the view from the Empire State building in New York to be dwarfed into insignificance and noth-ingness; to look out from the rim of the Grand Mesa and see the mountain ranges many, many miles away; and to pause in the Grand Valley where the silver Colorado flows, and pick a peach from a tree and taste its unbelievable flavor. How much more is this true of the kingdom that is at hand. We must never forget our purpose, our dedication, and our opportunity of letting our eyes be opened so that we can see and begin to experience the wonders and beauties and glories of the kingdom that is at hand.

Meanwhile at 100 Mile House the group was revealing increased understanding in moving as an effective body with Martin and under his guidance. He commented, in a service on April 21 entitled "Pneumaplasmic Body":

> The initial phases of this ministry have been designed to permit the gen-eration of that necessary pneumaplasmic substance so that the patterns may be set by which the formation can continue to develop and be brought forth in form. How foolish, then, for human beings to think they are in position to judge the procedure of its development.

He further elaborated in a service on his birthday, April 27:

> There have on occasion arisen critical attitudes on the part of some who do not share our immediate program here, with respect to you. When I hear

those who look in from the outside, judging you because you do not conform to some concept they have devised, I have no patience with them. I am not inviting you to start judging them, or criticizing! I do not want to give that any weight either. Observing what we are here in the world to accomplish, there is the necessity to keep up the pressure, so to speak; we cannot afford to sit back. We are here to finish the work victoriously, and if the situation in this fallen world is going to be wound up in any case, it would seem that in this day and age human beings do not have very much to lose! The victory is impossible in human strength. All things are possible with God, and our responsibility is making available to God that which we are.

I remind you of these things partly because it is an anniversary of my birth, partly because of the feelings of my own heart. No one can do the job alone. Uranda cannot do it. I cannot do it. Any one of you cannot do it. But all together we can! But we must be together. If we contend with each other the life force is wasted, nullified. The amount of life force required for any particular manifestation of contention between two individuals cancels itself out. Or if you contend with yourself inside yourself, that measure of life force utilized is wasted, cancelled out. And of course it is the contentions within yourself that cause the contentions with others. We need to be all together, with one purpose, with all our facilities directed into that one purpose, and then we can do the job. Uranda's ministry is virtually meaningless, just as our Master's was, as is mine, except as there are those who share in it and give it form.

Martin often availed himself of opportunities to spend a few hours, or days, on the tractor, experiencing a satisfaction and pleasure in an area which, incidentally, he shared with Uranda. Regarding work, Martin said:

> *Recreation* is an interesting word. Re-creation! That is our purpose on
> earth, to permit the re-creation to take place. Therefore everything we do can
> be enjoyed—recreation, re-creation, regardless of how you pronounce it.

Conrad and Rosalie O'Brien-ffrench of Banff arrived at 100 Mile House with Rollo and John for a visit, with the intention of possibly joining the Unit. Vivien Humphries and son Glenn (later resuming his name Lockie) came from Vancouver to share in the program. Edith Brownlee returned from Saskatchewan with her mother, Margaret, who was blind and became a permanent and beloved member of the family, living with her daughter in a little log house, still Edith's abode. A valuable addition to the 100 Mile complex was an upper storey to the "Annex," later named "Evergreen." Working on the job, Lloyd Meeker Jr. fell through the ceiling—practically into the arms of Jessie Stuckey!

The Emissary Society was able to take over the operation of the 100 Mile House Ranch by reason of the cooperative attitude of Alex Morrison, ranch foreman. This man proved to be a great asset in the performance of his many duties, as well as being a good friend to Martin over the years. With the arrival of various families from Ontario, the labor situation in the store was relieved, releasing Ernie Taylor and Morley Giffin for work on the ranch. Jack Horton helped with the milking. Ross Marks and David Oshanek had been doing the spring farm work.

Dave Robertson moved to 100 Mile House from Ontario with his wife and two daughters and established a clothing store in the Village, "Robertson's Ready-to-Wear."

In the second annual meeting of the Society at 100 Mile House on June 26 the President, Ross Marks, noted some current developments: There was an increase in numbers, the unit was operating the store in the village, services were being tape-recorded, with a library of Uranda's and Martin's tapes begun. *Northern Light,* an official organ of the Society, was playing an important role, and Sunday School was well established.

On Sunrise Ranch Uranda entitled a talk given on June 20 "Shekinah Magic":

> The sound you hear in the background of this recording is very pleasant to our ears, the motor of our water-sprinkling system which is throwing water on the knoll in the pasture, north of the little Prayer Chapel, the highest point in relation to our problem of irrigation. That sound testifies to the fact that water from the canal irrigation project (extending from Carter Lake to Horsetooth Reservoir) is reaching every part of our land. We thank God for that sweet sound, and in the days to come let all who hear this recording share in appreciation of what this background music represents.

On July 3 in a Class entitled "Shekinah Pattern of Being," among other things Uranda spoke of his love for horses and experience working with them, and continued:

> The processes of integration must be characterized by that which is fitting or wise in relation to that particular person, creature or thing. If I drive an automobile my concern is to establish a pattern of integration with me insofar as that automobile is concerned. I do not just step into it and mechanically drive it down the highway. I have an awareness of its parts, its tendencies, its weak points and its strong points. This integration does not stop with respect to the car I am driving but extends to other vehicles. If I can take over control for the moment, temporarily, and save a life, that is well and good.
>
> That happened two or three years ago going toward Loveland. I was driving a big Chevy truck, and in the car in front of me a mother was driving, with her baby on the back seat. She turned around to tend to the baby and I saw the

car swerve. It wound up against a telephone pole. Noting the erratic quality of her driving I had known she was not integrated with her car. Once you know what I am talking about, you can tell whether a driver is dangerous. I had established a pattern of integration in relation to that car, to which she responded. She was saved from a head-on collision with that pole. I helped her out, and then the baby, which had fallen down and was jammed into a corner, but it was all right. It could have been a very different story.

The pattern of integration can extend wherever there is response, wherever there is opposition, and wherever the individual simply for the moment ceases to have control. I am not talking so much about hysteria, although it works to some degree in that sense, but about those emergency moments when people do not know what to do, when they stop thinking. The individual who is opposing is not necessarily being integrated with you, but his actions are integrated, in spite of himself, with your pattern. It may take a little time, but by the very reason of his fighting he defeats himself. When we hold steady and function correctly, opposition permits us to take hold of the pattern.

Uranda prefaced a Class on July 8 with a word about Africa:

A situation has developed over there that presents a problem. According to this letter they have two hundred members interested in this work, considering themselves to be members of the Church of Emissaries of Divine Light, and are like babes in the woods. They need leadership, and I do not have anyone to send to them. They want some things, but sending them things is not the answer. They have been patient, working to the best of their understanding. Two hundred in one group in Africa! The first Church built anywhere on the face of the earth specifically for this Service was built in Africa, by the native people, on faith. And they request authority to organize another church.

What can one do? We need so many Servers in so many places. Before we can send someone to Africa we have to be in position to finance their program. We cannot just send someone out to Africa and drop them in the dust, so to speak. They will have to be backed up, and that includes money. These are just some of the things that I must consider day by day, the "calls from Macedonia," the needs, the things that cannot be achieved until we have the right pattern here, the right people to go and to do, the problem of writing the right words to those children of God in Africa. It is so easy to say something that is misconstrued. Of course they are getting the lesson material all the time, and studying it to the best of their ability. There are those among them who can read the English language, and they proceed—but there are two hundred in one group waiting, waiting. And they are a drop in the bucket. There are many in other places, far and near.

We cannot move any faster than the reality of the development of our basic program here. I wish, sometimes, that those who are inclined to get a little self-centered and move into petty fields of action, could see with my eyes.

In a service on July 16 entitled "A New View of Shekinah," he recalled as a boy hearing the word, "Every secret thing shall be revealed," and that it struck terror to his heart:

I did not know what I had done to sin, but that it must be something terrible, something even secret from me. The idea was presented as a means of causing fear: if you do something wrong, if you slip somewhere, it will be revealed, you will come before the judgment bar of God with all the evil revealed and be known for the miserable creature you are.

But now, and for many years, this text has been a source of great assurance, with the expectation of something very wonderful, to be greatly desired. I reached a point of comprehending something of the reality of being and discovered that the evil that men do, and think to hide, cannot really be classified as secret; they reveal it. The secret things are the things of God, secret only because human beings have not been willing to see, consider and give heed to them.

There are those who teach that the mysteries of God cannot be known, that there is so much that we are not supposed to know. I do not agree with that. We are supposed to know all that we have the capacity to know, as much as may come to focus in us; and if we begin to know the truth that is within the range of our potential comprehension we will find that range is enlarged and the secret things of God are being constantly revealed in our own lives and in the lives of others. One of the many secret things which needs to be revealed and made known in and through you has to do with the reality of your individual relationship with God, which has been a secret thing. But the promise is to you, if you will receive it—every secret thing with respect to your relationship with God in a personal sense shall be revealed.

In a Class on July 18, "Enoch and Moses, Elias and Jesus," Uranda said:

I was in my early teens when I could no longer accept the idea which the religious folk around me were trying to impose upon me, that of a god in the so-called Christian concept, an old man with a long white beard sitting on a throne, waiting to wreak vengeance on some human creature who makes a mistake. I rejected it all and assumed that that made me an atheist. Of course I found out later that it did not; it only gave me an opportunity to begin to know God. But what do most people have available to them, except the old husks that have been offered through the ages, or reject them and be atheists? If we truly look at the stars in the sky we must recognize that surely there is intelligence back of them. We have a part to play in the body of the cosmos, but the earth is not the center of it. We have come to have a new vision of God.

In a Class on July 21 Uranda spoke of the chapel on Sunrise Ranch:

Under this flooring there are two-inch planks; this chapel is strong. Many times I've seen this shell of a building from the outside, and wished we had the wherewithal to finish it. Many times I have flown over it and looked down upon it before there was any roof, but finally, here it is. It took patience to reach a point where we had the manpower to do it. A good deal of the material is used lumber, scrap lumber, but it does the job; and now as seen from the air it looks like as good a roof as you can find anywhere round about. It has been six years since we started this building. It took patience and perseverance, and when we could not do anything about it, we did other things. But now we have the job done to this point.

We have been using it like this for several months for classes. It is perhaps finished for the moment, a cycle completed, but there is always opportunity for something larger to appear. Expert opinion may say that you are weak, that the building process is impossible under the circumstances. But if you don't know enough to believe it, you can be strong—it can be done.

At 100 Mile House in a service on July 26, "Perfection," Martin announced:

The armistice was signed in Korea, and the fighting is supposed to finish in about ten hours. We give thanks to God that the active killing of man by man in this particular field of conflict is to cease.

Not so long ago this log house, our chapel, was a carpenter's shop, built for that purpose. There were benches around the walls and a large stove in the middle of the room. It was built by a craftsman, who used it for his carpentry work, which continued until about six or seven years ago. An interesting coincidence, one might say—a carpenter's shop reminding us of the activity in which our Master was engaged for a period prior to His ministry.

While we are touching upon so-called coincidences, we might note another in connection with the development of the Unit at Sunrise Ranch, and of our whole ministry from that point onward. At the time of the summer session in 1946, shortly after the acquisition of the property, there were very few buildings on the ranch, everything in a run-down condition. One of the best buildings was the big barn, the only place where a number of people could be accommodated for services, etc. So during that summer and fall services were held in a stable, the point of initiation for the Unit there, the one here, and developing now in other areas. That was not the starting point of the ministry, but of the manifest form as it is appearing. A coincidence! Our Master was born in a stable.

Strangely enough, amongst the livestock that were present during that summer session was a large bull snake. A bull snake is not a poisonous snake, but they grow to quite a size and are friendly to man. They keep vermin down and kill rattlesnakes. This one would occasionally attend the services. What an awesome sight it was, to see that large snake come in, go up to the front of the chapel, and curl up underneath Uranda's chair—the most natural thing in the world. There was, you may recall, a snake in the Garden of Eden, a serpent in the tree of the knowledge of good and evil in the garden as it was created. There was nothing wrong with that serpent. It was placed in the tree for a purpose. It was only when that purpose was violated that the trouble began.

In a Class on July 28, "Dealing With Response," Uranda spoke of receiving a letter from a man who

knows absolutely nothing about us and does not *want* to know, in which he said, referring to the Ranch, "That wild bunch out there has a sprinkling system now." Well, we have a sprinkling system. But on what basis are we called a wild bunch? The peace officers have never had to come out to quell a riot or a fight. That is what will stand. Do not let yourselves get trapped into resenting. The truth will stand, and the lies and prejudices will pass away.

In a Class on July 30, "My Attitude Toward Those Who Serve," Uranda said:

We made our beginning here with those who had the courage and willingness to set aside their concern with respect to worldly position and gain or security, for a pattern that from any ordinary standpoint offers no security or assurance of success. My attitude has always been that those who dared to make the change and share such a pioneering experience were to be accepted and commended, regardless of limitations. I have never found it in my heart to find fault because the material I had to work with was not of a higher quality in some respects. I knew that in the outworking, step-by-step, individuals would reveal themselves, either grow and come nearer to the divine design, or they would eliminate themselves from our program. And that has been the case.

If I had insisted on men and women who were perfect, never did or said anything that wasn't exactly right, so that no one observing from an external source or coming here with a critical attitude could jump to wrong conclusions or indulge in condemnation or judgment, where would they have come from? If I were to take the position that I am going to have only perfect individuals in the personnel on Sunrise Ranch, and dismiss all who did not function on an absolutely perfect basis within, say, thirty days, I suspect I would be here alone at that time. And then, if I were to look out into the field to find those who could come in and fill their places, ready and willing to devote themselves, to forget their own self-centered interests, I wonder where I would find them. I have never found them among the critical ones. I have never found them anywhere I journeyed across the land in the United States and Canada. Perhaps I should have looked in Europe, or China, or maybe Africa. Maybe they are hiding in the Andes in South America. I have not been able to travel all over the world to find out.

I would like to see some of those who have criticized put to the test to see what they would do on a day in and day out, week in and week out, month in and month out basis, facing the issues, daring to live, trusting God and letting it work. Time after time the Treasury has been down to two or three dollars and the next purchase of food had to be done on faith. Time after time we here have had to hold the line when there were discordant patterns in the field. We remember the Master's statement, "Judge not, that ye be not judged; for with what measure ye mete, it shall be measured to you again, and with what judgment ye judge, ye shall be judged." Those who find fault, in the field or anywhere else, cannot do so with impunity.

At 100 Mile House in a service on August 9, "Almsgiving," Martin spoke of the recent initiation of a new technique in attunements, that of radiating through the eyes:

Our Master asked, "Why beholdest thou the mote in thy brother's eye when there is a beam in your own eye?" It is impossible to see clearly as long as there is a mote or beam in the eyes of spiritual perception, just as it is impossible to see clearly if there are distortions in the physical eyes. We recognize the need then of undertaking to deal with the motes and the beams. If one is to see clearly, the beam needs to be taken out of one's own eyes.

In a Class on Sunrise Ranch on August 11, "The Glory," Uranda made specific reference when he said:

Sometimes the one who seems least likely to be of value will turn out to be the most valuable person you ever met. A number of years ago, back in the depression days, there was a certain little lady who lived in a little obscure place down in Arkansas who finally contacted me and my ministry by mail. The monetary situation wasn't good and I can remember getting a nickel, and a dime, once in a while, in her letter of response. The first year or two it didn't look like there was any comprehension of the lessons, but she kept writing and soon she began to get the idea.

Her family began to be included in the picture, and the greatest blessing of my life came into manifestation because of that little lady. She's my mother-in-law! Of course Dad has to be included; he certainly played his part. My wife has two sisters, whose function on Sunrise Ranch has been of inestimable value. When there wasn't anybody to do the cooking so we could get a start, Roz and Billie did the work. I have known Billie to cook three meals every day. Those three sisters came out of a little home in Arkansas where if one went by appearances it would seem very unlikely that anything of great value would emerge. Never judge or be quick to come to a conclusion. Keep on serving and giving, and if you really cast your bread upon the waters, not as if you were just going to let a little crumb go today—be generous—it will come back. If you are a citizen of the kingdom of God you can afford to be generous and you certainly cannot afford to be stingy. Give and serve. And it will come back.

"The Vibratory Turmoil, Tension and Misery" was the title of a service by Uranda on August 20:

Many human beings simply do not know how to have a meeting point with another person except on the basis of illness, operations, misfortunes, tragedy; and if we are going to find a point of relatedness we may be forced to acknowledge something of that nature—but we must not dwell on it. If we are functioning on the basis of reality we are looking for that which is right.

A good many years ago, in the early period of the depression, I got into a very difficult circumstance, financially, etc., and I was persuaded by some well-meaning friends, finally, that I ought to go to the Welfare Department and get a little help. I was having difficulty feeding my family, finding enough income to barely keep alive, and my whole soul rebelled against the idea. But finally I decided that for the sake of my wife and baby I must not let pride stand in my way. So I went, into an atmosphere that was utterly repulsive; the attitude was that if I was not some criminal, scoundrel or ne'er-do-well I would not be looking for help. I stood it for a while, then got up and walked out. The whole thing began to make me appear worse in my own eyes than I was and I rebelled.

Another time back in the middle Twenties there was a situation when I was ill, with no one to care in the outer sense. In desperation I got on a freight train and wound up in a little town in Oklahoma—Pritchard, I believe, a mining town. I looked for work, but found none. I'd had nothing to eat for two or three days and sought help through the usual channels. The whole thing roused every rebellious, independent streak in me. I am pointing out that all too often this thing that is called service is not service. It is contemptible, something that takes away any bit of dignity, any residue of meaning, there may be left. We need to see that any real service must be on the basis of that which is, and not on the basis of what is not.

After leaving Oklahoma I got to Joplin, Missouri, and went up one side of the street, asking each restaurant if I could do something, wash some dishes, for a bite to eat. No. They did not even offer me a crust of bread. Going down the other side of the main street I got pretty well down, and wondered what I was going to do. Terribly hungry, and getting so weak I could hardly walk, I went into a little hole-in-the-wall place. It specialized in a stack of pancakes and a cup of coffee, and I asked this man if I could do a little work to get something to eat, and he said he didn't have anything. There was a man sitting at the counter and he looked at me and tossed a dime on the counter and said, "Give the kid a stack and a cup of coffee"—some of the sweetest words I ever heard in my life. That was real service.

The Master repeated it three times: "Feed my sheep." Feed the body, feed the mind and feed the heart. Feed the three phases of being in those whom you serve, and be alert to ways in which you can feed them. I have seen so many starving people treated as if it was their just desert to starve, and not just physically. We feed the hungry, not with ostentatious display but with a comradely attitude, a meeting point that reaches into the heart. It seems to me that if our togetherness in this little valley is to have any meaning we need to meditate upon these things in relation to a world that is starved for love, for truth, for the bread of life. As God has been patient with us, let us be patient with others, and we will find that there are many who are eager and waiting to help us build the form of the kingdom of heaven on earth.

The Commencement exercises, on August 27, began with a violin solo, *Meditation*

From Thais, played by Ode Bainbridge. Kathy Meeker sang *The Lord's Prayer* by Malotte. Uranda spoke then, followed by George Shears, the members of the faculty, Martin and each member of the graduating Class.

One of the graduates, Alice Kuykendall, presented Uranda with a monetary gift from the Class and spoke of the miracle of being able to walk to the front of the chapel, having spent the past year being served, "night and day, in profound love," by Uranda. She thanked him and all in the Class and expressed her commitment to service.

Uranda enlarged on Alice's experience. Having suffered from polio and attendant complications as a very young child, and undergoing amputation of a leg in later life, she offered a response so complete to Uranda that a remarkable healing occurred. She had spent most of the summer in Uranda's home with daily attunements. What were called "attunements" were not in any sense limited to the physical level but involved true spiritual psychiatry, with resultant healing of the whole person. Alice was an outstanding example of this and used by Uranda for radiation into the body of mankind.

Perhaps through a few words by Frank Protzman, another member of that Class, you may catch a glimpse of the whimsical quality that endeared him to the "family":

> I have allotted myself six minutes [each was told to take three] on account of my better seven-eighths, Betty, being absent. Is that all right? I have criticized myself in the public speaking class and my greatest fault was talking through my nose. But what is the matter with that? We are all just one big happy family.
>
> I want to tell you that when the Class develops into thousands—in another building from this!—helicopters will be more popular than the horse and buggy ever were, or the automobile ever will be, because they will be propelled by atomic energy and they will land over in the field and will only cost between 35 and 38 cents—am I talking through my nose?

And on he went.

Frank and Betty, with their many talents and backgrounds of extensive experience, radiated a contagious atmosphere of happiness. Effective attunement servers and capable workers in field and office, wherever the need arose, their contributions were a vital part of the magical substance that characterizes Sunrise Ranch. Each day of their long lives was joyfully productive.

In a service on September 12, "Anniversary Meditation," Uranda spoke of the significance of the anniversary of his ordination and the initiation of this ministry, twenty-one years before:

> I was not seeking to *be* a leader, I was seeking *for* a leader. But, finally, in

that experience which unfolded I came face to face with the terrible awareness that I had the responsibility of *being* the leader for whom I had been seeking. Instead of refusing it or saying, "Lord, I can't do it," I took the attitude that if the Lord asked me to do it, then the Lord would make it possible for me to do it.

The moment you really accept responsibility in ministry with me you share, to some degree at least, my commission, because that commission was not limited to me. It was something in which any number of men and women could share, and it was my job to find them. Many who should be sharing in the Program are gone. We cannot waste time in vain regret, but we must do our part, and it takes a lot of filling in for those who are not here who should have and could have been. If we function effectively and correctly, there will be others come to share the work which must be done.

On the morning of September 13 Uranda, continuing his "Anniversary Meditation," reviewed the outworking of those three days in 1932 which initiated his active ministry:

At the conclusion of that experience I knew the answers to questions which in that sense have not concerned me since that day. What *has* concerned me is the question of application in service to humanity.

There was established in my heart a deep and abiding desire to help others come to the realization that man does not need to go somewhere else, to wait until he dies; for the door which leads to the kingdom of heaven is at hand. I suppose my inexperience at that time had its influence, but somehow I had the conviction that I could convey that truth to others in a way that would cause untold thousands to be drawn into that awareness. I was to find, through sad experience of many years, that human beings tend to be deaf to the word of truth, busy with such important business of their own that they have little time for our Father's business. But, finally, we have come to the year 1953, and we find ourselves here in a little valley at the foot of the majestic Rockies, various factors having worked together to make it possible for us, not only to have our regular services but a Class dedicated to the study of the principles of reality.

In a service on September 27, "Our Purpose, and Divine Commission," Uranda spoke of the urgent need to consider expansion, of our responsibility to the people of the world, and that "regardless of financial situations we are going to enlarge the borders of our tents. You have had a few lessons in learning to swim, but the time comes when we move on a sink-or-swim basis. I hope you all swim."

In a Director's Meeting at 100 Mile House on September 29 it was reported that

$1,000 sent to Sunrise Ranch should be considered a gift, rather than a loan.

Martin considered the fact that with the drive-in theater closing, the space above the garage could be fixed up to pass the fire marshall's requirements and a theater operated a few nights a week, with proceeds after operating expenses utilized to liquidate various accounts. This was successfully achieved, and I remember well watching *Arsenic and Old Lace* in the drafty but cozy old building.

Murray and Leato Weatherald and daughter Gail arrived on August 5, with Earl and Lela Weatherald, to take up residence. Charles and May Arnold arrived September 17 to join the program.

Marcia Harvey, a beautiful young woman with a crown of red-gold hair, arrived at 100 Mile House from Summerland (in the Okanagan region of British Columbia) to teach in the local school. She was drawn to participate in activities in the Unit, and in season married Ross Marks. Greatly loved, together they have provided substance of inestimable value in the development of the ministry. They have two sons and two daughters. Kevin was the publisher of the *Free Press* newspaper for many years, having worked in various areas as he grew up in the Unit.

In a Board meeting on Sunrise Ranch it was reported that the Ediphone Voicewriter Equipment and Model 543 Mimeograph would be sold, no longer needed since the advent of tape recorders and Multilith. The payment on Gateway property of approximately $1,500 was made on time. Eighty-four acre-feet of water was applied to our farmland. It was necessary to postpone the pond undertaking until early the following spring, to benefit from a substantial reduction of cost.

Uranda and his party left October 6 for 100 Mile House and Vancouver for about five weeks, to share with the sister unit the achievements in the recent gathering on Sunrise Ranch. In a service on October 11 entitled "Creative Principles," he expressed joy to be again in the well-loved Log Chapel, thankful that the Canadian Headquarters was making excellent progress and, above all, profound appreciation for Martin:

> As we all recognize, it is only by reason of that dedication to our commonly accepted cause and the spirit of God's leadership made manifest in and through him that it is possible for you to be here, and for us to share this hour.

In Uranda's lecture in Vancouver on November 2, entitled "The Creative Life #2," he said that most people have far more riches available to them than they are enjoying because their eyes become riveted on their problems, the things they think they want, they think they do not have. Busy looking into the void of a bottomless pit, they never see the things they could be enjoying. But the minute that is valued, appreciated, understood and lived with, a creative cycle is set up and the returning substance enriches life.

On November 4 in "The Creative Life #4," with a subtitle, "Emotional Control," he emphasized that the conscious mind is supposed to be the guardian angel, and illustrated with a story:

> One day the devil, having certain imps under training, decided the time was ripe to give them an opportunity to test the principles of deviltry. So he said to one of them, when a certain man came walking jauntily down the street, "Go get him." The imp raced over, jumped up on the man's shoulder and whispered in his ear: "You are discouraged. You are terribly discouraged." And the man said, "No, I'm not discouraged. I haven't got anything to be discouraged about." "Oh yes," the imp persisted, "you are terribly discouraged." "Well," the man said, "maybe, come to think about it, I do have a little bit to be discouraged about—yes, I guess..." His shoulders drooped and he went slowly down the street. Thereupon the imp popped down and went gleefully back to the devil. "I got him," he said.
>
> Soon another man came walking down the street, and the devil said to the other imp, "Go get him." So he raced over, hopped up on the man's shoulder and started the old routine. "You are discouraged, terribly discouraged." And the man said, "No, I'm not discouraged." He threw his shoulders back a little farther and walked with springy steps on his way. No matter what the imp said, he would not listen. Soon the imp dropped down and with his tail between his legs went slowly back to the devil. He said, "I'm sorry. I couldn't..." The devil asked, "What was the trouble?" And the imp said, "I did like you told me, I kept telling him he was discouraged, and when he wouldn't listen to me—I got discouraged."

He related another version of the story, where the devil took a likely candidate to view his headquarters, an enormous storehouse where the seeds of evil were kept. There were the sins of hate, fear, jealousy, many kinds. A tremendous bin covered the entire back of the building, and the devil said:

> "We use this seed more than any other. People who will not let us plant any other seed of evil in their lives will let us plant this one. You might think we were going to have the largest amount of sin in the bin of hate. No. We use that, but we have to start with something else before we can ruin a human life. The seed that we use more than any other is the seed of discouragement. Once this is planted we can plant any seed we want."

16

EXPANSION IN THE FIELD, AND AT HOME

November 1953 ~ April 1954

*U*randa and his party returned to Sunrise Ranch, and on November 20 in a Board meeting the financial situation was reported. Steps were being taken to sell the Bellanca and purchase a Piper Tri Pacer airplane, some gifts toward the purchase of which had been received. Three thousand dollars had been borrowed— $1,500 toward the payment of a loan and $1,500 toward purchase of the plane. Seventy-five dollars, which formerly was sent monthly by the 100 Mile House group, plus the $150 the Lodge had been contributing to reduce the former loan, would now be applied toward the new loan with its approximate unpaid balance of $1,800. The price of the new plane was $7,200.

It was anticipated that increased revenue would appear as a result of Uranda's expanded ministry made possible by the new airplane. An allowance of $2,500 on the old plane was to be applied against its purchase. The average cruising speed was a little over 120 miles per hour and would handle four 180-lb. passengers and 100 lbs. of baggage, plus a tape recorder weighing 23 lbs. and oxygen equipment for high altitude flying at a weight of 29 lbs. The backseat could be removed and the plane used as a cargo ship, or ambulance ship, with 500-lb. capacity. A stretcher was added later.

In a service on December 5, "Air Navigation—Its Principles in Living Life (Part 1)," Uranda spoke of the need for the pilot, after he has made his calculations in relation to his position, to trust his compass, and of the following tendency:

> Due to magnetic effects in the earth the compass goes haywire and one gets lost, to imagine that the compass is wrong. There is an urge not to fly in that direction, and yet the compass says yes. Check and double-check the variations and deviations, but fly the compass.

He related his experience flying back from Chatham toward Toronto, where there was a terrific thunderstorm:

> If I had yielded to the impulse to turn off I would have been going out over the wilderness of northern Ontario, sooner or later run out of gas, reached a point of no return, landed if possible, and been stuck. But I flew the compass, no matter how it looked.

> The Lord has provided us with a compass. I understand the impulses that come as we move along the way because one is not perfectly oriented for the moment, but if we yield to them something is going to go wrong. Live today. We cannot live tomorrow, but we must learn to look ahead while we live today, and if the tendency to a tangent pattern comes, don't yield to it. You know the course, the direction of movement, and you have a compass.

In a Board meeting on December 14 President William Oshane reviewed the Bishop's explanation of the Board's function, that of representing the mind as it relates to the Church body of responding ones. As the conscious mind is supposed to be the guardian angel, with regard to what is permitted to go into the unconscious realm of mind and heart, so it is with the Church Board. The initiation of new ideas, in conjunction with the Bishop, the spiritual head of the church, for the welfare of the Unit or the entire church body, should rightly originate in the Church Board. It is here, as in the mind of the human body, that a sense of selectivity and discrimination must be exercised whereby new cycles may be initiated in harmony with the principles of reality.

In a service on "Organization" on December 24 Uranda spoke of the centering of organization being at Sunrise Ranch and 100 Mile House, and extending into the various groups and servers in the field. He said:

> All things represent organization. We can observe that in the smallest forms of life, even a single cell. Organization means a coordination within a pattern for a single purpose.

> Another year is at hand. The pages of the book of this year shall soon bear the record of 1953 into the past, and whatever is written is written, whatever

has been done has been done, whatever has been said—in jest, in love, in anger, in hate, in resentment, in understanding, in whatever form, shall have been carried into the record. What shall the New Year bring? We trust a great increase in service, but if it does, it will be because we have organization. I have worked within the scope of the circumstances as they are, with the material and response available. I cannot force you, or anyone, into the pattern of the divine design; I can only invite and inspire. In the development of this organization it has been and is essential that we should achieve the greatest possible flexibility.

Sometimes people waste time resenting, speculating, thinking about themselves, what they want and what they deem to be fair and desirable, instead of learning the lesson that is inherent in every situation, learning to do well that which is at hand to do, without resentment, without concepts of justice or injustice, but the spirit of God working to achieve that which is beyond human vision, which human eyes cannot immediately see or comprehend.

In his "New Year's Eve Service" on December 31, Uranda said:

That which is of truth, of the divine design, God's love, all that is established in the pattern of reality, these things endure. If we are not aware of them it does not change that fact. That which God has established from the beginning still is. Its form of manifestation may have been distorted, or lost, but it still is. And when God made it, He looked upon it and saw that it was good; and when we look upon it we should see that it is good.

The enduring quality of the divine is something human beings need to more deeply realize, for the human tendency is to see with darkened vision, assuming that because the things which man has made pass away, the things of God likewise pass away. But that which was true in the beginning of creation, that which was true in the days of the patriarchs and the prophets, that which was true of the time our Master walked upon earth, that which has been true in any moment of time, is still true in this hour. With an increased consciousness of that we find ourselves standing upon a sure foundation.

The foregoing is a profoundly moving expression when viewed in the light of what occurred in the year that followed.

Uranda expanded on the process of "Letting it Work Out," in which the idea that this involves passive, irresponsible function was addressed.

It requires an impersonal and objective attitude, to see the factors, weigh and consider, check and double-check the trends, the influences, and be aware of the impulse of movement in a certain direction. A possibility may begin to emerge in consciousness, along with some improbable aspects of the development, suggesting distortion. It may be that *if* everyone concerned worked correctly, that ideal could easily be reached; however, the individual patterns of those involved are checked, and a sub-point, not the ideal, begins to surface. The world must be accepted as it is, something less than what might be possible, to get it in the realm of what is possible on the basis of the present situation. When the envisioned goal is reduced to that point it will still be far beyond what most people think to be possible.

I have been accused of setting impossible goals. I do not believe it. What I did was to see a goal that was possible if all had coordinated correctly, but I never set that as the immediate goal. I always brought it down to a point where it would simply require the best of each one, expecting a reasonable degree of centering. Always, so far, we have fallen short of that. In other words there has been a third point. Generally speaking, I did not even mention to you Point One. I only mentioned Point Two, and then we landed at Point Three! It was possible, but it seemed impossible to some, so we did not even get to Point Two.

When you say you are going to let it work out, what is *it?* The vibrations of the outer world pattern are going to work out into the circumstance and spoil it? You are just going to watch it and see which way the winds blow and the waves toss? Or does it mean you are going to let the vibratory factors which are of God work out into the realm of form, the field of action, through *you?*

In a service on January 3, 1954, "Think on These Things," Uranda announced that he and his party anticipated leaving in a few days on a proposed tour.

This business of leaving you here at Sunrise and journeying forth is something I feel very deeply, and there are indications that you feel it also. We have long recognized that we were moving forward, first toward and then finally into a cycle of expansion in our service, and long ago I pointed out that when this time should come there would be a certain degree of testing and it would be shown, in the outworking in far places, as to whether or not we had built soundly and well here at Sunrise. Certain stress factors tend to manifest when it is necessary that I journey forth from you. If you did not feel it when I left you, if it made no difference at all, you would not be of much value in our Lord's service. That which we feel in the pattern of oneness of spirit is essential if there is to be a centering, a drawing together, that holds the pattern safe and secure through the various cycles that are necessary.

On his tour, which began January 7, Uranda addressed the Kiwanis Club in Hunt-ingburg, Indiana, on January 11; his talk, entitled "The Living of Life," opened with a typically frank introduction by George Shears:

> Friends, before I introduce our distinguished speaker I think I should introduce myself. About four years ago I changed my methods of seeking to serve people, and experienced a change in my entire outlook on life as a result. I am no longer known as a Chiropractor. I am known as a G.P.C. Server.
>
> A few years back a book, *Man the Unknown,* by Alexis Carrel, was published, in which he said that the next great development in the history of mankind would be in the spiritual realm. The purpose for G.P.C. Servers is to serve in that realm. They are vanguards, forerunners of a new kind of service on earth. All G.P.C. Servers everywhere are under the guidance and direction of Bishop Lloyd Meeker. Your first reaction, never having met or heard him before, might be to try to classify him in one of the many secular cubbyholes in which the Christian world has divided itself. But I assure you, friends, he will not fit.

Uranda said:

> The phenomenal changes that have been worked out in the world in the past fifty years are almost beyond man's comprehension, and recently I noted a statement by a scientist that in another fifty years we would be able to go from coast to coast in one hour. That symbolizes the fact that we are living in a world of speed and great change. Where there is this increased tempo and we are required to undergo constant adjustment to the conditions of life, there develops tension, which is a primary factor in the increase of heart problems and many others—underlying conditions of emotional and mental distortion.

In Toronto on January 27 the subject was "The Creative Life #8," and he used the analogy of the atmosphere, or air pressure surrounding the earth:

> At sea level we have around fourteen pounds of pressure on every square inch of our bodies all the time. You are conditioned to that pressure. If you go to some elevation in the mountains, where you are a mile higher, you have a mile less of the thickness of the earth's envelope above you and you have to go through a process of reconditioning to get used to it. The highway just back of Sunrise Ranch goes up to 12,180 feet above sea level, quite a little over two miles. The atmosphere becomes thinner, there is less oxygen, not nearly as much pressure. So you adjust. You move slowly; you take it easy.

If we recognize that there are right patterns of tension and are not subject to the abnormal which brings about a tension cramp, so to speak, and lose control, tension is not going to hurt us. But it is these tension cramps that come through the emotional realm which produce a condition that is called heart trouble. The high tension in the modern business and professional world, etc., takes its toll. We can work under tension as long as we are in control, a pattern greater and stronger than any of the tensions in the unreal world. It will not hurt anyone who is willing to yield to the spirit of God, but it will crumble ill conditions. It will cause the walls of Jericho to fall down.

The next stop was Chatham, Ontario, where Uranda spoke on "The Creative Life, #11" on February 2. There we were beautifully hosted in the home of Ray and June Lloyd. As often happened, Uranda's presence proved to be a magnetic attraction, and in this case he was interviewed by a reporter who accompanied us to the airfield, with the result that a photograph of us with the plane appeared with the article in the Chatham newspaper.

Back at the Ranch, in a report on February 13 Uranda spoke of the recent trip in his Piper Tri Pacer and invited Albert Ackerley, who with his wife Edna had accompanied him and Kathy, to say a word about it. Albert closed with this comment:

Moving out into the world from this blessed place is like moving into a vacuum. You feel as though you were a breath of air moving into an empty place. Going out there is no picnic, certainly not for Uranda. The vacation is in coming home.

Uranda remarked:

When traveling I often wish it might be possible to gather you all up and set you down where you could see for yourselves and feel what it means to the people whom we contact in such a journey. The speed with which many allow their lives to be changed is marvelous. But if you, and those who share the responsibility at the Hundred, had not let those changes come in you and established a pattern to which they could move, those rapid changes would never have taken place.

Our first destination was Spencer, Iowa, on January 7, where we visited with Don and Izetta Buchan. We flew from there in bitter cold, about a hundred miles to Mason City to get gas, and then made a nonstop flight to Huntingburg. On Tuesday morning, after sharing a rewarding time with some very responsive friends, we flew south, over Nashville, Tennessee, the place where this ministry began, dropped in at Huntsville, Alabama, for gas and went on to Columbus, Georgia. Eddie and Helen Hoffman have carried on the work alone there and done some wonderful work. They have a plot of land that has tremendous potential and would be an ideal spot for the development of a program in the southeastern United States. Tremendous opportunities are opening before us, more rapidly than our personnel can handle them. I look forward eagerly to the time when we can inaugurate such a program.

From Columbus we flew to Myrtle Beach, South Carolina, where Harold Tibbedo and his wife Billie have chiropractic offices. Our plane was housed in a dirigible hangar, the airfield having been part of air force activities during the war, operating now for a few private planes. On Tuesday we were informed that there was fog north of us. We wanted to get on to Toronto, so we flew out on top of it; of course we had our navigation instruments. (Albert had gone back to Toronto at this point.) We got as far as Harrisburg, Pennsylvania, where we got word of freezing rain ahead, so we stayed over that night. We contacted Gladys and Eddie Miller at Berwick and they came down and brought Mabel Hagedorn, who is helping them in their center; her little son Danny was also with them.

We got away about noon the next day. The fog was right down on the river, the way we were supposed to go, but had opened up on a direct course out over the mountains. So I changed my flight plan. It is a bit of an experience to fly over some of those Pennsylvania mountains. Gracie has a little smile of satisfaction at my having to admit there are some mountains back in Pennsylvania! [Uranda was always rhapsodizing about the Rockies!] Within ten or fifteen miles from Buffalo, New York, we had to turn back because of the fog and finally landed at Arcade, where we found the airport absolutely abandoned. I had to leave the ship out in the cold. There we met a most cooperative and friendly man, Mr. Wilson. He stood out there in the bitter cold, with the wind blowing, while I sat with the ladies in his car where it was nice and warm. He brushed down all the frost off the wings, did a thorough job of wiping down the whole ship, and put in gas. And then of course it would not start.

He went into town and got two batteries. He got me some heavy boots, which he had from his days as a flier in the Air Force. I do not believe there is a fraternity more closely knit than pilots, all across the land. When one of them meets another he lends assistance, all having known what it is to be in a tight spot.

He had to take the seat out of the plane to hook up the batteries in order to get a tandem line. With all that booster battery back of it we started the ship. He did all that work, and he let me pay for the gas but that was all. He is a manager in a big plant there, but he took almost a whole morning off his job, to see us off the airfield. He stood there until we were airborne, and waved us farewell.

We went to Toronto that day, and then to Chatham by train and back. It was beautiful around Toronto when we left to come back home, but the nearer we got to the river, the border, the lower the clouds became. We flew into weather and eventually landed at Buffalo in a snowstorm where we stayed that night. The next day the air was rough and we got to Fort Wayne, again staying overnight. The next day we had a strong headwind from Fort Wayne into Ottumwa, Iowa. From there to Grand Island it was a very nice flight.

We had cold weather on the entire trip, even in Georgia, all the while hearing about the nice weather back at Sunrise Ranch! We took off from Grand Island, the final day, with wind gusts reaching 43 knots. But it lessened by the time we got down, the other side of Imperial, Nebraska, and we began to get into warm air. The flight across eastern Colorado was the smoothest air we had on the whole trip, though there were a good many flights that were pleasant. It was smooth as velvet, and I thought, "Wonderful air for coming in."

We got out here ready to come in on Loveland field. I was up 7,000 feet and started coming down. I was crossing the field at a much higher altitude, and was surely thankful I did. In order to check the wind direction, I did not come in on pattern level. I could see evidences of wind around and I wanted to double-check things. We got in a down-draft out there south of Loveland field. I threw that engine. I do not mean to ordinary cruise throttle; I mean full throttle, every ounce that baby would take, and we were still going down. I had all the climbing attitude I dared give it because if I fly under 80 miles an hour on a climbing angle it begins to get down to a stall point. So I have to keep the ship attitude so that you can keep at least 80 miles an hour. But I was down to that range and as slow as I could go with safety with the load I had. I was still a thousand feet over terrain, doing my best to stop coming down.

We were down to within 600 feet of the ground before we gradually, on a long swing, managed to climb it up, back to the 800. And it was the roughest air; I had to practically make a full power approach against that terrific, gusty wind. I put on the flaps, and with full power on I could not hold altitude enough. I had to take off flaps in order to come in against the wind on a power landing and keep control. I deliberately put her in firmly and held her nose down—and there we were. We swung around and taxied up to the Loveland gas pump—home after quite a journey!

I have skipped over many things that might be interesting, and it does not begin to tell you about the meaningfulness of the trip itself, the wonderful hospitality we received, the remarkable way in which the program worked out in Toronto, the fine response there. We had 200 at one meeting. There was good attendance everywhere, but that was the largest group I have talked to in my personal ministry, other than in a church, etc., for a long while, which was gratifying. In spite of the fact that we were traveling in the east where winter weather is weather, we covered a tremendous lot of territory, with many blessings wherever we went.

Minutes of a Board meeting on Sunrise Ranch on February 12 reported that a new Class was tentatively scheduled to begin April 2. Cash receipts for January were $1,407.37, consisting of $504.21 from students' income, $404.35 over and above expenses from Uranda's ministry in the field, $133.50 servee income, $320 loan from Home State Bank, and $45.31 miscellaneous income.

On his birthday, February 25, Uranda entitled his service "From Womb Unto Womb." With a depth of heartfelt thanksgiving he spoke of the fact that in his forty-seven years he had received much response and love, recalling that Jesus had said, "The birds of the air have nests, the foxes have holes, but the son of man hath not where to lay his head." He said that the Master was not speaking merely of a geographical location but a place where His spirit could come to rest and that he, Uranda, was greatly blest to have such a place:

When I meditate upon the wealth of response that I am privileged to receive in the name of our King I feel that we have made some very real progress. And yet I cannot forget the untold tens of thousands of those who are hungry and thirsty for what we know. I thank God for you who walk in the vanguard of those who are beginning to come, company upon company, into the sphere of this service. If my memory turns back, twenty years for instance, to the early part of my ordained ministry, there were those who were responding, and considering the circumstances it was good response, yet to such a high degree I was alone. I was working, serving, and waiting patiently for you to come and share the labor and the joy, the heartache and the satisfaction which comes to those whose lives are dedicated to the service of our King. In the intervening years, step by step, one here and one there, sometimes by remarkably unique events, you came.

As I waited for you then, working and serving the while, we now wait for others yet to come. We must not be slack in the performance of those tasks which are now possible, but there is that which we cannot do until others come to share with us. There is a world need. Important opportunities are opening before us, and we do not have the personnel or financial resources to take advantage of them as rapidly as they are appearing. This is not in any sense a complaint, but emphasis on the importance of being about our Father's business. Compared to some organizations our undertaking is small in form, but the greatness of anything is not determined by its physical size. Greatness relates to potential, that which can yet be achieved. It is written, "Where there is no vision the people perish." There must be a great vision if we are to permit the development of a great restoration.

In his service on March 11, "No City to Dwell In," Uranda quoted from the Bible:

"He blesseth them also, so that they are multiplied greatly; and suffereth not their cattle to decrease. He turneth rivers into a wilderness and the watersprings into dry ground; A fruitful land into barrenness, for the wickedness of them that dwell therein." This was a dry and barren place when we came here. For many months we hauled every drop of water we used, from down near the Big Thompson School. There was no electricity in this valley except at the Filter Plant. We brought in R.E.A. We drilled wells, put in pressure water systems, etc.

In those early days we took the attitude that if we functioned in righteousness the land that was barren should become fruitful, and there would be water. We have already shown it to a great degree—wonderful wells, and the standing water. Is that not the biblical way of saying a pond? A little lake is being formed down here. There were those who said we would never have water. We do, and we are going to have more.

In a Board meeting on March 12 there were some financial reports. Cash receipts for the month of February were as follows:

*Students Income	$ 1,270.17
Servee Income	173.00
G.P.C. Servers Training School	1,000.00
Miscellaneous	67.87
Total Receipts	$ 2,511.04

*Included $408 from Uranda's ministry in the Field

Pertaining to the trading of the Piper Tri Pacer plane for a 1953 used Cessna #180—which had unanimous agreement from the Board—a letter of March 9 from Clinton Aviation Company was read, outlining the terms of the deal. They would give us our full purchase price credit of $8,000 for the Piper Tri Pacer and we would pay $6,450 in cash, making a total of $14,450. There were about 225 flying hours on the Cessna 180 on which they allowed $6 per hour, or $1350, and we would allow them approximately $522 covering 87 flying hours on the Piper Tri Pacer.

After paying $6,450 in cash for the Cessna 180 we would have a balance of approximately $3,550, to be used to pay the following bills:

Note due Home State Bank	$326.00
Real Estate Taxes 1953	825.00
Installing pond	750.00
Due on Skelgas	514.00
Total	$2,415.00

There was a remaining balance of about $1,000.

Bishop Meeker was authorized to negotiate a loan of $10,000 at the Home State Bank, offering as security a mortgage on Sunrise Ranch.

The new greenhouse was in operation. Work on the pond would begin shortly by Mr. Coulson, with excavating and moving about 3,330 yards of earth at the rate of 15 cents per yard, total $500. (By comparison, the 100 Mile House Unit paid 60 cents per yard. This was under the Government Support Program, with the proviso of a one-half refund next spring.) Arrangements were made for free trees in that area, and for fish to go into the pond without charge to us.

Uranda expressed thanks to God for the way our whole program was shaping up, with mention of progress being made at the Hundred, adding that he expected to make a trip there with the new plane, to be gone about a week, inasmuch as Martin and Uranda needed to get together.

"Our Pattern of Relationship" titled Uranda's service on March 13, in which he mentioned the pleasure he experienced in a significant conversation with Rev. Woelber of Loveland that morning and the way in which he was sharing the meaningfulness of ministry.

> He is a Lutheran minister, and from the standpoint of what might be called religious differences we are content to say nothing. Our pattern of relationship is based on those things in which we have agreement, not on our

differences. We are concerned about those things, and they are many, in which we stand together in the service of our Lord, and when I talk with him I have the feeling that I am in conversation with a man of God.

On the evening of March 18 Uranda gathered the group in the Chapel, and proceeded to address Kathy, Lillian and me as though no one else were present. Assisted by the three of us, he conducted what he called an experiment with a "little instrument" that would reveal the characteristics of a person, said person's name having been drawn at random and known only to Uranda. Then he put the slip of paper with the name into his "instrument," a simple little box, and concocted an assortment of numbers and combinations, which I then wrote on the board. The one whose name he used for analysis did not receive a result on the "right" side of the ledger. The whole thing was conducted as though the group were not present. Later the man involved in the experiment told Uranda he recognized that he was the one being scrutinized, and intended to undertake some constructive self-examination. This was entitled "The Qualities That are Present in a Human Being"—a unique experiment, with a constructive result, but never repeated!

A Directors' Meeting at 100 Mile House on March 19 reported that the gross income for the year ending March 31, 1953, amounted to about $24,500, to be divided among 23 partners. Bishop Martin Cecil stated that the chief purpose of the meeting was to consider the building program. The new garage was finished, and the shop and warehouse were nearing completion. It was decided to make no new addition to the Lodge at present but if necessary to increase dining room accommodation by removing the wall between the staff dining room and ping-pong room. Due to limitations of manpower and finances it was decided to postpone building of the Bishop's new house. It was approved that a cabin be built for Vera Parsons which could double as a music room.

One of the most beautiful expressions I have ever heard was in a service given on Sunrise Ranch on March 21, "The Reality of Form," in which Uranda said:

> I think those who have artistic ability would be the first to acknowledge the vast difference between the flower as God made it and an artificial one, a form that is not alive, which imitates the invisible essences. The delicate details of the form itself are not there. One could presumably put some perfume in it; but the perfume, the essence, of the flower is absent.

> We can have the form of human beings, but if we are simply imitations of what God intended us to be—no matter how well the imitation may be worked out or delude someone who takes a casual look—there is a difference. Is it the genuine thing? Is the form the true revelation of that spiritual essence, which includes life, which includes so many things that can hardly be described?

The other evening we saw a picture of a mariposa lily, just one of the exquisite things, comparatively rare, that grows here in Colorado. I wonder if anyone would like to try making an imitation of it. It would be difficult—the subtle differences, the colorings. Under a magnifying glass the imitation does not look so good, but under the magnifying glass the real thing looks infinitely more lovely. And what of this thing we call life, this process of living in which we are all engaged? Is it not the magnifying glass which causes the real to be even more beautiful in its manifestation? And the unreal, when it comes out where it can be seen, looks uglier under the magnifying glass than it does to the casual glance.

Once we begin to accept, deep in our hearts, that the physical body was made by God, not as a prison for the soul but as a means by which He could be revealed on earth, by which His love, wisdom, knowledge, understanding, all the joys of life, every lovely thing in heaven could be translated into the earth, what we *are* can appear. The physical body is spiritual, a part of the divine process of spiritual revelation, so that what is coming down from God out of heaven may find form in the earth.

If the process by which this is achieved were fully understood and practiced, there would not be one ugly word ever pass the lips of anyone here. There would not be any act which, when seen under the microscope of the process of living, would not be beautiful. I have looked into the heart of a mariposa lily with a magnifying glass, and those delicate shadings of color, the exquisite form, almost leap out in a still larger and more detailed perfection when they are clearly seen. So it is with that which is divinely ordained, divinely designed, for you. And if there is that which is not of such perfection, there is an imitation.

"Divine Control, Significance of a Control Pattern" was the title of a service on March 18, in which Uranda said:

It is a mockery to be concerned about establishing control out there somewhere while we refuse to accept those conditions which would establish control here. The Master asked us to pray: "Thy will, O Father, be done in earth"—what is that but a control pattern?—and then "It shall be done of my Father, which is in heaven." I have spoken of agreement before this group many times, and one of the things that I am hoping and praying for is that before the year 1954 shall close I shall have achieved in the ministry this one thing, that this little group shall have accepted the divine control pattern so that they can come together with one accord in one place and allow, for the first time in over nineteen centuries, the real manifestation of the power of the Holy Spirit.

On April 1st Uranda spoke of "The Challenge of the Hydrogen Bomb." He had brought with him an article from the *Denver Post,* which contained pictures of the first hydrogen blast about two years before that. Two explosions, much greater than the first, took place later in 1952. After reading the article aloud, outlining the tremendous destructive capability of the hydrogen bomb, he said:

This emphasizes the need for a definite forward movement in the understanding of spiritual things. The tremendous power to destroy needs to be counter-balanced by a tremendous power to create and to control. I am not talking about merely the world need but of our putting aside those things that have hindered or prevented our movement. There has been in some a deepening understanding of the reservations which human beings impose upon the machinery of the Lord. This machinery of reality is more delicate and marvelous than the mechanical brains which man has made, the huge calculating machines with their great capacities and mechanisms.

The world recognizes that teamwork is important. In the Army, Air Force or Navy we find coordination, each man in his place doing his part, and every other man in the crew depending, often for his life, on each one. It should be much more so with us. We all depend upon each one. You, individually or collectively, may say, "We are depending upon you," meaning me. And in the name of our King and through the working of His spirit I accept the challenge of that trust. And I must depend upon you. It is in a pattern of teamwork that we can allow the development of the machinery of reality through which we truly let our Father's will be done in earth as it is in heaven.

The G.P.C. Servers Training Class of 1954 began on April 2. In his talk entitled "Opening Day" Uranda asked:

Why are we here? In brief I would say we are here to learn to know the truth, that the truth may make us free, to accomplish that for which we came into the world. Then the next steps follow naturally, and you find yourself stepping free from the limitations that have beset you. You will learn to know the futility of trying to contend with limitations, and step up out of that old level of consciousness to function in a higher level. And this will happen more than once. You do not shed the old skin, the old pattern of life, all in one operation; and these step-by-step processes by which you emerge are called the cycles of rebirth, or illumination.

At first it may seem difficult to distinguish between the aspects of long-ing. Some may think they are not supposed to want, to experience any hun-ger, to be controlled by this or that desire. That is the state of blindness in the pattern of perception at first.

Uranda then related a story about himself as a toddler, when his family had just moved from Iowa to North Dakota, living on the prairies in a sod house, natural to that time and place. The inside was whitewashed to make it look nice. He evidently had a physical hunger and would crawl under the table where he assumed nobody could see,

and proceed to start eating the house, digging out chunks from the sod wall. Obviously the hunger was translated on the basis of the idea that my body's craving would be satisfied if I ate that earth. There is some truth to that; my body needed minerals, so I turned to the only source available. There was nothing wrong with that hunger, and there should have been something else, minerals and vitamins that my body needed.

There is no condemnation against anyone because of a need to change a pattern by which a normal longing and hunger can be satisfied. There is a tendency to say that if I try to correct you and stop you from doing some-thing, it proves that I do not understand your longings, your need. But I do, and when I say, "Let us not do this," I am not denying that, but pointing you to a way by which that longing may be truly satisfied, the hunger filled with-out eating your house down and destroying yourselves.

Martin repeated the verse from Psalm 127 which had been acknowledged from the beginning of the Class pattern as its motto: "'Except the Lord build the house, they labor in vain who build it.'"

In a service on April 3rd Uranda said:

Man's capacity to bring destruction upon himself has so increased that it would be possible to produce one bomb capable of destroying all life in the United States. He now has the technical know-how; but he has many others, the destructions which he produces by wrong patterns in the living of life.

Uranda waxed poetic in a Class on April 6 entitled, "The Basic Steps That You Uti-lize, Making the Way Easy":

A little later, when spring has opened up more, we will probably as a class go back up in the mountains. I can tell you something about Estes Park, or Horseshoe Park, Hidden Valley, Many-Parks Curve, Trail Ridge Road, or Tim-berline, perhaps even Grand Lake or Bear Lake. I could tell you *about* them, I might even conceivably show you a picture, but until you have gone there and stood on the shore of the lake or looked out from Many-Parks Curve, or rested for a bit in Hidden Valley, until you have seen for yourself you cannot say "I know." My function and that of your other instructors is not to make you feel that now you know so much about, you do not need to take the trip yourself. I want what I say about the truth to make you want to go for yourself.

The Narrows—have you seen it in the moonlight, have you seen it in the spring, in the summer, in the fall and in the winter? Have you seen it early in the morning, have you seen it late in the evening, have you seen it at midday? Have you seen it when it was cloudy and when it was bright, have you seen it fanned by a rainbow in a spring shower? How have you seen it? Just a bunch of rock, the vertical strata? Does it ever impact you with the tremendous power in some distant past which turned all that mass of rock up on its end? What about the moss and the trees growing out of the crevices, and the stream that runs below? Oh, I can tell you about it but you will have to go and see it for yourself some day. And if you have seen it as many times as I have I do not think you will say "I now know all about it." Class dismissed.

Uranda admonished, in a Class on April 7, "The Application of the Basic Steps," that care be taken, in a class or service, not to be distracted within oneself when some point is presented which particularly interests or brings up a question. Trying to figure it out or make application with respect to it will cause what follows to be missed, whereas continuing to listen would, perhaps a minute or two later, clear the entire question.

The death of our dear friend Frances Brown was reported. She led the way for those without physical sight, had attended Classes and established the department of Braille translations for our material.

It was noted in a Board meeting on April 9 at Sunrise Ranch that work was begun on the dam in preparation for the pond. The management of the Home State Bank changed hands, with Harold Pickler and Vern Manahan leaving the First National Bank and purchasing the interests of Gordon Christensen (not the Gordon who was part of our family) and his father. Uranda felt that with the new management a mortgage should not be put on Sunrise Ranch in the deal with the new airplane and he would try to obtain the money from some other source.

Other matters demanding attention were enumerated: the 1953 real estate taxes of $825 must be paid by May 1, the most pressing item at the moment. Also, irrigation water must be ordered and paid for by April 30. Water is costing us $2.65 instead of $1.50. Two hundred cubic acre feet @ $2.65 would amount to $530 or a total of $1,350 for the two items. It was noted that inasmuch as our pastures are coming along slowly we had to buy hay.

Cash receipts for March were as follows: Students Income $1,194.11, Servee Income $172.50, Kathleen Van Haersolte $100, Sale of Towner Disk Plow $75, Misc. $29.12, Total $1,570.73. The purchase of a Model 2 Rototiller and an electric Rototiller, also a sprinkler system for the garden was approved. Thirty-four fruit trees were purchased.

The sad and difficult situation with Edith, Martin's wife, came to its natural conclusion with her death in Vancouver, the funeral being held on April 2nd. Martin had continued to provide for her comfort through the years, letting her abide in the assurance of his love, which was always present.

17

PORTALS OF HEAVEN—MAGIC

April ~ June 1954

*I*n a Board meeting on April 13 there was discussion regarding covering for exterior walls of Stable Gables, the big barn at Sunrise Ranch.

This has insulating qualities, carries a 20-year guarantee, Good Housekeeping seal of approval, has a 5/8" overlap, center is basic fibre 5/8" thick, fire resistant but not fireproof, carries lowest fire insurance rate, has special type of adaptors to prevent need of furring—30 to 40 percent saving in fuel. Walls will be vapor proof and material take warpage, cracks will not appear. Two skilled men could do the work in three days. The regular price was between $1,400 and $1,500 but to us $1,000, delivered without down payment, extending payment up to 18 months.

The Board approved the project.

A Message by Uranda, to be released to the School, was read to the Board, dealing with the raising of $15,000 within the very near future, from those in the field who had stewardship over funds which they could lend the Church, on which we would pay interest at the rate of 5% per annum. Smaller loans with a minimum of $50 would run one year, larger up to five. This had unanimous agreement.

The new airplane deal was postponed until June 15, Uranda going to British Columbia at the end of the month with the Piper Tri Pacer.

In a Class on April 14 entitled "Ontology, Server's Training," Uranda cautioned the students that they would be embarking on the school of experience and that, all together, there was a definite movement in an expansion program, which included right terminology. He had previously introduced the name "The Universal Institute of Applied Ontology," and added that the *Funk and Wagnall's Dictionary* definition for *ontology* was "the science of real being."

> *Pneumaplasm* means substance that relates to spirit. *Pneumatology,* a word in the dictionary, means "the doctrine of the nature and operation of spirit, or a treatise on that science, the science of spiritual beings or existence." That is what we are studying, the means by which spirit which originates in God may have practical meaning in this realm where we live. So we have a department of pneumatology in The Universal Institute of Ontology, and that is where you are today, learning how to serve man by bringing him into attunement with his source of life. To begin with, you are not a pneumiatrist but a pneumatologist.
>
> [These terms were never used, and did not replace the title "server."]

He then spoke of the possibility of developing a trademark in the form of a triangle: The U I of O, with a cross in the center, for possible use on letterheads. This came to the same end as the terms mentioned above. These seeming failures were never a source of discouragement. Richard Thompsons's fruitful mind and imagination found a definite place in the unfolding design of the ministry, but such things were always seen in the light of experimentation—"So be it."

Again the hunger in Uranda's passionate heart resounded through his words on April 18, "Rebirth":

> I come to the close of another Easter day with a poignant sense of inadequacy. I would not deny what has been achieved nor can I ignore it. All things must grow in their true cycles in the processes of development, but I feel that individually and as a whole there is need for a greater acceptance of inspiration. We could say that we need to draw nearer to God, but that has been repeated so many times that even though it is true it means little.
>
> Only in the days to come can we see and know and share in the harvest of the seed that has been planted in the good ground of our hearts and minds in recent days, to bring forth fruit. I do not think there is any shallow ground here. There may be a few briars left, a few thorns which tend to choke out the good seeds; there may be a few birds left that eat the seeds, the self-active

thoughts that keep them from germinating. I also know that there have been some very deep patterns of realization, deeper dedication, forward movement and illumination.

In a service at 100 Mile House on April 25, "The Spirit of Truth," Martin Cecil spoke of the necessary recognition of Uranda in his place, referring to the words of Jesus when He said that the Spirit of Truth would come and teach you all things. He said:

> You who have had opportunity to hear Uranda speak on every conceivable subject may have come to the realization that there is nothing within the scope of the sphere of his responsibility of which he cannot speak the truth. If I have that which is made available to fill your needs, where does it come from? It is not mine as a human being, but it springs forth from that same spirit. As you share in letting that same spirit express through you, you know it too, and you find that there is that which is ample to every need.

A Class on May 4 was entitled "Stimuli—Learning Control," in which Uranda spoke of resurrection out of the level of reaction to external stimuli, into the level where we deal with external factors on the basis of intelligence and right action, the flow of the life force from the source into the realms of form through words, deeds and attitudes. Gradually as you let this process work correctly in yourself, people will begin to accept the green pastures and the still waters which you offer to the hungry and thirsty ones.

> I am reminded of an incident when I was a boy in my early teens. I was in the mountains, coming out from the trees into an open space, a valley. And there, on a little rise, was a buck deer and three or four does, standing with their heads up. The buck, although I was evidently down wind, had perceived something and had given the initial warning, but they did not know yet which direction to go. A remarkable thing about deer is that they depend on the judgment of the buck. The buck that is at the head of a flock of deer will raise his head, listen, smell the air, and not move until he knows the direction from which the danger is coming. I have wished sometimes that human beings had more of that! That beautiful buck was standing there with his head up and his nose in the air and when he perceived the direction from which I was coming and that I was not carrying a gun, danger was not in the air, they did not just break and run. They trotted off. It was a beautiful sight.

"The True Spirit of Home" was the title of a service on May 9. Uranda said,

> On Mother's Day we could note that its significance depends upon the significance of birth. God the Father, God the Mother, had a purpose in bring-

ing forth that which you are—you the man or the woman. I remember certain lovely things with respect to my mother, and when she left this realm there was a loneliness, a deep sadness, and yet an acceptance of the situation as it was. As time passed, the greatest need in my being was for a sense of the meaningfulness of my own life. At that age it appeared that the years before me, stretching toward adulthood, were unspeakably long and endless, and I had some vague concept that when I had reached manhood I would then have meaning.

I remember hours on the barren wastes of the White Water Country, and in the high mountains and Grand Mesa, and particularly certain hours when after a long day's work the time for milking came. There was no milking shed on top of Grand Mesa—a corral under the tall evergreen trees—and there, with the wind moving through those trees, the mountain stillness and chill in the air, the whole atmosphere so far from the haunts of men, no sounds of civilization in the dusk, certain feelings came that cannot well be described; but I think it was a longing for home. Yet my mind could not turn to any geographical location on earth and think of that as home. There in that vast loneliness there was a sense of communion with nature, and yet a longing for home.

Human beings have produced a substitute pattern of home, not wholly satisfying but providing something of an anesthesia, trying to somehow be content with the geographical location called home. And there may be certain factors in a location that produce that sense of home, which is a sense of meaning. Home is the place of personal meaning, and we think of mother as the one who provides the deepest and most consistent sense of that. Yet many mothers, regardless of their fine qualities, have faults or limitations; and in many cases the sense of personal meaning becomes overshadowed by a sense of duty, because of the fact of physical relationship, resulting in conflicts that distract from the true significance of home and mother. Perhaps my early experience instilled deep in my being a longing for a spirit of home on earth for all mankind, regardless of race or color or creed.

In a Class on May 10, "Co-owner in the Father's Business," Uranda spoke of investments in the body of humanity through particularized persons when it may seem there is no return through those specific channels, by way of appreciation, etc.

But we know that as we sow, so shall we reap, and the field is the body of humanity as a whole, and the spirit of God working through that body will establish somewhere, somehow in the cycle a return pattern. What we do in relation to persons is never lost. As far as those who turned away were concerned it was loss; as far as I was concerned it was not.

About ten years ago it looked as if the investments I had made would never pay off. We went through a cycle where it looked as if there was nothing but failure and the things for which I had worked collapsed all around and I had to make a new start. Because I did not quit, regardless of who came or went or what anyone did, the investments that I made all paid off—not necessarily through the persons in whom they were made, but through the body of humanity, someone, somewhere. And if they have not already paid off, they will. The mind wants to know just how and when and where and in what amount the investment is going to pay off, and if you work on that basis you will lose out, because you are not making your investment in persons alone.

Actually, you are sharing in the results of my investments through the years. You have made your investment, and I am not belittling that, but there needs to be the right attitude on the part of those who share or they will take things for granted, expect me to pull rabbits out of a hat, fail to share in the results of their own investments in the lives of others as well as mine. We cannot assume that the blessings we share are all the result of our own personal substance or endeavors.

On May 14 a Board meeting on Sunrise Ranch reported the negotiation of a 90-day loan from Home State Bank in the amount of $850 to cover 1953 real estate taxes. Bulldozing work on the pond cost $500, on which $300 had been paid. An extra job of bulldozing cost $70 and price for smoothing out a landing strip for our plane $55. Two hundred twenty-five acre-feet of water was purchased at $2.65 per foot, also 600 feet of pipe and fittings, part of the garden sprinkler system which could also be utilized as fire prevention equipment, pumping water from the pond. A 60-foot well had been drilled at the Bishop's residence.

The recent message sent to the Church members regarding raising funds through loans resulted in special gifts of $2,280 and offers of loans of $6,650.

The Piper Tri Pacer plane was sold for $7,460, which was applied as down payment for a Cessna 180 airplane, N 2972 C, with complete equipment. There was a chattel mortgage for $7,862. The purchase was unanimously approved, at $15,311.50, also insurance coverage at annual premium of approximately $1,100.

Uranda spoke of "The Significance of Opportunities" in a service on May 15, and suggested that if someone appears to be a little edgy, off-center, it provides an opportunity either to be edgy in return, or to be serene, tranquil, patient, unmoved by the irritants which have appeared. He said he could not remember

> even in times of deepest loneliness and inadequacy, ever being bored. I cannot recall a time when there was not something I needed to do. A state of boredom is a state of failing to have any interest in that which comes within the range of comprehension. If the mind is centered in one direction with respect to a hoped for opportunity, then we ignore the opportunities at hand, the pattern of vivid interest is not stimulated, and without that we move like automatons, merely existing, because the opportunity we think we would recognize seems to be unattainable.
>
> One of the particular opportunities which I feel has not yet been adequately explored here on Sunrise Ranch relates to the human factor, the opportunity to understand one another, to observe, to listen, to examine, without immediately attempting to act as if one had a full comprehension of the situation.

In a service at 100 Mile House on May 16 by Martin, "Evidences of the Spirit of Action," I see an interesting correlation with the one above delivered by Uranda on the previous day on Sunrise Ranch. Martin said:

> If we find an individual staying within narrow confines, in the attitude, "This is my field and I won't look over the fence on either side," there is evidence that he is insisting upon keeping his mental capacity in a narrow channel. The working of the spirit of truth can increase the capacity of the mind; God is even capable of doing that! But, first of all, we have to use the capacity we have. The working of the spirit of truth produces a healthy curiosity. I don't know of any place that has more scope for healthy curiosity than right here at 100 Mile House!
>
> When I first came to this country twenty-four years ago I had absolutely no experience, no background, in relation to any of the activities here. I was supremely ignorant, and that's a pretty good starting point to learn something! I had a background of sorts, but mostly to do with the sea, boats, water. There was some water here, but most of the activity was definitely on dry land. Therefore I was forced to have a healthy curiosity, and during the course of the last twenty-four years there is no field of activity in our pattern here that I have not worked in—not merely because I had to, although there were those times when there simply was no one else to do it.
>
> If you are to be in position to provide leadership you are going to find it necessary to do things just because you have to. What causes that "have to"? The spirit of God's love in your heart. If that is not there to hold you steady you will

duck out—"I don't have to put up with this; I don't have to do this sort of work"—and thereby prove that you are not trustworthy, capable of standing up under pressure. How many slip out from under, because God's love has not come into their hearts to hold them steady, so that they simply have to do the right thing; they cannot do anything else. I have heard it said that it is so hard to do the right thing. It should be impossible to do the wrong thing! Something that is impossible is very, very hard. When that centering in God's love is found, there is something solid and the individual cannot be moved.

Uranda spoke, in a service on May 16, "The Heaven, and (Then) the Earth," of the early days of his ministry, pointing out that it never took any real form until the beginning on Sunrise Ranch, the manifestation being purely in spirit at first.

Out of all the vast areas on this planet finally we managed to get 120 acres of the earth's surface, here in this little valley, and let it be dedicated to giving form to this heaven, this spirit, this atmosphere, which has been to some degree recognized and accepted. The beginning was in spirit, with every one of you. A person can come here and stand among our buildings and speak to us, and if he does not first feel and know and share the spirit that is here he cannot share the form of it.

Only heaven can recognize heaven. Hell can recognize hell, easily enough; and heaven can see the little scars, that actually mean very little but are hell for those who respond to them. Hell does not look very dangerous to heaven, or big or difficult, but not so to the person in hell, because he cannot see the heaven. Heaven can be right there, closer than hands and feet, and it cannot be seen by hell. Before long various ones will be coming through the gate. They expect it to be a heavenly home, and we can make it that. Finally there is the beginning of the body, and the spirit and atmosphere of the body, the heaven and the earth.

A few days later Uranda and his party arrived at 100 Mile House, where on May 24th he spoke about "God Principle":

The evening before last while attending the Regional Conference of the Civil Air Patrol at Ogden, Utah, Kathy and I had the pleasure of having dinner with two C.A.P. Chaplains, both of them Roman Catholic priests. Incidentally, our national chaplain in the C.A.P. in the United States is a Protestant. His Deputy-Assistant is a Roman Catholic priest, Chaplain Madore. He and the Wing Chaplain from Montana were present. In fact we three were the only chaplains present and shared two very interesting hours. We carefully avoided the subject of religion, as begets a good chaplain, and found many points of mutual consideration.

I was particularly interested in the comments of one who has traveled extensively in various parts of the world and particularly in Europe, regarding communism. I said that if we here (and I included Canada with the United States) where we have what we call a Christian civilization, were to recognize that we harbor within ourselves as nations the rootlets of greed, fear, hate and all the rest, and allow them to be cleansed from our lives, we could establish something which would very rapidly take the force out of the communistic movement. The chaplain answered something like this: "I believe that communism is so well entrenched, so widespread, so well organized, that even if we were all to become as good as angels overnight it would not make very much difference." I did not reply specifically, but it was amazing to me that someone highly placed in the Roman Catholic Church, holding the second most responsible position in the Chaplaincy of the C.A.P. should have so little real comprehension of and faith in spiritual power.

On May 26 at 100 Mile House in his talk, "Understanding the Absence of Something," Uranda said:

With each specific development of man, with his so-called advance in civilization, how much has his nature changed with the changing of the times? If we go back fifty years, before aviation produced such an impact upon all of our lives, and examine human nature then and now, how much has it changed? Very little. Man himself has not kept pace with his own pattern of development in his circumstance. Right there is the breakdown, and the gulf becomes wider as we move into the atomic age. We are trying, with respect to understanding spiritual things, to function on the basis of the oxcart days in relation to jet propulsion.

This chasm between must be narrowed and finally closed, because if progress of circumstance and condition outruns too far man's progress in relation to himself he will have a Frankenstein monster on his hands which will in turn destroy him. [More than forty years later one would be blind not to see the spectacle of hysteric, accelerating movement in the world of computers and related electronic inventions, and note the fulfilment of the "Frankenstein monster" prophecy becoming an increasingly common item on the evening news.]

Man was created in the image and likeness of God, endowed with the capacities to allow God principle to operate through him. It is in the practical living of life that this must become active. So our purpose is the revelation of principle in this world, not in some far heaven but right here where the design is in accordance with that purpose on a controlled basis. And true control must be established, first, in oneself.

A Board meeting on Sunrise Ranch on June 11 reported that

$5,000 had come in on the promised loans, $2,000 of which had been applied on the purchase price of the Cessna airplane. Bishop Meeker was authorized to negotiate a one-year loan of $6,000 with Home State Bank for liquidation of the balance owing on the airplane.

A new engine for the field irrigation system had been purchased for $745, converted to Butane gas; also additional pipes for the garden sprinkling system, $300. A new well had been drilled west of the Ranch kitchen, $320. The new well at the Bishop's residence, drilled to 60', did not produce enough water, cost being $200. It was felt that further drilling to about 90' would produce adequate flow.

The Gateway Inn property was leased to David and Rosa Groves, at a fee of $1 per annum, in order that they might operate a barbecue enterprise. They followed through with this venture, and it provided a homey, attractive spot by the spectacular falls, with travelers stopping in for a refreshing snack—and sharing real family with Dad and Mother Groves.

Bishop Meeker spoke of the need to send one of our number to our Church in Africa at the earliest opportunity.

He spoke, in a service on June 13, "The Activation of Ideas":

The so-called Iron Curtain would crumble without the firing of a shot or the dropping of a bomb, if we would let the right spirit activate us, men and women, we who are the ideas given form in the flesh out of the mind of God. As long as we are subject to the same spirits as are contained behind the Iron Curtain we may call ourselves the free world but the events which unfold day by day make that claim a mockery.

Unless we begin to do something about it right here, in the homes, in our communities, in our towns and villages and in our great cities, we will pay the price, and it will be an awful one. The Iron Curtain could crumble before the right spirit. Once we have that conviction and turn our attention to that, we will not be merely on the defensive; we will take the aggressive position in world affairs, not so much with guns and bombs as with that which can truly change the future of mankind.

A few years ago an incredulous world witnessed the dissolution of that vibrational curtain dubbed "iron," following swiftly the "concrete" fact of a crumbled "Berlin Wall." These are outer evidences of the working of the Law, which is absolute, and are not seen by most as such. They are not happenstance, but the result of consistent, day-in-and-day-out function on the part of a number of dedicated people. The work is done in the invisible realms by those in physical form on this physical planet, wherever thay may be, and the power brings about the visible evidence in its own way and time.

In a Class on June 14, "Hallucinations," Uranda dealt with the vital subject of magic, both black and white. He spoke of the advertising methods used in newspapers, magazines, radio and television, referring to them as being

to a large degree in the pattern of black magic, emphasizing the spirits that are not true to divine or heavenly magic. Actually, black magic is a very weak thing, easily nullified. The communistic program of Red Russia employs black magic in a wide field of application. There are certain churches that claim to be Christian that fundamentally express black magic because the controlling spirit is fear.

One who is involved in a fear pattern or difficult situation struggles to overcome the wrong forces at work which he feels but does not understand, and is caught in the web of black magic. On the other hand, in the field of white magic, or I prefer heavenly or divine magic, it is all too often not keenly felt or perceived. It tends to be obscure except in certain moments of life. But what is the nature of this magic? If one sees a glorious sunset and is caught up with the sense of its beauty, there is magic, something beyond description.

I might illustrate with a little incident from our recent trip. After clearing Customs into the United States at Bellingham, Washington, our flight plan called for following the airways to Portland. But we got down south of Tacoma and there was weather over the mountains, heavy rain over Olympia, many of the mountains absolutely hidden. So I flew west and picked up a little valley, running out toward the coast. We flew down this under very dark clouds, almost like night. But as we approached the end of the valley out toward the ocean, there was a glorious opening, a pattern of light. There were some lighter clouds out over the Pacific, but there were glorious fingers of light carrying tints of rainbow color. The light, the delicate colorings, the ocean, all combined to provide a sense of magic, exquisite beyond description but very real, penetrating all the avenues of awareness and perception. *That* is magic. Kathy described it as something like the portals of heaven.

There are moments of sharing the sweet essences of friendship with another, all sense of adverse pressures gone, peace within and without, and *that* is magic. When we begin to sense and know and abide in God's love, let it fill body and mind and heart, something utterly exquisite, *that* is magic.

In a Class on June 16, "The Necessities of Correction to Maintain Balance," Uranda said:

As we examine into the natural processes in what we call nature we will find that balance is emphasized over and over again in relation to all things, from the tiniest organisms up to the mammals of the ocean, the great whales. If things begin to get out of balance, sooner or later other factors come into play which restore the balance. There is an ebb and flow, a pulsation.

If I am flying in somewhat turbulent air I do not grab hold of the wheel and grip it, trying to keep the ship absolutely level all the time. I let the ship ride the waves of the air. If it begins to go too far I make the correction, but I do not fling the wheel over and jerk the ship. It is an easy, natural, fluid movement. If we let the natural processes, which will produce correction, take most of the load, then if there is a movement out of balance you can be sure that if you function correctly you will find something working somewhere to help counteract that movement.

18

THE THRILLING THRESHOLD

July ~ August 1954

*I*t was in a Class on July 1st, "Fruits of the Garden," that Uranda first used the words, "The Art of Living," which have continued as a title for classes and work shops to the present time.

In a service on that day entitled "The Right Environment," he spoke of the many different types and natures of people encountered on his journeys, emphasizing the fact that "there is no way to force anyone to turn heart and mind to God," and that in each one there were compulsions at work engendered by the circumstances brought upon themselves by their attitudes and patterns of life. "Some were in a state of desperation, and some asleep—not a true sleep; a narcotic-like hypnotic sleep, a self-righteous, false sense of security." He observed signs that some people were being compelled by circumstances to awaken, to recognize them as opportunities.

He then referred to a lecturer he had once heard who used a jar about two-thirds filled with nuts, all kinds mixed together, to illustrate a point. He would casually pick up the jar and shake it. Every nut in the jar was shaken with equal force, with the little nuts going to the bottom and the big ones to the top. He said:

> We all have the shaking. Some people feel their lot is worse than that of

others and get so lost in a contemplation of their own ill conditions that they go round and round in circles, spiraling down until there is no hope. Others, facing the issue like men and women, learn the art of living, arise and return to the Father's house. What kind of a nut are you, a little one or a big one?

On the morning of July 4th Uranda spoke of "Freedom" and the weight of responsibility faced by the President of the United States at that time, accentuated by ever-ready criticism, which seeks to counteract whatever may be done.

There is a mass tendency not to center attention upon that which is, but to search diligently for what is not and rebel against that. Selfish interests, personally, nationally or worldwide, defeat any movement toward peace. Many human beings are driven like dumb creatures under the whip of fear, while others become lethargic and fatalistic, convinced there is no way but to make the best of it, and let whatever happens happen. But things do not just happen; they are produced by action and non-action, and if we don't like what has been produced we should share the work of changing it. Causing right things to happen means that we do not live haphazardly, subject to causes beyond control. We are not so concerned about escaping disappointments, problems and suffering, as we are about learning to meet them creatively, that others may begin to see a ray of hope in the situation as it now is.

Regarding shame, Uranda said that without the realization that one has done something wrong, and a vision of how not to do it again, repetition of the action, or non-action, produces a conflict within, resultant upon the inevitable sense of shame. Then one feels he must learn to live with it because he sees no way by which he can live and not produce it. This is a critical point in relation to attaining individual and collective freedom.

That evening Uranda, in his service, "The Thrilling Threshold," spoke of a higher freedom of expression than the one "so near and dear to our hearts [that of our country] by which we may discharge our responsibilities and enjoy our privileges as citizens of the world as we stand together at the thrilling threshold of a New Day." He expressed profound appreciation for noble men and women since the dawn of history who have labored that this hour might be possible to us, an opportunity bought with a price and not the product of chance.

Uranda's words always carried an emphasis on right anticipation, characterized by a readiness to receive whatever God might bestow, inherent in which was the element of surprise and also one of challenge—to exercise capacities to the full in giving form to the garden planted by God, eastward in Eden. *Eden* is the whole world, not just a section of Mesopotamia or somewhere else. Eastward? Out of the east come our tomorrows.

Uranda made a brief trip to California, a profitable journey that cost about $250. It included a valuable contact with Dr. Bernard Jensen at his Health Ranch near Escondido, a pioneer in many fields of healing. Drawn by Uranda's work, he had visited Sunrise Ranch and shared his own wealth of knowledge and experience in several class sessions.

Also, on that trip Uranda became a distributor for a product called "Derit Food Wafers" designed to help people from becoming tired (spelled backwards). He had a vision of using the profits from this venture to help defray the costs on the plane and the Gateway property, as well as real estate taxes due shortly. The Church was not to be involved in this venture, which continued profitably for a season.

Another result of that fruitful trip appeared in the form of five machines called "Dr. Pivot" at a cost of $9 each, to be sold for $15. A simple wooden structure upon which one stood and could turn the body effortlessly in any direction, it was to be used in conjunction with attunements to assist in loosening the spine. Along with "Derit" it contributed, though not spectacularly, to the coffers of the ministry.

In a service on July 10, "Reciprocity," Uranda noted that those who have a disregard for the welfare of others are accepting for others the condition which they experience, and in so doing also accept it for themselves. He said it might take a little while for it to work out, but outlined some interesting examples in world conditions.

> Looking back a little in history, we can see that if there had been some real encouragement, real help, not necessarily financially, from the United States and Great Britain and perhaps a few others, to the German nation when it undertook to become a republic after the First World War, that government that was able to exist for only a few months would not have been upset and lost through the activities of Hitler and his gang. The young democracy, established with the intent of taking its place in the family of nations, had not been given any real backing and, without an appreciation of what was happening, the other nations accepted for the people of Germany that action on the part of Hitler and let the revolution take place.

> As a consequence, what did we finally get back ourselves here in the United States and Britain, from Hitler and his program? So many lives lost, so much property damage. We accepted that change for the German people, without being willing to put forth the effort to help a young democracy, and it cost us thousands of times more than it would have if we had refused to accept for the German people what was imposed upon them. We could have stopped Hitler before he ever started, and it would have been easy because Germany had launched forth on a program of democracy that could have avoided the tragedies to the Jewish

race and to the whole world. But we accepted for Germany something we did not want ourselves and finally had to defend ourselves from it.

In a Special Service on July 11, "Uranda's Responsibility and Ours, Atomic Power," he said that man has reached a point where increased power is available for his use. While there are those who would use this for constructive purposes, control on that basis is absent, and those who do not recognize the sanctity of human life have a high degree of control. "And the world trembles."

In a Class on July 12 on "Attunement Technique," Uranda spoke of a prevalent limitation in the function of servers, thinking they needed to feel what some other one felt, server or servee.

> Do not imagine what you think you should feel and then try to feel it. It can take a variety of forms, and Albert Ackerley still thinks he seldom feels anything when he gets an attunement. It was six or seven months after George Shears was giving attunements before he was aware that he felt anything. If for any reason you should not touch someone, or if there is a complication with respect to the law, you certainly do not have to touch to give an attunement. It does not improve it, and in fact many people can feel the current more if the server does not touch.

In a service on July 12, "Learning to Welcome Changes," Uranda said:

> Sometimes changes seem long in coming. The fact of change should give us joy, assurance, confidence. If we hold steady, maintaining the right atmosphere, the changes will be according to God's choosing. We need to welcome and learn how to use them. Many people fight against changes; others wish for changes for the better but continue to do those things which reproduce the old circumstances. Instead of fearing and resenting it, as we learn to welcome change and use the opportunities which it brings, we maintain the evidence of newness, of growing.

> I know so much love and loyalty, a sacred gift. We are getting close to our 22nd anniversary. Twenty-two years ago no one knew, to all intents and purposes, that I was alive. How did it happen that I began to receive so much love? I must have expressed some, somewhere, somehow, consistently, whether people loved me or not. No matter what people said or did, it had to be there, and finally I began to receive back some love, trust, loyalty. And now you are here in this room, because you perceived the presence of something from God and because you are invited to share in bringing forth the evidence of that presence. The best that is in you is challenged. Learning to actually do it,

not just dream about it, not just talk about it but *do* it, is the evidence of the presence of the One who dwells.

"The Shepherd's Psalm (Questions and Questionings)" was the title given to a service on July 17, in which Uranda said:

> If we haven't the spirit of home here we have nothing. What difference does all the vaunted wisdom by which you might think to answer questions make if we do not have the spirit of home, of love, of rest, of understanding, into which we welcome anyone who comes? The things that are past are past. If I have to touch on them to help a person let go of something some day, leave it up to me. Must you fix it up so quickly? Let it alone. Let it work.
>
> What did the father do with the prodigal son? Run and greet him and say, "It is good to see you, son, but now before we do anything else you sit right down and tell me all that happened to you. I want to know everything. Tell me all about the girls you met, the swine you fed, all of it"? No. He just said, "Welcome home, let's have a good dinner, come to rest, my son, welcome." He did not have a lot of questions to ask, he did not expect him to have a lot of questions either. It was just good to be home. And if we cannot produce that kind of atmosphere, so that people can let go of their questions and just relax, we might as well dispose of Sunrise Ranch. Either it is that or we have nothing. It takes time, yes; it is not perfect yet.

In a Class on July 19, "What Makes a Champion? Attunement Technique," Uranda spoke of coming to the point established by the limits of personal potentialities and being at home there.

> Then in that atmosphere you will be in a place which no other can fill. No one else has the peculiar combination of factors, personally and in circumstance, that will allow arrival at that place which you and you alone can fill. And only then can you function effectively and correctly as a cell in the body of God.

Meanwhile at 100 Mile House Martin was diligent about the Father's business, and in a service on July 22, "Uttermost Devotion," he dealt with the subject of taking for granted that which is priceless. He stated that unless it means more to us than anything else on the face of the earth we do not have what is essential to experience the renewing of a right spirit in us.

> People can be caused to do tremendous things for a million dollars. What would you do for that which is priceless? Fifteen years ago I made contact with the Third Sacred School, after shopping around in various fields of so-called metaphysical thought and collecting a number of concepts and ideas

which were contrary to the truth. For a while I received the first mailings and they brought great joy to me, but there were certain things in them that did not seem to fit with some of the ideas I already had. It was not long before I had to come to a decision as to whether I was going to hang onto those or let go and see what was here. When I did that the way began to be easy.

He recalled the effect the sight of "one of those long white envelopes, with Emissaries of Divine Light written in the corner" had on him—"not all that different from today." He would drop everything and read it, and after about a month there was a red-letter day when two large packages of material arrived—prior mailings covering three or four years, with instructions, etc.

I read and read. Eating and sleeping did not mean anything. This which I had found satisfied my hungering and thirsting, and at the same time increased my appetite. Those words burned themselves into my consciousness in letters of fire, and I knew where my treasure was.

He spoke of the tendency in many to feel that reading or listening to something is all that is needed: everything else will happen automatically. Just to pray, "Create in me a clean heart" and expect God to do something without regard to oneself won't work. The heart must be used to contain the right spirit, and the mind used to consider the truth, and then the truth begins to be one's own. The absolute requirement is uttermost devotion, without the distraction of fictitious, false values.

Uranda spoke of the same thing in a different way, in a Class on July 23, "Attunement Technique—Primary and Secondary Cause." He defined an attunement as being "attunement with basic cause, disregarding all effects, regardless of their nature." The attention must not be sidetracked by any effect, good, bad or indifferent. Attunement is with cause, and if a secondary or distortion pattern of cause enters in, there is illness, chaos, a lack of peace.

In "Blind Spots," a Class on July 29, Uranda shared a humbling observation:

If as a leader you have gotten far ahead of those whom you are leading, you need to back up to where your people are. You might have to explore and do a little scouting on your own, but don't be brash; don't jump in and commit yourself in some fashion that is almost certainly going to make you back up. But if, because of various factors working out, or some failure on your part, you get on a tangent and find it is not working, do not become desperate and struggle to make it work.

Back up. There is nothing wrong with that. Come on back, leave your pet idea, leave all that seems to be so intriguing for the moment. Come on back to the realm where you know where you are, where you have your orientation and true starting point. If you think you have the true starting point and keep winding up in exactly the same spot, having tried it two or three times, it just could be that you are wrong. Do not come to the conclusion that you are right if you find yourself coming out on a variation pattern consistently. Come back and remember that you, right at your starting point, are failing to calculate something with respect to your course.

I might illustrate with a little story. Up at 100 Mile House the compass heading reads 26 degrees from the true direction. The pilot has to know what this difference is in his locality in calculating his course. There was an instance where the pilot did not stop to double-check his course. He flew out, and when he was not heard from they checked, flying over the route he was supposed to have taken. They could not find a sign of him. Then some bright pilot got an idea. At this particular point the compass reads 30 degrees from the true direction. This fellow said he was going back to where the pilot left and assume that instead of adding he subtracted. He set up his route on that basis, flew on it, and right there at the end of his gas supply, sixty degrees from his starting point, he found the plane that was down. The fellow had followed his course, marked it out on his map, but had failed to check and remember whether it was add or subtract. He made that mistake before he left the ground, with tragic consequences.

With respect to all the moves we make, there are factors which must be taken into account, and if we do not calculate them at the start, as far as we can be aware of them, we are not going to go in the right direction, and then when we get lost we say, "I have tough luck; it doesn't work out right for me."

He continued using flying to illustrate his points, and said that at first the fledgling pilot's primary interest tends to be with the feel of the ship. He wants to get out and fly! But some ground school is necessary before he can go soaring into the air.

I know you want to try your wings. You feel that sense of joy and accomplishment of working in the current of the spirit and are beginning to stretch your wings in that sense. But do not say, "If I can fly in the air of the spirit, if I can just feel the current working through me, I'm all set." Are you? Perhaps you have allowed a pattern to open up which allows the actual flowing of the spirit of God through you, not your full potential but it is there and you know it. But do not forget the compass.

God provided the capacity for intelligence, and the mere fact that somehow you are letting something of the spirit of God flow through you does not guarantee that you will be doing God's will. There is a tendency, at first, to imagine that everything works on the basis of feeling. "I feel this way about it. I don't feel right about that. I don't like that, and I think I like this." Feeling has its proper part and place, but the intelligence factor must be used. The mind is there for a reason, and if it has a blind spot you do not have the starting point and are going to spoil it sooner or later.

On July 29 in "Hallucinations and Blind Spots," Uranda referred to the basis of spiritual psychiatry. He spoke of the need to let the distortions or blind spots that have become buried in human consciousness be cleared away without the necessity of the usual process of trying to dig them out one by one. He said:

> It may be necessary sometimes to specifically consider some basic blind spots, a cycle of consciousness with respect to a particular experience, but we do not need to go through this process by which we probe around inside to bring to the surface all these things.
>
> From the usual viewpoint the endeavor is to uncover some ill condition which must be approached from the standpoint of psychiatry. The best the psychiatrist can hope to do is establish in consciousness a new or different idea, substitute one idea for another. Some people have been helped to a degree by this process, but admittedly it is incomplete and not altogether satisfactory. When man is depending upon his own wisdom, his own idea of what is normal, of what is best for himself or another, there may not be too much improvement even if there is a successful substitution of ideas.
>
> The power of God has been used by the human mind without regard to the will and the wisdom of God. When we see the problems that relate to a state of guilt on every hand, we realize they cannot be worked out without definite, specific intelligence. The Master said: "And ye shall know the truth, and the truth shall make you free," the state of freedom from sickness, disease, ill conditions of every sort in body, mind and heart, in circumstance. If most of the things we know relate to those ill conditions, then our knowing is of a nature which produces a state of slavery. If a person tells you how he knows what it is to suffer, what it is to have ill conditions of various kinds, what it is to have losses, how inconsiderate, how foolish someone is, and needs to be corrected, almost all of the expression with respect to what he knows relates to the state of slavery, not to the state of freedom. And he wants you to understand *why* he has accepted a state of slavery. A great deal of the talking about is designed to make you see why people cannot help it.

Remember what God said at the time of the Flood. "The imaginations of men's hearts are only evil continually."

A child knows the difference between the realm of make-believe and the realm of what is real, and it is not a concern. But when he begins to get older and lives continually in this realm of hallucination and make-believe, he destroys his effectiveness in life. Once we begin to reach the realm of this blind spot, and the individual is willing to see the truth without regard to all his ideas and beliefs and concepts and so-called experiences, then that truth can penetrate into consciousness and immediately it becomes a governing factor in an underlying field where it exerts control. And we do not have to go back into the whole slimy mess of evil imagination and try to figure it out, try to find out why this person has this quirk and why that person has the other difficulty and what is back of his hallucination.

As long as you struggle and fuss and fume and fight with respect to all these vain imaginations in the realm of not knowing, you are not going to have very much faith in me when I say to you, "A problem? There is? That's no trouble. All you have to do is let it alone." Only as you come to know the truth can you let the truth make you free.

When human beings work too long from the standpoint of not knowing, they become so accustomed to the realm of make-believe that they never get tired of playing the game; and then of course it is hallucination. All we have to do is begin to know the truth without regard to all these figments of fancy, and as you know the truth you begin to let it evolve in consciouness. Not trying to get it all at once but coming as a little child, developing more and more away from the realm of make-believe into the realm of knowing, you realize you are maturing—a thrilling threshold. And that is such a good feeling, no longer lost in the mist of not knowing but living in the realm of the truth that makes you free to Be and share in the creative processes of Becoming, which is called *living*.

These were the last words of Uranda spoken in the Chapel to his beloved family on Sunrise Ranch in Eden Valley. A few days later, a trip having been scheduled where some opportunities for service were beckoning, he flew from the Loveland airport to California. With him were his wife Kathy, Billy Van Duzen, Sharon Call and Albert Ackerley. On August 4th, enroute for home, after take-off something happened to the plane over the Bay area in Oakland, and before it could make the return journey to Sunrise Ranch it plummeted with its precious cargo to the earth, and the Bay.

All were killed instantly.

On that day I was in my little house, working at my typewriter, endeavoring to "line-up" or justify the margin of the service entitled "Freedom." This would be the first to appear in booklet form, and I had my wonderful new IBM Executive typewriter, which could do this magic work. I found the process to be a fascinating one, but in that hour I was, unbelievably, absolutely incapable of getting two lines to come into alignment. What was the matter?! Before me was an entire page with the same two lines, each spaced differently but not one of them lined up with the other—over and over. Incredible! I just couldn't make it work.

As I sat there, wondering what was wrong with me and why my mind was functioning in that strange manner, Rose Forker came to my door. Standing there she hesitatingly, reluctantly, finally managed to tell me that she had just heard over her radio that a plane had crashed in Oakland, California, and landed in shallow water in San Francisco Bay, that all five people had been instantly killed. She felt sure it was Uranda's plane, though names were not yet released.

I was highly indignant. The idea! This could never happen. So she left, realizing there was no way I could accept what she was saying. "That's not possible!" I insisted—words that I was shortly to repeat when I was called to answer the telephone in the Bishop's residence. The man was calling to inform us that the plane had crashed and all were killed. Even though he gave their names, I repeated the inane words, "It's not possible." There was no substance in my being that could accept the burden of his words. After several repetitions he kindly said, "Lady, I know you are deeply affected by this news, but it is true." Finally, I had to let an area inside open up enough to absorb the awful actuality.

Lillian and I then put through a telephone call to Martin Cecil at 100 Mile House. Could anything more traumatic, more suddenly fall upon the shoulders of this man than was conveyed by that phone call? Closer to Uranda than anyone could imagine, he heard that he was no longer walking on this earth, would never again speak the wondrous word of truth. And then, when that could be tolerated, came the shocking realization that he was now responsible, in that instant, for this body which had been built by Uranda and was expanding into far places, with promise of covering the face of the earth. It was a moment that called for all the preparation he had known in those fifteen years with his beloved, to don his mantle, the title now his, "Bishop of the Church of the Emissaries of Divine Light."

Later we were told by those who were with Martin at the time that upon hearing the news he paced up and down the room. Then he called for the ones who had been closest to him, the first necessity being to establish a nucleus whereby the lines of force could be drawn together into fitting form for what was to come—in the next moment, to say nothing of a future that seemed to stretch into infinity. But this great man took up the work that only he could fulfil, and through the many ensuing years provided inspirational leadership for the body so beloved by Uranda, its creator. There was no room for question, should there have been any, as to who should fill that place, due to the impeccable wisdom of Uranda seven years before when he ordained Martin, in Riverside, California, the Second Bishop of the Church.

Martin flew immediately from the Hundred to Oakland, as did Lillian and I, also Lorraine Cowan, from Sunrise Ranch. There we were met by Martin. Uranda's daughter Marjorie, with her husband Chuck Horne and small daughter Diane, who lived in Oakland at the time, were also there. We saw the wreckage of the plane in the water near the shore and stayed until the necessary arrangements were made for cremation. Then we all flew to Sunrise Ranch, along with the ashes of the bodies of our most beloved ones.

Three precious children, Nancy, Helen and Lloyd Meeker, were orphaned; Lillian and I were left without our beloved Billy and Sharon; Edna Ackerley was widowed with two young boys fatherless—and all who had found the answer to their hungering and thirsting for the truth through Uranda were called upon to prove the strength of their devotion to the Lord. Remarkably few were found wanting.

19

WITHOUT A BREAK

August 1954 ~ February 1955

The transition from the leadership of Uranda to that of Martin was without a break in the vibratory pattern. The magnificent spirit that found expression through each of these great men was the same. The Truth is true and cannot be changed, though the manner and nature of the forms necessary are infinite in variety. The movement of the body of which Uranda was the founder, and head for many wonderful years, found continued smooth movement, without a ripple, because of the provision of Martin Cecil.

In a service on August 7, "Facing Facts," Martin acknowledged his fifteen years with Uranda, seven of them shared with him as Second Bishop, and the enormity of the task so suddenly his, of leading the cherished flock which Uranda had gathered in his forty-seven years.

> My heart is full, and I know yours is too. We need to remember that tragedy is never God's will. This is not something imposed by God. But, seeing that it is so, for whatever reason, it is necessary that we face the facts, in the sure knowledge that it can be a means of bringing forth blessings as we let it be so. We know something of the blessings that were brought forth by reason

of that which man imposed upon our Master, and human beings have scarcely touched them. This need not remain a tragedy. What needs to be accomplished can be, by reason of the circumstances as they are—and there is much already accomplished.

Our Master spoke some words almost twenty centuries ago: "And your sorrow shall be turned to joy." There is a natural and proper cycle of outworking in which we may share, if we will. Neither do we need any attitude of self-judgment or self-condemnation. I do not wish to induce a sense of discouragement, or guilt, on the part of anyone. Human beings, functioning out from under the control of the spirit of God, produce patterns and situations which cause tragedy. It is futile to try to place the blame, try to find some specific point, some scapegoat to pin it to. We would have to go way, way back if we were to find the starting point for such things, but there is responsibility in that regard in every generation. We cannot blame anyone particularly but, facing facts as they are, begin to be in position to let the blessing appear.

There is the prevalent attitude that God works in such mysterious, hidden ways that they simply cannot be understood. On the basis of present function on earth human beings have not understood, but that is not God's will. The first creative act in the beginning found focus in the words, "Let there be light." And there was light. The light shines in the darkness of human minds and hearts, and the darkness does not comprehend it, but that is not God's fault. God intended that human beings should see and understand, that the mystery of God, and all other mysteries, should be finished. So while we may recognize, to start with, that we are in a state of darkness, and there may be a tendency to reiterate the question "Why? Why? Why?" God is willing to show us why if we are willing to understand and comprehend the answer. But we cannot if our hearts are filled with turmoil and grief, rebelliousness, resentment or self-pity. Heart must be still, and mind tranquil, before the light can shine and understanding come, because there always is an answer, always a reason.

There are reasons for this particular accident. Certain investigations have been going on in order to determine what mechanical failure was involved. I was speaking to the Commander of the Naval Air Station in the Oakland Airport and he had an idea with respect to the cause. Apparently the conditions were just right for icing of the carburetor, which may have been a contributing factor.

It seems that human beings will not move in the direction in which they should go, under the influence of the spirit of God, without being compelled to do so. We find ourselves faced with a certain compulsion. I found myself faced, particularly, with a very vivid compulsion. When Uranda was here with us in person he carried the primary responsibility in relation to the development and expansion of this ministry. I shared that with him. And you know well enough that he had more than he could possibly do. Those of you who were associated with my part in that pattern know that I have had more than I could possibly do. If there was more than two people could possibly do, how much more it is than one person could possibly do! But you share this ministry with me, and we are in position to do it together—which is what Uranda emphasized, over and over.

We all depended a very great deal upon Uranda as a leader, as a friend. Did you ever experience a time when he let you down? No. And do you think that in the situation in which we now find ourselves he is going to let us down? We can trust God. Uranda proved that we could trust him, some of us over long, long periods of time. We came to know him, because we experienced in our own lives the working of the spirit which he revealed and exemplified.

I am speaking particularly concerning Uranda. He was not alone in the outworking of this tragedy, but all of them—Uranda, Kathy, Al, Bill and Sharon—shared in that dedication which Uranda brought to focus. Even the children shared in that same spirit, all of them a part of his ministry. These loved ones have no form in an individual sense through which to manifest on earth any more. Do you think that Uranda's dedication to the purposes of our King is any less now than when he had a form on earth? How, then, is the fulfilment to be known? Through the forms which we provide for the manifestation of the same spirit. It requires a body of many members, dedicated as his individual body was dedicated, even as the body of Jesus was dedicated.

After that tragic outworking in our Master's life, His disciples found themselves in a situation where they were compelled to do something, under great pressure. It was not necessary that they had to be compelled; I do not believe it should have been necessary for us, but that is the way it has proven to be. It is always easier to take the way God first provides, but if there is not that vibrancy of response to the spirit of God which permits the individual to play his part, then the requirement of compulsion arises, not because God wants it that way but because human beings insist upon it. "The works that I do shall ye do also, and greater works than these shall ye do, because I go unto my Father." Human beings have professed to believe on Jesus Christ, century after century, but where are the works of God made manifest? It requires the instrument, a body, by which His spirit can be revealed on earth. No other way will work. Human beings have had plenty of time to prove it, and there is not much time left.

So we can let our hearts and minds be stilled to the point where the possibilities, the potentialities, with respect to this situation begin to come into focus so that we can see in the light. I do not think that Uranda, Kathy, Al, and the children—or those whom we only knew as yet as children—are any less with us in this moment than they ever were. And there is that current of compulsion which can permit the fulfilment of that to which their lives were dedicated while they were with us in person, and are still dedicated while they are only with us in spirit. We have the opportunity of sharing it, not only those here present but responding ones of every nation, kindred, tongue and people.

The funeral service was held on August 8, at 2 p.m., conducted by Bishop Martin Cecil.

We are assembled here on this beautiful Sunday afternoon in the Chapel on Sunrise Ranch to undertake a most holy and sacred task, and to give honor and pay tribute to Bishop Lloyd Arthur Meeker, head of the Church of the Emissaries of Divine Light, and his wife, Kathleen Meeker; also Albert Ackerley, one of the outstanding leaders in this ministry; and the two children, William Van Duzen and Sharon Call.

Our Bishop was a Chaplain of the Civil Air Patrol under the command of Chaplain Maxwell, whom I now ask to provide the opening prayer.

Chaplain Maxwell: "Heavenly Father, grant us the consolation of Thy spirit, that in this time of darkness we may be raised above the shadows of mortality into the light of Thy living presence... We pray Thy blessing upon the ministry that has been accorded through the work of this brother and his companions, and we pray somehow that Thou wouldst speak to us through Thy word, that the blessing that may come to us in this hour shall undergird and direct us. We thank Thee for the ministry of this Chaplain in his work, for his fidelity to the task, for that kind of devotion. As we think of the others who have gone, we pray that their ministry and their lives may serve to remind us of our constant daily duty and concern. Amen."

All sang a hymn that Uranda loved, *This Is My Father's World*. Then Martin used some of Uranda's favorite passages from the Bible, beginning with the 23d Psalm, followed by an excerpt from the 2nd chapter of the Song of Solomon, and concluding with some words of the Master:

"And ye shall be sorrowful, but your sorrow shall be turned into joy.

"A woman when she is in travail hath sorrow, because her hour is come: but as soon as she is delivered of the child, she remembereth no more the anguish, for joy that a man is born into the world.

"And ye now therefore have sorrow: but I will see you again, and your heart shall rejoice, and your joy no man taketh from you." (John 16:20-22)

Rosalind Hooper and Billie Cable, Kathy's sisters, sang *The Lord Is My Shepherd*. Martin continued:

Always when we come to times of parting, there is a sense of loss. To many, there is a seeming finality about what is called death. Is that not because there is such a seeming gulf, a thick veil, between what is called visible here on the surface of the earth in relation to physical things, and a realm here or anywhere which is supposedly invisible? People put so much store by the outer manifestation, the appearance. We recall our Master's words, "Judge not by the appearance," and in relation to this particular tragedy there is an appearance which has caused some to judge and speculate.

The physical body is very important, but it is given meaning by reason of what is revealed through it. There is the tendency to let the physical form blind us to the fact that we have this direct contact with what is invisible. The characteristics that make an individual life worthwhile are invisible until we can see them because of some physical action, some word. Once that true expression of Being is absent from the physical form, the form has no more meaning and there is a need, decently and in order, to return the substance to the realm from whence it came. That is part of our task this afternoon but a very small part, for that which has real meaning in our loved ones is no less a reality now than it was before. Recognizing this, our cause for sadness is merely a personal thing. And perchance there is a certain sadness insofar as they are concerned because they do not have the instrument, the body, by which they could be with us in person. But that should be the extent of our sadness, because the reality is not lost and is as surely present now as it ever was.

Martin spoke of the characteristics of each of them that made their lives so meaningful and beloved: of Kathy's beautiful expression of true womanhood, and true manhood through Uranda. He stressed the qualities of faithfulness and dedication in Albert. Of the children, Bill and Sharon, he noted the "precious evidences of their reality taking form."

He concluded:

We do not give honor and pay tribute to these our loved ones just by sharing an hour such as this. The real tribute is in continuing to reveal that which we saw exemplified in theirs. Let us make sure that their lives are not in vain. This is the true meaning of our service today. We are not really parted from our loved ones; they are here. And do you think they are any less interested in the purposes for which their lives were given when they were here? Human beings have been inclined to cause our Master's life to have been in vain. Let us not make the same mistake again, that neither His life nor the lives of our Bishop and his wife, Al and the children, may have been in vain.

This was followed by a beautiful prayer, the singing of *The Song of Praise*, and a benediction.

The pallbearers, each bearing the ashes of one of the departed ones, led the group as they left the Chapel for the cemetery for interment. The urn for Bishop Meeker was carried by Chaplain Maxwell of the Colorado Wing of Civil Air Patrol; for Kathleen Meeker by George P. Shears; for Albert Ackerley by Edward Miller; for Billy Van Duzen by James Wellemeyer; and for Sharon Call by Oliver Latam.

Beside the little grave prepared to receive the ashes from all five urns, at the top edge of the cemetery just at the foot of the rimrock which crowns the valley, Martin spoke:

We stand here in this beautiful green valley which our Bishop and Kathy, Al, and Billy and Sharon loved so well. We bring the remaining substance, that it may be returned to the elements from whence it came, and become a part of this Sunrise Ranch. Even as that is given the opportunity to share in the second resurrection in forms of life made manifest, so also may the true expression of Being revealed through their bodies while they were here be caused to be resurrected in us in the expression of our lives, that we may share together in letting this which is our Father's world be returned to Him. So we return this substance to the dust from whence it came.

A prayer brought to conclusion a deeply moving service commemorating what could indeed have carried the atmosphere of hopeless tragedy, with hearts deeply wounded and arms empty of such dearly loved forms. This man caused the ache in the sorrowing spirits, including his own, to be bathed in the light of firm resolve to carry on the work begun by our adored Bishop. How quickly he had our love as we resolved to fill the great void suddenly left in his and our world.

Later, there were many expressions of appreciation for the fine service extended by Kibbey's Funeral Home, their loving gestures of consideration going far beyond the "call of duty"; also for the wonderful spirit of cooperation shown by our neighbors and residents of Loveland. Instead of a floral tribute, the Parent-Teachers Association of this district established a scholarship in any of the Colorado colleges for one of the Sunrise Ranch children.

In a service on August 8 on Sunrise Ranch entitled "The Precedent of Victory," Martin reminded us, as he would in all the years of his ministry, that this was a good starting point, on a firm foundation, but that

> it is easy to be uplifted and feel ourselves to be dedicated in an hour of inspiration, but it is the minutes and hours, days and nights, weeks and months, that truly tell the tale, what is revealed in our living consistently. It is that which permits sorrow to be turned into joy.

In "A Message to You From Your Bishop" of August 11, Martin announced to the Church and School the fact of the crash of the aircraft and the consequences. He observed that the funeral service was attended by large numbers of people from near and far, the largest assembly yet gathered in our little valley. After instructions regarding letters, etc., he spoke of the tremendous task before us, giving thanks, during this period of testing, for all, with emphasis on those who shared positions of specific leadership with him, on Sunrise Ranch, at 100 Mile House and in the field. "There is no question in my mind," he concluded, "nor in the minds of any of us, that under the blessings of our Lord and King and in the power of His spirit we shall finish the work which He has given us to do."

In a Board Meeting on Sunrise Ranch on August 13, President William Oshane read a resolution which confirmed and approved the appointment of Martin Cecil as Bishop of the Church of the Emissaries of Divine Light, such appointment having been made by Bishop Meeker in 1947. This had unanimous Board approval.

A payment was made to the bank on the plane insurance money. Oliver reported that the insurance covered medical expenses, also $15,000 on the plane—$225 deductible and $30,000 on the passengers. Six thousand dollars was due on the plane, also a number of outstanding accounts, the Gateway balance amounting to $8,000.

Martin suggested that he, Oliver Latam and Grace Van Duzen be appointed as temporary guardians for the three Meeker children, to act as executors if necessary. He suggested that the house which Richard Thompson had begun to build should be completed for Edna Ackerley, Richard and his family being well established in Vancouver. This was quickly finished and became a home for Edna and her sons, Alan and David.

"The Universal Institute of Ontology" was noted as the official medium to be used by the Church for its educational program. William Oshane proposed that inasmuch as Martin was not a resident of Loveland, whenever present he take his place as Chairman of the Board.

In a service at 100 Mile House on August 22, "Sacred Fulfilment," Martin used a text from Matthew 24: "And the powers of heaven shall be shaken," noting that the power of heaven manifests through those who take responsibility for it, and that it certainly was a time for shaking. He said that he and Uranda had shared an agreement, a line stretched upon the face of the earth, a lifeline, the base of a triangle.

> There is a line now just the same, to him and to the LORD of Lords. There has been no change in that respect, except that it does not manifest on earth. There is a line on earth, the maintenance of which is your responsibility, and of those on Sunrise Ranch, because that line stretches between you and them now. Now it is up to you to hold your end of the line. An open door has been set before you.

In that service Martin announced that Lillian Call would become his wife, and drew attention to the fact that she had "played her part in a pattern of focalization which Uranda had established."

Martin continued to gather the threads of his ministry together, constantly clarifying, and in a service on August 30 he revealed his personal feelings regarding leadership:

> If I consulted my personal preferences I would not assume a position of responsibility, but there is something more important to me than my personal preferences. I know I have a job to do. I am not doing it for you, or for anyone else; I am doing it for my Lord, and Him only. I might say, as Uranda said a time or two with regard to himself, that if there was anyone who came into position to be able to handle the job, I would certainly be delighted to hand it over to him. I do not say that because I want to escape, but as an indication of my personal feelings. But a deeper feeling is so strong that these other things carry no weight.

> We are here together to establish the essential machinery by which the purposes of God may be fulfilled now, and it is God's way only. When Uranda was here, if it was needful that we come into agreement, yet the pattern was set by him, I never questioned it. I did not even consider what I would have done if I had been in his place. I let him do what he would do in his place, and if he presented the picture and I had anything I might add I did so, and we came into agreement. That has been a stumbling block to some, not only in relation to this pattern but out there in the world; and it applies with respect not only to my position but to all positions of focalization. The one who is focalizing the pattern is responsible for it, and it is up to those who are focalized to cooperate, whatever they may think. If you do not come under control, how can any control extend through you to others?

Lillian became Lady Martin Cecil in a civil ceremony in Kamloops on September 3rd.

Present were Michael Cecil and attendants, Conrad and Rosalie O'Brien-ffrench. This fulfilment was a joy to Martin's heart, then and always. Martin and Lillian made their residence at 100 Mile House, Martin's home since 1930. A great deal of their time would be occupied with many trips to Sunrise Ranch, which was also their home, and other centers in the field. Upon their return to Sunrise the Unit gathered in the Inn overlooking the falls at the Gateway property to share in a beautiful celebration of the union of these two beloved ones.

The third year's session of the G.P.C. Servers Training School had been in progress at the time of the airplane crash. The remaining faculty carried on, completing that course, with Martin participating in the final sessions. In a Class on September 22 he said, "I anticipate that we will continue to use the term 'Server,' regardless of what may develop from the standpoint of 'Ontologists.'" The latter term gradually disappeared into the mists. Martin concluded with the reading of "The Server's Code."

In a Class on September 23, "The Basis for Agreement, Eternal Triangle," Martin referred to

> a time, not so long ago, when I personally would have considered it impossible to stand up here and speak to you; but where there is the right centering and we are not controlled by what is impinging upon us from external sources, there is that available from within which provides a pattern of assurance in expressing what is essential. It may not appear the way one thinks it should according to an idea of what sort of impression should be made on others, for instance. The fact is we do not know. The Lord knows, and when one is centered in the Lord, it may not be perfect all at once but it unfolds and brings forth what is true to one's own expression of being, step by step.

In a Board meeting on Sunrise Ranch on September 24 it was learned that a clause in the insurance policy for the airplane had been invoked by the insurance company, stating that a private pilot's license does not permit the owner to do any instrument flying. This particular flight plan recorded visual flight with instrument flight through the overcast; therefore they contended that the policy was rendered legally null and void. However, there was a possibility that the bank loan of $6,500 would be taken care of.

Concern was expressed about a considerable sum owing in outstanding accounts. The $1,000 payment due on the Gateway property was paid on September 24 by Bishop Cecil out of funds from 100 Mile House. The interest on this, amounting to $480 was paid by the Church.

It was noted that William Martens moved to Milwaukee, and his resignation as Trustee and Secretary was accepted by the Board. William Oshane moved that Emery Stofferahn be appointed as Trustee. Appointment of a secretary was tabled.

Mabel Hagedorn with her two children, Lois and Danny, also Eddie and Helen Hoffman and their sons, Jimmy and Jeptha, arrived for permanent residence.

In the concluding Class on the final day of the Servers Training School of 1954 Martin said: "You are Servers. What does the word mean? We might define it in various ways but basically it means just exactly what you as an individual cause it to mean by your own expression of life, that which others find manifest by reason of your presence."

Speaking of "Sacrifice" on October 3 Martin spoke eloquently on the subject of accepting an established pattern of control, likening it to the point of conception where there is one cell, with the subsequent manifestation deriving from that.

> The embryo, to start with does not particularly resemble the human being that shall appear in due season; it does not even resemble the babe at the point of birth. There are obviously controls established in relation to the development of the physical form, the embryo, the fetus, eventually appearing as a babe. The initial appearance is very different from that which is to be. We are under the necessity, always, of utilizing the material that is available at any point of development. You and others who share this ministry are the building material for the form that is needful. I do not complain about it. I know very well that we need more, but we use what is available.

It was reported in a Board meeting on October 8 that a loan from 100 Mile House, requested by Martin, made possible payment of outstanding pressing accounts. He suggested an account be opened for special gifts and allowed to accumulate as a reserve fund for urgent financial obligations, such as installments on the Gateway property. A tenth of the monies for our current account should go into this special account as a tithe. This introduced a vital new element in our financial procedures.

Genie Pierce purchased the house on the hill above the Gateway property for $4,000, paid on a monthly rental basis. Mary Mackenzie of 100 Mile House and Norman Tizzard of Toronto were to be employed as resident members of Sunrise Ranch in the capacities of nurse and gardener. Grace Van Duzen was appointed Secretary of the Board. It was approved that the old rototiller and caterpillar tractor, also two printing presses, be offered for sale.

Mrs. Marjorie Horne, Bishop Meeker's eldest child, had submitted a petition to Mr. McCreery, attorney in Loveland, asking that the court appoint Bishop Martin Cecil as guardian of the three Meeker children—a necessary procedure in the outworking.

A Board meeting on November 12 reported that we accepted an offer of $400 for the salvagable portions of the Cessna airplane. All obligations in the bank had been taken care of, excepting the amount outstanding on the airplane, on the Nash automobile, and

Edna Ackerley's house. Also, $1,800 was paid on the $1,900 note in connection with the trip to Oakland, and funeral expenses. There was a note on the barn siding, $43.50 per month, final payment June 1.

The financial report for October included special gifts from the School of $1,195 toward liquidation of obligations. Checks were issued in October in the amount of $7,765.75.

April 4, 1955, was selected as the opening date for the fourth term of the Servers Training School.

In a service at 100 Mile House on December 6, Martin introduced a program coming to focus under the Universal Institute of Applied Ontology. Uranda had written a paper of introduction and the first in a series under the title, "Thoughts in the Night." Martin took up the challenge, as always, and wrote three more, continuing the series.

In a Board meeting on Sunrise Ranch on December 10, it was suggested that a fire- and moisture-proof vault for storing Uranda's original manuscripts should be constructed. This was accomplished without delay. It was arranged with REA in Fort Collins to have all our electric meters registered in the name of the Church. A previous suggestion by Martin to have the Church incorporated in the state of Colorado was consummated, with a Certificate issued December 3 and Affidavit filed on December 10.

Oliver deposited with Harold Pickler, Manager of the Home State Bank, $3,000 received from Martin to be applied against a note held on the plane if the insurance company did not pay their claim, the money to be held until the matter was cleared. Mr. Pickler, a proven friend through the years, said he would not be charging the 8% interest on the balance of the note.

The financial report for November was as follows:

Student Income	$1,308.78
Servee Income	29.50
Other Income	153.48
Total	$1,491.76

Checks issued for November were in the amount of $1,528.47; Special account, $730.20.

In a service at 100 Mile House on December 26, "Becoming Selfless," after a brief review of the movement of the ministry up to the time of Riverside, Martin observed that Uranda came to 100 Mile House for the first time in the fall of 1947. He regarded that as the initiation point for the cycle in relation to the Unit, which had been developing ever since, with the focus centered in the Log House, where services would be held thereafter. He noted the "distinct difference" between that which was rightly focused on

Sunrise Ranch and what was done at 100 Mile House and emphasized the importance of the latter's opportunity for direct contact with fields of activity which make up the world "out there," through close proximity with the Village.

It was reported in a Sunrise Ranch Board Meeting on January 14, 1955, that the airplane salvage check amounted to $400, received from the Gee Bee Aero Company of San Jose, California. Receipts for December amounted to $5,027.50, which included a loan from 100 Mile House of $3,000.

In a service at 100 Mile House on January 14, 1955, Martin used a text from the third chapter of II Peter:

> "Knowing this first, that there shall come in the last days scoffers, walking after their own lusts,
>
> "And saying, Where is the promise of his coming? for since the fathers fell asleep, all things continue as they were from the beginning of the creation."
>
> The theories of science are based largely in the idea that things had always been operating the same way down through the ages. The theory of evolution, for instance, is based on such an attitude: "All things continue as they were from the beginning of the creation." Human beings do not know how they were at the beginning of the creation, and their calculations and estimates based upon what is now possible of determination in the world as it is are not a sound approach, because man is not the way he was first created. Because the creative processes in relation to this world have been virtually at a standstill since man removed himself from his proper place, mankind's present condition is seen as having always been that way. That is not true. What has been possible to man in his limited state is not comparable to what was possible when he was functioning correctly.
>
> You are here to learn what it means to let God's will be done through you, and the conditions here are ideal for that. Human beings think it should be some other way, less pressure here, a little more independence, some other place. The question is whether we are going to come under control or not. Unless we do, or someone does, how can the spirit of God control in the world? It appears through human beings who accept it, and then God can do something on earth.

In a service at 100 Mile House on January 19 Martin baptized John Valentine O'Brien-ffrench, second son of Conrad and Rosalie. On the 22nd he spoke at the Palliser Hotel in Calgary on "The Initiation of a Cycle."

On January 27 at 100 Mile House Martin shared his deep concern that the affairs of men are moving steadily and rapidly toward a point of climax. Fallen man has a little circle of his own which he tries to operate on earth. It is entirely of his own devising and is based primarily in the spirit of gettingness. When the individual responds to God he brings this circle along with him, and when he begins to be connected up in the circle above he finds it is revolving in a different direction and at a different speed to the one which he has devised. There is a feeling of discomfort, and perhaps the sparks begin to fly. He must stop trying to operate his own circle, let it come to rest and move in the proper direction, connected with the circle above. [He likened the process to wheels within wheels.]

Martin's service, "Leadership and Infallibility," on January 30 at 100 Mile House highlighted the fact that human beings let themselves be cursed much more easily than they let themselves be blessed, because they feel so strongly about things which are a curse, whereas that which would uplift and bless is generally passed by with very little feeling. He also spoke of leadership, using the structure of the atom as an example.

There is a nucleus and there are electrons revolving around the nucleus. In the case of hydrogen, the nucleus is composed of what is called one proton—a positive charge of electricity, if you put it that way; it is more than that—one proton, one electron; and that produces an element we call hydrogen. When we approach the other end of the scale we have uranium with a nucleus composed of 91 protons and 92 electrons, and a state of balance under such circumstances. When they are in a state of balance, all the elements have in their structure the same number of electrons as there are protons in the nucleus. Yet that nucleus is actually one thing. It is often illustrated as though it were a collection of billiard balls, but in fact it is one thing fused together.

The growth with respect to this ministry must be on the basis of the Law. There must be a positive point of centering, a nucleus, which is absolutely stable, unified in its positive point, we could say in God. All humanly produced nuclei will break and fail sooner or later, because only what is centered and has accepted the higher point of leadership can itself provide stable leadership and centering in relation to that which is below it.

Some have supposed that this meant an arbitrary dictatorship of some kind, but it does not. I have to make many decisions, direct the course of affairs day by day. On what basis do I do it? Do I say, "Well, I am inspired by the spirit of God; everything I say goes"? You have not found me taking that attitude. As far as I am concerned, whatever is done will take into account all the factors which I am capable of observing. If in any situation there are factors which I cannot see I will avoid making a decision as long as possible in order to allow them to become apparent. On occasion I am not in position to wait; therefore I make the best possible decision on the basis of the circumstances according to the principles of truth.

Speaking of "Single-mindedness" on February 6 at 100 Mile House, Martin said that most people think their mountainous troubles, problems and sufferings are more important than anything else. They may be important in the sense of being stumbling blocks, but once the individual accepts that which is supremely important his troubles take on their true proportions.

> Individual troubles are very little compared to that which needs to be dealt with in the world, evidences of the absence of what should be there, nothing of themselves except as one makes something of them. We cannot retain our troubles as points of extreme importance and get rid of them at the same time. Accepting the control of the spirit of God as our own, it is done; there's no other way.

20

A YEAR OF CHALLENGE

February 1955 ~ March 1956

The minutes of a Board Meeting on Sunrise Ranch on February 11 reported that two typewriters were available for shipment to Africa—a miraculous and soul-satisfying outworking in those early days. The initial connection with that great continent came about thus, in the words of Timothy Oluwafemi Olagunju:

Away back in 1953 the captain of a ship brought one of Uranda's booklets to Nigeria and dropped it on the ground; maybe he was not interested. And a Nigerian named S. A. Adekolawole picked up the booklet and after reading it wrote to Uranda, who replied. The ministry started, with S. A. Adekolawole the leader. On one beautiful Saturday morning in 1954 I went to the post office in Ilesha and there I met this man Adekolawole holding some booklets of Emissaries of Divine Light and some posters to be pasted on the wall announcing the establishment of this ministry in Ilesha. I stopped and read it and asked him if he could give me one of the booklets to read and he was happy to do so.

I told him I was a school teacher and he said he needed people of my type in the ministry. After going home and reading the booklet I came to tell him I was interested. Then I went back to resign my appointment as a school teacher and joined the ministry as organizing secretary. A lot of people came as I did. At a certain stage Mr. Adekolawole began to introduce something different, and some who could read and write refused to be in agreement with him because they said he was not doing the right thing. We wrote to Lord Martin Cecil and informed him about the rift.

In a service at 100 Mile House on February 13, Martin read a letter received from Nigeria, "the General Secretary as the Head of Nigeria Branch." Six leaders, "Pioneer Pastors," were mentioned, and the amazing fact that they intended building churches in five different cities. Martin utilized the occasion to clarify attitudes toward superstitions in peoples of cultures other than those with which we are familiar.

In a Board Meeting on Sunrise Ranch on March 11, James Wellemeyer was appointed to membership on the Board, consequent upon the resignation of Emery Stofferahn. On March 26 James was ordained a Minister of the church in a service by Martin, who used the text from Revelation with reference to the seven golden candlesticks, saying that all people have the privilege of sharing in ordination, the angel incarnating for a specific purpose. He drew attention to the fact that few yield to the influence and control of the spirit by which they would become aware of that purpose. There must be a willingness to accept the ordination of our own beings, without question as to the results. Then all things can be used to advantage by the angel to accomplish, not necessarily what is hoped for, but what can rightly appear moment by moment through his or her expression.

We come to this solemn and joyous moment, and I would read to you some words of our Master: "Ye have not chosen me, but I have chosen you, and ordained you, that ye should go and bring forth fruit, and that your fruit should remain." This reveals the nature of ordination.

On April 2nd Martin spoke on "Freedom Within Limitation."

There are those who are forever going through cycles of clearing. They go through one clearing, then another, and another; and it will go on forever and the individual will never clear. Why? Because that one is still seeking to be cleared *from* limitations. And the individual never is. Until we learn to be free *in* our limitations we will never become free from them; we will never know how to function correctly in any other way. "And ye shall know the truth, and the truth shall make you free," in your present circumstance. As long as there is the idea that one must have a different state of physical health, or circumstance, in order to function correctly one will never know true freedom. It is dependent upon identification with the spirit of

God, regardless of limitation, physical or otherwise.

There are those who have moved into positions of leadership in our ministry because they were willing to function on the correct basis within the scope of their limitations. This has caused a stumbling block for some because of judgment that the form of leadership should have been what they would call perfect, which it was not.

"And ye shall know the truth, and the truth shall make you free" in your present circumstance. As long as there is the idea that one must have a different circumstance in order to function correctly one will never know true freedom. It is dependent upon identification with the spirit of God, regardless of limitation, physical or otherwise.

The 1955 Class of the Servers Training School opened on April 4, with seventeen students in attendance. That year the "Story of Man" was incorporated into the Class program. Shortly after the airplane crash the previous year, some of those on Sunrise Ranch initiated a weekly gathering to share what anyone might wish to offer, supposedly on new or different subjects, with preparation beforehand. I had been reading the Bible one evening and thought it would be interesting to read the story from beginning to end. It was a fascinating adventure and I presented it (in one hour!) on one of those evenings. Afterward William Oshane said to me, "You should give a class on that," whereupon Martin, within hearing distance, commented that it would be a good idea.

So it was begun, and continued throughout Martin's ministry. Related material from sources other than the Bible was included which added to the color and magic of the story. A beautiful large oil painting by Conrad O'Brien-ffrench occupied the space in the chapel/classroom next to the blackboard. It portrayed the geographical area of the biblical story, created specifically for use in my classes. It added an exciting and artistic dimension of inestimable value. In season there were others in many places qualified to instruct this class, which proved to be a vital and most enjoyable aspect of training over the many years.

Among the attendants of the Class of 1955 was Roy Kuykendall (Kirk) who, with his wife Alice, moved at that time to the Ranch from Loveland. He had experienced miraculous healing following a stroke before coming to Class, and spent many hours on a tractor in the fields. He said it was a good place to meditate. Always alert and conscientious, he delighted in presenting, or accepting, new ideas and ways of getting the job done.

Bill, son of Kirk and Alice, shared much pioneering activity on the Ranch for many years and had an unusual background knowledge of the native people of the area and its land, which he loved. I was intrigued by his account of the name the Indians had given to what is called "Horsetooth Mountain," within view of the Ranch. Their interpretation had to do with the wounded heart of a warrior. Seen from the angle where the appellation "horsetooth" applies, it does look like a heart that has been pierced.

Of special interest to me was Bill's comment that the blood from the heart ran out and covered the earth round about. That reference to red is contained in the story of the Exodus when the rivers "turned to blood," a phenomenon explained by Dr. Velikovsky in his work as an aspect of a great cataclysm, the result of near collision with the planet Venus. Since that event was worldwide, it was thrilling to find what to me is evidence of its effects in this valley. There are many evidences of the past here, an abundance of ancient flint arrowheads, etc., and a few years ago the unearthing of the remains of a creature whose name ends in "saurus," one of the monsters that roamed the earth in an era preceding ten thousand years ago—and this a few miles from Sunrise Ranch, up Masonville way.

Conrad and Rosalie O'Brien-ffrench, moving toward a separation, were members of that 1955 Class, after which Conrad made his home in Vancouver for a number of years. Eventually Fairholme was sold to the Canadian government to be incorporated in the Banff National Park. From Vancouver, Conrad moved to Sunrise Ranch where he built a uniquely beautiful home on Green Ridge, one of the foothills of the Rocky Mountains just behind Sunrise Ranch and part of its property. Dearly loved by his family there and countless visiting friends from all over the world, he found home and spent his many remaining productive years overlooking the wondrous beauty of Colorado and communing with the birds and squirrels, chipmunks and any other visitors that happened along in his spot on the "mountain."

A Board Meeting on April 8 reported the moving of two small cabins from the Gateway property to Sunrise Ranch; that the Church had purchased 180 acre-feet of irrigation water; and that the lawyers had been given authority to proceed against the insurance company for settlement of the hull damage on the aircraft.

The group was gathered by the Little Chapel on the hill just before Easter morning's annual sunrise service on April 10. Martin spoke in the dawn's stillness.

> As we stand here, has the battle passed from our valley? Is it out beyond? Have the dry bones come together, bone to its bone, and the flesh and the sinews come up upon them, so that there is the evidence of that which may reveal the glory of life? Has the decision been made, so that insofar as we are concerned it may be said, "It is finished"—and we are ready for the rising of the Son?

On April 13, in "The Function of Focalization," Martin said that our Master provided the point of focalization of deity on earth, and that what is provided and needs to come into manifestation on Sunrise Ranch is a focalization in relation to the whole ministry. He said,

If one cannot function correctly at Center he cannot function correctly anywhere else. If he can function correctly at Center he can move to any position, anywhere, and continue to function correctly.

He then spoke of a suggestion for a form of ministry made by Uranda as a basis for letting these principles have application. The individual would privately set up some empty chairs and in the current of the spirit express to those who were symbolically occupying them, in the recognition that in season, as the spirit was allowed to control, those chairs would be occupied. This practice was carried out by several, an outstanding example being Bill Bahan, a prominent and successful chiropractor in Epping, New Hampshire, who recognized the magic in Uranda's words. In the process of initiating the change from a chiropractic to attunement center, he established his service seemingly alone in the outer sense, and eventually, after an entire year, first one, then another and another, were irresistibly drawn to fill the "empty" chairs with the physical substance necessary to build a body for the Lord's use on earth. Bill provided a most needed and deeply appreciated right-hand man in the field for Martin.

Along with some other chiropractors who were drawn to the Servers Training School, Bill had previously resonated with a strong note of reality sounding through B. J. Palmer, head of the Palmer School of Chiropractic in Davenport, Iowa, and son of its founder, Daniel David Palmer. This man integrated the spiritual component in his teachings and emphasized the spirit in each one as the source of all healing. The word *innate* became the by-word of his school. It was the influence of George Shears, related by marriage to the Bahan family, that caused Bill and his brothers to become chiropractors. Walter, the youngest, and also their sister Shirley, with Bill became powerful and stalwart members of the Emissaries of Divine Light. Some years after the death of George's wife, "Pa" Bahan's sister, he married Naomi Wellemeyer, widowed mother of three children, two of whom were James and Betty.

A Board Meeting on Sunrise Ranch on May 13 recorded Bob Palmer's observation that the house on the hill at Gateway purchased by Genie Pierce was situated partly on our property and that the deeds would be altered to correct this.

Through the years the young people on Sunrise Ranch participated in the 4-H Club, acquiring valuable experience in the field of animal care and training, cooperation with their peers and focalizers, and in many other ways. They loved it. The four H's represent head, hands, heart and health—mental activity, physical doing, emotional experiences, and the well-being of the whole. It was rewarding, and fun, to share the joy of a youngster or teenager when their pig, calf, goat or whatever gained a pound or two. It also included other areas, involving skill in cooking, sewing and operating machinery, etc.

In a service on May 22, "The Light of the World," Martin said:

> Our program is a very small pattern of ministry amongst hundreds of thousands of others—some large in the outer sense—and we are reminded of the statement in the Book of Revelation in relation to the woman who was given the two wings of a great eagle that she might fly to her place in the wilderness, and the serpent sent forth a great flood from his mouth in order to carry her away. We have evidence of that great flood, a plethora of ideas, concepts, teachings, philosophies, churches and denominations, religions of all kinds—everything under the sun.
>
> It is obvious that if there is to be that which will do the job it must be incapable of being broken. The fact that we run into pressures along the way—judgments and condemnations seeking to destroy—permits the development of a little strength, courage, that in the days to come we may be in position to stand, no matter what comes. We do not blend with anything else; we do not even touch the forbidden fruit. We *know* the truth. Human beings are inclined to flirt with the devil—just listen a little and wonder a little, and it begins to seem reasonable. "Perhaps it is right"—and soon the individual is knowing the devil, having union with the devil, and the results appear. That is what breaks the pattern. It is only when we know the truth, the whole truth, and nothing but the truth, every day, all day long, that we begin to have the essential embryonic formation of a candlestick upon which the light may be set. And that light cannot be hid.
>
> We do not need to try to persuade people to recognize it, or go out and pound it into them. Once there is a candlestick there is a light, and those who respond come to the light—and there is the basis for expansion. When we decide that all our knowing is going to be of the truth, there is nothing that can break the pattern thereby established. It is a manifestation of the rock, the stone, which the builders rejected, but which becomes the head of the corner. It cannot be broken externally, no matter what anyone does; it can only be broken from within. When we know the truth it cannot be broken—we cannot be broken—and we provide a candlestick upon which the light of our Lord and King may be placed once more on earth.

In Martin's service on May 28, "The Responsibilities of Ministry," Martin pointed to the futility of having four hours of class in the morning and then four hours of class in the afternoon, thus reducing the term to three months, with the idea that it would be the same as having four hours of class every morning for six months.

It would be completely inadequate and to a high degree a waste of time, because the four hours in the afternoon—and in fact the rest of the twenty hours—are essential for allowing the practical application of those principles being learned. How quickly the results appear when our supreme concern is to make right use of the opportunities that are with us day by day. The way opens so easily and there begins to be something that can be seen of men.

Martin and Lillian left on June 4th for a two months' stay at 100 Mile House, accompanied by the three children, Nancy, Lloyd and Helen Meeker, also Mary Mackenzie and Alan Ackerley.

On June 26 Martin spoke of "The Nature of Loyalty," and said:

We are few in number, and if we are called to provide a centering through which the world body of humanity—not all at once, immediately, but company upon company—may be lifted up into the state of being what they ought to be in the design established by God, then there is going to be a down-drag upon us. We are going to feel a weight that need not be a burden if we function correctly. I have seen a load just dropped, dumped on others, without regard to anyone. Perhaps the individual just does not show up. Of course if no one showed up to perform the necessary tasks we would not have a program at all. And, you know, the external manifestation of this Unit is not indestructible. The divine pattern is indestructible, for which we thank God, but the external manifestation is not. That remains in form as there are those who are sharing wholeheartedly in the program, and we have marvelous opportunities of training in learning how to accept responsibility.

On July 28 Martin clarified a vital aspect of our purpose in a discourse entitled "Serving the Multitudes." He quoted from the 5th chapter of Matthew: "And seeing the multitudes, he went up into a mountain: and when he was set, his disciples came unto him." He spoke of the

very rapid expansion of that which is of the world pattern. Unless our expansion keeps pace with it, the opportunities we have here will be lost. If the control manifest with respect to this environmental pattern continues on the proper basis in relation to the overall pattern, we have in miniature exactly that which is needful with respect to the world. If we lose this opportunity, I wonder where we could find another comparable to it.

If, looking back, you see the care with which the Lord prepared all things by which this opportunity might be made available, it is a wonderful thing! Do you think that, anywhere along the line, He is going to say, "Well, that is about as far as I can go"? No. But as we move forward to higher levels we must conform with the laws and principles of being if the unfolding cycle is to be carried to the point of completion where it may truly be said that we have finished the work we have been given to do.

If the provision does not appear, if our disciples do not come unto us, why is it? It is because we have not been brought up into an high mountain apart, not out of the world but apart from the controlling influences of the world, so that we might get set and allow our environment to be filled with that which comes from God, and then the power of God works. The Lord's provision is boundless, and all will come into place, filling the need, permitting the greater opportunity, the enlarged range of service. But it comes in God's way and if we refuse to walk in His way, there must be failure. Yielding to the vibrant, moving spirit of our King, we may share with Him the reality of victory.

On the 4th day of August, a year after the airplane crash, Martin entitled a service given at 100 Mile House, "A Year of Challenge."

A year ago today we were faced with a challenge. Meeting a challenge in the spirit of God permits a release of power and permits growth and progress in the cycles of maturing. Unless we are willing to meet such challenges as arise, our supposed dedication in the service of the Lord means nothing. I cannot feel badly or ill treated because I have voluntarily made a choice to serve God. That is my choice and I accept the responsibility for it. And if I frequently find myself doing the things that I probably would not do other-wise, and not doing what I perhaps would do otherwise, that is still my choice, and I cannot blame God or anyone else for it. That should rightly be the atti-tude of all who have dedicated their lives to God: "We have done it, and that is that." Because we have made that choice there is a compulsion which we ac-cept, and which on no account will we violate.

Martin emphasized the importance of the function of the two Units and his respon-sibility of moving from one to the other.

The two units properly should provide two points upon which to stand by means of which there may be accomplishment in the world beyond them-selves. Today is a day of challenge as surely as this day one year ago.

At this point you should be so identified with being, regardless of the necessities of the becoming processes still working out in you that when I come it is not to straighten out personal problems, to clear vibrational tur-moils and confusions in the Unit, but to bring inspiration and encouragement and assistance in the actual field of achieving; for you are here to achieve something, as surely as I am in my place to achieve something.

Martin's service, "Blessing the Multitudes," on August 14 continued a theme begun a few weeks earlier.

> How can you tell what the elements in your environment should be, through which your particular expression of ministry can manifest? Accept that which comes as your means of contact with the multitudes, with which you have to work. "His disciples came unto him." Insofar as I am concerned, you are the material with which I must work. I am not objecting to it, but that is the fact of the matter. I cannot pick and choose, nor do I wish to.

> Our Master never rejected anyone. The world rejected him, but he never rejected anyone. Let us not reject what naturally comes to us. God provides that which is needful, right and proper, for filling the environmental needs. Seeing the multitudes, we would serve them, but only in God's way.

It was reported in a Board Meeting on Sunrise Ranch on August 19 that in the six-month period ending June 30 debts had been reduced by approximately $2,500. We had filed a lawsuit in California within one year of the date of the accident, as advised, in the amount of $275,000, supposed to come up about six months later. It was agreed to pay $700 in monthly payments of $75 to Charles and Maude Strikwerda, in repayment of claims that they had lent said amount to Uranda or the Church.

Martin made it possible to pay off the $3,000, plus $296.88 interest, owing to the bank on the balance of the plane, the bank retaining the note in the event it would be needed later at the court case. William Oshane thanked Martin, as was his wont in all such instances, for his unbounded generosity.

Total irrigation water used up to August 19 was 113 1/2 acre-feet. This left 66 1/2 acre-feet to be used, paid for.

The Weld County Farmers Protection Association Insurance Policy was renewed to cover $2,000 on the barn, $1,500 on household and personal effects anywhere on the Ranch, and $1,000 on shop tools and equipment. Oliver had added $1,000 on farm machinery and $500 on hay or grain in stacks. The premium was $10 a $1,000 for five years, so our $6,000 worth of protection cost us $60 for five years.

In a talk entitled "Out of Prison" on September 4, Martin emphasized the point that one can be subject to a "good" concept as surely as any other, and referred to the attention given to changing a nutritional pattern, with the caution that while dietary factors are certainly important they should not allow an inflexible attitude to enter in. Balance was the theme of his address.

In a Board Meeting on Sunrise Ranch on September 9, it was decided to put in our own water line at the Gateway property, rather than sharing one with Genie Pierce.

For several years after Uranda's departure the attendance at Classes dropped appreciably but soon regained, and exceeded, the numbers in the first three classes.

It was about that time that Martin wrote a booklet, *An Open Door,* to be used as introductory literature. This proved to be a very effective tool, the perfect size for tucking into purse or pocket—an important detail, as we were to discover.

Martin, Lillian and I left Sunrise Ranch on October 5th for a three-week tour of service in various places, primarily in Canada. At Toronto we were met by Jim Pogue, who with his wife Mary served for many years and focalized a group there. In addition to conducting his work in Court, he participated in the Attunement office. Hugh (Mac) and Jane Duff were primary figures in those beginning days, and still in the Unit at 100 Mile House. I recall memories of a weiner roast at their farm property, a very large bonfire and the stars shining in the early evening. Music was provided by Bill Martin and his accordion, assisted by Percy Briggs with a peculiar self-constructed instrument consisting of an extended cigar box and one string, which he played with a violin bow—not bad! Singing accompanied all this.

The next stop was Montreal, where we spent Thanksgiving Day, with about forty people attending a public service the following evening. Phyllis Carter and Allan Egleston were most helpful in that location for a number of years, with Phyllis later spending some time at the Hundred. After a return to Toronto and a public service there, the party continued to Chatham, where services were held in the attunement office. Don and Elaine Hodges focalized the group at that time. Also, we had a lovely visit with Ray and June Lloyd in their home. Martin and Lillian then took a side trip to Milwaukee where they had an opportunity to touch in with Lillian's family, before returning home.

In a Board Meeting at Sunrise Ranch on October 14 it was reported that Martin and Bob Palmer had made an agreement with respect to the boundary lines between the properties at Gateway. The Universal Institute of Applied Ontology was incorporated in Colorado on October 6. William Oshane announced that he had taken a position in Denver and wished to have a leave of absence from the Board. David Groves reported a harvest of approximately 400 lbs. of honey from the bees that year.

In a service on October 18, "The Spirit of God Is One Spirit," Martin said:

> You cannot receive the kingdom from God for yourself. The only way you can receive it is to offer it to others. The blessings you have received have been through others. The blessings that others receive should be through us. What we allow to be given through us we have, while it is moving through us. We do

not have it to hold on to. This was portrayed by the story of the Children of Israel when they were fed in the wilderness by manna and were instructed to gather it each day and not save it. Also, we pray, "Give us this day our daily bread." There is the provision in the moment; we cannot store it up for future use. That which is of the spirit of God is constantly flowing, constantly moving.

Another vital point was emphasized:

Some who contact this ministry take the attitude that what is presented may be all right but so-and-so does not live it, and he is supposed to represent the ministry. That may seem to be a good excuse for not paying attention to the truth oneself and living it, but we cannot rightly deny the truth because someone else does not live it. If something is true, then surely we should acknowledge it, regardless of what anyone else does, and allow it to find expression through ourselves. Actually, no one else can prevent you, no one but yourself.

Martin dealt with a core issue in his service "The Right of Free Choice," on October 30:

Insofar as our ministry is concerned, it is impossible to join it. We have a name, we are legally incorporated; but you know very well that whether that is there or not makes no difference insofar as the reality of our ministry is concerned. We cannot rightly go out into the world and say, "Come now, you should join our church." "Many are called, but few are chosen." God has called all people, but few of the human race are chosen, because so few are willing to surrender their right of free choice. What is it that properly gives identity to our ministry? Not because it is incorporated and has a name. No. It is because of the Spirit which, when it is allowed to express, permits the formation to appear.

That evening he spoke again of leadership. After sharing the incident in his Navy days when he was commissioned to drive the captain's car when he had never driven before, he emphasized the need to be versatile if one is to experience true leadership.

While it may be wise to indicate a lack of experience in a situation, there should at the same time be the attitude of willingness to do what is required.

Are you afraid to do things that you have never done before?

On Sunrise Ranch in a service on November 2nd, "In the Spirit of the Living Christ," Martin told the assembled group that since he had come in August there had been progress, with much accomplished.

The greatest opportunity for progress is when I am not here. We have spoken of holding the line, which has perhaps tended to establish an idea that when you are on your own the best that can be expected is to dig your toes in and not lose ground. There may be occasions when that is about all we can do for the moment, but those should be exceptional. You can move forward. You can achieve that which is properly within the scope of your sphere of responsibility regardless of whether I am here or somewhere else. This is vital, so that it is not a matter of your feeling that all that is necessary is just to keep things turning over until I come again.

"Giving the Kingdom" entitled Martin's service on November 10, in which he again commended the group and spoke of the increase of response noted in the cities visited on his recent tour, naming Toronto, Montreal and Chatham. He had been deeply touched by the hunger in human hearts for the truth.

> That is why there is so much success in the evangelistic field today. And yet, what is being accomplished? Hundreds of thousands of hungry and thirsty ones are being offered—what? Is it fresh and new, vibrant and spontaneous? Or is it the same old hash warmed over and served up again? If it has not satisfied hitherto, why is it going to be more successful today? Perhaps some may find what is being offered in those fields to be a stepping-stone along the way. But usually people are channelled back into the same old patterns, offered through churches and otherwise for centuries. Obviously something more is needed.

> Our Master said, "Fear not little flock, for it is your Father's good pleasure to give you the kingdom." We have recognized that the kingdom indicates divine control and dominion, divine government, and the correct design with respect to the living of life. Human beings think they can manipulate the external things, get them into shape, and when everything is just right, everything is set in their environment, that will produce a more heavenly state within. Of course it does not work that way because the external manifestation, the earth, is the result of the heaven and not the cause of the heaven.

Minutes of a Board Meeting on Sunrise Ranch on December 9 revealed that application had been made as a charitable organization for tax exemption from the Department of Internal Revenue.

A delightful and greatly appreciated custom had been initiated, and continued for many years, of giving our delicious home-made bread as Christmas gifts to our business associates in Loveland.

In a service on December 18, "Your Brother's Keeper," Martin spoke of "the tragedy which took place in the vicinity of Sunrise Ranch last Thursday, a car accident in which Eddie Hoffman and his little boy Jepthah were killed. Helen, his wife, is in the Loveland Hospital in critical condition, with a fractured skull and also a broken leg." Their other small son,

James, was not in the car. After much repair work, which included extensive dental surgery, Helen survived, to spend many productive years on Sunrise Ranch with Jimmy.

At the close of that year a project was undertaken at the Log Chapel at 100 Mile House to remove as much as possible of the office material (for the most part literature of the Third Sacred School) into another building, to make space for the increasing numbers attending services. Built of massive logs, about 20 by 30 feet in size, it was used in earlier years as office and sleeping quarters for John Oshanek. No longer needed in that capacity and not fitting as a storage place for literature, it would henceforth be used solely as a Chapel.

On January 2, 1956 Martin ordained John Oshanek a Minister of the Emissaries of Divine Light. The decision had been made to accept his prayerfully considered offer to go to Nigeria and minister to those people, incessant in their pleas for leadership and eager to be trained in the way of service to the Lord.

The Chapel was filled with an atmosphere of deep feelings of love for this man as Martin spoke. He referred to the words of Jesus which describe His body as a vine, with emphasis on love as that which binds it together. Then, with John kneeling before the altar, he ordained him, and read the "Certificate of Appointment" which John would take with him, as the "official representative of the Church sent to the American Church of Divine Light Mission in Nigeria." He was authorized to assume the position of Super-intendent of the Mission,

> providing such spiritual instruction and assistance to the members as will permit them to live practical, useful and honorable lives as valuable citizens of Nigeria. God bless you, John. The spirit of benediction that is extended through all your fellow members of the true vine on earth rests upon you.

John's sojourn in Nigeria was very brief, terminated in an illness contracted in that faraway land. He died on February 10th. A year later, speaking of it in a service in Vancouver, Martin said:

> His ministry was cut rather short but it has borne much fruit. The comment was made by one who worked closely with him over there [Timo]: "He spent twenty-eight days in Nigeria and did twenty-eight years' work. He was equal to ten people, a hard worker, peacemaker, a wing of healing. We are proud that he had finished the work he had been sent to do on earth."

> Some of our brothers and sisters in that country have been associated with this ministry for many years, and since John was there their understanding has increased. Their zeal, their enthusiasm has grown. Recently there were 1,762 present at a conference in one of their cities. They have been waiting

patiently for someone else to come, but thus far we have not been in position to send anyone. I have done what I could through personal letters, and they receive our mailings, which keeps the pattern moving in the right direction. I suggested it might be possible for them to send some representatives to our Class on Sunrise Ranch this March and they offered to send two of their number. One of them is the Pioneer Pastor and the other has been the Secretary, both members of their Board of Authority. These two anticipate attending the 1957 Training Class.

They added that after they have completed the school term they may serve in Nigeria or anywhere else on earth—wherever the need might be. All the way through I have found a remarkable openness of response, a willingness to give of themselves freely to the service of the Lord; all the more remarkable because they do not have a broad understanding of what we teach. But they have touched the spirit of what we offer, and that is good enough for them. No matter how much we may study, no matter how much we think we know, it is all of little value if there is not at the same time that deep feeling response which touches something above and beyond what may immediately be perceived with the mind.

Later Timothy Olagunju, speaking of John, said:

When John Peter Oshanek came to Nigeria I was made his secretary. We ate together, slept together, and when he spoke I translated. And then, suddenly, he had died, and Lord Martin Cecil wrote to the Board of Authority of the ministry in Nigeria to send two people to the U.S.A. to attend the Class on Sunrise Ranch. The Board picked Adex and me to attend Class in 1957 and we were both ordained as ministers. We have been able to establish seven groups in Nigeria.

At 100 Mile House on January 8, 1956, in his service, "Healing and Restoration," Martin answered the question which has shadowed the hearts of men and women through the ages as to why mankind is in its miserable state.

God certainly did not create man to experience the woes that are presently his common lot, and anyone who imagines that so much misery and suffering, disease, conflict, hell on earth, is God's will has very little understanding of the meaning of God's love. These things are not God's will but evidence of the fact that His will is not being done. This state of human experience has been present in the world so long that it is thought to be a natural condition, part of the so-called evolutionary process by which man reaches some exalted state over a period of millions of years.

Man provides God with the capacities for the divine expression on earth. If men and women do not offer those capacities to God, He cannot use them, because mankind was created in the image and likeness of God and consequently has the right of free choice. And when man chooses to give himself to God so that God may make use of his capacities, the divine expression appears and God is revealed on earth. It is not just a matter of what you are doing with your conscious mind. There are many patterns throughout every level of human consciousness, subconscious, heart, all hooked up, and it is necessary for a reconditioning process so that these things may be replaced by the true design in mind and heart.

In his service at 100 Mile House on January 15, "Maturity," Martin touched on the nature of the subconscious mind in the sense of subjection to some destructive feeling moving through a crowd, for instance fear in the presence of a fire in a theater.

If there is one person there who will allow an adequate expression of the spirit of God to appear so that there can be a stable point established, and there is quick action by that individual so that attention is moved from this mass feeling and a centering begin to be there, the situation can be changed and brought under control. The same principles operate in relation to the environmental factors around the individual at any time. But it must be a consistent thing.

On March 17 on Sunrise Ranch in a service, "Thine Is the Power," a beautiful tribute was paid by Martin to Lillian and me:

I thank God for that response which I have received from you and others, and for the privilege of ministry granted to me thereby; but, in actual fact, if it had not been for two who serve closely with me I doubt very much if we would still have one. Those two are, firstly, my wife Lillian, who has stood at my side with me and served so faithfully, playing her part and giving herself freely, fully. I thank God for her, and so should you. The other one is my secretary Gracie. She has been doing her job, holding the line with Lillian and myself. But for these two we would likely have very little ministry. I feel at times there has been a lack of recognition or appreciation of that which they have done. I know something of the weight of responsibility, a vibrational weight, that has rested upon them.

If there is failure to fully realize what has been accomplished by reason of their ministry with me, that tends to prevent a proper harmonization in the formation which is in the process of developing as an instrument in the hands of the Lord. I would that all of you might recognize that here we have the manifestation of a little stone cut out without hands, not arbitrarily established by any human being. It is a reality because there has been a willingness on the part of each one to accept the particular responsibilities which are individually required.

March 21 on Sunrise Ranch Martin spoke of "Unit Potentialities and Responsibilities":

We have an embryonic form, and we need to recognize the needs of that form so that we function in proper relation to them. Each of us is required to function in patterns which are not truly natural to us. Some have been inclined to feel that in order to find themselves and their own fulfilment they must move into some pattern which allows the inherent qualities that should be developed to find expression. We are here to contribute what is necessary to the needs of the developing embryonic formation and not primarily to find some sort of satisfactory state for ourselves. That satisfactory state is only possible when the formation comes to the point of adequate maturity.

I read a little story this morning, supposedly about Abraham when he was a boy in his father's house. His father had a great many idols and one day when his father was out of the house Abraham undertook to smash all the idols except one. He put the club which he had used in the hands of the one remaining idol. When his father came in he was horrified, and Abraham said, "This idol with the club did it." His father said, "How on earth could that be? He is just made of stone. He could not do anything." Abraham said, "If the idol cannot do anything, why are we worshiping it?" Let us remember that all power belongs to our King, and have no other gods before Him.

Can we allow the garden of God to manifest as it should in Eden Valley? Is it an embryonic manifestation of the garden of God or merely a miniature of something we can find anywhere in the world? We have to let go of the idols, let go to God, and then we have to let that which is of God appear.

21

PRIVILEGES AND RESPONSIBILITIES

March 1956 ~ January 1958

O n March 23 Martin spoke to the men on Sunrise Ranch, seeking to further ensure a firm foundation for the Class, bringing out the fact that there had never been a perfectly clear pattern regarding the acceptance of the man in position of focalization.

> Certainly the ones in positions of leadership have not been perfect. If we had to wait for someone to be perfect before we could appoint him to that position what would we do? We might as well quit right now. The one in that position has to grow, but by the same token those who are being focalized have to grow too in order to learn how to follow, to learn how to let themselves be coordinated. We must all work together in this.

Easter was on April 1st that year and in the evening Martin clarified many points relating to age-old concepts of sin. He quoted a story about President Coolidge, a man of few words, who came home from church one Sunday and his wife asked him what the sermon was about. He answered, "Sin," and she said, "Well, what did the preacher say?" The President replied, "He was against it." Martin said:

> Let us not imagine that because something is classified as being good,

therefore it is not sinful. It is the nature of the control in the individual life that tells the tale as to whether that which is expressed is right or wrong. It is not the classifications of good and evil which human beings place upon things which determine the answer.

On April 11 Martin undertook to consider the name "Emissaries of Divine Light." He said:

> We have what might be called a motto, some words our Master spoke: "Let your light so shine before men, that they may see your good works, and glorify your Father which is in heaven." He also said, "Ye are the light of the world." We would that every human being on earth would realize that he or she is rightly an Emissary of Divine Light simply because he or she belongs to God. I am not suggesting that all human beings must belong to this particular organization but nevertheless all should be emissaries of divine light; for human beings were created in the image and likeness of God that they might be light-bearers on earth, angels of light in the world. Let us remember who we are and to whom we belong, that we may ever be true to our calling, letting our light so shine before men that they may see our good works and glorify the Father in heaven by letting their lights shine.

It was reported in a Board Meeting on April 13 that Bert Gray, a resident near Gateway, had built a new house and was considering selling the old one to us for a reasonable price if we moved it off the premises. This was done in season and, with alterations and additions, provided a home in the center of Sunrise Ranch for many years for Jim Wellemeyer and his family. Later it was the home of Donna Bahan.

Martin presided at a Men's Meeting on Sunrise Ranch on April 16 and informed the men that Oliver Latam, who had been functioning as Ranch Manager, was going on a trip to Toronto and asked to be relieved of his duties as focalizer. He and his wife Millie, Edna Ackerley's sister, had filled vital positions in the operation of Sunrise Ranch for three years. Oliver brought his experience in the field of accounting—and whatever else was needed—and Millie provided a much needed focus in the functions of the office.

Martin said:

> At our men's meeting less than a month ago I suggested that each one, after careful consideration, write on a slip of paper the names of their first and second choices to fill this place. It was an interesting experiment. In the meantime I have come to a decision. I was pleased that there were those willing to offer themselves, one of whom I have chosen, namely Kirk (Roy) Kuykendall. He was not sure whether his own affairs would permit him to do

it, and there may have been a few doubts in relation to filling the position—
which I'm sure would be true of anyone. Kirk will be taking over while Oliver
is still here, as there are many things he will no doubt wish to learn about his
responsibilities.

It might be said we function here under certain handicaps, which I see,
rather, as challenges. In the world pattern if you need someone to do a certain
job you go out and find a man who is proficient in that and you hire him, and
you say, "Do this." And if he does not do it you probably fire him and hire
somebody else. In many fields of our function here we do not have particular
backgrounds of knowledge or experience. But it seems to me that in virtually
anything one undertakes with that rather rare commodity "common sense" it
does not take long to determine the right course of action. And one can use
one's intelligence to glean information from others who know.

Those words were truly spoken from personal experience. The circumstance upon
Martin's assuming the responsibility of the property at 100 Mile House required that he
function in areas with which he had previously no remote proximity. Rather than complaining, "I don't know anything about this sort of thing" and looking around for a non-
existent helper, he proceeded to take such action as was available. And he made it be
available. Researching the sources of such information and training as was required of
him, he gradually acquired a library of books on "how to do" just about everything. I
marveled once, when I came upon some books in Martin's office on how to install and
repair plumbing, of how one could possibly be self-taught in that way. It looked like a
complicated maze to me. But he learned—and not just plumbing—and constructed the
Lodge in that way, a beautiful building still standing, which he called "a monument to
my inexperience." But it stands, solid and sure, a symbol of what was built in every realm
because of his steadfast, meticulous spirit which allowed the design of the Lord to appear in the substance available.

Martin continued:

The one who occupies the position of focalization in this pattern does not
thereby become superior to anyone else, but there must be a recognition of
his position if there is to be coordinated function. Kirk will require your backing
and cooperation, as does any other in a similar circumstance. Oliver has done
an excellent job, and while he may give a sigh of relief when Kirk moves into
that position I trust he has not found it too onerous a task.

He suggested that it would be helpful for the men to meet and share a devotional
period whenever possible, allowing the daily activities to be imbued with the atmo-

sphere of the purpose for which they were there.

Kirk expressed heartfelt appreciation for the new opportunity, followed by Oliver whose words revealed his ongoing steadfast spirit in service to the Lord. Martin thanked God for the dedication manifest in both these men.

Wesley and Dorothy Jones moved to Sunrise Ranch the beginning of May. They brought their furniture and made their abode in several places, one of which was Martin and Lillian's home in their absence, where they took care of the children, as well as the house. Following that, they occupied a house at the Gateway property. Inside and out, over a period of years, there was much cleaning, repairing and painting required. The addition of a bathroom was by no means a minor item, and all was achieved with the high degree of exceptional decorating genius of those two, a truly beautiful home. Gigi, their little dachshund that had shared the journey from Canada, had its own little house.

Dorothy had worked in the florist business, and our flower arrangements hence-forth were unexcelled. Wesley, a fine organist, brought his electric Hammond organ with him and provided exquisite music in Eden Valley for services, the choir under Lillian's direction, and occasions of all kinds. I loved presenting plays with the children, also adults, and Wesley simply needed to be at the organ during dress rehearsal to do an amazing job of providing the perfect accompaniment at the final performance!

The organ had a particular history, purchased in 1953 by Wesley when he was living next door to the ministry's service center in Chatham, Ontario, with its first tape re-corder which operated on a 60-cycle alternating current. Chatham, however, was still using the 25-cycle frequency, so Wes's organ was called upon to furnish the needed gen-erator. This was just prior to Uranda's visit in 1954—hence Wes's introduction to Uranda!

A Board Meeting on Sunrise Ranch on May 2nd dealt with various matters, one of which was whether we should lease the Inn on the Gateway property. After hearing from the members, Martin said it was evident that the long-range view revealed its purpose to be for the expansion of the ministry. There was unanimous agreement that it not be leased outside of the ministry. Martin reported the need for another IBM Executive typewriter and other office machines: a cutting machine, folding machine, etc., and ex-pressed appreciation for the recent move of Claudia Romanick to Sunrise, a capable and efficient office worker. Her marriage later to Ted Black enhanced the vital contributions of both of them. The resignation of William Oshane as President of the Board of Trust-ees of the Church was read and accepted, and James Wellemeyer was voted the new President. Richard Cable was declared a Trustee of the Board.

In a Class on May 9 Martin utilized some passages from an article in *Chamber's Journal* (June 1954) which related to the wonders of radionic photography consequent upon experiments in the Delawarr Laboratories, Oxford:

"These scientific discoveries demonstrate where true science and religion meet; where complete harmony is reached with the designs of the creator, the will of God. These scientific laws and forces divorced from the will and mind and purpose of the creator—that is, science divorced from religion—are a body without a soul. In view of the epoch-making discoveries it might seem to the materialist that physical science alone applied in medicine could eliminate disease, but the spiritual element in man enters into all forms of healing whether he is aware of it or not, and as an essential component."

The patterns which they are finding it possible to photograph in this way relate to what we call the underside of the pneumaplasmic body as it relates to the particular manifestation under consideration. It does not penetrate through to the design as God established it. It reveals a design as it is taking shape next to, and will be reproduced in, physical substance. [Martin emphasized that the design as it first came from God was perfect but by the time it reaches the level where it may begin to take form in physical substance, it has in various ways been distorted. The attention then is entangled in the distortions, disease, the ill condition, and there is the effort to try to correct it.] In giving attunements if we are primarily interested in what is wrong we will fail. The starting point must be in what is right, so that the true design may begin to move through the pneumaplasmic body all the way to the physical.

We are not wrestling with flesh and blood, as Paul put it. We are dealing with the invisible factors present in the realm of pneumaplasm. God has provided the perfect design, and it is the clearing of the patterns in the pneumaplasmic substance that makes possible the perfect reproduction of the divine design. When human beings cease being controlled by external things and reactions to them, a condition may begin to be established in the pneumaplasmic body which will allow the perfect design to reach all the way through. The radionic instrument which man is, is the means by which God makes the corrections, and only as man is radionically attuned with God can the instrument be used effectively.

Man is beginning to perceive things now which have been beyond the scope of his conscious awareness and consequently there is an ever-increasing need for right control to be established. It does not take much imagination to conceive of the ways in which this could be used that would be anything but a blessing, which emphasizes the necessity for control and our responsibility in it.

In a service at 100 Mile House on June 7, Martin used the subject "Man, the Capstone," in which he likened mankind, individually and collectively, to the symbol presented by the Great Pyramid of Giza. He said the invisible capstone is the only complete pyramid and as long as it is missing, the mass of the pyramid is not a pyramid.

> The capstone should be composed of physical substance, that contained in the bodies of human beings. And when man is lifted to the level of the capstone he is lifted out of the body of the pyramid and consequently out of the realm where what he imagines to be tribulation is a natural thing. No matter how he struggles and strives, suffers, he cannot make the state experienced in the body of the pyramid anything other than it is, the place where the transmutation process is going on. We do not need to change that. There is the necessity for the experience of resurrection, the process by which man is raised out of the body of the pyramid into the capstone so that the capstone may take form.

> The capstone itself is a little pyramid which reveals the fact that focalized in man are all the essences of that which is present in the rest of creation, all the kingdoms—mineral, animal, etc.—and only when men and women are in place can the kingdoms of this world become the kingdoms of our Lord and of His Christ.

In his service "To the Church of Thyatira" at 100 Mile House on June 14, Martin spoke of the heart as a means of perception.

> If you perceive something with your heart that needs to be changed, does that make your heart impure? Not unless you react to it and are controlled by it. Many feel those things and don't know what to do about it. They feel they have to raise hell in some fashion in order to blow off steam, to get rid of it. They try to escape by various means, go to the movies, or somewhere, or do something, to get out from under it.

> Suppose I acted that way when a particular vibratory focalization I have been feeling all day came upon me and I tried to escape and run away from it. "I don't like it!" That is a call coming from out of the world, human beings needing strength, encouragement, something stable in their difficult situations. Am I going to duck out and just let all those people go hang? I have been endowed with a heart in order to perceive such things, to hold steady and offer what I can to those in such great need. You share that responsibility with me in relation to our brothers and sisters out there, and beyond them to all mankind.

Kirk suggested that the name, "Emissaries of Divine Light, Sunrise Ranch," be painted on our pickup truck, so that people in town would become more accustomed to the name.

On June 16 in Kamloops Hospital, British Columbia, a baby girl was born to Martin and Lillian. I recall the delight in his voice when I answered the telephone at Sunrise and Martin said, "I have a daughter. Her name will be Marina June." This little one added a precious element of joy to our household over the years.

That same year a son, Kenneth, was born to Ross and Marcia Marks; and Barry to David and Carolyn (Marks) Oshanek, the latter couple having been married several years, with a daughter Susan to welcome her brother.

Meanwhile at Sunrise the inspiration to have the interior of our Chapel be "finished" before the return of Martin and Lillian was voiced by me and found immediate and vigorous agreement with the members of the group and also the Class. A Board Meeting was held on June 8 in which Eddie Miller, a Class member, presented a plan whereby the works could be facilitated at once and offered his services as a plasterer. An experienced expert in that field, he sent for his tools to be shipped from Pennsylvania. In the meantime Gladys wrote to servers in the field, inviting them to share in this project, with the result that little if any contribution was needed from the Church Treasury.

So, pronto! all hands were busy. Meanwhile classes were held in the "little red school-house," where the first Class had been held. Window framing, carpeting, especially the lining of the raw cinder-block walls, and all the things which make a house a home were under way in the Chapel. Just a few days prior to Martin's return, the men went all-out to finish the ceiling in time. Several crews were set up, working all day and late nights. The ladies scrubbed the floor each night so the plaster would not stain the boards. The ceiling was insulated with fiber glass for the cold winter months and hot summer days, and covered with white insulating board, which added a glow, enhanced by beautiful lights, a gift from the Class. Men and women shared, in shifts, in painting the walls a delicate green, with natural wood trim. The transformation was perfect, with beautiful wood panels at each window carved by Class member, artist Egon Milinkovich.

It was all achieved in record time and imbued with the love that made it a truly holy place. Never was there an expert job more lovingly done. Eden Valley vibrated with a high pitch of excitement when Martin and Lillian, with baby Marina, returned on July 31. We thrilled to see their surprise and joy as they were escorted into the Chapel. The people had gathered, alert to a prearranged signal, and Wesley was playing the organ, which looked as if it had been there all the time, but had barely been set in place. *All Things Bright and Beautiful,* an old favorite of Martin's, was sung lustily, and I read Solomon's prayer in I Kings when he dedicated the magnificent temple of old. Martin expressed his deep thanks for the gift of those who lived in that Home, saying that for the first time he felt all were with one accord in one place, and that I had made it possible—music to my ears.

As he and Lillian, with Marina asleep in her arms, stood before the group, Martin said, "We bring with us a new Emissary. She is relaxing into a little sleep and has been a very good traveller. She symbolizes something, which has come to birth here on Sunrise Ranch, in the center of our ministry." As she was held up for all to see, the beautiful babe opened her eyes and gazed calmly around.

At 100 Mile House the new Food Centre replaced the old general store, an example of the accelerating pace of progress in the whole area. Martin's son, Michael, recently out of school in England, found himself in the position of managing the big store. He did an excellent job and spoke, in *Northern Light,* of sitting in his

> plush office, set on a mezzanine in the right front corner of the store and watching the crowd go by. The various departments are all linked up to the office by an intercom system, proving very useful and saving steps. The staff wear green coats with buff trim, to match the surroundings, and the whole area is brilliantly lighted, with spotlights marking various displays.

Meanwhile in Calgary, Alberta, Roger de Winton had continued to move ever more closely with the ministry, and with his two small daughters, Diana and Dallas, visited Sunrise Ranch in August. The following year he attended the Class and was invited by Martin to move to Headquarters if he wished. He returned to Calgary, terminated his employment in the banking world, settled his affairs and moved to Sunrise Ranch where he has made his home ever since. Diana and Dallas have continued to live in our central Units, Diana finding her home on Sunrise Ranch where she has focused the music program for the ministry and contributed in many other vital areas. Formerly married to David Gilbert, Dallas lives at 100 Mile House with her husband Robert Vaillancourt and daughter Christina Gilbert. Coming as little girls with their dedicated father, Diana and Dallas have contributed in immeasurable ways to the Lord's work.

On September 12 George Shears was ordained a Minister of the Church of Emissaries of Divine Light by Martin.

In a service on September 19 Martin spoke at length on the subject of "Women." Among other things he said:

> It is truth that has been lacking on earth. It is often imagined that we must do something about increasing love. But, whatever measure of God's love is now flowing into the world, it is virtually all distorted because it has to pass through human beings, and as long as the truth is not allowed to have meaning in their lives every ill spirit is a distortion of the spirit of love. There is a range of all the ill spirits, from the most degraded and lowest type to man's highest concept of God's love. Perhaps one could say that some of the

higher levels have a relatedness, but are not the reality until the truth is in operation.

Perfect love—the father, God's love; the mother, God's truth. The child of these two is the manifest expression of life here on earth. The tree of life is supposed to grow here on earth; the river of life is supposed to flow here on earth. God created this world to be a living organism, a whole thing filled with life. Presently it is a long way from that creation, a little trickle of life compared to that, because what appears now is all that can get through the distorted pattern established by man.

There is inherent in human beings a feeling, a memory, a longing, an assurance that somehow, somewhere, there must be something more. Because they could not recall it properly, resultant upon wrong function, they have decided it is not related to this world and must expect its fulfilment after they die and go to heaven. But that isn't it at all; it's a memory of the Motherland. Interesting—the Motherland. A particular country may think of itself as the fatherland, an arrogant assumption. The heavenly Fatherland has continued, but the Motherland, of which we have spoken, disappeared beneath the waters of the Pacific Ocean many thousands of years ago. Why? Because the Mother was gone. God created man male and female, to make possible the manifestation of Mother God on earth. Man was placed in the Motherland—male and female, the two elements of truth, control and design. All created living things were given form by reason of mankind, the mother, which includes both men and women.

Now we see something emerging of the relation between the two elements of truth in male and female—control and design. The control aspect relates specifically, with respect to this pattern, to the male; and the design aspect to the female. At the point of the fall Eve proceeded to exercise control. She decided to act regardless of divine control. Perhaps it seemed a little thing to her at the time, but she undertook to impose that control on the man. Of course the man let it be established and he followed Eve. There are many concepts of what it means to be positive, from the standpoint of the male. It is not rightly an arbitrary thing. There is thoughtfulness and consideration, a willingness to move this way or that, to provide a pleasing pattern in relation to his wife.

Women have been inclined to feel that it is essential to the universe that they should maintain control, that otherwise everything would go to pieces. Men and women alike need to remember those elements of design and control, within each one and between individuals. Woman has her wonderful place, and there she can be truly content, truly herself, truly a woman. I am speaking particularly of the ladies, not because something does not need to be said to the men—perhaps I'll get around to that—but our time has slipped by, so that must be it for now. Let us begin to see the truth again, that we may come to know, and be restored to, the state of being divine men and divine women on earth.

On September 26, in "Our Privilege and Responsibility on Sunrise Ranch," Martin spoke with deep feeling of his appreciation for the privilege of living on Sunrise Ranch, suggesting that others search their hearts to see how much was being taken for granted.

> If our service requires it we go out into the world and serve in whatever field necessary, but at the same time we are aware that there is this spot on the face of the earth, this little valley, in which something is established of the kingdom of our King, in which all of you are enfolded. You may forget it on occasion but it is here nonetheless, something established into which responding ones may come. But those who dwell here have the responsibility of tending and keeping this garden planted eastward in Eden insofar as the world is concerned, for it is that which is coming out of the future for the world. What is brought forth here should be seen as that in which the whole world of mankind may share in season.

In an exchange with Kirk at a Sunrise Ranch Board Meeting on October 12, Martin acknowledged the depth of wisdom Kirk had acquired regarding methods of plowing, organic handling of the land, etc. He expressed appreciation for the contribution of the Millers to the Unit program during the last six months as they prepared to return to Berwick, Pennsylvania. (They would be back in season.) The offer of Myron and Elsie Fausey's 70-acre farm near the Miller's home for use in the ministry if someone could go there and operate it was noted. It was a great offer, fertile land, good equipment, but no one in position to take over the job.

In a special meeting on November 8 the pattern of focalization during Martin's absence from Sunrise Ranch was addressed. Jim Wellemeyer would carry the primary focus in the spiritual field with the assistance of Dick Cable, Kirk would focus the men's activities, and the Church Board would function as always. Billie Cable would continue as a focus for the ladies. Martin emphasized that each one is called to be a leader and this period of his absence presented opportunity for growth, for proving faith in God and in each other.

Responding to the urging of the editor of *Eden Valley News* for a contribution from him, Martin submitted the following:

Poetry

I'm not so good at rhyme, it seems,
Yet, if a man indulge in dreams,
Let him apply himself to do
The thing his yearning tells him to;
And he will find, to his delight,
That as he works with main and might
Ways open up before his view
So that his longings may come true.
To prove this fact I do my part,
And while my rhyme may not be art,
It seems to me that I can do it,
Despite the fact I'm not a poet!

A profound and consistent blessing on Sunrise Ranch for many years was the frequent presence of Bobbie (Carolyn) Garrett. Her husband Ed, the Mayor of Loveland, soon accompanied her on many occasions, this regardless of any opinions that might exist on the part of friends, or otherwise, in town, and also of church affiliations—none of which, by the way, ever provided a problem but resulted in deepening those ties. These two beautiful and genuine people were dearly loved and contributed greatly to the growth of Sunrise Ranch. One aspect was Bobbie's work with the children in Junior Training School, which included several books written by her. When their individual sojourns on this planet were completed, at their requests the funeral services were held in our Chapel. It was a remarkable sight in Eden Valley to see the long line of cars filled with many people from town and area slowly wending its way through the field to our little cemetery nestled under the rimrock.

On November 19 at 100 Mile House a subject of paramount importance, separation, was considered by Martin, emphasizing the fact that the newness of heaven and earth merely relates to a recognition of that state which already is, and that separation identifies the old heaven and old earth which will pass away. "Heaven is not complete without the earth," he noted, "any more than the earth is complete without heaven. It requires both in oneness."

He spoke of the general recognition in the scientific view that the final word has not yet been spoken with regard to anything. On the other hand in relation to what is called religion, the assumption is that the final word was spoken back along the way somewhere, the authority established, the pattern set, with nothing more to appear in the future.

How shall this gap between heaven and earth be dissolved so that the fact of oneness may be known? In relation to you, what barriers stand in between? We speak of the necessity for clearing away limitations. First, we need to realize that there are limitations which are right and proper. We could say that an automobile has limitations as an aircraft. If we wish to fly we use an aircraft; if we wish to go upon the water we use a boat; if we wish to drive on the highway we use a car. We can see limitations in nature. Trees, for instance, were designed for a specific purpose. There are natural limits in relation to human beings. However, we need not be concerned about them, because no matter how much we may think we have achieved I do not believe we have come anywhere near those natural limits.

"From Fancy to Fact" entitled a service on November 28, in which Martin spoke of the serpent that was described in Genesis as more subtle than any beast of the field.

The mind of man, symbolized by the serpent, has exhibited a beguiling subtlety which has deceived human beings in ways without number. Few are willing to take an honest look at themselves, lest they have to acknowledge their own state of self-delusion and admit they have been fooled into action that betrayed their highest aspirations. Yet unless there is an honest examination of the truth, mistakes acknowledged and attitudes changed, the deceit of the serpent will surely bring the individual—and the world—to disaster. In this ministry we learn that the practical nature of the truth which is taught must be proven in our lives if anything worthwhile is to be accomplished.

No matter how much might be achieved by segregated individuals scattered upon the face of the earth, unless the truth is capable of practical application to a group it would be of no value to mankind. This emphasizes one aspect of the vital importance of our two Units. There are other factors, but none more important. Some, coming to the two Units, found that the actual experience in the pattern did not conform with their expectations. Probably this would be true of virtually everyone, because concepts and ideas on the subject are colored and distorted. Past experience cannot be changed, but it is important that there be a facing of facts now and in the days to come, that all may be left without excuse. It is not the Unit that is on trial, but the individual. Regardless of what changes need to work out in the Unit, the individual's attitude to the Unit and his own responsibilities therein must be proven. He is faced with a test; he is on trial; not because anyone placed him in that position but because of the nature of the situation.

> Neither of the Units was expected to be perfect the moment the programs were initiated. At any point along the way the group was what it was supposed to be just to the degree that those composing it were letting the truth apply them to the living of their lives in that setting according to the particular level each one had attained in the cycles of his or her progress. Could any of you presume to undertake an accurate analysis of each member in this regard?

Martin deposited the sum of $2,000 in the consular office in Vancouver toward transportation for the two Nigerian students for the Servers Training School, Timothy Olagunju and Adex Adewole.

On February 16, 1957, Martin discussed the "Care of the Body," in which he spoke of his feelings when, in that area where there was considerable lumbering business, he would watch a tree being felled.

> Some of these big old trees are several hundred years old. Trees were put on earth for a very specific purpose which man ignores—not so that he could build houses out of them. That is the bright idea of the devil. Man has destroyed so much of that which God put on earth. We have many desert places in the world which once were covered with trees and vegetation. He puts off the evil day of reckoning somewhat by his so-called scientific knowledge, but it comes in the end.

> God's way is not a way of destruction, but that is the tendency of human beings, is it not? It is so easy to tear down, knock down, push down, destroy. You can destroy in five minutes what may have taken five hundred years to build. That is true in relation to the things of God, a body built with infinite, meticulous care for millennia, only to be torn down in a matter of minutes.

Some interesting observations were noted by Ross Marks in the 1957 edition of *Northern Light,* among them the fact that the population of the town of 100 Mile House had grown from about twenty in 1948 to three hundred and fifty, an increase of almost twentyfold in eight years. The need for expanding facilities was obvious, primary being the water system. The following report by Ross accurately depicts the changes necessary in every field as the town grew:

> Back in 1946 the ranch, under the direction of Martin, installed a wooden pipeline to supply an elevated storage tank of 1,000-gallon capacity, the line linking the tank to a high spring located on a hillside about a mile southwest of the townsite. This provided the ranch buildings and the Unit with an entirely

adequate supply of cold spring water, delivered by gravity at no cost, and heralded the beginning of a water system for the town that was to develop.

As houses, businesses, etc., began to appear following the development of a lumber and logging industry in the area, new lines were run out and water was delivered to the fast growing population. Even then it was becoming obvious that a water system was vital to the continued development of the town, its availability from the beginning having influenced people to settle here. Two wells were developed, one drilled to a depth of 90 feet and equipped with an electric pump in 1950; and the other hand-driven to a depth of 18 feet and operated by a gasoline engine pump in 1951. These, together with the spring, provided a fairly adequate supply until this year. This past summer the shallow well began to produce quantities of rusty looking water—no doubt a result of overpumping—and there were reports of washday "reds" from some complaining residents.

We had advanced from wood pipe to galvanized, and then to plastic, easy to install, etc., up to 3-inch diameter. Meanwhile, with the town growing by leaps and bounds the original 1,000-gallon tank was looking increasingly miniscule, and in the summer of 1951 we erected a 12,000-gallon wood stave tank elevated on a timber structure and constructed an insulated wooden building around it as protection from the elements. This is now rapidly becoming inadequate.

We turned our attention to a stream just east of the townsite. After study and engineering consultation we proceeded to construct a pumping installation, and during the fall months an intake system, pumphouse and electric pump capable of delivering up to 5,000 gallons of water per hour to the storage tank were installed. In the few months prior to this David Oshanek, John Fraser and I, with a big assist from visiting Jim Wellemeyer, installed some 3,200 feet of 6-inch asbestos cement water main and several hundred feet of plastic line, linking the pump site with the rest of the system, and servicing a new subdivision and other developments in the community. With our own ditching machine and bulldozer, we were able to complete the job largely on our own—a pipeline company!!!

Of interest is the fact that British Columbia's first natural gas pipeline, from the Peace River country to Vancouver and the United States, wends its way right past 100 Mile House [and through our property]. The company responsible for this section of the line decided to locate their construction camp and trailer court immediately south of the village and of course wished to have water piped in. This meant a touch-and-go situation for some time for us until the new pump began delivering, but we did it! The camp has some 80-odd trailers, dining hall, etc., as well as a population close to that already in town. Future plans? Thus far it has worked to meet the situations as they arrive.

Ross also spoke of another vital addition to the town.

Until just recently the cry "Fire!" would have resulted in someone dashing for the nearest pail of water. Today we have our own volunteer Fire Department, and the result would be someone rushing to set off the village siren, albeit a small and rather ineffective one. A further result would be, if in the wee hours, men in various stages of dress and undress streaming from various quarters toward the fire hall, after which a gleaming red truck (a good buy of a used fire engine from a small town near Seattle) would emerge and, mustering all possible speed, red lights flashing, dash to the scene.

In that same issue Conrad O'Brien-ffrench spoke of the inauguration of an Art Class at 100 Mile House, with a pupil from the Village, long-time friend of Conrad's, Steve Smele, posing for his portrait.

Martin and Lillian and family moved into their beautiful newly finished house, set in a secluded and spacious surround at the top of the hill from the Lodge and Unit buildings. It provided a true home for the remainder of Martin's life, a tribute to his meticulous design, combined with Lillian's imaginative contribution. There were exciting additions and changes through the years as the family grew.

Martin welcomed the 1957 Class on Sunrise Ranch in his Sunday morning service on March 24, "The Initiation of a Cycle." That was followed in the evening with "The Source and the Word" in which he extended a special welcome to Timothy Olagunju and Adex Adewole, our two friends from Nigeria, Africa, and emphasized the significance of their representation of so many hungering and thirsting ones. I remember when Martin, Lillian and I met them upon their arrival in Denver. We had gone to welcome them after their long journey, meanwhile availing ourselves of the opportunity to see the movie *The Ten Commandments*. Their plane arrived early and they were met at the airport by Jim Wellemeyer and Bob Patton who brought them to the theater. We experienced a special thrill upon unexpectedly seeing those two beaming faces amongst the crowd in the lobby.

Timo came from Ilesha. His father had been Chief Ogboni of Ipole, who ranked third to His Highness the Owa of Ijeshaland. Timo could have assumed the position of his father upon his death, but found his life in the Emissary ministry. With a very adequate command of the English language he had functioned as both school teacher and interpreter. Today our literature has been translated into fourteen different languages. Timo, together with Adex at that time, led the vanguard in this field. The first foreign tongue to carry the Word was that of Nigeria, in Yoruba, a very ancient language. Millie Latam was a vital key in accomplishing this complex and intricate project.

Among other outstanding members of that sixth Training Class were George and Naomi Shears from Huntingburg, Indiana; Michael Cecil from 100 Mile House; Roger de Winton from Calgary, Alberta; and Chris Foster from Vancouver.

Born in Dulwich, England, Chris attended college there and while working as a junior reporter with a newspaper, at the age of eighteen was offered a post as assistant to his editor cousin in Salisbury in southern Rhodesia. Two years there were followed by a visit to Australia and New Zealand, and eventually back in London he got a job as a junior reporter with the *Daily Express.* He loved sailing and found relief from his work in a 16-foot sailing boat which he kept on the Essex coast. He came to Canada and met Richard Thompson in Victoria, British Columbia, where he had worked as a reporter. Shortly after a sail in his 21-foot sloop he was en route to Sunrise for the 1957 Class. He later worked on publications in the ministry and found his home with the 100 Mile House family.

It was reported in a Sunrise Ranch Board Meeting on April 12 that a Multigraph Exposure Frame had been purchased for office use. Work had begun on walls for a new office building and storeroom at the north end of the Chapel building, and the Class had undertaken the project of putting a tile floor in the Chapel.

On the 5th of June, in his service, "Thy Going Out and Thy Coming In," Martin announced that he and Lillian would be away for a little season and said,"I am giving you a gift; I am leaving Gracie with you and she will continue to carry my spirit to you. Her place actually is with Lillian and me but she is staying with you." This happened on occasion, and I found that such times presented special opportunities for growth, in me and also in the group.

Jim and Nell Allen with their children Susan and David moved to the Ranch from California on June 18, their trailer arriving shortly after.

In a Board Meeting on August 9 Martin offered a reminder of the September payment coming up of $1300 on the Gateway property. He also brought up the matter of the insurance case on the airplane and suggested the best thing to do was to drop the case. It was so agreed. Regarding eligibility for tax exemption, the Commissioner of Internal Revenue had said there would be a need for reorganization. The possibility of making two separate organizations, the Church and the Ranch, was discussed, and Oliver was to look into the matter with Mr. Rellstab. Martin commented that we did not have any up-to-date by-laws in our Church and that the ones used at 100 Mile House could probably be used here. He advised waiting to see if we could make the above-mentioned change before the 1st of September.

A water tank had been acquired, traded for hay. Chairs for the Chapel, new to us and in fine condition, were purchased very reasonably from a theater under renovation, and a new chair, gift from the Class, for Lillian's use in the Chapel.

Roger de Winton and Edna Ackerley were married on Sunrise Ranch on August 9. The Ackerley boys, Alan and David, were enfolded in that family unit. It was not to be of long duration, however, for after only a few months of happy union, Edna's health showed signs of a deterioration that had been in progress for many years and it was not long before her time on earth was finished.

A special meeting of the Board on September 2nd acquainted the personnel with the fact that the Board of Trustees of the Church would be the Board for the Joint Enterprise, Sunrise Ranch. A unanimous motion completed the transaction.

In a Board Meeting on the 11th of November Oliver Latam reported that he had found application for exemption dated 1941 and also a copy of form 990 for 1942, proof of exemption. He had written to Washington and Buffalo, New York, and the reply from Buffalo was: "Under date of March 10, 1943, your organization was ruled exempt by the National Office. Unless changes have occurred in the organization that ruling is applicable." It was decided that Oliver should write again to Washington, advising them that we had the exact date, and await their reply.

On January 12, 1958, a baby girl was born to Martin and Lillian in the Kamloops hospital whom they named Janine Dawn. The precious spirit of beautiful little Janine was a delight to those of us who knew her, during the short time she was to be with us, leaving in May of that same year. A complication with the function of her heart presented a very different situation in those days from that of today, with advances in technology in every field. The correction of the problem would be ordinary procedure in today's hospital, but then it meant that a very dear little person left a bereaved family and friends—so quickly.

In the 1958 edition of *Northern Light* Gordon Marks, the magistrate of 100 Mile House, described the Village as it was when he, his wife Emily and daughter Carolyn joined their son Ross, who had preceded them by a year, to contribute a vital family element in the Unit. He said,

> When we came in 1949 there were three or four dwellings, a garage, a
> store, a coffee shop and a telephone office, and from that it has developed into
> one of the beauty spots of British Columbia. In and around the area are over

100 sawmills and logging outfits, with lumber the chief industry, although cattle ranching is the oldest by far. The smallest village in British Columbia, we have a real honest-to-goodness sewer system—which works! There is a modern hotel, and recently natural gas for cooking and heating has been piped from the Peace River district from the far north. Our power is presently generated right here, but later it will come from Quesnel, about 120 miles north.

This part of British Columbia is generally referred to as the "Cariboo," in the County of Cariboo. Years ago caribou roamed these parts, as the deer, moose and bear do today. Hunters arrive annually to hunt their winter's supply of meat. Some are successful; others spend their time lost in the bush! Grouse, ducks and geese are plentiful in season.

As nature reveals the beauty of the Creator by being what it was created to be, so we have the privilege and opportunity of being what we were created to be—the instrument on earth through which the glory of God may be revealed to His children.

Gordon was fun-loving and delighted in playing a good-natured joke on his fellows now and then. He relates an incident:

As magistrate one of my jobs is to dismiss, remand or commit those who come before me on various charges, small and large. Usually I take a look in the cell room to see whom the long arm of the law has brought in. We have an Indian reserve nearby and some of them like their firewater and often spend a night in our little jail.

One day I received an urgent call from one of our police officers asking me to come to the jail where they had a man behind bars who knew me and wanted me to bail him out. On my arrival I could hear the cry, "Let me out! Let me out!" and the constable said, "Take care, this is a tough character, but he says he knows you." When the door to the cell was opened, such hair as I have left stood on end! There before me was my son, my only son Ross. Sometimes your jokes come back to you. We all had a good laugh. The RCMP (Royal Canadian Mounted Police) really do always get their man!

That was the centennial year for British Columbia, and as part of the celebrations Martin lent the stage coach, which had been part of the property since his arrival, to the Centennial Organization. It made the trip from Victoria to 100 Mile House, and then the 190 miles to Barkerville, carried on a truck between the towns, one reason being consideration for the feet of the six-horse team traveling on paved highway. Jack Turnbull was the driver, accompanied by a guard. Six passengers, dressed in appropriate costumes, would ride in the coach, which was "held up" in each town along the route.

This old stage coach has been like a mascot for the Lodge and Unit. Painted a bright red, with "B.C. Express, No. 14" in gold lettering on each side, it has yellow wheels and a green luggage compartment at the back. It rode on leather "thoroughbraces" which served as shock absorbers and springs. It has remained in remarkably good condition considering it was taken out of long and useful service in 1917, having made countless trips up through the Fraser Canyon—in those days a perilous trip, depending on weather, narrow treacherous roads, etc. Its last trip was made in 1917, between Ashcroft, eighty miles south of us and Prince George, two hundred miles to the north. This symbol of pioneering days in that wild and gorgeous country still occupies a place of honor in the courtyard of Red Coach Inn.

The Early Years

Lloyd Meeker (Uranda), age 21, Kansas

Uranda, age 25, in Nashville, Tennessee

Uranda's boyhood home in Palisade, Colorado, as it appears today

Uranda in California, 1930s

Fern Meeker

Marjorie Lee, daughter of Uranda and Paulene
(Foster)

Uranda in St. Petersburg, Florida, 1940

Uranda speaking in California, circa 1939

1941, Uranda during Summer Session in Pittsburgh, Pennsylvania

Group in attendance at Pittsburgh Summer Session

Uranda at Sylvan Dale Ranch in Colorado

Dorothy Cameron (left), Fern Meeker (right) at Pittsburgh Summer Session

Summer Session at Sylvan Dale Ranch in 1944

Chaplain Lloyd Meeker, Civil Air Patrol

Hanya Oshanek, Irving Harwood, John Oshanek and Uranda

Sisters: Billie Groves, Rosalind Hooper and Kathleen Groves

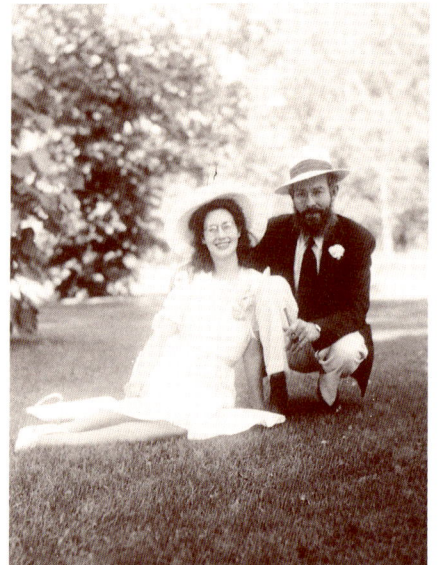
Wedding of Uranda and Kathleen Groves

Sunrise Ranch ~ 1946

Sunrise Ranch, purchased in late 1945

Rosalind Hooper

Bill Kuykendall, William and John Oshanek, Dorothy and Richard Thompson

Tent, part of early accommodation on Sunrise Ranch

Grace Van Duzen, Uranda, Byrdie Jane Dahl, Bernice Kain, Norma and Albert Christiansen, Richard and Dorothy Thompson—a drive up the mountain

Drilling a well

Uranda laying the cornerstone of the Chapel

Ready to go!

Charles Strikwerda

Riverside, California ~ 1947

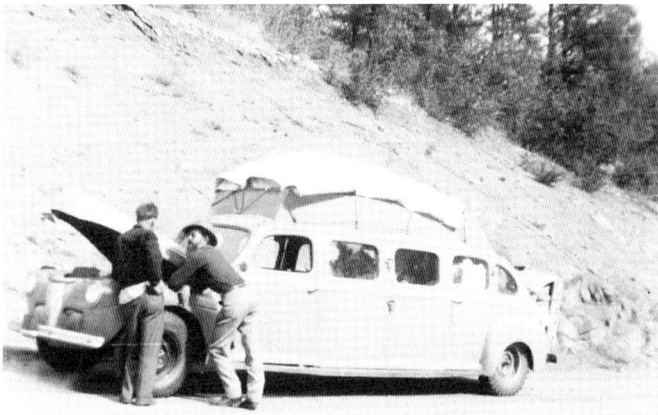

En route from Sunrise Ranch—one of many interruptions

Milking Mossy

Uranda and Lord Martin Cecil

Conrad O'Brien-ffrench with Uranda and Martin

Gordon Christianson, Frances Acheson, Conrad O'Brien-ffrench, Martin, Grace and son Billy, Lucy Twining, Mabel Gulliver, Marjorie Lee and Uranda

Salinas, California ~ 1947-48

Accommodation at Gabilan Ranch

Sulky racetrack at Gabilan Ranch

Martin and Uranda

Grace and Uranda

At the beach—Grace and Billy; Uranda, Kathy and Nancy; Edna Henderson; Mabel Gulliver and Sally Bainbridge

Uranda and Kathy with Nancy and Lloyd—also Tippy

Billy, Nancy and Sharon

Storytime—Groves (Ralph) Hooper,
Billy Van Duzen, Sharon Call, Nancy,
Uranda and Lloyd

Four generations: Lillian Call with
daughter Sharon, her mother Marie
Johnson and grandmother Jennie
Olsson of Milwaukee, Wisconsin

Dictation—Grace and Uranda

Uranda giving service in the old Ranch House

On the mountaintop, Estes Park

Canal begun behind Sunrise Ranch—Government Irrigation Project

Richard Thompson and William Oshane, laying blocks

More water! The new pond was initiated as a swimming hole

Uranda in the
Bellanca

From left:
William Oshane,
Martin Cecil,
Richard Cable,
Don Buchan,
Richard
Thompson—
with Uranda

Richard and Dorothy Thompson with
daughter Mary

One of many meals outside

Alice and Roy Kuykendall

Muriel and William Oshane

Frank and Betty Protzman

Richard and Billie Cable

Dorothy and Richard
Thompson

David and Rosa Groves

Burghley House, Stamford, England

Burghley House

William Cecil, The 1st Lord Burghley, Lord High Treasurer to Queen Elizabeth I

The Fifth Marquess and Marchioness of Exeter (Martin's parents)

Martin enjoyed riding at an early age!

Romayne, Martin, Winifred and David Cecil

Martin Cecil—the Royal Navy

Wedding of Martin Cecil and Edith Csanady

"The Heaven Room" in Burghley House

Uranda, Lillian, Grace and Kathy, with plane, in Chatham, Ontario

James and Mary Pogue,
Toronto, Ontario, Center

Hugh (Mac) and Jane Duff,
Woodbridge Center, Toronto

Drs. Edward and Gladys Miller,
Berwick, Pennsylvania, Center

G.P.C. Servers Training School and Faculty

First six-month Class, 1952, Sunrise Ranch

Dr. George Shears, founder of G.P.C.

Dr. Albert Ackerley

William Oshanek and Richard Thompson

Richard Cable

Dr. James Wellemeyer

Uranda and Kathy with their children

Albert and Edna Ackerley, with sons Alan and David

Nancy, Lloyd and Helen Meeker

An outdoor Class with Uranda

God planted a garden eastward in Eden. It does not say He transplanted something already formed from another place into the earth.

We see those who neglect what God has planted, and with a frenzy try to plant their own seed and cause it to grow, and the seed from God never has a chance to sprout.

URANDA
Founder and Leader
of the
EMISSARIES OF DIVINE LIGHT

*The seed is already here. It is for us to provide the right atmosphere for its growing. It is for us to dress it, to give it form, to let it grow and come to the point of harvest, and **keep** it, not throw it away, not let it be meaningless in the days of our yesterdays.*

— Uranda (July 4, 1954)

Marie and Roy Johnson

Lord and Lady Martin Cecil

Early residents of Sunrise Ranch: (from left, back row) Norman Tizzard, Robert Patton, Roy Kuykendall, Millie and Oliver Latam, Alan Ackerley, Edna Ackerley, James Wellemeyer, Elsie Sierck, Fred Sierck (just visible), Geneva Hooker, David Groves, Marjorie Christiansen (Murray), Martha Whitcomb, Tom Crouch, Robert Lecen. (Second row) Frank and Betty Protzman, Alice Kuykendall, Richard and Billie Cable, Lillian and Martin Cecil, Mabel Hagedorn, Nadine McKenney, Mareda Murray, Albert Christiansen. (Seated) Fern Meeker, Helen Hoffman, Lorraine Cowan, Grace Van Duzen, Bertha Meyer, Rosa Groves.

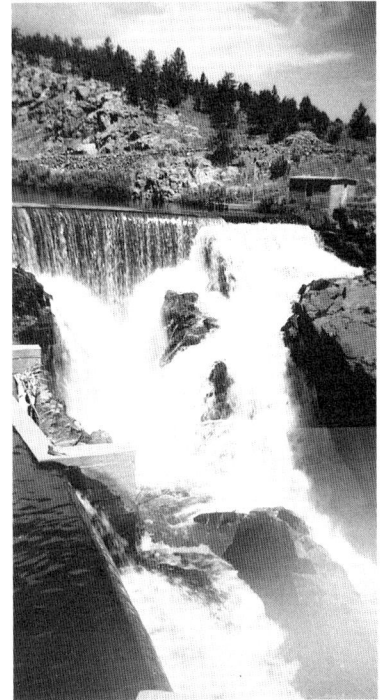

The Falls, at the Gateway property

Anne and James Wellemeyer

Dorothy and Wesley Jones

Grace with Sunday School (JTS) Class

Naomi and George Shears

Timo and wife Rachel in Nigeria

Rev. Timothy
(Timo) Olagunju,
from Nigeria

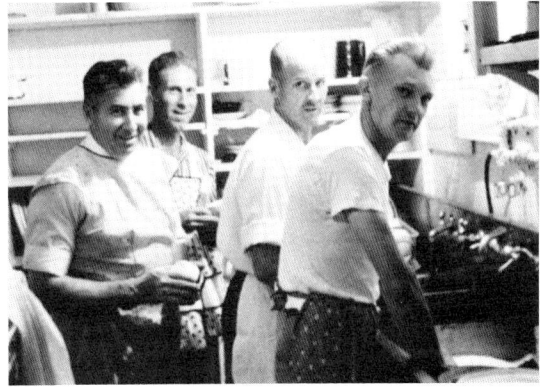

Edward Miller, Bob Schmeer, Mac Duff,
Floyd Conell

Adex Adewole and Timo with James
Wellemeyer

Lorraine Cowan, Nancy Meeker,
Lillian Cecil and baby Marina

Marina Cecil with her parents

The Gilbert family: (clockwise) Norman, Marjorie, David, Brian, twins Michael and Mark, and Wendy

Early New England group, with resident servers Dr. Walter and Joan Bahan, and Dr. Bill Bahan, in center front; Lillian, Martin and Grace behind them

Lillian, Martin and Grace at 100 Mile House

Ross and Marcia Marks

Martin with flight instructor Terry Field

Martin and Ross shared the pilot and co-pilot seats

Swami Premananda and Martin

Martin at the Awake O'Man Convention at Love's Retreat

Mahdah Love, Love's Retreat (Atlanta, Georgia) and Grace

From the Hundred—on the landing strip in field at Sunrise Ranch, Martin greeting Ross and Marcia Marks

Martin received the key to the city, in the office of the Mayor of Baton Rouge, Louisiana: (from left) Dr. Frank Ault; Grace; Martin; Lillian; Mayor of 100 Mile House, Ross Marks; Mayor of Baton Rouge, W. W. Dumas; Conrad O'Brien-ffrench; Dr. Bill Bahan and Dr. Kenneth Lim, Coordinator of activities in the South.

Dr. Jerry and Olive England, Mobile, Alabama

George Bullied, founder of the Twin Valleys School, Ontario

The first Supreme (Executive) Council gathering, with Lillian, Martin, Grace, Michael and Nancy Cecil, Donna and Bill Bahan, in the home of Dr. Jerry and Olive England in Mobile, Alabama

Martin with ministers Michael Cecil, Roger de Winton, James Wellemeyer and Bill Bahan

Stamp Crew at 100 Mile House: (back) Jim and Grace Moore, Helen Ames, John Fraser, Gary Brooks, Nowell McGuire; (seated) Heather Pinchin, Margaret Hawkshaw, Angela Seiberling, Judy Repar, April Britton

Dictation, Martin's office on Sunrise Ranch

A Story of Man Class

Sharing the joy of living—from the lectern

Lillian presiding at one of the frequent musical performances

Gathering in West Chapel on Sunrise Ranch, advent of video era

Lake Rest Hotel, in the Catskill Mountains, New York

Dr. Louis and Bridget Rotola with daughter Allison, Dr. Frank Reale

Fayetta Gelinas (Fay McKay) was a prominent star in Las Vegas, Nevada

George and Joelle Emery

Meeting Dr. Immanuel Velikovsky in Toronto, Ontario

Grace with Dr. and Mrs. Velikovsky in their home in Princeton, New Jersey

Grace's visit to Israel, accompanied by Donna Bahan and Johanna Walters, in the home of Richard and Barbara Dash, Jerusalem

Work on the Dome Chapel

Martin at the site

A living ladder

Finished!

Martin's vision completed in form

Artists Conrad O'Brien-ffrench, Bill Talkington, Michael Gress and Bob Ewing

Sculptress Nancy Hadler from Canada with Bill and Michael

Deborah Grace (Foreman), Joy and Chris Foster, in India

Rob Cass and Achal Bedi

Group in India, gathered with Joe Houlton and Bill Bahan (center, second row), and Deborah Grace (third from right, second row from top)

Jim and Pat Miller, Alberta

Paul and Libby
Blythe, Australia

Bill and Doreen Thompson,
Powell River, B.C.

In Sunrise kitchen: Chef Max von Hartmann, Fay Gelinas and
Chef Jake Koellen

Bob and Beverley
Purdom, London,
Ontario

Ron and
June Polack,
B.C. and Ontario

Dinner in the dining room on Sunrise Ranch: (clockwise) Glenn Lockie, Anne and James Wellemeyer, Sally Taylor, Marie Johnson, Jeffrey Newman (South Africa), Marina Cecil, Lillian, Martin, Grace, Princess Lida Radziwill (Italy), Peter and Tina Kafka

Luncheon in the home of LeAnna Moore: (clockwise) Mary Lou Patton, Selma Valentine, Nadine McKenney, Della Bever, Madeline Maynard, Anne Laflam, Mabel Hagedorn, LeAnna, Hazel McKenney, Marjorie Murray, Betty Dice, Mary Schmeer, Marie Johnson, Toni Wing

Ranch Manager
Peter Castonguay
with Martin

Martin—at home on his horse,
in the Cariboo

Bridge Creek Cattle Ranch

25th (Silver) Wedding Anniversary of Lord and Lady Exeter

Their home in the Cariboo

Martin with daughter Marina at Milque Ranch

Helen Meeker and Estralita at a Jumping Clinic at the 108 Riding Arena

A visit to Burghley House: Martin's brother and wife, Marquess and Marchioness of Exeter (David and Diana), with Martin and Lillian

Four generations: Marie Johnson, Lillian, Marina and Majessa

A gathering of musicians: Ellen Roos, Lillian, Nancy Cecil, PenDell Pittman, Carolyn Rhodes, Meridy Migchelbrink. (Seated): Jason Hall, Peggy Gretsch, Betsy and George Hanson, and Donna Bahan

Eunice Taylor on Sunrise Ranch

Helen Vorstermans, Marjorie Spears, Nancy Cecil
(Uranda's daughters)

Nancy Cecil and
Janine Romaner

Anne Fees, Grace, and Liddy
Martin, in Hawaii

The McKenney family made frequent valuable contributions to Sunrise Ranch, in many ways. From left: Maynard Ludwig, Edna McKenney, Bart McKenney, Roy Bever, Nell McKenney, Marilyn Ludwig, Joanne Knaub. Seated: Della Bever, Hazel McKenney, Nadine McKenney. Not pictured: Ben Knaub.

Sky Pilots

Pilot Charley Kitchens, and his wife Asti, air hostess

Pilots Frank Frazier and Alan Christie

Barbara Frazier later filled the position of hostess

Conrad O'Brien-ffrench, long-time friend of Martin

Hugh Malafry at the lectern

Ann Foorman in her show
Catch Fire With Me

Michelle Johnson, Holly-wood!

Jim and Wendy Hoffman with twin sons, Japeth and Jeptha

Bob and Judy Hollis

David Lynch

Shareen Ewing and Grace at work

Mack and Leslye Fontenot, preparing a
Cajun dinner

Healing Arts Clinic, Loveland: Dr. Michael Iacoboni, Lillian, Martin, Grace, Dr. Laurence Krantz, Dr. Cecil Taylor

Roger and Dorothy de Winton with daughters: Melanie Isenhour, Diana de Winton, Dallas Vaillancourt

Alan and Jean Hammond, Judith Aranow

Marie Louise Radziwill with her sculpture in process, model Martin in background

Ted and Claudia Black

Attorney John and Carol Amey

Jim and Georgene Higerd with daughter Lindsey

Yujin Pak

Bob and Mary Schmeer

Emissary International Congress, 1982
Fort Collins, Colorado

Addressing the throng

Martin, with pilot Eber Wright, arriving on Sunrise
Ranch from EIC

On World Tour, service in Australia—it was hot!

Martin breaking ground in South Africa

In Africa: (back) Michael and Nancy Cecil, Gary and Glennifer Gillespie, Lillian, Martin, Grace, Tino and Lynn Stefano; (front) Rupert and Tessa Maskell, Leon and Judy Bekker, Howard and Marian Goodman

Native Zulu
performance

Martin with our Zulu friends

Home again to Sunrise Ranch—and sharing the adventure

Martin with a vintage Burghley automobile

Martin about to enter the House of Lords, London

Martin with painting of his mother and photograph of his father in Burghley House

Pub lunch in London—with Rupert and Tessa Maskell

Part of the group representing our worldwide ministry, gathered to construct the Pavilion on Sunrise Ranch: (back) Bill Dice, Frank Moore, Jim Greaney, Paul Senna, Ray Skinner, Rory McNamara, Don Hynes, David Ward; (front) Joel Appel, Pat Fitzsimmons, John Miller, Mark Novins

Entrance to completed Pavilion

Dinner in Executive dining room in Pavilion (beautiful table a gift from African group): (clockwise) Conrad O'Brien-ffrench, Tessa and Rupert Maskell, Marina and Peter Castonguay, Shareen Ewing, Iris and Bill Becker, Marie Johnson, Lillian, Martin, Grace, Bob Ewing

First meal in Pavilion dining room, before completion, with view of executive dining room and family room (with fireplace)

Glen Ivy Hot Springs Spa,
Corona, California

John and Pam
Gray, Glen Ivy

Stan and Linda Grindstaff
with daughter Jenifer,
California

Executive Council—
relaxing!

Martin and Lillian at Glen Ivy

Tennis

Executive Council: Alan and Jean Hammond in front, James Wellemeyer, Nancy and Michael Cecil, Rupert and Tessa Maskell, Lillian, Donna Bahan, Roger and Dorothy de Winton, Martin and Grace seated

Michael and Nancy Cecil with Angela and Anthony

Peter and Marina Castonguay with Majessa and Dylan

The Vorstermans: Luke, Benjamin, Rebecca, Helen and Stefan

Lloyd and Paula Meeker with Lloyd James

The Dome Chapel—standing room only!

The joy of serving the Lord together

Easter Sunrise Service at the Little Chapel,
Sunrise Ranch

On the rimrock, viewing new reservoir in the Valley

Facing the sun

After service in the Dome Chapel

The Little Chapel

View of Sunrise Ranch from the irrigation canal

The Sculpture Pond
fountain, memorial to
Martin on Sunrise
Ranch

22

Overseas

April 1958 ~ December 1960

*I*n his service on April 19, "An Aspect of Leadership—Mutual Respect" and "A Review of Our Ministry," Martin shared a consideration of our ministry from his standpoint.

Those who participate in our program here on Sunrise Ranch have the primary responsibility for the ministry which extends on out into the world. That responsibility is shared by the Unit at the Hundred but primarily it centers here. Its nature has not yet been fully appreciated, but you are required to provide the example, release the power, reveal in action that which we present through the spoken and written word. If that is done we have a true center. I do not wish to produce too much of what we might call Unit introspection. I feel we should look out from the pattern here to that for which we are responsible out there. How many individuals would we have to contact to find one person who would carry through into the pattern of a true Emissary? We do not expect multitudes to respond and follow through, but amongst them are those who recognize and accept the fact of the Lord's choosing.

Therefore those who are to be true Emissaries in the service of our King find that the level of their contact is on the spiritual expression plane of being, and there must be something released on that plane to them if they are to find it. There are many people in the world sending out what is supposed to be help, instruction, educational programs of various kinds, primarily on the mental level, and there are millions who respond to that. But insofar as that to which we are ordained is concerned, such response means nothing unless it carries to the spiritual expression level.

"Exemplary Intercession" was the title of Martin's service on April 20.

I wonder how keenly aware you are of what we might call the "borrowed time" upon which the world of mankind, ourselves included, is living. There is only one hope, and that centers in God and His action on earth, which can only manifest through human beings. The world is in need of intercession, that the results of man's ill action may be turned aside. The nature of that intercession has been seen by some as the particular responsibility of Jesus Christ, that he is interceding with his Father, presumably to prevent this angry God from obliterating the human race. We see what it is that could obliterate the human race, but it is not the action of an angry god. It is the inevitable result of man's own choice, his violation of God's laws.

Martin spoke of "The Heavenly Atmosphere" on May 4:

God's will is done in heaven. If it is to be done on earth, heaven must be present on earth. To imagine how God's will would be done in heaven and then try to do that on earth produces a counterfeit; that is eating of the forbidden fruit, judging good and evil. God's will is done in heaven because the control in heaven is in God's hands. God's will is not done on earth because the control on earth is presently in man's hands. Because of that we find a great deal of the manifestation of hell. God's will cannot work except in heaven. If it is to work on earth, the atmosphere of heaven must be a reality here, the atmosphere of love, truth and life, available for expression through men and women.

What is the atmosphere that surrounds you, which you inflict upon others by your presence? Is it heavenly—stable, dependable, trustworthy, strong, loving, understanding? If there is something wrong that needs correction, a mess that needs clearing up, it cannot be done until the heavenly atmosphere is there. Man vaunts himself on his great intelligence, but the world itself reveals just how intelligent man is. Human beings can hardly solve the simplest problems in their own lives, let alone world problems, and the chaos and confusion increases because man's intelligence is not intelligent at all. He has so little awareness of that which is behind him, of what would make possible the manifestation of the atmosphere of heaven.

According to the record in the Book of Revelation, John turned to see the voice which spake with him, and being turned, he saw. In other words, it is evident that there was the capacity present in him as a human being to be aware of that which was behind—behind him as an individual and behind all manifest things. Only as we have that awareness of what is behind us can we begin to understand what is in front of us and act intelligently in relation to it.

In a Class on May 10, "The Spoken Word," Martin announced that two of last year's Class members, LeRoy and Nonna Jensen, were providing focalization as servers in Powell River, British Columbia. LeRoy, an artist, had made contact through Egon Milinkovich. The group in Powell River had been previously well established following a talk by Richard Thompson on June 10, 1956, after which the members continued to meet regularly in their various homes. Definite points of leadership emerged from within the group, primarily through Bill and Doreen Thompson. Monthly visits by Richard and Dorothy from Vancouver were welcomed in those early days.

On May 28 Martin ordained Roger de Winton and Richard Cable Ministers in the Church of the Emissaries of Divine Light.

A beautiful wedding ceremony was held in the Chapel on Sunrise Ranch on September 13 for Rev. James Wellemeyer and Anne Broddy, of Toronto. Michael Cecil and I were attendants.

In a service on October 15 on Sunrise Ranch, "The Expression of Practical Perfection," Martin shared a report from George Shears of a meeting where he spoke to a group of chiropractors, some of whom were his nephews. The Chiropractic Association in New Hampshire had expelled about twenty because they were practicing the G.P.C. principle. The Bahan brothers had experienced remarkable success in their program and were putting fifty-eight students through Palmer School of Chiropractic in Davenport, Iowa. This was disturbing other New Hampshire chiropractors who were concerned that these would come back there and practice.

A service on October 25, "The Challenge of the Present Moment," contains gems of truth, such as:

Whatever you are doing, in that moment it is your life work. Give to it all you have and are, that you may prove the power of God in action on earth, having accepted the challenge with which you are faced. It isn't some challenge out there somewhere, some day. Oh, we see this great task with which we are faced, but where is it? It's right here—in the pattern where we now are.

That does not need to limit the vision; there is something greater beyond, yes, but that isn't here now. What you are doing now is here. Moving on from that, unless I have been accepting what I am doing now as my life work, or have been doing all along the way, I shall not be able to accept the greater challenge when it comes.

Sixteen attended the Class of 1958 on Sunrise Ranch, among them Edith and Margaret Brownlee, Max von Hartmann, Martha Whitcomb, Jose Bruce, Jim and Mary Pogue, Gail Pogue, Floyd Conell and Della Bever. At that time there were fifty-three resident on Sunrise Ranch, fifteen of whom were children.

On February 22 Martin introduced a new song in his service, *Come and Behold Him*. He had written the words a year before and said:

Just a few weeks ago the vibrational pattern came to point so that the process could be initiated by which the music to the words might take form. Lillian carried through and wrote the music, which you heard sung this afternoon by the choir. The song extends an invitation:

Come and Behold Him

The Word of the King is spoken on earth,
"Come near unto me,"

The gate of His Kingdom is opened on earth;
Come, enter thou in,

The Way of His Love is prepared on earth;
Come, walk with rejoicing!

The River of Life is flowing on earth;
Come, drink of it freely,

The mystery of God is finished on earth;
Come and behold Him!

This exquisite expression has been an integral part of our service in true worship since that day.

In the 1959 issue of *Northern Light* Emily Marks paid tribute to Lillian's and my function in allowing old patterns in women to be loosed and made new, "in order to bring forth the manifestation on earth of the One Woman, including all."

It was at that time that Max von Hartmann joined the family at 100 Mile House, coming from the Class on Sunrise Ranch. Max, of German origin and with an intriguing background of experience in that country during the Second World War, has proved that the spirit of God is indeed available for His use, in all who will let it be so, to unite the body of mankind in love. Besides that contribution, he is a trained chef (the best!), and a stalwart pillar in the temple of our God.

Upon arriving at 100 Mile House from Sunrise Ranch Martin spoke in a service on June 3, "Foundation for Progress," of the degree of true oneness achieved by the eighth Class of the Servers Training School in session. He felt that personal difficulties had not been allowed to interfere with the Class as a whole. "That is absolutely wonderful. These things establish precedents and make possible forward movement, not only for the Class but for all concerned."

On July 29 at 100 Mile House Martin ordained three men as Ministers—Ross Marks, David Oshanek and Michael Cecil—

> into the ministry of the Lord on earth, that in oneness of spirit and purpose you may accept your individual responsibilities in ministry, no matter what they prove to be, and serve faithfully in them, letting God's will be done, concerned alone with the divine purposes, yielding all to the Lord. So is it established unto you in this hour and through you in blessing to all who will receive and share the ordination of the Lord on earth.

In the course of Martin's travels, in early August he and his party stopped in Coeur d'Alene, Idaho, where we met Dr. Victoria Carbury, the Minister of the "Church of Truth" there. Originally from Ireland, she and her husband had lived in Coeur d'Alene for about five years with their two children. She had a radio program with a national hookup every Sunday. Victoria and her husband had undergone some terrifying experiences during the World War in England and lost two young children, at which time Victoria sustained deep injuries herself. After moving, first to Canada and then the United States, two other children were born to them. The bereaved mother felt these replaced their great loss and were an answer to her prayer while in the midst of an inferno. A woman of indomitable spirit, it was a privilege to know her and her family and to stop there on a number of occasions, where Martin spoke in her church several times. Later we were delighted when she visited Sunrise Ranch.

There were seven couples in the 1959 Class which numbered twenty. To name a few, who contributed much through the years: John and Pat Summerbell, Mac and Jane Duff,

Harold and Win Pym, Bob and Edith Schmeer, Carl and Helen Kelly. LeAnna Moore (then Harman) has been a resident on Sunrise Ranch for many years, remarkable in her steady contribution, as were Bob and Edith Schmeer. Bob is still on the job here and married to Mary, formerly Milinkovich, nee Thompson. Another future and valued member of the Sunrise family was Clayre Withers.

On August 22 Martin carried a gift into the Chapel on Sunrise Ranch, a beautiful eagle in flight, in bronze. It was placed on the wall directly above the chair occupied by him or whoever was giving the service. A fitting symbol of the spirit of truth, the eagle has a great span of powerful wings, a tremendous range in flight and speed, all the while maintaining perfect control and accurate vision in its freedom in the rarefied atmosphere of high altitudes.

That year marked a vital addition on Sunrise Ranch. The upper story of an Army Air Force Barracks building was transported in two halves from the Cheyenne Air Force Base. The foundation had been dug and prepared, and then what a sight to watch the capacious structure turn majestically into our road. It was placed expertly on the foundation, the second half coming close behind and backed into place to form a truly beautiful and adequate new dining room. Decorated tastefully, with new tables and chairs, it marked the beginning of a cycle for the appearance of many needed buildings in Eden Valley.

The building which housed the Chapel also provided accommodation at that time for a printshop and office.

Bill Dice had a remarkable ability to find incredible bargains at auction sales—a building, or vital piece of machinery, furniture, anything that was needed, at a price we could afford, and often less!

Of interest, in the minutes of a Board Meeting on Sunrise Ranch on October 9, are references to people focusing centers in widely divergent places. Mac Duff reported on a new center in Toronto; Bud Murray in Bowmanville nearby; Bob and Edith Schmeer in Hazleton, Pennsylvania; Anna Drury in Pittsburgh; and Timo and Adex in Nigeria. Chris Foster was making contacts in England, Dave and Rosa Groves in Ohio, and Carl Kelly in Chatham.

Martin and Lillian embarked on a journey which was vital in the unfoldment of our overseas ministry. Martin commented that this had never happened while Uranda was here and was the first time under his own leadership. Lillian later wrote a glowing account in *Northern Light* of her initial visit to England and Martin's family, from their departure in Denver on October 15. After stops at Toronto and Montreal they flew TCA with about 70 passengers and crew to land at Prestwick Airport in Scotland for customs, etc. Then on to London where they were met by the chauffeur from Burghley House, Martin's birthplace and boyhood home.

This was a fulfilling time, for Lillian to meet Martin's parents and family and for Martin to bring his wife "home." Some time was spent in London, with a service also in Tunbridge Wells. The return trip was via BOAC Britannia. Turbulent weather necessitated a stop at Gander, Newfoundland, and a late landing at Idlewild Airport in New York. They enjoyed a day in the big city, hosted by a chiropractor friend, Dr. Jim Chresomales and his wife Penny.

The following day they flew to Boston, where they were met by Bill Bahan and stayed two nights with his parents at their home in Methuen, Massachusetts.

The Bahan family consisted of five sons, all chiropractors (the George Shears influence), and four daughters. At that time there were thirty-six chiropractors in New Hampshire serving on the G.P.C. principle, and fifty-two in the whole of North America. The Bahan brothers operated two clinics: one in Salem, Massachusetts, the other in Derry, New Hampshire. This connection was most significant, with the youngest members of the family, Bill, Walter and Shirley, playing vital roles in the ministry.

A meeting was held in the home of Walter and Joan Bahan, with about twenty-five in attendance. With their three children, they provided a center in that area over many years, which eventually occupied a beautiful estate given the name "Green Pastures." It nestled amongst wonderful ancient trees, with roomy old houses, barn and other buildings. Bill, with his wife Ruth and three children, provided vibrant leadership in that area, with an unequalled passion for "bringing in the sheaves," sometimes whether they wanted to come or not! Bruce Valentine, functioning on the G.P.C. principle, served in the New England area with his wife Selma, as did Bob and Alice Spaulding.

On the 6th of November Martin and Lillian flew from Boston to Chicago, and finally home after an exciting and rewarding trip. It was a joyful reunion with Marina at the Denver airport.

On November 25 on Sunrise Ranch Martin brought a new element into "A Service of Radiation," in which he utilized the golden bowl, which had its special place on the altar in the Chapel, as a symbol which represented those present. He spoke several names to be included in radiation in filling special needs, then encompassed "all those responsive needs that rise up in your minds and hearts, held together by the substance of God's love."

In a service at 100 Mile House on January 24, 1960, "Putting God First," Martin spoke of the differences in function between the Unit there and the one at Sunrise Ranch, in part resulting from the varying proximities to the towns in which they reside.

> We have a program here which is vital to the Lord's ministry on earth,
> from the standpoint of each of you undergoing training as servants of God. It
> is vital from the standpoint that the Lord has made available considerable

funds for His purposes, through our businesses, etc. A substantial sum goes to Sunrise Ranch from here. If it had not been for that, the way things have been, the ministry would have had to be curtailed tremendously. So obviously there is a vital ministry here in that respect.

On Sunrise Ranch the program is different. There is no source of income other than gifts received. The uses to which such funds are put are almost entirely devoted directly to the ministry itself. As far as the personnel are concerned, very, very little has been done to improve their quarters. All the printing is done there and so a printshop had to be built. Considerable money has been invested in equipment and we shall be needing more. We have had to buy a stapling, and then a folding, machine and another IBM Executive typewriter at $595. With the increase on our mailing list, in which we greatly rejoice, there is the constantly increasing need for more printing, more paper, more stamps, more envelopes, more everything.

A new dining room was required, not for the personnel on Sunrise Ranch [though it was becoming crowded!] but because of the increase in numbers during Class and Conference times. A great deal of money has gone into that and we are most grateful for contributions, from here, Vancouver, Toronto and other places. But as far as the operating expenses are concerned a rather small proportion is used for providing food to eat or improving their living quarters. There has been wonderful improvement in the Bishop's residence, and I am richly blessed both here and at Sunrise in that regard. I do not believe any of you here or there have a grudging attitude in that regard, and that is well. Yet I think you know that I do not serve because I have a nice house. There is no plumbing on Sunrise Ranch, except in the Bishop's residence and Bertha Meyer's house. We look for the day when there will be, but there are so many other needs directly relating to the ministry of the Lord.

Perhaps there has been a tendency here to lose sight of these things. It is so easy to look out into the community round about and see the things that people have. By the same token, we can see the vital things they do not have. Let us not be deluded by the relatively insignificant things which they do have. We are not competing with the world, endeavoring to have all the world has. That is not our purpose. Our purpose is to serve God, to let His will be done, to increase the manifest expression of His ministry.

I think sometimes in relation to the children there is an attitude that the town children have this, that, and the other. They do not have what we have here. If we ourselves put more emphasis on the external things as being important, our children will do likewise. As I have said before, there is nothing wrong with having things, or with the things themselves, but there can be something very, very wrong when they take too prominent a position. We are supposed to be revealing the worth and value of the things of God to each other, to our children, and to those, anywhere, who have eyes to see it.

In Martin's service on January 27, "Jehovah," he spoke of the

free, unfettered working of the spirit of God through the name *Jehovah*, the true name of God in action on earth, in which there are no consonants, all vowels. [In the language from which the name was interpreted, "J" does not carry the consonant sound, and the word consists solely of the five vowels.] It is one sound, unlimited; and until there is that manifesting through the human being God is not in action.

In a service on February 14, "The Capacity to Be Governed," Martin said:

It has been stated generally in the Christian world that mankind's fall took place because human beings ceased being governed by God in the divine design and descended to a level within themselves where that government could no longer adequately operate. Man (men and women) was created to provide the connecting link between heaven and earth, between God and the rest of creation in the world. With man in place at the apex of the creation God's dominion could readily manifest through him in relation to all created things, and there was control.

Man first left his place in relation to his own being but in so doing left his place in relation to all created things. He began to identify himself with his body and its consciousness and the results appeared round about. He was functioning at a level which correlates with the animal kingdom where the dominion was designed to work through man, as was also true with respect to the other levels of creation. When man came down to the vibratory levels directly related to the animal kingdom he was no longer in position to exercise dominion, because dominion was designed to come to that level from God through him. Therefore all attempts to raise himself up to be something of importance, while remaining within the scope of the levels to which he has fallen, is futile! He is supposed to share the action, not be subject to it.

We are not, for the moment, concerned with the pattern as it was in the Motherland but with what is the case now. There were many levels of education, and we have spoken of the Seven Sacred Schools, for instance. If there is to be a return to the divine state there must be the learning which makes it possible. It will not appear by chance or by some peculiar magic. There must be discipline, and the primary thing to be restored in consciousness is obedience.

In the story of Noah, in spite of all the wickedness, violence and conflict around the world [sound familiar?] he was still able, because of his training and practice in obedience, to receive what was necessary from the Lord. Because he followed directions before the submersion of the continent, after the great cataclysm there was preservation of life sufficient for a new beginning, for what we might call further colonization. There was a particular movement to Egypt, for instance, with the Great Pyramid and the Sphinx established before the Flood.

The Bible was written—much of it—not only to tell a story of what happened in the past, but to portray the principles for right function in the days to come. That was also the reason the Great Pyramid was built. The story of the Flood, while it has some historical significance, indicates what is necessary to those with eyes to see it now. We recognize the necessity of the construction of an ark, not necessarily a boat covered within and without with pitch, the oil of love, but certainly permeated by God's love.

The way the story is written it seems as though the Lord spoke to Noah. But how? Noah was obedient. His body and mind and heart were moving under the dominion of God, and consequently they expressed that which was from God. It is not a mysterious process. It does not require fanciful imagination of some mighty figure thundering out of heaven telling Noah what to do. When there is internal government, that which is required from the divine standpoint appears through the capacities designed to convey it into the world. If they are not obedient, deluded into imagining that they are something of themselves and can produce something of themselves, they know nothing of that which the Lord is offering. It is all present, available, and we are here, to learn and practice true obedience.

Martin touched on some points relative to the foregoing in a service at 100 Mile House on March 5 entitled "Training in Responsibility":

Before what is called the fall, humanity as a whole carried a very great responsibility both with respect to the divine purposes here on earth, the rest of the forms of creation on this planet, and also to the greater sphere of things in the solar system. The earth is certainly not unrelated to the rest of the solar system. Man was the connecting link between the creator and creation. There were necessarily those who had particularly great responsibility, but each individual was handling his or her own specific field of responsibility.

There came a time when the creative currents from God were not allowed to work through the whole of mankind, and troubles began, distortions appeared in the pattern. For a considerable period of time control was maintained through those who were permitting the divine design to continue to manifest, but finally there came a point when divine man ceased to be on earth and at that point the creative currents from God had nothing through which to move except fallen man. There followed tremendous upheavals because that over which man had had dominion was thrown out of polarity. Man was seeking to establish his own dominion, and the earth, and even the solar system, were affected.

There is the general view that this planet has been moving around the sun in much the same orbit, in the same way ever since its creation. Therefore, in this hypothesis, a lengthy period of gradual processes of evolution was provided—around five billion years, I believe. But of course many things remained unexplained. I read the other day the suggestion that periodically, for some reason, the earth gave a sort of shudder and because of that the ice caps began to move down over the continents. Well, the earth has shuddered all right, subjected to the unnatural stresses and strains imposed on it by man's failure. And fallen man lost his vision. It was blotted out; it did not take long; and he also lost his sense of responsibility to God.

The purpose of this ministry which we share is achieved to the extent that it becomes a means for God's dominion to be reestablished on earth. That cannot happen without the restoration of some human beings to a state where they begin to remember from whence they fell and to find again that sense of responsibility to God. Once God has that, the creative currents can move according to the design established for the earth and the entire solar system, and dominion be restored.

At this point, Martin spoke of his responsibilities in his early days at 100 Mile House:

I do not like to talk much about myself, but it may be profitable to look at the tremendous growth that has taken place here at 100 Mile House in the last thirty years and the wonderful opportunity for training I have had during that time. There was a total of about fifty thousand acres, and I was running some two thousand head of cattle, with at one time two thousand head of sheep. The Lodge was here; the ranch was here; the store was here, which also housed the post office and the telephone and telegraph offices.

When I arrived there was no running water, no electric light. I was responsible for these things if they were to take form; there was no one else. I ran the ranch and did a good deal of the actual work. I ran the Lodge—I have waited table. I ran the store, looked after the post office, telegraph office, the telephone exchange, kept the books for the Lodge, the store and the ranch; and there were always forms to be made out in relation to the telephone, telegraph and post office. I also had outside interests and was president of the Cariboo Cattlemen's Association from its beginning, until I resigned after many years. And there were other functions dealing with provincial associations.

Responsibility! It was all interesting work, but because of my rather unique position, just about everything fell upon my shoulders. If the plumbing froze up I had to thaw it out. If the light plant broke down I had to fix it. If the beavers built a dam across the creek and shut off our water supply I had to go and dynamite it, sometimes in the middle of the night. Often, returning from a trip to Vancouver I would arrive late at night and find that all the power was off and would work all night to try to get it going. Wonderful training! If I did not do what was required, it would not be done, and so I did it.

When we had sheep they gave me my baptism in many ways! I spent many sleepless nights trying to figure out how I could feed a thousand head of sheep when there was no hay, and winter coming on. There was no market for them; you could not *give* them away. What to do? I could not sit there and just watch them die. Suffice it to say, the Lord provided a way and we saved the majority. Then later we had a little bunch of sheep around and they usually lambed in February. I acted as midwife, because you cannot leave a newborn lamb even in the barn when it is twenty or thirty below zero for fifteen minutes before it is frozen solid. So I spent many a night in the barn, watching those sheep and then bringing the lambs up to the Lodge Apartment where I put them on sacks around a little heater to dry out.

With respect to all these activities, there was an initiation of baby cycles which have expanded. Why? Oh, we may say the lumber industry came in, etc. No. Because those baby cycles were taken care of, handled. None of them were let down. What needed to be done was done, and for the most part I did it. What else could I do, and keep my integrity? The thought might have occurred on occasion that it was not worth it, but there was the job to do, and I thank God for that training. I was not always too happy about it at the time and there was always seemingly more than I could possibly handle. But I always handled it. I have suffered from most of the ills to which flesh is heir, in one way or another, but looking back I cannot remember ever staying in bed for a whole day—not that I would not have liked to many times. I am still here.

My responsibilities have not grown less. All that back there was child's play. There are many things taking place of which you are quite unaware, but which I have to handle every day, and I have this responsibility in relation to the whole of God's creation, something trusted to me. Can it also be trusted to you? How much of God's dominion is operating in you, in relation to your immediate fields of responsibility? What is your attitude when something is required of you? "I will accept this responsibility; I know it can be done"? Or do you say, "Oh well, there are others who can handle it; I have too much to do already"? Weak, wishy-washy nothingness! We are looking for those who are strong, who let the dominion of God manifest, who answer, "In the power of the Lord I am capable of handling anything." As long as you can say, "Not yet," you will never come to that point. Oh, it may start in minor things. The world certainly would not have stopped if I had not handled my responsibility. But you would not be here if I had not.

Dominion! What mountains human beings make out of molehills! They cringe before things over which God has ordained that His crowning creation should have dominion. I thank God that there are those who are sharing in the reality of dominion with me, in those things which are at hand to do now.

In a Board meeting on Sunrise Ranch on February 26 there was consideration of proper handling of distribution of tape mailings for sale to our people, and the possibility of other items produced on the Ranch in the future, such as organically grown foods and flour, which might be sold and need separate classification for commercial opportunities.

On March 15 in another Board Meeting Martin recommended that some action be taken with respect to grave markers, with the result that six small and one large one, in red granite, were ordered from the American Beauty Company.

Two outstanding and greatly loved friends left this sphere in 1960, one at Sunrise in the person of Roy Kuykendall and the other at the Hundred, Gordon Marks. Bright spirits, lifting the hearts of those around them, the absence of these two men was deeply felt, combined with profound appreciation for their wonderful qualities of leadership.

It was on April 16 that Kirk was out in the field on the tractor and came back to the Ranch, saying he felt the need to share an attunement and to rest. Lying on his couch in the living room, he quietly left this sphere of things. His last years, working as Ranch

Manager, were rewarding, for him and for the "family," who would miss his infectious joy and ready laugh. It was through the friendship with him and Alice that the Mayor, Ed Garrett, and his wife Bobby found their way to Sunrise and Home.

Gordon Marks was a true pioneer in the beginning days of the Unit at 100 Mile House. Previously a linotype printer, he found a multitude of areas awaiting his talents. His wife Emily laughingly commented once, "We arrived one day, and the next day Martin told us to take care of the Lodge business, and immediately left for England!" Gordon's presence filled a very large place in the Unit, in a way similar to that of Kirk's with a jolly mien that did not depend on the way he might feel, physically or otherwise. Very active in the development of the town of 100 Mile House, he held the first position as Magistrate.

There were eighty people from the Village of 100 Mile House sharing a memorial tribute to their friend Gordon, and many townspeople from Loveland were present at Kirk's funeral on Sunrise Ranch.

In a service on Sunrise Ranch, April 24, "Let There Be Light," Martin referred to the fact that there are some seventy vibratory octaves of radiation of which human beings have become aware.

The physical spectrum occupies less than one octave, and yet there is no real distinction between any of these levels except the vibratory rate. Just because man has the equipment to perceive with his eyes a very limited range of these radiant vibrations does not cause that which he is able to see to be different from all the rest of the range; it is all one thing. We have the equipment to be aware of a certain range visually; we are aware of some more through the sensation of heat. We call it heat in that range, we call it light in a little bit higher range, and all these various radiation bands have been given names by human beings, but fundamentally they are all the same thing, that which is referred to as light.

It is this radiation, which comes primarily from the sun as far as this earth is concerned, that activates the design established in relation to the forms of life on earth. If the earth was suddenly excluded from the radiation from the sun it would be a dead planet almost immediately.

For that true manifestation of life which is supposed to appear through man revealing God on earth there is the necessity of that which is symbolized by light, a vibratory radiation at a level different from the levels of which man is aware either through his own senses or through equipment that he has been able to develop. As long as he excludes himself from this radiation by insisting that his life be governed by the determinations of his own mind he condemns himself to disintegration. Mankind has not, obviously, completely excluded it-self from all the radiation coming from God; it is a partial eclipse we might say.

All that the mind is required to do is let go and yield the design of life to God. When man begins to yield to that which is of God there is a range of vibration of which he may be consciously aware but there is also a range of which he is not properly consciously aware which moves through the deeper levels of his consciousness. We have taken note of the terminology used in the Bible, the "Holy Ghost." There is a range of radiation which properly fills the whole void of man's being which has been for so long empty of the things of God and filled with the rubbish produced by the wrong uses of his own mind, and it has stood as a veil between himself and God. When the spirit of God is allowed to move upon the face of the waters of man's own being, then the creative word is spoken, "Let there be light," and the radiation which actually comes from God may activate the design established in man so that it begins to become functional again.

The title of a Class on Sunrise Ranch on April 25 was "The Organization of God Beings Composing God." Martin specifically clarified the point, sometimes challenged in Class, of focalization:

While God is one being, that fact is consequent upon all the parts being in place. God is composed of all the God Beings in the whole of the cosmos, and the parts of God Being fit together. We do not need to concern ourselves with anything beyond our own solar system, but, more specifically, with anything beyond our own planet. In relation to this planet there are God Beings who are responsible for it, and insofar as we are concerned the sum total of those God Beings constitute God, in that context composed of perhaps some seven billion individual God Beings. These are referred to in the Bible, by various words: the angels of God, for instance.

Obviously, if this body is to function in a manner that does not produce conflicts, there must be an organization, a pattern of some kind which coor-dinates all beings into one thing. This organization is made possible by rea-son of the principle of focalization. All things are drawn to a point some-where, and we have utilized the triangle as a symbol of this principle. The triangle has an apex and a body. That which is of the apex focalizes the es-sences of the whole triangle. You can keep reducing its size; it is the same triangle, only a different size. Gradually, as you approach the apex it becomes smaller and smaller, but within that smaller triangle everything else of the whole, larger triangle is focalized. We begin to know what it is when we let that point expand and become whatever the form may be.

That apex focalization contains within Himself everything that may be expanded into the triangle as a whole. That apex focalization is one God Being. We have spoken of Him as the LORD of Lords and KING of Kings. Contained within the rest of the triangle are the Lords over whom He is LORD and the Kings over whom He is KING.

There are God Beings incarnate on earth and those who are not. There are those specifically responsible in relation to the inner plane aspect of this world and those specifically responsible for the outer plane aspects. We may see that truth portrayed in these candles: three candles on either side of the central one. The three on this side represent the inner plane pattern and the three on the other side represent the outer plane pattern; the one in the center represents that which provides the essential vibratory factors which unify the inner and the outer.

LORD of Lords, He is, in turn, the representative of the higher focalizations of God Being as they are established in the solar system as a whole, specifically in the sun, the highest point insofar as this world is concerned. That God Being incarnated on earth in the body of Jesus, a revelation of the apex of God Being in relation to this world. We can recognize that, from the words which He spoke, either as referring to the God Being incarnate in His outer form or as an expression by the LORD of Lords with reference to the Father, the higher point of focalization of Deity which centers in the sun.

We may recognize one individual God Being bringing to focus each plane insofar as this world is concerned. The seventh plane is the highest. We sometimes speak of the LORD of Lords as the Lord of the Sacred Seven. These candles represent the sacred seven. There is a focalization for each of the three inner planes and one for each of the three outer planes—either the focalizations or the planes themselves. The seven are spoken of in Genesis as *Elohim*, a plural word for *God*. "Let us make man" was an expression coming through the Elohim, the seven rulers of this world.

There is an ultimate point of apex, what we might call the GOD of Gods, a central focalization of Deity for the cosmos. But there is an uninterrupted pattern extending from that point throughout the whole body of God right down to us here. The divine organization is not a haphazard affair. Angels do not just flit around wherever they please, according to the human concept. They have definite places and responsibilities—not an arduous business but the most wonderful thing, providing the experience of fulfilment in each moment throughout eternity; and there is a shifting and a changing, to a certain extent. Obviously, there was a starting point in relation to the creation of this world, and there was something that went before. And when that for which this world was created is finally consummated, there is something that will follow. There is plenty of scope in the divine provision.

The six God Beings on either side of the LORD of Lords are responsible to Him. Those focalized by the six are responsible to the particular focalization under which they serve. So the whole body of God is brought to the apex on the basis of focalization. There are those God Beings who form the base of the triangle, and they fill the whole triangle to complete the One God insofar as this world is concerned. Individual God Beings have specific places in relation to that divine pattern, and it is that place which needs to take form through each of us and find application in our living, so that we know it, and not just in theory.

In Martin's service on May 28, "The Seventh Angel," he spoke of the seventh spirit before the throne of God, mentioned in Revelation, as being the Spirit of Love, at a particular time finding outer form in the body of Jesus. He dealt masterfully with references in the eleventh chapter of Revelation, closing with the words:

God's love is irresistible. You can look at that two ways. For those who respond it is irresistible and draws the human being back to God; if there is any true response in the individual he cannot get away from it.

On the other hand, if the dominant element in the individual is one of fighting against God's love, resisting it, refusing to be moved by it, then it is irresistible in its power to repel that individual into what is described as outer darkness, where there is "weeping and gnashing of teeth"; a painful business, not in some obscure hell somewhere but right here on earth. So a process of separation occurs. It is not an arbitrary thing; each person decides for him- or herself. Surely we have found the power of God's love to be irresistible, and being returned to our rightful place with God we find that the kingdoms of this world become the kingdoms of our Lord and of His Christ.

On June 12, in "The Journey," Martin said:

I would like to tell you a little story. Yesterday Michael and I took a little journey. The objective was to go to a place about twelve or fifteen miles due west of 100 Mile House in a rather untraveled part of the country to look at some property. The so-called road which leads to it is not very good, so we selected the jeep as our conveyance. The first part was through familiar country, which has been changed because of recent logging operations. Once very beautiful, untouched, there is now evidence of devastation on every hand, an unholy mess: skid roads radiating in every direction, piles of brush, logs lying around, most of the green ground cover destroyed. We may say that such logging activity is an essential part of man's world. Perhaps it might impress upon us the importance of letting the pattern established by human beings be changed.

As we drove along the road we were under the necessity of cutting various trees that had fallen and blocked our way. Finally we came out of the logging area into the more or less untouched countryside, where the beauty of the land was revealed again. What a remarkable transition! We had previously flown over the territory. Distances are rather deceptive when seen from the air. There cannot be the experience of that which is known by the actual movement on the surface of the ground; it can only be imagined. Being on the ground the beauty of things close at hand may be appreciated, the spring smell of the woods, and the sounds.

We came to a very muddy place and, perhaps putting more trust in the four-wheel-drive than we should have, we stuck fast. The frame of the jeep was resting upon the mud, and the wheels were not gripping. How to get out of that one? We had a shovel of course and could shovel out a little around the wheels, but in that gooey mud with water running constantly it was very difficult to get the dirt out from under the frame. The wheels just sank deeper, so we undertook to raise the jeep and place a firm foundation under the wheels. It took about two hours in that mud hole, but eventually we were able to back out and go around it and continue on our journey.

How important it is as we move along that we make sure when we approach any hazard that we have a firm foundation and are not standing on sinking sand. If we get caught in a morass we have to back up and, before that, reestablish the firm foundation. Have you ever found yourselves caught in a morass, floundering around in a muddy place, sinking and struggling and getting dirty? It is necessary to find the rock foundation. When we got stuck yesterday the material was there available to enable us to get on. There is always the material available, particularly for you who have come into a greater understanding of the laws and principles of being. There is the One Law. Orient! Find the firm foundation. Back up out of the mud hole and go around it. There is no sense in plunging into it. If you plunge into it once, back out but do not go plunging into it again.

At one point we came to a stream. There was a bridge that you could hardly see because it was covered with water. After careful inspection we agreed to proceed and reached the other side and went on. There needs to be the agreement between the two of you—heart and mind—if you are to keep moving. After a while we came to the same stream again and there was no bridge, just a ford, probably two or three feet deep in the middle, so we left man's machine behind and proceeded by foot, without getting too wet. Man's machinery will take you just so far. Finally we came to our destination after a mile or so and walked on to a lake I wanted to see from the ground, not just from the air. What a beautiful place!

It seems to me that this could be a portrayal of that journey which all who are moving toward the garden planted eastward in Eden must take. It is necessary to move through an area where man's devastation of things divine is seen on every hand. There is a trail; others have gone before and we are most thankful that they built that bridge, for instance. Others have marked it out, but we do not know it unless we travel it. There is a goal but let us not imagine that when we have reached it the purpose is to stay there. We can be of no value as servants of our Lord in providing that which is necessary to others until we have done it ourselves, following through every step of the way.

On September 17 Martin performed a marriage ceremony in the Chapel on Sunrise Ranch for Harry Jerome and Helen Jones, sister of Gladys Miller.

A baby girl was born to Jim and Anne Wellemeyer on September 21st, to be named Lana.

Twenty eager men and women composed the Class of 1960. From New Hampshire were Walter and Joan Bahan, also Bob and Alice Spaulding; from 100 Mile House, Ross and Marcia Marks, Emily Marks and Dorothy Hughes; from Ontario, Winifred Moore, mother of Dorothy Jones and Jim Moore; also from eastern Canada, Violet Gibbs and June Lloyd. Vivian Grindstaff and Bob Moore, of Sunrise, contributed much, as did others.

On September 26, Martin and Lillian, accompanied by Roger de Winton, departed on an extensive motor trip to visit the many groups fast materializing on this continent. Marina and I were passengers on the first leg of the journey, affording Lillian's parents a visit with their granddaughter. The first overnight stop was in Lincoln, Nebraska; the second in Iowa at the home of Mike and Dorothea McCann, with daughter Pam, a warmly welcoming stop. At Davenport, Iowa, the following day Martin spoke to a gathering of students in the Palmer College of Chiropractic. The next four days with Lillian's parents, Roy and Marie Johnson, in their home in Franksville, Wisconsin, provided a pleasant and relaxing time for all of us and particularly a prelude to Martin's very busy trip. He, Lillian and Roger then left for Windsor, Ontario, after seeing Marina and me off for our return trip to Denver—a very special experience with a little girl's first airplane ride, which she thoroughly enjoyed. So did I.

Martin's speaking tour continued, recorded by Lillian on their return:

> We proceeded to Chatham, staying with Ray and June Lloyd, where a public meeting was held with eighty-five in attendance; the next stop London, Ontario, where little Chipman, son of Bob and Bev Purdom, was christened; on to Toronto with Jim and Mary Pogue and a public lecture in a hotel attended by two hundred thirty-five. [Martin commented later that he never mentioned God in that talk and there was excellent response, also interest on the part of reporters who requested an interview.] A meeting of the group was held the following evening in their new center. There were brief stops at Port Hope [scene of Richard Thompson's early teaching days in Canada at a Boys' School] and Ottawa. The next visit, to Montreal, was memorable, with Jack and Helen Stubbs and family. [Incidentally, in view of the steadily increasing number of their offspring, they were once asked the question, "Are you Catholic?" to which the answer came, "No, just passionate Protestants!"]
>
> The next stop was North Conway, New Hampshire, at the clinic of Bob and Alice Spaulding with their group of about fifty, followed by a visit to the Bahan Derry Clinic and overnight with Bruce and Selma Valentine in Andover, Massachusetts. Martin lectured at the Phillips Academy. A lobster dinner with Wally and Joan Bahan was memorable. After a visit in Nyack, New York, with Daniel and Grace McGaurn, there was time for some gift-shopping for the children. Then to Pennsylvania and Bob and Edith Schmeer's center in Hollywood, and Berwick to stay with Eddie and Gladys Miller at their center. A service that evening, October 16, was most welcomed by the friends there, also a public lecture the next evening. Myron and Elsie Fausey showed us their farm. Our visit with Howard and Evelyn Bittenbender in their home was the first of many to follow in years to come.

Howard and Evelyn contributed in consistent and invaluable ways to the welfare of the family on Sunrise Ranch. Besides their generous monetary donations, on occasion a box of clothing (the best) would be received, and distributed with great joy. One day at Big Thompson School one of our little girls was wearing a "new" dress and one of her friends said, "That's a pretty dress. Where did you get it?" The answer was, proudly, "In a box!"

Lillian continued:

> A brief stop and lecture in Pittsburgh, Pennsylvania, at the home of Fred

and Mildred Raupach was followed by several days in Huntingburg, Indiana, with George and Naomi Shears and time for some well-earned rest. A public lecture there concluded the "ministry" trip, with excellent turnout and interest. After an overnight stay with George and Jean (my sister) Stabler and family in Belleville, Missouri, followed by one in Seneca, Kansas, and a long drive of 550 miles, we arrived *home.*

And that evening—tired or not!—was spent sharing the trip with the Sunrise family.

Incidentally, I was surprised to read, in the 1960 issue of *Eden Valley News,* that I had conducted "most inspiring services" on the Ranch "to coincide with Martin's lectures" during the above-mentioned trip.

Floyd Conell had married Gail Pogue and they were busy establishing their abode on Sunrise Ranch and also their family, eventually three sons and a daughter. Floyd had lived in Loveland with his parents before moving to the Ranch, where he worked tirelessly in the position of Manager—and in the fields—for many years.

Tom Crouch, a devoted follower of Uranda and his teachings, was leaving for Thermopolis, Wyoming, having accepted a teaching position. In later years Tom purchased a small hotel in Strasburg, Colorado, and developed a group there, running the hotel and developing a successful honey-making business. Sunrise could always depend on Tom and his group for support. Today two very capable and dedicated members of that group, Marsha Bogolin and Bill Crosman, fill vital roles on Sunrise Ranch.

That year saw the initiation of a two-story Apartment Building, which has provided vital accommodation in Eden Valley ever since. The site was leveled and John Summerbell was drawing up the plans. John's talents and ever-ready spirit of happy willingness have proved to be invaluable in countless areas of our ministry, without regard to boundaries such as oceans—either one! It was anticipated that the building would house at least 170 people. Designed to have three wings, it would be built in sections, part of the first, running from north to south, to be completed in time for the 1961 Class. When finished it would form an open "U," facing the county road.

Other pressing needs were considered, including finishing an apartment in the old ranchhouse, to be used by Alice Kuykendall, who after Kirk's passing was moving from their tiny quarters in the Chapel building. She contributed funds for the installation of toilet facilities in the old house, and an adequate heating system was under way, including sufficient insulation. There was also room for an office as she had become proficient in helping with the increasing work at Headquarters. It was not long before Alice's talents and irrepressible spirit made it a very "new" ranchhouse. There was always a welcome—and a hearty laugh!

23

CLEARING THE AIR

January 1961 ~ January 1963

*I*n the 1961 issue of *Northern Light* Michael Cecil wrote an article entitled "Our Ranch" which portrays some of the history and atmosphere surrounding life in the Unit at 100 Mile House through the years.

Almost a century ago in the pioneer days of the Barkerville gold rush, the first white settlers moved into this area and built a stopping house on the gold rush trail, where miners and freighters rested on the journey north. A ranch soon developed in relation to the stopping house, including a big barn where horses could be fed and rested. It later burned down and was replaced by the large structure which still stands today. Built to stable forty teams of horses, now it is useful for feed storage, ranch horses and for milking a number of cows.

The outfit changed hands several times through the years until in 1912 the Marquess of Exeter bought the place on speculation. In the meantime many other ranches had opened up in the area, being excellent ranching country producing much of the best beef in the Province of British Columbia. The Marquess, who had large interests in England to keep him occupied, had a manager run the ranch and store and stopping house until 1930 when Martin, who was his son, came out to take over the property for him. Martin has been here through the years, and has owned the place since 1950. Under his wise and loving guidance the land has flourished, bringing forth much fruit after some bleak years in the 1930s.

Now a busy village has sprung up on the best wheat field, the area is full of people and many unimagined activities. A mighty gas pipeline runs through our back yard on its way to the western states. Electricity spans 130 miles to reach us from the north and a smooth superhighway rushes through the village, stretching from Vancouver to Dawson Creek—a far cry from the ruts and bumps of the old trail. But the ranch itself, covering more than 12,000 acres, stays much the same in all its natural beauty and peace, reminding us of the nearness of the Creator and His handiwork.

For so many years it was Martin's own particular joy to work hard and ride through all the miles of this God's country, and now it is my lot to manage the ranch, with the able assistance of our trusted foreman Alex Morrison; for our Bishop is well occupied in larger fields of service. It is a land of vast forests—pine, poplar and fir—rolling out like a great green carpet across the country. It is also a land of hills and valleys, of fields rich with sweet grasses, of rippling singing brooks filled with cold refreshing waters that dance down to a thousand lakes or wind silently amid the willows through the fields. What a joy it is to till the field, bring in a harvest of hay in tight green bales, watch the steers fatten on the summer grasses, and see a multitude of fresh young calves appear, dancing in the sun.

A large part of the ranch, being forested, is used mainly for shelter and grazing. The cattle are let loose among the trees and in the clearings throughout the summer. There are, however, several hundred acres of cultivated land, much of it near the ranch headquarters. Hay is the main crop, with clover and alfalfa prominent. A considerable amount of swamp hay is also put up from the fertile but wet areas down by the lakes. A good deal of hay must be taken in because of the long cold winters, occasionally down to 50 degrees below zero, though it has been milder in recent years.

By utilizing only the topmost levels of the soil to prepare a seed bed it is anticipated that a much better use of nature's riches can be made, with a resulting increase in yield. We are seeking to find ways and means to avoid violating the integrity of the soil, with chemicals and destructive methods becoming so common. This has carried through to the raising of the cattle themselves that are fed and doctored in as natural a way as possible. They exhibit remarkable health. Our steers are sold to the local supermarket here (we have our own slaughterhouse) and we are happy to note the marked preference of customers for Bridge Creek beef!

About 700 head of cattle are presently carried and this is being increased due to recent purchase of good haylands. An ever more efficient operation is being worked toward so that every inch of that which we have may be used to the full, no waste. New methods of farming are being worked with, new buildings planned, new yards and fences. Yet without doubt it matters little what we shall do in this regard insofar as the nature of the country is concerned: it shall remain the same. As long as the Lord is allowed to be in this place the loon shall cry his haunting cry upon the stillness of the lake down the valley, the smell of fresh-cut hay shall come to us from the fields upon the mellow summer air, and the silent silhouette of the pines upon the hills shall stand out in the clear distance of this north country, night after night, to remind us that all of this is His, and we are His, and there is a job to do for Him in this place.

On April 30 on Sunrise Ranch Martin spoke on "The Willingness to Be Different":

The little baby is concerned solely with its own physical needs; if it is hungry, uncomfortable, wet, whatever, it makes its displeasure known by crying. It would seem that this manner of filling individual needs is never completely outgrown by most human beings. If something does not please them they make their displeasure known by yammering in various ways. In the unfolding cycles of growth, that self-centeredness which is concerned with the apparent physical needs begins to expand in relation to the desires of mind and heart.

In the world of man, in order to make it possible for human beings to live together without a constant battle, certain checks and controls are provided to prevent self-centeredness from going to an unreasonable extreme, and human beings conform to this pattern, which is accepted on the basis of the majority idea. Some break out of it in criminal activity; others would like to break out of it but dare not for fear of what would happen to them; some do it up to a point if they can keep it concealed from their fellows. But all this is contained within the pattern of human self-centeredness. Generally speaking people do not like to be too different from their fellows. Up to a point there may be distinctions that are acceptable, but most do not wish to stand out beyond the accepted norm of the group.

There is a fear of being different, and yet the evidence of increasing maturity is revealed in the greater manifestation of the true individual differences—not based in self-centeredness but differences based in divine nature. From the divine standpoint, each one is different; therefore the very fact of being God-centered permits these differences to be revealed in the expression of life.

By April of 1961 the new Apartment Building on Sunrise Ranch was occupied, with siding still to be applied to the second story and other finishing to be done.

Minutes of a Board Meeting on May 5th noted that the addition of a room to my little house was under construction. This meant I would have a bedroom, separate from office/livingroom. Great! Work on a cloakroom in the dining hall was also begun. A Miller Trojan Sharpshooter camera had been purchased for $1,041 and delivered, plus about $60 worth of supplies to start a darkroom which would be located in the west room of the Chapel building. A vital need was presented for an electrical appliance shop, which had "once again been set up in the entranceway of the Barn." Things were humming on Sunrise Ranch!

In his service on Sunrise Ranch on May 7, "Sacred Honor," Martin spoke of the man who had been sent up into space a few days before, of the intensive training for a long time to make it possible, and of the participation of thousands of people to work on the rocket equipment used to project the capsule.

> Everything had to be just right. Millions of lives were involved, that this particular outworking should be successful. We need to recognize the same principle at work insofar as those who are aspiring to be truly honorable in the sight of God are concerned. Everything must be *exactly right*. Millions of lives depend upon it. And how little real recognition there is of this fact. How casually those associated with letting the Lord operate on earth often are: "It doesn't matter if I make a slip now and again; who cares?" If there had been any slips made in this recent venture into space there would have been a lot of people who cared. The same thing, only on a much greater scale, is true of you. What a priceless thing is honor, and how little it has been known in the world.

The name Henry Gross, an excellent water diviner, had been introduced in an earlier Board Meeting by Bill and Walter Bahan who offered to pay $1,000 to bring him on the Ranch. He arrived on May 11 and stayed a few days. We had sent him aerial photographs by means of which he divined water at 154', with a depth of 260'. Harry Hersh, the driller, was presently working through solid granite.

On May 13 Martin spoke of his first visit to Sunrise Ranch:

> I came here first in the spring of 1946, about this time of year. I travelled down by bus and the bus got caught in a blizzard between Laramie and Chey-

enne. I spent the night in the bus, on top of the mountain with drifts all around, and it was cold.

He then continued with a service entitled "Significance of Water Divining":

> A dry farm, run-down, with weeds everywhere, Sunrise Ranch neverthe-less looked to Uranda like the land of promise, and he gave assurance that there would be water. We hauled water from the vicinity of the Big Thompson School for our domestic use. Since then there have been many changes. Fa-cilities were made available whereby we could drill some wells. The canal was built. And there was indeed water on Sunrise Ranch. It is beginning to look green and lush, so different from its appearance not so very many years ago. We have reached a point now where there is need for more water for domestic use, and so another step has been taken.
>
> The last couple of days we have had Henry Gross here divining for water. He has come a long way to do it. According to his perception, except for some seepage the waters which flow right under this building and in the vicinity are the only veins in the whole valley. There is another vein close by the Big Thompson River, but nothing much between and nothing to the north of us. Yesterday in Class he touched upon this ability he has and put forward several reasons therefor, settling on the final one which was sufficient for him, that it was a gift from God; so he prefers the use of the word *divining* to *witching,* a term often used in black magic, something done without regard to the divine source. Henry's ability is not limited to water but other substances such as oil, uranium, gold.

Martin proceeded to use the symbol of a pyramid to illustrate the pattern or design of creation, with the mineral kingdom as a layer at the base.

> Out of that vibratory level of being springs the vegetable kingdom, then the animal, with man at the apex here on earth designed to bring all these things to a point of focus, the capstone. And that capstone has a capstone.

Henry had said that he needed to "blank his mind" in order to experience his remark-able subconscious contact with the water under the earth, and Martin pointed out that

> each kingdom has mind at its particular level, a key to the oneness of all creation.
>
> These things which are being discovered are interesting, but there is also an atmosphere of the nucleus of the atom, something which shines forth from the nucleus into and around and through the electrons. Whatever that is, we can call it *mind.*

On June 5 in Boston, Massachusetts, Martin delivered the "Three Hundred and

Twenty-Third Anniversary Sermon" of the "Ancient and Honorable Artillery Company of Massachusetts." He shared his experience in a service at 100 Mile House on June 10.

The way it worked out was rather interesting. Alan Shephard, United States astronaut, comes from Derry, New Hampshire. The five Bahan brothers, all members of the Ancient and Honorable Artillery Company, have one of their two chiropractic clinics there. Bill is also on the Speakers' Committee. After Alan Shephard's flight into the blue yonder it was suggested that it might be fitting if one of the ministers from Derry preached the anniversary sermon this year. Bill was asked to suggest someone and he said he did not think any of the Derry ministers would be suitable, but he did know somebody whom he thought he could get. So I received the invitation and accepted, leaving Sunrise on Sunday. I was met at Boston by Bill and Walter, Bob Spaulding and Al Valcourt. That evening we had a service, with forty present, in Walter's house where I was staying.

Monday was the big day; so Walter, Bill, another brother Paul and their father and I drove to Boston where we took a room in a hotel, then went to the armory which is in the old part of Boston down by the water. The armory is called Faneuil Hall, a very old building; in fact I believe the War of Independence started there. It is a very high structure and the Ancients have their facilities at the apex. It has been proclaimed a fire-trap, with only one staircase going up to the top and a very small elevator which holds three people.

Upstairs the Ancients, resplendent in their uniforms—more diverse I have seldom if ever seen—and others were gathering for lunch. There were contingents of similar organizations from other States, some from way back dressed in their ancient outfits. A very good buffet lunch was served to a large crowd, after which they assembled outside in the street in order to march to Copley Square, over a mile away, mostly uphill, where the Old South Church was situated. Some were mounted on horses and there was also a contingent of mounted Boston police. Bill and Paul were to participate in the march. Walter was my personal bodyguard, so we went by taxi, together with Mr. Bahan, partly because we needed to set things up to record the service.

The taxi driver took us to the wrong church, then said, "Oh, you mean the *new* Old South Church," which proved to be a very fine Congregationalist Church which would probably hold a thousand people. There is no altar, just a stage at one end, with the lectern and backdrop with a cross, and above a beautiful stained-glass window covering the entire end of the building. At the other end was a large organ in a loft. We set up the recording equipment and prepared for the parade to arrive, which it did in due course, escorted by two bands playing different tunes, which made it a little difficult for the marchers. Crowds assembled on the sidewalks to watch, and in front of the church one of the bands stopped, turned around and played *Onward, Christian Soldiers.* Then contingent on contingent they marched into the church with their standards and swords and rifles, down the middle of the church into the pews. Some were quite elderly gentlemen. There was a large number of high-ranking officers of all the services, some dressed in proper uniforms—Air Force, Army, Marines, Navy.

In the meantime I was escorted by an Army Chaplain to my seat, up on the platform where there were four thrones. I sat in one; he sat in one on my right; and Walter who was to read the ode composed by his brother Paul sat on my left; and beyond the chaplain was the Recorder of the Ancients who was to read the lesson. A bugler came and stood beside me on one side and a drummer on the other. The Chaplain asked me if I knew what the procedure was and could I get in what I was going to say in fifteen minutes. I said I would see what I could do. The church was half full, with quite a number of the general public. The marchers went up and set their colors on either side of the platform, then all sat down at the order and took off their caps. The service began.

My portion ended in exactly fifteen minutes, without a conscious effort on my part to "fit it in." There was a period of complete silence. I could have gone on of course, but did not wish to disrupt their program. Afterward they had the commissioning of officers for the next year, that ceremony held in the square outside with the governor of Massachusetts officiating. They fired a nineteen-gun salute and later loaded an ancient cannon dating from revolutionary times. Everyone stood back, and there was a blinding flash and clouds of blue smoke. This was repeated five times, about all the cannon would take! The extraordinary event concluded with a great banquet in the hotel.

At Martin's invitation, Michael Cecil participated in the service on June 25 upon his return from a visit to England. He said:

One of the primary purposes of my going to England was to be at our ancestral home, the estate at Burghley, to find out what was going on and see what the feelings were in those parts. It is an estate of twenty-seven thousand acres in the middle of England, with many attached businesses and extensive influence in various ways, going back to the time of the first Queen Elizabeth.

My uncle has a great desire to provide leadership for the people of England, and he and his family are aware of our program here, somewhat concerned about it. One comment was made to me, in defiance, "You will never change the English! You'll never cause them to conform to your pattern!" It is not a matter of trying to do something, there or anywhere else, but of living. One is deeply aware of what is extended from Center when out there, and that something is being accomplished.

Minutes of the Sunrise Ranch Board on July 7 revealed that on the morning of June 28 the drilling of the well had reached a depth of 270', at cost of $10 a foot starting at 190'. Six more feet were drilled at an hourly rate of $10 plus bits, and then the drilling operation was halted until further word from Henry Gross. He called collect from St. Thomas, Virgin Islands, and had a Mr. Bailey speak for him. Advised that Henry would contact us immediately upon his arrival home, July 6, we were still awaiting his call. We agreed to pay Harry Hersh $100 of the $742 we owed him. From Minutes of the August 4th Board Meeting: "Henry Gross has advised that with fifty more feet of drilling we should hit more water."

The Class of 1961 consisted of thirty-one eager men and women, numerically equally divided, with ten married couples. There was a remarkably similar representation from the two countries, United States and Canada, also Kenneth Lim from New Zealand. After the completion of the Class, Sunrise Ranch was blest with the return of Bill and Betty Dice and their three children, with the intention of making it their permanent home. Bill was instrumental in locating and procuring equipment of various kinds, as for instance the Miller-Trojan Sharpshooter Camera, which was required to handle the increased material having to be retyped, etc. Then, of course, a darkroom was the next necessity and a base for the camera, all of which was built by Bill, assisted by several Class men.

In the summer of 1961 word got out that Martin and Ross were taking flying instruction at 100 Mile House. It was a training program offered by the local Flying Club and Aero Club of B.C. The instructor was Terry Field. In September Martin introduced the new venture for consideration at Conference, "so that all concerned are willing to let me fly." He pointed out that he and his household had made twenty-nine trips by car between the Hundred and Sunrise since 1954.

So it is the intention, if we can find the finances, to invest in an aircraft capable of making the journey between the two Units in one day. We could also move personnel back and forth with greater ease. The symbolic aspect appearing at this time is a factor of which I have been very conscious. Our ministry is beginning to be spiritborne. In other words, there is in relation to our whole program a far greater measure of function from the standpoint of the spiritual expression plane than ever before, and this which is working out is related to that.

It is not something which has been forced. It is not in any personal sense because I had a great hankering to fly an aircraft, although I don't object to it. Since I have been doing it I enjoy it. It has simply unfolded on a natural basis. In fact, when I went to the Hundred last spring I had no anticipation that I was going to participate in that flying program at all. It came up one day and I enrolled the next, because it was right at that point. So we can continue to let it be right all the way through, and I give thanks for the spirit of support and willingness to let whatever is right take form.

So it was that seven years after Uranda left us while piloting an airplane, Martin felt it right, and necessary, to open that cycle of travel in our ministry. In November of that year the first edition of a monthly newsletter, *Newslight*, was released, and on its cover page was a picture of Martin standing in front of the plane, with a short article by me entitled "Clearing the Air":

From out of the blue it came—right over Sunrise Ranch! It dipped its wings in salute to our Bishop as he stood down below [Lillian, Marina and I with him] looking up at the beautiful aircraft gleaming in the bright October sun. Gordon Maitland, a former bomber pilot and president of the 100 Mile House flying club, and Ross Marks flew 1,200 miles to Sunrise Ranch, leaving October 1st in the four-year-old, four-seater Cessna 182, CF-JYE, painted silver with red and black trim, and with a cruising speed close to 160 m.p.h.

It was a joy to see Martin take the plane into the air, to see him piloting it during the four days it was here, *and* a thrill to go up with him! The weather was perfect. We rejoice in this movement into a new cycle of ministry.

In her column, "Seeing Sunrise," Alice Kuykendall announced that the waiting room in the Attunement Sanctuary was extended—

indeed a thing of beauty, with its one wall of native stone and the other two covered with a mural in oils of mountain scenery, created by our artist of highest caliber, Conrad O'Brien-ffrench. Roger de Winton's office was paneled in walnut, and the addition of two attunement rooms and a restroom enhanced this very precious facility.

Also noted by Alice was the "flexibility and versatility" of the office staff who met with me after lunch one day and decided to prepare the evening meal that same day in honor of the kitchen staff, an annual affair usually planned in advance.

Due to a very full agenda it was decided to just *do* it that day and not wait any longer. In thirty minutes the menu was decided upon (not entirely based on what we learned in Lorraine's nutrition class). While Bobby Garrett and Oliver Latam rushed into town to purchase 35 pounds of ham, 35 pounds of sweet potatoes, 3 gallons of peas and 5 gallons of ice cream, the rest of us invaded the kitchen and with gales of laughter, fast repartee and seeming confusion, utensils and supplies were soon organized by teamwork into a smooth operation which produced a feast replete with candlelight, flowers, dinner music and clever place cards conceived by Grace at 3 p.m. and executed by Jim in the printshop at 5 o'clock. A great success—and fun!

Another of her items:

"School bus is coming," shout our 25 children each morning as they rush from the diningroom. Helen Kelly sees them safely off, waving until the bus is out of sight. At 4 o'clock Helen has a snack prepared for them, at which time they meet with her and Jose [Bruce], and the young folk are allocated work activities. After the 4-H chores are finished a ball game is usually played before dinner. I've never decided from Jose's frequent "Wows" whether he wins or loses!

Exciting developments in other places were reported in that first issue. News from Toronto noted the increasing value of people who were carrying on the ministry in the absence of primary servers Jim and Mary Pogue, also Mac and Jane Duff, who were attending Conference on Sunrise Ranch. Named were Ron and June Polack, Ron having changed his chiropractic center at Donlands to attunement service; also Gordon McEachern, Mamie Martin and Bob Barber, who included such areas as the West End, Oshawa and Hamilton. The new headquarters center in Toronto at Roslin Avenue had been opened the previous fall, with upstairs apartments and two large basement rooms nearing completion for Junior Training School. John Summerbell was busy finishing this excellent provision, with auxiliary kitchen for social activities.

In Vancouver, Richard and Dorothy Thompson moved from the old house on Pender Street which had provided a temporary center for the group, to the recently purchased one at 2506 Cornwall Street, in the Kitsilano district. A beautiful house and property, with the ocean in view and close enough for a swim, it became a true home for the Vancouver family, and also for Martin and his party when in that city. The basement was spacious enough for services until such time as public accommodation was necessary.

The Servers Training Class of 1962 numbered twenty-eight, among them Ernie and Virginia Taylor, Egon and Mary Milinkovich, Joy Westren, Kenneth and Virginia Morrison, Ronald and June Polack, Hugh and Kaye Unwin, George and Aili Helander,

George and Marika Horvath, and Fayetta Gelinas, a popular performer, later to be featured in Las Vegas by Liberace.

On February 21 Martin spoke in the Public Library Auditorium in Vancouver, at which reporters and photographers from the Vancouver Sun and the Province newspapers were present. The subject of his address was "Ontology—Key to Life," and he dealt masterfully with the difficult task of clarifying the dictionary definition of "Ontology, the science of real being." He said:

> That is a very true statement but somehow it tends to leave one without much more awareness as to what Ontology is. It is a science; it has something to do with the intellect, something reasonable; but it is also an art, and this has something to do with the heart, the feeling nature, the emotional realm. It is both a science and an art to be what one really is.

He went on to say that it is not a religion, a philosophy, a political system, an economic system, a social system.

> I do not think you can classify it, because when a person is what he really is in the expression of his life, he is different from everyone else. We would have to have a classification for each one, and that becomes complicated; so let us not try to classify it.

The little plane, CF-JYE, was used to maximum advantage by Martin in those days, with trips from 100 Mile House to Sunrise Ranch in March of 1962; Calgary in June; to Sunrise Ranch again in August; to Wisconsin from there in October, on to Huntingburg, Indiana, and Berwick, Pennsylvania; Toronto and Chatham, Ontario; Detroit, Cedar Rapids, and last hop Sunrise Ranch. In November the faithful little machine *and* its wonderful pilot took the party from Sunrise to 100 Mile House—in time for Christmas, and a white winter! Of course there were many flights within British Columbia, to Kamloops, Kelowna, Powell River and Vancouver.

The trip to Calgary in June included opportunity for Martin to speak on several occasions and a pleasant stay with Ralph and Vivien Pekary, serving then in that city. The passengers on that flight from Sunrise to the Hundred were Lillian, Lloyd and I, with Ross and Marcia driving Nancy and Helen Meeker, Marina Cecil and Diana de Winton by car.

On July 7 Martin spoke on "Ontology, Key to Life" at the center in Kelowna, focalized by LeRoy and Nonna Jensen:

> People say they are only human. But we are not only human; we are human beings. In other words, there is the being aspect as well as the human aspect, and being relates to that which is back of the external factors of which

we are aware from the standpoint of our physical senses. Something causes these external factors to be.

> One of the most outstanding characteristics of being, evident in what we can observe, is what we might call "order." We can look out into the solar system and see the sun with the planets revolving around it, and other systems beyond. Who can look up into the heavens on a clear night and not sense an orderliness? And it is the same with the very small, in the field of the atom for instance; we see orderliness there too. And what about the human body? How did it appear? Just on the basis of the physical factors, just from the standpoint of what are called genes? They have a part to play; something must appear in the physical level, but how is the human form so beautifully integrated and brought forth as a wonderful organism? Because there is something back of it, because there is a design, there is being in relation to each one, that which is quite capable, and has the intelligence, the wisdom to operate a physical body, the wisdom to operate a mind and the emotions. Relinquishing this idea of being just human, we will find resources within ourselves of which we never dreamed.

Going on to Powell River, where the center was ably focused by Bill and Doreen Thompson, Martin spoke on July 14, continuing on the subject of Being, which he said is the source of order, and that where being is neglected and concentration is on the human, chaos is the result, with the big fat human ego thinking of itself as so important that it must be saved.

> Most people have very little awareness of how much they are controlled, manipulated, by influences arising from human sources. People think of themselves as being independent, the supreme goal often to be entirely independent. Do you know what an entirely independent person is? Dead. We have, on the international scene, conferences galore—pushing and pulling to get a state of order, and all we have is more chaos, which is the absence of order.

In his service at 100 Mile House on July 22, "The Attitude of Life," Martin referred to the use of the drug Thalidomide by pregnant women to alleviate morning sickness, the awful results of which were then becoming apparent, the absence of arms and legs in the babies, etc.

> Now they are trying to do something to correct the damage, but cannot. Human beings disrupt things because they do not know the ultimate repercussions of anything they do. Anything one does is like a stone dropped in a pool; there are ripples going out. It is not only physical. Any thought that moves through the consciousness, any feeling in the emotional realm—all

these have effects. But there *is* a way of functioning by which blessings may appear, and that depends absolutely upon the expression of God, of Being, through the human form. God knows what to do, how to do it, when and where, and if we learn to let that come through, it will be right, regardless of what human beings think about it.

Eden Valley News had an article on our method of printing in those days, having graduated from a small A. B. Dick machine to a Multigraph, all the subsequent operations, gathering, folding, stapling, trimming being done by hand. This included literature in the form of booklets, for which there was increasing demand.

The Chapel was enlarged that summer, with the major portion of the work being done by the men of the 1962 Class, spearheaded by Egon Milinkovich, who later commented:

> The most acrobatic part of the operation was the changeover from the old Chapel section. This involved wrecking the wall between the old and new, tearing down the old roof, putting new trusses in place and so on, all within a space of 48 hours. We held one morning's class in the Attunement Sanctuary, but the next morning everything was in place and we continued our class work as if nothing had happened. We were now sitting facing west, in a Chapel measuring 24 by 48 feet instead of 24 by 27. Then the work continued on the extension without disturbing class and service activities.

On the 5th of August CF-JYE returned to Sunrise Ranch. What a thrill it was to fly over the Ranch, dip our wings and land on our own airstrip just beside the cornfield, near the rimrock on a warm summer day in Eden Valley. It was not long before it became apparent to our pilots that the space was too limited for a safe landing strip, but that day it was a thrill—to be followed by another, the sight of our beautiful new Chapel. That evening in a service Martin commented that the change in our Chapel structure was evidence of a change that had been working out through our whole ministry, the orientation changed from north and south to east and west.

> I face toward the east confidently expecting something to appear through you and all who share in this ministry out of the east, out of the future.

> Lillian and I noted that this is the fifth building in which services have been held on Sunrise Ranch. It was the barn first, the ranch house, the "little red schoolhouse," then finally the Chapel, completed sufficiently to hold services and now enlarged and refurnished. Even now, when it appears to be finished, we know there will be more to come, incorporating the old. All that was meaningful, that could be used, all that was right in the old is still present in the new. We share an opportunity to recognize these things and see a larger

vision of something which is being builded, the body built upon the Rock which is the living body through which God works on earth.

In an article in *Eden Valley News* Chris Foster acknowledged the "indescribable" experience of oneness known in the Conference, an annual event attended by Servers from all places in our ministry. He said:

> There was the priceless blessing of coming to know the one who leads us as we have not known him hitherto—by sharing God's gift of life. Martin indicated, before the Conference began, that it was not his desire that it should be the same as previous sessions, and it surely was not. "I am come that they might have life" were words that took on actual individual meaning for each one, server and visitor alike.

Noted also in *Eden Valley News* were celebrations of birthdays and other occasions, one of which was highlighted by a barbershop quintet and "an amazing drum solo." Frank Protzman had an impressive array of hidden talents, not the least being his expertise with the drum and fife. Like his father, a Civil War cavalry veteran, Frank loved his country and, wishing to show it in a way that others could feel it, had organized and led the "Pioneer Fife and Drum Corp" of Morgantown, West Virginia, and later Pittsburgh. It was the finest in the country, and Frank marched in uniform with the group of twenty to thirty men in parades in many towns and states. It was a rare treat when he indulged his appreciative family on Sunrise Ranch.

There was a service of Ordination for James Pogue of Toronto at Sunrise Ranch on August 29.

The Sunrise Choir presented a concert on August 30, which was enhanced by the participation of servers attending the Conference, such as Doreen Thompson of Powell River and Betty French from Calgary. This became an annual event, under the direction of Lillian, later assisted by Bob Patton. Wesley Jones at the organ and Lillian at the piano with duets and solos provided memorable experiences.

On September 18 a baby daughter, Melanie Lynne, was born to Wesley and Dorothy Jones.

On Sunrise Ranch on September 19 Martin spoke poignantly of the need for increased response.

> The most important thing is to stay steady, centered, so that nothing can drag you out of your place. It takes practice, application, because of dedication. Over and over again coming back, centering, holding it steady, you are in place, you are of value, you are building. Anywhere else but in that place you are plucking it down with your hands and you are foolish. Over the years

I have been concerned with this matter of building. I have builded, and builded, and I have also watched my building being torn down, many times just about as fast as I was building it. It requires patience to watch such things happening, knowing that if the building was left alone and there was a gathering instead of a scattering abroad, it could quickly take expanded form. How quickly the house of the Lord could begin to be really known on earth.

In a service on Sunrise Ranch on October 27, "Emergence Out of the Cloud," Martin reviewed a tour just completed by him and Lillian, with Norman Gilbert. They stopped at Huntingburg, Indiana; Berwick, Pennsylvania; Manchester, New Hampshire; New York City; Toronto, Hamilton and Chatham, Ontario. "Annihilation or Ontology" was the subject of Martin's talks on four occasions.

How many more seconds have we got, do you think, before annihilation? They are ticking away, one by one. Annihilation is certain, unless the cause changes. Through whom will that happen? Only when we say "through me" does it have any meaning, and that takes backbone, something which apparently most human beings simply do not have or are not willing to acknowledge.

Martin continued that theme in a service on November 3, "Consciousness of Divine Being":

The human pattern of things is to pass away, to be annihilated; and there is movement toward that point of climax. It is a converging movement. The human pattern of things could not come to that point of climax if it were not for the fact that divine being was present. So while there is movement, which we can see, toward this destructive climax of the human pattern, we may also recognize that there is movement toward that same point of climax of divine being. People sense that movement and see it as a disaster.

If we have divine vision we see something more than that. If the greater intensity is becoming known as the human pattern moves toward this point of climax, then there is the greater intensity also of divine being; both converging toward this meeting point. If nobody has any consciousness of awareness of divine being, it might as well not be there as far as human beings are concerned. And that's that—annihilation! ultimate disaster! But if there is a consciousness of divine being adequately present on earth in human form, then there is a means by which a hand is taken with respect to that climactic point, a divine hand.

After two years of planning, and exercising a marked degree of patience, Wray and Anne Laflam arrived on Sunrise Ranch, to participate in the forthcoming 1963 Class.

With them were David, 13; Margaret (Mickie), 12; and Debra, 11. Through the ensuing years this family provided vital elements in the substance and growth of Sunrise Ranch. Today Anne and Debra still live and work in this home of the Lord on earth.

Up north significant expansion was occurring in British Columbia. A vital addition to our Canadian family was located in Kamloops, a town with a population at that time of 20,000, situated 125 miles south of 100 Mile House, with an orchard and fertile farmland. Right on the bank of the Fraser River where it curves, we named the property Riverbend Orchard, and over many years this provision was the source of vegetables and fruit, and later sheep, for the family at the Hundred. The primary factor in production was the difference in altitude and weather conditions. It was a treat for different ones from the Hundred to spend a few days there, helping in the garden or just relaxing.

Several had been gathering to share services for about a year in Kamloops in the home of Murray and Leato Wetherald, who had moved, with their young daughter, from eastern Canada. Roger and Marion Harvey's home was also available for that purpose, and Micki Kalten provided a point of firm support. In season, as the numbers grew, the meeting place was moved to the TraveLodge Motel. Michael provided a focus for the group there and soon found himself increasing his visits to twice a week, sharing services and attunements. Martin spoke in the Kamloops Library building in June.

In October Egon and Mary Milinkovich, fresh from their Class experience on Sunrise Ranch, moved in, with their three little girls, as permanent servers at Riverbend Orchard, about nine miles out of town. That became their home for many years. Egon, an accomplished artist and sculptor, was constantly building additions to the little house, which gradually assumed a shape characteristic of the builder's unique realm of imagination. Mary added in countless ways, imbuing the place with the welcome of her enfolding spirit.

Newslight related, in November:

> After a 14-hour drive from Vancouver in a rented truck filled with just about everything, including the kitchen sink! plus furniture, a bathtub, hot water tank, large pieces of marble and an air compressor for Egon's sculpturing! Egon and Mary, with Egon's brother Bruno, also LeRoy Jensen from Kelowna and Ross and Michael from the Hundred, arrived at the Orchard on October 18 to establish a service center for this area. [Egon and Bruno had immigrated to Canada from their native country Hungary.] That evening Egon and Michael held a joint meeting at the TraveLodge Motel, with 23 in attendance. Egon held the first meeting at the Orchard the following Sunday.

In addition to his trips to Kamloops, Michael also visited, weekly when possible, another location opening in British Columbia. Prince George was 206 miles in the other direction from 100 Mile House. For the past year Ellen Richmond, of the 1961 Class, had provided a dependable point there, her brother Carl sharing the first few months before moving to a place of service in Toronto. Prince George, as is also true of Kamloops, is situated at the junction of two mighty rivers: in this instance the Nechako and Fraser, with a population at that time of about 20,000—large numbers in those days for British Columbia. Interest was beginning to appear also in two other, somewhat smaller, towns in that general area, Williams Lake and Quesnel.

Northern Light opened with an article by Michael Cecil, "The First Supper," in which he spoke for many in a touching tribute to his father:

> The evening meal is ready and the waiting people turn and begin to make their way toward the serving counter. But in their hearts they are thinking of more than food: Martin is here! And then the door to the dining room opens and there are Martin and Lillian with Grace and Marina, and suddenly the air is charged with radiant happiness, as greetings are exchanged. Martin is here!— our leader, wise, thoughtful, strong, kind, come to be with us for some time to lead us into larger vision and understanding of the way, the truth and the life. Food is forgotten, for what in this moment could be more important than to welcome this one, the friend of God on earth? With simple words and gracious gesture each one conveys his love and reverence to Martin, whose face shines with that special affection he knows for his people.

At 100 Mile House on November 25 Martin spoke on "Things That Are." He recalled a statement made by Uranda many years before in which he described himself as a pool of clear, still water.

> And one, looking into that pool, might see something he did not like, in which case he would be inclined to blame Uranda, whereas it was a reflection of the individual who begins to look into the pool. As awareness of the things that are increases, the individual begins to become aware of himself as he really is. Finally the pool changes and becomes an open window through which one begins to see the Lord. In the measure that you begin to become what you truly are, you can look into my pool and become aware of the reality in relation to yourself.
>
> You begin to become aware of what you are in reality but perhaps not yet adequate in expression, so that when you express something which is not a true portrayal of what you really are, you know it. There are human beings with thick hides who do not have any sensitivity or awareness of anything

divine in relation to themselves, and they can express almost anything and it does not bother them. To the extent that we begin to become aware of the reality because of our response to the spirit of God, we certainly begin to be troubled when that which finds expression through us is not fitting to the reality. Of course humanly established concepts are not the divine reality. That reality is, and in response to the spirit of God, having the opportunity to look in the jade stone, the mirror of self-revealment which is offered to you, you begin to see what is there.

In a service at 100 Mile House, "Look and Consider," on December 2 Martin said:

We might for a moment touch upon some of those groups in the United States and Canada of whom we have a direct awareness. In most places where there are groups it is carried by a server and his wife, working together, and those who share closely with them.

In this province, British Columbia, there are groups in Vancouver, Powell River, Kelowna and Kamloops. There are other groups or potential groups in other places—Prince George and certain locations on Vancouver Island. Focalizing the group in Vancouver, Richard and Dorothy Thompson make regular visits to Burnaby, New Westminster, Crescent Beach, Victoria, Nanaimo, Port Alberni and Seattle, Washington.

Moving across Canada, in Alberta there is a group in Calgary and something moving in Edmonton; in Winnipeg, Manitoba; and coming to Ontario, there is the Toronto group, Orillia, Hamilton, Oshawa, Peterborough, London, Chatham and Windsor. In Montreal, Quebec, a group is in the process of development again.

Sharing with us in a central pattern of responsibility is the Unit on Sunrise Ranch. Moving out from there we have a group in Hammer, South Dakota; Huntingburg, Marion and Muncie, Indiana; Berwick, Pennsylvania; Salem and North Conway, New Hampshire. There are many places where there are individuals and no groups and some where the occasional group gathers. Our program is not circumscribed by the oceans which surround the North American continent but reaches out into Africa, Europe, Australia, India, Indonesia. All these depend upon me to stay in place, in character, faithful and true. You who participate in the pattern here and those on Sunrise Ranch are also looked to with me in a more direct sense to extend something which is constant and dependable, so that there may be the sensing of the Rock.

As I look forth into the ministry of the Lord I see those whom I could well call my children. There are other lambs of my flock who are not presently included directly in this pattern of our ministry who are nevertheless an essential part of that which is unfolding in the fulfilment of the divine purposes. One point in this field relates to Swami Premananda, and beyond all this there are many others. I share these things with you that you might let your vision harmonize with mine, so that you do not limit your viewpoint to that which is around you. This Unit has meaning because it is willing to move under my hand in the fulfilment of those purposes which relate to the greater whole.

On December 19, "Give" entitled a service in which Martin said:

I have mentioned the origins of this building, the Log Chapel, before, but it is evident that the man who built it back at the beginning of this century undertook to do a real job. He thought he was building it for a carpenter's shop and it was indeed so used for a number of years. But he was actually building a chapel. People very often have ideas with respect to what they do, imagining that they know what the purpose is, but it turns out to be something entirely different. This particular building has served as a chapel for a number of years. It has been well built, because the builder put himself into it. How much do we put ourselves into what we do, whether or not we know its true purpose?

In a service at 100 Mile House on January 12, 1963, "Crisis," Martin said:

In the early morning hours of Tuesday, the first day of January, this ministry moved through a point of very particular crisis. It came to focus in my physical body. If the members of this ministry are dependent on me this gives indication of the fact that I am dependent on them. To the extent that you have felt the possibility of an awful gap in the pattern of this ministry, you have a recognition of the extent to which my continued manifestation on earth is dependent upon you. I am still here with you, and I would say it is primarily for your sakes.

I would draw something to your attention. If there is a recognition that this ministry could be in rather desperate straits if I should no longer be here, then it should emphasize the point that there is something, if not wrong, at least inadequate. In order to come to this point it has been necessary for me to accept into myself the vibrational factors present in the developing body of our ministry. I have carried this with me ever since Uranda left. This constitutes a vibrational strain which is constant. My physical body has suffered accordingly. Somewhere along the line this developing body should reach the point where it is capable of taking responsibility for itself, of assuming the vibrational load in itself.

A week later Martin spoke, in a service at 100 Mile House, "Server or Servee?", of a change in the pattern, explaining why he had not been giving as many services, adding that it was not entirely because of his physical condition. He said:

> I would like to bring it to a more direct point with respect to the individual. Each one rightly carries the responsibility of the Lord's ministry—each one of you, for instance. It is easy to say in a collective sense, "It is *our* responsibility," but what would it be to say, "It is *my* responsibility," because unless it is the individual's responsibility it is no one's. It is true that the body as a whole carries a responsibility, but there is no body without the individual members of it.

A conspicuous number of Unit members held office in the Village affairs, as for instance President of Chamber of Commerce by Ross Marks, later David Oshanek; Norman Gilbert, Treasurer of Cariboo Tourist Association, etc. Ross was Treasurer of the 100 Mile Flying Club, was the first Fire Marshall, and occupied the position of Mayor of 100 Mile House for twenty years. His father, Gordon, had been Magistrate, the position before incorporation of the town.

Ross was also the local agent for Inland Natural Gas Company since its initial installation in 1957 when a gas pipeline was laid from the Peace River in northern British Columbia southward to Vancouver on the coast (a section of it running close in the vicinity of Martin's house), a great boon to many communities in the interior of the Province, certainly to 100 Mile House, eliminating the reliance on a supply of wood or sawdust for the heat supply—an unspeakable blessing to the housewife cooking meals.

On a number of occasions Martin acknowledged the vital part played by Ross Marks in the development of the Unit but equally in that of 100 Mile House. Interviewed in Vancouver once by a reporter from The Sun, he was referred to as a midwife who had seen the birth of a town, the population of which had risen in ten years from about 20 people to approximately 700, described as the fastest growing community in Canada, with more airplanes per capita than anywhere else. Ross became active in Canadian politics, an area in which he felt at home and enjoyed. Today the town of 100 Mile House services the town and surrounding area with a population of 17,000. On one occasion Martin reminisced: "Way back we invited all the townspeople over for either Christmas or New Year's dinner, and Emily reminded me that there were thirty-two who sat down. That seemed like a large number then."

A few notes from an Aircraft Log Book give a bird's-eye view of a flight from 100

Mile House to Sunrise Ranch on January 19, in CF-JYE with the two pilots, Martin and Ross, plus John Fraser (in the back seat with maps, clothing—and lunch!). They left at 10:40 a.m. and landed first at Penticton, B.C. A direct line route was impossible because of overcast; nevertheless good time was made.

They left Penticton at 12:35 and eventually flew over the last mountain range to the vast flatness of the prairies, landing at Great Falls, Montana, at 4:00, where they intended to stay the night, which turned out to be two (not uncommon when flying small planes). The temperature was 10 below! On January 21, after complications with the oil cooler because of the cold, they took off at 11:25 and landed at 1:00 at Billings, Montana. Further complications prevented take-off that day. January 23 presented a most welcome change in weather and they took off at 11:00 with a smooth flight to Sheridan and Denver, making a low pass over Sunrise Ranch just before 2:00. The flight was culminated at the Denver airport at 2:30, with arrival at Sunrise by car at 5:00.

That was a short visit, and the plane took off on January 24 from Denver to Ogden, Utah, and Pendleton, Oregon, the next day completing the journey to Penticton and 100 Mile House. It was "a breeze" by comparison, with slight turbulence but no real problems. Ross's comment was, "It provided most valuable pilot experience for Martin and me, and I am looking forward to doing it again—in the summertime!"

The first Server's Conference of British Columbia Servers was held at 100 Mile House January 25-27. Attending were Richard and Dorothy Thompson, Vancouver; Bill and Doreen Thompson, Powell River; Egon and Mary Milinkovich, Kamloops; LeRoy and Nonna Jensen, Kelowna; Ellen Richmond, Prince George; also present was Roger de Winton from Sunrise Ranch.

The forthright directness of Martin's expression when necessary was a trait I admired in him. The title of a service on January 26 was "Mind Your Own Business," and in it he spoke of the universality of curiosity in the minds of human beings "which causes man to eat freely of the forbidden fruit and penetrate into realms where he does not belong." Phrased differently on occasion by Lillian: "Everybody doesn't need to know everything!"

One day Norman Gilbert noticed that the old stage coach, in its position of honor outside of the Lodge, was beginning to show signs of age, a bit of loose canvas here and a paint job needed there, with evidence of decay in its joints, whereupon he took action. Norman related, in *Northern Light*:

> It was discovered that the structure of the undercarriage was good, so in the spring of that year the chassis was removed and underwent major surgery, with strict adherence to preserving the original design. Each defective part was used as a pattern, with facsimiles being made, even of the original oak ribs.

As this coach was built on the same lines as a ship, with no square corners or straight lines, we had to make templates of each of the panels out of thick paper stapled together for the area involved. The panels were then cut out of varying thicknesses of plywood, laminating, etc. With perseverance each panel was trimmed to shape and screwed to the ribs—in some cases a new piece needed to be shaped. The finishing was done with auto body plastic paste, also used to fill in some of the original wood that had been marred. While this was proceeding, and the undercarriage had received three coats of yellow paint, Martin and Grace started painting the fancy trim, which included the lettering, using the exact design and colors as in the original, a delicate job requiring much patience. Harold Box, with experience in upholstering, redid the interior.

In the fall there was occasion to test our handiwork when we were visited by the Lieutenant-Governor of B.C. in his official capacity as representative of the Queen. We thought that with his experience in the cavalry he would enjoy his tour of the area in the stagecoach. A local rancher brought in his team of four coach horses and was the driver on the tour, which was a great success, General Pearkes being thoroughly delighted. The coach seemed to enjoy it also and to our breath-held satisfaction returned from its jaunt in perfect condition. Later a roof was built over it, with open sides, to protect it from winter weather.

This beautiful relic of the history of that country still stands in its place of honor, now outside of Red Coach Inn, a mascot lovingly cared for, its original design intact. It has been photographed and admired by countless visitors to the Cariboo over many years. An original Concord coach, it was on the run from Lillooet (which marks Mile One in the numbering of the "Houses") to the gold fields at Barkerville in the latter part of the last century.

That gold rush was parallel with the great one at San Francisco in size and date. A relic of those days, the tiny town of Barkerville is annually visited by tourists. Along its one street are the old shops, inhabited by startlingly lifelike wax figures of clerks, a doctor, a dentist, etc. The original theater is open and functioning in the summer months, and offers fine performances by excellent artists transported to the Interior from Vancouver. A show of a different kind reveals, with vintage equipment, the fascinating methods of gold-mining in use in those days.

24

FLYING NEWS

February 1963 ~ July 1965

*I*n the February issue of *Newslight* the "Young People's Column" featured sixteen-year-old Jim Miller, then of 100 Mile House, who persevered in his love for the Word, serving in many places and presently with his family in Calgary, Alberta.

"What's that again?" was the frequent reaction to what came "out of the mouths of babes." For instance, in the cafeteria line at suppertime at 100 Mile House little Johnny Hooper answered Marjorie Gilbert's question, "How much of this fish loaf do you want, Johnny?" with the sober reply, "Just enough to last me till I finish supper."

The Financial Report in a Board Meeting on Sunrise Ranch February 1st stated that we would pay taxes amounting to $1,399.84 in full by April 30 and start laying aside the money now in a reserve account.

Minutes of the meeting on March 7 recorded the arraignment of Bobby Patton regarding the incident of the death of Susan Allen, who was shot by Bobby when he was out hunting rabbits, over on the rimrock. As a result, this young man in his early teens moved through a period in prison where he took advantage of the opportunity to learn the lessons that had been neglected in his very early days. His father, Robert, had been unaware that his wife, who left him and took the infant with her, had died not many years later and the boy was on his own in his vulnerable formative years. The death of the young teen-age Susan was a tragedy indeed, and her parents exhibited a remarkable depth of understanding in that time of crisis. It is rewarding to note that Bobby let his future be changed and has since lived a fruitful life with his wife and children, also providing loving care and home for his father in his latter years.

In the 1963 edition of *Eden Valley News* Roger de Winton included a history of the old days of the area prior to our appearance on Sunrise Ranch. It was inspired by a visit in early November from Gustave A. Poirot, then 76 years of age and living in Platteville, Colorado.

Gus had homesteaded 160 acres on Green Ridge just above the Ranch in 1911 and later took up 40 acres more. His cabin was immediately above the Ranch and some red stone slabs can still be seen there which he brought up from the rimrock to use in roofing one of his buildings. About that time Gus married Nellie, daughter of Ed Berry, who was living on what we call Sunrise Ranch in the old ranch house. Up to that time Ed had arranged for the clearing of 20 acres by someone else, on which land he grew oats for a few cattle. Homesteading was allowable on the basis of living on the acreage for five years, with seven years to prove it up.

During those years, up to 1919, Gus built the barn from timbers taken off the Ridge, brought down on a two-wheel logging cart which had, passing down its length, a long spar with enormous spikes in it. The trees, trimmed to some extent, were placed on this spar and chained to it; then with a team of horses the cart was dragged down Green Ridge, the log itself moving down the slope acting as a brake. A steam engine and sawing outfit from up the Buckhorn was rented and brought onto the ranch for cutting the timbers. Then Gus, with Ed Berry and a carpenter from Campion, Mr. Strickland, proceeded to build the barn as it stands today. The lean-to on the southwest was used to house a six-foot grain binder and a 1914 four-cylinder Oldsmobile which Gus purchased from his first major sale of grain off the ranch.

With a grub hoe and an axe he cleared the remainder of the acreage upon which we now farm—all but the 20 acres originally hired out for clearing by Ed Berry. Clearing was quite a job as there was a good deal of buckbrush which had a very heavy and extensive root structure. There were many rocks in the valley which had to be removed on a stoneboat, and much of this was used to fill in a washed-out draw south of the barn.

The acreage immediately north of the old ranch house was given to a cherry orchard and an alfalfa field. On the other side of the county road Gus raised fair crops of corn and wheat and at one point rented the property immediately north of us, now farmed by the Wilders. Early during the First World War he harvested 80 acres of wheat, running around 43 bushels to the acre. On his own acreage up on Green Ridge in the tableland he raised oats and took the six-foot binder up for harvesting. During this period, between 1914 and 1919, when all these acreages were being operated, he was running, with Ed Berry, about 60 to 70 head of cattle, which were carried for their calf crop.

At that time the stone quarries were very busy, employing up to 300 men at one time. However, when cement came in, many of the quarries closed down.

The land in the valley throughout this period was held as follows: that now occupied by Eden Valley Institute, by Chris Olin; the Wilder property, by Miss Lulu Kane; the present-day Sunrise Ranch, by Ed Berry; and the properties on the south, by Chasteens and Phil Boothroyd. Gus Poirot left the valley in 1919 and farmed near Kelly in western Kansas until 1930, then returned to Platteville where he has been ever since.

I note that the time of Gustave Poirot's initial appearance on this property, destined in season to be the International Headquarters of the Emissaries, coincided with the purchase by Martin's father in England of a plot in British Columbia which would be the future home of the Canadian Headquarters.

At 100 Mile House, having received an invitation to join the Sovereign Order of St. John of Jerusalem, the Knights of Malta, Martin flew to Langley, B.C., on March 16 to attend a meeting. The necessity of taking any vows was waived, and he accepted the invitation. Conrad O'Brien-ffrench was a Knight of Malta, the Papal Order. There were a number of different orders, many branches having appeared following the breakup of the original. Both Martin and Conrad spoke at the meeting, and there was much agreement expressed with Martin's emphasis on the necessity of obedience to the First Great Commandment, before the fulfilment of the Second Commandment, that of serving others, was possible.

A new hangar was built for our plane at the 100 Mile House Airport, a small but very busy place in that air-minded town. Martin was being trained for special instrument and night flying in Kamloops by Helen Harrison, and Michael Cecil and David Oshanek were taking flying lessons from the same instructor.

In the words of Ross Marks:

It became evident, late in 1962, that the time was approaching when JYE should wisely be replaced by another airplane. We soon became aware of the possibility of acquiring a 1962 model Cessna 210, in use by the Vancouver Cessna dealer as a demonstrator and charter aircraft. Early in 1963 one of the salesmen brought it to the Hundred on a demonstration basis and in spite of atrocious weather conditions we were impressed. In April we found ourselves the proud owners of Cessna 210, CF-NZL.

We have noted many advantages, perhaps the greatest being speed. With increased horsepower, plus retractable landing gear, we are now able to cruise easily in the 180-mile-per-hour range, and this puts Sunrise Ranch just one day from the Hundred at virtually any time of the year. Previously the single-day trip was possible only during the longer summer days, and that took a really full day.

Another advantage is increased room and comfort in the cabin, also more room for luggage, and the cabin noise level is low enough to permit conversation at normal speaking levels. It's beautiful too!

A notable and beloved visitor that year was Swami Premananda, of Agra, India. It was the time of the Hindu New Year, "Festival of Lights," and he found himself at 100 Mile House via some mutual friends in Vancouver. He had met Martin previously and experienced a unique and instant oneness with his spirit, a freedom that removed any obstacle relating to differences in background of country, religion, etc., and joyfully acknowledged it. Swami was preparing for an upcoming gathering in Atlanta, Georgia, and invited Martin to participate, which he accepted. Swami's contact with Martin was a point of initiation for what was to follow in later years of communion with other countries that transcended the superficial levels of culture. Swami visited 100 Mile House on two other occasions and spent a day on Sunrise Ranch during a tour which included centers in Toronto and New Hampshire.

Late July saw the triumphant opening of a swimming pool at the 100 Mile House Unit. The "heaven" for this had been established by Norman Gilbert who diligently followed through to make sure that the "earth" aspects appeared. In that northern climate a heated swimming pool in your own back yard is an inestimable blessing. It had an adjacent little one that invited the tiny tots to indulge. Its location in a lovely spot just behind the Log Chapel has provided the scene for many outdoor meals for the family.

Martin, Lillian and I toured the eastern United States and Canada in July in NZL. The first stop was at Love's Retreat in Lakemont, Georgia, an exquisite spot in the Blue Ridge Mountains not far from Atlanta. This introduces Mahdah Love, a dear and colorful friend. She and her husband, then deceased, had established their home as a center into which representatives from every conceivable variation of thought and practice were invited. And they came.

Swami Premananda was focusing an "Awake O' Man" convention, the title of his presentations as he traveled about the world, in the Dinkler Plaza Hotel in Atlanta, July 26-28, which we attended. Also present were a judge, the bishop of a church, several ministers, doctors, all prominent in their fields, and it was a wonder to observe how the Word found its way into hungry hearts regardless of background or position. That proved to be the first of some interesting visits to Mahdah's home. In season she attended Class on Sunrise Ranch and provided an easy connection between aspects of "New Age" she-nanigans and the truth she loved, so lucidly articulated by Martin.

It was at Love's Retreat that William and Myrtle Byl met Martin, and after hearing him speak Myrtle was overheard to emphatically announce: "That's the first sensible thing I ever heard in this place!" They did not let the contact fade and soon became Emissaries in the true sense of the word, moving before long to Sunrise Ranch where they made their home. One day Bill, an immigrant from Holland and worthy sea-farer in his day, said, of their daughter, "Our Donna will be here some day." And Donna did come, via Bill Bahan, whom she later married.

There was another member of the 100 Mile House Unit with experience in the field of aviation. A flying instructor in the R.A.F. during World War II with almost 2,000 hours to his name, Norman Gilbert brushed up his abilities and renewed his license. So in October he occupied that seat "up front" with Martin as co-pilot on an eastern tour, which included Lillian. Lectures were held in Huntingburg, Berwick, Derry, New York and Toronto, the latter including a few other Ontario cities.

In *Northern Light* David Oshanek spoke of the change of the name of "Tip-Top Radio Shop," in which he played the major role, to "Tip-Top Radio & TV." He explained: "We made the change when TV came to the Hundred a year ago. And now a dream comes true, with our move from the Bridge Creek Estate building to our new quarters on Birch Avenue."

Junior Training School was a joyous and effective activity in those days, both on Sunrise Ranch and 100 Mile House. At Sunrise I had a Bible class for the Seniors (not very old!), Richard Cable an Intermediate class, Claudia Romanick and Helen Hoffman the Junior section, and Gail Conell the Primary group. Beginners gladly gathered with Carolyn Garrett, better known as "Bobby." There were fifty-two members. The name JTS replaced "Sunday School," the latter initiated over a decade before when my young son Billy came home from school and asked if he could go to Big Thompson School on Sundays where they were having a Sunday School. All I needed was Uranda's raised eye-brow for me to get the message, so I started Sunday School on Sunrise Ranch, which made our little ones happy to spend Sundays in Eden Valley.

The old facility for printing on Sunrise Ranch was replaced by an A. B. Dick offset machine, model 360, equipped with chain delivery and receding stacker. This could accommodate paper from 3" x 5" to 11" x 17" and turn out 9,000 sheets an hour, as compared with the former 6,000.

The November issue of *Newslight* announced the purchase of a farm in New Hampshire covering 67 acres, of which about 25 were beautiful, rolling fields. Two houses were on the property, one a three-story building with ten bedrooms and attached two-story garage, the latter ideal for JTS or other groups in one section, and a Chapel in the other. The second house, across the road, offered ample family accommodation consisting of seven rooms with an attached barn. Picturesque "Green Pastures," with its historic atmosphere, huge trees and stately buildings, provided a home for the rapidly growing ministry in New England.

On November 9 and 10 another "Awake O'Man Convention" was held, this time in the Statler Hilton Hotel in Buffalo, New York. *Newslight* reports:

> Under the combined inspiration, guidance and direction of Swami Premananda of India and Bishop Martin Cecil of Colorado and British Columbia two productive and wonderful days were shared by over two hundred from many places in an atmosphere of expansive togetherness. Dr. William Bahan was chairman of the Convention, and author W. Clement Stone contributed to the proceedings.

On November 23 at 100 Mile House Martin spoke of the assassination on the previous day of John F. Kennedy, President of the United States, with the comment that the mass reaction of people is always something that can be used to advantage by those who are in position to serve: "With respect to anything that occurs, the attitude of a true Emissary of our King will be, 'How can this be used to advantage in the service of the Lord?'"

A Conference for Servers in British Columbia, which included some who lived in the Unit, was held at 100 Mile House January 24-26, 1964. Michael wrote his impressions of the occasion in *Northern Light*, a few of which I include here:

> What superb leadership was provided through Martin, with Lillian and Grace in close accord. Their own *knowing* of what true communion is gave all of us the foundation upon which to move. Martin's words were seen with new appreciation; what keys they all provide! Lillian and Grace spoke also, and their words were pure gold, blending so completely with Martin's own expression. By this were we all inspired, drawn closer to them in oneness of purpose and experience. Thus must it be for all mankind.

The story of Pentecost has come down to us as the symbol of the release of great power through the agreement of a group of people in an upper room. This agreement must have been a rich and intimate experience for those who shared it. Not less was the outpouring of the Holy Spirit known by us. How wonderful to reach the point where barriers vanish away and judgment and limitation are allowed to evaporate; for in such a state of dedication and love true oneness is found, and through that accord the release of unending blessing in effective service surely comes.

A new wing was added to Martin and Lillian's house, a lovely apartment which provided special accommodation in many ways, including temporary quarters for the newly married (Michael and Nancy, later Lloyd and Paula Meeker), for guests, and later an office for Martin, which left the large one he and I had shared to be occupied by me.

The 1964 Servers Training Class on Sunrise Ranch numbered 22 and included such shining lights as Stanley Grindstaff, Howard and Evelyn Bittenbender, Louis Rotola, Bridget Lee, Frank Reale, Joe and Norma Maynard, Helen Reynolds, Nowell McGuire, Susan Traff, Patricia Kristie and Margaret Stanley.

On April 25 Martin dealt with a vital subject and entitled his service "Anti Attitudes." He referred to an article by Richard Thompson, "Pacifism and Peacemaking," in which he sought to evoke a realization of the responsibility rightly shared by the entire body when an individual member undertakes specific work to achieve the common purpose. Martin said:

> We do not always consciously know what is going on but we need to be in position to support the various functions of the body as they find focus in each one. We are in agreement, in the sense that our attitudes are harmonious to the spirit of God and the moving currents as they are working through the body.
>
> Many people claim to be "against war," and are classified as pacifists. In Richard's approach he makes the distinction between being "against war" and being "for peace." Being against war is not being for peace. Physical action is usually considered the most effective means of gaining human ends, but there is economic, political and ideological warfare; there is the cold war. It is all warfare, and of course the desired ends are always considered to be good.

On Martin's birthday, April 27, I presented in the dining room on Sunrise Ranch a skit that hit an all-time high in comedy (with a purpose). For belly laughs it has had no peer. In the words of *Newslight:*

> Fayetta Gelinas portrayed a certain woman who could not resist eating a certain apple, and Joe Maynard [whose girth at that time was on a par with Fay's] was cast as a certain man whose initial reluctance turned into voracious appetite at the first bite.

It was presented in pantomime behind a screen so that only their "naked" silhouettes, in tight-fitting clothes, were seen, also a tree trunk with a few branches, on which hung an apple, and in which the hose of a vacuum cleaner, with folded paper napkin for head and two large matchsticks for fangs, twined itself, an incredibly realistic portrayal of a serpent! The unbelievable title was "Neath the Shade of the Old Apple Tree."

I changed the conclusion of the story (a practice I found effective in dramatic presentations) from one of failure to victory, achieved by a momentary blackout during which the two figures of Adam and Eve were replaced by the svelte ones of Stan Grindstaff and Pat Kristie (blissfully unaware of the serpent or the apple).

The former "Gateway Inn," purchased in 1953, became "RimRock House" on May 3, 1964, culminating many hours of painting, wallpapering and decorating. The roaring waterfall, re-christened "Great Falls," imbues that spot with a sense of awesome power as well as beauty. Gifts were on sale to the public, who often frequent the place, especially on sight-seeing Sundays. It featured unique items handcrafted by personnel from Sunrise Ranch and other Emissary groups. Bill Kuykendall's fertile imagination and expert handiwork produced juniper wood lamps and other works of art, with small cards carrying pictures and descriptions of same, thanks to Bill Dice's photographic ingenuity. There were stuffed dolls and other items on sale as well. Wes Jones coordinated the retail phase of the program.

Dr. Robert Bradley of Denver, a pioneer in the Natural Childbirth movement, spoke at the 1964 Servers Conference on Sunrise Ranch, at the invitation of Lillian who had a keen interest in that area which was just beginning to become popular.

On May 27 at 100 Mile House in a service entitled "Wise Stewardship" Martin referred to the manifold duties that had constituted his daily agenda, both before and since inheriting the place of leadership for the ministry. He had other inherited duties, such as his place in his family, being heir presumptive to the Marquessate of Exeter.

> These all come within the scope of my responsibility, just as your relatives do, to the extent that there is a proper vibrational attunement.
>
> We didn't come through the experiences and backgrounds that have brought us to this point without some reason; it wasn't just by chance. Because we may not immediately see the reason doesn't mean there isn't one. We don't have to see everything, but we do have to learn to handle our stewardship wisely, because it all belongs to the Lord and we represent Him in these circumstances. We were put in the position of handling these things and we take care of it all in His name.
>
> We need to have a balanced view in this regard, so that we are not afraid of

anything. Someone recently tried to make it appear that it was terrible for me to have responsibilities over in England. Why? We are in the world but not of it, not controlled by it, and extend the control of the Lord into these things. I have stewardship. All of you have stewardship too, and as you become trustworthy it all comes into the body. It all blends in with the whole, with each one having a specific responsibility in the whole. As we learn to trust, and become trustworthy, the power of life increases within the body. It brings increased health of body, mind and heart, and an intensification that permits victory to be experienced.

Martin, Lillian and Marina visited Burghley House in Stamford, England. They left 100 Mile House on June 29 and returned to Sunrise Ranch on July 11. It was eight-year-old Marina's first visit to her ancestral home, meeting her paternal grandmother and numerous other relatives. Martin shared realizations experienced on that trip to great advantage, in a service on July 12 (with scarcely time to recover from jetlag!).

Returning from a journey into a far country, there are always a number of things to be learned from the experience. Many people who are responsible for handling the affairs of men do it to their highest vision, and in such case it is evident that to some degree at least they are under the necessity of forgetting themselves. They must set on one side their personal affairs in order to effectively function in the field of their responsibilities. This we have emphasized from our standpoint. The moment we become overly concerned about the things of our personal sphere of function we separate ourselves from ourselves and become a house divided. If those things that are working out within us become dominant in our view we prevent the right outworking.

We need to have the wide vision. If we are under the necessity of considering our personal affairs on occasion, which is true enough, then we need to see them as they relate to the greater whole. They are virtually meaningless when we consider the vast whole, and yet how big and fat human beings make them, as though the world would stop going around if first consideration wasn't given to those things.

Out there in the world there are millions of people, each with personal problems. If we are involved in ours, of what earthly use can we be to anyone else? There needs to be someone on earth who is capable of seeing beyond themselves to what is needed with respect to others. Only as we have forgotten ourselves in the human sense can we experience ourselves in the divine sense.

In a service on Sunrise Ranch on July 18, "Position," Martin described the Seven Spirits before the throne of God.

Beginning with the Seventh, "The Spirit of Love"; then the Sixth, the "Spirit of the Womb" which enfolds sacred things to keep them holy and safe.

The Fifth, the "Spirit of Life," of vibrancy; the increased expression of that which is divine on earth.

The Fourth, the "Spirit of Purification" which enables those things which are responding to come up and move over into the divine design, the divine pattern. This relates to the fourth plane, the connecting link between the first three planes and the fifth, sixth and seventh planes. Everything that ascends must pass through the fourth plane. It relates to the flaming sword, that which purifies. Coming up out of the world, the outer three planes must pass through the purifying flame to come into the divine design, established from the higher planes. We are concerned to so function that all that comes to us is purified by reason of its coming to us, and not defiled; caused to be lifted up, changed, become meaningful.

And then the Third, the "Spirit of Blessing"; extending something of blessing constantly, one is identified with this Spirit.

The Second, the "Spirit of the Single Eye," with which we find attunement as we maintain centering in this Spirit.

The "Spirit of the New Earth," the First, is something which is known through actual experience in living, not a constant feeling of going down and down and down, but coming up, moving higher, into something fuller and freer.

All these spirits permit us to find attunement with and experience of the "Spirit of Love" in a manner that is creative and constructive.

In a service on July 22 on Sunrise Ranch, "Welcome Pressure," Martin said:

We are not interested in dissipating pressure. Our concern is to let it build because we are centered in the truth, and that which is not true, which is distorted, will be cleared out. With this attitude we can go anywhere and do anything, move into any realm of function. We can deal with human beings in any sphere and are not limited in our attitudes as to how things should be handled. We are not limited in our approach to any particular method.

We say, "Attunements can clear anything." What do you mean by an attunement? Holding your hands thus and so? That won't clear anything. It may be a channel through which the power of God can work, but if we insist that's the only channel it can work through we prevent the power of God from manifesting except in a limited condition and maintain a distortion pattern. Using the word *attunement* to indicate the process by which human beings are restored to their right relationship with God, I wonder how many methods of giving an attunement there are—I'm sure vastly more which you know nothing about than those which you do know about. Every time I give a service I give an attunement.

I accompanied Martin and Lillian on a tour of eastern United States and Canada which began August 28 at Love's Retreat in Lakemont, Georgia; proceeding to Huntingburg, Indiana; Berwick, Pennsylvania; Epping, New Hampshire (Green Pastures); Long Island, New York; Toronto, Ontario, where there was a large gathering in the YMCA; then a visit with Lillian's parents Roy and Marie Johnson in Brookfield, Wisconsin, and home to Sunrise Ranch on September 25.

My response to that journey's experience was contained in a poem which appeared in *Newslight*:

> *For the joy we shared together*
> *All along our eastern way,*
> *For the lovely, clement weather*
> *Greeting us most every day,*
>
> *For the lighted eyes quick-lifted*
> *At the sound of truth's clear ring,*
> *For the sight of dark clouds rifted,*
> *Bringing life's new song to sing,*
>
> *For the wondrous new beginning*
> *Instituted in each place,*
> *For the strong, compelling, winning*
> *Love that shines from Martin's face,*
>
> *My heart thrills with deep thanksgiving*
> *To the Lord for all His ways*
> *And abides with you in living*
> *His eternal loving praise.*

Rev. T. O. Olagunju announced that the Emissaries of Divine Light Church in Nigeria would be opening an approved primary school at Itiya, a village seventeen miles from the Ilesha headquarters, early in January of 1965. There would be two classes, each with at least forty pupils; two teachers, paid by the government; with grades from Primary One to Six. Help was needed for the building project.

A marked changeover at 100 Mile House in January was from the old hand-crank wall telephone system to the new dial system.

On January 31 Lillian shared a service with Martin at 100 Mile House entitled "Here I Am," in which she offered a touching tribute to Swami Premananda, in collective radiation to our dear friend who she felt was in need of our specific support, and emphasized the responsibility of the whole body with respect to him. She closed with his words in the last edition of his *Awake O'Man* magazine:

> "Live with yourself. Love yourself. When you retire at night and wake up in the morning, send a thought of love to the whole world. When you can sincerely love everything and everybody you will be astonished at the results, for love is the magnet that attracts the best of everything. Love and praise your body and mind; think what a wonderful machine it is and how agreeably it responds to every demand. Your body is the temple in which Divine, your Lord, resides, and your mind is the worshipper. Keep both pure and happy. Do not be critical of others and do not be impatient with their mistakes. Always send out thoughts of joy, love and life. They will come back to you laden with their kind. Live and smile each day."

Lillian spoke of her sensing that Swami might feel a bit "stuck" in India.

> I wonder if we could help un-stick him, to be free to move whithersoever the Lord wishes him to be. Do we, in our own hearts, feel him free, let him be free? If, in our hearts, we let our neighbor be free, the one sitting by us tonight, then we let Swami be free. I would open my door that he is free, that all peoples are free. This is my purpose in life: to let the Lord be free on earth and all peoples be free in His kingdom. Then I feel that I AM indeed manifesting. We haven't arrived, and yet we can say, "I AM."

In a Board Meeting on Sunrise Ranch on February 4 Martin opened up the consideration of a new Chapel to be built on Chapel Hill, which would leave the present one free for class activities and fill an increasing need for a lounge for young people. This was the initiation in the heaven for the magnificent form to appear in due season on that site of which Uranda so often lovingly spoke.

The contract for the purchase of a tract of land from Eden Valley Institute had been signed, and registered in the County Clerk's Office in Fort Collins. It included twenty acres on rimrock and two parcels of land, one just west of the garden and the other by Martin's house, together covering eight and a half acres, We agreed to their $10,000 offer with the understanding that they have the twenty acres on rimrock surveyed. A $2,500 deposit was made, another $2,500 to follow in a month's time, and the remainder in ninety days.

It was established, with a ten-year permit, that we could have water pumped out of the canal west of Martin's house for irrigation purposes, etc., through a pipe, with meter attached, making it possible to do away with the present ditch leading to the land south of the barnyard. A private telephone line was installed on the Ranch.

"Grow up!" was the title of a service at 100 Mile House on February 6, in which Martin spoke of the persistent indulgence in self-centeredness.

> It is natural for a child to be childish and self-centered; it is growing toward maturity and is in the process of evolving. We have used the word *evol* in this sense. If, however, it is carried over as the individual grows toward what should be maturity, then it is turned from evol into evil and becomes a destructive thing. A very few have accepted the means by which this evil state may become the state of evol, by stopping this futile and useless attitude which maintains centering in self. I have heard it said that when it comes to doing some work, young people are like mules.

> As far as I know, there has never been a mule that put its own harness on, backed itself to the implement it was going to pull, and gone to work. However, if someone comes along and puts the harness on and attaches the implement, the mule, if it is handled rightly, will be content to go to work. This is applicable to all who are still childish or self-centered. The mule-state, as I have described it, is the childish state that is moving in a cycle of evol. The person will go to work and do a job, maybe quite a good job, but it only happens when someone else does something about it. The immature individual never backs himself into harness but stands around waiting for someone else to do it, and that is childishness. Maturity is not waiting for someone else to do what can only be done in fact by the individual himself—that is, if there is ever to be an emergence out of the self-centered state.

Roy and Marie Johnson had been anticipating the happy day when they could move to Sunrise Ranch, pending the sale of their home in Wisconsin. And after two years of patient waiting, on April 16, it happened. They made it Home in time for their golden wedding anniversary. They had bought a large mobile home, which was placed at the end of the driveway which was the entrance to the Ranch. These two provided a place of welcome typical of Eden Valley and contributed in many ways. Marie worked at RimRock House, in the Library, and later instituted the Commissary, making many lasting friends in town while shopping for it, and pricing things within the range of the Sunrise citizens. Roy worked in many other areas.

Marie's father, John Nordland, had come to Wisconsin from Sweden and experienced a close friendship with Uranda when he met him. Jennie, her mother, also knew and loved Uranda and what he brought. Precious friends to everyone, Roy and Marie lived the remainder of their fruitful lives on Sunrise Ranch. Their house was, in a very real sense, everybody's home!

On April 23 Swami Premananda was killed in a motor accident in India. He uttered one word as he left this sphere, one we had heard him say many times in love and reverence: "Aum," or "Om." Ever a beloved friend to Martin, he had a deep conviction that his and our purpose were, and are, one. I have a poignant memory of the last time we shared with him, at the "Awake O'Man" Convention in Buffalo. Seated beside him at the dinner, I asked him what the *ji* meant when he was addressed as Swami-ji and he said it was like saying "Beloved Swami." When we said our farewells as he departed for his homeland he said, "Goodbye, Gracie-ji"—a gift that has remained in my heart.

On May 9 in a service on Sunrise Ranch, "The Heavenly Home," Martin emphasized the vital part played by those who work in the kitchen.

> This does not eliminate other fields of activity. Obviously the right atmosphere and influence need to be extended in all departments, but the measure of our progress as a ministry is determined by what occurs in the kitchen on Sunrise Ranch. It is not just a matter of preparing food. Some of the physical problems that have arisen here are directly attributable to what we might refer to as vibrational poison which has been folded into the physical food.
>
> The attitude of those who partake of the food is important too. We have had some rather despicable attitudes at times in this regard, critical of both quality and quantity. And of course it is somewhat dependent upon the extent of our budget. But if the wrong thing is going out, the substance doesn't come back, and maybe we'll have to go hungry! We are here to inspire by reason of right attitude, accepting the control of the truth, so that we are considerate of one another and not so concerned about ourselves in a self-centered sense.

In a service, "Heavenly Appreciation," on May 19, Martin noted he had been away for over two months and that on May 12 Richard Thompson completed his ministry on earth. Stopping in Vancouver on the way back to the Hundred, Martin had spoken to the group there, expressing his keen sense of loss in a personal sense.

He used the illustration of a tree, which draws some of its nourishment from the soil.

> Its roots are in the ground, firmly embedded in the earth; therefore it seems as though the earth was the most important thing to the tree. Well it needs to be there of course, and about five percent of what is required by the plant or tree for sustenance comes from the soil. Ninety-five percent comes from the atmosphere. This emphasizes something tremendously important to us, because as human beings in the fallen state we seem to be rather deeply embedded in the earth.
>
> The tree has been used in the Bible to portray man's relation with God—the true vine with its many branches, and the tree of life. In the view of the vast majority of people, external, material things occupy almost a hundred percent of attention, and yet it relates to only five percent of the individual's real being. There is another ninety-five percent which concerns more immaterial, intangible, atmospheric things that can't be immediately touched and handled or even seen. If it wasn't for the atmosphere around the earth there wouldn't be any life. Because of it the radiation from the sun, including much more than light, reaches the surface of the earth in a manner that is not destructive. We know this in theory, but the same principle is at work with us.

In July of 1965 the Village of 100 Mile House was incorporated, the result of a 61 percent majority vote of leaseholders. The villagers could remain leaseholders or buy their land at a later date. This meant a shift in responsibility for the management of town affairs from Bridge Creek Estate to the villagers themselves, represented by a five-man commission. However, though Estate Manager Ross Marks declined nomination as chairman because of his unique position, the townspeople insisted he was the man for the job and elected him by a landslide vote. A Village office was opened with a full-time clerk, and taxes which once went to the provincial government were channeled back into the Village.

25

COORDINATED ACTION

August 1965 ~ October 1968

*P*rior to the establishment of Headquarters on Sunrise Ranch the office personnel mimeographed mailings in small rented offices or private homes. In 1945 the "office," focalized by William and Muriel Oshane, was moved to a house in Loveland, and the following year to Sunrise Ranch. Staff and equipment grew steadily, with such additions as offset printing press, paper cutter, commercial camera, etc. But the office staff was scattered over the Ranch, with typists working in their homes or tiny individual offices. In the summer of 1964 I turned the first spadeful of ground for the foundation of the new building, and members of that year's Class and Conference participated in the beginning construction.

In 1965 the Administration Building was completed, a beautiful edifice which provided, for the first time, a spacious office where all the departments could function together under one roof.

In May the staff moved into the "promised land," which included tape-recording headquarters with room for storage and supplies. There were individual offices for Oliver Latam and Betty Protzman in bookkeeping and related areas. The downstairs housed printing equipment, facilities for sorting, folding and packaging, plus a photography darkroom, and office for Bill Dice and Bob Moore. Officially opened on August 2nd, this was just one of the uniquely individual structures that took form under the inspiration of Martin at the helm of the constantly expanding ministry.

A few words from *Newslight* impart a sense of the activities shared by those in "administration" and their joy in it:

> In one month two Emissary and two Ontological mailings are prepared, sixteen servers' mailings, two issues of *This Is Why*, one issue of *Newslight*, and JTS material for four weeks. In addition many commercial jobs are accepted each month, annually *Eden Valley News* and *Northern Light*, as well as Christmas cards and Hasti-Notes stationery for RimRock House.

> Many steps are involved in bringing the word to its finished form. Martin's services are transcribed from tapes and each one is checked, first by Martin and Grace, then again for accuracy by office personnel before being handed to Jim Wellemeyer for printing, after which they go to the ladies for folding, addressing and stamping. [The typists were Julia Kelley, Claudia Romanick, Clayre Withers, Marjorie Christiansen and Martha Whitcomb, all under the capable direction of Millie Latam.]

One gorgeous day in Eden Valley, early in September, Martin and I were walking past the golden fields where hay lay ready to be gathered. He observed that it needed to be baled immediately and brought in. As always, he suited the action to the word and the state of affairs was swiftly ascertained (a broken-down baler). A baler was borrowed and manned, while all other available men proceeded to the field with pitchforks, plus tractor and trailer. Martin worked through the afternoon with the men, and suppertime found the entire fields cleared. It was a simple but powerful experience. How ripe is the harvest today? Awaiting the gathering? It must not spoil in the fields. Quick, decisive, coordinated *action* can save the day. And He works right with us.

At 100 Mile House another magnificent building was in process under Martin's hand. The Red Coach Inn was being constructed, with the first wing of twenty units nearing completion and the foundation laid for the hotel complex. In *Northern Light* of that year Max von Hartmann wrote:

> It seems only right and fitting that 100 Mile House should have one of the finest hostelries found anywhere. After all, it had its beginning as a roadhouse on the old Cariboo wagon road in the days of the Barkerville gold rush, when most traveled by horse-drawn coach or on horseback. Since then the public hospitality business in this little community has changed considerably.

> In 1931 Martin opened the door of the 100 Mile Lodge—by old-timers

recalled as the finest hotel in the Cariboo—to the public, which had just begun to use the automobile extensively as a means of transportation. With the growth of 100 Mile House and increased traffic in the rapidly developing North of British Columbia—over the new and paved Cariboo Highway—came the need for additional and better quality accommodation, soon provided by the 100 Mile Motel in 1952 and the Exeter Arms Hotel in 1956, both in the Village. Even so, still more accommodation is needed, with emphasis on the more luxurious type of motel unit, together with first-class restaurant and catering facilities.

Under Martin's direction a design for the new enterprise was gradually developed by the architect for the project, Colonel Alan Gray of Vancouver. It shows, to quote the latter, "a quietly colorful lodge-type building, blending the use of beams, wood siding, plaster, shakes and stone into an inviting structure that expresses the ranch and historical theme of the Cariboo." The tentative name "Red Coach Inn" may well be its final one. And so it has proved to be, and stands today the most attractive and inviting "home" between the Coast and the vast interior on the Alaskan Highway.

At that time the population of the town of 100 Mile House was approximately 850, with a general trading area of about 5000, about 45 business establishments and an airport that boasted 3140 feet elevation, runway length of 2100 feet and 12 to 14 aircraft to call it home base.

Another momentous happening in that eventful year was the acquisition of our next airplane, the Cessna Super Skymaster, SBX, Model 337, a twin-boom aircraft (one engine behind and one in front), making for greater safety in the air, excellent stability, with a cruising speed at 10,000 feet of 191 mph and range of 865 miles. Martin and Ross took additional training to obtain license endorsements, and incidentally on a rescue flight early in November were able to spot the tiny fire of a hunter lost in dense brush, enabling the RCMP ground teams to bring him out by following the plane's directions as it circled overhead.

Winter sports were natural at 100 Mile House and the provision of a skating rink afforded much fun and exercise, not only for the Unit members but on occasion a party was held which included people from town, enjoyed by the bank manager, high school principal, Herb Auld of the service station, and many others.

At that time George Bullied made his connection with our group in Hamilton, Ontario, where he provided a haven, called "Wayside House," in which food and lodging, love and leadership saved many from the "asphalt jungle" who found their way to the door of this beautiful old red brick home halfway up Hamilton Mountain. Later

George and his wife Pat established a center in Ontario which they named "Twin Valleys" and continued their wonderful work. They had a son, Adam, joined before long by a little brother.

October 12th heralded the advent of Bill and Ruth Bahan with their three children to provide a focus for the group in Vancouver. They moved into the Center on Cornwall Street which had been home to Richard and Dorothy Thompson and their large "family" in Vancouver. It did not take long before Bill was attracting new and different elements from near and far. On the 22nd of October the authors of the Journal of Modern Subjectivism, Robert Dolling Wells and Constance Rodger Emerson, came to the Center at Bill's invitation.

On January 20, 1966, Roger de Winton accepted the position as overall coordinator of men's activities on Sunrise Ranch. There was a strong pattern of male focalization, with Jim Wellemeyer, Bob Patton, Roy Bever, Floyd Conell, Bob Moore and others.

On February 21 at 100 Mile House the Red Coach Inn opened for business. Nine rooms, part of the rear wing of twenty-two units, were readied, including the executive suite. Martin was often seen on the premises during the building of the Inn, and members of the Unit and many visitors helped with the final cleanup and furniture moving. The first customer was Jerome Worthen, of Vancouver, given Room 49, a special reservation for that first guest.

Four months later all twenty-two rooms, licensed dining room and luncheon area, spacious lobby, lounge and unique porte-cochere were in operation, with further construction continuing under John Summerbell's direction. With Ross Marks and George Coutts as co-directors, John had formed a building contracting company, Pioneer Development, which expanded into the building supply business to great advantage. He later dealt with "Irly Bird," a group of independent lumberyards in British Columbia who functioned on a cooperative basis. An ex-RCAF pilot, building contractor, health food store proprietor and real estate salesman, John had almost become a minister, eventually finding his lasting home and place for his talents in the Emissary family.

Max von Hartmann was the Manager of Red Coach Inn. He came to Canada from Germany in 1951 and owned a small restaurant in Vancouver. Later he managed another, where he met Richard and Dorothy Thompson in 1956, and by 1958 was on his way to Class at Sunrise. He had been in the restaurant business in Germany, as well as on the road as an entertainer, in literary cabaret and as a magician. His ready wit was always an attribute in his role as congenial host.

Hanya Oshanek was the head cook, Greg Archambault assistant manager, with a rollaway cot behind the desk in the manager's office where he slept at night. Nancy Meeker was one of the desk clerks and Shirley Stephen a waitress in the dining room, later to be on the desk. Lloyd Meeker was the engineer in charge of the dishwashing machine whenever necessary. Nowell McGuire did a great job looking after the motel units. This marked the end of the Lodge's function as a public facility, with a few rooms kept for boarders and some for our own visitors.

A thirty-bed hospital was opened in the Village on July 15.

The completion of a large Esso Service Station by the Imperial Oil Company in 1966 was a milestone in the development of 100 Mile House. Situated directly south of Red Coach Inn, it was managed by George Coutts, a member of the 100 Mile Unit, and served the public throughout the ensuing years.

The Log Chapel, one of the oldest buildings in the area, built at the turn of the century, and once used as a blacksmith shop, had received a new roof the previous year and now a furnace and vestibule. The floor raising, six inches to lay the pipe, was held on Easter Monday when most of the men were home to give a hand. A platform was added to the front of the Chapel, raising the altar. Conrad O'Brien-ffrench had donated a bell, which was ready to be hung. The original logs have remained intact and sturdy to this day.

At that time the home of Ross and Marcia Marks, originally Martin's, received a much needed addition of two bedrooms, bathroom, furnace room and extra room upstairs.

The 100 Mile House *News Herald* did indeed herald the ever-expanding news media in that Village, with Chris Foster and Joe Maynard playing vital initial roles.

In the Sunrise Ranch Chapel on April 20 Bill Bahan was ordained a minister in a special service which closed with Martin's words: "Certainly the spirit of giving is characteristic of Bill, and all of us have long recognized the fact that he is a minister in the true sense of the word."

In May a new avenue of service opened up when Martin, George Bullied, Alan Hammond and Dick Cable flew to Canon City, Colorado, to speak to the Alcoholics Anonymous chapter in the state penitentiary. George, who had worked in AA for many years, continued weekly speaking engagements at the prison, often to large groups of over a hundred that were participating in the prison's guidance and rehabilitation program.

A Center was opened by Fayetta Gelinas at her apartment in Denver, where Bill Bahan focalized weekly meetings, accompanied by his wife Ruth and several of the Sunrise family. A few of that first nucleus were David Lynch, his mother Mary Lou Sleichter, sister Ronnie Lynch, Ben and Joanne Knaub, Tom and Helen Crouch and Gisela Kroeger.

Fayetta, a talented comedienne known professionally as Fay McKay, divided her time between Denver and Sunrise Ranch. Her talent, also in singing, is an integral part of her generous and loving nature and she has charmed audiences throughout the world. Fay's gift of a beautiful Hammond organ was placed in the Chapel on Sunrise Ranch in May. It had the latest features, such as percussion, split vibrato, reverberation, etc., to say nothing of its rich tone and handsome cabinet work. And Wesley Jones, our resident organist, was the best. The organ which he had brought to the Ranch in 1956 was then installed in the Denver Center.

On July 20 in a service entitled "Sunrise Ranch" Martin spoke of the supreme opportunity and privilege to be in this place, a part of that manifestation of Center which is here. Once it is experienced you know there is no higher field of service anywhere. Some perhaps have taken the attitude that they didn't feel their place of service was on Sunrise Ranch. If that was the way they felt, of course it wasn't. And if any of the personnel on Sunrise Ranch have such a feeling they have no business here. It has seemed terrible to me that a person could be so blind, so insensitive as to fail to recognize the potential that may be actualized by accepting that responsibility. Not everyone should be on the Ranch, but it should be the highest aspiration to be privileged to serve here.

Without what is here, there would be no ministry. We only begin to get somewhere when there is participation in the divine plan, divine design, when there is a willingness to leave all and follow our Lord and King. That's all that's needed, and yet the human mind can put up a barrage of excuses as to why not, and human beings have fallen for it generation after generation.

I rejoice in the response which comes to focus in the hearts of all of you. Years ago, when I first came to Sunrise Ranch for a visit I said to Uranda, "I would love to serve here." He said, "Maybe you will one day." And so I do. So we all, without exception, carry the responsibility of being an inspiration to all our fellows, whether here or anywhere else.

In a service on Sunrise Ranch on September 4 Martin spoke of the atmosphere that characterizes a true home.

A home is in one sense a private place. While many may be invited into the home, nevertheless there is something private and personal about a home, which is right and proper. One of the unpleasant aspects of some so-called homes is what is called "back-fence gossip." We don't have a true home where there is prying. One of the evidences of divine being is the ability to keep one's mouth shut. Even within the home not everything is said to everybody. It would not be fitting. How quickly the truly stable point of being can be dissipated by unwise talk, gossip. And anyone who truly serves in the home will immediately meet any expression of gossip in a forthright manner, either by turning on their heel and walking away, or saying, "Shut up!" I'll back anyone to the hilt on that.

In a service at 100 Mile House on October 15, "Journey in the East," Martin shared an outline of a trip, in which he was accompanied by Lillian and me, and Roger de Winton, to the eastern United States and Canada.

We left Loveland airport in our plane on September 6 and arrived at Watertown, South Dakota where we were met by Selmer and Sylvia Hammer. That evening we were joined by others in the group at Hammer, the town bearing the name of Selmer Hammer's forebears. The next day we flew to Green Bay, Wisconsin, stopped for fuel and a bite to eat, and continued on to Marion, Indiana, where we stayed overnight with Harry and Helen Jerome. The next morning we flew to London, Ontario, and landed for Customs. We were welcomed by most of the London group at the airport and were driven to the home of Bob and Bev Purdom and later to the center, in the home of Bob and Alice Barbour. Then we flew to Toronto via Buttonville Airport.

On Friday, September 9, I conducted the wedding service for George Bullied and Pat Kristie in a hall near the farm of Hugh and Jane Duff. Subsequent sessions were held there, conveniently close to Toronto. With over forty of our own people in attendance, sessions began the next day, morning, afternoon and evening. Lillian, Grace and Roger participated with me, as well as Bill Bahan, Jim and Mary Pogue and Joe Houlton. About a hundred attended, with many more at the Sunday morning service which was open to anyone. The time in Toronto concluded after a service night on Tuesday where people were packed in. On Wednesday the 14th we just got as far as Syracuse because of a storm. So we drove to Albany and stayed the night. The next morning Ken Morrison and Bill took us to Salem, where we stayed with Bill and Ruth.

The next day, Friday the 16th, New Year's Day for our ministry incidentally, the sessions began at the farm at Green Pastures in Epping, New Hampshire. A number came from New York and other places. Sessions were held in the chapel with about a hundred people. On Sunday evening I had a lecture at West Townsend where Al Reida had made arrangements in a small hall, jampacked with people. Bill introduced me, as was usually the case.

About 150 attended the public meeting in Lynn, Massachusetts, on Monday the 19th in the Oxford Club. On Tuesday Bill and Ruth drove Roger and me to Keene, New Hampshire, and I finally got our plane, which had been held up because of repairs and later weather; then to the Lawrence airport.

Wednesday we could not fly—weather again! five inches of rain and blowing a gale. We drove to New York, leaving early with Bill and Ruth. En route we stopped at Westport, Connecticut, for a meal and connected with Ricci (Mary) Cardiff. Then we had an interesting visit to the Famous Writers' School, noted for their excellent correspondence course which Grace had been taking. It was an experience for her to meet a few of her instructors in person and we all enjoyed a tour of the place.

We reached the home of Lou and Bridie Rotola in Brooklyn without delay in spite of the weather. We stayed there, and that evening a group of about forty gathered for a meeting, to the accompaniment of the elevated railway trains that passed every ten minutes—it was a warm evening, so the windows had to be open! The next day we visited the United Nations and were able to get tickets to go in to the General Assembly, after which we had a very interesting tour of the U.N. buildings. Charles Lo Giudice drove us back, and after setting off in the opposite direction to our destination we had an extensive and unexpected tour of Brooklyn, seeing Coney Island and around the coastline and finally, about an hour and a half later, arrived at the Rotolas. It should have taken twenty minutes!

That evening a public meeting was held in the Famous Restaurant. Not a very large room, it was covered with mirrors and set up so that I would have my back to a mirror and the audience would be looking at themselves. So we quickly reversed the arrangement, which put the door from the street just beside me. People continued to arrive throughout the meeting and chairs were brought in from next door, until the place was filled to the brim. People were standing, and there was a constant shuffling while gentlemen gave their seats to ladies. It was rather distracting, with people coming in until about ten minutes before I finished. One of the last arrivals, a lady came up to me afterward and said, "Would you please give me a summary of what you said?" Surprisingly, though, in spite of all that it was a very good outworking with about 140 people in a room for 75.

The next day I had some appointments, then we all went to downtown Manhattan, the ladies shopping and Bill and I walking to the top of the Empire State Building. After a dinner together we enjoyed a play in the Big City. Back to Westport the next day, where we stayed overnight in the home of Don and Mary Cardiff, with a public meeting in the evening attended by forty people. The following morning, the 25th, we were in Lawrence again where we greeted Wally and Joan

Bahan at the airport before taking off in our plane for Berwick, Pennsylvania. There we stayed at the lovely home of Howard and Evelyn Bittenbender. Evelyn's family had for years provided a focus for the 7-UP company in that part of the country. She and Howard have always been most generous in their support of the ministry. We had most of our excellent meals with Eddie and Gladys Miller at their center/home, with a well-attended meeting on Monday.

The weather had been fairly good up to that point, but on Tuesday, the 27th, it began to deteriorate. There was a storm to the south, which was the direction we were going of course. We got as far as Harrisburg, not very far, and had to stay overnight, trusting the reports that the weather would improve the next day. We waited at the airport until almost one o'clock and took off, hoping to fly via Pittsburgh down to Huntingburg and get behind the storm. We followed the Susquehanna River to the north and then the Juanita River as far as Altoona.

There is a three-thousand-foot ridge west of Altoona and it was covered with cloud. We circled several times looking for a way to get by and got into a thick cloud close to the ridge. We climbed as rapidly as possible while turning and hit the top of a tree, which came upon us suddenly. The plane never faltered, just went right through the top of the tree. Still climbing rapidly we went up another five hundred feet. The instruments and controls seemed to be all right except for a roughness to the forward engine, which proved later to be due to the front prop being slightly bent. The rear engine was fine. It took off the step and did some damage to one of the wings, the struts and tail assembly.

In about five minutes we were over Johnstown. I radioed in—they don't have a tower, they have a unicom—and asked them to check my landing gear. They said it was all right, so we landed successfully and were met by a delegation of very thoughtful people who were helpful in every way possible. It turned out that another airplane had just landed on the golf course close by and been completely demolished, the people unhurt. Soon there was the TV camera and radio people, and everybody else, out on the airport.

[I would interject something of the impact of that experience, on the part of all of us. Lillian and I were in the back, Roger up front beside Martin. Visibility was nil after take-off, that cloud dense. As Martin was seeking to climb his way out of it, there was a jolt that shook the whole plane. It was, of course, the tree, but we had no way of knowing what it was at that point. A little later we could see, on my side, the trunk of a tree jammed into the wing. It was a miracle that it did not upset the balance of the plane with its added weight and thrust. We were as close to hitting the mountain as the height of that tree! As it was, with its upper part embedded in the wing, we, amazingly, landed safely.]

We were due in Atlanta the next day. Fortunately there was a commercial flight coming in shortly and we got space on that, having just had a glimpse of ourselves on the news! We flew to Pittsburgh and then Atlanta where we stayed in the Dinkler Plaza Hotel, the setting for sessions to follow. We proceeded to Love's Retreat, a two-and-a-half-hour drive, where we stayed Friday and Saturday with lectures each evening and a service Sunday morning, with excellent response. On Monday we drove to Atlanta where we now have a center in a house given to us for two years by someone who contacted us at Love's Retreat. It had not been lived in for a while but the house is fine, close to one of the main streets and opposite a shopping center. The lawn had grown up into a hay field, and being downwind from the shopping center was filled with an accumulation of paper and rubbish. So about a dozen of us got busy and took care of the trash. Bill and Myrtle Byl will be there for the next few months and Mahdah will go down every week. So something is on the move in Atlanta.

On Monday, October 3rd, we flew to Denver via Chicago and arrived on Sunrise Ranch after a very eventful journey which covered just about a month. Something was achieved where the public was concerned, and there was an experience by our own people there for the first time. Paramount in this was the fact that we had a team in agreement; this presents an impact. Another factor was that there was something strong and stable back of us from the standpoint of those on Sunrise Ranch and you here. The home fires were kept burning.

People everywhere are more open than I have experienced heretofore. There is a greater hunger, an awareness that what is known and experienced is not adequate; there must be something else and may well be quite different—which it is. Of course there is always a need for follow-through. Human beings are not generally self-starters, nor do they maintain their fire very long on their own. You may know something about this. I would name a few with special responsibilities who are keenly aware of this necessity to maintain the movement: Jim Pogue, Mac Duff, Bill and Walter Bahan, Lou Rotola, and their wives, the Millers and others, an impressive list.

There was delight in Eden Valley when, on September 24, a Conference was held, not for Servers or Class members but for Sunrise Ranch personnel—a first!

For several years Wesley and Dorothy Jones had been separated, in agreement that their paths lay in different directions.

A dearly loved member of the family, Mary Close, passed away at the age of ninety-three. This still-beautiful woman had pioneered as a young girl, defending herself in a covered wagon on her journey to the West. Her independent spirit prevailed and she could be found in the kitchen, laundry or anywhere helping in any way she could.

From *Eden Valley News:*

> The Little Chapel on the hill has stood for many years, a rather lonely symbol of all that man has looked to in ages past—and present. This year the Class of 1966 undertook the joyous task of bringing new life to this beautiful little temple. Inside and out it was made clean and new, with the addition of a rock planter surrounding it on three sides. Here are planted lovely juniper trees. Now there is a stone walk leading from the road to the Little Chapel, and a charming wooden gate. Seven steps comprise this inviting walk, the first of which is outside the gate. Sunrise Ranch and that symbol are connected as never before in oneness of purpose and creative achievement. The road is plain for all to see, the steps invite "Come. Come and See."

In a service on October 12 Martin brought with him an issue of a journal, *Encompass,* by Bob Wells and Connie Emerson and referred to an article dealing briefly with what was being called Reality Therapy by Dr. Glasser, in which the conclusion was reached that much of psychotherapy is useless. Martin quoted:

> People do not act irresponsibly because they are ill; they are ill because they act irresponsibly. We have been concerning ourselves with the necessity of accepting divine responsibility in the expression of our lives. To try to correct ill conditions in body, mind and heart without first accepting divine responsibility is a futile undertaking. There may of course be a patching-up process or delaying action in the cycles of disintegration, but the experience of the true state of health is impossible without the acceptance of divine responsibility first; and we cannot do that without accepting our own divine being.

> Why would there not be as much feeling with respect to identification with what one knows is the truth as has been customary to give to the state of being involved with something wrong? Why should we look upon the truth as merely an intellectual concept? This has been used as a very convenient excuse to avoid the necessity of coming to the point of being identified with the truth. Why not identify with that rather than with the mess? To become responsible we must become emotionally involved with the truth of our own beings. Here are our deepest feelings, with the beauty, nobility, rightness, strength, stability of our own divine being. But this never hap-

pens unless we do something deliberate about it.

We are going to accept identification with something; that's the way we are made. Most people are bogged down in human nature, their feelings open to various states of illness, weakness, irresponsibility. Then they struggle to correct them through various means, which provide all kinds of excuses—we couldn't help it because of all that happened to us. But the fact of irresponsibility in the past does not need to be the fact in the present. We can consciously assume responsibility for ourselves, regardless of how our parents behaved or how the hereditary influences came down to us from our ancestors, or regardless of our environment. We can still be responsible for what we express, for our own thoughts, for body, mind and heart.

On October 23 at 100 Mile House Martin invited Alan Hammond to share the service with him. Alan had left his native England for Canada as a young man and played a vital role in the Ontological Society at the University of British Columbia. When only seven years old he miraculously survived a severe traumatic accident. Terribly burned, he found himself in the hospital, at that time filled with troops of the British Army returned from Normandy. Physically shattered, they displayed a courage and comradeship that Alan, who was in bed for two years and had to learn to walk again, never forgot. "Some of them went up, and others down, and it wasn't their injuries that determined it."

Alan provided inspiration himself, and was chosen from sixty applicants to teach during the summer in the British Columbia Penitentiary. He had other ideas than teaching English and convinced the prison authorities, which resulted in the forming of a new class. It was so successful that he was asked to continue through the winter. "One of our most terrific meetings," he said, "was when the men began to see they weren't so terrible after all, and people outside were really just as crooked as they were. It was a matter of a change in the perspective of their views." Alan's influence has been immeasurable in the forming foundation of education in the ministry.

Accepting Martin's invitation to share his service on October 3rd, he said:

Since leaving Class I have started work (this is continuing an old pattern of service) in a prison. At Conference Martin spoke particularly of the probable opportunity this ministry has of offering something to people addicted to drugs and alcohol. I applied to a new twelve million-dollar drug addiction center, forty miles from Vancouver called Matsqui, where people are sentenced to over two years, so they are the really bad ones, users and traffickers in drugs. I decided to go straight to the top, so I phoned the warden and reminded him that I had worked for him eighteen months ago when he was warden of the

B.C. Penitentiary. He remembered me and I was interviewed.

I told him I knew there was only one answer to drug addiction, which was to somehow convince those men that life is more wonderful, more fulfilling, without drugs than with them. He agreed, and I knew we were well on the road.

The main personnel are what they call counselors, who counsel the inmates. The main therapy is that you get twelve or fifteen men sat in a room with the counselor who encourages the men to criticize each other. For example, they say, "Now, what's wrong with Fred over here?" So everybody looks at Fred and they find his weak spot and agree on it and talk about it. They try to keep it down to practical everyday things, so Fred is subjected to criticism, revealing that he is in fact a selfish swine and is made to really know it.

The idea is that he will stop being selfish. However, what they are finding is that Fred is not even listening, because as soon as he hears his name spoken he goes into a shell, and some of his friends will not criticize someone they have been friendly with in and out of jails for twenty years. The men are realizing that this stirs up their hostility. The psychologist says they are deliberately doing it so that they will begin to feel insecure. Well, it's working on some of them!— four were removed to Essondale (mental hospital) in the last five months.

My basic approach is diametrically opposed to this. I am a teacher and called that. I teach academic subjects in the schoolroom during the mornings, and in the afternoons have my own "educational discussion groups," where I present a subject which is obviously educational. I may show a film on the population explosion, or the plight of the underprivileged nations, and then we discuss and develop it from there. It is a huge place and there is a women's section, which I visit on Wednesdays, with some academic courses in the morning and in the afternoons we talk.

It is impossible for me to achieve anything until I have had an adequate experience of the nature and qualities of my own true being. This applies to each one of us and also on a group basis. The principle works dramatically, like gravity. Before I tackle anything out there I have to resolve the very things within myself.

Alan then shared some experiences he had in the prison, which revealed that he had indeed done his homework and was seeing lasting transformations in the lives of others.

At 100 Mile House the directors of Red Coach Inn decided that, though the business had actually been in full operation since July, it would be fitting to show the place to the public and honor those who had played particular parts in its development. So on November 19 a gala event was enjoyed by the townspeople, with fifty-one guests invited to, first, a cocktail party in the Manager's suite, and then an elaborate dinner in the main dining room of the Inn. The architect, Alan Gray from Vancouver, and lawyer David Rogers from Kamloops shared the head table with other notables. A feeling of home was dramatically conveyed in that public opening, an atmosphere that has continued and been acknowledged by many through the years.

Following dinner, Fay McKay entertained in her inimitable style which delighted everyone. One Hundred Mile House had never seen or heard the like in their midst! She made the trip for the occasion, the previous day appearing on Kamloops TV to tell viewers about Red Coach Inn.

Nancy Meeker enjoyed a year attending the newly opened Simon Fraser University, set high upon a hill overlooking the beautiful city of Vancouver.

Early in January of 1967 Martin and Lillian went to get our plane which had been left to be repaired after the accident in Pennsylvania in September. Martin took it up, and discovered several important things that were not right. It took a while before they were corrected and he was satisfied to fly it. Even so, the inspection at the Canadian border discovered the need for another vital correction to be made. Finally it was right, and back home again.

In a service at 100 Mile House on January 22 entitled "Rejoicing in Heaven," Martin said:

> I have a special announcement to make this evening. Michael and Nancy have indicated their desire to walk together in the fulfilment of life's purpose for them. This, to me, is a remarkable outworking in fulfilment in view of a number of factors, presumably the chief one being that Michael is my earthly son and Nancy is Uranda's earthly daughter, besides being our daughter. Something is emphasized to me with respect to what one might call the inexorable unfoldment of the creative purposes of God.

On January 25th in the banquet room of Red Coach Inn Chris Foster and Joy Westren were joined in marriage, a union which proved to be of inestimable value, and delight to all who knew them. Relatives attended, from Toronto and other places. The wedding ceremony was followed by a reception which included the Unit family and others from surrounding areas.

The first Emissary Conference at 100 Mile House was held on February 4th, with about 140 attending. The hall in the basement of Red Coach Inn was quickly finished, largely through the efforts of Geoff Tisch who came from Vancouver. Many areas were represented, with Jim and Mary Pogue from Toronto, Bob Spaulding and Robbie Robinson from New England, Eddie Miller from Berwick, and Stan Grindstaff from Los Angeles. Claudia Romanick arrived early from Sunrise to help with preparations. Others came from Prince Rupert, Banff, Saanichton and Vancouver Island. A Greyhound busload came from Vancouver. It was a Saturday and Sunday to be remembered.

LeRoy Jensen had moved from Kelowna, B.C., to New York City to serve there.

It was around this time that a grouping of chiropractors in the Deep South were considering a motivational speaker to invite into the area, in hopes that it would enhance their practices. Those doctors included Jerry England, Irv Shepherd, Bill Gallagher, Ernest Whitman, and Glenn Doty. None of them had heard of the Emissary program or Sunrise Ranch, but they had heard that Dr. George Shears was an excellent speaker and proceeded to inquire about his availability. As it turned out, George recommended that Bill Bahan come instead. Bill travelled to Louisiana that spring, and consequently the Emissary program caught fire in the South. Martin and Lillian spoke at a symposium in Shreveport in the fall.

The marriage of Michael Cecil and Nancy Meeker took place in the Chapel on Sunrise Ranch on May 3, 1967, and was conveyed via telephone hookup to 100 Mile House. Martin officiated, with Rev. James Wellemeyer and Rev. Roger de Winton sharing in the service. To the chorus of the Wedding March, played on harp and organ, Nancy walked down the aisle on Martin's arm and took her place beside Michael. The attendants were Diana de Winton, maid of honor, and Rev. Ross Marks, best man. Following the ceremony the wedding party went to the Little Chapel for a private ceremony, after which a reception was held in the dining room.

In *Eden Valley News* Roger de Winton reviewed the achievements in the past year. With the constant need to accommodate increased numbers of visitors and Class members, additions were made to the Apartment Building, with washroom space for both men and women, a utility section on each of two floors; also there were two new family dwellings.

> As the spring opened up further we found ourselves with a valuable gift of a linotype machine and related equipment needing to be housed, and so quickly we laid down a concrete pad beside the Administration Building, and then built around the gift on the pad, connecting the structure with our main printing section.

> A water tank with capacity of 7000 gallons, from the 100 Mile House Unit, had been awaiting reconstruction for some time and this we erected after first laying down a concrete base of very special shape and varying thicknesses, which required expert thought and framing. This provided much needed storage to back up our wells at peak load periods during the day. Our greenhouse, of ancient vintage, needed major reconstruction to be usable any more, and we were offered the funds by one of our members to provide for a fully modern structure with plexiglass top and sides.

The roofed-in patio by our dining room was in need of screening, which we provided in paneled sections and also adapted a large number of extra windows, which we obtained when we bought our dining room years ago. So the whole patio can now be closed in during the winter and early spring. That construction removed our root cellar which is relocated east of the dining-kitchen building using straw bales protected by plastic covering and held in place by poles and heavy chicken wire for roof and walls.

Bountiful rains brought more moisture than had been seen for many years and we had bumper crops of hay and grains and a fine garden, while our irrigation equipment lay idle for most of the season instead of running much of the twenty-four hours from May to September. Our herds of cows and goats provide milk, cottage cheese, yogurt and butter. Chickens, turkeys and rabbits fill many needs. We mill our grains for bread and cereals. We have a fire department with pumping equipment, which has been used on occasion to save neighbors from being burned out, and there are various types of fixed warning systems and extinguishers.

It is a wonderful experience to play a part in this miniature town, all together doing what is required to keep it moving in an orderly and expanding way.

Dorothy Jones reported, in that issue, on

Freezing:

Chard	800 lbs. or 32 cans
Peas	1,632 lbs. or 68 cans
Green and yellow beans	1,200 lbs. or 75 cans
Corn	1,532 lbs. or 60 cans

Canning:

Apricots	522 cans
Peaches	570 cans
Pears	178 cans
Tomatoes	525 cans
Pickles and relishes	171 quarts
	1 barrel dills

Famous for pickle-making, Hazel McKenney, her sister Della Bever and daughter Nadine filled Sunrise shelves with their delectable concoctions. Hazel provided the cu-

cumbers, and all kinds of vegetables and garden produce, over many years.

In a service on June 4th at 100 Mile House, "The Umbrella of Love," Martin cited two comments, one by Paul Hellyer, Canadian Minister of Defense, when he said that the value of military force was to provide an umbrella under which something might be worked out between nations. This was to permit a sphere of relative calm in order that the processes of growth and maturing could take place to the point where there was no need anymore for the umbrella. If nobody took advantage of the umbrella, of course, the opportunity would be lost.

The second comment was by U Thant, Secretary-General of the United Nations, when he was speaking in eastern Canada. He indicated that the moral and spiritual state of human beings needed to advance very rapidly in order to catch up with the advances in other fields that had already been made. Martin said:

> We have recognized that the part which religion should properly play in the lives and experience of human beings has been left way back in the stone age, so to speak, while technological advances have carried us into the space age. Far from being reduced, the gap has become increasingly great. The dislocations in human experience consequently have become more marked. We are concerned with a different sort of umbrella, not maintained by force but by love, an atmosphere provided in which young and old alike may, if they will, grow into the reality of manhood and womanhood. That has to some extent been provided right here and on Sunrise Ranch.

At 100 Mile House the historic Concord stagecoach, mascot of the Lodge for many years and responsible for the name of Red Coach Inn, played a key role in the Centennial celebrations held on August 11. Jim Keller, a ranch hand with Bridge Creek Estate cattle ranch for a number of years, took the reins, while Alex Morrison, foreman for almost twenty years, rode "Shotgun." A bevy of Red Coach waitresses sat inside the coach, while Miss Odian, a young lady of "Miss Outriders Club" stood on the driver's seat, entrusted with the ticklish task of hooking the mailbag onto the rope which would be lowered from a helicopter. Two sturdy Belgians pulled the coach into the big meadow behind the Lodge, where a crowd of spectators, photographers, reporters, etc., were expectantly waiting.

After twice bringing the Canadian Centennial helicopter down low and spooking the horses, the pilot Frank Ogden succeeded on the third attempt and at just the right moment Miss Odian hooked the mailbag onto the dangling rope. There were over two thousand letters in the bag, with former prime minister Lester Pearson and Premier Bennett of B.C. among the recipients. The ceremony was completed with the helicopter landing at the newly opened Centennial Park, and later in Victoria, B.C.

In a service on Sunrise Ranch on August 19, "Known to Unknown," Martin spoke of mass amnesia, a subject introduced by Dr. Immanuel Velikovsky in his books, whose view was that there have been disastrous occurrences worldwide in which all human beings were involved and vast numbers died. These cataclysmic events were so terrifying, so horrible, that the conscious memory of such things has been shut out in mass memory.

> We know this happens in the individual person who may have a terrible experience and pushes it down into the subconscious mind. But it is still there, a controlling influence in the individual's life. Whether he realizes it or not, it is so in his waking state and may erupt in his dream state, perhaps waking up screaming. Those who experienced these things at the time, on a worldwide scale, had no awareness of what was happening, and because it was so fearful the memory was pushed down to the subconscious levels and hidden from view. If there was a record it was destroyed, and the eruptions come out through myths, stories that are told about the submersion of continents and things of that nature. We have the story of the Flood in the Bible, and people are inclined to say, "Well, that's fiction." Any records are looked upon as myths, although there has been evidence uncovered which gives irrefutable authenticity to them.
>
> We recognize that the amnesia relates to more than those cataclysmic events. It may be that this amnesia obscures the awareness of man's divine origin. Perhaps these events are the barrier beyond which human beings cannot go. The fear of the unknown may well be rooted in this state of what could be described as amnesia, something that mankind as a whole doesn't want to remember. If we are to move into the experience of the divine state, obviously we have to move into the unknown. It is contradictory that there should be so much resistance to this process of moving into the unknown when it is our avowed goal. And perhaps it is because there are some rather terrifying memories in the subconscious mind which need to be exhumed so that we can get beyond them and they do not form the barrier which prevents us from allowing the experience of the divine state to be restored to our remembrance. I am not speaking of this restoration as relating just to something we remember in the sense of an experience of long ago. The memory is reactivated by the experience of it now.

After noting the varied locations where new Centers were opening up, Martin said, in a service on Sunrise Ranch on September 17, "What Choice?":

> I think, having observed what is moving in various places across the land,
> there may be a sensing of something very powerful, irresistible, on the move.
> There is nothing from the human standpoint that can stop what is moving,
> whether anyone is aware of it or participating in the process or not. If there
> are those participating, perhaps unconsciously on the part of some but con-
> sciously on the part of others, there is a basis for a controlled outworking in
> the affairs of men. Otherwise there still is nothing that can stop it but it will
> not be particularly constructive in the experience of mankind. If we ourselves
> begin to sense something of the irresistible nature of this which is moving, it
> is because we are emerging to a level where we consciously work with it.

Martin spoke of "Instant and Total Commitment" at 100 Mile House on December 10.

> The year 1968 is at hand and we will be celebrating the twentieth year of
> our Unit program here. There are two present who were on hand at that sig-
> nificant moment when the Unit program was initiated, Jessie Stuckey first,
> followed shortly by Ross Marks. Not long after, others arrived who are still
> here. I am most thankful for those who have carried the heat and burden of
> the day during this extended period and for those others who have come from
> time to time to provide their support and precious spirits to maintain and
> augment the unfolding program. I am certainly thankful for those who have
> played their parts on Sunrise Ranch and in other places; however my initial
> responsibilities were centered primarily here and while I had been associated
> with this ministry for eight or nine years before the beginning of the Unit, I
> tend to date things rather from that important year, 1948.

The Class of 1968 enthusiastically adopted as their Project the construction of a
swimming pool on Sunrise Ranch, one that had been waiting in the "heaven" for a
number of years. Funds donated by the Class paid for the excavating (done by a local
contractor) and basic materials such as cement and reinforcement steel. Class men
did all the leveling, surveying and other work, using Saturdays and "after hours"
projects daily.

"1968—an explosive year on Sunrise Ranch!" wrote Dorothy Jones in *Eden Valley News*:

> Needing more accommodation, instead of one apartment wing we added
> two—twenty-four rooms in all. Thirty-nine pairs of drapes were made and
> countless pieces of furniture sanded and painted or stained. Chairs and couches
> were reupholstered, all to be ready by March 1st for Class members. We didn't
> stop building come March but started another two-story wing on the Apart-

ment Building. There were other areas of explosion as well: a new tractor for the garden, new equipment for the administration building and kitchen. A new well was dug. A magnificent swimming pool was built and a two-room commissary remodeled, with a new root cellar and storage room in process. Our canning operation has boomed, the numbers of cans of fruits and vegetables greatly increased over last year.

There is an explosion in the office staff, with many hours spent meticulously preparing mailings, *Newslight*, *This Is Why*, two new books, *As of a Trumpet* and *Labor of Love*, to say nothing of the bookkeeping department and receptionists. I salute the men's pattern and their multitude of jobs, and those women who care for the needs of the home. The explosion has taken place, is taking place, and shall continue to take place, because the Lord builds the house and we labor in love.

Bill Porter and Lois Boutillier were united in marriage in the Center in Vancouver on February 4. These two played major roles in many areas, one of which provided an effective focus for the Toronto group during a critical period of its development.

In March, I accompanied Martin and Lillian to Fort Walton Beach in Florida, where we were hosted by Cecil and Eunice Taylor. After their marriage on Sunrise Ranch they contributed much together in service in the South.

There was another extensive tour in the fall of that year, with a most interesting visit on October 4th to Martin's cousin, George Cecil and family in Asheville, North Carolina. George's father, brother to Martin's, had left England and married the daughter of Cornelius Vanderbilt. Their beautiful home is designed as a French chateau, one of the show places in this country, open to the public. Martin followed that visit with others, maintaining a contact with that branch of the family.

On that tour Martin received the key to the city of Baton Rouge, Louisiana, from the Mayor, W. W. Dumas. We were treated to coffee in his office—Cajun! Martin participated in many ways in that state: a radio program in New Orleans; a lecture at Northwestern State College in Natchitoches; a symposium at Louisiana State University, sessions at Colonnade there; and a TV program in Baton Rouge.

Martin spoke of that tour in a service on Sunrise Ranch on October 19, "Men in Agreement," citing the disintegration evident in the realm of politics,

emphasized in various ways on this journey by contacts with people who were important in the political area, searching rather desperately for something that would provide a basis for constructive movement. Finally there are some who are realizing they are faced with a blank wall. If there is to be a change in the realm of effects there must be the initiation of true cause at the level where the effects appear. This is our business.

In the Little Chapel on Sunrise Ranch on October 17 Martin officiated at the wedding of Roger de Winton and Dorothy Jones. Jim and Anne Wellemeyer were the attendants. Lillian and I were also present. After the beautiful ceremony we went to the Chapel, where the assembled company awaited the arrival of the newlyweds. Rev. Wellemeyer represented Sunrise Ranch in a beautiful expression, as did Rev. Marks for 100 Mile House. A reception was held in the dining hall.

26

THE WORLD ENCOMPASSED

October 1968 ~ June 1970

Bill Dice described, in *Eden Valley News*, the advent of a fire truck, to replace the portable pump, with suction hose and pressure hose, mounted on a two-wheel trailer, which will do a job, but too much time is lost in setting it up and getting it to the location. Late in September Roy Bever handed me a sale catalogue and, sure enough, in a mass of old used equipment there was a fire truck on sale. After much deliberation and in view of the fact that bidding was closed on October 8 and the truck had to be removed by October 28, Martin suggested that Ross Marks fly me and Bob Schmeer to Window Rock, Arizona, six miles from Fort Defiance where the truck was. We flew—five hundred and twenty-five air miles in three hours!

Window Rock is the council seat for the Navajo Indian nation and Fort Defiance is also part of the reservation, with government schools, etc. The old fire truck was used by the maintenance department for their buildings. There she was, sitting in the Arizona sun, a 1942 Ford, 1 1/2-ton, with a front mounted 500 G.P.M. Champion fire pump, a rear mounted hose reel, a 150-gallon water tank, two ladders, six flat tires, broken head and tail lights and, to top it all, the driver's cab full to overflowing with Gravy Train dog food for the dog pound. Inspecting our treasure, we found the gas cap gone and the tank with several gallons of water. Removing the eight spark plugs we found two cylinders full of water even though the radiator and engine drains were open. The truck hadn't been run for about two years.

After much draining, hooking up a battery to turn over the engine which had been rusted tight, supplying gas and oil, new head and tail lights, blew up the tires (actually in good condition!) and filled her with water, the engine started. Joy! One more trip to Window Rock, port of entry, got us an Arizona permit to drive the truck to Loveland. After our 650-mile journey and two days on the road, we drove into the Sunrise Ranch shop at 1:30 a.m. and staggered home to bed.

Bob and I have worked several hours on the truck and sucked water out of the canal and pumped it out of the rear 140-foot hose, also filled the 150-gallon tank and pumped it out at up to 225 pounds pressure. It has many interesting features, with much potential to unfold in days ahead. By the way, ask Bob how he felt when I wound up the siren in the middle of the Navajo desert. He didn't know it worked till then!

As of a Trumpet, an exquisite expression by Martin, appeared as a book during the 1968 Servers Conference. Printers Bill Dice and Bob Schmeer found the task of working with Martin on the setup of the book to be exciting. The Class shared enthusiastically in Martin's reading of it, as did the servers at the Conference, and a third reading followed during the Special Session. Later the members of the Unit were alert to their responsibility and under Roger de Winton's direction undertook to consider passages on a daily basis. With people thoughtfully expanding its contents in their individual expressions, the experience proved to be highly enlivening and most effective. All this was done just prior to Martin's return from a tour, along with Lillian and me, and, as it was put in *Eden Valley News,* "We were ready to receive them on the mountaintop." This book is a timeless expression of truth, and the one instance where Martin used the name "Aumra," in the same way that Bishop Lloyd Meeker used "Uranda."

"Extending Creative Dominion" was the title of a service by Martin at 100 Mile House on November 3rd.

There is a design. It has emerged to this point, not because anyone undertook to beat it into shape or organize it in some fashion. It has appeared on the basis of the fact that the spirit of God, the nature of cause, has been of primary concern to those participating in the process. If it wasn't of primary concern they didn't participate for very long. And there has been a weeding-out process, because it was only possible to the development of the form for those to remain associated with it who were wholly given, to their highest capacity of the moment, to the acceptance and expression of true cause. We are here, and others are in other places—all a part of this one thing.

We don't need to speculate about the design but we are capable of observing the fact of it. Some have looked at this design, usually from outside, and said it should be this way or that way. Some have wondered what has been achieved by reason of what has occurred, but are we content that it has occurred? We should be in the recognition that it doesn't stop here. There is a continued unfoldment of design and it becomes more meaningful, more comprehensive, as it includes more of those who are supposed to form the body of that design. In just the same way, the little embryonic form in the womb doesn't reveal the nature of the grown man and woman. So here we are with this much design.

His service on November 10 was given the title "Divine Light" and clarified many points.

"Emissaries of Divine Light" is the name given to our ministry. To some the name wasn't acceptable. If the human mind could think of a name that was acceptable it is unlikely that it would be true to the truth. As we have moved in the unfolding cycles the accuracy and perfection of the name becomes increasingly apparent.

The radiation describable by the word *light* indicates the true nature of creative cause. It is used to describe an electromagnetic phenomenon, but it is also used to describe something even less tangible. If we say a person saw the light we think of increased understanding, awareness. For instance, what radiates from the sun of our solar system is far more than visible light; there is a total radiation. This is a striking symbol of the reality of God, that which shines forth from true cause and is behind the reason for the whole cosmic scheme of things. It is that to which we refer when we use the word light in our name. *Christ* could be used but I think there would be even more human mind objection to that terminology.

We use the adjective *divine* to describe the light because we make a distinction between visible light and this light. This radiation, which may be said to be a cosmic phenomenon in the realm of cause, must be translated, made active and operative, at this particular level on the surface of this planet. What more accurate description of those who let themselves be engaged in this undertaking could be given than that of Emissaries of Divine Light? We are charged with the conscious expression of the creative radiation of true cosmic cause, at the level where further creation needs to take place on this planet, which we may describe by the word *re-creation* at the moment because there is obviously something that went wrong and needs to be set right before the true continuation of the creative process relating to this planet may occur.

The creative radiation from true cause we have called the spirit of God. Where it comes to focus and is given specific expression it produces effects. The effects in toto we describe as the cosmos. The effect closest to us is our own physical form, the evidence of a creative cause. What that cause is has been a mystery to human beings, even though some may have described it by the word God. Others may attribute the cause entirely to factors observable in the realm of effects, as for instance an awareness of genes and various chemical substances and combinations which relate to the formation of the physical body. The process by which the chemicals themselves exist begins to lead into the realm of invisible creative cause.

Contained within that which is back of your physical form are all the essences of whatever may have appeared in the whole cosmos, and whatever may appear in the future. There is nothing that can appear in the realm of effects that is not already present in God. It is beyond the comprehension of the human mind how there could be something without limit as to scope; yet in essence it is already present in the point of origination and proceeds from that point through this radiation which has an effect: positive radiation, negative response. The negative response of which you are most keenly aware is the formation of your own physical body, the evidence of the working of the Law—negative response to positive radiation. Response, attraction, union, unified radiation—in other words a new expression of radiation occurs at the level where the union has taken place. If it all works as it should the physical form is drawn into union with the light which produced it in the first place, and that union permits further radiation at the level for which this physical form was created to carry divine responsibility—the world, or all that is present on the surface of this planet.

This extended radiation we speak of as the human mind, the consciousness of the physical body. How does that consciousness appear? Where did it come from? The physical substance of which the body is composed did not have it before it was in the body. It could be described as a reflection of the original radiation which produced the form, with no substance or being of its own but is an effect of the working of the Law. The consciousness of the body includes various levels, just as white light includes the colors of the spectrum. If there is to be white light, there is a balanced blending of all the colors of the spectrum. If some of these reflected levels are missing or inadequately present the consciousness will not be that of divine being, which has obviously been the case in human experience.

The higher levels of consciousness have been the ones mostly lacking, so that the experience of that light has been dominantly at the red end, the blue end largely missing. The symbol of the color red has been used in relation to the activities of human beings, particularly where there is evidence of intensi-fication of self-activity. You may "see red," for instance, relating to a concentration at the lower end of the spectrum, and the effects appear accordingly. The middle of the spectrum is green, the symbol of life. Both ends balance each other, and in the middle is the experience of life itself. Then the white light can appear and the radiation achieve what is needed in the realm of surrounding effects. The specific focus points for the reflection of the invisible light relate to the endocrine system, referred to as the seven seals.

The purpose of Emissaries of Divine Light is to reestablish the creative radiation, which includes the whole spectrum in balance—white light. When that finds expression the effects will appear accordingly. "Let your light so shine before men"—allow all this to occur. It is not some vague, undifferentiated thing; it is very exact and relates to specific levels of consciousness and experience. God is not a permeating divine fog of some kind. There is specific design inherent in the essence of whatever God is, and this divine character takes form by reason of the union of the physical body of man with the creative cause of that body. When that union is complete, there is unified radiation, and that is the mind which was in Christ Jesus.

Reported in *Eden Valley News* was a development of prime importance to the farming program on Sunrise Ranch, begun on October 15 and completed on December 1st. It was the underground, pressurized irrigation pipeline in the fields east of the County Road.

The project was coordinated by the U.S. Department of Agriculture, which also furnished a percentage of the cost. The Interstate Irrigation Company of Greeley was the contractor. Work was done primarily by Floyd Conell with the use of a neighbor's backhoe, plus a few sticks of dynamite to loosen stubborn rocks.

A cement structure houses the motor and pump (which previously had to be transported to the various locations). The canal water flows into the housing through the open ditch, as before, and is pressurized to obtain a constant flow to any valve along the line. These are located every 240 feet with the sprinklers attached to the valve openings, with or without feeder lines, for thorough coverage.

From the pump house the line extends east, parallel to the lane, approximately 850 feet, south 1,000 feet and west 480 feet. This giant U-plan will efficiently provide for all fields. The propane motor is the same that has been in use for years and is capable of speed changes to compensate for pressure requirements. In other words, one set of sprinklers can be used at the northeast valve at the same time as one at the southwest. Floyd estimates the motor has run the equivalent of 1,500,000 miles!

The present installation is a good basic foundation for future additions. When the pump and motor housing are moved to the irrigation canal, exact measurement of water feet used will be possible and no necessity to order water twenty-four hours ahead. Underground lines will run to the present site, with north and south extensions for lawn and garden watering. This new system is part of the changing cycle on Sunrise Ranch, not just to make it easy but to free substance, that the greater works may be done.

On Christmas Day at 100 Mile House a practice was initiated whereby Martin's service was heard at Sunrise Ranch, Toronto and Vancouver. Via a telephone hookup an additional 175 persons shared Martin's words. The group at Green Pastures and the Rotola home in New York City were unable to make the connection in time, no doubt due to the fact that it was the busiest telephone day of the year. This means of extending the Word has been of inestimable value since that first exciting experience.

The January 1969 issue of *Newslight* reported that Ross Marks was re-elected to his third term as Mayor of 100 Mile House.

The Village was incorporated in July 1965 and the population has increased ten percent per year to top the 1,000 mark. In 1966 the Village Office was built, also the Hospital, with much expansion in all areas including the residential. An interesting feature in the northeast end of town was underground wiring and servicing of all utilities, including telephone, electricity, gas and water.

There was increased activity in England. Returning from Class, Doris Hunt, with Odim and Georgina Mkpa of Nigeria, were holding meetings in Rupert Maskell's apartment in London. [Helen Turner had been Rupert's initial point of contact with the ministry.] Ann Prain, from Suffolk, and Doris from Dorset were consistent in their support.

That year Lloyd Meeker, who was attending the University of British Columbia in Vancouver, focalized the meetings held there for students.

In a service at 100 Mile House on February 16, "New World, or No World," Martin quoted from 11 Peter 3, beginning with the third verse:

"Knowing this first, that there shall come in the last days scoffers, walking after their own lusts.

"And saying, Where is the promise of his coming? for since the fathers fell asleep, all things continue as they were from the beginning of the creation.

"For this they willingly are ignorant of, that by the word of God" (the action of primary cause working through the consciousness of human beings) "the heavens were of old, and the earth standing out of the water and in the water.

"Whereby the world that then was, being overflowed with water, perished."

This is a descriptive passage referring to the rise and fall of land masses relative to the ocean, something describable in allegorical terms as the "flood." We recognize that there was a colossal catastrophe which disrupted the entire pattern of the world, including the climate, and massive sheets of ice formed over various parts. What had been before was obliterated, all a result of the working of the Law because man's consciousness was not permitting the expression of true cause but was responding to the environment, which brought the outworking cycle to a point of no return. The state of affairs was so far removed from the true pattern that it could not be restored to divine cause and purpose. The obliteration was not entire insofar as the human race was concerned because, after all, we're still here—but a new start was required. There is a point of no return, where the plunge becomes so precipitous that the crunch inevitably occurs. The civilization that man had built vanished from the face of the earth, now scarcely remembered. According to man's sciences it did not exist, and is recalled in mythology, and in the Bible.

"But the heavens and the earth, which are now, by the same word" (by the same working of primary cause through the consciousness of human beings as they now are) "are kept in store, reserved unto fire against the day of judgment and perdition of ungodly men."

What is an ungodly man? We think of those evil people who live someplace else I suppose, but an ungodly human being is one who is not expressing the qualities of divine being, and it doesn't matter how he may be judged according to human standards. The day of judgment is every day because we reap what we have sown, but it also moves beyond the point of no return to an ultimate climax. I would suggest that that point is long gone. There is no return for mankind in the world he has made; he cannot reform the world. It is either a question of obliteration or of a new world, and I would suggest that it is some of each. It doesn't take a keen discernment to recognize the blank wall with which mankind is faced, nor that there is bound to be immense loss of life, as it is called. The human race finds it has painted itself into a corner. There are things that are coming, and in some measure already here, of catastrophic proportions.

I don't wish to engender fear, because fear achieves nothing—constructive at least. It is obvious that there are those who sense the dissolution which is at hand. There are those who align themselves with the destructive forces which mankind itself has set in motion. Of course that doesn't do them any good but it does play into the hands of the Lord because the harvest of man's own sowing is at hand. The Law is at work and part of the fulfilment of divine purpose now is the obliteration of billions of human beings. Recognizing something of this, some may say, "How could there be a God of love to permit such a thing?"

God is a God of love, but love operates according to Law. The Law works according to the choices of human beings, and those choices have been long made. The generations of today find themselves in the position of reaping the whirlwind that was sown a wind. But mankind is one; we are part of the body of mankind and there is a need to face this fact. Instead of complaining about the harvest, we need to concern ourselves with what can be done in this situation which is, after all, the fulfilment of divine purpose—maybe not the way that it might have been.

I recall our Master's words when He wept over Jerusalem. The way was open, the opportunity there, but rejected; and the house is left desolate because the nature of the causes that were set in motion must find their inevitable fulfilment if no opportunity was taken along the way to allow the direction of movement to be changed. The point of no return is passed and the world is faced with the inevitable by reason of man's own choice, but not because of what God did. God offered every opportunity to the children of men. The day of judgment is here; it has always been here but it moves to a climax.

"But, beloved, be not ignorant of this one thing, that one day is with the Lord as a thousand years, and a thousand years as one day."

It seemed for quite a while that there was a very slow movement, very slow change. It didn't seem as though the harvest was really being reaped. Perhaps not consciously, the idea was that people were getting away with it. Not so. In these latter days the movement is much more rapid. Only a couple of "days" have passed since our Master was on earth.

"The Lord is not slack concerning his promise" (in other words, the Law works regardless of human time elements) "but is longsuffering to us-ward, not willing that any should perish" (if there is perishing it is the human choice) "but that all should come to repentance" (experience change). There was an extended period of time, seventeen, eighteen hundred years, when there could have been a change, but there was not.

"But the day of the Lord will come as a thief in the night; in the which the heavens shall pass away with a great noise, and the elements shall melt with fervent heat, the earth also and the works that are therein shall be burned up" (the inevitable result, however interpreted, of the seeds of ungodliness sown by mankind generation after generation).

"Seeing then that all these things shall be dissolved, what manner of persons ought ye to be in all holy conversation and godliness,

"Looking for and hasting unto the coming of the day of God, wherein the heavens being on fire shall be dissolved, and the elements shall melt with fervent heat?"

The way this is written, it seems as though these godly people are going to be just sitting on one side and observing what is happening to all the ungodly, that the godly really don't have much to do with it. This is not the case of course because it is only by reason of the godly people—in other words those who are permitting the divine expression, true cause, to appear on earth— that there can be a new world. If there are none of those, then there is no world insofar as mankind is concerned, because the very nature of the processes of obliteration would take the human race out of circulation. It is through the consciousness of men and women who are expressing divine being on earth that the true cause is established and the true effects appear.

The heavens relate to the realm of cause, the earth to the realm of effects. The realm of cause in this world is the realm of man's consciousness and it is evident that it is taking fire, mostly uncontrolled, which is destructive. Emotions run high, emotions control. There is an intensity of feeling building up in the consciousness of human beings everywhere. They have their causes and they feel so strongly about them. The fire is burning. Whether it is a destructive fire or a creative fire is the question.

The way it is burning in the consciousness of human beings in general is obviously destructive. It causes people to do insane things, to destroy, to tear down, to kill. This insanity is intensifying on earth, a fire out of control. By the same token, that fire is the creative force, the means by which there may be a new world. But for a new world to appear, the fire must be under control; in other words it must be love as it really is and not the distorted patterns that human beings espouse in their own consciousness. Some of those are hate, but it is a strange contradiction that very often human beings indulge in hate with the idea that the end results are going to be love. Destroy all the wicked people in the world—depending on where you sit as to who they are—and, having hated them to death, the world will be a lovely place. Ridiculous! The fire would burn itself out completely and the consciousness of man would be dissolved from the face of the earth.

But there is something else. There is the true fire which comes down from God out of heaven, the fire of true cause, the fire of love. It works according to design and under control, according to the truth. It is the flaming sword which turns every way. Back of it is the reality of life, the meaning, the purpose and fulfilment of life, which only appears as the qualities of divine being permeate the consciousness of men and women. Then there is true cause on earth where the creation needs to take place. Behold, I create all things new—a new consciousness, a new heaven; and the result of that, a new earth. "Nevertheless we, according to his promise, look for new heavens and a new earth, wherein dwelleth righteousness."

Martin spoke of "The True Qualities of Leadership" in a service on Sunrise Ranch on March 30.

A leader is looked upon as a man who can offer some sort of program, political, military, religious, economic, etc., designed to produce beneficial results. In what is called a democracy we have the opportunity of looking over the programs to decide which ones we favor. This is a difficult task because there are aspects about all of them that we don't favor, so the choice is the best of the evils presented. But it all emerges out of the old state of consciousness, where there is no answer. It has been assumed that we can develop a political system which will reproduce heaven on earth. It is not put in those words but many look hopefully to the future on that basis. But it doesn't really matter what system is offered. The answer is not in the consciousness of human beings centered in human ego.

What is important is the state of man's consciousness, because the world will reflect it. The New Jerusalem coming down from God out of heaven, prepared as a bride adorned for her husband, is a symbol of that changed consciousness. A bride is beautiful. Why? Because she is filled with love, and in that experience love is supreme—a description of divine consciousness.

In May the first issue of a journal, *Ontological Thought,* was released, referred to in *Newslight* as representing the culmination of creative cycles initiated many years ago. There had been *Why* magazine, changed to *This Is Why,* which provided an excellent foundation for this new form of communication.

A "Free University" group at Colorado State College in Greeley was attending a weekly class in Ontology on the "campus" of Sunrise Ranch under the inspiration of Bill Bahan. The Free University was innovated by state-supported universities to meet demands for broader and more student-oriented curricula. Also, a series of lectures was opened at various universities within a forty-mile radius of Sunrise Ranch, using the name "Ontological Society." The initial one was by Bill, with lectures held every two weeks. Alan Hammond and Ted Black from the Ranch also participated in them. Several CSU students, including David Lynch and Michael Cardiff, were instrumental in the creation of this new endeavor. Denver played a prominent role in the expanding picture, with services by Ted Black, Frank Reale and Charles Lo Giudice.

Peter Kafka, bearing the title "king of the hippies," met Bill Bahan in Boulder and attended his lectures. Peter had an extensive group of "hippies" in those days, many of which followed his lead in finding a source of inspiration through the words of Uranda and Martin. Peter later married, and he and Tina lived on Sunrise Ranch where two sons, Joel and Jeffrey, were born. Later they functioned as servers in New York City and Hawaii for many years.

Elizabeth Sciple joined her family, as she would call it for the remainder of an already long and fruitful life, on Sunrise Ranch after attending the 1969 Class. Coming from Atlanta, Georgia, she brought the finest of the South's qualities of graciousness and charm, her presence a reminder of the refined substance of living, not limited to external niceties. Her love for Martin and his Word inspired others in her vicinity. Before long she was in her own apartment which she called "my lovely little doll house built for me by so many loving hands."

Jim and Pat Miller were married that year. Both grew up and attended school in the 100 Mile House area. They focused a Center in Calgary, which included surrounding areas, for many years. Their ministry carries a robust quality that successfully embraces the business world.

John Summerbell and Rene Egger were married in Kamloops on June 8th. They participated in the Unit on Sunrise Ranch for a number of years and later made their home at 100 Mile House where they were valuable members of the group. Rene had a young son Michael, and later a lovely daughter, Gabrielle, was born to John and Rene.

A Musical Workshop was held at 100 Mile House in July under the leadership of Lillian. Participants were Bill and Doreen Thompson from Powell River; Marjorie Gilbert and Nancy Cecil of 100 Mile House; and Wesley Jones, Fayetta Gelinas and Bob Patton from Sunrise Ranch. At that time the organ which Wesley had brought to Sunrise was delivered to 100 Mile House, where it found its final home. Years later, replaced by a new one, the original was moved to the Log Chapel where its sweet tones are still heard, often at weddings and other special occasions.

In July, Geoff Tisch, a native of New Zealand, established a summer preparatory school for boys on Holden Lake, near 100 Mile House. With his assistant instructors David Selby and Jim Miller were twelve boys in their mid- and late teens from Vancouver and Powell River who participated in the seventeen-day building program. Margaret Stanley of Powell River cooked and served meals, largely prepared in advance by the Lodge. It was anticipated that classes would be held in July and August the following year, two 26-day sessions with thirty boys in each.

Geoff said:

> It is not a youth movement, but a situation which will provide the means for the young person to become aware of his own potential, demanding self-discipline, integrity, honesty, teamwork, fortitude, tenacity, imagination and intuitive perception. The training is severe, but does not demand more from any student than he can give, being based on a high conception of honor. The school will have an experienced and well trained group of instructors in charge.

Upon this foundational building block has been constructed the Educo Program for young people that has been carried all over the world by a staff of capable and dedicated leaders.

At that time Block Brothers, a fast-growing, publicly owned B.C. real estate company, purchased the large 108 Mile Ranch to build a grand-scale recreational development. In two months they laid nineteen miles of roads, many miles of fencing, put up for sale the first 1,500 of a possible 5,000 homes. A development of approximately 26,000 acres, it established a vast summer and winter playground with such outdoor activities as boating, fishing, golfing, horseback riding, skiing, skating and snowmobiling.

On the rolling hills edging two lakes, an 18-hole professional golf course was built which was completely irrigated to ensure summer greenness. A mile-long airstrip was in operation and expected to accommodate daily flights to and from Vancouver. Plans for a hotel and condominiums were under way and homes completed, with many more under construction.

This was originally a large cattle ranch of 35,000 acres owned by Lord Egerton of Tatton, England. Known as the Highland Ranch, it extended from 105 Mile House to 114 Mile House and was managed by Martin from the middle 1930s until 1948 when it was sold. He used to swim and sail his small boat in the lake that now borders the golf course. Henry Block and his group did a commendable job of building a place that enhanced rather than detracted from its natural beauty. Of course it brought in many people, and the occasional wistful expression on Martin's face was attributable to the fact of many changes occurring, there and everywhere, losing something of a private, perhaps even solitary, oneness with the silent, enfolding countryside.

Martin's love for that part of the world, which included 100 Mile House and was known as "The Cariboo," was shared by Ross Marks who extolled its beauty in a *Northern Light* article. He quoted author Bruce Hutchinson:

"The Cariboo plateau is the only place where the size of British Columbia can be glimpsed, where distance is not shut out and the next valley hidden by a mountain or forest. It is a varied country of forest and range land, valley and hill, adorned by many lakes and threaded by mighty rivers and seasonal streams. It is a country rich in resources, land-oriented where people are engaged in forestry, ranching, mining, farming and tourism. It is a land where every stretch of earth and water is important and people are proud to say they belong to The Big Country.

"The Cariboo country covers an area of some 40,000 square miles and is populated by about 30,000 people or a little less than one person per square mile on an average basis. The region is bisected by the mighty Fraser River, with a large portion of the area to the west referred to as the Chilcotin country. The extremities of the western section reach to within a few miles of Pacific Ocean inlets, while the eastern boundary is tucked into the Cariboo mountain Range which lies against the North Thompson River.

"The population is generally concentrated in a relatively narrow band in close proximity to the Cariboo Highway, the only through-transportation artery, running some 180 miles north and south through the region. Several thousand people live within a thirty-mile radius of 100 Mile House. To the north are the larger centers of Williams Lake and Quesnel. Other smaller communities dot the map in the farther reaches of the district. Although the inroads of 'civilization' are very much in evidence, only a few miles beyond city limits one is aware of the frontier spirit. An abundance of lakes and streams attract summer visitors and tourists, as well as large numbers moving in on a permanent basis, convinced that it is a land of opportunity."

In a service on Sunrise Ranch on July 27 Martin spoke on "The True Ecology." He recalled something of

a very far-distant memory, when the world was a garden. Man was in it, and the creatures, vegetation, the state of the mineral earth—very different from the present state. We have evidence in the mountains just back of us of some violent upheavals which took place through the ages. But man in the garden, with divine consciousness, knowing himself and the part he was to play, recognized that his physical form and the capacities of mind and heart were all included in this whole pattern of what we now call nature. When nature is spoken of nowadays it excludes man—he's out of it somehow. But then he knew he wasn't out of it but an essential link in the whole system.

In that state the earth itself was a living thing, just as the cosmos is a living thing, not a machine as some have supposed. Our solar system is a part of that living organism. Human beings go up to the moon and, incidentally, leave some garbage there, polluting it, and look around and say, "Oh, here is a dead planet, there's no life here." But the moon is a part of the ecology of this planet, even as earth and moon together are part of the ecology of the solar system. And the solar system in its completeness is part of the ecology of the galaxy. Nothing is dead. It only appears so to the ignorant human intellect.

The forms on the planet then were not the same as those we know today. The creation wasn't finished at that point. There was expansion to take place on the basis of the living, integrated form that had appeared on earth, in the recognition that what was being developed was not unrelated to the galaxy, to the whole cosmos. Therefore man had a very particular and delicate part to play because he had to provide the connecting link of conscious understanding as to how this living organism could operate and expand and achieve what it was created to achieve while still being held in the integrated pattern of the whole. Made in the image and likeness of the Cause of all this, whatever he did would have to be done with a conscious understanding of what was necessary to be harmonious to the ecology which was already operating. Man was never required to do anything to disrupt nature in order to fill his own needs. Nature was supplying his needs and he was supplying nature's needs.

Here is the true system, complete in itself and yet part of something greater. Man did not have to destroy anything to build. He destroys constantly to build his civilization. The trees have to be cut down to provide lumber to build houses, and the minerals are torn from the bosom of the earth to create all kinds of things—automobiles and airplanes, all these "good things of life." Man's concern, in the true state, is to increase life, to multiply the forms. In his present state he cannot envision the possibility, for instance, of his own dwelling place being alive and consquently self-renewing. His house is always falling apart; we're always having to patch it up and paint it and get it in shape, renew it one way or another; but eventually it is going to pass away.

It was a living world, a green world, and as long as man worked on the basis of his centering in what was above him the control could be extended to what was below him. There was a control in operation in relation to the processes of procreation, so there was no possibility of the cancerous growth of human beings that we see today. So instead of being willing to go back into the true control, man tries to invent controls of his own in this field. He makes a pill, and finds there are repercussions involved in everything he does.

But we are looking to a more pleasurable picture, one of beauty, truth made manifest, divine men and women, and all the other kingdoms in harmony, in balance, under proper control. There is a very vague and far-distant memory of this, deeply buried down through the ages. It was said, however, that the spirit of truth would call all things to remembrance—the state where the morning stars, the new creation of consciousness in man, sang together and all the sons and daughters of God shouted for the joy of experiencing true identity and sharing a creative process.

The answer to the problem of destructive man is divine or creative man. The answer is not in the environment. That will reflect the answer when the answer is given by man.

What the restoration to the divine state will be is unknown to the human mind. We share God's knowing, in divine identity, to the extent that the knowing is needful to fulfil our own personal responsibilities. We don't need to know it all, even if we could. But if each one knows what he or she needs to do, everything will be done and the answer reflected in the environment. That is salvation. We are interested in saving it for the ecological purposes of the cosmos. There is something beautiful and unique to be experienced on earth. We all have the opportunity of playing a part by which this may be brought to pass. The impossible takes a little while, but it proves to be possible.

On August 28 Roy Johnson, Lillian's father, passed away after a brief illness at the age of seventy-three. His robust spirit and encompassing presence were greatly missed. He and Marie brought a special substance to Sunrise Ranch.

Fay McKay's career rounded a significant corner when, during a trip to Los Angeles, she stopped in Las Vegas and made a few contacts. Things moved swiftly and before long she found herself the featured entertainer in the Night Hawk Lounge in the tower of the Landmark Hotel. Martin, Lillian and I were her guests there in September and enjoyed her performance.

An event of fathomless blessing occurred September 30 on Sunrise Ranch, when George Shears arrived from Huntingburg, Indiana, and settled into his new mobile home. With him was Alice Wellemeyer, second cousin to Jim. George had practiced chiropractic for fifty-two years in Huntingburg, where he and Naomi lived until her death earlier that year. Her son Jim was resident on the Ranch to welcome George, who never tired of telling people that Sunrise Ranch was "the headquarters of the kingdom of heaven on earth." George and Alice found a natural field of service together in the area of attunements with people in far places, in answer to letters and phone calls for assistance.

Floyd Conell, manager on Sunrise Ranch for many years, passed away on October 27. The attendance at the memorial service by a large number of Loveland residents was a tribute to the esteem in which he was held.

On November 16 at 100 Mile House on the weekend when the British Columbia servers were gathered for a conference, Martin used the opportunity to set the theme for the ministry, and indeed the world, for the decade of the 1970s. He closed the service, entitled "The Truth, Internal and External," with the words:

> As we move to the conclusion of this decade of the '60s ['69 marked the incredible experience of looking up at the moon, knowing that one of the inhabitants of this planet was walking on that bright orb in the heavens] we may move away from the mere consciousness of the hopelessness of the human state into a vivid consciousness of the absolute value of the divine state, because we are in it and exemplify it. The stress then begins to be placed more particularly upon the right state rather than upon the wrong. This is fitting and right as we move into the '70s.
>
> I do not think anyone would be inclined to deny that the world is at a very critical point. There needs to be a steady hand at the helm. That's what we're

responsible for. There is only one thing that is not in the hopeless state, and that relates to what we know. We need to be very conscious of this fact so that we maintain the experience of the right state in our momentary living. What else is there? Nothing! To put it the other way, what is there? Everything! Everything, when we offer it!

One day, while I was working at my desk in our shared office, I happened to notice Martin writing what seemed to be a note. My attention was caught, a little later, when I saw him drop something in the wastebasket.

Later, emptying the basket, having forgotten the incident, I was intrigued by a tiny bit of paper with his handwriting, and read it. I have always been glad I saved it from extinction, after he agreed with me that it might be of use. It was a poem:

Any Moment

Any moment of hating,
Any moment of lying,
Any moment of resentment,
Is a moment of dying.

Any moment of loving,
Any moment of giving,
Any moment of thankfulness,
Is a moment of living.

All our moments add together
Like the digits in a sum,
And the answer tells us plainly
Whether life or death shall come.

Michael and Nancy traveled to the Kootenays in November where, at Slocan Park, they held a meeting in the home of Bill and Natalie Voykin. Cyril Demoskoff operated a sawmill with his brother Walter, and Nick Podovinikoff and the Dergousoffs were also very active in that area. These people were Doukhobors, with the background of Russian immigrants who had settled in that part of Canada. We enjoyed our contacts with them for many years.

Martin traveled to England December 18-23, to visit his family. Rupert Maskell and

Odim Mkpa, with Georgina, were focalizing the ministry there and arranged the gathering of the group for the night of Martin's stay in London.

Fay McKay flew to 100 Mile House December 29 to put on a sensational performance as star of the Red Coach Inn New Year's Eve Party. The next day she and the musicians, the Paul Martin Sound Factory from San Francisco, performed especially for the Unit. She returned to Las Vegas on January 29 to a twelve-week run at the Landmark, with a further twelve-week option.

In April she flew to London, England, for rehearsals and meetings with Liberace and Engelbert Humperdinck and taped a show, the latter to be telecast to the United States. She did two concerts with Liberace at the London Palladium and returned to the Landmark with a contract running through the end of July. When that concluded she embarked on an extended nightclub and concert tour with Liberace in the eastern and midwestern states.

An Ontological center was opened in La Have, Nova Scotia, at the mouth of the La Have River and overlooking the Atlantic Ocean. Helen Turner, who focalized activities there, was assisted by Bob Ewing from Green Pastures in plastering and painting the house in preparation for meetings. Meanwhile Bill Bahan spoke to a group at the home of Helen's sister, Dora Smith, in Bridgewater, Nova Scotia.

The year 1970 opened auspiciously, with Martin's service conducted at 100 Mile House on January 4 shared via telephone by over five hundred people in thirteen centers throughout Canada and the United States.

On February 4 in a service, "The World Encompassed," Martin welcomed those who had come for the ten-day annual Conference and reminisced:

> Regardless of what you may be feeling, I wonder if you have any idea what I am feeling.
>
> Forty years ago in April I arrived at 100 Mile House, which has constituted my home ever since. Of course latterly my home has expanded to include other places, particularly Sunrise Ranch. But then 100 Mile House was scarcely on the map. I arrived in company with my father, who stayed about a month and then I was left alone; of course not literally because there were about a dozen people at 100 Mile House, but in many ways alone. I knew very little about anything that was happening here. Unbeknownst to me, it was not only a period of training for me but the beginning of the creation of a heaven for what should come thereafter.
>
> Ten years later, again in April, I had the privilege of meeting Uranda, in Vancouver. Many things have happened in the subsequent three decades, and

everything that has occurred at 100 Mile House was designed to permit our gathering in this facility tonight. [The new dining room was being used instead of the small chapel because of the number involved, which represented the entire ministry.] Many of you have come from far places. A strong compulsion has brought us here to be with one accord in this place and the intensity of feeling is indescribable.

On Sunday morning, February 8, during that Conference, Martin introduced the service by reading a poem he had composed a few weeks before:

Thus It Is

From age to age
Love's word rings forth,
"The truth is true and all is well,
Unconquerable life prevails."
Oh, man, whose strident dreams
Lead gravewards,
Return to calm and noble
Character of life.
Blaze forth pure virtue;
Depart false ambition's restless schemes.
Busy thought and troubled feeling
Trespass not in virtue's wise serenity
Where firm control and awful power
Eternally abide.
Here earth's pains are healed
And cruel chaos of mind's spawning
Is called again to order and to beauty.

"The Language of Love #1" entitled his service on February 22, in which he read the story of the Tower of Babel in Genesis. It began:

"And the whole earth was of one language, and of one speech." This story may be seen as indicating the evolution of the language of the human race. If that is the extent of the vision it means very little. We have the opportunity to recognize the reality of a universal language which comes to us through the spirit of all that we may observe. It speaks of oneness. Oneness is love. It is, then, the language of love and speaks of life.

The languages that have evolved in human experience may have sprung from the one language, of which we have some faint awareness, but they were devised as substitutes for it; for the one language has been ignored and there has been concentration upon the many tongues which have appeared in the body of mankind. These are not only in the sense of English, French, Italian, Russian or something else, but there are languages within languages, peculiar jargons at different levels of society. Young people have a jargon, somewhat incomprehensible to their elders, there is scientific jargon, all kinds, and the more proliferation the less understanding there is between people.

People imagine that through their own intelligence they can build a state on earth that would be worthwhile, where there would be peace and harmony and everybody would enjoy themselves and it would be wonderful. There are different ideas of how it will be done—political, economic, all kinds of systems, at variance with each other. When the word God is used it usually engenders ideas and concepts which belong in human language, in the many tongues. Each division has its own god, no evidence that anyone is listening to the universal language, but the ones invented by human beings. This is not limited to religion but is true of every field.

Until there can be communication with what is higher than man, there cannot be communication between people. What is true of the state of affairs between people is a reflection of what is true of the state of affairs between mankind and God. Trying to understand each other does not produce worthwhile results. There is the first necessity of discovering what it means to communicate with God, to return to this one language. That communication is through what has been called spirit. Becoming aware of the spirit of what is higher and loving it, rejoicing in it, we are undertaking to keep the first great commandment to love the Lord with all. Yielding to that spirit, we begin to find ourselves in communication with God. True understanding of each other then is the natural result. The mind may experience through right communication in this universal language a consciousness of God, and so the ability to communicate.

In a service on Sunrise Ranch on May 3rd Martin offered a definition of "Wisdom," which is not something

merely of the intellect, but relates primarily to the heart, to what is spiritually discerned. It is a sense of the fitness of things, a perception of the true design of being, so that one may be aware of what it is that is true to that and what isn't. It relates to a sensitivity to a true note. If we lack wisdom we are tone-deaf in this sense and don't know what is fitting to the true design of things. Design and control are the two primary elements of truth. If we lack wisdom we lack the perception and experience of the truth. There is an obvious need in people everywhere for this, and we would acknowledge this in us too, to come into position to discern what is true. The instruction was to "Ask of God, who giveth to all men liberally, and upbraideth not."

At Sunrise Ranch a new and successful business venture, operating under the name "Eden Valley Enterprises," had emerged from the carpentry shop. It all began in February of 1970 when Louise Green, longtime friend, expert weaver, and owner of nearby Greentree Ranch handicraft items, asked if we could make a few experimental models of a small hand loom for teaching weaving to school children.

Bill Kuykendall, interested in opening up a money-making outlet for Ranch craftsmanship, and Ralph Mitchell were the two who were qualified to answer the request. Making the first one was one thing; producing in quantity was another. Bill soon produced a set of jigs and fixtures to hold loom parts while they were being shaped and assembled, and with Ralph's expertise in design a prototype emerged whereby they were able to fulfil the request for fifty "right away." Then there was an order for a hundred! A friend of Mrs. Green, Barry Schacht, appeared on the scene with ideas galore, and soon they were making two different looms and an intriguing rope maker. Over six hundred units had been manufactured and sold at that time, primarily to elementary schools to teach the art of weaving. A new shop was set up for production, and when tools were not available they were beautifully made by Roy Bever. This project was a portrayal of love in action.

"Minister to the Disenchanted" was a title assumed by George Emery, a minister on the staff of Christ Chapel, United Methodist Church in Tempe, Arizona. Divorced and with a family, he and his new wife Joelle Sturgeon heard about Uranda from Anthony Brooke when he visited them in Arizona. They came to the Ranch over the Easter weekend and George said he was delighted by the wonder of being enchanted by the truth of love, and that he and Joelle were busy sharing it with others.

Not quite a year old, a group was established in a Center in Westport, Connecticut, under the leadership of Ricci Cardiff in her and her husband Don's home. A meeting had been held in the University of Bridgeport and things were on the move.

On June 3 Martin conducted a service, "Man, a Part of the Whole," in the Victoria

Center, home of Jack and Mary Dockar. He said it was the first time he had the opportunity to speak in the capital of his home province. It was a picturesque trip to Vancouver Island via Horseshoe Bay and Nanaimo.

> The province of British Columbia loudly proclaims the beauty of the world we live in. So often the idea is how we can use the beautiful countryside for our own pleasure and recreation, as though the earth is there simply for the benefit of man, the beginning and ending of everything. He couldn't even exist on earth if it wasn't for everything else. He is not isolated from the whole; he is a part of it even though he apparently does not know it.

27

EXCITING DEVELOPMENTS
June 1970 ~ September 1973

There was a memorial service for Jessie Stuckey on June 6, in which Martin paid loving tribute to a dear friend:

> We come here to cherish and delight in the memory of Jessie. I am deeply impressed with the vibrancy of life which she brought. Her passing during this past week came at a most fitting moment, early in the morning, the sun rising and the birds stirring themselves, the beauty of life springing forth into a new day.

Originally from England, Jessie had come to 100 Mile House from Winnipeg in 1948 at Uranda's suggestion, the first member of what would be the Unit. Others appeared shortly but Jessie took the lead, which required a certain amount of courage and gallantry, which she had. She went with Martin to Sunrise Ranch in 1952 where she attended the first Class. Upon her return to the Hundred she worked happily in Martin's home for many years.

On August 9, 1970, a son, Anthony John, was born to Michael and Nancy Cecil at 100 Mile House.

Twenty-five instructors, students and cooks embarked on the first month-long regular program of Educo in August, with Geoff Tisch as director. Born in Auckland, New

Zealand, he had his own cabinet-making and construction business at the age of twenty. Later, after compulsory military training with the N.Z. Medical Corps, he decided to "see the world" and traveled to distant parts. While working on Alice Tannar's house in Vancouver he met Bill Bahan who asked him to put a new roof on the Ontology Center. There he worked with John Summerbell who invited him to join him in a job on Red Coach Inn and 100 Mile Lodge. Geoff said, "The job was really subterfuge. I came up to see what everybody was talking about and was very impressed with what I saw, but particularly with Martin."

He attended Class in 1966 and a report to Martin caught the attention of Alan Hammond, who was a graduate of Britain's "Outward Bound," the forerunner of many schools now using wilderness programs to develop young men. It was through the dedicated efforts of Alan and Geoff that Educo was born. Bridge Creek Estate offered an ideal site at Holden Lake, fourteen miles from 100 Mile House. Jim Miller was added to their staff, with June Higdon of Vancouver and Florence DeWitt of Hamilton as cooks. In season Geoff and Flo were married, and later were blessed with two beautiful children, Daniel and Kathy.

In Montreal, Quebec, a Center was thriving in the home and under the leadership of Jack and Helen Stubbs with their large and energetic family.

Peter Castonguay came to 100 Mile House at that time. The previous fall he was a picket-carrying student demonstrator at Simon Fraser University when he attended a lecture by Michael Cecil. Peter said he was "overwhelmed culturally to find four people there the same age as my parents who had vibrations the same as I was moving into. In fact, this experience terminated my mental set about the older generation." He saw the fallacy of his position of conflict as a radical and after a trip home to Ottawa at Christmas packed his bags for 100 Mile House, drawn as if by a magnet to be close to the people in the Unit.

"If you go around trying to fight it and change it and worrying about the state of things, like Martin said, you're going to be just that, a fighter and a changer and a worrier," he explained later. He worked in a machine shop in the Village and then moved into a small cabin in the cattle-grazing country near Exeter Lake. For company he had a horse, his means of transportation, a goat and a dog. He did gardening, skinned and tanned leather and did wood carving when not working on the Bridge Creek Cattle Ranch. His next move was to Vancouver for a period.

Joe and Norma Maynard, with daughter Kinah, after a cycle of focusing the ministry at the Orchard in Kamloops, moved to Sunrise Ranch. Arriving from Hamilton, Ontario, to take over from the Maynards were Carl and Anne Richmond.

In September and October Martin's tour included groups in Louisiana, Illinois, New England and New York. With us were Bill Bahan and Donna Keister. On October 6 we visited our new property, Lake Rest Hotel, near Livingston Manor, New York. In the heart of the beautiful Catskill Mountains, the huge old hotel had been witness to illustrious guests in the past, a focus for the culture in that part of the world. One day, in the midst of renovating procedures, the removal of some wall covering revealed an age-yellowed program of a show there which depicted Eddie Cantor as the star.

Purchased through fund-raising efforts of the New York, New England and Berwick Centers, the hotel consisted of a main building and three bungalows on nine and a half acres and could accommodate up to a hundred guests. With 450 feet of frontage on a clean, spring-fed lake, there was swimming, boating and fishing to be enjoyed. To be out on the lake in a canoe in the autumn, surrounded on every side by the vivid color of trees of many varieties in their glorious hues, repeated in their reflection in the clear water, was like being in the center of a scintillating jewel.

The clientele of past years was expected, and welcomed, to continue spending their vacations in that mountain spot. Norman and Vicki Tweiten coordinated the management of the hotel, assisted by Bob and Carol MacEwen. Three long-time employees, including the chef, were retained, the remainder twenty-two staff to be drawn from the ministry, which offered an opportunity to some of our young people.

In a service at 100 Mile House on November 1st, "From Concept to Reality," Martin introduced a new word, in the phrase "pneumatomenal world," as compared with the phenomenal world: the world of spirit and the world of form.

He used it again in a service entitled "High Frequency" on December 27, in which he said:

> When we accept the yoke of reality in the pneumatomenal world we are no longer subject to the yoke of the compulsion of the phenomenal world and experience a state of ease. Remember, the true yoke is easy! So we experience a state of ease rather than dis-ease. This relates to healing, the restoration to the true state.
>
> They tell us scientifically that there is nothing faster than light—186,000 miles a second. Light as it is understood by man relates to the phenomenal world. We recognize that light provides the connecting network throughout the whole cosmos. The velocity of light is quite incidental to the pneumatomenal connection exerted through this network. One could portray something of this by looking at a snowy slope upon which someone is skiing. Obviously there is a great deal of activity going on in the snow. There are atoms present, in which there are electrons buzzing about at high speed. Yet

the movement of the skier over the snow has little if anything to do with what's going on in the snow. He makes his passage easily over the surface of the snow which is the connecting substance between the top of the slope and the bottom. Light forms a connecting substance, which provides the medium over which the pneumatomenal perception and creative action can work.

When divine action is considered in relation to one's immediate field of responsibility, there is some reference to light. Before that it is something else, perhaps heat. "The heat's on," can be heard. Well, let the frequency of your response be raised a bit and you will find that the heat turns to light. Some people spend their lives in the hot place! When the frequency has been raised to the level of light, beyond the infrared range, then we are flooded with the light. "My burden is light." Then this high-frequency radiation is available to others. It is there in the phenomenal world but imperceptible to most; halos are not visible to people generally. An emissary of divine light is not known because he looks like a blazing comet; he is known because there is this radiation released to the extent of the frequency of response. There must be a rising pitch through this intensifying frequency which then becomes the vessel receiving the coordinated frequency of radiation.

As high-frequency response becomes a consistent thing because we have accepted the new yoke, the light comes within the range of our experience, and on the basis of that light we know, we perceive what we should perceive, and this is the healing of the earthly pains; it is also the healing of the earthly pleasures. That new yoke makes all things new. It brings the phenomenal world back to God, the phenomenal world for which we have responsibility in the name of the Lord.

On January 8, 1971, Rupert Maskell was welcomed to Ghana by Rev. Oral Kingsley as a special guest. Pokoase, Kumasi, Sunyani and Accra are some of the places he visited.

In a service at 100 Mile House on February 14, "The Quality of Honesty," Martin referred to the experience of Moses when the Children of Israel were given the opportunity to move quickly into the promised land and did not do so.

That was their choice and determination, with the result that they wandered in the wilderness for forty years and perished. That generation stubbornly maintained their complaints, their disputes among themselves against Moses and Aaron and everybody in general. Some arbitrary God did not say "No!" They themselves said "No!"

I think it was quite a shocking thing years ago to Uranda, who had the vision to see the ease with which it could be done, faced with such incomprehension, such unwillingness on the part of people. Something could have worked out so quickly, and it's the same thing today. The change can happen so easily and quickly when there is a willingness to accept the new state which is peculiar. Those who accept it are peculiar in this sense. If we don't become emotionally involved in all the things that everybody else is involved in, we are looked upon as being inhuman. It is simply that we are not interested in continuing to be subhuman. Let us remember that this is a new state and therefore different, and we cannot stay in Egypt and come out of Egypt at the same time. We may give ourselves with assurance to the experience of the new state and know that is what we are here on earth to do.

On March 1st Martin, Lillian and I departed on a cold wintry day from Vancouver on a trip to Hawaii, a gift from Fayetta Gelinas. In twelve days we visited four of the islands. We saw steaming remains of volcanoes and flaming blossom-covered trees against the multihued blue of Polynesian skies on Hawaii, the Big Island. On Maui the Iao Needle rises 2,250 feet above a valley that lifts the heart with its vast wonder. It was on Kauai, with the superb view of Nawiliwili Harbor, that we enjoyed a day of relaxation on the beach. And on Oahu there was the Nuuanu Pali, a precipice where the wind indulges in awesome fantasies. A land to remember is Hawaii, with its delectable food, lovely hula girls and haunting music.

In 1971 on Sunrise Ranch, under the direction of John Summerbell, an attractive functional building, the "Fourplex," located to the east of the Chapel, was completed. It consisted of four apartments, each with three bedrooms, living room, bath and kitchen. The initial inhabitants were the Bob Blacks, Dices, Moores and Morrisons. The addition of the north wing to the Apartment Building was just completed, part of which was the town house built by Elizabeth Sciple.

A large extension to the Administration Building provided the Accounting Department with their own wing. Dan Hagedorn did most of the construction, also focalized the job.

Anything else that remarkable year? Yes! Using beautiful native stone, the Class artistically built a base around George Shears' home, under the direction of Lloyd Meeker. The Class project also included the building of a sun deck by the pool.

The Conference on Sunrise Ranch was held April 5 through 16, with a record attendance of seventy-five servers. Forty-nine Centers and groups in the United States and Canada were represented, directly or by area coordinators. Rupert Maskell, recently returned from Africa and the European continent, provided a representation for many in those areas.

Bill Bahan had been divorced from his wife Ruth, and on April 16 he and Donna Keister, daughter of Bill and Myrtle Byl, were married in a beautiful ceremony conducted by Martin in the Little Chapel on Sunrise Ranch.

A venture to warm the hearts (and stomachs!) of those who lived on Sunrise Ranch found its origin in the South, through Jerry and Olive England of Mobile, Alabama. What a great gift it was when they drove into our Valley in April with that freezer filled with five hundred pounds of frozen food, such mouth-watering items as shrimp, crabmeat and other delectables foreign to this Western mountainous clime. It was a labor of love, and they planned for greater amounts of specific foods needed by Sunrise to be provided by the southern groups, already eagerly anticipating the trip next year.

"The Significance of This Moment" was the title of a service at 100 Mile House on May 23, in which Martin outlined occurrences on Sunrise Ranch over the past two and a half months.

> A Short Course was completed, with over fifty present, followed closely by Conference, with seventy-five servers. Thereafter the Regular Class was initiated, with fifty-seven. Concurrently, it appears that the physical extent of Sunrise Ranch will be doubled by the addition of a hundred acres or so to the west on Green Ridge. We looked for land to the north and to the south, but the Lord provided it from the west! Also the Chapel is overtaxed these days, which holds a hundred and fifty people. We have had to use the adjacent lounge and elsewhere, indicating an urgent need for a larger chapel facility. We trust something will take form this summer.

> "Where there is no vision, the people perish." This is not a threat, merely a statement of fact. How keenly aware are we of the significance of this moment?

Martin continued to share his vision of the pressing need for expansion to accommodate, not only with regard to material needs, the growing numbers of responding ones covering the face of the earth.

Closing a period of discussion after a service on June 27 at 100 Mile House, "The Immanent Spirit," Martin said:

> Whatever the universe is, whatever the whole is, it is already in operation, already working, and everything moves with that working. Sometimes there is the idea that there is a difference between what is called animate matter and inanimate matter. There is no fundamental difference at all; it's all animate in fact. It is considered, for instance, that what is occurring on the surface of this planet is something remarkably different from what is occurring from the standpoint of the operation of the solar system or the galaxy, as such, but it is

not different. It is all an expression, an evidence, of the nature of God.

We have the capacity to be aware of the working; not to try to direct it but aware of what is working. All aspects that are not aware of the working are nevertheless participating in it. This is the unique position, this capacity to move consciously with what is working. Seeing what was working, man also had the opportunity to decide that he would like to impose his own workings on it, which he has done, and lost the consciousness of the working. But he still has the capacity to have a consciousness of the cosmic operation as it relates to this earth if he is willing to relinquish his own concept of what that is.

A symposium was held in London, England, on July 17 in the St. Ermins Hotel in the heart of Westminster with sixty in attendance. "The New Sense of Self" was its title and five speakers initiated this important step in that great city. Rupert Maskell was assisted by Anthony Brooke, Odim Mkpa of Ghana, and Bill and Lois Porter.

On Sunrise Ranch there was the first closed-circuit TV broadcast of Martin's service, from the Chapel to the lounge which accommodated the constantly accelerating overflow. This ushered in a vital and appreciated medium in the entire ministry, which enabled a greater number to see Martin as well as hear him.

In *Eden Valley News* Ted Black wrote of an area which he initiated and has tended over many years. He entitled it "Right Translation":

In the past couple of years another phase of Emissary service has opened up, coordinated from Center but participated in by people from various places. The Word, so wonderfully presented by Uranda and Martin to us who comprehend the English language, is being translated and made available to others. This is not entirely new but renewal and intensification of a pattern begun some years ago with the translation of many booklets into Yoruba (Nigerian) and several into French, Danish and Polish. Frank Caputo initiated something in Italian in New York and Suzanne Core and I finished it, bringing Lida Radziwill of Rome into the picture.

Several in the 1971 Class had fluency in other languages, so Ursula Schlueter and Hilda Armstrong worked on German translations, Maria Frid and Rena Cassidy on Spanish, and Nel Van Dommelen on Dutch. Later Karl Lembcke and Jack Gallach provided assistance in the areas of German and Spanish, and Bill Cordes on Dutch.

Martin, Lillian and I journeyed from Sunrise Ranch to Lake Rest Hotel at Livingston Manor, in New York, for the final two weeks of the Short Course there in September. The first Class to be held off the Ranch, this initiated an exciting new cycle in our expanding ministry, with fifty eager people participating and Bill Bahan, Lloyd Meeker and Lou Rotola on the faculty. Martin conducted the final classes of each day, and I thoroughly enjoyed sharing the Story of Man in that beautiful setting.

The first business year at the Hotel looked good. Norman and Vicki Tweiten focused the new unit under the overall coordination of Lou and Bridie Rotola. Mae Vallee played a vital role, and there were others. Steve Tashiro, who came via the Army, Vietnam and the California Center, filled many vacancies, as well as being the correspondent and photographer. Jack Caputo and John Flood started an organic garden. It was a busy place!

Majestically situated high up on a hill, it was a perfect place for relaxation, with hours to be spent boating on the lake, or miles and miles for walking through woods—and just a hundred and thirty-five miles from New York City!

On the weekends caravans brought people from New York; Berwick and Reading, Pennsylvania; Westport, Connecticut; Green Pastures and other cities in New Hampshire and Massachusetts; as well as other places in the United States and Canada.

While in New York and preparing for our next stop scheduled for Canada, Martin received a phone call from Bill Porter who focalized the Center in Toronto, informing him that Dr. Immanuel Velikovsky would be lecturing at a university there while we were in that city. So on October 18, after driving from Lake Rest that same evening, we found ourselves in a room in the university awaiting the entrance of this man whose works I had been using in my Classes and who had answered my letter of response to his latest book.

As we sat, waiting, a touch on my arm by Martin caused me to look up and I saw a very tall, white-haired elderly man, his regal bearing proclaiming a natural authority which did not deny profound humility. After his talk we met him, and Martin invited him to share lunch with us the next day, which he did, with his wife and granddaughter. Sitting beside him in the lobby of the hotel, he turned to me at one point and said, in his wonderful Russian accent, "You could be my secretary?" What an offer from this great man, at a time when there could be no question as to my chosen path of service!

On several occasions in years following, when we were in New York on tour, I went to Dr. Velikovsky's home in Princeton, New Jersey, and visited him and his wife. I counted it a great privilege to know that remarkable man who contributed greatly in clarifying the truth as presented in the Bible in conjunction with other scientific fields.

In Toronto we stayed at Eden Place. On October 19 Martin spoke to over a hundred at the newly finished Roslin Center. It was exciting to visit the new farm property recently acquired by the group, not far from the home of Joe and June Houlton and situated on a hill, surrounded by beautiful wooded land. This would eventually be known as King View.

The condensing of Classes had begun with the six-month Class shortened to three, then the one-month, held first on Sunrise Ranch, followed by one at Lake Rest. Less than a month passed before the second Class held off Sunrise Ranch took place, this time at 100 Mile House with forty-four in attendance and coordinated by Michael Cecil and Alan Hammond, with Ron Polack giving anatomy lectures. Martin, Lillian and I arrived at the end of October and participated in the last two weeks. As always whenever Martin was present, he offered the final class of the morning, drawing together the material in the previous presentations. In his absence, often the material used was a recording of his or Uranda's. My Story of Man class was included, the length being adjusted to the shortened periods of the courses.

The Phoenix Ontological Center was established in sunny Arizona under John Gray's direction, with the first Sunday evening service held there on November 21, public meetings continuing on Tuesday evenings and Junior Training School classes begun.

Fay was enjoying a successful cycle, appearing five times on the Mike Douglas Show, six on Merv Griffin's, also on Dick Cavett's, Engelbert Humperdinck's and Mickey Finn's, and was in national radio and TV commercials. After thirteen months at the Landmark Hotel in Las Vegas, she co-starred with Liberace for fifteen months. She was the star of Theater Royal in Australia for three months. On December 24 she opened at the Dunes Hotel in Las Vegas as star of her own show in the "Casino de Paris." Frank and Patricia Caputo were with her there and assisted in many ways. A Southwestern Servers Conference was held in Fay's home.

The year 1972 saw much activity on Sunrise Ranch in connection with the newly purchased acreage on Green Ridge. With it came the water-right to ten acre-feet from the canal behind the Ranch. Amounting to 5,500 gallons per day year round, it filled a long-standing need for additional water for domestic use. Bill Dice oversaw the purchase and installation of a surplus U.S. Army water filtration plant, capable of filtering 1,500 gallons of water per hour. The filtered water was pumped up the hill on the new Green Ridge property to a 16,000-gallon redwood storage tank, custom pre-cut in Denver and assembled on our hill by Bills Dice and Kuykendall.

There was also the need to fence the property, which was done, under the supervision of Bob Moore. The materials, including steel posts and 24,000 feet of barbed wire, were supplied by Maurice Jessup, owner of nearby Sylvan Dale Ranch whose land abuts ours up there on Green Ridge. The Jessup family have been cherished friends and neighbors of Sunrise since they met Uranda.

A beautiful home on that hilltop was being built by Conrad O'Brien-ffrench. Working with him were his son John, John Summerbell, George Hanson and Bob Patton. Through the years Conrad delighted in entertaining his countless friends, often at breakfast on the deck overlooking the valley and miles and miles beyond. Creatures of the wild lost no time in recognizing a real friend in this newcomer and made themselves wholly available.

Behind Stable Gables, on the west, Jim Hoffman created a unique garden, an inviting spot to pause for a rest or meditation, and eventually equipped it with a gazebo.

A sign of things to come on Sunrise Ranch took the shape of a geodesic dome, about twenty feet high, with a number of thoughts as to its proper usage, which proved to be a unique and beautiful playschool for the very young. However, the primary purpose for its creation was to acquaint the builders with geodesic construction, just in case the new Chapel would be built along those lines of design. The spherical construction of triangles in such a building releases its own special energy.

The women on Sunrise Ranch had undertaken, in the winter months, to open up new avenues of expression in themselves by creating handcrafted gift items. These were artistic and professional-quality products, which included ceramics, china painting, knitting, crocheting, art, loom weaving, candle making, sewing, leather work and sculpturing, to be displayed later in the year in a small gift shop located on the Ranch. Ingenuity was exercised in obtaining the materials for the various items. Scraps of cloth and leftover yarn were transformed into aprons and place mats, for example. The items were for sale, with servers attending the April Conference offered first selection.

Visitors were generous, and the money for their purchases was placed in the donation box in the dining room. The proceeds were to provide the means for further projects.

At the sunrise Easter Service in Eden Valley on April 2 at 5:50 a.m. Martin noted that it was the twentieth annual gathering on the knoll beside the Little Chapel, with only a few times when it was transferred inside the Chapel because of inclement weather. He said:

> This year there is a difference. We have a P.A. system and recorder, so I don't have to exercise my voice quite so much and Grace doesn't have to take the service in shorthand. Also a sundial has been added, in its place just against the Little Chapel.

Previously from Toronto, Len and Irene Polack with their three sons moved to 100 Mile House. Irene was responsible for the fine Library in the town, which is in operation today. She and I agreed that such an institution would fill a need in our group also, and she generously contributed her expertise to establish and operate a fine Library in the Unit, initiating it with a gift of the Dewey Decimal book. Joy Foster was the librarian, with Marcia Marks assisting, to be followed by others, particularly Helen Ames in latter years.

It was around that time that Queen Elizabeth visited Canada, and included in her itinerary was the town of Williams Lake, to the delight of all who made personal contact with that very gracious lady, which included Mayor and Mrs. Ross Marks. Ross, Mayor of 100 Mile House since 1965, was elected president of the Union of British Columbia Municipalities at their annual convention in Vancouver, an honor not only for him personally but for 100 Mile House, the smallest community ever to be represented in that position. With a membership of about 140 municipalities plus 24 regional districts, the UBCM has a direct responsibility to virtually everyone in the province. Previously vice-president, Ross was appointed by acclamation and while in Vancouver was interviewed on radio and in the newspapers, giving his views on some of the challenges to be faced in the coming year.

In Vancouver our Center was under the direction of Dale and Susan Maranda who were expanding the area of influence to an enthusiastic group of thirteen in Seattle, Washington, 150 miles south. In Rogue River, Oregon, 600 miles from Vancouver, eleven people met, with the expectation that Stan and Linda Grindstaff from nearby Ashland would provide leadership.

I attended a Velikovsky Symposium at the Lewis and Clark College in Portland, Oregon, August 16 through 18, accompanied from Sunrise by Ted Black and joined at Portland by Michael Cecil and Lloyd Meeker from 100 Mile House. Prominent men from all branches of science, art and history participated, including a representative from NASA. There was opportunity to have a little time alone with my friend Dr. Velikovsky.

I accompanied Martin and Lillian on an eastern tour in September. After a stop in Boston we had a few days at Green Pastures, where Martin spoke to almost two hundred in the new dining room, a beautiful structure capable of accommodating the increasing numbers being drawn to that place. The following day he spoke to about sixty people at the Center in Westport, Connecticut, Ricci Cardiff's home, and a few days later held two services at Lake Rest with two hundred and forty people in attendance, from New York, Pennsylvania and elsewhere. Also fifty-five had just gathered for the Short Course.

We returned to Sunrise Ranch for a week before setting out on a tour of the Southwest, this time with the addition of Ross Marks who had brought our airplane to Sunrise from 100 Mile House. Martin's first service was in Sapulpa, Oklahoma, at the home of Bill and June Gallagher. From there on, flying our plane, "weather permitting" would be a conditioning factor in our schedule. Heard on occasion was the comment: "Time to spare, go by air!" The next visit was to Dallas, Texas, with a stop at Shreveport, Louisiana, where a group had acquired some property, called Paradise Plantation. Martin said, "We have a ranch and a farm and an orchard, and now we have a plantation." After Dallas, with a service on the 28th at the home of Irving and Mary Shepherd, we flew to Phoenix, Arizona, where there was a substantial, active group under the leadership of

John and Pam Gray. Services were held there on October 1st, after which we went to Las Vegas and saw Fay's show at "The Dunes." After that, home to Sunrise after a month of extensive traveling, with many hearts deeply touched and lives changed.

On Sunrise Ranch it was time for the second trip from the South, bearing its wondrous burden of food, laden with love. Jerry and Olive England, assisted by Cecil and Eunice Taylor of Atlanta, Georgia, loaded 1,800 pounds of food, fresh and frozen, into a camper truck and trailer for the 1,600-mile trip from Mobile to Sunrise Ranch. The food was collected by the groups from Fort Walton to Dallas, covering a five-state area: Florida, Alabama, Mississippi, Texas and Louisiana. After loading potatoes, sausage, honey, okra, black-eyed peas, shrimp, and 400 pounds of Louisiana raw cane sugar in Mobile, on September 10 the Englands took their departure with the truck and car, and stopped at Baton Rouge, Opelousas, Lake Charles and Shreveport, adding strawberries, jams and jellies. There they unloaded the overburdened car into the second pickup provided by John Waskom of Natchitoches, Louisiana, and driven by Marynell Whitman.

The two trucks made their first stop in Dallas, where they added cantaloupes and squashes—and a night's rest. After an 865-mile drive the next day they arrived at Sunrise. The food totaled about 2,300 pounds. Those generous and adventurous servers of our King then anticipated making a similar trip at least twice a year.

In Natchitoches a group formed under the leadership and inspiration of John and Sara Waskom, with their family. They had purchased 49.5 acres of beautiful farm and pasture land containing a peach orchard, pecan trees and some plum and pear trees. Situated on the beautiful Cane River Lake, the old home was being renovated and plans were in progress for a new home. They hoped to clear off 440 feet of land along the Cane River for a park area, with boating, swimming, etc. That was a unique group, with the entire family of four sons and later a daughter continuing to provide a true community in a pattern of unified dedication. John's rich mind and heart revealed a remarkable union of the mystic and down-to-earth, with his love for all kingdoms and especially the mineral (he talked to the rocks), divine geometry being as natural to him as A-B-Cs to the rest of us. I listened to him by the hour when I had the opportunity; and, however much I understood, it was magic.

The Apartment Building on Sunrise Ranch, begun twelve years before and progressing in sections, was finished that year and formed a giant U around the pool and lawn area, scene of many special family occasions over the years.

The fall of 1972 witnessed the installation of a vital feature on Sunrise Ranch, a 144,000-gallon Extended Aeration Sewage Lagoon, situated near the county road close to the entrance to the Ranch. A hole 54 feet square and 12 feet deep was dug by Loveland

Excavating Company, after which it was "all hands on deck!" as thirty men quickly pulled the liner (30 mil. Butyl rubber) over the top and into the hole. It weighs 1400 pounds and prevents sewage from leaking into the ground water. It was an awesome sight to behold a chain of men being lowered into that hole, each ankle being securely held by two men on top.

In tribute to one who has contributed beyond measure on Sunrise Ranch over many years, I quote from *Eden Valley News,* November 1972:

> Six years ago when David Lynch was about to graduate from high school his counselor told him it was no use thinking about college, his grades and aptitude were not good enough. The following spring Dave attended Class on Sunrise Ranch and upon its completion had an interview with Martin. It was decided he should go to college. Enrolled at Colorado State University with his major in forest range management, he took a part-time job and began his school work. When the grades came in they were tops, and continued so consistently excellent that David was granted scholarships each year. These, plus his job, enabled him to carry through financially, meanwhile holding Ontological meetings at CSU.
>
> When asked what caused the change from mediocre grades to top ones, he stated, "Change of attitude: whatever you do, do it well—the result of my agreement with Martin. It became a matter of the utilization of my time for the Lord."
>
> David spent the weekends that summer working on Sunrise Ranch and the other five days in the mountains working for the U.S. Forest Service. After his five years he found that the wealth of study and experience could be put to use on the Ranch, and he began by studying the cattle-feeding program and pasture conditions, suggesting improvement in the practices. He made soil tests to determine nutrition needs for various crops.

It was a joy to observe Martin's profound appreciation for the self-initiated development of this young man whose dependability and outstanding capability have continued to this day to play a most vital part on Sunrise Ranch and in the expansion of the ministry.

The first Class of three months' duration was held on Sunrise Ranch in 1973 under the leadership and guidance of Alan Hammond.

One day I was taking dictation as Martin answered his correspondence, which covered every conceivable range of human activity with accompanying questions. I felt an urge that others, with similar problems, might share the healing wisdom, rather than limit it to one person. So I submitted the following to Martin, with the result that he included it, with the title "A Word of Grace," in the next mailing:

"As Martin's secretary there are times when I feel strongly that an expression of his which is directed specifically to one of his flock would be of great benefit to many. And so, subject to his approval of course, I may share some of these with all of you from time to time."

Letters dealing with questions of a personal nature went out with the mailings for decades, shedding welcome light and lifting spirits in countless hearts. Later, these were compiled and released under the heading, "Letters for Living."

Hugh Malafry was a personal assistant to Martin, and contributed much to the wealth of literature and music. In the Administration Building work was begun on publishing the *Third Sacred School* volumes, which Hugh compiled—a monumental undertaking—after reading the complete writings of both Uranda and Martin. This labor of love resulted in 18 volumes of the laws and principles of being, easily applicable in the effective, victorious living of life. Ted and Claudia Black played a vital role in the editing aspects of the production. Robin Reily, in Illinois, arranged for the printing of the 18 *Third Sacred School* volumes, as well as numerous other publishing jobs through the years.

George Emery, with his wife Joelle, was very busy spreading the Word. A typical sample: on March 1st they traveled to the Seattle area where George spoke at the University of Washington, at Fort Lewis to a group of drug counselors, and to one hundred at the University of Puget Sound. A public meeting was held on March 7th in Ashland at Southern Oregon College which Carl Romaner was attending. George spoke in Grants Pass at the Neuman United Methodist Church to over two hundred, then shared an hour in the Cave Junction Methodist Church and in the Wilderville Church. On March 13th the "Pied Piper" addressed a group at Adams High School and that evening initiated a new cycle at Oregon State University.

Two weeks later the Emerys were joined by Gib and Donna Curry of Ashland, Warren and Mickey Brown from Phoenix, and the Harringtons from Loveland—all on their way to the Class at 100 Mile House. Also leaving for Class were Moira O'Connell (later Malafry) and David Ish. After a gathering in Portland of seventy-five from Tacoma to Ashland, George and Joelle, with George's young sons Buddy and Tim, departed for Sunrise Ranch.

Services continued at Portland under the leadership of Rick Dunn. This became a very busy Center, with an attunement group on Monday night, Tuesday at Lewis and Clark College and Oregon State University, Wednesdays at Portland Community College and Portland State University, Thursdays in Monmouth, and Fridays in Tacoma at the University of Puget Sound.

Another tour!—this time southeastern. On March 24 Martin, Lillian and I flew from

Denver and were met at the Miami Airport by Bill and Donna Bahan, following which there was a motor tour of our Centers in Miami, Florida; Atlanta, Georgia; Mobile, Alabama; and New Orleans, Baton Rouge, Natchitoches and Shreveport in Louisiana. It was always a special delight to share the beautiful home of Al and Betty Romaner in Miami, to be welcomed by Cecil and Eunice Taylor in Atlanta; Jerry and Olive England in Mobile; Ken and Ronnie Lim, John and Sara Waskom, Irv and Mary Shepherd, Ernie and Marynell Whitman in Louisiana. Martin gave public lectures, spoke to capacity audiences—and then there were "open houses"!

George Bullied described the unique institution of which he was the founder:

> Education in our world is geared to preparing our young people for the market system. This fact is brought home by a question often asked of me: "Are you preparing our young people to make a living?" My dream is to show them "how to live." My agreement was first established with Martin, through him to Jim Pogue, and with Michael Cassidy and Bob Purdom. This brought all the divine potential, character and talents needed to allow a vision to take the form of Twin Valleys School.

George Bullied was the director, Les Kerr focalizer of Opal Acres community, Ken Nicholls agriculture supervisor, Dianne Brancato teacher, David Pasikov principal and Tony Viocchi vice-principal. Gordon Orr was the director of the academic area, and Jan van Dommelen focalized the administration. Barbara Center headed up the English portion of the school, Alan Lange taught the technology of chemistry and physics, and David Pasikov biology, hydroponics and yoga.

George and his wife Pat chose a site in the center of southern Ontario, one hundred acres of hilly, partially wooded pastureland that was markedly devoid of human habitation. The cows graciously shared their land while ten pioneering students, along with the family, began the task of providing buildings, wells, electricity, phones and roads. Meanwhile the residents called a small trailer and a variety of tents home. A hastily constructed classroom-kitchen combination appeared first, followed by a set of two-story geodesic domes serving as dormitory, classroom and library. A nonprofit charter for the school was drawn up, the Board of Directors consisting of George and Pat Bullied, Jim Pogue, Robert Purdom and Michael Cassidy, later replaced by Oliver Latam.

The initial step in this outworking depended on a relationship which evolved between George and leaders in the Department of Social and Family Services to agree to provide financial support to teen-age dropouts who were seeking some kind of meaningful education that would give them a starting point in life. A second point of agreement occurred at the base line when Dr. Quintenton, a college president, was inspired by

George, who signed a contract with St. Clair College of Windsor to develop his vision under the college's protective umbrella. Each academic level was termed a consciousness level, one to four, which gained a totally new place in education, designated by the Department of Universities and Colleges as a "social preparatory program."

Soon the core group was joined by June Lloyd and Mary Birch to focalize women's activities, followed soon by Bill and Bev Robertson, Larry Gagnier and Marlene Kereluik.

Home sites for the staff centered on the farm of Opal Acres, an additional one hundred acres of farmland purchased to provide housing and fill agricultural needs, trusting it would prove to be self-sufficient in providing food. It was already inhabited by eight head of cattle, six pigs, one hundred fifty chickens and a hundred rabbits. As George put it, "This family of sixteen adults and two children now offer their learning experiences in life to an eager group of thirty-five students who came to Twin Valleys School to learn how to live while learning how to make a living."

Concurrently the other youth-oriented movement in our ministry, Educo, was well under way, with its focus in Vancouver and Edenvale Farm in British Columbia, and King View Farm in Ontario.

Meanwhile on Sunrise Ranch, in the April issue of *Newslight*, Lillian Cecil said:

> I happily report that the musicwriter is now on the Ranch and during the past few months Bob Patton has been learning how to operate it. The Music Trust Fund was able to pay part of its cost, with the Church supplying the rest. Also some of the fund will be used for maintenance and repairs of our instruments, of which we have received some generous gifts. A good set of drums and a trombone came from the group in Peru, Indiana; two clarinets from the Kafkas; a viola from Ernie Taylor of 100 Mile House; a family heirloom violin from Marie Johnson; another trombone from Dan Hagedorn, Atlanta; a tenor saxophone from Selma Valentine of Sunrise.

> Diana de Winton completed the Choral Conducting Course and the Orchestral Course (necessary now that we have an orchestra). Choirs are rehearsing at Sunrise and the Hundred, also at Green Pastures, and groups elsewhere. And the orchestra keeps practicing! The recent tuning and care of all the pianos at Sunrise was done by a Class member, Martin Alexander. Behind the scenes many things move: practice, writing of music, teaching our youngsters, dance, offerings at symposiums, and on and on. We are most thankful.

In the Deep South much was on the move. The annual Escambia County Mental Health Workshop was held in Pensacola, Florida, May 2-5. Dr. Jerry England opened it with his lecture entitled "You Are More Than O.K." The audience of forty-five counselors, psychologists, school principals, teachers and nurses responded enthusiastically. One school principal said it for many: "It's the first thing I've heard in a long time that really makes any sense."

Cecil and Eunice Taylor were busily engaged, with monthly meetings at Love's Retreat with Mahdah Love and also in the Sautee-Nacoochee Valley, in addition to their full schedule in Atlanta.

In Kelowna, British Columbia, seventy people gathered on May 5th, coming from as far south as Spokane, Washington, and 100 Mile House from the north. Ken and Johanna Walters were hosts, and Michael Cecil brought to focus the speakers of the evening: Carl Richmond, Dale and Susan Maranda, Hugh Duff and Johanna Walters.

At 100 Mile House on May 20th a special supper was held in honor of Lillian's and Grace's birthdays in the new dining hall, memorable because it marked the first time a meal had been served in that facility, built for that purpose but used as a chapel until then. Large enough for the whole Unit family to be seated in one room and bedecked with fragrant lilac blooms, it was a colorful scene, with music and entertainment following the feast.

In *Northern Light,* Chris Foster wrote, with a smile of satisfaction:

> Quietly, without any fuss or production, a call is being sent out from our Unit Headquarters at 100 Mile House to people in countries as far apart as South Africa, Malaysia, Pakistan, India, New Zealand, Kenya, Argentina, Bermuda, Japan, Australia, Ceylon, and many more. The call is to men and women of integrity, whoever, wherever they may be, and whatever their backgrounds, beliefs, religions, race, color, age, or anything else.

This marked the birth of a publication, named *Integrity* by Chris, which elicited answers from people all over the world to the call that sounded, loud and clear. The resulting correspondence formed the inspirational content of the publication which continued for twenty years.

On May 28 Bill Dice, Bill Kuykendall and Jack LaRiviere left Sunrise Ranch for southeast Wyoming where a 160-acre property had been purchased to provide additional hay for Sunrise livestock as well as for sale. Situated about 97 miles northeast of the Ranch, 25 miles from Cheyenne on the Colorado-Wyoming border, it was named "Sunrise Farm." Bill Dice had contacted Bob Price through whose father the quarter section of flat farmland was acquired at dryland prices, with an irrigation well being drilled. The double-Bill, assisted by Jack, had been at work for weeks and the small four-room house and garage were in good shape to welcome Betty Dice on "leave" from Sunrise kitchen to offer her very welcome services. By early July the sprinkler system watered 130 acres; and 8,000 pounds of oat seed, 1,300 pounds of alfalfa and 150 pounds of orchard grass had been planted. Then the rains came!

On a Sunday, August 5, Martin dedicated the RimRock House Gallery, bringing to focus the initiation of a cycle in the ministry of the arts which had been held vibrationally by a few for many years. Many years previously the Gateway property, by the Great Falls, at the southern entrance to Eden Valley, was the original Dam Store when that twisting section of road was part of the main route to Estes Park. Later a restaurant open to the public, it was also used as a private dining room for vacationing ESA International Sorority members by Bob Palmer, previous owner and personal friend of Uranda.

Our first enterprise, "Mother Groves' Barbecue," opened in the summer of 1954, with Dave and Rosa Groves who personified Sunrise hospitality. Renamed in the mid-1960s, RimRock House was reopened as a beautiful gift shop. Later it was used for weekly meetings of the Free University program coordinated by Ted Black, a vital branch of our service with ramifications that expanded throughout the continent.

And now, on a beautiful Sunday afternoon in 1973, RimRock House was being dedicated to a new and lasting purpose, still so used. Three outstanding artists provided the foundation for this outworking and formed the faculty for the Gallery school soon to open. On display were thirty watercolor paintings by Michael Gress and a dozen bronze pieces by sculptor Bill Talkington. Conrad O'Brien-ffrench and I had shared a special agreement in the early years in the area of visual art, a vision substantially clothed with flesh and talent as the other artists appeared.

Completely rebuilt, RimRock House offered ideal conditions for classes, with the three artists in agreement (miraculous in itself!) participating in their special fields: life-drawing, painting and sculpture, with emphasis on the art of living rather than techniques. Lighting and other requirements were perfect. There were private studios for the two artists, Conrad's in his new home on Green Ridge and Michael's in his Masonville home near the Ranch which also supplied necessary framing facilities. RimRock House Gallery and the homes of Conrad and Michael formed a triangle, with Sunrise Ranch in the middle.

Richard Cable wrote, in *Newslight*, regarding the above incident:

> For many years Billie and I and our two sons have lived across the road from RimRock House and the Great Falls. Though the falls cease when freezing weather commences, one can be assured of enjoying this spectacular scene any time, night or day, throughout the summer. But midafternoon on August 5th the falls suddenly stopped for several minutes and rather than a steady roar there was silence—a pleasing silence, timed precisely to coincide with those moments when Martin spoke to dedicate the Gallery. Someone, somewhere, for some reason diverted this great volume of water into alternate

channels—the only occasion we've ever known it to happen in midsummer.

Perhaps a unique symbol of the magic of life.

On September 4th the attendees at the Conference on Sunrise Ranch were treated to a concert on the pool lawn presented by a 21-member orchestra. It was a rewarding event for Lillian, shared by conductor Diana de Winton and assistant Jack Jenkins.

On his way to that Conference, Rupert Maskell, whose service has always reached into far places, stopped off in Buenos Aires, Argentina, where he contacted *Integrity* correspondents and their friends. Flying from there to Rio de Janiero, Brazil, and then Caracas, Venezuela, he met other connections with *Integrity*. En route home he stopped in Ghana, West Africa.

Also attending Conference, Herman and Ursula Schlueter returned to New Zealand anxious to spread the Word; and Achal Bedi, resident of Colorado, departed for a month's visit with his parents in India, armed with a long list of friends to contact in Bombay, Calcutta, Madras and Sri Lanka in Ceylon. That vital connection with India through Achal has steadily increased through the years.

On September 5 a Center was opened in Long Beach, California (area of Uranda's initial center in very early days), the result of action taken by Steve Tashiro and the Riverside group.

A new home was found for the center in Powell River, British Columbia, on Tahsis Street, with two rooms promptly set up as music teaching studios by servers Bill and Doreen Thompson.

The Midwest hosted a tour, initiated with a talk by Martin entitled "The Irresistible Force" in a Holiday Inn in Minneapolis, Minnesota, on September 11. Mac (Hugh M.) Duff was providing focalization in that part of the country and introduced Martin. That was followed, on the 15th, by a Symposium at a university in Gary, Indiana, using the same title and focalized by Lee Martin. The following Sunday a service was held at Beverly Shores near the home of Mark and Mary Roser, where we were staying. On the 19th, again using the same title, Martin spoke at Newark, Ohio, where Bill and Betsy Plikerd were at the helm.

On September 14 James Hoffman and Wendy Morse were married on Sunrise Ranch, later the parents of twin boys, Jeptha and Japeth.

Up north, in September Ross Marks was reelected president of the Union of British Columbia Municipalities in a surprise vote at the federation's convention in Prince George. He had not planned to run again but his name was submitted from the floor and he was reelected over the nominating committee's choice.

At the home of Martin and Lillian fourteen goldfish were freed from their indoor aquarium into a pond built in the garden. Martin devised a warm-air intake from the basement and also put in a stock-tank heater, thereby enabling the creatures to survive the winters, which can be severe on occasion, and also incidentally eliciting a sigh of relief from Lillian who had a few small nightmares of transferring the fish-abode indoors come cold weather! They can be seen today swimming in their long-time home—unless sleeping on the bottom in the cold winter months.

Helen Meeker's love for horses found fulfilment in dressage training at the 108 corral with her beautiful Estrellita, who later presented her with a lovely little foal, to be followed by others.

Edenvale Farm, not far from Vancouver, had its first week-long seminar September 16-23, with twenty-five in attendance. Michael Cecil, Ron and June Polack, and Dale Maranda composed the faculty for that event, to be followed by many classes and seminars over the years, with a variety of faculty and class members. A beautiful Chapel, built to accommodate that first class, has served admirably ever since.

A service by Martin in the auditorium of the MacMillan Planetarium in Vancouver brought to fitting climax that seminar experience, which was followed two hours later by an event with the title "In Concert With Friends" in the beautiful and spacious Queen Elizabeth Playhouse downtown. Featuring the blended vocal and instrumental talents of Lloyd Meeker, Heather Pinchin, Harry Aoki, Judy Repar and Hank Anderson, it was a unique offering of classical, folk and jazz music, attended by approximately four hundred. In addition to providing funds for the new facility at Edenvale, this opened up new and exciting vistas of service.

In New York on September 15 thirty-two people gathered at the Brooklyn Center on Jerome Street for a symposium entitled "The Creative Power in You." Larry Krantz opened it and was followed by George Fuentes, Jack Caputo and John Flood.

John Flood was among those present at a lecture by Dr. Immanuel Velikovsky at Nassau College in New York on September 26 and became a close friend to him and his wife. He visited them in their home in Princeton, New Jersey, and assisted them in many ways.

Dr. Velikovsky often referred to his friendship with men like Albert Einstein and Sigmund Freud. The former had many discussions with Dr. Velikovsky and was reconsidering his own theory of relativity. Open on his desk the day he died was a copy of *Worlds in Collision*. Also, our friend Immanuel psychoanalyzed Sigmund Freud who he discovered had a father complex which had its roots in the story of Moses. It was, in fact, Dr. Velikovsky's scrutiny of the life of Moses in that context which led to the revelation that occurrences at the time of the Exodus of the Children of Israel had a basis in fact. He removed that, and other stories in the Bible, from the realm of fairy tales. The purpose of his work and life took an entirely new direction at that point.

During one of his lectures, referring to man's remarkable technological progress, he said, "But what do you say about a human race that has gone irrational, that has produced atomic devastation and continues to tread in this path?" He said the answer was "Know thyself." He stressed the need for scientists to love the true scientific method of investigation without the judgment and bias inherited out of the past. *Worlds in Collision,* his first book, found a place of honor as the Book of the Month. Nevertheless there followed instant reaction and judgment of the scientific community to the truth revealed through his work.

28

THE DOME CHAPEL

September 1973 ~ May 1975

*A*lice Kuykendall, greatly loved member of the Sunrise family, passed away on September 30. She and her late husband Kirk and their son Bill contributed a robust pioneer element most fitting to this place.

In October Rupert Maskell was in Nigeria at the time of the Convention/Seminar in Ibadan. One of the results of Rupert's visit was a greater closeness between Ghana and Nigeria. Following that, he spoke to over two hundred at the World International Sacred Peace Movement in Lagos, where Odim and Georgina Mkpa served in the place of focus. The value of Rupert's continued work in South Africa was inestimable.

What Martin called "a rather protracted journey for the last three months or so" in the Northwest came to its close with his talk in Portland, Oregon, on October 7, with the Emerys and Rick Dunn. That was followed by a visit to Seattle, Washington, where Dick Kezlan was the focus. Before returning to 100 Mile House, Martin spoke in Vancouver on October 10, where Dale and Susan Maranda provided the leadership.

In the November issue of *Eden Valley News* there were photographs of
a living circle, outlined there in the golden sunlight on the verdant hillside, of
men and women joined together by clasped hands. The wind blew free around

proud forms, faces lifted as in prayer to a dome of clearest blue. Thus was the
foundation delineated and established for the Chapel, the Lord's house, on
earth. These were His proven servers [gathered from the far corners of the
ministry at the annual Conference], presenting a unified temple of the living
God. The dome to appear shall ever be a symbol of that vast one high above
that enfolded and blessed on that perfect day when Martin, at the core of the
Chapel in essence, spoke the sacred words of dedication—a holy day.

Yes, in season the Dome Chapel took the dimensions outlined that day by the living
circle which represented the body of our King on earth, a tribute to the oneness of purpose shared by human beings in the living of their lives.

On November 1st our dear friend Rosa Groves passed away at age eighty-two, after
thirty-six years of participation in the ministry, twenty-four of which she and her husband David shared with their Sunrise Ranch family. These two contributed greatly to
making Sunrise Ranch a home, Dave with his expertise in gardening, well-drilling and
bee-keeping, and Rosa giving herself in any way that came along. Parents of Kathy, Roz
Hooper and Billie Cable, they were "Dad and Mother Groves" to all.

In New Orleans, Louisiana, a 26-foot offshore fishing boat, with a flying bridge, was
purchased by the Center there, assisted by contributions from others, to make possible
the weekend fishing necessary for the planned gift of seafood to be delivered to Sunrise
Ranch. Glenn Doty and Mack Fontenot were the fishermen.

There was increased and varied activity in far-flung places. Gregori Miller reported
that the Westport, Connecticut, group gave its first live performance of the musical
Godspell at Lake Rest Hotel in Livingston Manor. In the middle of the continent at Lisbon,
Iowa, Mike and Dorothea McCann hosted an Ontology group from Davenport, with
some intense sessions coming to a fitting climax via a videotape by Martin. And in Sapulpa,
Oklahoma, the ladies were busy, aided by the men who just couldn't stay away, and
produced a bake sale that won first prize for the most unique and impressive display,
presented by the largest shopping center in Tulsa.

"Without Prejudice" was the title of a service at 100 Mile House on November 18 in
which Martin spoke of hereditary factors.

Whether we approve of them or not these hereditary influences are present
in all of us and influence our daily experience. Regardless of their nature we
usually, particularly in earlier years, object to them. There is a feeling of being
trapped in what is inherently present, brought to us out of the past. I wonder
if I might be permitted a little reminiscence in order to portray something
which applies in principle to every human being but not in exactly the same

way to everyone; each one brings to focus something unique out of the past.

I was raised in a country which at the time was one of the great nations of the earth. Britain ruled the waves, and the sun never set on the British Empire. This obviously established a general background for almost everyone who was born in England, or in the United Kingdom, as it is now called. In my own case it was very specific, because I suppose it could be said that I had an overprivileged background. Being born into one of the so-called great families of England, a certain viewpoint and training were naturally experienced. This is true of everybody, isn't it?—not the same viewpoint but a definite one.

Also, later, a young officer in the Royal Navy—ruling the waves at that time, mind you—the point was further stressed. And yet, in my own experience there was this sense of resentment, as there is present in most everyone. After all, something—whatever it was—was seemingly imposed and one was trapped. I am quite sure that this element of resentment was part of the motivation that brought me to Canada, and it took me a while to come to terms with it.

Whether one is over- or underprivileged makes little difference. It may make a difference to the experience itself but not to the generation of a certain attitude of resentment that one is trapped in a particular state. This resentment may be used to advantage and I'm sure is, in my own case and in that of all of you sitting here. In view of the fact that in my own circumstance I had, along the way, an attitude of resentment toward it, I can understand when others resented me because of my background. Fundamentally it was the same thing: the individual felt trapped in his own background and found a convenient scapegoat in me to hang his resentment on. We find this pattern of envy which springs from the fact that human beings sense that they really are something, quite apart from their heredity; but the heredity is strongly, inevitably there, and it seems like a trap. Sometimes the resentment becomes extreme and there may be violent actions, but they are all based in this structured memory.

There is a way by which this may be cleared, as we have recognized, but certainly not by human effort of any kind. It is cleared by the working of the power of God, the irresistible force of love, the power back of, sustaining and governing the universe, when it is allowed to work in the individual's own life experience.

In the Sunday morning service at 100 Mile House on December 2nd, "Holy Unto the Lord No. 1," Martin spoke of the civilization on earth, a product of man's present consciousness, which is in the process of passing away.

What is now occurring is but a hint of what is yet to come, but "Babylon the great is fallen." In that regard the statement was made: "Come out of her, my people." The people of the Lord reveal themselves by coming out of the disintegrative aspect of the cycle. They come out of that into the integrative aspect. Those who heed the call to come out of that state of consciousness, which involves becoming fearful or trying to ignore it, find they have accepted a commission which relates to the integrative aspect of what is occurring. A new consciousness begins to come, in the awareness of a new identity.

Continuing his theme in the evening service, "Holy Unto the Lord No. 2," Martin admonished:

Let people be where they are, with the understanding they have, and if they are moving with the integrating aspect of the cycle everything is all right. If they are not, it's too bad for those concerned, but do you imagine that you can somehow do something about it and make it different? If you are a true priest or priestess in the holy place you have no desire to interfere with the working of the creative cycle. It is taking care of things the way they should be taken care of on the basis of the facts—whatever the facts are with people, that's the way it will work. There is some leeway but each must make a choice; it is impossible to make a choice for somebody else.

We trust the Lord, we trust the working of His creative cycle, and if it works out that some go down, well some go down. Our concern is that everybody should not go down. Generation after generation human beings have been going down. This disintegrative experience needs to be brought to its conclusion, and the more speedily the better. The days are shortened to the extent that the priesthood are true to their calling. The priesthood is distinct. The other parts of the body as they emerge are distinct. The whole body is put together in the working of this creative cycle. It isn't put together by any human beings organizing others; it is put together by God. We can't adapt it to our own desires; it is exactly what it is. But what a delight to move with the creative cycle instead of bucking it. We find that it all unfolds as it should.

On January 26, 1974, a group of sixty servers from the Colorado Centers gathered on Sunrise Ranch to share in a new experience, a workshop coordinated by Jim Wellemeyer who was assisted by Roger de Winton, Alan Hammond and Ted Black with their years of experience in various fields. It was a total success and presaged many of like nature in years to come.

Sixteen of Martin's services were published in a book, *Being Where You Are,* with the intriguing chapter titles: "The Cosmos and You," "Potential Released," "The Art of Peace in a World of War," "God—The Creative Compulsion," "The Snare of the Fowler," "The Worth of Work," "The Authority of Doing," "Unashamed to Praise the Lord, No. 1," "The Passing of Restrictions," "The Salvation of God," "What of the New Age?", "Heaven and Earth Are One!", "Your Significance," "Be Thou Perfect," and "Return to Being."

Two centers appeared in South Africa, one known as Fennmoor in Claremont, the other about two miles east, home of Lawrence and Sylvia King and family, renamed Sunny Lodge and located in Cassandra Road, Lansdowne.

Activity at the *Integrity* office at 100 Mile House was increasing, with new contacts being made throughout the world. A shortened version of Chris Foster's original letter was published in six newspapers, eliciting response from India, Switzerland and Germany. Sigridh Kiersch had translated the letter into French and German. It was also available in Spanish via Rena Cassidy of 100 Mile House and found its way into South America.

On the 14th of February Martin spoke on "The Living Universe," noting that from man's usual self-centered view it is considered that only here on the surface of the earth are there forms of life.

> If there is opportunity to examine what is present on the surface of the moon, then the view would likely be that there are no evidences of life. If the so-called evidences of life are discovered in rudimentary forms on one of the other planets, no doubt there would be much excitement. All this relates to the self-centered view of human beings blind to the fact that we are present in a living universe. Certainly there are peculiar forms of life here on this planet— the most peculiar perhaps man!—but whether we consider animal life, vegetation, the mineral kingdom, we are considering in each case forms of life. All forms in the whole universe are evidences of life. They would not exist if it were not for that cause. The cause is life.

> If we really begin to see this, then obviously it could be said that there is no such thing as death. Life is an animating principle, a creative principle, by which all things are. This of course relates it to what human beings refer to as God. Love and truth portray the character of God. They are inherent in what we call life, and life is the cause of all that appears in what we call form. There could be no form if it were not for life. We are more familiar with what we refer to as living forms on earth, but if we use those words it tends to give the idea that anything not a living form on the basis of this definition must be dead. Nothing is dead. We are part of a living universe, which is a whole structure, a living

organism, portrayed in a fashion by the human body itself, because certainly the human body contains within it representation of the other kingdoms. There are far vaster evidences of life in the universal whole than are comprehensible to man, and yet his own body is a portrayal of that vaster whole.

An outworking of vital import came to focus in March of that year at the beautiful Center in Theodore, Alabama, home of Jerry and Olive England. Participating with Martin in a special time of concentrated consideration of the state and affairs of the ministry were Lillian and I, Michael and Nancy, Bill and Donna. This initiated what would be called the Supreme Council, with other members included as the cycles unfolded.

Returning to Sunrise Ranch, Martin gave a service, "The Trumpet," on March 31 in which he referred to the gathering in Theodore as being

> essentially of the mouthpiece of the trumpet. There would be no point to such a gathering if there wasn't at least something of the trumpet attached. For that mouthpiece to be put to use requires the rest of the trumpet to be attached; so it was only when this state of affairs had become a sufficient reality in the dimensional world that something of the nature of what has occurred in recent days could be brought to pass. I had been looking to this day for some time, and all that has been occurring over the years has allowed this focus of creative expression to become more than a dream. I am thankful for the part you and others played in maintaining the vibrational setting, the connection, the enfoldment, so that the mouthpiece and the trumpet might be connected.
>
> The tone that is set in the mouthpiece is picked up everywhere else. The ability to encompass that tone in your consciousness determines the extent to which you are in fact part of the instrument which generates the tone in the dimensional world. This is the way it works! "Not by might, nor by power," not by any human manipulation of circumstances or events or people or anything "but by my spirit," by the generation of the true tone through the mouthpiece, throughout the trumpet, and consequently beyond in the substance of consciousness in the world, primarily in human beings. To find and encompass this tone—by this the restoration occurs; by this all things are made new.

A friend of the Sunrise Ranch family for many years, Ted Mettlen passed away April 23. He contributed much in the area of maintenance and repair, and he and his wife Helen with sons Tommy and Teddy were good neighbors, living "next-door" in the small town of Masonville. Ted and Helen operated the Masonville Post Office for many years, handling all the incoming and outgoing Ranch mail.

That year witnessed a "New Acquisition," as Bill Dice described it in *Eden Valley News:*

The South half of the SE 1/4 and the SE 1/4 of the SW 1/4 of Section 27, Township 6 North, Range 70 West of the 6th P.M. is part of the legal description of a piece of land approximately 75 acres in size. It can be seen looking north from Sunrise Ranch and has been known to us as the "Wilder property." We have looked in that direction for many years with the assurance that it would come into our direct area of responsibility.

Then one evening early in December 1973 we received a phone call from Harvey Wilder informing us that this land was for sale and he would give us first opportunity to purchase it. We took possession of the land in April of this year and began, as time permitted, to clean and change the facilities and let it become a valuable part of Sunrise Ranch. The first need was to build a turkey yard under the big cottonwood trees, with room for them to roam out of the pen and into the field for greens. The birds are moved in and thriving in this new location.

There are several buildings on the property, a lovely five-room home with a full, unfinished basement. George, Joelle and Tim Emery, and David Lynch are living there now. Dave's prime responsibility is the care of the animals. There is a milk house, which we have rebuilt for both cows and goats. The cows are milked three at a time in a herring-bone milking stanchion, raised thirty inches above ground and includes an automatic milk-line which delivers the milk directly to the separator. The goats also have a three-stanchion setup but are still milked by hand.

The cows have a ten-acre pasture directly south of the milk house and corral; the goats have a one-acre pasture, with housing included. The beef corrals have been moved to the new land and the remaining acreage there is being used for beef pasture and the storage of hay and farm machinery. The rabbit building is to be moved and a new chickenhouse provided, allowing removal of all the animals and birds from the old barnyard on the Ranch to the new land and a more organized setup.

Two dead cottonwood trees along the drive have been replaced with a row of twelve lombardy poplars. We have also planted nineteen willows in the dairy pasture. The small garden north of the house is full of tomato plants, heavy for the harvest. There is a flurry of delighted activity as Sunrise Ranch once again expands her visible borders.

That beautiful property has provided a home for our farm animals through the ensuing years, with David Lynch still in his place of expert husbandry, constantly alert to opportunities to extend his spirit and experience far afield, until today he plays a major role in many aspects of farming and ecology throughout the land.

On May 24 Elizabeth Sciple passed away, in the atmosphere of tender love shared with her many friends in Eden Valley.

That year marked the beginning of bringing into form on Sunrise Ranch the magnificent design that had been nurtured in Martin's fertile mind and heart and been outlined on the hill by a magic circle. He found great delight in working with John Summerbell and the others, together participating in the awesome emergence of a truly unique creation.

John wrote, in *Eden Valley News:*

> A truly beautiful structure. When we were considering designs for a chapel, prior to a geodesic dome coming into focus, we had some elaborate and different variations on square and rectangular structures. At that time we experienced some very high winds, up to 125 miles per hour and gusts exceeding that. On a square building, winds of this strength could cause very serious problems because of pressure on the windward side and a vacuum on the leeward side. A dome allows the wind to flow over and around it, thereby eliminating most of the adverse effects.

> The use of natural forces and the mathematics of the spheres makes domes stronger. In a dome, when a load is put on one strut, every other strut becomes stronger to support it. You can check out how the strength builds up in a dome by using a dull pencil, a wooden match or a pen. Place the object between your two index fingers and, holding it very lightly, increase the pushing pressure of your fingers. The more pressure, the stronger your fingers and arms get to support the object and the tighter the object is held in place. It takes much more weight to bend the object when more pressure is applied to the ends. Besides the strength factor, it takes less material to cover a dome than it does other shapes of comparable size.

> Working on this building has been an entirely new experience for all of us. Not one could say we knew how it would work out. We had to be continually flexible, experiment, think and rethink. Previous knowledge and experience needed to find a new way of building. Because of this we found new relationships, new intense patterns of producing in loving agreement, "leaping upon the mountains and skipping upon the hills"—energy released and

vibrantly renewed, strength and stamina multiplied by our rich agreement.

The first night, when we started pumping the ferro cement, working with lights after dark, Martin, Lillian and Grace and most of the family on Sunrise Ranch were gathered around the dome and a big bonfire. There were about fifty men on the job, mixing, operating the big plaster pump, caring for the two hundred feet of 2-inch hose used to pump the cement up to the top of the dome, and spraying the cement. The stage was set as the job of plastering began. At one point, after applying cement for forty hours straight, I became awed by the intense love and appreciation felt and expressed man to man and for all.

Geoff Tisch and Egon Milinkovich and I have been primarily responsible for the construction of the dome at certain stages. All were vital to the out-working, with a special word for Jim Higerd and Andrew Shier. We have all had varied experience in the construction field and count it a rich privilege to bring our individual experience and spirits into this unique venture.

This indeed is a Chapel, like none other on earth; and we who work closely with it, letting the design established by our Lord come into form, know great fulfilment in life's expression.

Jim Higerd, who focalized the operation under John Summerbell, said:

As I stood looking at it early one morning, the sunlight glistening off the fresh dew clinging to the dome, there was a deep sense of awe...of wonder...of love. The spirit of the crew is the most tangible substance, where the delightful work takes place. The crew consists of individuals from all types of backgrounds, running the gamut from a retired surfer to a draftsman, a cabinet-maker to a musician. This has been found to be a tremendous blessing. A building this shape requires a crew that can remain flexible and creative in their thinking. It was not specialized skills that were primarily needed but a real love by each one for what they were doing. It can honestly be said that each one involved has a love for Martin and his Word, and therefore a love for those around him, and the work as it unfolds each day, with the inevitable result of a rich experience.

The crew is not an isolated part of the body but a part of the whole. We are well aware that the necessary substance for this particular edifice is being generated by people of integrity everywhere—in the office, on the farm, in the kitchen, in businesses, in all fields of life. Together we are letting this temple of the Lord take form on earth.

Andrew Shier contributed his view as he worked on that unique building:

I soon discovered the necessity to be flexible. We were all learning as we went along, often changing previous designs and techniques. Wintertime at the dome was particularly a time for this, and the crew mainly consisted of Jim Higerd, now in charge of construction, and myself. There is only one way in which this experience of doing and redoing can be uplifting and fulfilling and that is through an agreement which underlies all superficial accomplishment and achievement. Jim and I became aware of this agreement; and what has been and still is transpiring is the most enlightening experience I have known. Because of the love I have for this man, there is no task or circumstance that may violate this bond of agreement—not even tearing down a wall you spent weeks building. Can you believe it possible to laugh at such an incident? It does not happen often but when it does it is freeing. Agreement with that which is higher has proven to be the key, and it certainly has unlocked many doors.

Glenn Lockie added his word:

The building under me is growing a little each day, the incompleteness of early construction being infilled. How to tell you of my deep love for this chapel crew and the Sunrise Family, of the beauty of being with these angels, the magic of working with Andy, Mike, Chaz and Jim, my brothers? Can men be closer than this? No critical word between us; coordination in unselfish harmony; agreement with Jim, and his careful consideration of each detail allowing an assurance of execution; the blessings left by the Class men who've worked as one with us, and the delight of visitors who offer a day or a week of labor. Jim is a wizard at drawing forth our talents, but we know we bring more to the Lord than expertise. The sacredness of His Word in expression is primary—the Lord builds the house!

Glenn Lockie composed a poem in *Eden Valley News* to share something of his feelings:

Ferro-Cementing the Chapel

'Twas the middle of beautiful May,
When they turned the hoses to spray
On the dome that we'd made
What those skilled in the trade
Call "mud" (that's cement, by the way).

For forty straight hours they toiled,
Undaunted crew—couldn't be foiled,
But they saw that this phase
Couldn't be done in two days
And rested with spirits unspoiled.

'Twas August when the job was complete,
And all knew that this marvelous feat
Was done in good time
With the Lord's true design
For turning abstract to concrete.

The wonder of the shared experience is also touched in Stan Waldron's words:

It has been my distinct pleasure to work with the Chapel crew in Eden Valley for the past few months. Outstanding is the agreement known by reason of focalization on the job site. Each one realizes the necessity of moving together in every moment if the plastering is to be accomplished correctly. More important than the form though is the magic of God's love that finds expression through this medium of work. At times it is very humorous—perhaps a cold squirt of water when you're not looking, or a splotch of mud on the neck as you're tying your shoe!

We learn the aliveness of being alert, for there is always someone to enfold and encompass—for instance, the men on top of the scaffold who walk in rhythm with the wobbly structure, or the fellows who transport the muddy concrete to the top, knowing their clothes will never be the same. Some days we begin work just before sunrise, discovering that God is the greatest artist as He quickly paints a brilliant sky. When the day is done we see the fruits of our agreement in a true sense of service. Something was built—along with this outer form is an experience that is stronger than ferro-cement.

As clear as the shining of the light in Eden Valley is the fact that the building of this wondrous Dome Chapel, unique in design and execution, has revealed a living temple of human beings true to the design ordained in the beginning of creation. In the first stages of its inception it appeared that the design might take the form of a geodesic dome, but as the pattern unfolded it portrayed, rather than the dimensions of the earth itself, the elliptical path our planet travels in the heavens around its god, our sun. This principle was conveyed most beautifully in the spirit of the men as they eagerly accepted the places naturally established in the project. "Except the Lord build the house, they labour in vain that build it."

Later, in *Eden Valley News* PenDell Pittman revealed some interesting facts pertaining to the Dome Chapel:

> The ceiling height was set at 24 feet. The basic structure was a wood frame using two-by-six lumber. Plywood was used to support the outside covering of ferro-cement. An elastomeric coating was then applied to the ferro-cement in layers—seven layers of neoprene embedding a layer of polyester mesh. Four more layers of Hypalon gave the Dome exterior its milk-white color and durability. This elastic covering allows a constant seal against leaking and cracking, which would otherwise be inevitable with the different rates of expansion and contraction between the wood structure and the ferro-cement.
>
> The Dome can seat 472 people, has a 38-foot by 14-foot stage area and uses retracting theater-style seats on a stepped floor. Broad windows offer a panoramic view of Eden Valley and the surrounding Colorado foothills. An "eyebrow" surrounding the base of the Dome roof catches moisture and is designed to provide solar shading in summer and solar heating in winter. Venting via a natural chimney effect is created using top and sidewall vents. Temperature is stabilized by fan-coil heating and central air conditioning. Extensive use of skylights provides plentiful natural lighting, with theater lighting accenting the stage area.
>
> The Dome hosts a Rodgers two-manual pipe/electronic organ with pipes speaking from the back of the auditorium. Also present are audio, video and teleconferencing facilities. The Dome is the largest, and most unique structure of its kind in existence.

A service given by Martin on the so-called temptations of the Master drew out my response in poetic form:

> *He stood upon the mountaintop—that vital triune day,*
>   *"Make these stones bread," his body said,*
> *"then you will know the way.*
> *Transfuse these cells with life—*
> *food, drink, right exercise;*
> *In unrelenting discipline's the secret to be wise."*
>
> *His word rang clear, eyes lifted up steadfastly to the hills,*

*"The flesh is but an empty husk till it the Spirit fills
And brings life overflowing to the hungry waiting earth."*

*Then quickly came the second step, mind swelling with its worth:
"Cast thyself down! Invulnerable, I shall not surely die!"*

*"Self-will and pride bring death and never life—all else is lie!"—
The answer rang throughout the mount as with a mighty thunder!
And with it every creature paused along its way—to wonder.*

*The third step—all the kingdoms and the glory of the world
Were there, before His loving gaze majestically unfurled,
All His—His own—so dear, enfolded, loved, caressed
From the foundation of it all, with His own Being blest.*

*Then what the need, what fever to possess, at such fierce cost,
What always was, and is, shall be, and never can be lost?*

*"Get thee behind me, Satan"—and the victory of His Word
Thrilled all that holy mountain, the Temple of the Lord.*

In a service entitled "Whence Are You?" Martin used a text from the 8th Psalm: "What is Man, that thou art mindful of him?... For thou hast made him a little lower than the angels."

Personally I feel a closer kinship with the angels than I do with an ancestry reaching back into the primeval slime. How about you? Whatever the fact may seem to be with respect to human heredity, a potential which transcends the earthy condition is inherently sensed by anyone of integrity. From whence does this assurance come? It certainly is of much more immediate impact than speculation about an amoebic forebear! Would it be less scientific to listen to the voice of this intuition than to trust the laborious processes of human thought tracing the speculative contradictions of circumstantial evidence?

What is man? The sad consequence of senseless chance? The most complex organism and therefore the highest form of life mysteriously evolved out of more elementary states of living matter? Or could the fact of his presence on earth stem from a higher rather than a lower source? How about looking up for the answer instead of down? The downward view is sustained by the endless acquisition of knowledge about the time-oriented phenomenal world. The upward view calls to remembrance the eternal nature of the present moment and the higher cause of what now is. That there is such a present cause is proclaimed by one's sense of transcendent potential: "I may not yet have realized all my potential but I inherently know it is here to be realized."

So much attention is paid to the appearance of things, to pleasures and pains, to the experience of the past and expectations of the future—in other words, to what is lower—that the transcendent angel vanishes from view. "There ain't no such animal!" is the skeptical view. But a person is dead inside himself when he has lost consciousness of his own potential of greatness—his sense of kinship with the angels. Yet virtually all human experience constrains toward this violation of integrity. Science teaches it—believe only what you can see and touch and measure; here is the real world, the true values; look down and you will go up. How ridiculous! But the angel is present, encompassing all the true values in human experience, which cannot be inherited from the past or acquired out of the world. They spring only from a higher source. When a person is the expression of the angel he engenders transformation in what is lower. This is the creative art of living.

Look to the angel! Loud and clear I hear that silent invitation—an irresistible compulsion beyond the call of ancestry and worldly circumstance. Man is made a little lower than the angels, that the angels may walk on earth in human form. Are you the angel alive on earth in a body of flesh? To deny the angel is death. To express the character of the angel is life. What you express you know—death from below; life from above. Whence are you?

In an evening service, "True Representation #2," on July 7 at 100 Mile House Martin recalled his consideration in the morning where he spoke of clouds which account for the separation of spiritual man and material man.

The sun is shining but it is dark under the cloud. Those who find themselves under the cloud, which includes everyone on the face of the earth, realize there is something wrong; otherwise they would not be so quick in their attitudes of blame. It is not at all difficult to find manifold devils who seem to be to blame for the multitudes of evils to be found the world over. There is a continuous endeavor to find what might be thought of as the ultimate devil, because no matter what particular kind of evil you may look at, and what particular devil you may find who seems to be responsible for that evil, there is always a devil behind the devil, and you can continue endlessly discovering new devils. If you want to whip up enthusiasm with the general public, you seek out one of the devils and lay stress upon him as being the cause for all the troubles of the community, or nation, or world.

The idea of a gallant and worthwhile male is that he should mount his charger and slay the dragon. That was St. George, wasn't it? Let George do it! There is a dragon all right, and he has numerous heads—you cut off one head and another grows in its place. I'm sure we recognize there is a need to come out of that state, and we do so first of all in the recognition that the condition under the cloud is the way it is because of the cloud. The cloud is simply the human malady of self-centeredness, to which all human beings have succumbed. It is one's own aspect of the cloud for which one is personally responsible, and while other people certainly have their own clouds to deal with, that's their business. We're not looking for scapegoats or devils as substitutes for our own self-centeredness, because if the cloud dissolves in our own experience we find that with it went the attitude of blame.

The building of a new Chapel was initiated at 100 Mile House in July, designed by Michael, which has proven to be a remarkable combination of beauty and practicality. John Summerbell and David Oshanek shared the foreman's duties, and some of the crew were David Waskom of Louisiana, Ted Aikman of Ontario, Doug Elliott and David Thatcher. With seating capacity for 324, rectangular in shape, 45 by 95 feet with a mansard roof, it has a sloping floor and a stage at one end. A full basement provides spacious accommodation for a choir hall, music rooms, library and storage. Washrooms are located in each end of the building, with a beautiful foyer at the entrance, also a lovely hallway in the rear where a stairway ascends to an upper level which provides space for three offices. Situated next to the Log Chapel, the flat-roofed design was chosen in order that it would blend in with the existing buildings and not overshadow them.

A tour of the Northeast by Martin, Lillian and me began on September 16 when we flew from Denver and were met in Washington, D.C., by Bill and Donna Bahan and welcomed by Jim and Maria Frid into their lovely home in Beltsville, Maryland. We enjoyed a tour of the United States capitol, which included the National Gallery of Art; the Kennedy Center for the Performing Arts; and Mt. Vernon, George Washington's stately home on the Potomac River. I was enthralled by the latter, sensing something intimately familiar in the atmosphere of the house, outbuildings and grounds.

On the 18th we drove to Lake Rest Hotel where we had our first tour of the newly acquired property across the lake, which Martin named "Clear Water." That lovely spot in the Catskills provided accommodation for classes and other sessions. On the 22nd, all fifty-two Class members had arrived and shared, with about three hundred others, Martin's services, "The Day of the Lord" and "Great Responsibility." The next day we drove, with Bill and Donna, to Floral Park, Lou and Bridie Rotola's home on Long Island.

In New York City we enjoyed an adventurous tour in a big black Cadillac limousine rented by Frank and Patricia Caputo and driven by Frank, our elegant chauffeur, cap and all! We went through Central Park, had a spiral stroll through the tiers of the Guggenheim Museum of Modern Art, lunch at Geiger's German Restaurant, a quick shopping trip through Macy's (very fast!), dinner at Brooklyn's hundred-year-old Gage and Tollner restaurant and, to top it off, an evening at Broadway's Plymouth Theater viewing Peter Cook and Dudley Moore's hilarious *Good Evening.*

Westport, Connecticut, was our next stop. There we spent a delightful time with Don and Mary Cardiff and later their son Michael, his wife Bari-Lynn and their two children. The following day Mary accompanied us to New Canaan where Martin met Nathan Keats, publisher of his book *Being Where You Are.* The next few days were spent at Green Pastures, with a visit to the Bahan Chiropractic Clinic in Derry. Martin's service was held in the beautiful new dining facility at Green Pastures, with its comforting capacity to enfold the steadily increasing numbers coming to its doors.

On our way again, we thrilled to the brilliant fall colors of the Green Mountains of Vermont en route to the new home of Bill and Gail Cordes on the outskirts of Montreal, Quebec. After viewing that city we had a quick visit with Egon and Andrea Milinkovich and family at Silver Bridge Farm, swung through Ottawa and continued on to King View Farm outside of Toronto for an overnight stay. Off again the next morning, we stopped in Hamilton to see Manning and Stephanie Glicksohn, then proceeded to Anduril Farm in London, Ontario, the beautiful home of Bob and Beverley Purdom, with a reception by the London group later at Ray and Norma Singer's home. We left the Purdoms on Friday the 4th and drove to Windsor, where we were greeted by Bob and Alice Barbour and their group at that Center.

After a brief stop in Chatham we moved on for our first visit to Twin Valleys and the home of George and Pat Bullied. We met the family there, which included some students. On Sunday, October 6, Martin spoke in Glendon College in Toronto, our last stop, to people gathered from all over Ontario, Quebec and many from the United States. The three of us stayed at King View Farm for a few more days and left on the 9th, flying to Vancouver and, several days later, home to 100 Mile House.

Down South, at the Theodore, Alabama, Center, home of Jerry and Olive England, eleven Class members began a new cycle of one-week classes on October 20.

The first week of December witnessed the arrival of twenty-four active Attunement Servers to Sunrise Ranch, with an overall theme based on Martin's service of March 10, "Re-creation in Consciousness." In agreement, Roger de Winton and Michael Cecil had laid the groundwork for this very effective outworking. A highlight was a service given at 100 Mile House the previous Sunday by Martin, entitled "Attunement."

A circular letter written by Billy Graham came to Martin's hand and he read a portion of it in a service at 100 Mile House on December 29, the last Sunday in 1974, entitled "The Two Cross-Over Points":

> "Christmas Greetings. This year has been one of the most critical years in world history. The scientists moved the atomic clock nearer midnight...an American President resigned for the first time in history...scores of countries sank deeper into an economic morass...the price of oil shifted billions in Western currency to the Middle East...leaders hung their heads in despair as the world plunged deeper and deeper into crisis. Natural disasters struck—floods, droughts, hurricanes, earthquakes. Millions live on the edge of starvation. Few leaders seem to be emerging anywhere. There is a crisis in leadership as the world looks for a 'leader' and a 'messiah.'
>
> "Diplomats are now openly using apocalyptic language to describe the current world situation. More and more people are seriously questioning if the human race can survive. How accurately the ancient words from Jeremiah describe our present world situation. Today, as then, people are saying, 'Peace, peace; when there is no peace.' Those who refuse to learn from history are condemned to repeat it. Today we are startlingly close to repeating one of the most tragic chapters in human history. The present world situation parallels in striking fashion the conditions which prevailed during the prelude to World War II...."

Martin continued:

> There is a looking for leadership, for a leader and a messiah. Of course most people think of this in terms of the manipulation of events; someone is going to arise with a brilliant idea as to how all the besetting problems of the world may be solved, and lo and behold, the answer will appear. Even in the expectation of the "second coming of Christ" this is the sort of view people have. Events are going to be manipulated; of course this is quite all right if it is done by Jesus Christ. But that is not the way God works. You don't see anyone standing around—I'm not sure where—manipulating the solar system so that it works the way it should, or the galaxies or the universe, imposing some sort

of tyrannical dictatorship. Yet things do work; there is evidence of a certain orderliness. And while some of the things that happen may not be adequately understood, there would appear to be a control in operation. Even with respect to the confused state of human experience there are evidences of control in operation. In spite of all the nonsense, our hearts are still beating, we're still breathing, and digestion is working after a fashion. What is the nature of the leadership, of the government?

According to the account in the *Bible* it should emerge through the cloud in like manner as it disappeared. Of course that has been translated simply in terms of one person. We realize there is no experience except in the present moment. Therefore the true government is of the present moment. It isn't coming; it didn't really come and then go. The government is here in this present moment. It may be behind a cloud insofar as the awareness of human beings is concerned, but let us not put so much importance upon what human beings may or may not be aware of. Let us be more interested in fact than fancy.

On May 10 forty musicians gathered for six days, the first of many Music Conferences to be held on Sunrise Ranch. Coordinated by Lillian, she was assisted by a steering committee composed of Diana de Winton, Donna Bahan, Ted Black, Bill and Doreen Thompson, and Marjorie Gilbert. From all over the United States and Canada, each brought a variety of musical talents—composers, conductors, instrumentalists and vocalists, and more! Specific workshops were headed by experts in their fields, including a session devoted to African music with its special rhythm.

An initiation of monumental proportions was a dental clinic on Sunrise Ranch, a gift by Dr. Michael Iacoboni who had attended the Spring Class and was in private practice in Elizabeth, Colorado, later moving to Loveland. It was (and still is!) located in the basement of a house which was then occupied by the Dice family, situated near the dining hall, Administration Building, etc. As expressed by Jeannie Sixkiller (now Kezlan) in *Eden Valley News*, "The dental unit, the chair, instruments, etc., would be of little value without a staff to operate them—and what a team we have!"

That team consisted of experts, primary among them (next to Dr. Iacoboni) Jeannie, an experienced dental hygienist working with a dentist in Loveland. She gave freely of her experience and expertise in the ease and enfoldment of her bright atmosphere. Dawn Blechman, a registered nurse and Sunrise resident, was a valuable assistant. In Jeannie's words, "Her love for life and laughter helps soothe even the most apprehensive patient."

Of Michael she said:

He makes going to the dentist almost fun. His enthusiasm for doing dentistry the right way is immediately felt by the patient and his artistic abilities in that field are matched by his patience and understanding. Mike truly gives of his time and talent to those in need of his services. It is my responsibility to make certain that everyone who comes for a dental checkup realizes that care of the mouth is a vital part of caring for the whole body.

One day, a year later in the fall of 1976, I was ensconced in "the chair" when a telephone call from Pennsylvania was transferred to me there. I was informed that my husband (we had been separated for many years) was dying and a friend of his was inviting me to come and stay with her to settle his affairs as he had no other living relatives. I did this, accompanied by Roger de Winton who was most helpful in the business procedures, an arrangement by Martin in his ever-present loving care and consideration. I mention this because as a result of some money left me at that time I was in position to upgrade some rather antiquated equipment, including the chair, in the dental clinic.

Through the years there have been others who ably assisted Michael, among them Debra Bobrowski, Anna Gayer and Diana de Winton.

Dr. Iacoboni continues to share his skill and love in that little office on the Ranch, an incredible and enduring gift to his Emissary family.

29

THE SETTING FOR THE JEWEL

May 1975 ~ December 1976

*A*nother of the wonders that appeared in 1975 was our Art Gallery in Estes Park. Following the river up Big Thompson Canyon, one comes upon this little town, a mecca for tourists, about thirty miles west of Sunrise Ranch and twenty-five hundred feet higher. It is surrounded on all sides by glorious mountains: Meeker (yes, named for Uranda's ancestor), Longmont, Twin Peaks, and myriad lesser but equally breathtaking rock formations. The town offers an intriguing stop before proceeding farther up, through Rocky Mountain National Park to enchanting places with names like Hidden Valley and Bear Lake, where one can observe all manner of wild creatures and thrill, in proper seasons, to the unique trumpet call of the elk. Ascending into increasingly rarified atmosphere, you eventually arrive at Trail Ridge, there on the Continental Divide where one seems to be perched on the peak of the world. The gallery was located at the end of Elkhorn Avenue, the main tourist shopping center. Fall River crosses under the street right in front of the gallery, and a huge waterwheel slowly turns.

Bob Ewing described it eloquently in his *Eden Valley News* article, "Founded Upon the Waters":

With the beautiful big waterwheel slowly turning, tourists pause to enjoy the lamplit boardwalk which leads up the rustic stairs to the WaterWheel Gallery. The display area is framed in a dramatic sky-lit, cedar-beamed upper room, the view from which is of Old Man Mountain on up the Valley. When Bill Talkington and I first arrived at the site to lease the art gallery there was only some cement poured, and blueprints of the proposed design available. It was mid-May and tourist season near. A finished gallery seemed far away, yet not impossible.

As we moved in the rhythm of the thing, many intricate factors that required a wide range of professional skills poured in. Roger de Winton drew up the legal incorporating documents, and from then on the Sunrise family fleshed out all the necessary factors, right up to June 11th, that last evening of preparation when we opened the doors to the public. Paintings were hung, sculpture displayed, signs up, lighting placed, carpet being cut by the Class men, refreshments. Lights—action! And in came over two hundred guests from the surrounding community, traversing up a safe but unfinished structure to welcome us.

Debbie Sims, an illustrator from Connecticut, assists me in managing the gallery. The initiating artists are Bill Talkington, sculptor; Michael Gress, watercolorist; Conrad O'Brien-ffrench, who works mainly in oil, as do I. Meanwhile the facility is being refined, the customers are pouring in, and business is accelerating. A mainstream of creativity is being opened through this developing facility, product of agreement between the artists (a rare commodity), with the loving guidance of Grace.

Terry Oftedal, member of the Class, observed:

On June 11th six men drove excitedly from Sunrise to Estes Park to help with the final touches for that evening's six-o'clock grand opening of the WaterWheel Gallery. Upon arrival, around 1:30, we found carpenters building a stairway to the second floor, so we climbed a ladder, to behold the smiling faces of Bob Ewing and Bill Talkington in the upper room of an artistically striking new building. Two rolls of carpet sat in one corner, doors propped against a near wall, and between was an assortment of furniture and construction equipment. Bill warmly welcomed us and announced that the lights worked, the art had safely arrived, and over six hundred invitations had been sent out.

Seven shining faces turned toward me—I was the head carpet installer. Without a thought from any of us as to how much could be accomplished we set to work clearing the floor. As the first length of tastefully selected gray carpet was cut and fitted into place, men began hanging the superb paintings of the artists. As the second length was put into place, some ladies appeared and began dressing tables with flowers and refreshments. Upon freshly painted pedestals Bill Talkington placed his sculptures—a collection of animals held to their bases by one or two hooves. I finally looked up from a last corner trim to see the stairway finished and a large waterwheel lowered by winch into the rushing water beneath our patio. I saw snowcapped Rocky Mountains, clouds closely overhead in a blue Colorado sky, and a living Gallery filled with radiant people. Bob brought out the guest book and said, "We did it! Thanks."

In early May, Bill Talkington had set out on the first leg of a Northwest Art Tour. Besides his own sculpture he carried Conrad's and Michael's water colors. He conducted shows in Oregon and Washington. On June 8 Michael and Antoinette, his wife, with Conrad, came together in Richmond, B.C., to take over the tour, while Bill flew back to Colorado to assist in the opening of the gallery. After a four-day show in a Richmond shopping center the artists, joined again by Bill, drove to Port Alberni on Vancouver Island. Three days were spent there at an outdoor fair, workshops and an exhibition in the Echo Center.

Antoinette said:

> From there the party went to 100 Mile House where a two-day show was held in the arena, arranged by Lloyd Meeker. A public lecture was entitled 'Everyone Is an Artist' and the three artists offered their techniques and their spirits that make their work so beautiful. The room was filled and the crowd delighted. Conrad then returned to Vancouver and Bill, Michael and I continued on to Prince George, where the show was held in a large hotel. There was not much artwork left for sale; indeed the tour was a great success in every way.

A daughter was born to Michael and Nancy Cecil at 100 Mile House on May 19. She was named Angela Kathleen.

In a service at 100 Mile House on June 1st, "The Furniture in the Holy Place," Martin spoke of the present stage of the

> collective body with many people, in the development of which it was necessary for everyone to be concerned with both bread and with spiritual expression; there was much to be done and each one did a very great deal. As the body has developed and there are more people, there begins to be a differentiation, so that there are those more concerned with the bread and those with the word. This doesn't make some better than others; it merely means the body is taking form. Obviously the physical heart has a specific function and does not go on a holiday and let the liver take over. There must be specific

provision in very particular ways. No one person is supposed to be capable of doing everything. This was necessary in the beginning, that one person should be able to do whatever was required on the basis of the development then. But now it is different; there has been a proliferation.

There have been those who looked at me, and perhaps also Lillian and Grace, and wondered what we do. No, we're not out there hoeing in the garden—not that one anyway—or in the kitchen washing dishes, etc. So satan may say, "You have it made! But look at us; we have all these things to do." That's what caused the downfall with respect to Job, satan beginning to judge. The three of us have been required to do things in times past that none of you will ever be rquired to do. I don't think you can do anything we haven't done, because it was necessary then; there was no one else to do it. Now there begin to be others and we can allow the specific nature of the operation to take form. It would be a very incompetent body if we were all doing the same thing! The competence comes because we all have our own fields of competence which need to be developed.

I have observed incompetence. It is very fortunate that we have such a tolerant employer in the person of the Lord, because I am sure every one of us would have been fired otherwise. He gives time to develop competence, but we have to use our opportunities, recognize our incompetence, and acknowledge our failures. Then we scout around to find how the lack may be filled.

I have never felt the need to become competent in the field of electronics; I know very little about it; but there are others who can do what is needed in that area. I have found it necessary to develop a competence in the field of my responsibility, and the same should be true of each one. When we do, we find we complement each other; we fit together. I've always welcomed people to move into my field. I don't imagine that it is such a narrow little thing that if two or three more people came into it there wouldn't be any room left for me. The field of our responsibility is vast and we've scarcely become aware of any of it yet.

Forty-one businessmen attended a seminar in the Log Chapel at 100 Mile House June 23-26. They came from points in British Columbia, Alberta, Quebec, New Hampshire, Arizona, Oregon and Washington. Twenty from our businesses at 100 Mile House shared in this venture coordinated by Ross Marks and Michael Cassidy. There was also a three-day convention of a sizeable group of B.C. Community Newspaper Publishers at Red Coach Inn. After a tour of the Lodge and grounds Michael spoke to them of the Emissaries of Divine Light program, which was followed by entertainment by Geoff Tisch and Sam Dice.

The Emissary replaced *Ontological Thought,* the content of the monthly journal having undergone substantial change along with the title. July dated the first issue.

Northern Light of 1975 carried a tribute to his father by Michael, who said:

> For many a visitor over the years the sight of the blazing fire in the Lodge lounge has been a welcoming first impression of the communal family at 100 Mile House. It is an impression that took on increasing significance with the years, for this is Martin's home—a place to which he came over forty years ago—warmed now by the strong, wise atmosphere of his person.
>
> Now a hundred people make up the group family here. Another fifty or so live nearby in the village in close association with us. In recent years much construction has expanded facilities. Three Classes a year bring one hundred and fifty students. A dozen businesses provide financially for the group and in the process provide a service to thousands of people. Yet in all this activity there is a serenity which shows in the eyes of the family—still pools of light, with a reflection of that blazing fire in the background. This is Martin's home, as is the noble white house set in trees on a hill beyond the main group buildings.
>
> Visiting his house on the hill, one is welcomed into a gracious home and finds warm hospitality, calmness and laughter, and everyday things done with love and exactness. The essence of integrity is here—Martin, Lillian, Grace, and Lloyd and Helen (Marina away in university).

> "Eden Valley Press, Inc." on Sunrise Ranch, proudly announced the welcome addition of a brand-new Royal Zenith 20-A printing press. Installed the latter part of August, it begins where our old press strained to produce. Far from disposing of our twelve-year printing veteran, we will use it for booklets, envelopes and many short-run jobs. The Royal Zenith will handle the mailings, some booklets, *The Emissary, Newslight, Eden Valley News and Northern Light.* Manufactured in Czechoslovakia by Adast Company, in business since 1360, the two-thousand-pound machine was a precision instrument and arrived direct from Europe via New York City. Men from the Denver franchise installed and tested it, which took five days.

On September 6, the day following the conclusion of the 1975 Conference sessions on Sunrise Ranch, Martin officiated at the marriage of Rupert Maskell and Tessa Welch. Their attendants were Alan and Jean Hammond. The wedding was well attended by Rupert's immediate family who flew from England, after which the couple left to serve in their home in Cape Town, South Africa.

Martin, Lillian, Marina and I toured the Southwest, beginning at Phoenix, Arizona, where Martin gave a service on September 21. John and Pam Gray coordinated the Center there and provided focus for the entire Southwest area. Four settings in Phoenix were included: Glendale, with the Grays; Broadmor House, with Mike Baim; Westside House; and the home of John and Carol Amey. A Sunday morning service was held in the Sheraton Greenway Hotel.

From there we went to the Riverside Center in California, where Richard and Karen Toal had the focus. We met eighty-three-year-old John Ostrom, an Emissary who had visited Sunrise Ranch when Uranda was there. The following day Bob and Alice Spaulding welcomed us to their Center in Anaheim, after which we had our first Disneyland experience. The next stop was San Diego in the beautiful Coronado Hotel where Gay Goodman was resident. She and Steve Tashiro were our excellent hosts and we enjoyed a time of relaxation on the beach, tennis court and in the swimming pool. Martin spoke to a group on the 28th.

Just ten days before we arrived in Los Angeles a new Center had come into form with Chris Jorgensen the focus. We enjoyed a dinner with twenty people in a beautiful house set in a garden filled with lush growth of fruit-bearing trees, and also visited Lou and Marian Novins in their home. Our next stop was in Santa Barbara, where Rob and Denise Cass welcomed us to the Center, located in the attractive home of the Kanes, Denny's parents.

From there we went toward San Francisco and stayed the night in a motel in Salinas. Before proceeding with the remainder of that journey, I interject Martin's words from a service he gave at Portland, Oregon later, on October 12, in which he was speaking of the trip:

We have been traveling the past few weeks, moving through Phoenix to the West Coast—California, and now we are in Oregon. This ministry was initiated by Uranda some forty years ago in Atascadero, California. Long Beach was the headquarters for some time, and then moved to the Bay area in San Francisco, around 1937. [Our present travel took us to all these places.] Subsequent to those early days Uranda was back in California and some vital events took place there. In Riverside in 1947 I received ordination as the second Bishop of the ministry at his hand. [We could not find, on our recent visit there, anything to identify the place where we had been; it was all built up and changed.]

The end of that year and most of 1948 was spent by Uranda and his party in Salinas, near San Francisco, a place called El Gabilan Ranch. It was a crucial time in the developing ministry, and Uranda held a session there in the spring, which I attended. On this recent trip we stayed a night in Salinas and had opportunity to explore the area to determine the location of El Gabilan if possible.

That part of our journey, almost thirty years after our advent in Salinas, presented me with an unexpected challenge. As we explored, we found ourselves on a road that led into an area that had remained remarkably uninhabited, the surroundings unspoiled. It was beginning to look alarmingly familiar to me. Yes, that word is descriptive of my feeling, because I had not given any weight to the possibility of the place actually still being there. Each day of my stay at Gabilan Ranch had been filled with intense feeling experiences, and as we rounded another curve in the road, memories crowded my whole body with breathless anticipation—of I knew not what.

And then—there it was, incredibly just as I remembered it. The driveway into the property was the same. And even a sign—El Gabilan. It was Sunday and there was a stillness that intensified the other-worldly sensations I was experiencing. It could have been yesterday that I walked down that road, with the motel-like building where we stayed still there, and the big barn. The only new structure I saw was an additional barn, which did nothing to change the effect of the panorama there in that valley.

It was like watching a movie which has been stopped and the scene frozen. Not a moving thing was in sight. Martin and I were the only ones who had been there previously and the others stayed in the car. He and I started to walk down the driveway, and halfway down I felt myself halted by his hand on my arm. "I think that's far enough," that wise man said. There was a hypnotic compulsion to go farther but I knew we had to stop, which we did, just standing there in an all-pervasive, thickly palpable silence. Then we slowly retraced our steps, I took a last look at the unbelievable scene, and got into the car.

Martin continued, in the aforementioned service:

> All these things have significance—clearing patterns, weaving things to-gether, so that what is occurring may be properly coordinated with what is happening throughout the whole world in the continued unfoldment of our ministry. *Ministry* is a rather limiting word, when what is actually happening is vast. It has broken surface, shall we say, within the range of our experience and we cannot separate ourselves from the whole body of mankind, nor can we separate mankind from all the other life forms that inhabit this earth, nor can we separate this earth from the solar system, or the solar system from the galaxy, and so on.

The next day we stopped at Boulder Creek for a visit with Art Hemple and his group, and finally arrived at the Center in Oakland, the beautiful home of Stanley and Linda Grindstaff which easily accommodated eleven of us. At San Jose we visited David Di Grandi at the Center there. A memorable and most enjoyable visit in that city was in the home of Marjorie Spears, Uranda's first child, and her husband Joe with their three daughters—another thread from the past.

On Sunday morning, the 5th of October, Martin held a service in San Francisco at the luxurious St. Francis Hotel. The President of the United States had just been there and been shot at, fortunately missed, and shortly after our visit the Emperor of Japan arrived, with the anticipated soon return of the President. We went on to the Center, where the Shulmans lived with several others, then flew to Medford, Oregon, where we had lunch with the Samples and others in their home before continuing to the Ashland Center. Grants Pass came next, in the home of Don Bryant, with the Padgetts as servers. Eugene was the next stop, where we visited Shepherd Hoodwin, then went on to Milwaukie, a suburb of Portland, and spent a few days with Eric Dunn and his group. The Huskeys were living in that area, as was Larry Krantz.

The Sunday morning service in Portland was held in the Ramada Inn, attended by about 170 people from all over Oregon and Washington. From there we visited the Auburn Center with Dennis Brown, and landed up in Seattle where we stayed in Miriam Saar's house, beautifully cared for by the Kezlans.

Approaching the close of our trip, Martin said:

> We were in many places, centers, different settings, each one different from every other. I don't expect to see repetitions all over the place. There was a time when some tried to reproduce Sunrise Ranch, which was impossible of course. Each center has its own quality, and doubtless the needed changes will happen as the jewel emerges with greater clarity. Any environment in which you find yourself is the setting for the development of the jewel. Don't object to it, don't downgrade it, don't complain about it. Rejoice that your present setting allows you to develop the expression of the true jewel which you are in reality.

> Those who have become aware of greater significance in their fields of ministry can look back and see how the circumstances of the past were absolutely essential to the development of the jewel of the present, and how the present circumstance is absolutely essential to the development of the jewel of the future. So we move together, thankful for this setting that provides us with the opportunity for the greater emergence of our shared spiritual expression.

Back at 100 Mile House, Martin shared the events of that memorable journey. His service, on October 19, "The Setting for the Jewel," was the first held in the beautiful new Chapel. After expressing his delight and great appreciation for the new building, he spoke of the Log Chapel, setting of services since the beginning of the group,

> built many years ago by a man who, with his brother, owned the 100 Mile House, "Bridge Creek" as it was called; and he did a good job, he was a crafts-

man. It was built for a carpenter's shop and was used for other things as well, until those who were in position to reveal the jewel put in an appearance. But the Lord had prepared the setting through various ones who were quite unconscious of the fact, and in the continuing unfoldment many are in position to play a conscious part in it. Of course the setting is not merely a building but includes the entire immediate environment of those who have assumed the responsibility for revealing the jewel, which cannot be revealed without a setting.

Michael Donck spoke, in *Northern Light,* of

the last two days before the first service given in the new Chapel. They were filled with many finishing touches, culminating a fifteen-month cycle of meticulous work. In the midst of much activity, Judy Repar practiced on the organ, with occasional interruptions by Richard Van Nus testing the PA and stereo systems. Spotlights shone brightly for a trial run of the video recording system. Jay Scott and a few others were polishing the wood of the pews, the upholstering superbly done by Bill Kuykendall of Sunrise Ranch. The heating system circulated fresh air, and a final cleaning of the tall, amber glass windows let the sunshine glisten through.

Final touchup was made to the walls, painted a soft spring green, blending with the grained paneling on the stage. Doors throughout are stable, solid-core. All this reflects the loving workmanship which has produced a building worthy of serving our King, our Chapel.

That winter Marcia Marks invited me to focus a Ladies' Meeting at 100 Mile House and I used some women in the Bible as my theme. This proved to be very attractive to those present, who wished to continue. We did, in the weeks following, until we had considered the lives of most if not all of the fair sex recorded in the Book. Thus was the series *Women in the Bible* born, recorded tapes of which have been used in many places.

In late November a communal home was opened in Loveland, Colorado, with Ken Adams assuming primary responsibility. His children, Bradley and Margaret, also Barbara Cotton, Lee and Nancy Salmon, were the residents in this first Center with close proximity to Sunrise Ranch.

January of 1976 found *Integrity* editors Chris and Joy Foster of 100 Mile House on a 25-day tour entitled "World Brotherhood Here and Now," in India and Sri Lanka, accompanied by Achal Bedi and Deborah Grace (later Foreman), both of Colorado at the time. Seminars were held in Bombay, New Delhi, Calcutta and Colombo, with attendance averaging between 25 in Colombo and 60 in Bombay. Public meetings were also held in Madras and Bangalore, where 120 turned out. It was special to have Achal's parents, who came from Jamshedpur, on hand in New Delhi. There were significant contacts throughout and Chris and Achal were delighted with the increased response since their previous tour in 1975, and acknowledged the vibrant element provided by Joy and Deborah.

Chris and Joy stopped in England on their way home. They visited Chris's parents in Pevensey and shared a seminar and meeting at the Center in London. Besides Manning and Stephanie Glicksohn, they were joined by Doris Hunt, Edith Hammond, Ann Prain and her daughter Elizabeth.

At 100 Mile House, Red Coach Inn prospered, with the evolution of the "Library Lounge," which transformed a beautiful room off the lobby, without previous specific use, into a bar where friends could share a drink and cozy time in front of the spacious fireplace. It also afforded opportunity for various kinds of entertainment.

In *Northern Light*, Moira von Hartmann observed that

the businesses of our Family have emerged as an outgrowth of the Unit. From a very small point, step by step a business develops. One such is Red Coach Bakery, which we might say is in its childhood stage. The seed was in the person of Lina Luscombe [then Lucyk] who came to the Lodge in 1948 to cook for the Unit, which numbered about ten. Her kitchen was always filled with delicious aromas—and her laughter and joy. Max von Hartmann arrived in 1958 and soon was assisting her in the baking of bread. Together they worked out recipes for specialty breads, such as Sprouted Wholewheat, Wholewheat and Honey, and Cheese Bread. It was these which eventually became the base for the products sold in the bakery business. Diners in the small public dining room in the Lodge proclaimed the goodness of the bread, and many loaves were purchased. Soon the Food Center in town was selling it on weekends and Max found himself baking late into the night to produce the 120 loaves for this outlet.

In 1966 Max became manager of Red Coach Inn, and "the little loaf" became famous. He began baking the bread used in the Inn and the small loaves served at each meal. The birth of the Bakery took place in the lobby of the Inn, a small shop being provided there to accommodate the growing number of requests. Soon tourists were spreading the news far and wide. In order to fill orders now being shipped to the interior of B.C. and Vancouver, as well as producing pies and pastries for the restaurant, it now sported three qualified bakers and at times entailed twenty-four hours of baking a day. So the Red Coach Bakery was designed, and established in the new Cariboo Mall at the other end of town in July of 1974. Peter Bono became the manager and full-time baker, a new role for him which he quickly learned. Because of the quantity of items produced, machinery was employed to a greater extent, but it did not do all the work.

This year, realizing the number of campers and tourists who pull into a mall for supplies during the summer and hunting seasons, Peter redesigned the "front end" of the Bakery to make room for a quick snack service, installing twenty-two seats and a hot-food and sandwich bar. Not only is it popular with tourists but a haven in winter for town people who come in for lunch, or coffee while shopping. David Selby came from Vancouver to assist Peter, having operated health food stores there. I assist in the front end. Wendy Gilbert comes from school each day and last summer Brenda Polack from Vancouver. Many of our staff come from the town and are part of the team, enjoying the sense of family. About eighty percent of the district population pass through our doors each week, coming in once a week for groceries, and expect it to be a memorable occasion. This summer we will grow out of the childhood state and eagerly anticipate the further changes around the corner.

Dearly loved by all who knew him, Frank Protzman passed away on March 8 at the age of 92 on Sunrise Ranch, the home so cherished by him and his wife Betty. Commenting on his "family," he had said:

Ever since 1898 I have been interested in character reading, and the expression of each individual here—in contrast to what one finds elsewhere—is something like the comparison between the old-fashioned tintype and the color pictures of today.

Jim Minardi spoke of the transformation in the residence on Sunrise Ranch which had housed Uranda and his family, then later Martin and his, through the years, intended to accommodate the leader of the ministry.

The structure was dismantled just one week after word was pronounced in late November of 1975. Rick Marwood, Jim White and Geoff Tisch came to assist, and under the direction of that expert, John Summerbell, work proceeded quickly. By Christmas the foundation was in and the first floor and basement decks laid. By mid-January of 1976 the framing was completed and Geoff returned to his home at 100 Mile House. Robin McKaig arrived, joined by David Ward. Plumbing, heating and electrical wiring were finished and inspections passed; then began hanging the dry wall. With the help of many attending Class it went up fast.

En route to the South on a tour during March and April (where Martin gave services in Miami, Atlanta, Mobile, Baton Rouge and Shreveport), Martin, Lillian and I stopped at the Ranch on March 15 for three days, during which time, as Jim says:

> John Summerbell estimated they had to make about five hundred decisions about the house; it also marked the countdown. The house needed to be ready by April 15 when the Bishop returned. Ceilings textured, walls primed, painted, trim and doors hung and finished, wallpapering, cabinets, flooring, light fixtures, outlets, bathrooms, etc., all had to be done in a month. The lights burned all night many times. With the help of so many in the final weeks we were able to accomplish it. Today it is finished and landscaped inside and out. What a joy it is to see a beautiful and safe home for our Bishop. I am most thankful for the opportunity of a lifetime to help in the building of this home.

A new communal home was established at Hooker Street in Denver and occupied by Bill and Lori Fullerton, Dan and Chris Boyle, Warren Allen and Danny Schnee. On March 8th a dedication service was held, following an all-day Colorado Servers Conference. Jim and Anne Wellemeyer and Frank Reale shared a service, with fifty-eight in attendance.

In a service on Sunrise Ranch on May 9th, "The Essential Point," Martin spoke of problems.

> There is no such thing as a problem; there are creative voids, which relate to the creative process. "The earth was without form, and void; and darkness was upon the face of the deep." That is always the starting point for any creative process, and there is nothing wrong with that. If we say that at that point God was faced with a problem we have no real understanding of the situation. The creative process naturally takes care of a creative void, but if human minds get in there and interfere with what is happening, then we have a deeper void.
>
> About ten days ago a lady from the Loveland newspaper, *Reporter-Herald*, phoned and asked if I would write an article of up to five hundred words. I agreed, and finally whittled it to something over six hundred. It was well featured in the May 7th issue and sponsored by a number of local businesses, entitled "Spiritual Orientation." [Martin read the very explicit and clarifying article.]

In a service on the evening of May 16, "The Living Tabernacle," Martin referred to those Emissaries who did not live on Sunrise Ranch.

> They are just as important as those who do. Sharing with you here now are those in the field who are taking care of things out there while the servers are present at this Special Conference. We may see concentric rings of a protective hedge which enfolds, mitigating distractions as much as possible. This hedge allows for the release of radiation, because there is a sacred place

in which those responsible may handle spiritual affairs. This radiation is unhindered by the protective hedge because it is actually made possible by it—a living tabernacle.

Early in the morning of May 28 the clarion sound of chimes were heard throughout Eden Valley. Celebrating the opening of the new Dome Chapel, the clear sweet tones came from the organ chimes played by Betsy Smith and broadcast from speakers set atop the Dome. It seemed as if the hosts of heaven had come to share in a song of rejoicing that this point of culmination had been reached. Its initiation was recalled by Martin as he repeated his words spoken on August 28, 1973, to those who stood in a circle on the hill:

> Here is the site of the holy place, outlined in living flesh. We come to this hour with the dome of heaven above us. The love that has been so evident in those who have played their part in building this structure has established an atmosphere, of which we are keenly aware, and we would henceforth let the holy place be filled with the glory of the Lord as we play our parts, together with many more, in letting it be so.

On May 30th on Sunrise Ranch Martin entitled a service "This Ministry." Among other things, he referred to those who took the attitude that they don't belong in this ministry.

> This may be true in the sense that there have been some rather restricted concepts as to what this ministry really is. If it is seen as a religious denomination or sect, certainly everybody doesn't belong in that; the fact is that nobody belongs in that. But if it is seen for what it really is, all-encompassing, all-inclusive, then the fact is that everybody belongs in that ministry.

A Bible Conference was held that week of May 30 on Sunrise Ranch, after General Council and before the 1976 Summer Class. It was a rewarding experience for me to focus this time with sixty-seven dedicated people eager to present the "Story of Man" classes. Ted Black said, in *Eden Valley News:*

> Free of the delusions of human religious concept, taking her cue from the truth expressed in living word and action by Uranda and Martin, Grace has scanned the Book with open eyes of spirit and touched the hearts and minds of many with the magic of its true implications.

Martin's brother and wife, Lord and Lady Exeter of England, visited 100 Mile House for four days in July. His first visit since 1947, the sixth Marquess of Exeter told of how he had seen a moose bagged by a ranch hand where a drugstore now stands—change! It was Lady Exeter's first visit, and she was thrilled with the beauty and vastness of the countryside. David and Diana proceeded to Montreal for pre-Olympic Games meetings and sporting events. Lord Exeter was once a competitor himself, earning a gold medal for the grueling 400-meter hurdles in the 1928 Olympics in Amsterdam. In 1932 he captained the British Team at the Los Angeles Games.

Shortly after Lord and Lady Exeter's departure, Lord Exeter's daughter, Lady Angela Oswald, her husband Michael (manager of Queen Elizabeth II's stud farm) and their two children, Katherine and William, visited Martin and family at 100 Mile House. Accompanying them were Michael Oswald's brother Patrick and their mother, Mrs. Rosemarie Oswald, both from Vancouver. Michael and Lady Angela had visited previously in 1962.

On August 8th at 100 Mile House in a service entitled "Shared Action!" Martin referred to a video of Dr. Immanuel Velikovsky speaking to a group of space scientists:

> Dr. Velikovsky indeed recognized the marvels that technology has achieved, but with respect to most of the scientists who were trying to increase understanding of the origins of man, etc., through probes to the moon and Mars, while he didn't use the exact word, he implied they were boneheaded.
>
> I thank God for this man who has such a wide encompassment of various scientific disciplines, so that he has been able to blend them instead of leaving them in isolated compartments, where they mean less than nothing. Because of his orientation in spirit he himself understands. He also tries to explain why people don't understand, why there has been such violent scientific reaction to what he has offered. Human beings are afraid, and I suppose you could say there is good reason for their fear, but why stay in the state where fear is the inevitable experience? If we are living now, not hooked up to the past, all that is essential is present and there's nothing to be afraid of. Earthly factors of heredity can be relinquished so that they no longer govern in our expression, coloring and distorting it.

That summer witnessed a catastrophic flood that swept through the Big Thompson River Canyon—two miles south of Sunrise Ranch. Completely without warning, it was as if the heavens burst. A deluge rushed down the Canyon, engulfing everything in its path. Afterward an observer commented that it looked as though man had never been there; not even traces of a roadbed remained. Our Ranch property was not in its path and RimRock House and our dwellings at Gateway were not damaged, though the bridge there and the huge siphon were completely demolished. After the two years it took to rebuild the road to Estes Park, signs were placed along the Canyon: "In case of a flood, climb to safety." That was the only recourse—and those who did, then had to hang on until rescued, probably by a helicopter. It was a *big* one!

"Unit Service" was the title of a service by Martin on Sunrise Ranch on August 25, which he had invited me to share. I used a reference in a little *Science News* magazine I had picked up just before the service. There was a picture of a zoo which had just built expanded quarters for their wild animals, some of which were enjoying it. But there was one very large expanse with a rhinoceros in the middle of it. He was pacing out the size of his old, little cage, over and over, and would not go beyond it. I asked,

> What about this expansive dome and what it symbolizes? The only borders are the ones we make ourselves, and they are all imagination. Those walls aren't even there. How wonderful to move into the vastness symbolized by this beautiful building. There are no limits to it, any more than to the dome of heaven. So let's not keep acting like there are, in a little cage in the midst of not only heaven and earth but all that is beyond.

Martin continued with the service:

> We have actually moved into a broad expanse. Maybe it takes a few blinks of the eye to recognize it, but if there is a continued pacing around in the size of the old container, what is the purpose? I have been aware of the fact that many tend to have what might be called "tunnel vision." They can see what is at the end of the tunnel clearly enough, but all the related factors round about are completely ignored. There is an unfoldment of the creative cycle. We have been inclined to think it is going to unfold just as fast as we let it unfold in us. Oh, no! It is unfolding anyway. If you imagine you have endless time to let it happen, you are wrong. We come to the conclusion of something and we're either ready or not. And the readiness is based in spirit.

The first concert held in the Dome Chapel on Sunrise Ranch was on August 27th and featured not only a glorious choir, with soloists, and Betsy Smith at the organ, but a string orchestra of ten talented men and women, all under Lillian's most capable direction.

On August 29th at 100 Mile House Emily Marks completed her time of ministry on earth. Coming from Ontario in 1949 with her family, her strong, joyous and wise character was an inspiration to everyone and she was cherished, not only by her large Unit family but many residents in the surrounding area of the Village. On the evening of her passing Martin gave a service in her honor entitled "The Coming Forth of the Angel," a beautiful timeless expression later published as a booklet.

George and Joelle Emery had just returned from a journey that included South Africa, Europe and Israel, and culminated in a week seminar in England. In Israel a fund was initiated, to provide finances for their return to that land to conduct a seminar.

In March of 1975 Michael Sieradzki had arrived in Israel, and established, in the interval, a solid foundation for what was to follow. At first he stayed with his parents in their home at Herzilya, just north of Tel Aviv. In order to further his contact with people he worked on a kibbutz called Givat Chaim, meaning the "Hill of Life." He soon filled the position of work manager, coordinating activities linking permanent personnel and transient volunteers. Another of his strong contacts was a moshav (similar to a kibbutz but less structured communally), Neve Illan, where he held weekly meetings. As he said, people come to that unique country from all over the world in their search for something more. Many whom Michael contacted attended our classes, with some participating in opening groups in Europe. Judaism, Christianity and Islam all claim roots in Jerusalem and are well represented in Israel. Then there are the atheists and the materialists, plus everything in between.

Michael described George Emery's time there as magic, which also applied to the way things had been happening in Israel from the time of Michael's arrival, which provided a dynamic setting for George. At that time Michael welcomed the helpful addition of Jeff Goldstein to the center.

That year, 1976, was very full, yet gave just a hint of the abundance to appear, year after overflowing year. September 19 found Martin giving a service in Livingston Manor, New York. During our stay there, at Clear Water, accompanied by Donna Bahan and John Flood I visited Dr. and Mrs. Velikovsky at their home in Princeton, New Jersey. Being in the presence of that great man was always a thrilling and rewarding experience for me, that time being very special as I talked with him as he relaxed in a hammock after refreshments on their lawn.

The next time Martin gave an address was on the 26th in the home of Eddie and Gladys Miller in Berwick, Pennsylvania.

The tour continued to Fort Wayne, Indiana, where Stan and Meta Prather welcomed us. Martin spoke there on October 3rd, and in Minneapolis, Minnesota, on the 7th.

It was around this time that Meta Prather opened up a new era in Emissary communications from the Emissary Center in Ft. Wayne, Indiana. She generously invested in audiocassette duplicating equipment and began handling the Emissary tape mailing service. This made services and classes more accessible worldwide. Meta and her husband, Stan, and family have continued to contribute in countless ways over the years.

On December 18 Roger performed a marriage ceremony for Mack Fontenot and Leslye Trope. Attendants were Alan and Jean Hammond, Leslye's sister Adrea from New Jersey, and Bill Dice. Other members of Leslye's interesting family from Miami were present. From a Cajun background in Louisiana, Mack contributed a vital element in the realm of finance on Sunrise Ranch, as well as the entire ministry.

Dorothy de Winton paid tribute to Eddie and Gladys Miller in these words:

They hold bake- and craft-sales and in other ways raise money so that they may offer in various ways to Sunrise Ranch. One of the special times here at Christmas is the opening of the packages that come from Berwick, all sizes, neatly wrapped and tied. Over the years the supply of stainless steel cook- and bakeware for our commercial kitchen has come from them—our Hobart mixer, meat-cutting equipment, our first electric milkers for the cows and goats, silver tea service, demitasse spoons, stainless steel creamers and sugars, salt and pepper shakers, tablecloths for all our tables. You can count on opening boxes galore of paring knives, kitchen gadgets, towels, and always money for the children—and so much more. When they visit us you can see Gladys looking here and there to observe possibilities to further clothe their unbounded spirit of givingness.

30

INTO AFRICA!

January 1977 ~ March 1979

I n the 1977 issue of *Eden Valley News* George Shears said:

Here on Sunrise Ranch we set a constant example before the world in concentrating upon *giving* in word, thought and deed. The truth is simple, the One Law is simple. We shall continue setting this example, knowing that getting into harmony with the Law is the only thing that can prevent mankind from committing suicide.

Also in that issue Shareen England (later Ewing) spoke of expansion in the Office:

Over the years much growth has occurred. A small office pattern formed, in the beginning days, under the loving hand of Grace Van Duzen, with a few people working in their homes transcribing services, typing booklets, JTS, letters, handling accounting needs, and much more. A printshop was established where Jim Wellemeyer, and later others, operated the press in the wee hours of the morning, after other essential responsibilities had been attended to. Services by Lloyd Meeker (Uranda) and Martin Cecil were sent out regularly to those on the mailing list.

In 1965 the Administration Building came into form, housing all these operations under one roof. As more and more people throughout the world became interested in what was occurring in Eden Valley the mailing list increased and it became obvious a few years ago that typewriters could no longer keep up with the amount of work; neither could our small but ever faithful press. A phototypesetter was installed, along with a new Royal Zenith 20-A printing press. What a blessing!

But we haven't stopped growing yet! Now an exciting new development is happening with the advent of a computer program which will enable an easy encompassment of many areas relating to our program worldwide, as well as at home. Donna Kimble, from nearby Loveland, has offered much of her time and expertise in assisting with the training of our personnel in the computer field. Mack Fontenot and Marty Worster are proving to be invaluable in this area.

With this increased activity it became obvious that an addition to the present building was needed. Steve Short set to work at once, drafting plans for accommodation of the new equipment. Another exciting innovation is the Ranch's first venture in solar heating: Lee Salmon has installed solar panels in the roof of the new addition. The true expansion is in consciousness. As there is an ever-increasing experience of the limitless nature of life, who knows what further developments may unfold in the days ahead!

In a service at 100 Mile House on January 1, 1977, Martin expressed his appreciation for Michael Cecil and Bill Bahan, both of whom were assuming greater responsibility in handling the rapidly expanding activities of the ministry.

On the south coast of England is a small summer seaside resort called Bexhill-on-Sea. There from January 23 to 29 the first Servers Council off the North American continent was held. The stately Granville Hotel, in all its fading Victorian splendor, housed a host of stars gathered from South Africa, Ghana, Nigeria, Israel, Italy, Germany, France, Norway, Canada, the United States and England, under the focus of Michael and Nancy Cecil, assisted by Rupert and Tessa Maskell, Manning and Stephanie Glicksohn. Thirty-one people came from eleven countries. While there, announcement was received of the publishing of Martin's new book, *On Eagle's Wings*, in Britain by Fudge & Company, to be in the marketplace in May.

Following that session Rupert and Tessa Maskell, George and Joelle Emery, were scheduled to hold a one-week Class at Findhorn in Scotland, also with Lindsay Rawlings' Genesis group. Groups were forming in Europe. Fred Palmer reported from Germany; Keith and Jeltje Anderson from Amstelveen, Holland; with a rapidly increasing interchange between the various countries. Noted for her ability in the field of translating,

Agnes Mura played a vital role, teaching English and French in Heidelberg and Mannheim and translating Hungarian films into German for a national TV station. Contacts were made in Switzerland; and Allegra Rousso from Paris, mother of Maryse Barak of Johannesburg, South Africa, was a faithful participant at services—wherever they were! Preparation was under way for the eagerly anticipated visit of Michael and Nancy on February 12th. Addie van der Kooy was an active member of the group in Holland; and of course frequent visits from Manning and Stephanie Glicksohn, David and Naomi Lesser, all of England, were vital.

In January Chris and Joy Foster, with Achal Bedi and Deborah Grace, ventured for the third time into India, Pakistan and Sri Lanka, for about a month's stay. Valuable additions to their staff were Barbara Frazier of New York City and Rob Cass of California. There was a seminar at Colombo, also a rewarding visit to Pondicherry. The initial contact with the Ashram there, which numbered about two thousand, mostly Indians, was made when Sri Madhah Pandit visited Sunrise Ranch the previous year. Related to the Ashram was the World Union International (where they met one of the original members, who had corresponded with Richard Thompson). The French woman who co-founded the Ashram and Auroville with Sri Aurobindo, said, "The conditions under which men live upon earth are the result of their state of consciousness. To seek to change conditions without changing the consciousness is a vain chimera."

On Sunday, January 30, Martin delivered the first service to be held at Glen Ivy, the new Southwest Regional Center. Attended by over two hundred from California and Arizona, this dedicatory address brought to a conclusion a weekend Media Conference hosted by Glen Ivy and focused by Alan Hammond. In sunny California twenty-two conferees considered the ins and outs of media as it relates to representing the true tone. An hour east of downtown Los Angeles, Glen Ivy had been purchased by the Southwest group. A historical landmark, the resort spa had a 22-bedroom hotel, 15-bedroom chalet, several mineral jacuzzis, mud pool, saunas, swimming pool, and other facilities. John and Pam Gray still focus this beautiful, long-established spot which has offered a welcome interval of "paradise" to many a wayfarer.

The Supreme Council was the name designating a small group of people who gathered on specific occasions to work closely with Martin in considering the affairs of the ministry. There were special meetings which included others, who focused different areas of the ministry: finance, education, art, etc. The gathering, held on Sunrise Ranch for the week beginning February 3rd, numbered eleven: Martin, Lillian and I, Michael and Nancy Cecil, Bill and Donna Bahan, Roger and Dorothy de Winton, Jim and Anne Wellemeyer.

February 12th witnessed the first marriage service conducted in the Dome Chapel on

Sunrise Ranch, with Martin officiating at the wedding of Chris Jorgensen and Donna Antell.

In March two week-long special sessions were held on Sunrise Ranch, in which servers from the Midwest, East and South joined Martin, Lillian and me, Bill and Donna Bahan—days filled to the brim with rapidly unfolding and expanding developments. It was exciting to be in the midst of the gathering of the "many waters" and hear its sound, through people like Joe and June Houlton, Mark and Andrea Anderson, Bill and Betty Hudson, Tony and Ruth Murabito, John and Sara Waskom, Bill and Iris Becker, Stan and Meta Prather, George and Pat Bullied, Norman and Vicki Tweiten, Eddie and Gladys Miller, from all parts of the continent—besides those already on the scene at home.

Dr. Paul and Libby Blythe and their children, Margaret and Joe, of Snowball Corners, Ontario, emigrated to Adelaide, Australia, where Paul participated in The School of Social Studies. They provided a most effective magnet for the drawing together of people who formed groups in many places on that great continent.

On March 12 David Lynch and Nancy Mello were married on Sunrise Ranch, attended by Andrew Shier and Sarah McQuillan, with Rev. Roger de Winton officiating.

The first one-week seminar on Sunrise Ranch was held April 3-9, with thirty attending from Colorado and neighboring states. Frank Reale, Jim and Anne Wellemeyer, Peter and Tina Kafka comprised the faculty, with a staff consisting of John Weins, Don Demmy, Jeltje Anderson, Mary Miller, Shirley and John Koellen.

Muriel Oshane, whose husband William was a member of the Emissary family since 1939 and among the pioneer residents of Sunrise Ranch, passed away in Loveland on May 23. William and Muriel made their home on Sunrise Ranch for many years. Their consistency of strong support for Uranda and later Martin enhanced the background of excellence in education and experience in their various fields. After Muriel's passing William continued to make his home in Loveland, close to Sunrise Ranch.

Della Robertson passed away on July 18. Before coming to Sunrise Ranch she had worked closely with George Shears in the Huntingburg, Indiana, area.

The Sunrise Family received as a gift from the 100 Mile House Unit an Advent Projector and the accompanying six-foot diagonal screen, for use in the Dome Chapel.

Up north the Vancouver Center moved into a beautiful twenty-five-room mansion on an acre of land in the Shaughnessy area overlooking the western part of the city. On July 15 Dale and Susan Maranda and their children, Richard, Sara and Janine, along with eleven others, moved into this elegant yet practical facility, built in 1920 and bought by the Mormon Church in 1961, now in Emissary hands. There was a beautiful large room, built as a private dance hall which proved to be the perfect setting for a chapel, with carved oak walls and beams, capable of seating 120 people. There were rooms for

JTS, attunements, offices, including Edenvale Enterprises, and lovely spacious rooms for guests. Ron Polack and Dale shared the first service there on July 17, attended by 120 people—with babysitting and JTS encompassed during service!

That month Edenvale, near Vancouver, hosted its fourth one-month Class for thirty-five representatives from Holland, England, Iran, New Zealand and North America, a unique blending of language and cultures. Ron and June Polack, who had contributed to the development of the ministry in Vancouver, made their home in that Center. Later they would provide a focus at King View in Ontario, with their five children also contributing in various ways through the years: David, Brenda, Rob, Russell and Andrew.

A little farther north in British Columbia the farm in Kamloops, River Bend Orchard, was flourishing under the hands of Don and Sherry Berger, who had spent some time in the hinterland of the 100 Mile House area, raising goats—and their children, Carol, Stewart and Holly.

On August 1st Rob Southcott, with World War II surplus equipment cramped beneath the back steps of #18 at 100 Mile House Unit, and Howard Silsdorf, with portable equipment in a motel room in the San Francisco Bay area, had the long-awaited fulfilment of hearing each other's signal come crackling through the ether. From that victorious moment the Emissary ham radio venture expanded to actively include many others: Bill Fullerton, Sunrise Ranch; John King, Twin Valleys; Bob Wallace, Lake Rest; Ken Morrison, Green Pastures; Eugene Kulbeck, Rainbow Farm; John Arkley, San Jose; and Mike Grassmeuck, Medford. John King served as its on-the-air coordinator, with the network under the hand of Alan Hammond. It provided a communications service for the entire ministry. PenDell Pittman later provided a focus for this area.

The Log Chapel, the oldest building in the 100 Mile House Unit, underwent transformation that summer. "The electrical wiring was updated to fill present-day needs, sometimes requiring drilling through huge logs with a 35-inch drill bit," related Michael Donck, who worked on the project along with Ralph Fossum, Steve Wright and others, under the direction of John Summerbell.

> Indirect, fluorescent valance lighting along the side and front walls replaced the old overhead fluorescent fixtures, adding brightness to accent the contours of the log walls. The noise of the furnace was eliminated by concealing it in a sound-containing room and using special material.
>
> A larger entrance to the seating area was made by cutting back the logs to put in an archlike opening from the foyer. A new window replaced the old one; a laminated, three-inch-thick cedar door was made for the side exit, and louvered vents beside it allow fresh air to flow in. The highlight is the plush green

velvet drapes at the front and on the window. Wall-to-wall carpet was installed and seventy-one upholstered easily movable chairs replace the theater seats.

Another building that was changed was The Lodge, with provision of a private dining room for various groups, a reception desk, mail center, and a store for an already thriving project, Wholesome Foods. Marina Cecil and Helen Ames were all set as storekeepers.

Something new!—a two-week session on Sunrise Ranch for visitors. Of the eighty-seven in attendance, thirteen came from South Africa and three from New Zealand. It began on August 4 and was coordinated by James Wellemeyer. A special feeling of freedom was shared in considering the Word, reveling in gorgeous Colorado mountain scenery. A particular soaring focus was experienced in the singing of *Sunrise,* a rousing song created by John Simituk which remarkably conveys the spirit of Sunrise Ranch.

In September a one-month Class was held at Lake Rest Hotel, New York, under Lou Rotola's direction, at which Martin, Lillian and I were present. We were touring the eastern part of the continent and Martin gave a service in New York City at the Statler Hilton Hotel on September 25; at Green Pastures in Epping, New Hampshire, on October 2; and in Toronto, Ontario, at the University of Toronto on October 16.

Back at 100 Mile House in a service on October 23 entitled "The Body of the Archangel" Martin said,

> It is not a matter of trying to get this ministry or anything else fitted into the structures of human consciousness. What is necessary is that we discover what the reality is in our own experience, and to do this we have to relinquish our structures. To know the truth we have to be related to the reality in our own experience; then all that needs to be understood will be understood, and it will be very different from the structured belief or concept one has held.
>
> Because there have been those willing to be associated with this reality, something has appeared to this extent. It has not been whipped into shape somehow by the imposition of fixed beliefs, or rules and regulations, or anything else. It emerges into experience by reason of the fact that there are those who begin to relate to the reality of spirit, what has been called the sounding of the tone. Then we find ourselves sharing a new state of consciousness, and that heavenly state is reflected increasingly in the facility of earthly consciousness, so that a new heaven and a new earth appear. This is the way, the truth and the life, which we are privileged to share.

A two-month Class was held at 100 Mile House, at which Rupert and Tessa Maskell assisted. On October 28 they flew into Salisbury, Rhodesia, where they were joined by Steven and Maryse Barak, Michael Boon and Debbie Friedland from South Africa. During a weekend seminar there Deborah Grace arrived from the United States via Barbados.

On November 10 Harold and Juanita Sturgeon moved into our house on the Gateway property, culminating nine months of work of transformation. Juanita wrote, in *Eden Valley News:*

> Bill Proctor, our server in Edinburgh, Scotland, was the architect, with the actual remodeling done under the direction of Cecil Taylor, assisted by many from Sunrise.
>
> The work included stone paneling, leveled floors and straightened walls, new rooms and ceilings, banister and fireplace.

This project resulted from the decision not to undertake, in the words of Joelle Emery, their daughter, "the enormous task of building a house above the Ranch on Green Ridge, but rather to enhance 3005 Waterdale Drive which had never been completed and might be just the place Sturg and Juanita could call 'home.'"

These two great friends and servers lived in their beautiful home for fifteen years, after which they joined Joelle (divorced from George Emery) and her husband Tom Schumacher in Fort Collins. Juanita took pleasure—and still does—in visiting "homes" where the elderly reside, playing the piano and sharing her vibrant spirit with them. Her presence at the front desk in our office provided an unconditional hearty welcome for many, and Sturg's cheery "Merry Christmas" has nothing to do with the month or the day!

In mid-November the mailing department on Sunrise Ranch announced a name change for the educational branch of our program: from the Universal Institute of Applied Ontology, "Ontology mailings," to "The Emissary Opening Series," to be sent from "The Society of Emissaries," the content essentially the same but with a different format.

Colorado continued to hum with activities, with another event on the CSU (Colorado State University) campus on November 20. Speakers were Roger and Dorothy de Winton, Jim and Anne Wellemeyer, George Bullied, Ted Black, Frank Reale, Peter Kafka, and George Hanson, master of ceremonies. Included were musical entertainment and a slide show of Sunrise Ranch, other Colorado Centers and Twin Valleys.

Larry Krantz, M.D., was established in his office in the Sunburst Building, Loveland, not far from Sunrise Ranch. The generous sharing of his services with his friends in Eden Valley has continued through the years.

Walter Bahan passed away on November 25, after eighteen busy years of service in the ministry. Based at Green Pastures Estate in Epping, New Hampshire, his area included five New England states. His brother Bill conducted a service in the Chapel on November 27, with 180 packed within its walls. Walter, with his wife Joan and their three children, Sally, Web and April, provided a true atmosphere of home in that beautiful spot.

In a different part of the world Leonard Polack, another dear friend, died on December 21st. With his wife Irene and three sons, Len had moved from Ontario to 100 Mile House in 1968 where he managed a store in town, Pioneer Development. He became very active in community organizations and contributed substantially to the spirit and atmosphere of that place in the "Cariboo." Ross Marks conducted a service in the Emissary Chapel, with the opening devotion by Len's brother Ron. It was attended by 120 friends.

On December 15 the computer world announced its presence on Sunrise Ranch in the form of a Data General CS/40 Computer. With a 64K memory capacity, it was expandable to 512K memory; in other words open-ended to serve our needs for years to come. It had four CRTs, a printer, and was connected to a Graphic Systems IV Photo-typesetter. This would allow much to take form, the *Third Sacred School* volumes being a vital one. It acquired the name F.R.E.D.—Friendly Ranch Electronic Digital (computer). Marty Worster was the head programmer and Sandy Baran resident fix-it man. FRED's little "beeps" became a familiar addition in the atmosphere of the Administration Building and it did indeed prove to be a valuable friend.

Martin commented, in a service entitled "Unification Through Focalization" at 100 Mile House on January 15, 1978:

> Handling situations in a mature manner is not requiring other people to do what one thinks they should be doing, and providing what one thinks one needs for oneself; that's childishness. Maturity is to be in position to handle any situation, including that of focalization, rightly; and that requires the right spirit, the right attitude. Certainly that would not be apparent if one said, "Oh, I'll do it," giving the obvious impression that one would rather not do it. No. We accept the point of orientation in one spirit, so that it becomes one's own. Then you won't require the situation to be some certain way; you'll simply handle it the way it is but in that one spirit. And then we stop judging each other, stop trying to make each other conform to some human concept. Allowing things to be the way they are, we bring to bear this creative expression of spirit into the situation.
>
> For the most part, what you see coming back to you is simply a natural result of what is going out from you. Anyone functioning from the standpoint of a judging human ego can never see another clearly. His own judgments come bouncing back to him. "Oh, I know it's this way," he says. It just seems that way to him. There are those who describe others to me and how they look to them. They don't look that way to me at all.

A week later, at the beginning of his service on January 22 entitled "The Hand of the

Lord," Martin shared news of some current activities:

> Michael and Nancy have initiated a two-week class at St. Albans, north of London in England, with forty or fifty attending, principally from a number of European countries. The two-week class in South Africa has now been completed and Ron and June Polack are journeying north toward Durban, speaking in various places as they go. Chris and Joy Foster and party are at the Sri Aurobindo Ashram at Pondicherry, India, having finished the week seminar at Bangalore last week. Closer to home, Bill and Donna Bahan are in Atlanta, Georgia, with Jim and Anne Wellemeyer. We may note that there is a touching into the consciousness of mankind on four continents: Europe, Africa, Asia and America.

> The Lord begins to rest His hand upon the world in a more particular sense. Of course He has never been absent from the world but such contact as has been present has been at a subconscious level, comparable to children playing their games in the automobile while it moves along the highway. The highway is not recognized; objects outside the car are not seen. Using this analogy, of course it does not mean that there is no highway or objects outside. It merely means that the consciousness of the children is totally occupied with what is going on in their immediate games. Our concern is with the movement of the car along the highway, the secondary is that the children's games should not become too obstreperous so as to jeopardize the automobile.

Wonderful things were occurring at the southernmost tip of the mighty continent of Africa. In Cape Town a beautiful hotel, the Hohenort, meaning "High Place," was in our hands, operated by Michael Boon and Valerie Morris, with Mia Euvrard, Myndy Itzigsohn and Vicki Edwards in the "hot seat," the kitchen, anticipating the arrival of Max von Hartmann in October to add finishing touches. An extensive staff was rapidly forming, with Renee Fouchee, Debbie Friedland, Dave Ellinger, Graham Laurie, Charlotte Euvrard, Joan Laurie, Peggy and John Norton. Negotiations were under way to buy the house next door to provide a home for Rupert and Tessa Maskell, core figures in that part of the world. It was declared that "All hotel staff should rightly be able to speak both English and Afrikaans." A few "native" workers were still there, such as Benjamin, headwaiter, his wife Dolores, housekeeper, and in Tessa's words, "our lovely Xhosa man, Moses," who worked in agreement with Peggy Norton in the garden.

This all came about because, after Rupert and Tessa returned from Council the previous year, it became apparent that the greatly appreciated facility at Helenasvlei farm was no longer capable of providing adequately for further classes and seminars, as municipal regulations prevented the addition of buildings on that property. The Hohenort

Hotel, a one-time family mansion in the heart of Constantia, one of Cape Town's loveliest suburbs, appeared in our orbit, and Rupert signed a ten-year lease with option to purchase. The farm was soon sold and business began in earnest at the Hohenort. Its twenty-five bedrooms and separate staff quarters provided a perfect setting for classes, the first held June 17-23. Assisting Rupert and Tessa with that class were Bill Comer, Liz Horner, Judy Wurtzel, Neill and Mary Ovenstone and Michael Boon.

Sunrise Ranch provided the setting, February 9-11, for the first Healing Arts Seminar. Coordinated by Dr. Larry Krantz, Dr. Bill Bahan, Rev. Jim Wellemeyer and Rev. Roger de Winton, the areas of medical service, chiropractic, dentistry (Dr. Michael Iacoboni), psychology/psychiatry, nutrition and attunement service were directly represented by some forty participants from throughout North America. Larry Krantz, editor of *Healing Currents*, the health-oriented newsletter, introduced the developing area of patients' classes. These professionals brought a clarity and unity to this vital field of healing, and what was achieved reached far beyond those immediately involved.

Supreme Council met February 22-28 on Sunrise Ranch.

Shortly after this, on March 3rd, a journey was begun which transported the ministry in a specific way to far places. It marked the departure of Martin, accompanied by Lillian and me, Bill and Donna Bahan, also Eddie and Gladys Miller, from New York, with Cape Town, South Africa, the first destination. Rupert and Tessa Maskell accompanied us on the journey in Africa and provided invaluable guidance and assistance. Of paramount importance, this venture introduced a decade of travel which transported Martin to many places around the globe, offering those in "foreign" countries the priceless opportunity to hear the truth which found beautiful and meticulous form through his lips—and living. We witnessed the birth of groups under the magnetic influence of his presence, and its galvanizing effect on those already established.

We stayed (all of us) for eight days in the lovely home of Neill and Mary Ovenstone in Constantia, with Table Mountain in full view (on occasion with its "tablecloth," the name given to a thick cloud layer which often covers its surface).

There was a capable and loving staff of ladies who cared for our every need: Glennifer Gllespie, Peggy Norton, Mynda Itzigsohn, Mia Euvrard, and others. There was tennis and swimming—and teas!

We shared memorable experiences, such as a glorious summer day's cruise on the Ovenstone family's luxurious tuna-fishing boat, *Marauder*, along the Cape peninsula's spectacular coastline. Martin thoroughly enjoyed taking the wheel, at the invitation of Doug, father of that most hospitable and caring family. Neill's sister Rosalind organized, among other things, a trip to their family's huge game farm, High Noon. What a thrill to have a giraffe pass right by the car window and look inside—at me!

Our visit to Cape Town was highlighted on Sunday morning, March 12, by Martin's service at the Athenaeum, with over three hundred in attendance. In his introduction Rupert noted the significance of sharing Martin's first service in the southern hemisphere, and also the fact that "it was seven years ago that the Emissary ministry was initiated in South Africa and this seems a most wonderful culmination of that cycle." Martin referred to "what we might call heart involvement on the part of these [African] people" and the specific opportunity therefore of relating to that aspect in people throughout the earth. The following day a specially invited group enjoyed further time with Martin.

From that exquisite part of the world we flew to Port Elizabeth, about 450 miles east, where a group had begun to form. We stayed at John Rushmere's family hotel and enjoyed dinner at the home of John and Shirley, afterward joined by others of the group. The next morning we took off for Durban, in Natal, arriving in time for lunch. Met by Bingo and Joan Cramb and others, much of our traveling time there was spent in a small bus, called a "kombi." We were ensconced in the Tongaat Beach Hotel, on a rocky coastline about twenty miles north of Durban. While there we enjoyed a tour of the huge sugar estate which had been the home of Rupert's mother's family for several generations.

It was thrilling to be spectators at a dance by natives in their familiar setting, Zululand, and rejoice in the extravaganza of sound, movement and vivid colors. Occasionally a special sight as we drove along was an African woman by the side of the road carrying a bundle of logs on her head.

The exotic flora of that part of the continent is breathtaking, with trees and flowers rampant with color and fragrance. Every bit as remarkable are the animals, inspiring renewed awe of the Creator—and His sense of humor! Colin and Bev Bertram, servers in Empangeni, Zululand, about 120 miles north of Durban, made arrangements for us all to spend one night at Hluhluwe, South Africa's oldest game reserve. It was a new sensation, being in close proximity to herds of rhino, buffalo, wildebeest, varieties of buck and zebras. What a sight at dawn to behold a herd of giraffe silhouetted lumbering along on the distant horizon. The night was spent in thatched cottages after a delicious braaivleis (barbecue). Phil and Sue Richardson were right in there, helping Colin and Bev.

We made it back to Durban by the weekend, where Bill Bahan gave a talk on Saturday night. The next morning, March 19, found us in Kloof, with Martin giving a service in the public library, after which the fifty in attendance gathered at the Crambs' home for lunch.

It was a short flight the next day to Johannesburg, South Africa's major city. Steve and Maryse Barak focalized the Center there, which housed the nine of us comfortably. Some of the personnel had moved elsewhere to make that possible and joined us for the evening meals, at which there were never less than two dozen seated. Martin conducted his third and last service in South Africa in a hotel there on March 22, speaking of angelic function:

> When we begin to find ourselves associated with angelic expression on earth we have no reason to be defensive, no reason to take the attitude anymore that we are surrounded by a hostile world. This is the state of affairs everywhere when human beings are identified in the realm of effects. This visible realm which surrounds us on every hand occupies so much attention that there is a tendency to completely exclude the realm of cause, which is invisible. If we are angels in fact, incarnate in human form—but also in expression—we are no longer governed by the realm of effects around us.

Our departure from South Africa was on "Good Friday," an hour's flight northwest to Bulawayo, Rhodesia's second city. It would not be long before Rhodesia (named for Cecil Rhodes) would be changed to Zimbabwe. There Rod and Joan Williams held a strong point of representation for the ministry; the contact appeared nine months before through George and Joelle Emery. We stayed at the Holiday Inn and dined with Rod and Joan at their home where we were joined by about twenty-four friends.

The next evening we flew to Salisbury where we stayed in a beautiful hotel, accompanied in that city by Joan Williams, Bill Comer, Dr. Rowley and Dawn Glieman and some others. Martin's service there was on Easter morning, March 26, in which he spoke of "something occurring of political significance" and of the need to be "much more concerned with what is back of that surface appearance, whether in relation to Rhodesia or to any other part of the world, or indeed the world as a whole." It was a beautiful and potent culmination of that cycle in southern Africa.

This was my first trip "overseas" and I found that just the act of crossing an ocean changed much in my consciousness. There were incidents strange to all of us from North America, such as the searching of the ladies' purses when we left and reentered the hotel (in Rhodesia). Also, on one occasion in the lobby as we were on our way out, everyone was told to get back against the walls. A suitcase had been left in the middle of the floor, unattached to a human being, and until its contents were ascertained as being harmless we were quite still!

Having bid a profoundly appreciative good-bye to Rupert and Tessa in Salisbury, we landed at London's Heathrow Airport around noon on March 28. Manning Glicksohn and Peter Garrett delivered the Bahans and Millers to Serena Newby's accommodation in Kensington, while Martin, Lillian and I were chauffeured to Burghley House in the family Rolls Royce. This part of the trip was a great adventure in my life and I have always felt that it revealed the depth of generosity in Martin as he freely shared his life and family.

That was a treasured time, to stay in the palace built by William Burghley centuries before, in the room which Edna, the housekeeper, proudly informed me was where Prince Philip slept when he visited. I lived in another world for a few precious days, enveloped in the atmosphere into which Martin had been born and lived with his remarkable family. It was most enjoyable to relax into the warm welcome of the Marquess and Marchioness, David and Diana; to tour the rooms where Queen Victoria, Queen Elizabeth and other royalty had slept; to stand in hushed awe in the exquisite chapel.

On March 30 we traveled by train to London and settled in at the Kensington apartment, which would subsequently provide the base for future visits to that city. It was exciting to look out the window and see the Kensington Palace just across the way! In London's largest hotel, the Penta, on Saturday evening, April 1, Bill Bahan spoke to an audience of 175. Afterward a tea was held at the London Center for about forty visiting European Emissaries, which afforded an opportunity to meet them in person. The next day, Sunday the 2nd, Martin spoke in the same room at the hotel to a gathering of 115 which well represented Britain and Europe:

> The principal purpose of this journey, one might say, was to bring a greater sense of unification to all concerned. Our effectiveness is based in the fact that we are one. While geographical distances may be great, there is just one spirit, which we all know. And we are here to allow that one spirit to initiate a creative process which is unique.

We thoroughly enjoyed sight-seeing and shopping, also an Agatha Christie play on Monday evening and lunch on Tuesday at the home of Don and Anna Factor by the Thames in Chelsea.

Wednesday, April 5th, was departure day, with the Bahans and Millers leaving in the morning for New York and we three for Chicago in the afternoon. Back at Sunrise Ranch Martin gave a service on April 9th:

> Obviously a specific creative cycle has unfolded during this period and I am sure all of you, besides many others on this continent, have felt a closeness with respect to that. There was indeed a consciousness of your participation in it.

A monstrous snowfall in May went down in the history of Sunrise as the *big* one! Wrote Jim Minardi in *Eden Valley News*:

> All three electrical phase lines went dead by midnight Friday. Wet and heavy, the snow took its toll on power lines, trees and roofs. Around the clock, shaking trees and shoveling roofs saved much property. Morning brought more than three feet of snow. The big Ford 5200 tractor plowed through to tow the generator up from its berth at the Ranch House. Shortly it was hooked up to

the water plant, where we started purifying and pumping twenty-six gallons of water a minute. Shifts were set up among Stan Waldron, Bruce Rogers and me to monitor it. By midnight the tank was filled and we rested.

By 11 a.m. the next morning the snow had stopped and all was set for Sunday morning service in the dining hall. That good old GMC Army generator came through again. When I first saw this eyesore in 1973 I asked myself if it would really work. However with me on the engine and Lyle Davis on the generator we had the thing ready in no time (if you consider three months no time!). By four on Sunday afternoon the power was restored. Heat! Joy! We can bring the goldfish back in from the gas space heater, drink the watery ice cream and clean out the refrigerators. Looking like a gray moth-balled battleship, the generator lies still in its slip of green weeds. Will she be needed again? Maybe not, but she's ready to go at the flip of a switch!

[Martin's Sunday evening service in the dining hall was imbued with the magic glow of oil-lamp and candlelight.]

Nancy Lynch added her word:

It was interesting to have a snowstorm of the heaviest sort here in May. Its size and severity took us by surprise. As hours of moisture-filled snow fell on our ready-to-bloom valley and the electrical power (which provides most of our water supply) went out, the real power came on.

Here at the farm things changed fast. Animals were confused and chilly. Milking had to be done by hand, and lights needed to be provided for new brooding turkeys and layer hens, tiny chicks too. There were roofs to shovel and trees shaken. Most important of all, there was thanks to be given for this unusual circumstance. As 3 a.m. approached and soggy men gathered in our tiny kitchen to savor hot chocolate and friendship, a sweet essence was shared. The power of agreement experienced by people who love and serve the Lord is surely the greatest power of all.

Bob Ewing, artist and veteran of the Vietnam War, and Shareen England were married on July 6. In 1979 a son Kyle was born to them. Shareen's eleven-year-old son Lance completed the picture, and this family has provided an integral and cherished element on Sunrise Ranch.

That summer, reflecting on the sustained expansion of business in the WaterWheel Gallery, Bob Ewing surveyed the scene:

Martha Miller and I sell the art. Mack Fontenot, accountant and business advisor, enfolds all in his careful way. Conrad ffrench, prestigious "Renaissance" man and artist of great depth, is most prolific in capturing the integrity and rhythm of his world. Michael Gress, a flowing watercolorist whose controlled emotions capture the subtle essences of beauty, paints luminous settings. The beautiful, sleek and very Scandinavian Design jewelry by Kari Bye of Norway graces our display cases. David Ward's belt buckles reveal true precision of craftmanship. I blend among these talented artists, managing the Gallery, which includes board meetings, sales, public relations, business connections in the Estes Park community, and painting. My paintings of late are of mountain landscapes, depicting the drama of the Rocky Mountain peaks.

Other artists presently showing at WaterWheel Gallery are Bill Talkington [his remarkable sculpture includes a rare depiction of animals native to Africa, of native Americans, animal and human, and much more], Shirley Beers, Frank Brown, Pat Howe, Larry Brown, Ellen Milan and Gael Wallace. Shirley Beers, from Dallas, Texas, spent three weeks doing her expert work in portraiture in the Gallery during our peak July traffic.

Each summer several million tourists pass through Estes Park. Michael Gress takes our artwork to shows across the land during the winter months and, with Conrad, director of the RimRock School of Art, conducts classes. The spirit of agreement permeates this art movement. Recently Conrad, Mike and I painted a scene together, depicting a range rider nobly trotting through the ponderosa valleys of the High Country, symbolic of our agreement in fulfilling the singular vision of the Lord through this provision.

Eager students were attending classes at the RimRock School of Art at RimRock House, with a workshop the first week of October at Elkhorn Lodge in Estes Park, at which twenty-three participated. Conrad offered lessons in drawing and Michael in watercolor. It was a special time, with the powerful sound and sight of the falls, surrounded by the glorious handiwork of the greatest Artist of them all.

A unique event was recorded in *Eden Valley News* by PenDell Pittman and Diana de Winton:

On August 5 the Dome Chapel proved the perfect setting for the weeks of precise rehearsal time spent with the Sunrise Unit choir during the spring and early summer. Fourteen hymns had been chosen from our hymnal, *Songs of Praise and Thanksgiving,* and Diana and PenDell had the expert assistance of Michael Wayman, Jean Hammond and diction coach Ann Foorman. Singers from the summer Advanced Session joined the choir, forming a recording ensemble of forty-five voices.

Bill Dice and Sandy Baran spent many hours regulating the organ, which enabled Betsy Smith, our accompanist, to choose the proper tonal settings needed for each hymn. Engineers Bruce Brunson of Radiant Star Recording Studios in Loveland and Rob Cass, of Santa Barbara, California, spent time considering the "sound" of the dome as it would be heard on record, and then placed the seven mikes around the dome appropriately. In the days following the recording session Bruce and Rob, with producer PenDell, would spend sixteen hours performing the "mixdowns." This process involved blending the sound of the seven audio channels into a stereo rendition of the original sound as heard in the dome.

"Tape rolling." In the keenness of that moment before the first downbeat— dome silent, choir poised, baton lifted—how could we take time to marvel at the events that had brought us to this point? Later we would pause to appreciate the substance that filled the dome by reason of twenty-three years of musical participation by many musicians under Lillian's hand. Later we would appreciate the fact of the abundant sound of the Lord's music on earth. Certainly it grows ever more powerful, having had its beginning with a few in a choir on Sunrise Ranch many years ago, then the composition of hymns, the publication of our hymnal, and now the release of the Lord's music "on record."

Wednesday, August 23d, was a beautiful day, and under a brilliant double rainbow the "Spirit of Sunrise" landed at the Fort Collins-Loveland Airport. Eleven members of the Supreme Council (having just completed a session on the Ranch) were there to greet the beautiful airplane and its pilot Charley Kitchens. The cream-colored twin-engine Cessna 421 seated eight people and had an average cruising speed of 250 mph, at an altitude of 20-25,000 feet. Passengers could relax in the comfort of its pressurized cabin, complete with stereo headphones, tables, bathroom facility and refreshment center.

Charley and his wife Asti, the perfect hostess on the plane, lived at Sunrise Ranch. Toby Taylor, a licensed mechanic who resided at the Loveland Center was responsible for maintenance of the plane. Charley, a widely experienced and most capable pilot, said:

The acquisition of this aircraft is the result first of the agreement and secondly the groundwork of many people over the past year or so, visible proof of the working of agreement. Its purpose is to transport members of the church on ministry business. The primary purpose of this aircraft is to bring the living Word wherever it needs to go.

Forms for scheduling flights were given to servers at General Council, then in session, an annual gathering eagerly anticipated by Servers from all over the world, highlighting a year of faithful day-in and day-out service to God and fellowman.

At that Council's close, in a service on September 11 Martin drew attention to the fact that this ministry was initiated in 1932, much having occurred since.

> There were occasions when everything seemed to disintegrate and there appeared to be nothing much left; but obviously the disintegration was not complete or we wouldn't be here this evening. In other words there is evidence of a compulsion of spirit which is moving, in spite of the shenanigans of those associated with the movement. If there is so much evidence of the capacity of this power to achieve what has thus far been achieved in spite of the resistance, the murmuring, the objection, all the judgments indulged in by virtually everyone, how irresistible it must be! It is for us to be aligned with the force that is irresistible.

On September 28, Martin, Lillian and I left Sunrise on a tour of the West Coast, traveling in the Spirit of Sunrise, with pilot Charley Kitchens and hostess Asti. Our first stop was Glendale, Arizona, with an overnight stay in the home of John and Carol Amey and visits to the other Centers in the Phoenix area. Then on to Glen Ivy, where we landed at the Riverside Airport. Martin spoke on Sunday, October 1, to a gathering of 294. On October 4 we went to the Auburn Center where Rick and Karen Toal had a gathering waiting, and a refreshing repast, before continuing the flight to Oakland, where we stayed in the home of Stan and Linda Grindstaff, and shared with many there. There was a uniquely arranged dinner in a hotel which went by the name, "His Lordship."

The flight from Oakland to Portland on October 6 took us to Still Meadow Farm. On Sunday the 8th Martin gave a service at the Red Lion Inn which was attended by over two hundred. Via a telephone connection, over a hundred more listened in Vancouver, which included the Class at Edenvale. October 9 saw the flight of "Spirit of Sunrise" from Portland to Abbotsford, B.C., where the Edenvale Class was at the airport and greetings were happily exchanged. Then on to the "108" airport and home to the Hundred.

King View in Toronto was the scene of a gathering on October 25 of thirty-six "Spiritual Leaders," in the fields of business, health and education, with a faculty, led by Alan Hammond, including Bill and Lois Porter, Lindsay Rawlings, Jeffrey Newman, Paul Price, Robin Newman and Tom Cooper.

A Wholistic Education Seminar was held on October 28 and 29 in Toronto with 150 teachers eager to acknowledge their common denominator and accept increased responsibility. John Waskom journeyed from Louisiana to join Alan Hammond and the group and share his magic in the world of spirals, rhythms and patterns that reveal the design

of life in all creation. Bill Porter, Tom Cooper, Jeffrey Newman, Barbara Coffman, Anne
Gagnon and David Pasikov shared the podium, and there was a delightful interlude of
music and mime provided by Rod Conway, Donald Harvey and Barbara Young, accompanied by David McMorrow and Richard Heinberg.

Dr. George Shears passed away on Sunrise Ranch on a Sunday evening, November
12, after eighty-eight fruitful years. George had pitched for the New York Yankees as a
young man and gave up baseball after a back injury. He entered Palmer College of
Chiropractic. Responsible for many becoming chiropractors, or practitioners in one of
the other healing arts, he provided a shining example in his unwavering dedication. He
treasured the last nine years in his home at Sunrise, which he constantly referred to as
the "headquarters of the kingdom of heaven on earth"—and meant it.

In a service at 100 Mile House, less than two hours after George left, Martin paid
tribute to him:

> He was a prince of the kingdom, a man of stature, not merely referring to
> his considerable height in the physical sense but to a spiritual stature. Years
> ago there was a particular occasion when Uranda was under considerable pres-
> sure, and George was the one to stand with him in that situation. He was in
> agreement with the Lord and those who have represented the Lord over the
> years. I am deeply thankful for George and for what he has provided on Sun-
> rise Ranch. Here was a particular focus of that spirit which we are all begin-
> ning to know with increasing clarity.

George could be seen making his rounds with his lawn mower almost to the day of
his departure and was heard once to comment, in his slow voice which seemed to arise
from the depths of his being: "If anybody ever finds my body, I want to be the first to
know." The twinkle was always in his eye, the humor bubbling forth.

Richard and Barbara Dash provided a radiant point of centering for a group in Israel
for many years. They moved to that unique place on this planet which has focused in
microcosm what has occurred throughout the ages in the whole world.

Two children were born to them, a son Immanuel and daughter Talya. The consistent and selfless service of this family has been a blessing beyond measure, in and through
that land to all people everywhere.

Newslight reported that the Israel family had moved into a new center, twenty minutes north of central Jerusalem, an Arabic hotel called the Samiramis. They occupied the
top two floors of the three-story structure and had held their first seminar in June, with
twenty-two students. Lee Salmon and Deborah Grace from Sunrise joined them, also
Manning Glicksohn from London. On the faculty were Richard and Barbara Dash,

Michael Sieradzki, Don Milan and Jeff Goldstein, with others visiting. A total of forty people shared the week.

Special appreciation was voiced in *Newslight* from Twin Valleys for two families: David and Dianne Pasikov with son Michael; and Fred and Irene Scott with their three daughters, Dorothy and Diane in other Centers and the youngest, Cindy, with her parents.

A cross-continent trip in the *Spirit of Sunrise* piloted by Charley Kitchens began with departure from 100 Mile House on February 22, 1979, with passengers Martin, Lillian, Helen Meeker and me. After a few days at Sunrise Ranch the first overnight stop was at the new Center in Shreveport, Louisiana, with Frank and Dot Moore. The next day we were met at the Ft. Lauderdale airport by Allan and Betty Romaner in whose North Miami home we stayed for seven great days. Also at the airport were Bill and Donna Bahan from Boston, and Ken and Ronnie Lim from Baton Rouge, all of whom accompanied us on the tour of the South. The Lims' car provided easy travel for local trips, with luggage, etc. Brian and Leslie Lanes contributed much to the care and comfort of the entire group and shared their home with the Bahans and Lims. Martin gave services in Miami, Atlanta, Baton Rouge and Dallas, each preceded the evening before by public lectures by Bill and Ken.

Our stay in the Miami area included a trip to the Florida Keys, a day at an air race show in Homestead, and a flight to Freeport, Grand Bahama Island, just sixty miles east of the Florida coast. I enjoyed the contact there with some native people and was impressed by the bluest water I had ever seen. A patio supper at the Miami Center was a great way to meet many people. Helen and Charley spoke to the Miami group at their regular weekly meeting at Parkway General Hospital. There were many opportunities for swimming and tennis, and the entire time was a welcome change for those from the cold North!

On March 7 we flew to Atlanta where we were accommodated at the Center by Jim and Jane Gensheimer and the group there which included Jim's mother, Betty. The public meeting and service were held at the Hyatt Regency Hotel downtown. We enjoyed a tour of Life Chiropractic College by Dr. Joe Maynard, assistant to the president, Dr. Sid Williams, which was followed by a visit to the Center in Marietta.

The next overnight stop was Baton Rouge, Louisiana. On that flight we met up with a "front," a wall of changing weather which pilots avoid if possible. We left Atlanta at 11 a.m. Saturday, and after a stop at Mobile, Alabama, took off again, found ourselves in a thunderstorm and landed at the New Orleans airport in a downpour. We drove a rented car ninety miles through torrential rain to Baton Rouge—just in time for dinner. Charley went to New Orleans the next day to get the plane, to the delight of some of the Baton

Rouge family, who flew with him. The meeting and service were at the Capitol House, a hotel overlooking the Mississippi River. We stayed in the home of Mark and Andrea Anderson, one of the three Centers in that city.

The next stop was Edgewater Acres in Natchitoches, Louisiana, where the Eastern Area Coordinators meeting was scheduled. Attending were Bill and Lois Porter from King View Farm, Bill and Iris Becker from Green Pastures, Lou and Bridie Rotola from New York, Ken and Ronnie Lim from Baton Rouge, and Hugh and Christine St. Onge from Rainbow Farm. The beautiful forty-four-acre farm, with hosts John and Sara Waskom, provided a most fitting and unique setting for our sessions.

March 14 marked the final stop, at Dallas, Texas, where we all stayed at the Center, home of Irv and Mary Shepherd. The Lowes Anatole Hotel in the heart of Dallas hosted the meeting and service, with about two hundred in attendance.

The trip on March 16 was different! It was a demonstration flight in a Cessna Executive Jet, Citation II, which deposited us after two thrilling hours in time for lunch back home on Sunrise Ranch. It was a fitting symbol of the ending of one cycle as another began. And "it was good."

31

CONQUEST!

July 1979 ~ December 1980

*M*artin spoke, in a service on Sunrise Ranch on July 15 entitled "Absolute Trust in Absolute Spirit," of the Dome Chapel as quite a prominent feature in this valley, both from the ground and from the air. Its geographical positioning may have some significance. I doubt if it is at the actual center of gravity for the land mass of the North American continent! But here is the location in a particular sense of the spiritual center of gravity for the world. Making that statement doesn't prove anything and I have no doubt there would be those who might dispute the point, but from the standpoint of our vision and outlook this is properly the case because we ourselves have assumed a certain spiritual responsibility. If I speak of a spiritual focus for the world I do so simply to emphasize a responsibility which must be accepted by some human beings on earth. By reason of the fact that we have a certain vision in this regard, then we can only assume that we are the ones.

A service by Martin on Sunrise Ranch two weeks later was entitled "Right Use of Existing Forms" and shed light on some vital areas.

Some of the leaders of various cults have not thought that I was much good because I didn't indulge in a lot of mysticism. My approach was: "Is it practical? Does it work? Is it good common sense?" That's not mystical enough for many. But mysticism is mostly a cover-up for ineptitude. The person doesn't dare come out from behind the mysticism because he would be found to be so hopeless and helpless. We don't need mysticism to cover up the truth. True mysticism is the expression of spirit in living. As I say, that also might be seen in terms of the practical, down-to-earth way of handling things at all levels, not just the physical. We need to be as proficient as is necessary at that level certainly, but there are also many other levels where we need to be proficient if we are to handle people who function on those levels.

On the 5th of August Martin's service, "Implications," opened with a word about being on time.

Year by year I have given many services, spoken to many gatherings, provided what was needful at classes and assemblies. I do not remember ever being late. I know there have been some occasions when I arrived somewhere, after driving, just on the dot. Last evening John Waskom was talking about credentials; perhaps this might be seen as one of my credentials!

If I have been on time all these years I suppose I must have thought it was important. Perhaps something is portrayed here relating to the matter of being where one should be when one should be. If one has developed a habit of being on time, then here is part of a foundation which will prove to be very valuable in being in place when you are not consciously trying to keep an appointment. Obviously in each moment we need to be on hand; we need to be where we should be.

In August there was a four-day seminar in Ghana, composed of those who had been in close contact with the ministry for years, with seven from Nigeria. Present were Rupert Maskell, Keith Anderson, and Odim and Georgina Mkpa. Five people, including Hardy-Francis and Grace Akuamoah, formed the nucleus of the Emissary Center in Accra, with almost a hundred people on the EDL and Opening Series mailing lists. Hardy-Francis and Grace were anticipating attending a Class.

In the October *Newslight* of that year Marina wrote:

Recently a whirlwind tour of the burgeoning Midwest was taken by Martin, Lillian, Grace and Marina. We took off from Loveland on September 11 in the *Spirit of Sunrise,* with our friend and pilot Charley Kitchens, for a gorgeous flight to Kansas City. There we were met by our hosts, Bob and Judy

Hollis, and the rest of our entourage, Bill and Donna Bahan and Hugh and Christine St. Onge. We enjoyed swimming, boating and tennis at Charles and Beverly Rensenhouse's beautiful home on Lake Quivira, followed by a lovely dinner. Also present were Sharon Rensenhouse, Tim Bahan and Deborah Grace, the latter present at most of the following stops. Bob Hollis gave us a guided tour of Kansas City which included his office and farm. He and Judy hosted an open house for the group that evening.

The five of us then flew on to Milwaukee, Wisconsin, and spent a few days with Lillian's brother, Robert Johnson, his wife Mary, and their family—and a tour of Lillian's childhood stomping grounds! Next was a flight to Rainbow Farm where we met the rest of our party and spent a few relaxed days, with Hugh and Chris our welcoming hosts.

On Sunday we all drove to Fort Wayne. There Martin gave a service in the Telephone Building where Stan Prather works. Many people from many places were in attendance for this vital time together.

We were in Davenport, Iowa, on Tuesday where we had a tour of Palmer Chiropractic College. Martin had not been there for nineteen years and noted many changes. We had lunch with Dr. Crowder, friend of Bill Bahan and president of the Alumni Association. That evening Greg and Susan McDonald, along with their vibrant household, held an open house in their home, Integrity House. Our next flight included a stop in Marshalltown to visit Ercil and Maxine Beane and their family and a quick drive to Ferguson, Uranda's birthplace. We carried on to Elgin, Illinois, where Robin and Pam Reily were our caring hosts and treated us to a grand tour of downtown Chicago. Again an open house allowed us to meet and greet many friends, both old and new.

Then on to Minneapolis where George and Joelle Emery took us to our hotel. We did a little shopping in that booming city, enjoyed a dinner theater one evening, and shared time in the Emerys' home with their group. Martin and several of us took in an afternoon of sailing at the invitation of Rhoda Brooks. Bill and George spoke on Saturday evening, setting a tone for Martin's service Sunday morning. Many from near and far attended both. On Monday morning, September 24, we packed our bags again and the five of us flew to Colorado while Bill, Donna, Hugh and Chris started back across the Midwest. It was a special time, with vibrant people sharing the greater vision of life.

In a service Martin gave at Fort Wayne on September 16, the forty-seventh anniversary of the ministry, Martin related Uranda's experience of illumination, and added:

> Insofar as Uranda was concerned it was a calling to remembrance. Something that was already present, already existent, began to emerge through his consciousness and he acknowledged the fact of it. He undertook to provide spiritual leadership in this matter of calling to remembrance. We are aware that this was the task of the spirit of truth: calling all things to remembrance, things that already exist for us as individuals and for us all together, something long forgotten to emerge into consciousness in this world. Heretofore it has tended to be a matter of belief rather than knowing.
>
> Most people are trying to remember it on the basis of an intellectual idea, but it can't be remembered that way; it is lost that way. It is only remembered when it does actually emerge; then there it is! No question, no argument; nothing else is required but that particular expression in that particular moment. And when it's there you know it and it isn't a belief. There's no need to shop around. There's no need to follow out all the peculiar ideas and concepts and beliefs that people have, because this is merely piling form upon form and producing greater and greater obscurity, less and less understanding. Knowing is life. One of the first indications that was offered in this bringing to remembrance was: Let go. Let go! The knowing that is required is of the truth, and the truth is only known in expression.
>
> So here is the reason for the existence of what we call this ministry, to call something to remembrance so that those who are stirred a little bit and begin to hear something may be assisted into a larger remembering, a larger expression of life, because the actuality of this remembrance comes when the quality, the reality of life is in expression, physically, mentally, emotionally, spiritually, a total expression.

The West Chapel on Sunrise Ranch underwent further transformation, after thirty-one years of constant use. New carpeting and chairs were purchased, the walls replastered in a scalloped pattern, new wiring, video lighting, doors, ceiling speakers, evaporative cooling system and hot water heating (eliminating a noisy heater). Michael Gress designed new windows, and Bruce Rogers, a wood-working genius, made a new lectern and veneered the existing altar with walnut wood. There were plans by Hymie Jacobson for another wing to be added to the east.

The spirit in Martin found further form in:

The Angelic Proclamation

How shall man in this day restored be?

Let it be by the Word of God.
Let it be by His kingdom, by His power, to His glory.
Let no human desire remain.
Let no human doctrine be kept,
or belief sustained.
Let all human religions and temporal systems
pass from the earth,
leaving only God revealed in man restored.

This is the Word of God spoken this day
by His angels in agreement on earth:

Glory to God in the highest!

Martin gave a service in Vancouver on December 2nd on one of our many visits to that city. There were occasions, while in that vicinity, when we enjoyed an overnight stay at Harrison Hot Springs on the way home to 100 Mile House, with friends—Bill and Lois Porter, often Ron and June Polack.

In the 1980 edition of *Northern Light*, John Summerbell wrote of

a new living complex being built at 100 Mile House. There was a need for apartments for the Duffs and the Traffs, also more accommodation for visitors and classes. Michael Cecil drew a sketch of possible types and sizes of rooms, then passed it on to Andreé Vaillancourt and me and suggested we go to work on them. The result was a beautifully shaped structure, something like a butterfly with open wings. We then had to draw up floor plans, elevations, sections—always with emphasis on energy conservation. We were greatly assisted in this by Michael Donck. During our last two-month Class we had twenty-seven men available for afternoon work. During those days the building had quite a "growing" experience, and so did all of us!

In *Northern Light*, Doug Elliott reflected on the 1980 Ski Marathon, with its start and finish on our property:

The preparation was perfect...special time spent with friends. The excitement of the race built right to the start.... "It's cold, let's get going!" The confusion of the mass start—1,485 strong—changed to amazement at a shattered ski pole. Watching for frostbite was a great excuse to look in their eyes, talk, and laugh at their frost-lined beards. Steady going up, steaming and puffing, generated thanksgiving for the chance. Swiftly going down, breezing and relaxing, kindled the thrill of it all. After came the aches, the hot shower, comments to friends, a pledge to be in better shape next year—culminating in a sense of thankfulness for the activating spirit that allowed this 50 km event to be a part of the day's offering.

In "A Word of Grace" of February 21, Martin replied to a letter:

> I am sure you can easily see that this paragraph of your letter was totally confused. The question now is as to whether you love your confusion more than the clarity of the truth. Here is your choice. Here is the opportunity to let a transformation occur in yourself. You seem to wish that the transformation occur in me and this ministry. Where do you think it is most needed? In your mixed-up expression, or in the clarity being offered through this letter? It is your choice.
>
> The initial purpose of this ministry is to engender transformation and change in the consciousness of those who are on the mailing list. Be willing to let it be the way it is. Then confusion will be cleared and the truth become obvious. As you allow this to happen I am closely with you in spirit.

That year the Supreme Council held their sessions at 100 Mile House for the first time, to the delight of all concerned.

On Sunrise Ranch, May 6, Fern Meeker passed away. Her strong spirit was invaluable as she served, first with Uranda in the early days of the ministry and later for thirty years as a vital and beloved member of the Sunrise personnel.

In *Eden Valley News* of that year Ginny Hogan outlined the process whereby the dry and thirsty land became a well-watered valley. Initiating it was the well dug on our own property on January 27, 1950. Divined within a foot by Uranda, it yielded eight gallons of water per minute. In season eight other wells were drilled.

> The Northern Colorado Water Conservancy Board negotiated a contract with the United States for the construction of the Colorado Big Thompson Project, designed to bring water from the Western Slope. In 1947 the Adam's Tunnel through the mountains was completed, drawing water from the Lake Granby, Grand Lake area to Estes Park. By 1951 a series of feeder canals and reservoirs delivered water to the Cashe La Poudre River north of Fort Collins

and south to the St. Vrain near Boulder. The Charles Hansen Feeder Canal was run directly west of the Ranch and in 1952 the first water ran in ditches to irrigate our fields. In 1953 a pump was installed and sprinklers were introduced into the Valley.

That was just the beginning of the unfoldment of a creative cycle which has continued to this day. In 1953 the pond was dug as a storage reservoir, and became a home for Canada geese and mallards. In 1968 the swimming pool was built as a Class project. Soon after, underground sprinklers were introduced on the pool lawn. In the late 1970s a holding pond was excavated behind the Ranch farm operation to provide water for the livestock.

In 1978 a reservoir was constructed in the southern mouth of the Valley, holding approximately 559 acre-feet of water, to supplement the Loveland water supply. This reservoir in Green Ridge Glade has considerably changed the face of the land, supplying humidity in the air and moisture in the ground. Wildlife is in abundance and wood ducks find their home on its banks. [A representative of the Audubon Society makes periodic visits to our beautiful property, which has been designated a sanctuary for birds. She finds excited pleasure in the steadily increasing variety of birds that make their home here.] In 1979 a sluice was engineered to direct water from the Charles Hansen Feeder Canal into the reservoir. This forms a beautiful waterfall which runs between two of the houses which we recently purchased south of the Bishop's home. A waterfall in Eden Valley!

This year a new well was drilled, to a depth of 480 feet, which is yielding 17 gallons of water per minute. It is significant that this fresh flow of water has allowed us to cap all the other wells, and bring the water system under one roof—a gathering together of the waters into one river. Is it by chance that the desert blossoms like a rose? No, it is years of faithful movement with the spirit of God. It is interesting that no arbitrary effort was made on the part of anyone to produce water for domestic or irrigation purposes. It just appeared, unfolding over a period of time, in ways that were useful and esthetically beautiful. This is how the spirit of God can achieve when there are men and women allowing it to work.

[Isaiah knew. He said: "The desert shall rejoice, and blossom as the rose. It shall blossom abundantly...for in the wilderness shall waters break out, and streams in the desert. And the parched ground shall become a pool, and the thirsty land springs of water... And an highway shall be there, and a way, and it shall be called The way of holiness... And the ransomed of the Lord shall return, and come to Zion with songs and everlasting joy upon their heads: they shall obtain joy and gladness, and sorrow and sighing shall flee away." Chapter 35]

Laurence Krantz was in Medical School in New York, and had an irresistible urge for something more. He quit school in 1970, with the intention of traveling, reading spiritual literature, etc.

Following a possible leader of "new-age" thought, he set out for California. He stopped off at Greeley to visit a friend's brother, and through that connection came upon an introductory brochure of Sunrise Ranch, and drove there without delay. As with others of kindred spirit, when he entered the lane he experienced a feeling that his search was ended. He stayed there until 1972, met Jim Wellemeyer, Ted Black and others, helped build the Four-Plex, and took Class. He was ready, then, to return to Medical School and finish his course.

He had a residency for three years, 1974-77, in Oregon, with family practice training, following which he opened up a practice in Loveland. In company with Drs. Michael Iaconi and Cecil Taylor, Dr. Laurence Krantz opened the Healing Arts Clinic in Loveland in 1980. That institution flourishes to this day, with changes through the years and Dr. Krantz continuing his substantially enlarged and intensified practice. His gift of special service to the residents on Sunrise Ranch, greatly appreciated, has continued without a break.

Dr. Iaconi's practice has also been a constant in that beautiful familiar haven on the road between Sunrise Ranch and the town of Loveland.

Dr. Cecil Taylor provided wonderful chiropractic care in the Healing Arts Clinic, as well as in his makeshift office on Sunrise Ranch. Dr. Taylor also provided his expertise over many years in building construction and refurbishing on Sunrise Ranch. He and his wife, Eunice, moved to Sunrise from Atlanta, Georgia, where they had coordinated the Emissary center for many years. Eunice contributed her excellent culinary skills as Martin's cook and baker on Sunrise Ranch.

Dawn Blechman, R.N., spent many years as the registered nurse "on call" twenty-four hours a day on Sunrise Ranch. She also provided natural childbirth coaching (being present at many a birth) and was instrumental in assisting Lillian Cecil in the production of a booklet on natural childbirth, entitled *Labor of Love*. Her loving care and sense of humor has assisted many through numerous health situations. Later, Audrey LaBagh assumed the role of resident R.N., adding her special touch of love to all on Sunrise Ranch. Audrey has also assisted with the seniors living on Sunrise Ranch, and in the attunement field.

As well, numerous other health practitioners offered their services freely to the Sunrise Ranch residents, including Drs. Janet Lang, Susan Rosoff, Jack Caputo, and Jane

Anetrini; Joelle Schumacher; Lotus McElfish; Dr. Lynn Carlisle; and many others.

On the afternoon of June 5th in the 100 Mile House Chapel, Marina June Cecil and Peter Castonguay were united in marriage by the bride's father, Bishop Martin Cecil. Her brother, Michael, opened the proceedings with a prayer and reading from Isaiah; and later Lloyd Meeker proposed a toast to the bride. Sandy Castonguay, the groom's brother from Toronto, was the best man, and the matron of honor was Dorothy Hughes.

A reception was held at Martin and Lillian's home on the lawn. Music was provided by a small orchestra consisting of Ron Free, Lance Willis, Barry Oshanek and Grant Clarke, with soloist Christie McCullough. Egon Milinkovich, from Ottawa, had created an exquisite ice sculpture of two swans intertwined. The groom's parents, Mr. and Mrs. Nelson Castonguay, had come from Ottawa, and joined over 250 relatives and friends of the couple for the beautiful occasion.

In a service, "Weighed in the Balance," at 100 Mile House on June 8 Martin commented:

It may be said that every human being on the face of the earth is being weighed in the balance. It may not be so apparent as yet with the vast majority, but I think it has become clearly apparent to us in our own experience and also in our awareness of what is happening in the world as a whole.

On July 6, at 100 Mile House, in his service entitled "Heaven Is Supreme," Martin described conditions in the early days on Sunrise Ranch, which included dilapidated buildings, drought, not much food.

Presumably those who went there wished to be there more than to be anywhere else, not because they could not have been more comfortable elsewhere—that wouldn't have been difficult—but there was something in their own experience which transcended the immediate circumstances. Obviously if one were to judge the external circumstance it would be said, "This is not heaven." Human beings have a concept of what heaven would be and I'm sure that certainly wouldn't have been the concept. On the other hand, when a more luxurious, a more comfortable state puts in an external appearance, there is an inclination to mistake that for heaven, or an approach to heaven.

While I've no doubt there were complaints on occasion in those early days on Sunrise Ranch I doubt very much if there were more then than there have been since greater comfort has put in an appearance. I think the more comfort there is the more complaint there is, because the external things begin to obscure the reality of heaven.

Bill Dyer, with his wife Kaye, of Newmarket, Ontario, had been coming to Sunrise Ranch year after year since the 1950s, offering their expertise. Bill had upholstered mosquito bombers during the war and subsequently had his own business. That year he packed up his machine head and they drove the many miles to stay for several weeks, during which they upholstered seventeen pieces of furniture, further contributing to the beauty of the Sunrise home.

There were sixty-six eager participants in a Drama Conference-Workshop on Sunrise Ranch, with all areas of the United States represented, also Canada, England and Israel. A collective expression by Glennifer Gillespie, Ann Foorman and Ruth Buckingham declared:

> We all knew that each one of us had a part to play, that the areas of directing, producing, scriptwriting, acting, music, dance, video and stagecraft would blend to create the new form waiting to emerge... Miracles were achieved. We experienced a hotbed of creativity and brought forth an abundance of substance in the way of ideas and material, only a small portion of which was used or developed fully. We were all conscious of the fact that drama is living, and that what we had brought forth was simply a result of our collective experience of dwelling in the kingdom.

"Conquest!" exclaimed Suzanne Core in *Eden Valley News:*

> In both symbol and form, our brand-new 1980 Cessna Conquest Propjet exemplifies the spirit of victory as it moves with power, majesty and safety. This, the 159th Conquest to be built, is white, with red and gold trim. It will carry up to eight passengers plus the pilot. A door separates the main cabin from the aft portion which contains a flush toilet and luggage space. Forward, behind the pilot, is a refreshment center, with a stereo tape system which can be played throughout the cabin or over earphones. There are fold-down tables, and an air-cycling system that regulates heating and cooling of the pressurized cabin; oxygen is also available.
>
> It is equipped with the highest quality avionics available, has a cruising speed of 3-400 mph and flies at an altitude of 35,000 feet. It is a twin-engine plane, with a range of 2280 statute miles and could, with four people aboard, journey nonstop from Los Angeles to New York. The Conquest will fly from 100 Mile House to Sunrise Ranch in three hours and thirty minutes with eight passengers on board (adding an hour for customs stop).
>
> It is the most fuel-efficient jetpowered aircraft available and uses no more fuel per mile than the 421 did, while having greater capability and performance features, such as fast climbing, high altitude and high speed flying, plus added load capacity. Included in the purchase was flight training for pilot Charley Kitchens at Flight Safety in Wichita, Kansas, where an intensive

two weeks included simulator training prior to taking up the Conquest.

Martin spoke of the new aircraft in "Spiritual Transmutation," his service of July 20 on Sunrise Ranch:

> Back along the way there has been a creative cycle unfolding. There have been many aircraft relative to our program. After Uranda's time I drove around the sky for a period. I was trained to fly in a Piper Colt, a little putt-putt, and that was delightful I recall. I would not have undertaken it for my own pleasure. There was a need, and a Cessna 182 was acquired. Then we had a Cessna 210, which was faster, and finally the Skymaster, 337. But here was something developing beyond the fact that I myself needed to move from here to there less tediously than driving constantly. These aircraft were very useful. With increased traveling it began to get a bit wearing, with all the flying details as well as the requirements after reaching our destination. Something continued to unfold, and the 421 put in an appearance because Charley was on hand to provide the piloting of it. A relief!

> A transformation occurred from one airplane to the next, always improved operation, also safety. There was a kind of apex reached, insofar as the ministry was concerned, when the *Spirit of Sunrise* put in an appearance. It was a culmination of something that allowed easy movement. Now we are approaching the time of absoluteness from the spiritual standpoint. I would say that this aircraft is symbolic of what is happening. It is illustrative of the fact that it is necessary for whoever is capable, to function in this new space. Charley would tell you that in operating this new aircraft much of the experience gained in operating the types we had before, even the *Spirit of Sunrise,* doesn't fit. There is something totally different. Let us see this with respect to our own spiritual experience. Conquest!

Martin also used the arrival of a new organ in the Chapel, primarily for Betsy Giglio's use, to illustrate his point.

> Here is an essential part of what is unfolding at the core of our ministry. By the way, the Dome Chapel itself is an example. There was even a little resistance toward it along the way because it was an unknown structure to those who were responsible for building it. John Summerbell was praying it wouldn't be a dome. I don't know to whom he was praying, because it is a dome! He played a very vital part in letting it emerge in form, and is a special expert in this field because of it—an elliptical dome, which is rather rare I understand. [After the completion of the building, John was called on occa-

sion for consultation with experienced contractors interested in constructing such an edifice.] When we let whatever it is that should take form do so on the basis of spiritual expression it will be right. But it may take a while for this focus of spiritual expression to become sufficiently clarified, unified, for the creative process to work so that you can observe it, you can see the reflection.

The real value is not in the physical form, although that is essential, but in what is made possible by reason of the physical form and what it represents. Here is a form that is sufficiently true to the spirit that we can see that it is. "Behold, I make all things new." This is the Lord's business and it is marvelous in our eyes.

"Absolutely No Choice" was declared by Martin with great power on September 14 on Sunrise Ranch:

Lo, these many years I have represented the spirit of the Lord to this forming body, sounding the tone, that all who had ears to hear it might be moved thereby, awakening to the sound of that same tone reverberating within each one. The forming of the body is dependent upon the awakening of individuals to the tone of life sounding within themselves and not just externally.

In a sense I suppose it could be said that I have been playing a particular role in this regard, one of representation, not my own role. This was certainly required. I have had no hesitation in offering it over the years. But for me it has been something of a substitute pattern until the body awakened sufficiently to make possible the assumption of the spiritual responsibility of the Archangel on earth. When that happens, as it is happening, then I can begin to step increasingly aside in that role. The reality of what I was representing to all of you and many others comes forth through all of you and many others. As you do it I don't need to do it; but I still am myself and am released into an expression of who I am.

Some have supposed that as the new appears, the old is simply discarded. No. The truth was present in the old, just as it is present in the new. It is not a different truth; it is the same thing. So nothing that anybody really knows has changed. We have a foundation upon which we stand. It hasn't changed. It is the same today, yesterday and forever. But there is what is pressing to come forth because there is a larger facility by which this may occur.

A tour through eastern Canada and the northeastern part of the United States presented a golden opportunity to fly in the beautiful Conquest. Accompanying Martin, Lillian and me were Bill and Donna Bahan, Liddy Martin, Gail Moore and pilot Charley Kitchens. Gail wrote about the trip in *Newslight*:

Highlights of the tour through Ontario, New England and New York, with a week in each place, were the Sunday morning services, which drew more than a thousand people. On each Saturday evening there was a special dinner; also entertainment was offered through drama, music and dance.

On September 17 we flew from Loveland to Toronto, where Bill and Lois Porter drove us to King View Farm and we were joined by Eddie and Gladys Miller who traveled with us throughout. There were interesting visits with Helmut Julinot and staff at Starseed Farms, with the Pasikovs and family at Twin Valleys, with the Purdoms in Arva, and at Wells Hill with the Houltons and their group.

We flew to Ottawa on September 23 where Martin, Lillian and Grace were the guests of the Castonguays, and also attended an open house at the home of Richard and Marilyn Pfaff. The next day we flew to New Hampshire, with a stop at the Abbey St. Benoit-du-Lac in Bolton, Quebec, where we were graciously hosted by Father Chamberlain. The monks use Gregorian chanting in their services, which we were delighted to attend.

In New Hampshire Bill and Iris Becker were our hosts at Green Pastures. We enjoyed a drive along the rocky Maine coastline [lobster dinners a treat], a day in Boston, and a tour of our businesses in New Hampshire.

After a short flight to Long Island on October 1st we arrived at the home of Lou and Bridie Rotola in Garden City. There were trips into Manhattan, and a drive to Westport, Connecticut, and the Cardiff's home and San Miguel Restaurant, operated by the group there. [While in the New York area, Frank Frazier, Donna Bahan and I availed ourselves of the opportunity to spend an afternoon in Princeton, New Jersey, with Mrs. Velikovsky, our dear friend Immanuel having died recently. Richard Heinberg had gone to assist Dr. Velikovsky in his home in Princeton. Just five days later Dr. Velikovsky died suddenly, and Richard stayed to work with Mrs. Velikovsky in finishing some works already begun. Richard later moved to Sunrise Ranch, where he contributed through his writing and music. He has authored a number of books.]

On October 8 there was a refueling stop at the Quad-City Airport outside of Davenport, Iowa, where the party was greeted by Greg and Susan McDonald with a few others, and then it was home to Sunrise Ranch after a great trip in the Conquest.

Thanks to Dr. and Mrs. John Reichhardt, with other members of the Estes Park group, there were some timely renovations to the Sanctuary on Sunrise Ranch. They fitted each of the stained-glass windows into individual wood frames constructed by Will Carpenter. Clear glass exterior panes added extra protection and insulation. Another vital project was the remodeling of both the interior and exterior of the Commissary, one of the most frequently visited establishments on Sunrise Ranch. It was a year for uplifting, renewing and expanding. An attractive air lock entry building was added to the north end of the Stable Gables apartments by John Weins, Glenn Lockie and Jim Greaney.

Nick Giglio, Walter Wurst, Bill Dice and Richard Clark were instrumental in the installation of a new intercom system in the Administration Building. A gift from Walter, of Guelph, Ontario, it handled a total of twenty-four phones and was to be expanded to fill the needs of the entire Ranch in season.

A sauna was the unique Christmas gift, via Nick Giglio and Frank Reale, from the Colorado area groups.

An overseas financial tour was conducted by Mack and Leslye Fontenot beginning October 24 and ending December 20. Leslye reported that it started

> in Denver and New York, then we went to London, England, and on to South Africa. Time was spent in Johannesburg, Cape Town, Durban and Zimbabwe. In less than a week we encompassed Rome, Italy; Mannheim, Germany; Amsterdam, The Netherlands; Paris, France; and then spent the last ten days in Mickleton, England. There was a total of fifty-one hours in nine financial gatherings, with 270 people in attendance overall.

Holland was becoming active, with a weekend at the apartment of Kurt Schmidt in Eindhoven on November 15 and 16, with about twenty people from Germany, Holland and Canada. On the 22nd a church in Amstelveen was the setting for a public meeting entitled "Body, Mind and Heart," with Tienke Klein and Irene de Groof playing vital parts. There was a new development in Gorinchem, with meetings at the home of Lois Grisdale.

Beginning on November 27, regular fortnightly meetings were held in Cologne, West Germany, with mention of Annette Franke of Muelheim and Kurt Schmidt from Holland. Max von Hartmann was present for that occasion and read translations of writings from Bishop Cecil, Chris Foster, Alan Hammond and himself. He also showed slides of his visits to the Centers at 100 Mile House and Sunrise Ranch.

In December there was a festive occasion at Mickleton House where fifty-two friends gathered to welcome Lindsay and Esther Rawlings to England. The hotel was undergoing expansion—a larger garden room to enable ninety to sit comfortably theater-style. Digging the foundations was begun on December 4th with volunteer labor arriving from England and Europe.

Meanwhile at Green Pastures in New Hampshire a new home was in readiness for

Bill and Donna Bahan, also Gail Moore and her son Howard. It was named South View, "a beautiful, functional, comfortable, useful facility," in Donna's words—and her description was accurate.

As 1980 drew to a close Martin's services vibrantly sounded the tone of Truth. He entitled one on October 26 at 100 Mile House "Restoration by Unified Action," in which he referred to a song that had just been sung:

> These words, "Lord God of hosts," may be understood by you as something that is not separate from you at all. The hosts are those who compose the spiritual and flesh body of the Archangel incarnate on earth. The restoration of man comes by reason of the action of the Archangel through His body on earth. The fall and failure of man was initiated on an individual basis. The fall would never have occurred if it had remained simply an individual matter. It came to pass because others participated and agreed with those individuals who first failed. The restoration comes as it is initiated individually, but it never occurs unless there are those who associate themselves in agreement with the individuals who initiate it.

Martin reviewed the lives of great leaders in the past who initiated the plan of restoration:

> There was Abraham who found agreement in an active sense with the one called Melchizedek. This initiation of the plan continued on an individual basis through Isaac and Jacob. Through the sons of Jacob the collective opportunity began to appear, the opportunity for agreement with what had been initiated. To start with, there was not all that much agreement on the part of the sons of Jacob, but in spite of that, Joseph as an individual sustained the initiation of the cycle. He did not judge or blame his brothers but took responsibility for himself.
>
> Later there was a proliferation of the tribes of the Israelites in the land of Egypt, so that a collective body began to take form. It was not yet at all conscious of its own destiny or reason for being, until Moses, as an individual, came and proclaimed that destiny. The thirteen tribes of the Israelites were brought forth from the land of Egypt as a body, a body destined to be the hosts for the incarnation of the Archangel. We are aware that this did not occur; there was failure.
>
> Again, the plan of restoration was individually initiated by the one called Jesus. In the previous design the Lord had always been represented by certain individuals who carried the responsibility for initiating that particular opportunity. This new initiation under the hand of Jesus was not in representa-

tion but in person. The same requirement was necessary, namely that there be a collective body for the action of the Archangel. This body in its core aspects was composed of the twelve disciples...

Regardless of what human beings did to Him, love was incarnate on earth, the word of truth was spoken, and life was revealed. And there wasn't anything anyone could do to reverse that fact. It was done. Those who at the time had opportunity to share the building of the body for the incarnation of the Archangel on earth did not let it happen.

The same requirement remains now. The only way by which restoration may occur is as there is a collective body of agreement permitting the incarnation of the Archangel on earth so that the required action may be taken. It is not taken successfully by one individual; it requires the body. But if those who compose this body are pulling and hauling within the body according to their own ideas and concepts, according to the continuing patterns of their own human nature, their own fallen state, then the body will be confused: the Archangel on the one hand offering life and those who are included in the composition of that body trying to tear it apart.

I quote a few remarks from Martin's service at 100 Mile House on November 2nd:

There are two worlds. The infinitely greater world is the true world; and there is this place here in the universal whole where human beings imagine they live in a world which, in the true sense, doesn't really exist. It exists in their own minds and it operates according to the askew consciousness of human minds. They see it in this askew state as operating in a certain way. This operation is seen from different angles, one of which is called scientific, and it is assumed that the world operates in this way, and it seems to do so to the askew mind; but it is only a fantasy.

That evening he spoke on "The Way It Works":

Is it to be imagined that we have to know everything in a moment to know the truth? This is a concept in the askew state that many people have. They are going to get such enormous heads that they are going to be able to contain all this tremendous truth. The truth is indeed tremendous, but we have eternity to find that out. We're not going to experience the whole of truth in one moment. All we experience is what is needed in that moment. And that is a very simple thing; in a sense a little thing and yet it is the seed of what is to occur in the realm of events.

Martin emphasized vital points on November 9, in "The Currency of the Kingdom":

If there is a super-focus of manipulation in the body of mankind it can only exist because of the body of mankind. Individual human beings everywhere are both manipulators and manipulatees. It is only because this is so that there could be a focus for all this. Those who are low down in the body of this pyramid are inclined to blame those who are above them in the body of the pyramid, but the higher points of focus couldn't exist without having something to bring to focus. What is brought to focus is what is present in people everywhere, and so this godless pyramid has been built...

We have spoken about spiritual self-starters. Part of my task over the years, rather a wearying aspect, has been the apparent necessity of prodding people because they had not awakened to the state of being a spiritual self-starter...

Power is an individual matter. Perhaps you have looked at the forming body and said, "When this body is formed sufficiently then there will be power." How is it going to form sufficiently? Only because there are individuals who have experienced, individually speaking, the fact of that power; then they know.

Some have evaded spiritual responsibility by assuming greater material responsibility; but you can't handle material responsibility as it should be handled until you have first assumed spiritual responsibility. That relates to passing through the tests. We don't demand that someone else make our stony hearts into the bread of life. We accept the responsibility for handling it ourselves. How? By every word that proceedeth out of the mouth of God; there is the spiritual responsibility.

On November 23 Martin addressed over two hundred people in the Village's community hall. The occasion was a dinner sponsored by the 100 Mile and District Historical Society, at which Lord Martin was guest of honor and named "Pioneer of the Year." Many longtime Cariboo residents were present, some given the microphone and asked to offer recollections from the early days. An outline of Martin's background was given by Ross Marks: the purchase of the land by Martin's father in 1912, Martin's arrival in 1930 at the age of 21, the building of the Lodge in 1932, and much more.

The *Free Press* quoted some of Martin's words:

"Let us preserve what might well be called the pioneer spirit and not expect to be provided with everything by other people, particularly I suppose by the government these days; that is the direction which leads to abject slavery."

After stating his appreciation for the honor bestowed upon him that evening, Lord Martin said he had left "a rather restricted and structured state of affairs to come to British Columbia where I found a greater freedom and opportunity to be myself. In those days one had to depend upon oneself," the Village's founder claimed, "and there still is a need for this sort of character... This is a beautiful part of the world to preserve on the basis of our own integrity and willingness to take responsibility for ourselves. This building [Community Hall] meant that we lost a good hayfield! Years later, on what was once good agricultural land the modern Village has sprouted up, instead of hay."

A rapt audience followed his words. At the conclusion a hearty round of entertainment followed, including soprano Gloria Dow, a rhythm band, square dancers, and the South Cariboo Community Choir. There was a magical mixture that night, of people, time and experience. On their way out of the hall Lord and Lady Martin Cecil were greeted by broad smiles and warm handshakes. 100 Mile House had turned out in force to honor the man without whom none of this would have happened. It was truly an historic occasion.

On the 30th of November, in Vancouver, Martin spoke of "A Genuine Person":

The Emissary ministry has been very important, because it provided (and still provides) a facility of training for those who are awakening to a consciousness of genuineness, a consciousness of the truth. There was a need for a transformed experience in living and a consequently transformed outlook, that there might be perspective in our observation of external events. However, the important thing is not to be in position to somehow correctly translate all the external events that are occurring around the world; there is no need. Our sole concern is as to what it is that is being expressed by reason of the Word of God. External events will take care of themselves when the Word of God is spoken on earth and when there are those in position to do this.

We may, in genuineness, have an awareness that we are part of a genuine whole. We are not in little isolated genuine pockets; we are part of a genuine whole; but each individual is genuine for him- or herself. I don't recall that it is recorded that Jesus said he was a Christian, for instance. Such an animal didn't exist! And he gave no particular emphasis to his Jewish status. He was a genuine person, and others had to accept him or reject him on that basis. He did not claim support from any of the powers-that-be at that time, whether secular or religious.

It doesn't matter what is present in the external sense, one may still be one's genuine self. This is what we are here to do; this is the leadership for which human beings are looking. Our concern is with an in-depth touching, a permeation. It is not a horizontal nudging of shoulders but an experience of true friendship.

32

BALANCE AMIDST CHANGE

January ~ December 1981

*I*n January of 1981 from all parts of India, Sri Lanka and Indonesia twenty people converged on the Sneha-Jyothi retreat outside of Bangalore for the first one-week Integrity Shibir (a Sanskrit word which means "a special gathering") held in that country. The faculty from North America consisted of Chris and Joy Foster, Achal Bedi, Rob Cass, Deborah Grace and Dennis Brown. They were assisted by Janis Barker, Dr. Ivan Chou and Krishna Raju from India. Prior to this a weekend seminar attended by seventy-five had been held at Chandigarh by Rob, Dennis and Deborah. On that same trip Chris and Joy joined Sigridh Kiersch at Hamlin for an Integrity gathering in northern Germany, where they were hosted by Sigridh's parents. Sigridh translated the Fosters' English into German. En route home, in England Chris and Joy, along with Janis Barker, attended the Overseas Council.

Back at 100 Mile House a small group gathered weekly with Chris and Joy to consider the movement of Integrity. At one meeting a letter from Dick and Margaret Christie, then living in Poland, was shared by a group that consisted of people born in Germany, India, Israel, South Africa, Hungary, England and Canada (all attending a Class at the Hundred at the time).

A cherished friend, Betty Protzman, passed away on January 18, 1981. She had achieved the age of ninety-eight and was still active and productive in her beloved home on Sunrise Ranch. We were special friends, with our beginning days with Uranda and the ministry in Pittsburgh and then our first trip to Sunrise together. A radiant pioneer in the Lord's work, she was a leader in the healing realm of attunements and in many other areas of service, with a profound love for Uranda and Martin, dedicated to furthering the work of the Lord.

When I hear of "laundered money" there is an accompanying stigma of breaking the law. Betty resurrected that area of man's dysfunction, with no conscious intention of doing so. Working in the accounting office on Sunrise Ranch, she enjoyed washing and ironing dollar bills on occasion, which action bestowed a clean, crisp aura on a very murky area of man's world.

On February 20 at 100 Mile House, under the leadership of Ross Marks, Ralph Fossum, Carl Richmond and Terry Young, fifty-seven representatives from thirty businesses operating in western Canada convened at Red Coach Inn. Ross Marks closed the sessions the following day with emphasis that "the important thing is the penetration of spiritual expression in whatever is at hand. The experience of lightness, enjoyment and balance comes about because of our presence."

Ginny Hogan wrote, in *Newslight:*

An eight-week Drama Workshop led by Ann Foorman concluded February 23. Unit and Valley residents were welcomed to join a thirteen-member core group for an hour each Monday evening to explore the beauty and purpose of dramatic expression. Exercises included natural breathing and sound production, "Standard American" English pronunciation, and oral interpretation and text work with Ted Black and Dale Kvasnicka. The principles found practical application in the presentation of prose and poetry by the participants. The core group then spent an additional hour concentrating on character development, using classic scenes and a one-act play.

Hugh Malafry engaged the entire group in a consideration of the history, possibilities and intrinsic nature of drama. Special guests Kathy Jenkins and Sharon Andrews, from the theater community in Colorado Springs, introduced us to the world of auditioning and gave a riveting performance of Strindberg's *The Stranger*. Drama obviously transcends mere entertainment, and the individuals involved in the workshop were concerned to develop the expertise and flexibility which will allow them to use drama with active force in the creative cycles of today.

A tour of the southeastern United States was initiated on March 17 as Martin, Lillian and I flew in the Conquest from Loveland to Key Largo, Florida. We were met by Bill and Donna Bahan, and Ken and Ronnie Lim, who continued throughout the tour, also Brian and Leslie Lanes who were with us in Florida. We enjoyed the view of the Florida Keys from the Conquest en route to Key West, where we spent a few days. Our visits to Miami were made very special by reason of our dear friends and hosts, Al and Betty Romaner, and it was exciting to see the famous Lippizaner stallions perform at a Miami fair. On Sunday, the 22nd, at the Florida International University in Miami Martin gave a service entitled "To Worship God," attended by 117 people.

The next stop was Atlanta, Georgia, where an open house was held on the 24th at the Center, focused by Jim and Jane Gensheimer. On the 26th we continued on to Edgewater Acres in Natchitoches, Louisiana, with John and Sara Waskom and family for a few days, which included a trip to Shreveport. From there it was Baton Rouge with Mark and Andrea Anderson and family. Martin gave a service entitled "Heaven Now!" at Louisiana State University on the 29th, attended by over two hundred. On Monday, the 30th, the Conquest took us to Houston where we were welcomed by Jim and Priscilla Connor and had lunch at the Center, after which we flew to Dallas for an overnight stay, with an open house hosted by Irv and Mary Shepherd. The final flight of this tour was on the 31st, from Dallas to Loveland.

Meanwhile, as was his custom, Bill Dice was busy ferreting out needed equipment at incredible prices. The latest acquisitions, this time with the assistance of David Lynch, were a new seed drill, a manure spreader and a power side-roll irrigation system, the latter a big step toward automating Sunrise Ranch farm activities.

Thanks to bountiful provision that came through Judith Aranow's parents, Ed and Rita of New York, the Sunrise kitchen was enriched by a dishwasher, toaster and double convection oven. Gifts via these two open-hearted friends were constantly appearing in many places on the Ranch.

"Human Unity Conferences" were held throughout the ministry that year, extending the borders of our tent. Its initiation was in Vancouver, and Sharon Grundy reported:

> As residents of the hosting city, we feel a particular responsibility for the support of the Human Unity Conference. To fulfil that responsibility much "networking" is being done—that magical process that brings the right people together to provide the setting for the Conference in July.

That "networking" extended around the world. At Auckland University in New Zealand, for example, a Human Unity gathering was held on March 14; and at Glen Ivy in April "all primary activists of the area HUC movement got together for a ways and means meeting, with a strong focus of purpose."

The first two-month Class at Green Pastures was attended by thirty-five, with a faculty of Bill and Iris Becker, Bill Bahan, Jr., Dennis Brown, Tom Starrs, Gail Moore, Alice Penfield and Steven Floyd.

Through the years there were many who came to Sunrise, for varying periods of time, and offered freely of their substance and talents. Martha Whitcomb, an accomplished artist and cellist, was available in any of her varied capacities. You might see her in the office one day, on children the next, or anyplace else! One day a small child came up to her and innocently inquired, "Are you *on* us today?"

Anne Laflam's daughter, Debra Bobrowski, a fine artist, is still a vital member of the Sunrise Ranch staff. She assisted Donna Bahan in the E.O.S. (Emissary Opening Series) department for many years and later focused that area. She has also provided assistance to Dr. Iaconi in our dental clinic on the Ranch and plays an important role in other fields of health. Anne has continued through all the vicissitudes of change to this day, and reveals that quality of love for the Lord and trust in His ways that allows the needs of the whole to be filled, according to the immediacy of the present circumstance.

Mary Jane Taylor, from Oregon, and Miranda Yeager of California came to provide valuable assistance in the office. Ginny Hogan (later Ward) contributed her talents in photography and eventually found an outlet for her special talent in painting. France Turgeon from New York contributed in many ways and eventually married Mack Fontenot. Bob Moore offered his expertise in various places in the office—from accounting to publishing.

The April issue of *Newslight* noted that

> the Basic Tape Series, a selection of 24 services on 12 cassettes is available, complete with folding storage case, at a price of $100. A large number of other tapes are also available, as listed in the Emissary Cassette Catalog, priced at $1. The second printing of Volume I of *The Third Sacred School* should be ready toward late April.

A seven-year cycle came to a close that year. The Dome Chapel, begun in 1973, was completed with the refinishing of the downstairs area. These rooms, beautifully done, served as music office, musical instrument storage and practice space, video storage, and kitchen, the latter just one example of the quality woodwork produced by Dave Miller and Will Carpenter. Of course the main portion of the building had been in use for some time.

A new configuration came into existence, referred to as an Assembly, offering further depth of understanding and experience to those who had participated in a Class. The Spring Assembly opened on Sunrise Ranch on April 13 and concluded May 8, with fifty "stars" from all over the United States and Canada, Italy, Australia, England,

South Africa, Nigeria and Israel.

A Music Conference was held on Sunrise Ranch May 13-20 with 120 in attendance: from Nigeria, South Africa, England, Holland, and of course many from the United States and Canada. Kay Stockton wrote, in *Eden Valley News:*

> The week was actually the final filling out of what had been held closely in the hearts and minds of a few for several months prior, possible only because of what Lillian has nurtured for many years.

An event at 100 Mile House was reported by Andreé Audette in *Newslight* for May:

> Ambitious and alive describes the "Evening of Classics" presented to an appreciative audience of 230 by the 100 Mile Lodge Orchestra and Friends, with conductor Lloyd Meeker. The orchestra of 20 regular members doubled, as musician friends from Sunrise Ranch, Portland, Vancouver, Prince George and Kamloops joined our ranks for this event. [The choir and orchestra included members of the Unit and also of the community choir from the town and its director Greg Archambault.] Friendship was one of the highlights in the experience of all the musicians. As Jack Jenkins from Sunrise Ranch remarked, "Playing with friends and not merely with peers, to an audience of friends, gives a completely new dimension to the experience."

Jim and Grace Moore arrived on the scene at 100 Mile House, a wonderful addition to the Unit, their presence still a great blessing. Jim's initial project was renovating the propane system, and he found other endless jobs, as did Grace. A product of Jim's fertile imagination, a company with the title "Cariboo Stamps" emerged, fittingly with him as president. Advantage was taken of the fact that letters came from all over the world to Headquarters, bearing stamps of every variety. The first profits after the initial expenses were being sent to Sunrise Ranch. The beginning operation on a spare-time basis was in a cabin near the Lodge, where stamps were soaked, dried, sorted and arranged in attractive packages for retail sale. These were in outlets or awaiting consignment, and commercial outlets were emerging. Packages retailed at $1.25 to $1.50 and contained anywhere from thirty to sixty stamps. Sunrise Ranch supplied the attractive labels for the packages, with a historical note featured on special issues such as the RCMP. This project continued through the years under Jim's faithful and careful direction.

Green Pastures had a unique method of farming, which continued through the years, contributed by Jack Carver. His extensive knowledge of farming and expertise with horses made a tractor unnecessary. Jack offered to instruct any who wished to come and work with him and the horses for a period of time, in order to put the natural way of living with the land in practice elsewhere.

An article appeared in *Eden Valley News* by Bob Ewing, in which he said:

This past year, through the activities of WaterWheel Gallery, many diverse art-related events have occurred. A highlight was the initiation of the use of Clear Water in New York for a wide range of artistic activities. This came to focus in April in the first Emissary visual art seminar, where twenty-one artists came together in an exquisite blending. Disciplines represented included photography, architecture, print-making, sculpture, painting and commercial art.

At the Human Unity Conference in Vancouver a whole new combination of artists surfaced. A large gallery at the entrance to the meeting hall was filled with a wide variety of colorful and powerful paintings.

The group workshops emphasized artists coming out of isolated function to share agreement in a larger vision, the potency of color, and poetic intuitive function. Traveling art shows and classes took us to Kansas, Missouri, New England, New York, Arizona, California and the South. During the winter months RimRock School of Art conducted evening art classes, and new programs are emerging to include more instructors and play a more extensive role in the Loveland community.

WaterWheel Gallery continues to provide a mecca in the high Colorado Rockies for art-oriented tourists. We have incorporated into our display an elaborate print section, and are filling our slower season activities with the distribution of a new print brochure which allows us to advertise and reach out into a large field of retail and wholesale marketing.

That year Eddie and Gladys Miller moved to Sunrise Ranch. It seems strange to affix a date to their arrival; their presence was vibrantly alive in Eden Valley long before they drove up the road to stay. The gift of these two imbued every area on Sunrise with their lively and generous spirits. They were unexcelled in the realm of attunements, but just as great in the kitchen preparing something special for the entire family, or Eddie doing an expert plastering job on a ceiling—all vehicles for their consistent expression of the spirit of God in action.

Up North, June 1st marked the opening of "The Inn Shoppe" in the lobby of Red Coach Inn at 100 Mile House. Marina Castonguay was and is the manager of this very successful gift shop. She makes regular buying trips to Vancouver, Calgary and Edmonton, and offers items of a quality that is new, and welcome to many in that part of the province.

Lloyd Meeker and Paula Martin were married in the Chapel at 100 Mile House on June 10th. Martin conducted the wedding ceremony in a beautiful setting, redolent with garlands of lilacs that canopied the new altar of wood and marble. A string trio and brass ensemble provided the music. The bride's sister, Liddy Martin, was the maid of honor,

Michael Cecil the best man. The bride's parents, of New York, and her brother Josh from Minneapolis were present. George Hanson and Gloria Dow sang love songs from the '30s in the reception that followed. The Meekers left the following day on a five-week tour of Europe and South Africa. Their honeymoon included a "working holiday," on the faculty of a two-week Class of 26 at the Hohenort Hotel near Cape Town.

In a service on June 14 at 100 Mile House entitled "Spirit Is Supreme," Martin spoke of Uranda's initiation of the ministry through his personal experience, and said:

> There was only one form involved, and that was the flesh of his own body. The expression of that spirit by reason of that form opened the door for those who were in the vicinity to touch it for an experience of spirit. Now this which has developed over the years out of that first beginning point has had meaning and carries weight solely by reason of the fact of spirit in action. Obviously the reality of spirit has always been available to be known. It has never been withdrawn, but human beings have sunk to such a low depth that there is scarcely any real awareness of the nature of that spirit in a direct sense. That awareness is lacking because people are involved in forms. But when spirit is introduced because the Word is made flesh, in whatever measure, and the flesh is revealing the fact that the Word is there, then there is the impact of the spirit relative to people; and I am sure all of you have felt that impact.
>
> Often those who first make contact in this way with the Emissary ministry find themselves lifted into a new state, vibrant and clear. That lasts for a while, but then the translation is again made relative to form and gradually that fresh new spirit is squeezed out, because forms are being produced out of people from their hereditary background, their subconscious minds, which they are packing onto this spirit. Each person will tend to clothe it in a little different way. Then as the forms become more dominant there is a conflict between the forms, and the moment conflict begins to come, the spirit is squeezed out of the picture; it is lost, gone. A person may have a vague memory of something; where did it go? The person himself crucified it by building forms.
>
> Many forms have been made. They have been called Emissary structures. That's not true. They are not Emissary structures. They are the individual structure that a person builds for himself out of whatever is present in his own subconscious mind, and he plunks that down on top of what he had sensed of spirit. And of course the heavier the structure is, the more the spirit is squashed down and tends to vanish away. There are those who have said, "Well, I thought there was something there, but later I decided there wasn't." That was simply an

individual looking at his own structures, and there wasn't anything there. We clobber ourselves. It isn't somebody else, ever; it's what we do ourselves.

The Word is supreme; the sounding of the tone is supreme. Hear that, sense that, understand that. If you do, and that is what moves your own expression, you will find that the fitting form appears because of the spirit, and you don't have the form already there ahead of time. The spirit is the only stable factor. The spirit is absolutely sure, and it is this with which a person must be associated to know the truth. That truth relates primarily to one's own being.

"Love Is Here!" titled a service at 100 Mile House on June 21. After a rendition of "Surely the Lord Is in This Place" by the choral ensemble, Martin repeated:

"Surely the Lord is in this place, and love is here." What words can be used to convey the reality of that love, of that great Presence in this place? Such beauty, such creative effectiveness, has been kept hidden because human beings were merely about their own personal affairs. If love, which is the essential core quality of life, is to be known it must be brought forth in living... We are here to fill the world with the substance of love, the transforming power of love. Nothing can withstand that, and then behold, all things are made new.

Shortly after this, in early July, Martin, Lillian, Peter, Marina and I embarked on a tour of England. Donna Bahan and I met there and together we fulfilled a long-standing desire to visit Israel and Egypt. Johanna Walters from Canada joined us and we were guests in the beautiful residence of Richard and Barbara Dash in Jerusalem. Besides their young son Emanuel and infant daughter Talya, the household consisted of Nechama and Ruth Basson, Clarice Friedman and Richard Lamb. From the window in my little room I looked out onto the panorama of the Temple site with the Golden Dome, and beheld the centuries dissolving, to Abraham on Mt. Moriah, to Solomon's glorious Temple and then, after its destruction, Herod's temple. That was the place where Jesus walked and taught. Here from my window was the procession of the ages, in one tiny spot on this planet.

On our trip through the Holy Land, with Richard Dash the perfect guide, we magically touched (in spite of tourism) the spirit of places in Jerusalem, Galilee, Bethlehem, Bethany, Gethsemane, Mt. Carmel, and the Gethsemane tomb in its beautiful garden. The surviving remnant of the ancient temple, presently called the "wailing wall," carried a special impact; and the spirit of peace and blessing that can be felt at the Sea of Galilee is awe-inspiring— an atmosphere so pervading that has survived the centuries and all that transpired in the interval. Richard read passages from the Bible in the appropriate locations, which greatly enhanced the sense of connection. To sit on the Mount and hear the words of the Master spoken to His disciples, "...Blessed are the pure in heart, for they shall see God..." is to experience the blessed assurance that nothing is lost.

Five of our precious days were spent in Egypt. The two Richards flew with us from Tel Aviv to Cairo, with its Sphinx and the Great Pyramid. Standing on that sea of sand, in the midst of these wonders, I sensed that there was a vast wisdom, long lost, inherent in those who built them, in exactly that spot, center of Earth's land mass. We shared an unforgettable hour in the interior of the Pyramid, and my sacred experience in the King's Chamber is one that has not faded with time.

Then we flew to Luxor where we stayed in the Winter Palace hotel, a beautiful edifice built by King Farouk, and traveled to nearby Karnak to see the incredibly gargantuan structures that, again, cause one to contemplate the changes that must have occurred in mankind since the days of their construction.

Looking out the window in our room, I was sobered by the fact that across the Nile and in the distance, but visible! was the temple of Queen Hatshepsut (Queen of Sheba, thanks to Velikovsky). Magic! We crossed the Nile, itself an adventure, as were most events because of the native people with their own time "schedule" and system of barter. The visit to the Queen's temple was an outstanding experience. As we beheld the ancient paintings (with their colors still alive) on the walls of the wonderful portico outside, with its majestic columns (miniature copy of the great Temple of Solomon) Richard read the story of the great Queen from Velikovsky's *Ages in Chaos*—and for me three millennia were erased!

Then back to Cairo for a short stay and the flight to Tel Aviv. After a further brief visit in Jerusalem, Johanna left for Canada, and my heart overflowed with gratitude to our precious friends in Israel as Donna and I boarded the plane for England.

At Mickleton House there was a Weekend Gathering of 110 people on July 18 and 19—from Europe, Africa, England, Canada and the United States. Dining accommodation for that number was provided by a large tent which extended the Garden Room facility comfortably. In his service on the 19th Martin said:

> This morning we enjoyed what Grace and Donna had to say about their journeyings into Israel and Egypt. The thing that impressed me, amongst other things, was the continuity that is so very evident in what has been happening in the experience of the human race over thousands of years. It is all coming to a point of climax, one might say, in these days, where a conscious awareness once again begins to emerge for human beings as to why people are present on earth. Evidently there has been a lack of such awareness, so that human beings have had to invent their own purposes. But now something is beginning to emerge again and come to a point of focus. Most people haven't a clue as to why they are

here, but we have been privileged to become aware of something of the truth in this regard and it is increasing in consciousness as the days go by.

As the focus is provided increasingly, there can be the guidance offered in this process of coordinating the awakening ones who are coming in greater numbers within the range of direct influence. We are considering how we can individually play specific parts and how it all may fit together. We find that many things happen and come together without any particular awareness as to how it occurred. That does not mean that one can sit around hoping that things are going to come together because one is so spiritual! It requires definite work. Somebody has to recognize what needs to be done and do it. And when this happens, far more is influenced than that immediate thing, and many related factors that were unseen come together.

Martin then referred to the Human Unity enterprise, which was intended to attract and draw together people and groups of varied backgrounds and beliefs, and accomplished it to a high degree. He continued:

As I say, this HUC operation has been an opportunity for many people to learn that being an Emissary is not having a structured consciousness and a lot of concepts. It is being capable of handling people wisely and opening doors for them so that they may become aware of what it is that is finding expression through themselves. We're all in this business together.

There were visits to England's wonderful historic landmarks, such as Windsor Castle and Cambridge University. Rupert and Tessa accompanied us, and their impeccable care and assistance made for an easy and relaxed trip. A day with the London group up the Thames River in three boats provided something different. A visit of special note was at Dartmouth Naval College where Martin spent some memorable years in his early life. Then it was home to 100 Mile House.

The final session of the Human Unity Conference on the campus of UBC in Vancouver took place on July 26 and completed the Conference. Over nine hundred people had registered. A public gathering was held that afternoon in the Queen Elizabeth Theater. Both 100 Mile House and Sunrise Ranch were connected by telephone with Vancouver where George Emery, a moving force in that outworking, spoke glowingly of the "tremendous beginning" made. He expressed gratitude for the participation of Joelle, Bill Bahan, Michael and Nancy, Marilyn Ferguson and Dr. Jampolsky, and added:

There are about a thousand people here this morning. In 1982 the ninth Human Unity Conference will be in Brasilia, but the one in 1983 will be sponsored by the Universal Unity Foundation and will be in London, England.

Martin continued from 100 Mile House:

This particular Conference included representation, in one way or another, from virtually every country on earth; they were compelled. We know something about the nature of that compulsion, because it brings us together, and we share what is forthcoming by reason of the action of spirit. Another item related to the Conference was a gathering yesterday of thousands of people on Boston Common. The mayor of Boston had declared that day Human Unity Day, and George, Bill Bahan, Marilyn Ferguson and Dr. Gerald Jampolsky all spoke to those assembled in Boston over the PA system.

At 100 Mile House a baby girl, Rebecca Grace, was born to Luke and Helen (Meeker) Vorstermans on August 13.

Payment on the Conquest, as of July, was 98.22%. The remaining percentage translated into $17,168. Each issue of *Newslight* kept the current information fresh in the minds of contributors—and it was working!

On August 26 on Sunrise Ranch Martin addressed the annual gathering of the General Council and shared the seed of a vital new development. He mentioned the 49th birthday of the Emissary ministry approaching, on September 16, "completing the seventh of the seven-year cycles," and said that in the recent Supreme Council, held August 17-22,

something began to emerge in our unified consciousness which is of significance from the standpoint of form. We have had many gatherings over the years but we have never had an overall Emissary gathering, an opportunity for all who rightly should be present to be with one accord in one place. Any further expansion of these things which are beginning to put in an appearance, such as the Foundation, for instance, and the Whole Health Institute, is based in whatever occurs at the core.

The suggestion is that we could have an Emissary gathering this coming year which will obviate some of our other gatherings. While there are things which have been happening which need to continue, as the spirit intensifies and comes together through a means for its expression at the level where it's needed, the form will tend to change. And the particular way in which this seems to be occurring relates to this anticipated gathering.

The area in which Sunrise Ranch is located would seem to be the most appropriate and we felt the wisest location would be Fort Collins. There is a facility in the university there, with one period of time available that would be fitting for us, from July 29 to August 1, 1982. We thought it might be called "Emissary International Congress." Another aspect is that many people who have never been to Sunrise Ranch would have the opportunity to visit. The details are still in the heaven but there is sufficient evidence that this can actually take place. [The approximate cost was $130-$150, with anticipated chartered aircraft available. Alan Hammond was appointed the logistical coordinator, and a committee was formed to begin to set things in motion.]

An International Fair sponsored by the Integrity group was held on Sunrise Ranch August 30 in order to raise scholarship funds for citizens of Third-World nations to attend Emissary Classes.

The September issue of *Newslight* conveyed the news that the payment on the Conquest was "100 per cent complete. Hooray!"

Martin officiated at the wedding of Diana de Winton and PenDell Pittman on September 5th in the Chapel on Sunrise Ranch.

Known to her many friends as Bobbie, Carolyn Garrett passed away on September 9. In a memorial service for her Martin gratefully acknowledged her absolute dedication in serving the Lord in many and varied ways, and referred to a poem she had written a week before her passing:

> Here she poses a question directly to everybody, a valid question: "In what world do we live? It is our own choice." So through her spirit she brings something to our attention here and now.

On that same day on Sunrise Ranch there was a telephone hookup with Cape Town, South Africa, where a group of seventy people, from Johannesburg, Durban and the eastern Cape were concluding a three-day session under the leadership of Rupert and Tessa Maskell, recently returned from General Council. Martin's service was entitled "Honesty and Quick Repentance," in which he dealt with spiritual abortion.

> Over the years of this ministry I have been required to handle countless spiritual abortions. It's interesting that in these days abortion has become quite a political element. This may represent something but it's not the real question. The real question is the aborting of the creative cycles established by God. If that is taken care of, all the other things will be taken care of; but if not, then nothing else will be taken care of. We are here to cease aborting the creative cycles that are at hand, so that we may move with steady spiritual step, quick to repent as necessary. With quick repentance comes quick restoration.
>
> We have before us a year of fire, and that certainly relates to the emotional realm. The refining fire—what doesn't belong in the heart is dissolved. If you're hooked on what doesn't belong, you're dissolved. Our business is to reveal a level of maturity in the spiritual sense so that we can handle what comes, so

that we do not become subject through our emotions to what is happening externally. Many things are happening externally, with more to come. But what about our hearts? What about the heaven where we are rightly dwelling? Because we assume responsibility for maintaining it ourselves and accept no excuse for not doing it, there begins to be a man or a woman, evidence of the creative process of restoration, of resurrection.

On September 16, the 49th Anniversary of the Ministry, Martin's service was entitled "Special Focus of Significance," and after a brief introduction he said:

We have chosen this particular day as a beginning point, in outer form, of this ministry forty-nine years ago. It is not just a matter of celebrating a birthday but of participating in a creative cycle which rises to a special focus of significance at this time.

He said there would be a few others sharing the service, and invited me to the lectern. After a brief word about my joy in experiencing the ancient symbols in Egypt, I read some words written by Uranda on September 14, 1936, "The Sphinx Speaks," which ends thus:

Look out upon the earth, beloved, and thou shalt see that it is a melting-furnace wherein the fire of my love brings all to that white heat of transformation. The gold of being, responding to my hand, comes forth pure, and ready for the shaping of a higher realm. Now it is ordained that all self-consciousness may be only in the realms of Reality; and so it is that the flaming fire of my creative force shall work its will in peace and all tranquillity, changing the dross to purest gold until the whole world shall shine forth as a sun of glorious light in the universe where it is ordained to be.

Lillian was invited to speak, and after she placed a picture of Uranda on the altar, said:

My contribution tonight will simply be to speak briefly of Uranda. He was the opening door, the focus of the awakening, at this very special moment in eternity, forty-nine years ago. Grace spoke of those symbols in the earth today that represent the Lord. And they still stand, after how many centuries? I wonder how good a symbol we each are of the Lord on earth. Uranda brought this to focus, a living, vibrant symbol. I met him at very tender years and didn't have to be told that he was special.

As Betsy played the organ, I thought how thrilled Uranda would have been to hear this gorgeous organ in this beautiful building. And yet he was never daunted by the fact that the forms around him were quite less than we know: a little old pump organ, in a small building which we call the ranch house. But it was the same; it was joyous because the symbol of God was on earth and there were those awakening to that fact. And as we share this in our hearts and produce the living example in our living, his life was not in vain. Indeed it was the most glorious thing for thousands of years!

My words are simply to offer our collective tribute to the special life which Uranda portrayed. He could be very serious, he could be witty, he could drive the point home so that you squirmed, but you were glad to wake up and see the truth of being, available. He lived life to its fullest. And we remember the Master's word, "Follow me," and in everything Uranda did and said he issued that word also, to all people on earth, "Follow me." I am thankful that Uranda walked the earth and that his spirit continues, as it ever shall.

Following a chant and singing by the Sunrise Octet of *Thou Art Worthy, O Lord,* words by Hugh Malafry and music by Betsy Giglio (later Hanson) Martin spoke:

The way of salvation, of restoration, has been established on earth ever since the original failure on the part of man. The way of restoration is the same now as it was anywhere back along the way. The worldly circumstances may have changed but the way by which the restoration occurs is the same as it ever was. [He recalled instances in past history of the means utilized at those times, as with Jesus and his disciples, or as in the Day of Pentecost, or Elijah's contest with the prophets of Baal. He read the story of Elijah where he repaired the altar of the Lord that was broken down.]

This, seven periods of seven years, which brings us to this day, has been a time when the altar of the Lord was in the process of being repaired.

"Hear me, O Lord, hear me, that this people may know that thou art the Lord God, and that thou hast turned their heart back again. Then the fire of the Lord fell, and consumed the burnt sacrifice, and the wood, and the stones, and the dust, and licked up the water that was in the trench."

Here is a very different state of affairs to the state of a wet rag. What of your hearts? Ar they really turned back again? The very moment that this is so the fire of God does fall from heaven. We may see and know this in this moment. We also see and know and understand it as relating to this particular aspect of the creative cycle that opens before us: the fire of God falling from heaven, pouring forth to consume the lives of those whose hearts are turned back again, so that they cannot help but allow the glory of the Lord to be revealed on earth in the oneness of His body.

"And when all the people saw it, they fell on their faces: and they said, The Lord, he is the God; the Lord, he is the God."

Is that really what is being said by all those present in this Chapel this evening—"The Lord, He is the God"? Are there in fact no other gods before Him?

The Lord, He is the God in fact, whether anyone acknowledges it or not. But only with that acknowledgment, because there has been repentance and participation in the creative cycles of forgiveness, does this truth have creative effect in the world. These things may be brought to focus in our consciousness, that as individuals we may acknowledge the fact of failure and repent—no excuses whatsoever offered for anything that has happened in which we have been involved, no explanations needed, but simply a willingness to repent, that there may be full and free and wholesome participation in what is now emerging.

We see this casting its shadows before. We have a certain awareness of expected physical events this coming year. These have little significance of themselves except as there are those whose hearts have been turned back again, so that what is of this creative cycle now emerging may be allowed to take form because there are those present to let it be so.

"The Lord, He is the God; the Lord, He is the God." What say you?"

The congregation answered, "The Lord, He is the God." Noting that Martin was still expectantly listening, they repeated, with emphasis: "The Lord, He is the God."

Martin said,

That's better! There is a tendency, isn't there, to do things partially because we have lived in a partial world. I rejoice very greatly in this hour. "Rejoice, ye heavens, and ye that dwell in them."

A Western Tour began on September 18, with Martin and his party flying in the Conquest from Sunrise Ranch to Phoenix, Arizona, and from there to Riverside, California. The following evening the newly completed dining room at Glen Ivy was initiated with a large dinner party for Martin, Lillian and me, Charley and Asti Kitchens, the unit members and various Southwest servers. Entertainment included music by Rob Cass's Santa Barbarians. A group shared a three-day session with Martin, and then we had some time in the Spa.

There were visits to Laguna Beach, Santa Catalina Island and Los Angeles. Back at Glen Ivy we enjoyed hearing Charley Kitchens speak on the Conquest and the aviation world.

In a service there on September 20 entitled "Seven and Twelve," Martin spoke of a notice forthcoming in the next mailing announcing the Emissary International Congress in Fort Collins on July 29, 1982, and that

we have moved into the fiftieth year of this Emissary ministry; we could call it the year of the golden jubilee. It is also the first in a succession of seven years, which is characterized by the fire force.

Martin then spoke of balance necessary in what occurs.

> It is interesting to note that the anniversary of this ministry falls approximately, in the northern hemisphere at least, at the time of the autumnal equinox. This is a balance point, not only for the northern hemisphere but for the southern hemisphere, when the length of the day and the night are the same; the same thing in the north as in the south. This is indicative of a balance point...
>
> I am emphasizing this balanced position particularly because certainly the swinging will likely occur with greater vehemence in the world around us as the days and years go on, and we need to have very sure footing where we belong if we're not going to be carried with it. And we can see a cleansing process occurring on this basis. But let not everything be cleansed away! If half of it is flung this way and the other half that way, there's nothing in the middle. There needs to be something left, something that is stable and solid, and provides a connection for all those who are in the vicinity of it, not necessarily physical vicinity but vibrational.
>
> The Emissary ministry is the means by which the conscious aspect of the mind of mankind has been brought to focus. Isn't that a tremendous thing! Why deny it? There are those who are ready to understand; for them the door should be open.

After we left Glen Ivy we flew to Santa Barbara, had lunch and continued up to the San Francisco Bay area where we enjoyed a week with Stan and Linda Grindstaff. A highlight was a trip through the Napa Valley with Bruce Reyes—and a gourmet lunch outdoors, complete with expert chef and assistants, at one of the wineries.

The next stop, on September 30, was Medford, Oregon, where we were welcomed by Rick and Sandra Dunn, had lunch and toured the Ashland Center, home of David and Linda Gleason and ten others. Michael Cecil joined the party in Portland later that afternoon. There Still Meadow Farm provided a beautiful setting for three days of sessions with five couples from Oregon and Washington. Saturday evening Ron and June Polack and several servers from Oregon joined those in the sessions for a formal dinner, following which I showed slides of my trip to Israel and Egypt. On Sunday, the 4th, Martin gave a service in downtown Portland, attended by 150. The next day, after a stopover in Seattle, we flew to Vancouver; then home to 100 Mile House on the 6th.

Two specific Educo activities appeared in the October issue of *Newslight.* "Marine Educo" was the subtitle under "Educo School" and reported:

> A crew of people flew to Newfoundland October 14 to receive delivery of

the new Marine Educo vessel, an 81-foot schooner, and will be bringing it through the Panama Canal to Vancouver, B.C., on an approximately four months' journey. The crew includes Richard Hudson, Bill Dice, Andreé Vaillancourt, Roger Hockett, Teresa Radley and the captain, Michael Walsh. A marine Educo program will be conducted during the voyage.

In late fall twelve men took part in a seven-day canoeing expedition among the Broken Isles off the west coast of Vancouver Island, which event inaugurated "Educo of the Sea," later incorporated as a nonprofit society affiliated with the Educo School. Among others, a course among the Gulf Islands was anticipated.

"Adult Educo" was the other event referred to, accompanied by photographs of very rugged terrain, including a perpendicularly steep mountain being climbed by human (Educo) beings! Clifford Roberts reported:

> We came from as far away as Sydney, Australia, and Bangalore, India, and as nearby as Chilliwack and Kelowna, B.C.: ten men to share ten special days in British Columbia. When asked about my experience, I related some adventures and personal challenges: rock climbing, the two-day mountain hike, white-water canoeing, the discovery of unimaginable physical resources in oneself, and the great food provided by the staff ladies. However, what impressed me most was witnessing how a safe, creative atmosphere was built for the students through absolute agreement in the leaders. At one climactic moment in the canoe trip we were paddling through rapids in the notorious Black Canyon. The call was to go for it—no skirting around the sides where it was comfortable, but to go right through the middle. We all did and had the time of our life, in an adventurous and victorious attitude.

Newslight contained an announcement that had appeared in a publication in England:

> Lord Martin Cecil has succeeded to the title of 7th Marquess of Exeter with the passing of his brother, David. The 6th Marquess of Exeter died in England on October 22. He was a noted sportsman and member of the International Olympic Committee for many years, as well as being active in business and other fields, and a former governor of Bermuda. Lady Martin Cecil has become the Marchioness of Exeter. Michael and Nancy Cecil receive the titles Lord and Lady Burghley, and Marina Castonguay becomes Lady Marina Castonguay.

Sunrise Ranch hosted the main organizational meeting for the Foundation of Universal Unity in October. During the next six months the administrative office was located in Fort Collins, and Sunrise continued to play a strong supportive role. Besides offering secretarial assistance to the Emerys in their capacity as Foundation Coordinators and providing space for Colorado area gatherings, organizational and financial expertise was provided particularly by Roger de Winton and Mack Fontenot. At that time George and Joelle Emery settled into a newly remodeled apartment on Sunrise Ranch.

Rick and Linda Lathrop moved to the Ranch, and the Foundation office took up residence in a trailer provided for that purpose. Rick functioned as executive director, with the assistance of Diana Soto in the office. Alan Hammond accepted the presidency of the board of directors, and with Mack Fontenot's presence on the board consolidated the coordinating team on Sunrise. This made it easy for Michael Cecil and Bill Bahan to participate in the Foundation International Board of Advisors, and also provided a secure undergirding for George and Joelle in their world travels as founding directors.

Working on the utilities project on Sunrise Ranch, affectionately called the Trench Connection, were four Jims: Higerd, Hoffman, Greaney and Minardi. Along with others, they placed all the sewer pipe, electrical wires and intercom system underground, for esthetic reasons and in preparation for the paving. On May 27—*the paving!* What a project that was, as the Coulson Excavating Company rolled onto the Ranch with their huge graders and blacktopping equipment. The Dome parking lot, the Bishop's driveway, and the north and south entrances to the Ranch were topped, the job to be completed by the end of the summer when the two entrances were connected, making a full circle.

Jim Higerd reported later in *Eden Valley News,*

> Sunrise Ranch the past year witnessed the installation of 6,500 square yards of asphalt, designed and placed in such a way to allow walkable paths from all the main areas of the Ranch during the rainiest times, and with the least amount of flooding potential possible.
>
> The last paving done this year, laying of 3,200 square yards, took less than seven hours from the time the machines started till finish. This seven hours brought to focus work that has been going on for the last several years. People too numerous to mention have helped in preparing by assisting in installing new electric lines, water lines, propane gas lines, upgrading the sewer lines, all designed so that when the paving was layed the manholes would be at just the right height, not an inch above or below the paving.
>
> Now when I see people moving about the Ranch with ease I am glad they can forget all the mud we used to have. Of course I will always remember the time George was seen in ankle-deep mud between the dining room and administration office, hopping on one foot, looking for a missing shoe.

Teen-age Heidi Patton wrote:

> When I stepped off the school bus one afternoon and saw the beautiful

pavement that swirled around the Ranch, I just couldn't believe my eyes. It was like a dream I never thought would happen! Soon after that, the actual landscaping began. I could see all the men and women hard at work, laying topsoil one day and planting gorgeous bushes and flowers the next. It gave me such a wonderful feeling inside that I felt like inviting the whole world to the Ranch and saying, "Isn't this the most beautiful place you have ever seen? And hey, this is my home, and I sure do love it!"

Madeline Maynard said:

> There is a program going on now of dressing the earth—where there was dirt there are now beautiful flowers and grass. The most outstanding feature is the new pavement—no more mud to drag into the dining room, office and homes. The people are the most important ingredient of the whole outworking, for it wouldn't happen without them. They allow the expression of life to appear, releasing the substance needed to change the forms in this beautiful Valley of Eden.

Work was begun on the de Winton's new home the end of November. This beautiful structure is the first house south of the Bishop's residence. Some of the men who came to share in the project were Rory McNamara, Jim White, David Gilbert and Gerry Conway.

Meanwhile there were exciting happenings at 100 Mile House where the media was attracted after it learned that employees and management of a local sawmill, Ainsworth Lumber Company, had agreed to wage and price cuts in order to keep their mill operating in tough economic times. Even New York's *Wall Street Journal* telephoned mill management, also the union president, to find out how such an unprecedented action was possible.

Peter Bono, manager of Red Coach Bakery, was also an object of interest to the media, after he had inserted an advertisement in the 100 Mile Free Press announcing he was rolling back bread prices in a gesture of appreciation for the agreement between the mill and its employees. Pamela Martin, TV anchorwoman of Vancouver's major station BCTV, came for a filmed interview with Peter and other Emissary businessmen, Luke Vorstermans of Red Coach Inn and Marvin Schmunk of Pioneer Home Center, who had also rolled back prices on certain items.

The Inn reduced the price of a cup of coffee to the 1971 price of—15 cents! Other local businesses joined the movement, as did a sawmill in Vanderhoof, north of us. Cecelia Walters of the CBC National News also interviewed Ainsworth Lumber representatives, Peter Bono and others, and planned to publish the story during the Christmas season.

In *Newslight* John Simituk commented that these were

> relatively small acts in a big world plagued by galloping inflation and uncontrolled self-interest, yet these acts touched the heart of a nation, which is no small thing.

33

Circling the Earth—and Emissary International Congress

January ~ December 1982

The formal invitation to the EIC was sent in January of 1982, the next step in the cycle initiated by Martin in September of 1981:

This, the fiftieth year of the Emissary ministry, will contain a number of particularly significant events, not the least of which will be the first Emissary International Congress. To be composed of a substantial proportion of the Emissary body, the Congress will gather to provide the Lord with an unprecedented instrument for unified radiation. You are hereby personally invited to participate in this unique event, to play a direct role as the conscious focus of the Spirit of Life coordinates the climactic cycles moving in the earth today.

Dorothy Halliday Thompson passed away at the age of eighty-three on January 19 in Vancouver. Born in England, Dorothy, her husband Richard and daughter Mary crossed the Atlantic Ocean to Canada in 1936. One day, in John Oshanek's chiropractic office in Winnipeg, she was impressed with an article by Uranda and both Richard and John suggested she write to him, which she did. To their surprise she received a package with an abundance of literature. In the fall of 1937 Uranda accepted an invitation to speak in Winnipeg, at which time Richard and Dorothy eagerly joined him and his work. From

1946 to 1952 they were numbered among the early pioneers who established the foundation of the Emissary ministry on Sunrise Ranch, after which they focused the ministry in Vancouver, Powell River and Victoria. Dorothy continued her ministry in Vancouver after Richard's passing. Courageous, diplomatic, kind and with a bubbling sense of humor, she was a beautiful lady whose message was delivered by her noble presence.

In a service by Martin, "Spiritually Substantial," at 100 Mile House on January 31, Michael opened with some remarks concerning the nature of the ministry that

> has brought many things into our hands beyond the immediate Unit family... All these external areas of responsibility mean nothing, really, except as tools for creative action, the means through which the spirit of God may be released into the earth. If that is not the primary aim and concern, then there is a certain element of desperation sometimes in trying to keep the ship of state afloat when it is in the process of going down the drain with the rest of the world's ships of state. In these days of expansion we see the need to have a largeness of divine vision which encompasses the world.

Martin said:

> There is indeed this largeness of vision but it is more than that, because it requires a person who has the large vision, and that is a large person. There are larger forms putting in an appearance in these days, forms for which we are responsible in various ways. We always need to have a clear vision as to their value, which is not so much in and of themselves but because they allow a larger outpouring of spirit.
>
> All forms are composed of substance. The quality of substance of which any form is composed determines the value of that form. You can think of a beautiful sculpture in marble by some great artist, probably worth a lot of money. This artist could no doubt reproduce an exact copy of that sculpture in ice. You would have to keep it in the deep-freeze, and not too many people would be interested in going to inspect it. That is an example of how the substance, even in an inanimate form, determines the value of the form.
>
> In a gathering at my house after this morning's service someone asked what the correct response would be to the question, "What are Emissaries of Divine Light?" The correct answer is "I am." That puts you on the spot. The tendency would be to describe some form, some organization, but that isn't it. If you say "'I am" you also say, "Look no further, here I am." And if they see that you don't have horns and a tail they may look again. Let us be responsible people in our own individual worlds—the only one there to provide the

focus. We do not put it off onto somebody else, or some convenient form, such as "Emissaries of Divine Light." As a legal entity that means absolutely nothing if you withdraw all the people from the organization. What would be left? Just a husk. Our concern is with this glorious, living expression of spirit which is present and in action when there is substance for its accommodation, and its action makes all things new.

"The weather for the fifty-kilometer annual Cariboo Marathon for cross-country skiers was perfect, the snow superb," wrote Geoff Tisch in *Northern Light*.

The first one was held at 100 Mile House in 1977, and has become the largest event of its kind in Western Canada [the second largest in the country]. Our guests come from afar and are billeted in dozens of homes, and hundreds volunteer to prepare for the event... Eleven years old, Anthony Cecil skiied the first sixteen of the twenty-six miles. The oldest entrant to finish the race was an 82-year-old man from Vancouver.

Joy Foster wrote:

In its tenth year of publication, *Integrity* magazine changed its name to *Integrity International*—concerned with true character and a well world and its format, to give a broader, more newspaperlike coverage to people and events that show true character in action. Over the years *Integrity* has provided an initial means of touching the ministry for many people from all parts of the world, including India and West Africa particularly. With this background of experience it was a natural step for the Fosters to join with Karen Stevenson of Washington, D.C., to coordinate the intercultural and interracial affairs of the Foundation of Universal Unity under the heading, "The Tapestry of Mankind." Karen, who is the first black woman Rhodes scholar from the United States, and Chris have written a letter to newspaper editors, designed to make contact with the American Negro community. [Karen has continued to serve in countless ways and places, for many years in the center at Glen Ivy.]

Martin gave a service, "The Halo," at 100 Mile House on Sunday morning, February 21, with a telephone hookup with Sunrise Ranch, in which he announced that on Tuesday, the 23rd, he and Lillian and I would be setting forth on a world-tour journey.

There has been a sensing, on the part of many of you, of the importance of this journey, not so much for the physical movement around the earth, although this is obviously a part of it, but for the spiritual movement that relates to it. This spiritual movement is concerned primarily with a process of unification, of agreement. This relates to the conscious levels of the human mind, which are designed to allow the authority and direction of God to be brought to focus in action on earth. I rejoice with you all, knowing that you are present with us in our journey, just as we are present with you wherever you are.

So we began a world tour on February 23, with departure from 100 Mile House in the Conquest to Vancouver, "circling the earth," in Martin's words. There we were joined by Bill and Donna Bahan for the initial portion of our journey. The first stop was Honolulu, Hawaii, and after a brief stop, which included a delicious dinner with temporary residents Hugh and Moira Malafry, we continued our flight to Nadi, Fiji, where we stayed at The Regent of Fiji and enjoyed a few relaxing days in the tropical sun and ocean, which was at our doorstep.

In Auckland, New Zealand, we were hosted at the Center by Robert and Maria Middlestead. Lloyd and Paula Meeker were already there, en route to Australia. Martin gave a service at the Hotel Intercontinental which was attended by fifty people. (Through the years the name Kenneth Lim has always been associated in consciousness with New Zealand, as has that of Geoff Tisch, both vital pioneers in the ministry in that land.) On March 2nd we drove around Sydney, Australia, where Lillian and Donna enjoyed a tour of the famous Opera House. On the 4th we arrived in Melbourne where Dr. Richard and Wendy Hetzel provided the focus. We proceeded to Adelaide on the 6th and Gawler on the 7th. In New Zealand and Australia, Bill and Lloyd spoke at public meetings, usually the day before Martin's addresses, a pattern utilized by Martin on the entire journey with the particular one(s) accompanying us at the time.

Through the years Lloyd Meeker's contribution encompassed many areas: attunements, music, writing, and teaching classes. Primary servers for many years, he and his wife, Paula, provided valuable focus for people in many places.

On March 7th in the chapel of the Gawler Center, home of Paul and Libby Blythe, fifty-six attended a service by Martin which was connected by telephone with Sunrise Ranch. With the heat at its peak and the chapel like an oven, Martin rigged up a very workable system in lieu of air-conditioning, which consisted of a blanket soaked in cold water and hung in an appropriate place. He thoroughly enjoyed dealing with such immediacies as they arose, when there was no seeming solution at hand and time was short. *And* it was the only occasion when anyone saw him give a service in shorts! The following day there was a special session, with servers gathered from the area.

From Canada, the Blythes had been in Australia since 1977 and, in Paul's words, had
> sent over thirty people to Classes. We have a unit at Gawler with around 25 people, and centers in Adelaide, Melbourne and Sydney, also meetings in Perth, Maroochydore and Whyalla.

On the 11th we flew to Perth, a city on the banks of the Swan River at the opposite end of the country, with a beauty very different from that of the east. There we visited our chiropractor friends, Drs. Doug and Shirley Winter. Meanwhile Rupert and Tessa Maskell had been traveling from South Africa, by way of India and Singapore, and met us at Perth. These two would be our companions on the next part of our fascinating adventure.

On the 13th our flight took us to the Indian Ocean island of Mauritius, where we spent three days at a French-owned and run hotel right on the beach. It was an ideal spot for rest and relaxation before the busy schedule ahead. Martin and Rupert seemed to enjoy their rides in a pedalboat. I noted, at meals, the strikingly obvious cosmopolitan atmosphere. I had to be alert to hear English spoken, in a mixture of many tongues.

On the 15th we arrived in Johannesburg, South Africa, where we stayed one night in transit to Cape Town. Michael and Nancy were already there. At Cape Town the Hohenort Hotel played a prominent part in the six-day proceedings. Michael had a Planetary Initiative meeting, and an open house was held at Rupert and Tessa's home. Martin's Sunday morning service, "The One Language," was connected by telephone with Fourways in Johannesburg. Before he spoke, there was beautiful singing by first a black choir and then a white. In his service Martin noted that many people are learning English as a second language, and used that as an analogy to reveal the universal language of the spirit.

> There is the need to awaken to our first language. Most people want to learn the truth on the basis of their already existing language, the character of their experience heretofore. The already existing state of affairs must be relinquished in order for one to awaken to an awareness of the fact that one already has a language, and all these other human languages can then be understood for what they are. But no one speaking those languages can understand this first language. This is why you may have found a little difficulty at times in seeking to explain what "Emissaries of Divine Light" is, because here is a language that is not understood by anyone who doesn't speak it. And it can't be learned as a second language, which is what most people attempt to do. They're going to stay in their own language but they want to learn about this other one. It can't be done. Our concern is to provide what is possible to assist people to awaken to this one language, the first language.

Two days of potent special sessions were held at Hohenort, which included four other couples: Gary and Glennifer Gillespie, Howard and Marian Goodman, Tino and Lynn Stefano, and Leon and Judy Bekker.

On March 22 Michael and Nancy flew to Johannesburg while Martin, Lillian and I, with the Maskells, went to Durban. There we had lunch with forty others at Waterfall

Farm, our new Hillcrest property, after which Martin shared a heartfelt time speaking to the group. Later that day we flew to Johannesburg for the final two days of our South African sojourn.

In the spacious Fourways Center we were made very much at home by our gracious hosts Howard and Marian Goodman. They had arranged various events, such as a tour of our impressive SkyLark sunroof manufacturing plant, lunch and shopping downtown, and an open house at the Center, attended by about ninety of the family. Included was a large contingent from Impumalanga in Zululand. Their faces lit up as they met Martin for the first time. Among them were Rev. Amos Nxumalo, several women, Absalom and Grace Makhatini and their son Gideon. It was gratifying to observe Martin's joy as he spoke to them and see the light of understanding in their eyes in spite of the difference in language. Later they expressed their joy in spontaneous singing of some Zulu songs.

On the 24th we arrived in London. At Mickleton House on the 28th Martin gave a service titled "Agreement in the One Spirit," with a telephone hookup with 100 Mile House, in which he observed that it was

> exactly five weeks today since I was conducting the morning service at 100 Mile
> House, with a telephone connection to Sunrise Ranch, so that there were upwards
> of five hundred people sharing that service, an initiation before our departure.

He noted that there were 250 present at 100 Mile House, among them Lloyd and Paula, and Donna Bahan, which brought all the participants of the tour together in that moment, either at Mickleton or at the Hundred.

He spoke of recent experiences on the tour, one of which was his contact with the Zulu people:

> We couldn't speak the same language for the most part, although we had
> some interpreters present. But the sense of agreement came long before any-
> thing was interpreted, because there was a sharing of the same spirit. This, while
> it is becoming familiar to us, was somewhat surprising to the Zulu people and
> they were most interested, particularly one man, in discovering what it was. We
> have shared an association with people along the route who were awake or awak-
> ening to a greater awareness of what is actually required in the world.

I have always been drawn by the magic in ancient sites, a generous number of which are located in England. On this journey, while Martin and Lillian were occupied other-wise, Philip Maultby acted as a guide (well-informed and accommodating in every way) for me, and Janine Romaner, on a tour which included Stonehenge and Glastonbury.

Rupert's brother Miles hosted Martin, Lillian and me, Serena Newby, Michael and Nancy, and the Earl of Lindsay at an elegant luncheon in his business quarters in London.

There was a special event in London which marked a climactic time in our world-circling adventure. On March 30 Martin established his seat in the House of Lords, consequent upon the recent death of his brother David, Marquess of Exeter. It was a thrill to enter the Parliament Building and sense the centuries-old atmosphere that imbues its historic halls, and a rare privilege to witness the procedure as Martin took his place. There was an element of marriage of the old and new as he repeated the same words uttered, in the identical surroundings and atmosphere, by the long line of his predecessors.

Then, on the 31st, homeward bound, the journey ended as it began, with the three of us. Its conclusion signaled another "first"—from Conquest to Concorde. The flight in the Concorde symbolized to me the direction of expansion occurring in the ministry under Martin's hand—upward, breaking (sound) barriers, so that at the altitude of flight, sans clouds, this planet can be seen in its true dimension, not flat but with the curve of a beautiful sphere.

On Sunrise Ranch Martin spoke of the trip:

> In thirty-five days Lillian, Grace and I completed our journey, between Sunday, February 21 and Sunday, April 4, today. I gave the service at 100 Mile House on February 21, and those gathered in the Chapel here shared it over the telephone connection. There was a sharing of the journey both in form by some and in spirit by everyone. This journey is a part of the creative action of spirit achieving something which has very little to do with human expectations but relates to a transcendent purpose. We have tended to see this purpose in human terms through a rather garbled human state of consciousness, but there is an awareness of a transcendent purpose even if we haven't seen it too clearly, even if mistranslated at times. And that is on the move, in our own living in whatever measure we are accommodating the expression of the creative spirit.
>
> It may be noted, as we begin to bring these things more specifically into a larger context, that all the countries through which we passed were part of the British Commonwealth, except for South Africa, which was a former member. The British Commonwealth sprang out of what was previously the British Empire. It is said that the British Empire covered one third of the world's population. The Commonwealth now includes one quarter of the land surface of the earth and one quarter of the population of the world.
>
> If we go back in history a little we find the beginning of something, which developed into the British Empire later, at the time of Queen Elizabeth I in the 1500s. The treasurer of England at that time, and her chief adviser for a considerable period of her life, was an ancestor of mine, William Cecil, Lord

Burghley. Here was an initiating point in which he played an essential part.

He also played a part in consolidating the Church of England. The Queen, the Monarch, is the head of that church. Of course Henry VIII, for personal reasons more than anything, had started the process of division with the Roman Catholic Church, but it was my ancestor who provided a point of initiation in a particular sense with respect to the Church of England. This presumably was the highest view, even though it may have had political overtones, of spirituality at the time; so that there was a spiritual component in what was occurring and what began to emerge in form later as the British Empire. And out of that also sprang what is now the United States.

So in my earthly heredity I do have this background, and it has come to a particular focus now because, seemingly by chance—and nothing happens by chance—I have succeeded to the title which sprang out of what the original Lord Burghley initiated; so that in that sense at least I am in the same position that he was from the standpoint of what is occurring in spirit. We all have our earthly heredities; we bring them along with us willy-nilly; but there may be a right purpose to all this, because our concern is with the experience of the union of heaven and earth in our own consciousness. We are here, not to follow out something in imagination but to let a factual experience be known now, and that is found to be inclusive of something vastly greater.

We might take a look at what is called religion, which is a system of belief and of the worship of that belief. We probably relate it to what are commonly thought of as religions, perhaps Christian, Judaic, Islamic, etc., but it includes far more than that, because wherever there is a system of belief and a worship of the beliefs of that system, there is a religion. For instance, there is the religion of science. The beliefs in the religion of science are called hypotheses. If they are threatened, how quickly the members of that religion jump to their defense. Politics is another religion. There are various political systems in which there are beliefs, and people to worship them. The need for systems of belief is present because in the consciousness of mankind, factually, the world of form has excluded the world of spirit; therefore there has always been a sense of lack.

The British Empire, the British Commonwealth, the United States—it has all moved forward to the point where in myself this particular aspect of heredity comes to focus out of the past. At the same time there is something else that has come to focus, something with which you are more familiar: a focus of spirit which has made possible whatever has happened in the Emissary world. And these two come together in a particular way. It is interesting that at this present time the Queen of England, of the Commonwealth, is another Elizabeth, Elizabeth II. One may see certain elements coming together that are revealing of the union of the world of spirit with the world of form.

We may need to do many things, take care of our responsibilities. For instance, I undertook to assume my seat in the House of Lords, something to do with my earthly heredity. I was accompanied by a contingent of Emissaries, and a few others: Lillian and Grace, Michael and Nancy, Serena Newby, Miles Maskell and the Earl of Lindsay, also a member of the House of Lords and helpful because of his familiarity with the ways of that establishment. So we may rejoice to move together and bring our earthly background with us and let it be correlated correctly because we stand in spiritual identity, the one who has incarnated in this form with its earthly heredity.

On March 26 Myrtle Byl, a dear friend and valued member of the Sunrise family for fourteen years, finished her time on earth at the age of eighty-eight. Her husband Bill had come as a young man from the Netherlands and, eager to learn to speak English, joined a class taught by Myrtle. They were married, and one of their three children was Donna (Bahan).

Myrtle regularly reported to work in the office until a few weeks before she died. Whatever she did was done with meticulous attention to detail. Another facet of her generous and talented nature was in the field of art; besides painting, she gave art lessons to the children on Sunrise. She was responsible for the construction of several buildings, including the cozy residence in which she spent her last years.

The Supreme Council (Martin, Lillian and I, Michael and Nancy, Roger and Dorothy, Jim Wellemeyer, Bill and Donna, and Rupert and Tessa) met April 12-17 on Sunrise Ranch.

At an April Board Meeting on Sunrise Ranch, Jim Wellemeyer announced Roger de Winton's retirement from the Board after more than 20 years as President of EDL Colorado (at that time the international board). Great appreciation was expressed by all for Roger's years of steadfast dedication in this capacity. Bob Ewing succeeded Roger as President. Others on the Board at that time included Jim Wellemeyer (Vice-President); Mack Fontenot (Treasurer); Shareen Ewing (Secretary); Dorothy de Winton, Alan Hammond, Ted Black, Nick Giglio and Andrew Shier (all Directors). Roger continued as Advisor to the Board for a number of years.

In late April acceptance letters were sent out for attendance at the Emissary International Congress. Administrative teams for hospitality, child care, photography, audio/video, recreation, etc., were formed; the schedule for the Congress activities developed; and forum leaders were selected.

Martin, Lillian, Lloyd and I traveled to Colorado's Western Slope and visited the site of Uranda's boyhood home in Glade Park near Grand Junction—spectacular, unspoiled country under the shadow of the Grand Mesa, a land deeply loved by Uranda. There were a few remains of his original home there, and the tombstone of Uranda's mother in the vicinity.

Ken and Veronica Lim had completed a twelve-city tour of the South, their area of focus. It was sponsored by the Foundation of Universal Unity and the theme was "Let's Take a Fresh Look at Intentional Communities." They spoke of their ongoing experience at Edgewater Acres in Natchitoches, Louisiana. Victor and Carol Summers of San Antonio assisted in meetings in Texas. The invitation was, "Come see for yourself," and some who heard them did come—and attended the seminar at Edgewater in May.

Meanwhile in South Africa a significant event took place near Durban when a group of Emissaries met with about two hundred black members of the Church of Zion, made possible by Absalom Makatini of Empumalanga in Zululand. It was through Absalom that Rev. Amos Khumalo had met Martin during the World Tour, and the impact of the meeting was bearing fruit.

That year witnessed the purchase of Kingcombe in England, an exquisite property three miles from Mickleton, set in ten acres overlooking the town of Chipping Campden. A dignified, stone-built, ten-bedroom home, it accommodated Lindsay and Esther Rawlings, Serena Newby and others of the Mickleton unit. It was to serve as a home for Rupert and Tessa when in that area, as well as the three of us, also Michael and Nancy.

The Sunrise Ranch mailing department had two vital acquisitions: a Pitney Bowes postal meter and a NCI electronic calculating scale that weighs parcels and calculates their postage rates. Capable of doing other wonderful tasks, these additions were most welcome in that rapidly expanding department. In another area, we had become involved in data transmission between 100 Mile House and Sunrise Ranch, which allowed us to transmit information between computers via the telephone line. Martin's services were conveyed via this system, with many other exciting projections for the future, including transferral of accounting data.

Preparations for EIC continued nonstop at Colorado State University in Fort Collins, the date for its opening fast approaching. On the 400-acre campus, with its one hundred buildings, Coordinator Alan Hammond, Secretary Diana Soto and Frank Reale could be seen conferring on the campus with Bill Virden, CSU Conference Planner. Bill Bahan had been holding "Art of Living" meetings there for twelve years.

A thirty-minute drive northeast of Loveland, Fort Collins is one of the fastest growing cities in the country. Its colorful, friendly, college atmosphere provides a perfect setting for recreational and cultural activities. Gib and Sandy Charles were coordinating the Emissary Center there. Gib managed a landscaping business during the summer and ran an outdoor specialty store with Sandy in the winter, as well as teaching cross-country skiing for the city.

At 100 Mile House Martin spoke of the upcoming event in a service on June 6 entitled "Movement Toward the Congress":

> This Congress did not come about because we thought it would be nice to have a large gathering with as many Emissaries as possible, a social occasion. It arose because of a spiritual compulsion, because there was sufficient substance available collectively to initiate the cycle. But what was available to initiate the cycle is not sufficient to carry it to its point of consummation. There must be vastly more by then.
>
> If I mention the possibility of abortion I do not do so to generate tension or fear, but to indicate the vital importance and possibilities present. If disaster is possible, at the same time creative fulfilment is possible; and this duality is present in the world. We are aware of a movement toward the creative fulfilment and also the movement toward destructive disaster. As things come more and more to focus the two directions become more evident; and the way it goes will be dependent upon our behavior, our experience between now and then.

And so, on Thursday, July 29, it happened. "And God said, Let the waters under the heaven be gathered together unto one place, and let the dry land appear: and it was so." Emissary International Congress was a reality, with 1,500 friends gathered from the four corners of the earth. Such places as England, India, Israel, Africa, Korea, Australia, New Zealand, South Africa, Nigeria, Ghana and all parts of this continent were well represented. The 100 Mile family chartered a bus for the occasion, in which 55 exuberant members of the Unit traveled to Colorado. It was a memorable adventure, with mountains of luggage, and a pillow for each traveler. There were more who applied, worldwide, than could be accommodated in the facility, but the first view of that Hall with every seat filled had a breathtaking impact on me.

A welcome was extended by Michael Cecil and Alan Hammond, whose handling of the administrative aspects was a key factor in its outworking. They were followed by Jim Wellemeyer, Rupert Maskell, Roger de Winton, Bill Bahan and Michael.

Then Martin stood before the assembly, surveying the gathering, and with deep feeling said, "My, oh my! A room full of friends!" He emphasized that we were gathered to experience something which transcends agreement—union. We were not there to get or to give anything, but to *Be*. This precious time came to a close with a few moments of chant, and we moved quietly out into the cool evening.

On Friday morning the participants gathered simultaneously in eight different rooms, each with four TV monitors, to view a historical video of slides and movies, and a two-hour report with slides of the various areas in our worldwide program, all beautifully compiled and edited by Richard Cable. This was followed by fourteen others bringing history up-to-date with delightful commentary as slide after slide picturing many places portrayed the joyous unfolding of a story with great significance. A comment heard afterward: "As we came out into the daylight, we knew that we are a part of this great story and deeply sensed a point of new beginning."

On Friday and Saturday afternoons those attending were invited to participate in smaller group forums. The specialized topics, and forum coordinators, were: English as a Second Language (Hugh Malafry); Right Use of Media (Alan Hammond), with emphasis on open, honest communication amongst ourselves and others; Music (PenDell and Diana Pittman), in which Lloyd Meeker worked with instrumentalists and Judy Repar was official organist; Drama (Ann Foorman), with Stan Grindstaff, nine dramatists and a hundred forty participants; General Education (Alan Hammond); Attunements (Roger de Winton and Lloyd Meeker); Writing (Ted Black); Speaking (Hugh Malafry); Hospitality (Jean Hammond), attended by three hundred fifty with seventeen speakers representing many parts of the world and viewpoints; Health Professionals (Dr. Larry Krantz); Right Use of Technology (Charley Kitchens); Visual Art (Bob Ewing), assisted by a panel of artists, with Conrad O'Brien-ffrench demonstrating techniques, and a gallery displaying works of Emissary artists; Dance (Nancy Burghley), a Movement Forum which included aspects of folk dancing, eurythmy, Middle Eastern dance, and ballet; Business (Mack Fontenot and Ross Marks), where vital areas of finance were considered, such as the investment fund and construction projects; and Young Adults Forum (David and Nancy Lynch), composed of thirty-four young people who attended the Congress, which gathering proved to be lively and fruitful, including topics of discipline and relationships.

A huge map of the world covered the large wall behind the stage, a work of art in lively design and color by artists Pam Holloway, Bob Ewing, Tom Walsh and others. It served as a backdrop for some exotic presentations, such as a Singaporean Ribbon Dance by Linda Grindstaff, a dance by our African friends, and others. Timo Olagunju of Nigeria introduced his address with the words, "Black is beautiful!"—and it certainly was.

Many participated in the recreational program in the afternoons, which was coordinated by Andrew Shier of Sunrise Ranch. Most congregated in the courtyard of Corbett Hall, the main residence, where they played ball, or sunbathed and enjoyed watching.

The nearby tennis courts were in constant use, as was the indoor swimming pool.

In order for that number of people to attend, there had to be a representation of the (much) younger generation. There were seventeen babies, plus four children under the age of four. These were under the care and direction of LeAnna Moore of Sunrise. Quoting one of her assistants:

> Have you ever met twenty-one children in just twenty minutes? I have, but never before when ninety-five per cent needed comforting—*now!* Our staff was small, but with LeAnna's experienced ability we piled the children into carriages and, with two carriages apiece, strolled them up and down the hall! After a night's rest and the light of day, the children could be taken outdoors and we got acquainted; they began to relax. It was an adventure and gave every indication of the divine nature inherent in each one, regardless of age.

Max von Hartmann, with a team of four, expertly coordinated Food Service and Accommodation during the Congress. Five hundred dined in one cafeteria, the remaining thousand in another. Various interest groups met in smaller dining rooms, and Martin, Lillian and I dined in either cafeteria, which provided opportunity for closer contact with individuals. The campus food service staff was most helpful, and the friendship and agreement shared allowed for a smooth handling of the busy weekend—as Max observed, "graceful as a swan on the surface, and paddling like the dickens underneath!"

The final service of the Congress, delivered at CSU on the morning of August 1st, was entitled "Emissaries of Divine Light." A brass ensemble and organ accompanied the congregational singing, and PenDell Pittman sang *How Shall We Give Thee Glory* (music by him and words by Hugh Malafry), accompanied by Judy Repar on the organ.

Martin repeated some words from the song:

> "Holy art Thou, Lord of creation." Here is one body for Thy creative use in this hour and in all the hours and days to come. This is the concluding hour of our Congress, but it is also a beginning.
>
> In the beginning is the Word, and the Word is with God, and the Word is God. Without the Word is not any thing made that is made. In the Word is life; and the life is the light of men. The light shineth in darkness; but the darkness comprehends it not. The light must shine in the darkness and the light compels the natural creative process. It is not necessary that the darkness should comprehend the light, but it is necessary that the darkness be moved by the light. For this movement to occur there must be the light.
>
> We have been called Emissaries of Divine Light. Human beings cannot make the light shine but angels are characterized by light. Bodies and minds

and hearts can participate in this shining, but the shining, the light, is of the angel. An Emissary of Divine Light is not merely a human being but an angel incarnate and in expression. The place of light is a place where we have a conscious awareness. In this body we have a representation of all levels of the mind, in each one individually and in all collectively. Whatever the level of our conscious spiritual awareness now—and this one is necessary—there is always an awareness that is higher.

By the same token there is much that is lower, and some of that we don't need to delve into. This is an activity, the psychiatric field, where they are trying to delve into levels where the conscious experience should not be, thinking thereby to solve whatever the problem is thought to be. What is needed is one who lives in the light, that there may be a rising up out of the mess. You can't make the mess not a mess. It may be useful as compost; let it be compost.

There is the necessity for the resurrection, first the raising up of mind and heart to a level of conscious awareness that is above what human beings have known for millennia. We have the example of Jesus. Resurrection is thought of as relating simply to his physical body, and that occurred in the tomb; but the resurrection had occurred in the experience of his mind and heart long before the tomb experience.

So we come into a conscious awareness of the resurrecting body, because it is happening in us as individuals. We are moving with the creative cycle and it happens. Move against it and it happens too but in a different way; it dissipates, disintegrates. Well, we are not in the suicide business but in the business of resurrection. Because it occurs in our own experience the light shines and is available to others. So we move together in oneness of spirit as incarnate angels in these particular human forms and these minds and hearts, to make use of them, to do what we are here to do easily and naturally. We have had a delightful time together and what is happening is happening, whether we are all gathered in this ballroom in CSU or wherever we will be.

Martin closed his beautiful prayer, and the Congress, with the words:

So we share the responsibility with Thee of Thy creative work, administering the creative cycle here on earth with the absolute assurance that the fulfilment shall come; it shall be done. We ever abide with Thee. Aum-en.

An opportunity to visit Sunrise Ranch was an integral part of the Congress experience and in three afternoons over six hundred people were welcomed to the Ranch. Upon arrival from Fort Collins they were greeted by Nick and Betsy Giglio, then met Jim

Wellemeyer or Roger and Dorothy de Winton at the Dome Chapel, where Judy Repar of 100 Mile House provided organ music. Accompanied by two Sunrise tour guides, each group continued the tour on foot, touching the main aspects of Sunrise life. On the final day the three of us were at Martin's home to greet each one. The sight of Martin arriving that day, August 1st, in a helicopter, piloted by Eber Wright, which landed on Chapel Hill provided the perfect exciting climactic element to a most fulfilling and thrilling time spent with him at the Emissary International Congress.

That evening on Sunrise Ranch Martin gave a service entitled "In the World, but not of It":

> Welcome to the Dome Chapel. I think this is the first occasion when every seat is occupied, not to mention those who are gathered [and hearing the service] in the West Chapel. I'm sure you have sensed something of a shift occurring, brought to focus through the Congress but in fact by reason of the movement of the creative cycle with which we are associated. You recall the Master's statement, "I have yet many things to say unto you, but ye cannot bear them now." In order to hear the Word there must be the substance to accommodate it. What is heard will be dependent upon the quality of that substance in one's own generation of it, and that generation is dependent upon the quality of one's own living. The shift, which is occurring now in a rather more particular way, relates to an emergence in the awareness of mind and heart of a new state that has not been known heretofore. This relates to another statement with which we are familiar. We are in the world, but not of it.

> We have remained largely still a part of the world as it has been known to us and the rest of the population of the world. This has kept us, at least partially, in a trap where it is imagined that somehow the way of the Lord is synonymous with the ways of men. We have recognized that it is not a matter of improvement, and yet there has been an inclination to see everything on the basis of improvement. For instance, we did not come into the world simply to be competent in the running of a Congress, or a Human Unity Conference, or a Planetary Congress. We are in the world; we necessarily have association with all these circumstances, and we are here to use everything to the advantage of the Lord, which is possible only if one's first order of business is to be closely associated with the Lord, to let that connection be strong and consistent, so that everything that is done springs out of that connection.

General Council was held shortly after the close of the Congress, which made it convenient travelwise for the eighty-eight who attended and who had been at EIC, which included those from far countries as well as many from this continent.

It was not long before David Lynch announced, in *Newslight*, that as a result of the representative configuration of young adults in the Congress a special session would be held on Sunrise Ranch in 1983, June 15-27, for young men and women ages 18-21. The focus would be on expression of the Word, with participation a primary element.

Robert Middlestead of New Zealand stayed after the Congress to work on the Little Chapel. It had recently been remodeled with the addition of a tiled roof and cupola designed by Martin. Also a beautiful new door was installed, handcrafted of Brazilian mahogany by David Miller and Will Carpenter, assisted by Chris Bullock. Robert's contribution was two stained-glass windows, which he designed and constructed. Located at the top of the east and west walls, they transformed the interior of the Little Chapel. The eastern window depicts the sun rising over the Rimrock, and the western portrays the sun high in the sky over Green Ridge, where the sun sets. A leading artisan in his field, Robert used primarily European antique stained glass, and the mahogany frames were constructed by David Miller and Will Carpenter. These unique and exquisite gifts from Robert provided the crowning touch in that special sanctuary, which is filled with their glorious color throughout the day; and at night if the light is on inside, the outer darkness glows with the rich hues of "the evening and the morning" of a new day.

Martin, Lillian and I embarked on a tour of the Midwest on August 17 in the Conquest. Accompanied by Donna Bahan and Gail Moore, we were joined by Bill Bahan and Hugh and Christine St. Onge in Kansas City, Missouri, our first stop. That evening an open house, with 65 people, was held at the home of Bob and Judy Hollis, our gracious hosts. The next day we flew to Cartersville, Georgia, where our new Southeast regional facility, "Southwind," facilitated by Jim and Jane Gensheimer, was located. An open house was attended by 75, with many students from Life Chiropractic College. Knoxville, Tennessee, was next, on the 20th, where we were treated to a quick tour of the World's Fair. It was special to see "Up With People," a lively musical touring show composed of young people, after which Tim Houlton (son of Joe and June) who played a major role in that production, escorted us to other points of interest.

We had several days at "Rainbow Farm" (later Oakwood) in Selma, Indiana, and enjoyed the new kitchen and dining room facility, where 170 people from all over the Midwest were hosted to a grand sit-down dinner. That facility accommodated over 200 people on Sunday morning, the 22nd, for Martin's service, "Focus Points for the Creative Cycle."

The next day the three of us flew to Milwaukee, Wisconsin, for a visit with Lillian's brother, Bob Johnson, and his wife Mary. Bill, Donna and Gail drove to Lombard, Illinois, where Hugh and Christine resided. We joined them on the 25th for several days, and an open house there accommodated 60 people. On the 27th our party, which included Charley and Asti Kitchens, Robin and Pam Reily and Jack Stubbs, enjoyed a tour by boat—a unique way to see Chicago! Minneapolis, Minnesota, was our final stop, and on Sunday morning, the 29th, in the Radisson Hotel where we were staying, Martin gave a service, "The One and His Hereditary Clothing," which was attended by 100 people.

On the 30th the others drove to Lombard, and the Conquest returned Martin, Lillian and me to Colorado and Sunrise Ranch, after a very full two weeks in the colorful Midwest.

On September 1st Martin gave a service on Sunrise Ranch, "Programming and Reprogramming," in which he referred to the approaching anniversary of the ministry:

> In a few days' time this present golden jubilee year, the fiftieth of the Emissary ministry in its present form on earth, will draw to a close. However, this past year has been the first year in a continuing cycle of seven years. It will therefore be the beginning of the eighth period of seven years. The number eight represents the union of heaven and earth. The eighth creative day would be symbolized by the fire force. The fire of love is the power of transmutation, the power by which what is symbolized by base metal may be transmuted into what is symbolized by gold. Here we see something of what is available, in the creative cycles, to our experience in these years which are before us.

Martin then spoke of the programming "into an earthly state which has excluded heaven" shared by all human beings,

> thus programmed from the moment of conception. The initial programming may be described as intrinsic, present in the very flesh of the fetus, stemming from parents, forebears and the experience of the human race itself out of the past. This is usually thought of in terms of genes, but there is obviously more to it than the physical genes, just as there is more to it than the physical tape in the tape recorder. If that's all there is, then—no particular sound when it is played. But something is imposed upon the tape from some source if there is to be a program reproduced. There is this intrinsic program in each developing form; the music out of the past is there. But as soon as there is conception, something else comes into the picture. You might call it an extrinsic influence, which is fundamentally the state of the mother imposed upon the developing fetus.
>
> So there are these two aspects, the intrinsic and the extrinsic. During the time of uterine development the extrinsic is more or less indirect, but as soon as the baby is born then direct influences begin to be brought to bear, so that the extrinsic programming continues. All people are programmed in this fashion with these two components. We may see that the intrinsic is more basic,

deeper, almost untouchable. It is there; no one is exempt; it is a carry-forward out of the past. It has been described in the Christian religion as original sin, an intrinsic programming coming out of the earthly experience of the past. Superimposed on top of that is the extrinsic which subsequently ensues. The state of the world itself is simply a reflection of this programming. The surface aspects can be manipulated and changed somewhat as influences of various kinds are brought to bear, but the total package is hardly changed at all. Certainly the intrinsic aspect is not changed; it sits there in the very flesh of the individual, which includes what are referred to as mind and emotions.

The intrinsic program—I suppose you could say the main part of it—requires that human beings die. Everybody is programmed to die; that's why everybody dies. As long as that program exists there is apparently no escape, and of course there is whatever leads up to that ultimate point, which may come speedily or more slowly. But the programming is set and the result is consequently inevitable as long as that program is there. We have become aware of the fact that man was not originally programmed that way. It is something that has been self-induced back along the way; it is the state of affairs as it is now; and we deal with the situation as it is.

Bruce Allyn had some experience at Oxford University in England, and lived and studied for two months at Leningrad State University in the Soviet Union. He also visited Soviet Georgia and Moscow, and was currently working on a Ph.D. in Harvard's Soviet Union program, with plans to study in Moscow for a year.

Lloyd and Paula Meeker moved to Denver, Colorado, where they provided a focus for many in the group in that fast-growing area.

Martin was a builder! The magnificent Dome Chapel was a product of his divine vision, a sight to behold in Eden Valley. Another grand structure was taking form under his direction. A vital member in the initial stages of this building was Paul Van Vliet, who with his wife Sophie had come to Sunrise Ranch to participate in what would be called "Project 30." With their two children they had emigrated to Canada in 1958 from the Netherlands. They contacted the ministry through hearing Tom Cooper speak about 100 Mile House and were especially intrigued by the Twin Valleys School. Before coming to the Ranch Paul was involved in construction at Green Pastures, Clear Water, the King View Conference Center and Southwind in Georgia.

Paul's specific reason for coming to Sunrise was to work on the design for the proposed Dining Room/Kitchen Complex, otherwise Hospitality Center, eventually to be named the Pavilion. His esthetic architectural drawings of the 20,000-square-foot complex were most impressive, and he served as project manager, with Don Hynes as builder and Jim Higerd the engineer and liaison with the local government. With ground-breaking imminent, a construction crew was being formed, with an invitation extended to men from other places to come and offer their talents in the project. And they came, not all at the same time but as each phase unfolded—craftsmen superbly trained to perform the many tasks involved in a great undertaking.

Before very long the lower level of the Complex, with its concrete wall, was completed. What a sight that was! Its vast dimensions sent a message through the fibers of my being that the "house of the Lord" was indeed being built, dissolving the constrictions in consciousness. It offered an opportunity to share more deeply the vision of Martin, and before him Uranda, that was never content with what was on this side of the horizon.

Don Hynes said, in *Eden Valley News:*

> As men of the "Project 30" Crew, our work is our prayer, and it is a joyful
> psalm. Rhythm, intensity, persistence, fruition, relaxation, pulsation, rhythm—
> this is the cycle of our expression. And in this cycle there is an expansive place
> of respect and enjoyment for one another's spirit. It is a space of friendship,
> discovered and enriched in the rhythms of work, a dynamic and creative space,
> and a space that by its very nature is an invitation to all.

The initial crew, with Don Hynes, were David Ward, Rory McNamara, Frank Moore, Pat Fitzsimmons, Jim Greaney, Kit Miller. There would be many more as the work progressed.

In the midst of all this activity it was heart-warming to see the old laundry facility being expanded and modernized. David Miller and Ed Haimowitz were busy preparing a concrete foundation for the extension to house two new stacked commercial dryers. Also a new automatic washer was to be installed. This was no minor outworking in the eyes of the laundry ladies Sarah Haimowitz, Peggy Antell and Peggy Gretsch—and the many others who would work there in the future.

Another trip to England was in order, and Martin, Lillian and I again enjoyed the charming Cotswold countryside, the quaint town of Chipping Campden, Kingcombe and Mickleton, where we had a tour of the Three Ways Hotel. Some of our family working there at the time were David Gilbert of Canada, Valerie Morris from Africa, and Philip Maultby of England. During our stay Rupert and Tessa, our ever-thoughtful hosts, treated us to a delightful luncheon in the elegant Compleat Angler on the Thames.

34

THE FIRE INTENSIFIED

January ~ December 1983

O ur first seminar in Italy was held in January 1983 "in the heady Alpine atmosphere of Bieno, a tiny village overlooking a magnificent valley," writes Rupert Maskell in *Newslight*, "where the faculty (the Maskells, Marco and Lele Menato, Sarah-Jane Gluckman and Lida Radziwill) and a dozen seminarians gathered for two days, some of whom will be in England for HUC and visits to Mickleton. Lele and Lida did an excellent job of translating."

Rupert and Tessa took advantage of the trip to include seminars in Stuttgart, West Germany, with thirty gathered. They were delighted to meet many of Agnes Mura's friends from Mannheim. In Amsterdam, Holland, they held an afternoon meeting, after which Rupert said, "Again, a fresh, open spirit characterized the event. Europe, which to me used to seem a little gray and musty, resounds increasingly with life."

The year 1983 welcomed an increased number of Martin's and Uranda's grandchildren into the world. On March 3rd a daughter, Majessa, was born to Peter and Marina Castonguay; on June 2nd a son, Benjamin, to Luke and Helen Vorstermans; and on the last day of the year, the 31st of December, a boy, Lloyd James, to Lloyd and Paula Meeker. The end of the following year, on December 12, 1984, a son, Dylan, was born to Peter and Marina; and a few years later on February 12, 1987, a boy, Stefan, completed Luke and Helen's family—and the grandchildren!

Another spacious and luxurious (adjectives that were becoming commonplace) structure was taking form on the northwest corner of the Sunrise property where it borders our ranch/farm area. The contract was awarded to Kamtz Karpentry of Loveland and was being constructed for Judith Aranow, Mack and Leslye Fontenot, Keith and Melanie Fairmont, and Andrew and Susan Shier. It consisted of four townhouses, in two buildings, beautifully designed and executed, in an unpopulated area with breathtaking views of this gorgeous valley from every window. Paul Van Vliet's talents were incorporated in the early stages of this project. Each of the four "houses" was distinct in design and atmosphere, according to the unique character of the home owner.

Conrad O'Brien-ffrench celebrated his 90th birthday on Sunrise Ranch, surrounded by his Sunrise family. He wrote something for the occasion:

> We are here to celebrate my growing out of my 80s, during which everybody wanted to carry my luggage or help me up the steps. If I forgot my name, or someone else's, people said, "Oh well, he's 80, you know." If I put things away and forgot where I put them, or while shopping left my shopping list at home, it was okay because I was 80. If I acted silly, put shaving cream on my toothbrush or tried starting my car with my house key, it was understandable—"He's 80." At 60 or 70 some expected me to retire to my little house on the hill, or to Hawaii. But if you survive until 80 everybody is surprised that you can walk, let alone uphill, or can drive a car, or that you have occasional lucid moments. At 70 I was clumsy and made mistakes which maddened everyone. But at 80 they forgive you everything and think it is rather funny. If you ask me, life begins at 90.

The Loveland Choral Society presented a spring concert on April 15 and 17 in the Dome Chapel, conducted by our friend Jan Earle, owner of a local florist shop.

On April 25-29 there was a "Ministers of Finance Gathering" on Sunrise Ranch, with twenty-eight present, representative of the vital area of finance in our ministry. The coordinators, Mack Fontenot, Ross Marks, Gordon MacFarland, David Waskom and Bob Hollis met the weekend preceding the gathering. Ron Kirby and Marty Worster of the Sunrise Accounting Department demystified terms and procedures, so that the momentum for decentralization of data processing could develop quickly and with ease. The daily forum sessions were highlighted by visits from Martin, Roger and Michael, which permitted any parochial vision to vanish. As Mack lightly offered comments in guidance, he affirmed that we are "people persons, not money persons."

A "Festival of Human Unity" was held at the University of British Columbia in Vancouver on April 30. It was a day packed with intense creativity, with poetry, music, dance and drama interspersed with many speakers, panel discussions and workshops. Lindsay Rawlings, of England, Co-President of HUC 1983, was the featured speaker. Some others were master of ceremony Manning Glicksohn, Ron Polack, Anita Storey (secretary to Marilyn Ferguson) and Dale and Susan Maranda.

In a service on May 15 at 100 Mile House, "The Invisible Design Inherent in Spirit," Martin observed that others were moving into position to share the speaking platform with him, in whatever location, for which he was grateful.

> Collectively this is our reason for being on earth. We may allow spiritual expression, which emanates from one source; this is why oneness is possible. Human beings have tried to produce oneness without acknowledging the source which would make it possible. It has been generally assumed that somehow, by argument and discussion, a true consensus will be reached which will be characterized by oneness. It never is; it's always a compromise of human views.

> That one spirit, as we well know, rightly differentiates in manifold ways. There is no restriction or arbitrary conformity required, but you have a natural agreement which becomes so powerful in one's own experience that it becomes unthinkable that it could ever be violated. This is the true state. Apparently back along the way, for whatever reason, it became thinkable to somebody that it might be violated, and all human troubles stem from that initial point of deviation. That would have had no effect if someone else had not agreed with it. So it multiplied, and we have the human state of chaos, confusion, destructiveness and violence presently with us. There is one invisible starting point for everything and because of that, coordinated living design is a reality.

The 7th International Council was held May 29 to June 2 in Mickleton, England. Martin, Lillian and I were present, as were Michael and Nancy, and we stayed at Kingcombe. Shortly after arrival the Exeters (Martin and Lillian) and Burghleys (Michael and Nancy) drove to Burghley House, at which time Michael officiated at the opening of a pub in Stamford called "The Lord Burghley." He also read the lesson on Sunday morning in Saint Martin's church in Stamford.

The Council took place at Mickleton House. Almost 200 attended the Sunday morning service given by Martin on June 3, subsequently entitled "To Express the Truth." The next day we traveled to London where we spent five days. There Martin renewed his Oath of Allegiance in the House of Lords, and all five of us participated in a reception and dinner party given by Polly, Marchioness of Lansdowne, at her home in Chelsea.

About 30 people were present, including Polly's father, Viscount Eccles, a former cabinet minister in the Conservative Government and one-time Minister of Education.

Then—home, via another exciting experience on the Concorde.

A service at 100 Mile House on the morning of June 5 was entitled "The Rent in the Veil," in which Martin referred to the garden planted eastward in Eden, with man placed in it to dress it and to keep it.

> This garden indicates a state of heavenly consciousness. Eden simply refers to the earth. The garden is planted eastward in Eden—our tomorrows come out of the east. We might see this with other than a horizontal viewpoint which sees the future ahead, the present now, and the past disappeared over the horizon. The true viewpoint recognizes something of a vertical nature. It was described as coming down from God out of heaven, in the moment.

In the service given that evening entitled "The Seventh Sense," Martin spoke about the veil which, in the symbol of the tabernacle of old, and the temple later, separated the holy place from the Holy of Holies,

> a rather apt symbol of the human state outside of the garden. It is possible to allow the generation of some spiritual substance on the earthly side of the veil, so that there might begin to be a sensing of holiness, of the natural wholeness of oneself as an individual and of all people. We have such a sensing.

He spoke of the "sixth sense" about which people get

> a little bit hung up on—ESP: in other words a sensing a little beyond the ordinary gamut provided by the five physical senses. Well we can sense things in that way; but the habit has been to be controlled by what one so sensed, and this is the source of the trouble. The prince of this world comes and usually finds plenty. The senses are stimulated; human minds and hearts and bodies go along with it. There is always a certain amount of self-deception in this regard, particularly with respect to those who try to figure out what should be done on the basis of the stimulation occurring through these six senses. Nothing needs to be done on that basis.
>
> There is another sense, which makes it possible for the connection to be made into heaven. This seventh sense has rather atrophied in most people. It needs to be reactivated. Obviously many people are quite unconscious of any sense of this nature; nevertheless it may still be there and capable of being activated. The activation of this, wherever it is possible, proves out to be one of the responsibilities of the priesthood in the holy place. The seventh sense is still hidden for most. It has taken a while to begin to experience the holy place

collectively, but it is here. In this place we become aware of the veil of separation. Perhaps the veil itself glows; in other words there is a dawning awareness that there is something beyond that veil which is very, very bright.

In *Newslight,* under the title "Musica 1983," David Polack wrote:

Edenvale, in British Columbia, hosted Musica, June 21 to July 3. The tone was set Sunday evening, June 19, when over a hundred people gathered in the elegant setting of the Vancouver Center to share in "A Summer Concert." George Hanson, PenDell Pittman, Margaret Tlustos and Ann Fisher, accompanied by Margaret Christie and Betsy Giglio, together provided a performance that initiated the excellence that characterized these musicians throughout this intensely creative two weeks. On Tuesday, June 21, under the direction of PenDell and Diana Pittman, George, Betsy and Allen Dorfman, music filled every corner of Edenvale. Sessions were held in the morning, afternoon and most evenings, with the remaining time taken up with lessons and rehearsals.

Mrs. Immanuel Velikovsky passed away June 24 after a long life of devoted service with her husband. After Dr. Immanuel Velikovsky's death a few years earlier I visited Elisheva at their home in Princeton on several occasions. She was a remarkable and most talented woman, and to me a dear friend.

Martin gave a service at 100 Mile House on July 3rd entitled "Pure Radiation, Pure Reception" in which he referred to

a world gone mad! This is not merely a modern-day phenomenon. The crazy state has been with us for many millennia. But in this setting now we have awakened to an awareness of our ability and responsibility to provide the essential element of orientation. If mankind is irrational and consequently there is a crazy world, it may be attributed to a diseased state in the population of the earth. We might describe this state as a deficiency disease. In view of the fact that everyone suffers from it, it has not been looked upon particularly as a disease but is considered to be the natural state of human beings. When it gets more extreme, here or there, it may begin to be recognized as a deficiency in the sense of physical lacks: maybe malnutrition, maybe an inability to assimilate certain substances. Individuals have these conditions, but they are only evidence of a much more universal state of ill health.

It is a deficiency disease because of the veil. What is present the other side of the veil has difficulty coming through the veil, and so those who exist on this side find themselves lacking what would otherwise be present if there were no veil. In one way it could be described as anemia, since that has something to do with the blood, which represents the life. There is a deficiency in the flow of life, so the substances required are missing, or distorted and reduced by the fact of the veil. The rich quality of blood is not presently the general experience and the true state of health is impossible under the veil. If you have continuous pain you learn to live with it; if the pain is removed you may be startled to find what a different experience it is. The pain had been incorporated into the lifestyle, so to speak. There is a lack of ease in human beings generally. That is the reason for requests for seminars, and one thing and another, to deal with so-called stress, a lack of ease—which is dis-ease.

There is the endeavor to get rid of this stress syndrome under the veil. It is found, in fact, to be impossible. You may modify it, you may learn to live with it, but it doesn't vanish. It's still there, because there can only be a lack of ease when the greater part of living experience is prevented from coming through into one's own existence.

The veil is the impure human heart: human emotion wrapped up in the world that is experienced through the six senses. The six senses bring information as to this world. But below the veil, of what value is this information?—because there is nobody present who can interpret it correctly and let it be used rightly. Because of the emotional clutter, people are governed by their view of the information incoming.

Perhaps we could look at this matter of incoming information through the six senses. I have indicated before—and it is evidently being discovered now—that there are two aspects to the six senses: a positive and a negative aspect, the radiant and the receptive. In human experience it has all been deemed to be receptive. There has been virtually no awareness that the radiant aspect even exists. There are a few perceptive individuals nowadays who are awakening to the fact of a radiant aspect to the sense of hearing, for instance, or seeing, or one of the senses.

What is radiant will be dependent upon the state of the heart, what is able to get through from the other side of the veil. There is a flaming sword. Flame is radiant, and the sword is penetrating, so there is something which emerges by reason of the flaming sword. But it must be experienced by human beings through the state of their emotions. If the emotions are governed by information incoming from the six senses, this will establish the internal quality which conditions the radiation. Certainly the radiation is not coming through clear and beautiful; it is distorted, colored, by reason of the impurities of heart, because the heart is the means by which the heavenly radiation comes into the earth. If the heart is cluttered up, then there is a little trickle that is called life; we imagine for the moment that we are alive. It is existence in the darkness under the veil. One may have a certain consciousness of subconscious goings-on, but to be truly conscious requires that the veil be dissolved, so that the radiation out of heaven may be known in the earth. That is the only way anyone can know the truth.

On July 10th Reverend William H. Bahan, a great friend of countless people all over the world and a valued assistant to Martin in his ministry, passed away in Elizabethtown, Pennsylvania, of a heart attack. With his wife Donna, and Gail Moore, he was en route to a speaking engagement. Bill was the second youngest of nine children born to Arthur and Ada Bahan of Methuen, Massachusetts. He and his wife Ruth had three children, Christine, William and Tim. He graduated from the Palmer College of Chiropractic in Davenport, Iowa, in 1949 and, with four of his brothers, practiced for a number of years in their chiropractic clinic in Derry, New Hampshire. During the 1960s and early 1970s he focused Emissary Classes on Sunrise Ranch and traveled worldwide, lecturing and holding seminars on health and creative living. He was the founding director of the Whole Health Institute and served on many advisory boards of organizations concerned with wholistic living. His most recent home, with his wife Donna, was beautiful "Southview" at Green Pastures.

Martin paid tribute to Bill:

> There have been one or two, just a few, during these millennia, when asked the question "Where art thou?" answered "Here I am!"—no dissembling, but a straightforward answer, the one required of every human being. Bill established a precedent in this regard in his generation. He offered that vision to all who would receive it. If we love Bill and respect what he brought we will recognize the door which he opened wide and walk through it naked and unashamed, that we may be clothed, as he was, with the garments of light, of understanding, letting the word of truth be spoken in our living always, sounding the Tone of Life.

Consequent upon Bill Bahan's departure, Jim Wellemeyer accepted the responsibility of providing a focus at the Green Pastures unit in Epping, New Hampshire, and took up residence at Southview. Part of his responsibility was coordinating the eastern and midwestern areas of the United States—quite a task, and Jim was the man for the job, an inspiration and example of consistent spiritual expression.

At the regional Southwind facility in Atlanta, Georgia, a service of thanksgiving was held for Bill Bahan, with approximately sixty present, including family, friends and chiropractic associates. It was conducted by Southeast Coordinators Jim and Jane Gensheimer (Bill's niece). After Bill's passing, Donna Bahan was welcomed to join the family on Sunrise Ranch and assumed the position of Administrator of Education, working with Alan Hammond, Director of Education.

"A One-Day Seminar on July 17 in Lagos, Nigeria, served a number of purposes," began an article in *Newslight* by Georgina Mkpa, who focalized that area with her husband Odim.

> It celebrated the end of student life and the beginning of practice at the Bar
> for Emeka Emeh. Also, it was a send-off party for Odim and our son Drako,
> embarking for HUC '83 and the Young People's Week in England, respectively.

The 10th International Human Unity Conference was held at Warwick University in England July 27-30 and was attended by 655 people from 25 nations. Its theme was "Integrity in Action: Formula for a Well World." Rupert Maskell, Michael Cecil and Alan Hammond were primary speakers, with fifty other speakers and presenters. Keith Turner, and George and Joelle Emery, played vital roles throughout. There were various dialogues and interviews conducted on the stage, and sessions were complemented by music, drama, dance, workshops/forums and audience participation. The finest talent, in their various fields, was offered freely by Stan Grindstaff, Tom Cooper, Dale Maranda, George Hanson, Ann Foorman, Clive Riche, Mora MacLachlan, Linda Grindstaff and others. There was a half hour of the Ekome black dance group one evening, also an offering by Sir George Trevelyan.

> Other participants were Frances Horn, Jean Bradbery (of the Hunger Project), Sister Jayanti (from the Brahma Kumaris group), Peggy Brook, Polly Lansdowne, David Bohm, Don Factor and Hans Hoegh (Secretary-General of the Red Cross International).

On July 30 Martin's service on Sunrise Ranch, "The Completion of HUC 1983," included a report via telephone connection with England of the three-day Conference there. The speakers were Lindsay Rawlings, Rupert, Tessa and Michael. The setting was a beautiful theater, attendance approximately three hundred. Rupert said:

> It was a particular thrill for Tessa and me this morning to stand onstage
> and introduce Absalom Makhathini and Joseph Mkhwanazi, our two Zulu
> friends who had come all the way here to be with us.

He expressed his gratitude for the emergence of The Foundation of Universal Unity and likened it to a newborn babe which was

> beginning to exhibit a true function in service alongside its Emissary parents
> who gave it birth. And my thoughts certainly go to you, Martin, and to Uranda
> before you, who were the means by which this child could come into the earth,

a child which will grow in grace and stature to perform a very vital service in
the world, standing alongside its parents.

Tessa spoke then of the "beautiful image of a very large earth, in blue and green, held
carefully by a brown hand and a white hand which was the backdrop of our Conference."
Michael commented that

there was a profound influence extended in consciousness beyond this place.
I suppose it was especially poignant to consider this fact in terms of England
and Europe, the Old World, being touched by a hand of new light in which we
were privileged to play our parts.

There had been a telephone hookup earlier that day with Vancouver and South Africa, which marked "the advent of the first concurrent Human Unity Conference to be
held in South Africa," with 180 people gathered.

Martin spoke, from Sunrise, of

receiving what shall be offered in the days to come out of the body of humanity. The door has been opened. Theory must be translated into experience,
because only so is there present the creative light by which all may find their
way through the door. There are transformations occurring—far more presumably yet to occur. It is all dependent upon those who are indeed the door
and whose living proclaims that the door is open because the light shines so
vividly and intensely that those who are awakening cannot help but become
aware of it. This Conference has been an evidence of the fact that many people
are aware of that light. Because there is a certain shining, a certain experience
beyond theory, the awakening ones become aware of it and gather themselves
together unto one place, such as occurred at this Conference.

The Emissaries present were an essential ingredient, but also the many
others there without a direct awareness of what we are about, yet willing and
capable of coordinating with what was unfolding by reason of the spirit present.
And the spirit is no respecter of persons—everybody is included—and shines
forth through all concerned, to the extent that the restrictions of consciousness begin to dissolve. We may align ourselves in our own experience of living, with that which is new to human beings but has always been present,
available, and is now coming forth with absolute inevitability. The command,
"Let the waters be gathered together unto one place," is being heard.

Beatrice Perry passed away on July 31st on Sunrise Ranch, where she first made her
appearance in the very early days of the Unit. A remarkable lady, she was a poet, among
other things. I recall walking into the kitchen of the ranch house early one morning. Bea

was the only one there, and I heard the perfect words to initiate a bright atmosphere regardless of the weather: "It's a misty, moisty morning"—not just a drizzly, rainy day! She was an excellent teacher and at Uranda's suggestion taught two children on the Ranch for a year, Mary Thompson and Chuckie Strikwerda. Emissary education proved to be unlimited in scope; it included learning to crochet, doing lunch dishes, cooking and, later, weaving—all of which added up to spiritual education. Mary Thompson (Schmeer) was grateful, in later years, for the opportunity to take care of her when she was in need. Bea's love for children and language was reflected in her poetry. Whimsy was a delightful ingredient, as in these:

I stood on the shore at sunset,
When it sank into the sea,
And it made a long, bright path of gold
Right from the sun to me.

****

The wild geese! The wild geese!
Come, see them going by!
There they form a long V
Away up in the sky;
It is no use to tempt them
With grain and food, to stay,
For winds and wings toward the south
Are bearing them away.

****

Over the treetops
Far, far, far!
Over the mountains high
All I can see is
One bright star
There by itself in the sky.

****

Nightingale

I heard a nightingale sing in the palm tree
In a grove, in the half-light before it was morn,
And his notes, half-remembered, brought back to me Eden,
And things I'd forgotten, before I was born:
I rose from my couch in a soft-scented bower,
And opened my lattice to greet the new day
Before Time was. The Garden knew naught of the hour,
But fadeless and deathless, the earth stretched away.
And I too was fadeless. I too joyed in being
Perfect in a world where perfections belong,
While the nightingale took of the whole world of seeing
And scents, and sweet loving—and put them in song.

Marie Louise Radziwill, of Rome, Italy, daughter of Lida, is a very talented artist. Her presence on Sunrise Ranch that year resulted in a uniquely beautiful creation, a life-size bronze bust of Martin. He spent many hours in his chair in the living room, working as usual, while she molded an exquisite and very faithful likeness of his strong, almost rugged features. The sculpture graces the southwest entryway of the Dome Chapel.

A new 12' by 27' pool and patio area was installed that summer at the Bishop's residence on Sunrise Ranch, a beautiful, welcome and well-used addition.

Don Hynes was enthusiastic about a new Course entitled "The Foundation for Leadership: On Eagle's Wings," which had been held in Loveland, with the distinction of being the first to complete the full 18-week cycle. He said:

> The course style provides an opportunity to cultivate specific work skills in the area of spiritual expression, and this was a key to the success of the evening sessions. The format also proves an effective vehicle for enhancing the individual work which the course requires. Most vivid in my heart and mind is the provision through this medium for the experience of the qualities of truth that are so amply present in Martin's magnificent book, *On Eagle's Wings*.

The Northwestern Drama Workshop was held at 100 Mile House, with 53 participants who came from England, New York, New Hampshire, California and Sunrise Ranch. An intensive two-week period of preparation was shared by Stan Grindstaff of San Francisco, Ann Foorman from Sunrise Ranch, and Nancy Barbour from 100 Mile House. They were joined by Paul Batten, a professional actor from Vancouver, Doug Elliott from the Hundred, and Russell Brown from England. That team of six coordinated the energy-packed weekend workshop, which was characterized by the key word *process.* The requirement for participation was not experience but "willingness to move with the creative force."

A Young People's Week, the fourth to be held on Keith and Jean Turner's property at Brackenber, near the Cumbrian fells (hills) of northern England, was held August 7-14. The 24 young people, ages 11-16, carried an international flavor, as did the 12-member staff, coordinated by John Kurk. Activities included horseback riding, swimming, music, games and quiet times.

"Coordination in the One Body" was the title of a service on August 14. Following congregational singing, accompanied by Betsy Giglio on the organ and Zoe Brunson on the piano, Martin said:

> This is a very special day and hour as we all assemble in many places to participate in our service. I understand there are 66 places connected to us here in the Dome Chapel on Sunrise Ranch by telephone. These places are in 27 states, and one has slipped in from Canada; by some magic, I am told, King View is on the line. There are some 1300 people, which when added to those gathered here total over 1600. We may not put great store in numbers but there is significance to them.

> Just over a year ago the Emissary International Congress was in session in Fort Collins. There were 1500 people gathered then; so there are more today. Those participating now represent a great many more who could not be directly connected by telephone but nevertheless are doubtless with us in spirit. We do not really need to travel great distances when there are other methods and means of communication. This assembly is present today because of the effective action of the spirit of the living God, to allow that radiation to continue and be intensified. Here is a representation on earth of this one spirit, in this body of people assembled, wherever they may be in the geographical sense, revealing their association with the one body drawn together by this spirit...

> Human minds and hearts have been expert in justifying themselves, in sustaining the illusion that there is some sort of useful existence in a state of separation. Even those who have come to some vision and understanding of the truth—in theory—have all too often, in fact and experience, maintained their own separation, saying in effect, "Well I'm me; therefore I have the ability, and the right even, to decide how things shall be in my experience." If one is honest I am sure you can find areas in yourself where you function on that basis: "I'm going to do my thing." Well your thing may have some value, I'm

not sure—and you shouldn't be sure either—but you will never find out if it is of the slightest value until you have lost your life of trying to do your thing. Horrors! Most people feel they would lose all meaning; their thing is supreme. Blessed are those who have no thing! That may be pronounced "nothing." They have nothing to lose and everything to find, and the everything which is to be found is in that one body."

Supreme Council gathered August 19-27 on Sunrise Ranch. It consisted of the three of us, Michael and Nancy, Rupert and Tessa, Alan and Jean, Roger and Dorothy, Jim Wellemeyer and Donna Bahan.

On September 5 there was a "Harvest Gala" held in the Pavilion, the new dining room facility, with the Sunrise family and General Council participants. The music, dancing and mingling in friendship all spoke eloquently of the thanksgiving in each heart for that remarkable building nearing completion.

The Three Ways Hotel, in the Cotswold village of Mickleton, 100 yards from Mickleton House, passed into the hands of the Emissary family in England on a 48-year lease from September 1st. Managers Keith and Jean Turner were backed by a staff of 16 from the Mickleton/Kingcombe unit (to name a few, Nicola and Alizanne Clark, Kay Turner, Stephen Leckie and David Heaney). Recently refurbished, with 38 double rooms (all with bathrooms en suite) and a three-star rating, the hotel promised much in the future.

During a visit to New Hampshire, Martin gave a service on September 25 at Green Pastures entitled "Passionate Love for the Truth":

It is difficult not to be aware of the imminent and terminal danger which, like an ominous black cloud, envelops the human race. Many of the more honest and clear-sighted in high places on the world scene realize that virtually anything anyone may do can at best only delay the inevitable. Well may men's hearts be "failing them for fear, and for looking after those things which are coming on the earth." Nothing is gained by pretending these things are not so!

Yet millions blindly attempt to live as though the world continues to be as it has been. Ambition and avarice still prevail. Self-serving and self-indulgence remain the order of the day and are often equated with freedom. Fear, amongst other destructive compulsions, is the cause of what is now coming to culmination. Fear not! Behold, a door is opened in heaven. Come up hither. See and act from this new perspective. The former things are passing away. Let the radiance of spirit be the power of our living, that the new state may be unveiled by the passing of the old. Everything contained in the old state is now in the past. Is anything gained by analyzing and discussing it? Such action maintains identification with it. Let the former things pass away. Let them go or go with them! No one is exempt from the working of the creative cycle. The attitude to be taken in this moment springs out of passion for the truth, never from reactive judgment of people and circumstances.

This business of misinterpretation is like building elaborate castles of sand on the seashore. Some of them can be quite impressive—marvelous structures! Then of course the tide comes in and washes it all away. No matter how magnificent, how beautiful they may seem to be, how long according to human standards they may have existed, the tide comes in. It is more profitable to be associated with the tide than with the sand castles. The tide may represent the creative processes at work regardless of human beings. The tide is not designed merely to destroy something that mankind may have painstakingly built, but to make possible correct interpretation, so that what is brought forth, created by reason of that interpretation, may be true to the living design. You don't have to have an extensive education to know how to wake up in the morning; it comes naturally. The time has come for mankind. We are becoming increasingly aware of this fact by reason of the changes that are occurring in the consciousness of people generally.

I've been describing something in terms of interpretation of a vibrational field that is present for everyone, heretofore misinterpreted. And then the misinterpretations have been misinterpreted, ad nauseam. Can we not see what a waste of time it is to judge, blame, condemn all the wrong things we think we see? There are masses of wrong things, but to struggle with them, to keep looking at them, to think that somehow or other by this method or that technique we can make them over into right things, is ridiculous. It can't be done. It is a waste of time. Every time one judges, and consequently becomes aware of increasing numbers of wrong things to be corrected, one digs one's grave deeper. It is more sensible to dispose of the shovel and stop the nonsense, that there may be space in consciousness for the dawning experience of right interpretation. That is describable also as re-creation. The world has been created the way it is by human beings through misinterpretation. A genuine world can be created when there are human beings on hand to interpret the vibrational field correctly.

During October the Whole Health Institute conducted lectures and seminars in London, Paris and several cities in India (where Janis Barker was the hostess). Representing WHI on this tour were Dr. Larry Krantz and Ann Foorman of Colorado, Mark Anderson from New

Hampshire, and Peter Garrett from England. A thousand people attended the events.

Martin spoke at 100 Mile House, October 30, on "The Transcendent Power of Radiant Love":

> From time to time it has been emphasized that the time was short. There has been dillydallying along the way, with the idea that things would continue as they always have since the fathers fell asleep. But the impact becomes immediate now. What might be thought of as failure is, to me, unthinkable. I trust this is so to you also and to all who have awakened to the truth. Very rapid strides have been made in the field of nuclear weapons, for instance; they didn't exist forty years ago. The initiation of this ministry was before nuclear weapons. BNW! How rapid has been the development of true spiritual expression? I am sure that those who have given themselves to their scientific pursuits, out of which came nuclear weapons, did so with great zeal. Why should a consideration of spiritual experience have tended to be so passive? We are awakening now, I am sure, to the imminence of what we have for a long time recognized in theory was required.
>
> There is no more wonderful experience than to be on the job, doing what we are here to do. The Master said, "Ye are my friends, if ye do whatsoever I command you." As we do whatsoever the spirit commands, constantly, we are friends. To that extent we love one another and get the job done.

In Martin's service at 100 Mile House on the morning of November 6, "Fire at the Core," he spoke of the symbolism of fire as representing love.

> Symbols, and what is represented by them, are not in reality separate. They have become separated in human consciousness; for the reality has been absent from human experience, leaving only the symbol. The symbol is distorted in consciousness because the reality is not known, and so the symbol represents something imaginary.
>
> We are concerned with fire as it truly is. The reality of fire cannot be known until love is known. In these days fire tends to be correlated with nuclear fission, a fire which seems to be external to man and dangerous to his continued existence. There is what might be referred to as an internal fire which when released, under control in the true design, is creative. We might look at this matter of internal and external fire from the standpoint of the truth of the matter. Most people are aware of the potential of destructiveness, but that is not based in the truth; it is based in the distortion in human consciousness.
>
> Alan mentioned last evening something with respect to the fire at the core

of the earth, a factor seldom considered. We creep around on the crust with very little awareness of subterranean fire. Occasionally we become aware of it because a volcano erupts, an indication that there is something pretty hot at the core. That fire is the symbol of love; therefore love is present at the core—the core of the earth. The surface of the earth seems pretty crusty and, in a general sense, the core has been hidden away. Maybe that is symbolic too; human beings on the surface of the earth have had very little awareness of the truth of love; however they wouldn't exist without it. The fiery core of the earth may be recognized as symbolizing the negative aspect of love. This relates to the working of the spirit of God subconsciously; we would say through the heart.

We are very much aware of another body of fire in the person of the sun. This seems to be an external fire. The creative process on the surface of the earth is consequent upon the fire in the heavens, the sun (the positive) and the fire in the core of the earth (the negative). As these two meet in the vicinity of the surface of the earth, creation consequently occurs. There is a radiant aspect proceeding from the core of the earth which correlates with the radiant aspect being received from the sun, the design established, under control, by which life appears. It is the interaction between these two that allowed for the birth of life in form on the surface of the earth.

That evening, in a service entitled "Let the Fire Intensify," Martin said:

We live where the fire blends. We rightly provide space for that blending—space, it might be said, between the positive pole and the negative pole, space where the blended fire appears and the light shines. This is the true position of man. The fire, the light, that has been offered to you and others over the years has been evident as something external. It has correlated with what was rising up internally through each one individually. With that comes a new sensing, an increase of light at the conscious level and the awareness of a spiritual body, within which the focus of fire is present and becomes increasingly vivid.

As we share the consciousness of being one in the body, there is then the fire externally present to others who have no awareness of the body as a personal experience. There are those, for instance, who become aware of the body of Emissaries of Divine Light. Here is a positive pole of love becoming visible in the heavens. There are clouds in the human heavens which obscure the focus point of fire, but that is no indication that it is not present in the heavens. The clouds are clearing for some. Some no doubt object to it; others find that they are beginning to be warmed and illuminated by it.

From the standpoint of this collective focus point of the spiritual body it makes little difference to the fulfilment of the purpose whether there is objection or whether there is appreciation. In human consciousness people become troubled by the attitudes of others, which seem to be critical at times. Those who stay under the clouds cannot see. It makes no difference; it carries no weight. But those who come into the light and the warmth of the fire are welcomed. People have the opportunity of making their choices: to stay in the dark or come into the light.

"Sunrise Musica" took place November 8-13 on Sunrise Ranch. The faculty consisted of PenDell and Diana Pittman and Jack Jenkins, Sunrise Ranch; Carolyn Rhodes, Texas; and Wayne Irschick, King View. There were 19 full-time Musica members, which included the Sunrise choir and a brass ensemble.

It was about this time that Michelle Johnson, after a period of modelling, found herself in Hollywood and in her first movie, *Blame It on Rio*. It was just five years prior to that, at the tender age of twelve, that she first met Martin in our center in Phoenix, Arizona. She has never wavered from her devotion to the Word which he brought and has allowed it to be a major influence in her living. She has continued in the movie industry.

"Born of Water and of Spirit" was the subject of Martin's service at 100 Mile House on December 11, in which he spoke of

a birth which occurs by reason of something that happens without regard to human effort or human ideas as to what should happen. What a wonderful thing to reach a point where one is totally willing to say, "I don't know." More people are reaching that point, some in positions of leadership...

There are those—we're counted among them—who took a chance in assuming an attitude of no judgment, no blame of others, so that we might be free to allow some changes to come in ourselves; because if we are preoccupied with the awful things going on in other people, as we suppose, then we have no space left for anything to happen in ourselves. Putting aside blame and reactions, resentments, fears, we allow some space to come for the true state which has emerged in our awareness. If that stance is taken in the true sense, out of heaven, then one is not a cowering little mouse amidst this vast array of other mice on earth. Finally there begins to be a man and a woman—Man, male and female.

Renaissance in Business! Forty-two business people participated in a planning meeting December 19 on Sunrise Ranch for Renaissance Business Associates, Inc., a newly formed Foundation-supported consulting and seminar company.

35

THE RISING TIDE OF CHANGE

January 1984 ~ May 1985

Mary Mackenzie passed away in Winnipeg on January 13, 1984, at the age of 85. Mary pioneered in the forming Emissary body in the 1940s and lived at the 100 Mile Unit in the '50s. She built a small home, which was occupied by Uranda and his family on their visits and later was my abode when I was Martin's secretary, until he and Lillian built their house, which I was privileged to share. A practical nurse, Mary helped care for Uranda's children for a while after the plane crash. Her sister, Anne Pekary, visited her for two weeks in 1949, and stayed the remaining 37 years of her life, a valuable and energetic member who contributed much to the growth of the Unit.

All in the day's work! "I was installing an air-bubbler in Martin's fish pond," Mac Duff related,

> when suddenly there was a rush of little wings through the hedge behind me, brushing past my ears and shoulders. My first thought was that I had ventured too close to a nest, but that was impossible; nesting was over for the year. They settled down all around the pool, some even standing on my feet. Then—reward of rewards!—one bright little fellow landed on my outstretched hand. I never moved a muscle lest he flit away. But no, we examined each

other carefully, then he nonchalantly dropped down at my feet, drank his fill and was off again. You don't have to go looking for life's little adventures. They come to you in all their living beauty.

The guest speaker at a luncheon of the Rotary Club at 100 Mile House, Martin addressed a group of business and professional people:

It's interesting, isn't it, how we get used to things and then think there is awful hardship if we don't have them. But if you never had them in the first place, it isn't hardship.

He went on to recall his early days there. Water was being hauled from the creek in drums and there was no electricity. About a dozen people comprised the population, with a few buildings: the barn, a general store with post office, and the original stopping house. He revealed some interesting details relating to his building of the Lodge. It took two years with the assistance of "two or three equally rough carpenters," with much of the lumber sawn in the mill at the falls on Bridge Creek, and other material hauled by truck from Vancouver, 300 miles away. Martin designed the original water and power systems.

I suppose I might be forgiven if I have somewhat of a parental attitude toward 100 Mile House, because it was initiated as a baby and I was the parent. I had to take care of the baby—everything!—for quite a while.

In the local newspaper's report of the event:

Lord Exeter received a hearty round of applause after his address, after which the Rotary president quipped, "Now the expression 'Thank the Lord' has new meaning to me!"

On February 17 Alice Wellemeyer passed away. Having provided George Shears with a home atmosphere on Sunrise Ranch, she also shared his spirit of service, and many people, near and far, were blest by her fifteen years of participation with George. Her spirit of faithfulness was not one of laborious duty but a natural, untiring and joyful interest in doing what was needed.

The annual Easter Sunrise service took place beside the Little Chapel, even though a storm had just passed through and a white blanket of snow covered the land. Overhead the sky was crystal-clear. The sound of organ chimes played by Betsy Giglio filled the Valley, along with the Sunrise ensemble singing, *Now Is the Day*. Following Martin's words of inspiration and upliftment, everyone joined in a chant. The spirit of Easter was deeply felt on Chapel Hill and overflowed throughout the Valley.

On May 19 at Glen Ivy, 53 professionals in the media and entertainment fields gathered for the Responsible Communicators Conference. The hosting team included Barbara Lourgos, Michael and Mary Shannon Baim, Barbara Coffman, Christine Boyle, Stan Grindstaff, Bill Wilkinson, Tom and Nancy Cooper, and David Smith, president of the World Good News Network. Stan Margulies, the producer of ABC-TV's *Roots, The Thunderbirds* and *Mystic Warrior,* spoke of the need for substance in those who would create meaningful work, and paralleled professional integrity with care in close family relations. His words revealed his own genuine character as a pioneer in television and film. Marty Ingels, celebrity broker/actor/writer spoke over a phone hookup from Hollywood. A similar gathering of 30 was held in San Francisco the following week.

The Healing Arts Center building (located on Eisenhower Boulevard between Sunrise Ranch and Loveland) had undergone extensive renovation, and we enjoyed a tour of the premises. Practicing then in that facility which has proved to be an incalculable blessing to the Sunrise family, were Dr. Michael Iacoboni, dentist; Dr. Laurence Krantz, M.D.; and Dr. Cecil Taylor, chiropractor. It has expanded further through the years with inevitable changes in personnel, the constants being Dr. Iacoboni and Dr. Krantz.

Over thirty participated in an Assembly held on Sunrise Ranch July 7-19.

"In Ft. Collins City Park the day dawned, on July 14, to the active sounds of preparation for the 'Human Race,'" reported Sandra Joyce and Glenn Ackerson in *Eden Valley News.*

> The opportunity to participate in the 1984 Human Unity Conference and raise funds for it started with Mary Jane Taylor's idea to sponsor a foot race. After background information concerning such a project was gathered, and when Ed Haimowitz came up with the name 'The Human Race,' the word was 'Go!' What started as a fund-raising race turned into Ft. Collins Human Unity Day. Don Hynes, Mary Jane Taylor and Lou Rotola from Sunrise Ranch, along with Glenn Ackerson, Sandra Joyce, Chip Grant and Sandy Charles from Ft. Collins, were the main coordinating team. Our volunteer staff of 70 came from the Ft. Collins community, the Colorado area EDL family, and Sunrise Ranch.
>
> The day started with a 10K and a 5K race with 500 runners around the park. John Sinclair, world class runner, won the 5K race. The Father/Son, Mother/Daughter Derbies and Diaper Dash included many families in the day's activities. There was lively entertainment by the Calypso Band which included Clive Riche, Sanford Baran, Jack Jenkins and Donna Sigala. Ann Foorman and Joyce Krantz presented a skit, and the Singers, headed by Michael Wayman, sang *Oh, What a Day.* The speakers for Human Unity were Dr. Larry Krantz, Alan Hammond and Ft. Collins Mayor Gerry Horak. He and the City Council declared July 14 Human Unity Day and suggested in a proclamation that this spirit be expressed every day of the year. [The Race continues to be

an annual event, with consistent growth annually.]

Bonds of friendship and cooperation were enriched between the Ft. Collins area and Sunrise Ranch. Many local businesses and residents were touched by the spirit of giving they sensed, and gladly gave their time, energy and financial support. The generation of funds for the Conference was highly successful. On Sunrise and throughout the community we see people wearing "Human Race" T-shirts—a symbol of the ongoing spirit of human unity being shared more fully every day.

At 100 Mile House on July 15 in a service, "The Meaning of Restoration," Martin referred to the Garden of Eden:

There may have been some fanciful imagination about it, but it does convey the recognition that all was as it should be; everything was under control, the design was what it should be. It was a living design, a garden filled with life. Because the consciousness of man/woman was unified with the consciousness of God the world of his habitation was describable as a garden. It isn't that way anymore, simply because the consciousness of mankind is now separated from the consciousness of God and the world is of the nature with which we are all too familiar. But there is no difference insofar as the fact of dominion is concerned. It is because man has dominion that he is capable of doing this, but it comes out distorted by reason of his separation from that original oneness with God.

What then is the restoration? The reexperience of that oneness with God; that's all that is necessary. Human minds and hearts in their state of separation have seen a vast problem with which mankind is now faced. But the problem would cease to be there immediately when the oneness was known again. Obviously what needs to happen is not going to happen because of the efforts of the mind and the heart in the state of separation from God, even through the working of the minds and hearts of Emissaries! There is only one fundamental thing to happen, to reexperience the state of oneness, which is described by the word *love.*

It is clear why the focus of the restoration, in the person of Jesus, brought with it emphasis upon love, oneness with God. He said, "The Father and I are one." Some may say, "Well it didn't do much for Jesus; he landed up on the cross and in the tomb." Did he? I don't think so; he landed up in the garden. Of course the story makes it seem as though the tomb was in an earthly garden. But, whatever the experience actually was, it transcended the world which had before been present for Him and He found himself in a new world; one might say in the garden. Well, as the population of the earth is not in the garden, they found themselves separated from Jesus. It is usually looked at the other way around. He opened the door for the creation in consciousness of the world which results when man and God are one.

RBA (Renaissance Business Associates, Inc.) quickly gathered momentum as a potent force in the world of business. It was situated in "Foundation House" just down the road from the Ranch. Also accommodated there were "Emissary Foundation, International" and "WHI" (Whole Health Institute). Alan Hammond was the president of RBA, and the staff at Foundation House consisted of Elaine Gagné, Joelle Emery, Randy Sue Yeager, Diana Soto, David Gray, Dot Moore, Judith Aranow, Wray LaFlam, and Rick and Linda Lathrop. On July 17 Alan addressed 95 people interested in hearing about RBA, in the new IBM building in New York City.

"Man, the Tree of Life" was the title of a service at 100 Mile House on July 22. Usually before a service, there was music and often other forms of worship, such as chant. That morning the choir, with two dancers, performed. Martin spoke of the Human Unity Conference in Boston

> completed earlier this morning. At the same time there were other Conferences in other places, one in Vancouver yesterday. There were almost 400 people present, the main gatherings in the theater at UBC with smaller workshops in other rooms. Manning Glicksohn and Carol Whitley provided the primary focus, and Michael gave the keynote address. They had a teleconnection with Boston yesterday (where there were around 600 present) and also with Hawaii. Larry Krantz and Elaine Gagné spoke from Boston to the Vancouver gathering, and Chuck Spezzano spoke from Hawaii.
>
> The usefulness of such occasions comes to point at subconscious levels. There was a sharper conscious focus in the various workshops with fewer numbers. The whole occasion was not based in some superstars, because when that is so, people are inclined to move momentarily with whoever it is and then it is all forgotten. But where spirit is allowed to be present and active, the vast majority of what happens does so subconsciously, the conscious level rather a thin layer on the surface. So the workshops were quite effective. It was here that Emissary capability tended to emphasize itself.
>
> It seems that many people are anxious to work with us, particularly in the business field. One who was present at this 11th International HUC was Robert Muller, Assistant Secretary General of the United Nations; Jerry Jampolsky was there too. They will be going to Green Pastures for a little time. King

Goodwill and his entourage [from Africa] will be returning there also, for about a week. There was a relaxed blending of people contained within the active spiritual atmosphere provided by those who have some experience in this field. Clearly such conferences could be of very little value if it were not for this essential element.

He referred to a Democratic Convention in San Francisco attended by large numbers of people, with the same thing occurring in Canada, and added that

the populace seems to recognize that nothing is going to be achieved by these political procedures; certainly none of the parties have the answer. This tends to lead to a sense of futility, but if something real is on hand there comes an increasing awareness of some unknown direction in which to move.

The Human Unity Conferences this year had as their theme "The Healing of the Nations: A Personal Purpose." That is a clear indication of what it is that must come to pass. I suppose the healing of the nations is looked upon as curing the various groupings of human beings the world around that have conglomerated into what are called nations. It is not a matter of trying to patch up nations, any more than it is a matter of trying to patch up people. That endeavor has been going on for a long time and everything continues to fall apart. There is no point in doing it again, but to participate in this creative process in which we have joined together.

Sunrise Ranch hosted the wedding of James Foreman and Deborah Grace of Garland, Texas, on August 5. Rev. Roger de Winton conducted the ceremony, which took place in the West Chapel. The attendants were Hugh and Moira Malafry.

A beautiful property at Glen Ivy, home of the former owners of the "Spa," came into Emissary hands. It was to accommodate Martin and his party when present, and others of the unit in his absence. It would be called the "Executive Residence," or more commonly just "The Residence." A pool and jacuzzi, artistically designed by Martin with the assistance of Rodney Canes and John Gray, was built in the spacious court area, formerly occupied by a large fountain which former owners Axel Springborg and his wife were very happy to move to their new place. With some other revisions, this provided a home in an area apart from main activities, ideal as a meeting place for councils, etc., and accommodation for special guests. While at Glen Ivy that year we attended the 1984 Summer Olympics held in Los Angeles.

Betsy Giglio (Smith) and George Hanson were married in the West Chapel on Sunrise Ranch on September 13 in a ceremony performed by Michael and Nancy Burghley. It was followed by a luncheon reception in the Sunrise dining room.

On September 13 and 14 I held a session for instructors of the "Story of Man" classes.

On the 16th (the anniversary of the ministry) Martin spoke to over 400 in the Dome Chapel via telephone connection to at least 2500 more in 74 locations throughout North America, Europe and Africa. There were 42 in the United States, 18 in Canada, and 14 on the other side of the Atlantic. The evening service, "Innocence," had a different phone hookup, with Centers in Australia, New Zealand and Japan on the line, in which Martin shared a few statistics:

> From those places from whom I received reports there were a total of 1,424 persons in attendance. This did not include the 400 present in the Dome, nor 22 other places with which we were connected, several involving fairly large groupings. In total there were at least 3,000 people. This of course does not include those who are with us now by telephone in Australia, New Zealand and Japan, which makes a total of 81 locations. All this gives evidence of a fairly extensive inclusion of human beings on the face of the earth.

The final September event, the 17th through October 6th, was an Assembly. Thirty-seven persons came together for three weeks to experience an intensification of spirit in a new form. They had experienced a Class and were eager for whatever came next. Martin's spirit was always seeking for means to expand existing parameters; nothing could remain static.

In Vancouver Ken Walters and Gloria Diggins moved into the lovely house which had provided a very special home for Martin and Lillian and family to relax while in that city. After a day of shopping, visiting, or preparing for a service, it was an open-armed haven, spelled "heaven" in the midst of the big city. In the early '70s Lloyd stayed there during his time at UBC, and later Marina while at Langara College. In 1985 it was no longer an accommodation for Martin but set up as the "Emissary Guest House" with paying guests, in order to help finance the Vancouver Center which was in need of a new roof, furnace and redecorating.

On October 31 Della Bever passed away on Sunrise Ranch. She and her husband Roy moved from Montrose, Colorado, in 1960 to make their home on Sunrise Ranch. They appeared with a herd of cattle and tractors and offered it all, a timely gift which included their talents and priceless years of experience in practical living. Della's strong sense of purpose graced all that she did in her 84 years. With sister Hazel and niece Nadine, she spent many hours in the kitchen providing delicious meals, fresh apple pies, homemade pickles and sauerkraut. Della and Hazel also ventured into soap and detergent production, using rendered fats, and acquired the nicknames "Soapy and Sudsy." Roy is another story! A truly colorful and greatly loved character, he kept the machine shop going for many years.

Reported by Barbara Coffman and Craig Sarbeck in *Newslight*:

> The last weekend of October, 26 media-oriented people from the United
> States and Canada gathered at Sunrise Ranch, and by Sunday morning ARC
> (The Association for Responsible Communication) was born. It spoke its first
> words almost immediately in a statement of purpose: "The ARC is an associa-
> tion of communication professionals who provide leadership and support for
> the continuing emergence of communication as a responsible and unifying
> force in the world."

The first ARC was originated by Tom Cooper the previous year with several events
held under its auspices, and the time was ripe for a formal organization. The momentum increased rapidly, and on December 7 there was a Global Village Teleconference,
which involved 100 communicators from five continents, including Vladimir Posner in
the U.S.S.R.; Annie Locke, BBC in London; Chuck Alton, producer of Global Town Hall
and other international radio programs; and George Christie, AT&T tech exec and in-
ventor of the early satellite TelStar. Tom Cooper, Barbara Coffman, Barbara Lourgos,
Bill Wilkinson, James Hollenbeck, David Ish and Sunwha Choi (in Korea) participated.
The event was produced by Tracy Carrara and Space Bridge.

Dr. Larry Krantz and Joyce Ellering were married on December 1st on Sunrise Ranch.
Joyce's sister, Peggy Antell, was the maid of honor and Alan Hammond the best man.

In a service on December 16, "Doing, Knowing, Thinking," Martin described the
state in which human beings find themselves on this planet:

> Life should naturally be a consistent paean of praise and thanksgiving. If
> this is not so, then very little life is being experienced on earth. Someone men-
> tioned the ABC of human experience: accusation, blame and criticism—the
> reverse of what would be natural to the human expression of life. In every gen-
> eration, in all nations, there have been people of integrity and goodwill. On the
> other hand there have been those who were self-serving, venal and cruel. The
> mass of the population is somewhere in between, easily swayed without any real
> comprehension of what is controlling or manipulating them. There have always
> been the righteous and the unrighteous, the good and the evil. In fact, the gen-
> eral view has been of a battle between the forces of good and the forces of evil.
> This battle has swung back and forth down through the ages.
>
> Obviously, from the standpoint of the human view the conflict is no closer
> to being resolved today than it was a hundred years ago or a thousand years
> ago or at any time during the course of human history. It has evidently not
> been seen that the good and the evil are inseparable. You can't have one with-

out the other; they are the fruit of the same tree. It is a vain hope to imagine that eventually good will triumph. From the human standpoint, what would we do without evil? We could hardly have any TV programs! It is assumed that life would be flat, uninteresting, indeed boring. This is so because the state of conflict has become accepted. It is required, one might say, to provide a little color in a rather drab human existence. We need heroes and villains to stimulate our earthly lot. This state of affairs has become most acceptable, even though there is the continuing involvement in the ABC of human reaction. What would we do if we had nothing to complain about?

Martin shared his meditation on the foregoing in a service at 100 Mile House one week later, December 23, entitled "The Abomination of Desolation Dissolved." After repeating the concluding words of a song sung by Heather Gayle, "For by His power and glory, all the earth is healed," he continued:

About 37 years ago a line of agreement was drawn on earth between Uranda and me. This vibrational line was drawn between the forming Unit on Sunrise Ranch and the forming Unit at 100 Mile House. It is reemphasized now as we share this service with those assembled on Sunrise Ranch. We are keenly aware of the agreement in heaven which we know increasingly as we choose, individually, to give it form. This focus of agreement, initially very small, was and is designed to accommodate the rising tide of spirit which emerges out of heaven into the earth. This rising tide of spirit, well known in our own experience, brings change.

The change may be seen in terms of the passing of the old and the unveiling of the new. The old which must pass away is well described in the Bible as the abomination of desolation, which stands in what should be the holy place of human mind and heart. As long as this abomination is there, what should be the holy place is unholy. There is an unholy ghost present in human experience the world around. Human beings everywhere are haunted by this. As we become aware of the reality of the agreement in heaven, which we have the opportunity of representing on earth, then the abomination of desolation may be caused to depart from our own holy place of mind and heart. It happens individually.

The following Sunday, the 30th, in a service at 100 Mile House entitled "The One Way," Martin's words of wisdom shed further light on recent considerations.

There is just one way by which the truth may be known and the reality of life shared. It has been a popular view that there were many ways, and that they lead to the one way. There are many ways which have prevented many people from awakening to the one way. Because these ways looked good from the human standpoint it was deemed to be profitable to follow them. Perhaps in following them a person might come finally to the conclusion that none of them lead anywhere. Good and sincere people have been walking in them for millennia and they didn't lead anywhere. Why should it be expected that they will now? The point should have been proven long ago.

There is just one way. In a sense it's a way that cannot be defined, although we may use, and have used words to point toward an experience; because this one way is an experience. We ourselves have been concerned not only to find and walk in that one way but to *be* that one way. There was a man who said, "I am the way." He not only made the statement; he proved it out. Those words have meaning to us and to others to the extent that we ourselves prove out the reality of that way, that we have the experience of being the way.

The 1984 Christmas Concert at 100 Mile House was held on two consecutive evenings, hosted by over fifty performers, with an audience of four hundred. George Hanson conducted the choir, there were dramatic presentations, and some excellent young gymnasts from a neighboring community were the guest performers. Nancy Burghley conducted the audience after teaching them a round of her own composition.

The Christmas season on Sunrise Ranch was not complete without Marie Johnson's annual Christmas Stollen party, at which there was an abundance of her homemade pastry, topped with her inimitable presentation of humor and loving goodwill.

"REA: A Beginning" headlined the front page of *Newslight*. Another birth—and at Christmas time! An education conference convened on Sunrise Ranch during the Christmas school holidays, December 28-30, under the direction of Alan Hammond, president of the EFI (Emissary Foundation International). The 36 who gathered from across Canada and the United States (with international representation by Yujin Pak and his sister Vana Kim, originally of Korea), brought a wide range of talent and experience in the field of education, from kindergarten teaching through grade school and secondary levels to university lecturing and teacher training, and outward to counseling, library administration, Adult Ed., Special Ed., Phys. Ed.—all bases covered. The purpose, however, was not to discuss details of various disciplines, but to explore the spiritual agreement upon which we base our professional function and bring forth an organizational form to facilitate further interaction within the world of formal education.

The new association was an autonomous nonprofit corporation named Renaissance Educational Associates (REA), designed to provide a voice for leadership and integrity in education. An initial Board of Directors was chosen: Alan Hammond (president), Judith Green (executive director), John Waskom, Ken Walters, Norman Rose, Donna Bahan, Ted Black, Fred Scott, Kristy Clark, Jody Morrison and Yujin Pak.

"By leaps and bounds" might describe the exponential multiplication of events and associations in the Emissary body, and a movement with the title "The Rising Tide of Change" was initiated in 1985, which particularly exemplified that cycle of accelerating change. Bill Becker reported, in *Newslight*:

> The Rising Tide of Change, a single event divided into eight biweekly segments in 19 cities worldwide represents opportunity for great change for those associated with the Emissary program. It is not an educational undertaking but an opportunity to acknowledge the rising tide of spirit and to associate in a specific way with the many evidences of that movement that are appearing.
>
> Local coordinating teams have been meeting to prepare for the particular event to take place in their city. Generally scheduled for the whole day, the events will consist of plenary (whole-conference) sessions and smaller, forum-style gatherings we are calling parallel sessions. These will afford opportunity to review and consider the myriad ways life is finding release in the fields of human endeavor. While each event will reflect the unique character of its locale and participants, the overall tone will be one of responsible personal association with the creative spirit catalyzing the rising tide of change so evident in the world today.

"Themes" were suggested for use in the one-day events, the central one being "a world view in which all that we see occurring outwardly is recognized as evidence of the influence of spirit." Some of the topics were: Health—a statement of wholeness, The Business of Excellence, Communication, Education, Trends in Government, The Natural World, Man and Woman as Creative Complements, The Urge to Unity, Visions of a Golden Era, Artistry—the impulse to create.

The Tide of Life was the title of a rousing song created, words by Lloyd Meeker and music by Melon (Ellen) Roos, in honor of the "Rising Tide" events and to enhance their effectiveness, which purpose was indeed achieved. The tide that swelled in hearts and minds with the irresistible current felt in singing this song brought a conviction of triumph, of the victory of the Lord through human capacities.

On January 6th at 100 Mile House Martin spoke of "The Ordinances of Heaven Conveyed Into the Earth":

> This is the first Sunday in 1985. This is the year when the rising tide of change is more particularly brought to the attention of people through the

various days which will be celebrated around the world. It would seem that most people are quite aware of the fact of change. There are those who try to promote it and others who attempt to resist it, but change is a fact. We see it as a rising tide of spirit, emergent through human hearts and minds, bringing forth effects according to what is present in those hearts and minds. The effects are worldwide, of course, because human beings are worldwide.

Most of the attention is paid to the effects. There is considerable concern about such things and continuing attempts to manipulate those effects in various ways. We have withdrawn some of our attention from the realm of effects because our first love is the truth of heaven. Heaven relates to the realm of cause; it is here that spirit is at work. To the extent that we align ourselves with that working of the spirit we are aligned with the rising tide and we have no particular objection to the changes that may be involved. The rising tide is the spirit of truth rising up within the confines of human consciousness. Where the content of consciousness in the individual is set in concrete, stiffly structured, the effect of that rising tide is painful. Where there is flexibility and one is not wedded to the concepts, beliefs, habits of human nature, then this rising tide begins to bring a sense of fulfilment, of comfort, of understanding.

On January 12 two hundred friends and associates gathered "To Honor a Friend," as it was put in *Newslight*, "for an evening of wining, dining and entertainment in the 100 Mile House Community Hall." The purpose was

to pay tribute to—and have some laughs on—the village's foremost politician. Billed as a "roast," the celebration sponsored by Village Council and local Rotarians was in honor of His Worship, Mayor Ross Marks, and his twenty years of service as mayor of 100 Mile House. Politicians from all persuasions attended, including the Honorable Alex Fraser, provincial government representative and acting premier of B.C.; the mayors of Quesnel and Williams Lake; the Chairman of the Cariboo Regional District (of which Ross is vice-chairman); and a number of past and present aldermen. Tim Wood, the Village Administrator, presided.

Before the roast began in earnest, Lord Exeter addressed the audience, referring to Ross as his "close confidant for many years." He recalled welcoming young Ross to the village 37 years ago. "He came for a visit and has not yet overstayed his welcome." At the evening's close Ross commented that the celebration was not only a commemoration of twenty years of mayorship but also the twentieth anniversary of 100 Mile House as a village. "Perhaps I'm a symbol of that," he said, "and I'm pleased to fill that position."

In the evening service, "From Caterpillar to Butterfly," Martin suggested that a caterpillar state is a good analogy for the human state. A caterpillar presumably came out of an egg. It spends a little period of time as a caterpillar and then, through the urging of the creative process, attaches itself to a twig and is willing to pass away as a caterpillar, becoming what is present with a chrysalis. It has to move through the chrysalis stage to have the experience of the butterfly. In this analogy, human beings creep around on the earth nibbling at this and nibbling at that. According to the story in Genesis, after Adam had eaten of the forbidden fruit in company with Eve at the behest of the serpent, the Lord said: "Cursed is the ground for thy sake; in sorrow shalt thou eat of it all the days of thy life," indicative of the fact that man had now become an earth creature. He no longer had the same heavenly experience he had known before; his identity was centered in the earth, of which he ate until he died. This is a sad picture of the beautiful crowning creation which had been man.

The ground was cursed for the sake of this fallen creature, which might be interpreted to mean that a recreative process was available to be experienced. Things were the way they then were so as to open the door by which changes might come and eventually the heavenly state be reexperienced. It was for the sake of this now caterpillar creature that the creative process had been slowed down. If it had continued at the same intensity as before, the caterpillar who insisted upon being a caterpillar would have quickly perished. In earthly identity not very much creative intensity can be accommodated without rather speedy fatal results.

We can see the caterpillar as representing the collective body of mankind, and also the individual, an illustration of how the restoration to the heavenly state might come. First of all, the sluggish creature humped along, like human beings do. They no longer knew what it meant to leap upon the mountains and skip upon the hills, but directed their talents to trying to improve their lot in this rather miserable state. Some succeeded a little, some didn't, and in any case the state of affairs didn't last very long individually, but it has lasted quite a while collectively. The caterpillar is still around, still endeavoring by its own efforts to become the butterfly, of which there is a very faint memory. They wouldn't be striving for better things if there wasn't something in themselves to remind them of the fact that it is possible.

Presumably there is something in a caterpillar which causes the little creature to do what is required to be in position to become a chrysalis, and as far as I know they don't resist the process. If they did it would be fatal. And it works that way for human beings. There is a means by which this creative process may work in individual experience.

I am sure the caterpillar has no awareness of what coming events are in the chrysalis, but there is evidently a willingness to let it happen. The chrysalis can be seen as a womb for the butterfly or it can be seen as a tomb for the caterpillar. In either case the caterpillar ceases to be. Ultimately, like it or not, one is forced to relinquish one's hold upon the caterpillar world.

The chrysalis state has been seen in terms of a tomb: individually everybody dies. This has been interpreted as a transition stage: you go into the tomb and you come out sooner or later, presumably, into a butterfly state—not on earth, somewhere else. But the butterfly state belongs on earth. The urge comes to move toward the butterfly stage, which requires that we relinquish our caterpillar ambitions. We no longer put weight in the kingdoms of this world and the glory of them. They begin to become meaningless to us if we enter into the chrysalis state, which is a limbo state. It is looked upon askance by people observing someone who is moving toward the chrysalis state, because that person seems to be becoming meaningless in the caterpillar world. And that's the way it looks to another caterpillar.

But there is something moving. This relates to the rising tide of change, because heretofore over these last twenty thousand years there has been a soft-pedaling of the creative process for the sake of the caterpillar, so that it wouldn't perish before it had a chance to become the chrysalis. So things have been slowed down, but now in the collective sense the urge is moving in the caterpillar to enter into the chrysalis. This urge becomes something real in the collective experience of mankind because of those who are sufficiently sensitive to that urge to let themselves move into the chrysalis experience where there is no expectation anymore of attaining great things, even great spiritual things in this world. We have no aspiration to become spiritual caterpillars. The spiritual state is the state of the butterfly. You couldn't say that a butterfly is simply an improved caterpillar; it is something totally different. But that transformation requires that one pass through the intervening stage, which need not be a tomb but may as well be a womb, out of which the butterfly comes.

We saw a movie on TV recently of the transformation into the butterfly. What a miraculous thing, that transformation! Most of it is hidden but it occurs, and ultimately there is the evidence of butterflyness beginning to appear, and finally the butterfly stretches its wings and, after a little, flies away. Here is the cycle of restoration, beautifully illustrated. Man is as different from human beings as they now are as the butterfly is from the caterpillar. No matter how beautiful we may have thought ourselves to be as caterpillars, or as potentially brilliant caterpillars, it is necessary to reach a point where that has no meaning to us.

To the extent that we have taken the responsibility for letting this transition happen, something is beginning to occur in the collective caterpillar of mankind. Something begins to come out externally and the irresistible movement, which causes a caterpillar in the natural world to move into the cocoon stage, is happening with mankind. It doesn't mean going somewhere else. The chrysalis is in the same world as the caterpillar was, and the butterfly is in the same earth.

All that has been happening over these thousands of years has been to enable human beings to survive on earth in the caterpillar state, because there was no indication of any willingness to come out of it. So it had to last a certain amount of time, possibly to allow for the vast increase of population so that there might be a sufficient number who would be willing to come out of it. Whatever the reason, we don't need to delve into that; we just let it happen insofar as we are concerned, internally. And we are not expecting to sprout wings tomorrow and fly away as butterflies. No, this process is happening through the whole, and there is that which is left behind from the standpoint of the chrysalis and there is that which emerges as the butterfly. This is the way it works. As we trust, as we free up in ourselves and are content to be nothing in the human state, we discover what it means to be something in the heavenly state. We cease being earthbound creatures and rise on the wings of spirit in the fulfilment of the restoration.

On the 27th Martin's word, "One With the Rising Tide," dealt further with preparing the consciousness of those involved for that movement which was no longer on the horizon but very close at hand. He said:

There is an outline taking form as to subjects for consideration which may come up at the Rising Tide events, such as business, education, art, etc. But in coming to these events it is not that business people can discuss business, or educational people can discuss education, or artists discuss art. There are courses in all these areas all over the world; anyone can attend them. But there is something else which has not been provided; that is, to bring people into association with the atmosphere and creative action of spirit. So if they come because of interest in business (or any area), that's fine, but they don't come in order to learn more about business. They come in order to experience the creative expression of spirit in living. If they feel they can carry this into their business, and if it is actually done, the business is transformed and ceases to be what it was imagined to be.

The rising tide moved swiftly, bringing in wave after wave of fresh and exciting experiences. At an event at 100 Mile House there were some distinguished presenters. Dr. Ernesto Contreras, head and founder of the Contreras Clinic in Playas de Tijuana, Mexico, gave a public lecture in the Chapel on cancer therapy, emphasizing that doctors can assist the healing process as much with the heart as with science. Countless people have been helped by our friend Dr. Contreras. Dr. Robert O'Driscoll, author and professor of Celtic studies at the University of Toronto, also lectured, as did Dr. Frances Horn, author of *I Want One Thing*.

Michael Burghley was the keynote speaker at a "Rising Tide" event in Vancouver on April 13, with 580 participants. Presenters were: Robert O'Driscoll, Chris Foster and Lloyd Meeker. John Gray of Glen Ivy, and others, made valuable contributions.

With the tide there were vibrant Emissaries emerging from Mexico City, one of the noisiest, fastest-growing cities in the world. John and Pam Gray, with their daughter Melissa, were met at the airport on April 18 by Carlos and Malena Ramos, who had attended a seminar at Glen Ivy and were (already) old friends eager to prove the Mexican adage of hospitality, "Mi casa es su casa" (my house is your house—and so are my friends, my city, my country). Eighty people appeared for a meeting and the next day 35 of them returned for an all-day seminar. John commented that everything was said twice—once in English and again in Spanish. A new element was added in that visit, a "chispa de entendimiento" (a new spark of understanding).

On the 21st David and Gloria Arillo and family welcomed the Grays to Cuernavaca, "City of Eternal Springtime," where John and Pam attended an intensive Spanish language school, their third enrollment there. Agnes Mura had been a student the previous four weeks. A professional translator in several other tongues, her presence was useful in many ways and places. As John and Pam were flying back to Glen Ivy on the 28th, Gene and Doris Kulbeck and Bill Martin were leaving to drive south over the Mexican border into the Baja to Ensenada, where they had been spending a day each month with Dr. Luis and Lupe Rojas and other friends. In the three cities visited our translated literature was read and discussed, and attunements shared. The tone was one of open hearts and open doors, and brought a new spirit to fan the "chispa" to a blaze.

Cliff and Alice Penwell moved to Sunrise Ranch, after serving in various Emissary settings around the world. Cliff brought his writing and editing expertise into the office and Alice participated in many areas on the Ranch. They have remained active in Latin American activities, conducting councils and classes. Later they moved into the Residence, providing a wonderful atmosphere in that home.

For Lillian's and my birthdays in May that year we were gifted by the Unit on Sunrise Ranch with an exquisite mirror and table, which grace the foyer in the entrance to the eastern section of the Pavilion and enhance its atmosphere of elegance.

"Knowest Thou the Ordinances of Heaven?" was the title of Martin's service at 100 Mile House on May 19.

> There are many things necessary in the human nature world as long as it exists. One of them is the EDL organization, and in order for it to function effectively in that world there is the requirement for people to do certain things. If we are functioning from the standpoint of the ordinances of heaven we are not unwilling to play a part in this way. In EDL there are a multitude of boards, committees, what have you—too many I think—but still, some of this is necessary. We have to have the chairman of the board, or the president, in order to provide some sort of control in the meetings, etc. We need a treasurer, secretary, and you can think of lots of jobs. That's all fine, and necessary as long as the human nature world exists; but the roles have virtually nothing to do with bringing the ordinances of heaven into the earth.

> There are those who have felt they were important because they had some sort of position in the EDL organization. Well I suppose they are important to the organization but that doesn't necessarily make them spiritually important. What is required to bring the ordinances of heaven into the earth may be done regardless of the particular human nature requirement that one may be fulfilling. It is this that is revealing of the design, which only then begins to put in an appearance. If we think the design is that we must have boards for every state and every province and every country or whatever, obviously we have another think coming, because that is just a requirement in the human nature world.

> "Knowest thou the ordinances of heaven?" If we do we are capable of functioning in any external field. We don't have to have some particular recognition in the external sense; it doesn't make any difference. One doesn't have to be president of the board but if one happens to be in that position he can just as easily bring the ordinances of heaven into the earth as anyone else. We are concerned to let the ordinances of heaven be set in the earth the way it is now, the human nature world, and then watch what happens! It emerges through all concerned as there is alignment with the creative process.

The following Sunday, May 26, Martin spoke of "The Coming of the Spirit of Truth," in which he quoted the Master:

"Ye have not chosen me, but I have chosen you," and the same truth prevails today and always has. As we move along I have been discovering who it is He has chosen. I do not take the attitude that anyone is excluded or, for that matter, chosen. I let it prove itself out. I have every confidence that it will complete itself as it should. We need to share that attitude of confidence that there are present those who need to be present. There is a form through which the spirit of truth may speak and act. We have participated in the process of letting the Word be made flesh, and the necessity now is that the words be spoken and the actions appear through the means which the spirit has drawn together.

The opportunity has been particularly brought to focus by reason of these Rising Tide of Change events. Before they put in an appearance there was a seeming reluctance by those who have been drawn into the composition of the body of the spirit of truth to let the spirit of truth speak the Word and allow the pointed action of truth to be brought forth. In the initial stages of approach to the Rising Tide events there tended to be still the rather mushy attitude that prevailed before relative to the HUC events. We were looking for somebody else "out there" to say something of importance. But nobody has anything to say of importance, except as an instrument of the spirit of truth. That alone is what is required. So, gradually as these events have unfolded, it has dawned upon those involved that we were not depending on anybody else to tell us the truth but we were responsible for speaking the Word of truth ourselves. When this is done, there are those who are waiting to hear it.

This body, this form of flesh, drawn together by the spirit of truth for the action of the spirit of truth, accepts the responsibility of maturity, so that the truth of maturity may be made evident to human beings everywhere. Those whose eyes are cast down, examining the muck and the mire, will not see. But there are those who look up, some of them just occasionally, others with a growing steadfastness, into the heavens to see the Son of Man coming in the clouds of His glory, which is His life in the flesh on earth. Are there still such dark clouds around this coming that those who look can see nothing much, or is this body on hand, clear, stable, steadfast, letting the light shine so that the cloud is dispelled?

36

CLIMATE FOR THE GARDEN

June 1985 ~ July 1986

A situation arose with regard to the reservoir at the southern extremity of our Valley. The City of Loveland was proposing to extend its size, and the expansion would of necessity be in the direction of Sunrise Ranch. They came up with dimensions that varied as they proceeded with their discussions. At one point it would have engulfed our little cemetery lot, as well as some of the houses and possibly the road itself. Jim Higerd, active in municipal affairs, was invaluable in their meetings, with the threat to our cemetery, a "sacred" spot, an item used in their considerations.

Martin spoke of that outworking in a service at 100 Mile House on June 16, "The Focus of Spirit in Form."

So we have a situation where there has been a seeming threat to Sunrise Ranch. I don't look at it that way. From my standpoint it's rather a dangerous thing for anyone to challenge the Lord. However that's not the point exactly, because we are here to provide what is necessary through the focus, which includes the whole developing body wherever it may reside on the face of the earth but brought to focus in the core. And the core has a facility in which it resides, a body on Sunrise Ranch. We are here for a purpose, part of which relates to Sunrise Ranch as a focus of something in form. It is vital and has ramifications for the whole world. It isn't a little thing: "Oh well we can get along all right without Sunrise Ranch." Do you think so? We have an extension of the body at 100 Mile House, another at Green Pastures, but there is a core position, and this challenge is not known for what it is by the Water Board of Loveland or the Loveland City Council, to the human beings involved. But *we* know what is going on.

Certainly we are very supportive of the requirement that there be plenty of water for the citizens of Loveland, but let it work out on the basis of the way it would be achieved by spirit, not on the basis of the ideas and manipulations of human minds. We are right in the middle of this situation to provide that, and things move as they should when we are ungoverned by what is happening in the external sense. We know the action of spirit will bring forth what is needful if there is a facility through which it can be done, and that is composed of those who dwell on Sunrise Ranch, with all of us and others too.

Incidentally there have been over nine hundred letters written in connection with this matter, and I am sure most of them are excellent, revealing the quality of spirit inherent in this body. [The entire body of the ministry had been informed of the situation and advised that it would be fitting, if they so desired, to write to the City Council; hence the response.] Nobody in the City Council, I think, is going to read over nine hundred letters, which were revealing the truth. That's not entirely the point. Of course the fact that there will probably be a thousand by the time it's through is an indication of something in external form insofar as the authorities are concerned. But our concern is not to be disruptive or to feel badly done by because this is some sort of threat to Sunrise Ranch. It is something which inevitably would come up, one way or another, just as it comes to us as individuals. If we deal with these things individually speaking, there is no problem with Sunrise Ranch.

Do you think this is the last thing that is going to be brought to focus in this way relative to Sunrise Ranch? I would say it's the first, that the control of spirit may begin to operate on earth, springing out of that positioning of Sunrise Ranch, the tip of Mount Ararat perhaps, showing up in a sea of nonsense all over the world. Let the spirit come forth there, and whatever is necessary will happen, and the people of Loveland in the days to come will have water as long as they last. We are concerned with being sensible about it all, but we would never deny or betray the focus of spirit." [This matter is still, at this writing, under consideration, with no particulars yet decided.]

An undertaking of grand proportions was in full swing, reported in *Newslight*:

> The Black Canyon Inn, a much touted restaurant in Estes Park, Colorado, reopened on June 17 under the new ownership of Renaissance Business Associates in partnership with Gary Lodmell. Magnificent views of the Rocky Mountains and the lovely valley are seen from every window and create an unsurpassed setting for dining. The excellent standard of the cuisine has been maintained by the new staff coordinated by chef Tom Fallon, who has moved here from Glen Ivy. The dining room of this mountain lodge, replete with vast stone fireplace, massive buffalo heads and log walls and ceilings, is contrastingly furnished with numerous small tables set with linen, crystal, etc. Music plays while an attractive youthful staff headed by Victor Summers ably serves the needs of the diners. [Vital members of the staff, Bill and Betty Dice moved to Estes Park after twenty years on Sunrise Ranch, Bill in charge of maintenance and Betty offering her delectable cooking skills.] Philip and Mary Maultby, recently imported from England, are the charming hosts and directors. Philip has had years of experience in the hotel/restaurant industry in England and on the Continent.

> Around the building are 20 tiny cabins, and there is a facility currently housing several of the 12 live-in staff members. The aim is to create a setting and atmosphere capable of accommodating the numerous conferences and seminars being sponsored by the Emissary Foundation International and also to generate income from rental of the lodging and conference facilities to other groups and businesses.

On July 14 in a service at 100 Mile House entitled "Space for Accord #1," which began with a telephone connection with Hugh Malafry in Houston, Texas, at a Rising Tide Event, Martin said:

> The Rising Tide of Change events are evidences of the movement of spirit. They are not anything in and of themselves but provide a vehicle, a means by which people may experience in an intensified way the spirit which is already moving, referred to as a rising tide. This certainly is not restricted to particular locations or people. It is an occurrence worldwide with respect to human beings everywhere. The pulsations of that spirit are either accommodated in minds and hearts or resisted. There is integration on the one hand and disintegration on the other, all part of the same process. We are concerned with accommodating spirit. To do so there must be space. Spirit can be interpreted

in social, political, even scientific, certainly religious terms. Spirit is whatever spirit is and needs no interpretation by human beings.

At Sunrise Ranch "The Emerging Spirit of Truth" titled Martin's service on July 28. It contained some potent observations:

> We're all supposed to be grappling with issues. That is fatal. It has always been fatal in every generation as far back as human memory goes—trying to manipulate things into a shape that would be pleasing to themselves, fulfilling, satisfying, on the basis of the apparent assumption that everything in the external sense was produced for the benefit of human beings.
>
> There is a creative process in operation whether one likes it or not. The spirit of truth is emerging, and the only space it has to emerge, in this particular configuration on earth, is human consciousness. If there is no space there, then obviously the place where the emergence should occur is blocked. Is that going to stop the emergence, do you think? No, of course not. It is just going to push what resists it out of the way. One contends with it, probably not deliberately but by the attempt to maintain what one has already been experiencing. And human beings have produced massive systems of all kinds in order to create something which is now in the process of disintegration.
>
> This might be said to be a return to innocence. All this arrogant manipulation is a hideous state of affairs. I'm not just talking about the great leaders of the world but about every individual on earth; everybody has been doing it. What is required is honesty, to acknowledge the fact that we have all, humanly speaking, been playing the same rotten game and have thereby excluded the spirit of truth from the facility designed to give it expression. We are coming to a climactic point insofar as the total individual population, or mankind, is concerned because this unfortunate state of affairs, this sad and painful interlude, is passing away.

In July, Craig Sarbeck visited Dr. Ernesto Contreras's clinic in Playas de Tijuana, Mexico, and felt privileged to share an interview with the doctor, who had been treating cancer patients with laetrile and other nontoxic methods for over twenty years. "However," he said,

> after spending time with him in action, one is impressed not with the techniques and substances he uses but with the expansive spiritual vision of the man which embraces all areas including the practical. An atmosphere of wholeness and healing pervades the clinic.

Martin's service on Sunrise Ranch on August 25 dealt with "Symbols":

> The use of words is the use of symbols. Symbols are required to convey

what should be conveyed out of heaven into the earth. I am using words now, but there is something which transcends them. We need to recognize the value of symbols; for the most part they are taken for granted and used as though they were the thing. [Martin used the Dome Chapel to illustrate his point.] Because of its beauty, its design, it has provided a facility which enhanced the process by which the things of heaven could be brought into the earth. This symbol has taken form because of the substance in many people. I had a hand in designing it, because I was in the best position to perceive what its nature would be to allow the greatest conveyance of what was in heaven into the earth.

Prior to that we had what we now call the West Chapel: a rectangular box which served its purpose. The form that it took was based in the substance of the people over many, many years before the present design of that Chapel put in an appearance; there were several before. It had to grow, because of the increasing numbers of people. The seats in this Chapel have been filling up, and doubtless will continue to do so as we let this symbol be used to make possible the fulfilment of the purpose which it shares with us: to let what is in heaven be brought into the earth.

We have a rather massive symbol which has been putting in an appearance for a while in the new dining room/kitchen complex. People may ask, "What is it going to be used for?" They do not see it as a symbol but as a material object which has some material use. If it is a true symbol it will be used, just as this Chapel has been used.

Another symbol which could be recognized is the Citation. It has been looked upon simply as an executive aircraft for transporting people here and there. Someone may ask, "Is it worth it?" There has been a great deal of blindness with respect to symbols. To me the Citation is a symbol of something that is absolutely transcendent. We can recognize that we have had a number of aircraft—I certainly do, because I flew several of them and survived!—and have since graduated from these elementary mechanisms, which in themselves were always symbols in my sight, to symbols which went faster and higher. The present one, the Citation, goes plenty fast and plenty high. It transcends most of the cloud cover around, which the previous one didn't; in the Conquest we flew a good deal in the clouds. This is a symbol which very accurately portrays what is necessary if the heavens are to be brought into the earth. We must be able to operate in the heavens.

One of the main symbols is our collective body, or the fact of the vine, the fact that mankind inhabits the earth. We may recognize that mankind has been a barrier to the process by which heaven comes into the earth, but we also have an awareness that mankind is the means by which heaven *does* come into the earth.

The Spiritual Leadership Class No. 3 was held on Sunrise Ranch, with 26 in attendance.

Central Council (always a large gathering) convened on August 26 and ended September 4th. One afternoon Martin took all the members up to the top of the Rimrock for the ever-new and breathtaking view of Eden Valley. Later they enjoyed sharing discussions in the huge room in the downstairs of the Pavilion with Judith Aranow and Don Hynes regarding the interior decoration and proposed plans for completion of that building. It was "finishing time" and the work was done in a beautiful spirit of comradeship. They came from everywhere—Jim Greaney, Ted Kepple, John Cruickshank and so many more—to lay their gifts of expertise in love upon the altar of this magnificent creation, product of the creative genius of Martin. The head table for the dining room was made of the native wood of South Africa, a gift from the Emissaries there. A gift of vast proportions came through Judith Aranow and her parents Ed and Rita, in the form of grants, which covered many areas such as furnishings, etc.

"Opening Doors" was the title of Martin's service on September 1st on Sunrise Ranch, in which he observed:

> There have been those, in times past at least, who thought that the Executive Council, as this grouping of people has been called, was there to make decisions. That may have been the idea of some members of the Council to start with, but I trust it has totally dissolved. Those who attended Central Council may have imagined they were present in order to make decisions. I trust they are discovering that is not so. The only reason why anyone needs to make a decision is because the conscious mind is somewhere where it doesn't belong, and in that place there are all kinds of problems, difficulties, that appear to need dealing with, and so the conscious mind assumes that it is incumbent upon it to make decisions.

> Even computers apparently indicate, with respect to the larger world situation, that any decision anyone makes will only cause things to be worse. That is the fact of the matter. I don't know how the computer got to be that intelligent; it hardly came from human beings, did it? Decisions by the conscious human mind may turn out sooner or later to be destructive. They look good at the time but produce things never thought of when the decision was made, and it turns out to be part of the disintegrative aspect of the creative cycle. We know another influence, another compulsion, which sets aside human manipulation.

A hydroponic greenhouse proved to be a bountiful provision on Sunrise Ranch. Lettuce is planted and grown in a tube filled with peat moss, which absorbs nutrients from a controlled flow of solution circulating through the tube. The large, deep-green heads could be classed as gourmet and are a delectable part of Sunrise menus when the earth's multicolored nightdress of autumn has been covered with winter's white sheet.

It was a great day when the Sunrise Fire Department retired "Olde No. 1" after many years of faithful service and welcomed a "new" 1942 classic four-wheel-drive fire truck, a generous gift from Drs. David and Linda Criste of Steamboat Springs, Colorado, to the Sunrise community. David had spent five years rebuilding and restoring the vintage vehicle, with the final touch a coat of paint—fire-engine red.

We visited the eastern part of the continent in September, and on the 15th Martin gave a service in Toronto entitled "Genuine Significance." He spoke of our being in the midst of the three days which celebrated the 53rd anniversary of the ministry.

> Some have thought of this as an organization of some kind, rather few in number and quite insignificant. It has been rather tiresome to some people. But I'm sure we are all very much aware that it is not basically an organization. Some organization is involved, but it consists of people who have begun to awaken to a purpose which transcends human purposes, of which there have been a plethora down through the ages, and are present today. It is thought that one must apply oneself to these purposes to have any significance, which, as it has been known in the world, is rightly describable as synthetic. People have felt it necessary to prove their significance. Some seemed to succeed; others got lost in the shuffle; but the fact is that significance already exists. All that is necessary is to unveil it, reveal it, let it be brought forth.

Our visit to Glen Ivy in October was highlighted by several events of note. Martin loved sailing, perhaps partly because of his years of experience in the Navy; and on a beautiful sunny day John Gray, Greg Botz, George Carpenter and Achal Bedi had the pleasure of accompanying Martin who expertly piloted a boat they rented for the afternoon. We watched as they headed into the wind off Dana Point.

Martin gave two services at Glen Ivy, and we enjoyed a preview of a performing arts presentation planned for another venture appearing under the name "Way of Stillness," set for the 19th after our departure.

It was reported in *Newslight* that the Red Coach Inn at 100 Mile House

> has recently purchased the 108 Motorlodge [with 62 rooms] and will lease the facility's restaurant. The deal was struck in conjunction with a group of U.S. investors, who bought the restaurant, [large, professional-dimensioned] golf

course and numerous other parcels. The entire package, worth well over a million dollars, was to be auctioned off in many separate parcels November 1st. However, Block Brothers Realty, the previous owners, called off the auction after Red Coach Inn manager Terry Young and the U.S. investors finalized the sale one day earlier. The sale was front-page news and the talk of the town! Feedback from the village populace was decidedly positive. It is anticipated that most of the resort's forty employees will come from the 100 Mile area. The size and potential of this operation provide an exciting business challenge to the Emissary management team.

The 108 facility is the showpiece resort of the Cariboo, with multiple tennis courts, swimming pool, lounge and nearby riding stables. The view is nothing short of spectacular, summer or winter, looking out from the dining room over the golf course [or watching wintertime skiers], the beautiful 108 Lake and the forest beyond.

An Assembly at 100 Mile House in November was attended by 33 and facilitated by Alan and Jean Hammond. The beautiful Log Chapel afforded a homey atmosphere for the sessions.

In his service at 100 Mile House on November 3rd, "Identification With the Light," Martin used words from Isaiah:

"Arise, shine; for thy light is come, and the glory of the Lord is risen upon thee.

"And the people come to thy light, and their leaders to the brightness of thy rising...

"Then thou shalt see, and flow together, and thine heart shall yield, and be enlarged; because the abundance of the sea is converted unto thee, the forces of the world are coming unto thee."

"Arise, shine; for thy light is come." *Light* is a descriptive word which indicates what is present in heaven, the source of the creative process. The word light in this sense includes far more than what may be scientifically defined as light. It is the vibrational radiance by which creation occurs and all creation is maintained. We are aware of light in this sense. An Emissary of Divine Light is presumably one who allows this radiance to shine on earth.

We find ourselves present in a world of shadows. We have been shadow people in a world of shadows. Awakening, in whatever measure, to the fact of light, incidentally proven by the apparent fact of shadows, we recognize that our place is in identification with the light rather than with the shadows. Here

582   THE VIBRATIONAL ARK

is a transformation without precedent. I am thinking of this from the stand-point of ourselves collectively because certainly a precedent was set, in the individual sense, by the one called Jesus. But it has never been set in a collective sense. We have awakened in some measure to this opportunity and offer ourselves to whatever would allow the transformation to occur.

On November 13 at Glen Ivy Dorothea McCann passed away at the age of 79, after a long and fruitful life devoted to serving the Lord. A true pioneer with an indomitable spirit, she and her husband Mike lived on a small farm in Lisbon, Iowa, where they were noted for accommodating Emissaries who traveled that way. In 1977 they moved to Glen Ivy where they spent the remainder of their lives, a joy to all there, in particular to their daughter Pam and grandchildren Broc and Melissa Gray.

In a service on November 17 at 100 Mile House Martin spoke of those who have lived to or beyond what has been accepted as the age of retirement:

Do we switch off the light at sixty-five? For those who have been associ-ated in the creative process of spirit for longer periods of time, if that has really been consistent, a great deal of substance has been generated which is not present with younger people—no condemnation; they haven't had a chance to do so. But there is something of much more value to be provided by older people when a certain backing-away syndrome is allowed to dissolve. For myself, I am keenly aware that I have available to me now much more sub-stance than twenty years ago. Is it true of all you with graying hair? Or do you take the attitude that your days are done, when really you are just moving into immense possibilities? Older people always have a lot of experience back of them. Sometimes it wasn't all that hot, but if you have been associated with the Emissary ministry for any length of time you have had immense opportu-nity to allow the generation of a massive quantity of spiritual substance, of immense value, rightly for use by the spirit for which it was generated.

Martin's vision was always beyond the horizon of what could be observed in form, and the people were drawn, as by a magnet, who had the talents to clothe the designs in his heaven. It was an inspiration to observe the working of his brilliant mind, in no way a manipulation but an example of the true function of that vital aspect of our beings. The next glow to appear over the horizon heralded a creation which would be named Climate for the Garden, released after a year in the making. Working closely with him on this, "the first Emissary broadcast-quality video," were Stan Grindstaff, Craig Sarbeck, and Chris Boyle from Denver, in conjunction with David Smith of Cincinnati, Ohio.

Craig and Chris wrote, in the November issue of *Newslight*:

"According to the climate, so is the character and growth of the garden."
From this simple first line of an outline by Martin emerged a visual, narrative
and musical journey that engenders deep love for our beautiful planet and evokes
a strong sense of stewardship from anyone with an open heart. The video the-
matically goes beyond religious, philosophical and cultural barriers, demonstrating how the internal environment of a person or people determines the
nature of their experience. Within this theme the story graphically depicts the
beauty of the earth, the sordid pettiness of human beings which has wrought
such desecration on this planet, and the regeneration and return of the earth to
its natural state through restored individuals. Sunrise Ranch, although not identified directly, is used as a clear example of the wounded and abused earth returned to the garden state by garden-dwelling men and women.

From its inception to the final stages of copying, the creation of *Climate for
the Garden* has resulted from a smooth blending of individuals and their love to
share in a creative process. It has involved people from around the Emissary
ministry under the tight coordination of producer Stan Grindstaff and the loving hand of executive producer Grace Van Duzen. From a basic outline by Martin, Craig wrote a working script. Then, in meetings with Stan at his home in
Oakland, California, and at Sunrise, the script was polished, visuals added, and
music ideas tossed about, until a final copy was agreed upon. Meanwhile a call
had gone out to Emissary photographers around the world for photos to fit the
tone of the project. Stan combed through thousands of slides, eventually hand-
mounting over 700. By this time the project had moved into second gear and
Chris was brought in to add her skill. She and Stan spent hours in the news-
room of Denver's KWGN-TV selecting appropriate video footage from their
files [accessible because of her position in that department]. This, and the space
photography from NASA, were given free of charge.

"Only those who come in the spirit in which we abide here will be able to
see that which we see, and hear that which we hear." These words, spoken by
Uranda about Sunrise Ranch, were beautifully read by his son, Lloyd Meeker,
narrator of the program. While Lloyd recorded the script in Denver, Ralph
Kessler in Hollywood worked on an original score. His compelling theme music
and some synthesized sound effects were later recorded in the California studio of Charles Albertine, of the Association for Responsible Communication.
With the project drawing to completion, Stan and Chris flew to Cincinnati,
the home of David Smith, president of the World Good News Network. There

the three spent two intensive weeks shooting slides onto videotape, generating graphics and editing visuals and narrative together.

Finally, New York, where Stan, Ralph Kessler and Mark Hollis of New York [Bob's son, another genius who offered freely of his expertise] completed the mixing of visuals, voice and musical score. A broadcast-quality master was completed, several copies made, and *Climate for the Garden* is ready for the public. Because of the generous donation of expertise, time and equipment by many, this video was done at significant reduction of the cost for such a project. More importantly, those involved moved quickly and easily with the creative currents of the project. In this video the clear tone set by Martin Exeter was maintained and amplified by those privileged to work on it, and will sound ever louder as Emissaries touch the hearts and minds of many around the globe.

In view of the abundance of cooperation of those already employed in the areas involved in the production of this project, I am vividly reminded of Isaiah's words quoted by Martin in his service of November 3, that "the forces of the world are coming unto thee."

In his morning service on December 15 at 100 Mile House, "Identity in the Spirit of God," Martin remarked that the 1985 Christmas Concert there, held on December 12 and 13, was attended by many from the town and area, about 450 other than Emissaries, in the two days. He announced that on the 18th a concert would be held on Sunrise Ranch to which the people of the surrounding community had been invited.

The Dome Chapel is already overflowing, with more than 500 people. After the concert the reception will be held in the Pavilion. This is the first event for that structure of a public nature. The dining and living area is now completed, carpets laid, drapes hung, furniture in. So this is a valuable opportunity to acquaint the local community with the expansiveness of what we are about as Emissaries.

On the evening of the 15th Martin's service was entitled "With One Voice."

There is only one "I." We have been busy trying to maintain separation; but in the expression, the differentiation of the One, it is one that is being differentiated. We do not have a whole lot of separate, peculiar charcters— just one, so vast that there is indeed the opportunity for infinite differentiation. But it doesn't change the fact of the one. I am here with this equipment because it's exactly the equipment I should have. It provides me with what is necessary for what I have to do, and I do it—for a hundred years if necessary, or I do it now and do something else in the next minute. These tools and this equipment have no say in the matter but simply accept the One I am. By this means there is restoration. I accept all the circumstances that come to me. I love the One I am. I differentiate the One I am in the way I can by reason of this equipment, these tools. And I trust we are all in agreement in this matter. There is no distinction, no separation. It is all one.

The Seniors Assemblage, "A Pilot of Things to Come," convened for two weeks in mid-January 1986 on Sunrise Ranch. Thirty lively men and women who had been around for over 50 years were ably led by Roger and Dorothy de Winton from Sunrise Ranch, and Mac and Jane Duff and June Lloyd of 100 Mile House. The weather was obligingly Colorado-wonderful and Martin's service of November 17 set the tone for a unique time which magically infused the whole of Sunrise Ranch with a special vibrancy. The conclusion was in the Dome Chapel with a telephone hookup with Martin, Lillian and me, and Martin summed it up thus:

> The older fraternity and sorority are responsible for providing, in a strong and particular way, an assurance and inspiration that is close to and felt by the younger people, so that they may have revealed to them consistently the substantiality of heaven.

The Sunrise Pavilion had been used on several occasions before, but was completely finished and officially opened for use on February 15. In *Newslight*, under the heading "This Place of Welcome," Don Hynes, who played a major role in its creation, said:

> Everything is new, from how we receive and eat our meals to how the food is prepared and dishes are done. A real ease and adventuresome spirit is needed and is in evidence. Hundreds of men and women from all of North America and around the globe came during the cycle of construction to pour their living into this creation. Some came for years, some for weeks, days— even hours—but in truth there is no testimony necessary, only a loving and appreciative recognition of the true quality of spirit that was expressed in order to let this symbol of welcome for the whole of mankind take form and come forth here on Sunrise Ranch. Welcome!

After the last meal held in the old dining room, when touching tributes were made to its years of service, each person carried his or her chair to the Pavilion in a helpful and symbolic gesture.

Selmer and Sylvia Hammer of Rapid City, South Dakota, longtime Emissaries and friends of Sunrise Ranch, celebrated their 58th wedding anniversary in the Pavilion on the evening of the first dinner there. The spaciousness and genial atmosphere provides a perfect place to welcome guests and activities of countless varieties.

Frank and Barbara Frazier arrived on Sunrise Ranch from Long Island, New York, to provide the crew, along with Alan Christie, for the Citation. Frank, a former astronaut and Air Force test pilot, added an exciting new element in many areas and quickly became a special favorite of the young people. The presence of Barbara as hostess in the plane, with her spirit of caring, was a great blessing. Both of these two contributed in many other ways to Sunrise Ranch.

In March we were at Glen Ivy and on the 23rd Martin addressed the group on "The Passing of Bureaucratic Rule."

After acknowledging and welcoming those connected via telephone with Santa Barbara and San Francisco, he said:

> Today is the culmination of several weeks of intensified participation in a particular focus of spirit. There have been the sessions of the Executive Council, followed by those of the North American Coordinators, shared by many others close at hand and far afield.
>
> The tide of change continues to rise. It is interesting that the tides of the earth, of the oceans, have been correlated with some of the heavenly bodies such as the moon and the sun. Here is a symbolic portrayal of what it is that causes this rising tide of change occurring in human beings everywhere the world around; the cause is a heavenly cause. It is because of the action of spirit, Jehovah, in an invisible sense that visible effects have been produced. Various changes have begun to put in an appearance relative to the visible factors in our Emissary ministry. We have the responsibility of participating in the invisible spiritual processes proceeding out of heaven. The visible effects will take care of themselves in the way they should if we provide the invisible compulsion to this end.

"The Trend Toward Alternative Agriculture" was an expression by David Lynch, Farm Manager of Sunrise Ranch, in conjunction with an agricultural conference, in which he said:

> The move to reestablish sustainable farming systems is no longer a novelty attributed to the backyard farmer or a showcase effort attainable only to the hobbyist. It is finding its way into the heart of American farming through the work of men and women of considerable backbone and vision. Organic farming and gardening is mainstreaming into the agricultural scene and demonstrating its practicality as an alternative to faltering conventional methods. The emerging network of men and women of integrity on the agricultural scene is a sign for the future. Indeed the health and welfare of the earth's resources lie significantly in their, our, hands.

David referred to associations with whom he found agreement, and he has continued to establish a firm foundation upon which many others are now coming to stand with him.

Along those lines, Craig Sarbeck elaborated on the video, *Climate for the Garden:*

"The earth is a whole, a living garden." So begins the half-hour video. In a world of poisoned land, air and water, depleted soils, deforestation and desertification, such a statement seems either a vacuous dream of an Eden long despoiled or the wishful vision of ecology-minded futurists. Yet this short video depicts possibilities realized in the time-tested experience of individuals, and the simple generative principles that support the reality of the statement, "The earth is whole, a living garden." This premiered during the agricultural conference on Sunrise Ranch to an audience of men and women who are concerned, practicing stewards of our earth. The video depicts, in sound, music and narrative, the simple principles by which life on our planet is naturally governed, and the sordid pettiness and rampant greed humankind has demonstrated in violation of those principles. A further step is taken, however, and the viewer is taken on a forty-year tour of a dryland farm (Sunrise Ranch) that, once dry and desolate, is now verdant farmland, abundant with wildlife.

The "secret" of this farm's success, however, is not solely based in alternative agricultural methods, but in the spiritually based living of those who dwell there. It is a way of living shared by countless individuals who know the sacredness of life. This video sets a clear tone for those interested in letting the fact of earth's wholeness be factually demonstrated. It is a perfect adjunct to conferences and sessions devoted to agricultural stewardship, providing ample food for thought and discussion. It does not purport to provide magic solutions, but encourages the viewer to see the possibilities in his or her immediate environment.

Martin spoke of these things in an address on Sunrise Ranch:

We stand on holy ground. In the physical sense we can't move anywhere, walk anywhere, without walking on holy ground. We can see this in terms of the earth itself, the planet where we dwell; this earth is holy. At the same time we see how it has been desecrated by human beings for their own purposes. Yet even now, in spite of that, this is a beautiful planet. It is designed to support, to reveal, the beauty of God in action, which comes because of man. The statement that man was originally created in the image and likeness of God is an attempt to describe the truth of oneness. And we cannot return to oneness without having respect for how we tread upon this ground and what we do with it.

"The earth is the Lord's, and the fulness thereof; the world, and they that dwell therein." It exists that God may do what is made possible by reason of the fact that He does walk on the surface of the planet. Obviously there is an infinite variety of possibilities throughout the universe, but there is a very particular and specific one related to this planet. We are concerned that it should remain for the use of God. For this to occur there must be those present on earth who let human nature pass away because the true nature of man comes forth. This is our sole concern.

A unique and endearing addition to our farm was Shiloh, a llama that shepherds our sheep herd. It has been proven over the years that that charming animal does a superb job of protecting its flock. A reporter from KUSA-TV visited the farm and interviewed David Lynch about Shiloh, which merited a spot in the Denver "news." Incidentally, a very large llama farm has grown up in the vicinity. On the road to Masonville many of these beautiful creatures can be observed enjoying life in Colorado.

A memorial service was held in the Dome Chapel on March 29 for Helen Mettlen of Masonville, at which Roger de Winton officiated. Many of Helen's friends from Loveland were present as well as her Sunrise family who honored a dear and longtime friend and neighbor.

A Drama Conference was held on Sunrise Ranch April 22-26, with 49 full-time experienced performers and 14 part-time. It was initiated by Martin's words in his service on April 20, "Spiritual Genius or Emissary Roles."

> We are aware that drama, which has had a little compartment all its own in the human scheme of things, is factually the whole state of experience; it is revealing that there is someone playing a role. The roles are opportunities. As something is allowed release in the Drama Conference it needs to be seen as relating to everything that is happening, in every aspect of the creative process, the coming forth into accurate expression of the heavenly one who is present, utilizing yielded mind and heart to do so.

Much was achieved as the conference proceeded, with an increasing awareness of the usefulness of specific dramatic forms utilized in living as the age-old tragicomedy is played out on the world's stage. There was a coordinating team of Ann Foorman, Stan Grindstaff, George Hanson, Rodney Conway, Paul Batten, Nancy Barbour and Alexander Brown.

On the weekend of May 3rd Emissaries worldwide gathered, in response to an invitation to an "At Home" day, for all who would to come home. Because of over fifty years of movement in concert with spirit, this body was in position to be together for two days with the same radiant purpose. All the Centers where Emissaries gather throughout the world are homes where single families or groupings of up to 150 people live, and that weekend their doors were opened wide to the public and provided a rich variety of activities in which all could share. The home fires burned brightly, and there were tours, picnics, slide shows, forum discussions in many locations.

The highlight was the same everywhere: the time spent with Martin in radiant release of the spirit into the world. On Saturday night (Colorado time) or Sunday morning in other places, over 4,000 people from 96 stations spanning six continents were connected by telephone to the Dome Chapel on Sunrise Ranch, where Martin provided the focus in two services. On Saturday evening, it was entitled "The Invitation to Come Home" and he specifically referred to those connected with us on the other side of the Pacific Ocean—in New Zealand, Australia, Tokyo and Korea. John and Pam Gray, present in Korea, represented those in the Pacific Rim.

Martin said:

> All that is happening on earth is happening because of the working of the creative process, and it will go the way it goes according to the states of consciousness of all concerned. As there is at last a clearing state of consciousness through which the spirit of truth may emerge with authority, there is a means by which this disintegrating state in the world can be brought again to order and to beauty—a true homecoming. What greater purpose could there be than this, the creative purpose, which is the Word, which is God, so that finally the human entity separate from the creative purpose, from God, ceases to exist, and there is nothing but Man restored.

In Martin's service on May 18, "The Expanded Focus of Spirit," he spoke of the crucifixion of Jesus:

> The very fact that this took place set the stage for the crucifixion of the body of mankind in season. The body of mankind is rightly the body of the Son of God. The body of the Son of God in the person of Jesus was crucified. What was done to him established what should occur in the larger sense. "Father, forgive them; for they know not what they do." They set the stage for the crucifixion of the whole body of mankind. It is brought to pass in a variety of ways, and the point is emphasized by this new technology of genetic tampering. Of course it is only one thing but it portrays a general direction in which human beings insist upon going. Certainly there is need for forgiveness for the abysmal ignorance of clever human intellects. There can be no forgiveness without repentance. It seems there is as yet little inclination to repent: "Let us further develop what is possible to the human intellect"—no recogni-

tion of the need for forgiveness with its requirement of repentance.

> You are aware that there is a focus of spirit present on earth, to be expanded to provide what is necessary to the whole body of mankind. We may refer to this expanded focus of spirit as our body. The body of the King may become a reality to the extent that those concerned have the experience of how it works; not a theory, not a belief in some principles, but the actual experience of the working.

> The rising tide of spirit has brought forth a focus of spirit in a very specific way. I would acknowledge that as having been so in Uranda who provided a focus that I, amongst others, acknowledged and accepted. By reason of the rising tide of spirit continuing in its natural movement and unfoldment, this same focus came to point in my own experience and has subsequently been offered to you and to others, and is being accepted now in many places by those who know the experience of how it works.

Martin succinctly described an Emissary of Divine Light in his service at 100 Mile House on June 1st as

> one who lets the radiant outpouring from heaven be brought to bear upon the world. There will be response to such radiation, and also reactions of various sorts to it. Where there is yielded response, those are drawn to the light and experience its warmth and beauty. Those who react do so in resistance, and the experience is of cloudiness at least, perhaps even violent storms of various sorts. The essential concern is that there should be an Emissary of Divine Light present in the world. Whether this element is described by those particular words or some others makes little difference. It is the fact of the focus of spirit that is essential. There must be one who comes in the name of the Lord, which is another way of saying the same thing. And who is that one? The answer is very simple for each one: "I am."

"One Voice" was the title of Martin's service on June 15 in which he referred to the Master's statement that his sheep heard his voice, but many did not because they were not his sheep.

> This same voice resounds in the earth today, amplified in living expression as the Word is spoken. Those who are referred to as his sheep are those who have ears to hear, in other words whose living experience brings them into position to hear that voice. The only way to know the voice is to participate in the sounding of the tone of it and in the articulation of the words of it.

This expression carried Martin's poignant longing for leaders to emerge who would share his work of leading the sheep.

Bill Wilkinson reported in *Newslight* on some current events in Vancouver:

> On July 5 the ARC (Association for Responsible Communication) convened an afternoon communication seminar, "In Touch." Expo 86 was a major happening in that city, with the theme "Communication and Transportation—World in Motion, World in Touch." Generally, as is customary at World Fairs, the technology overshadows the content. While Expo 86 celebrates communication technology, "In Touch" focuses on the people and values behind the technology. The keynote address, by Michael and Nancy, emphasized the personal level of communication as primary, relative to global impact. A dialogue with Nancy Burghley and Bruce Allyn tied the microcosm of male/female relationships to the macrocosm of U.S./U.S.S.R. negotiations. Rashmi Mayur, an environmentalist from Bombay, India, conveyed a sense of the immensity of ecological problems afflicting our world. A highlight of the day was a teleconference hooking up representatives in Seoul, Moscow and Johannesburg. The 270 participants shared responsibility for focusing a radiant outpouring of a genuine communication between each other and beyond—and it happened!

Two very welcome visitors that summer were Joe and Marjorie Spears from San Jose, California. Uranda's first child, Marjorie has a deep and cherished place in my heart. Her spirit has maintained a steady rhythm of loyalty and devotion in the face of this world's challenges.

Also visiting Martin and Lillian at 100 Mile House that year were George and Jean Stabler (Lillian's sister) from Norfolk, Virginia, and they accompanied the three of us, and Liddy Martin who was a welcome addition to Martin's household, to experience Expo at Vancouver. It is always a delight to share the adventurous spirits of George and Jean.

37

THE BURGEONING WHOLE

July ~ December 1986

*I*n Martin's service on July 6, "When Judgment Ceases," he referred to a statement from the Bible:

"And there shall be no more death." That seems a ridiculous notion on the surface. One of the things that makes it seem ridiculous is that there are now five billion people on earth, and if there was no more death how many would there be in a few years' time? Of course this is still maintaining the idea that the world the way human beings have made it is going to persist. It isn't. It is going to pass away. That world is characterized by death. There is death-orientation in everything. The misnamed life insurance industry has done very well. It isn't life insurance; it's death assurance!

This afternoon I was sitting in the sunshine before the rains came and I wrote:

"Oh that it might be that when the sons and daughters of God come to present themselves before the Lord in *this* day, satan no longer comes also among them.

"Then may the morning stars sing together and all the sons and daughters of God shout for joy, as the Lord once again lays the foundations in the earth upon which the holy city may rest."

A week later, on July 13 in his service, "To Be the Focus of Spirit on Earth," he said:

> In accepting the focus of spirit which is mine I haven't done it to excuse anyone else from doing it. My friends are those who do it, and we find that we belong in the same design. The focus of spirit centers in the One we have referred to as our King, or the Supreme One, which is unknown until given expression in form on earth. Each individual has that responsibility. I can do it for myself, you can do it for yourselves. As this is done we become friends instead of trying to be servants by the sweat of our brows. We become friends because we have been drawn by love, the power of creation.

At 100 Mile House Anne Pekary, one of the early members of the Unit, passed away on July 10 after 37 years of giving in myriad ways which contributed to the development of that special home.

Mary Ovenstone reported in *Newslight*:

> With school out in June there has been a large influx of young people on Sunrise. All our youth programs have been filled to overflowing: nursery, playschool, Adenturers for grade-school children, and the Apprenticeship Program for teens.
>
> The Adventurers, currently coordinated by David Miller and me, hosted 26 children from as far afield as South Africa for Youth Visitors Week, which included a four-day "Base Camp" experience for the 10- to 12-year-olds (the five under-tens participated in activities appropriate to their age, including a one-day visit to the Base Camp). The theme for the week was the "Climate for the Garden" established in the beginning of the week with a showing of the video and a workshop conducted by Craig Sarbeck and the Base Camp staff. This excellent program was developed by Craig and Karen Stevenson to be used in conjunction with the video and is suitable for youth groupings of any age, in any setting. This gave the children not only a new understanding of the four forces but also a common vocabulary for articulating their deeper experiences for the rest of the week. The night before they left we enjoyed a family dinner with entertainment, and each child presented himself to the Unit.
>
> The Apprenticeship Program, under the direction of David Lynch and Judy Morris, assisted by Judith Green, will include about 20 teenagers in the daily activities of the Ranch for various lengths of time during this summer. As well as working alongside the adults, a variety of activities and outings are planned for them. It is remarkable to observe the clarity and beauty of expres-

sion in these young Emissaries and the quality of friendship they are sharing with the adults.

On July 13 the second annual "Human Race" was held in Old Town Square, Fort Collins. A family-oriented event, participants could run a 10K, 5K or a 2K wog, and it provided a symbol of the movement of mankind toward the reality of oneness.

The "globe-girdling cycle" of the Rising Tide of Change events in 1986 culminated in Fort Collins on July 27 at the Lincoln Center with 525 people in attendance and nineteen cities and six continents represented. Alan Hammond was the keynote speaker, and Gib and Sandy Charles were effective coordinators, ably assisted in myriad ways by Sunrise personnel and others from the surrounding area. Lou and Bridie Rotola, with daughter Allison, were the area coordinators for the Rocky Mountain Region and active in all that was occurring in the area.

"And a fitting conclusion it was!" commented Bill Becker.

> The deepening connections with old and new friends and the subsequent excit-
> ing ranges of continued relationship give evidence that the "Rising Tide" day
> did exactly what it was supposed to do: provide a point of invitation to the
> experience of true friendship and purpose. Our worlds widened and many rec-
> ognized the opportunity of leadership available in these days of rapid change.

Kevin Ovenstone, 13 years old at the time, wrote in *Eden Valley News*:

> This summer Sunrise Ranch children and others from around the area
> formed a youth choir and went to the Rising Tide event in Fort Collins to sing
> at the "Parenting and Education" forum. Before we sang I went to a forum
> called "The Urge to Unity." They talked about things going on in Russia, China
> and South Africa. It was a great experience for me because I came from South
> Africa. It was a great day and I loved it.

Another 13-year-old, Jason Morris, related his experience:

> I got there about noon to do my first session, "The Spirit of Athletics."
> After the youth choir sang, all the kids left except me and the teens. Then
> there was a general session in the theater and we had a phone hookup with
> Michael Burghley in Calgary. After that we had dinner and went to the closing
> session. Lots of people spoke and we all sang the *Rising Tide* song. I couldn't
> believe all the people who were touched that day. It was great.

One day some of our friends from Fort Collins came to Sunrise to assist in laying the sod in front of the Pavilion—a beautiful green lawn in one day!

Martin, Lillian and I visited some places of special interest that year, traveling in the Citation. One was the Smithsonian Institute in Washington, D.C., where Charles

Lindbergh's plane, *The Spirit of St. Louis,* had a particular appeal to our three pilots, Martin, Frank Frazier and Alan Christie. With us were Jim and Maria Frid and John Gray. We enjoyed a beautiful dinner with Van and Harry Brown in their home in Maryland, and spent several days with John and Sara Waskom and their family in Natchitoches, Louisiana.

The 1986 Music Conference was held on Sunrise Ranch from July 26 to August 2. In *Newslight* Joyce Krantz reported:

> The 112 Emissary musicians represented four countries and a wide range of experience and expertise. Under Lillian Exeter's expert direction, with the assistance of her Conference Committee (PenDell and Diana Pittman, George and Betsy Hanson, Nancy Burghley, Donna Bahan, Jean Hammond and Allen Dorfman) we began a delightful week of considerations in the Sunrise Dome. Our sessions took shape in many different formats: lectures, mini-seminars, forums and ensembles, the latter word chosen to replace the term workshop and indicate a more active participation. We each attended two out of the eight offered: Children's music, Synthesized Music, Conducting, Improvisation, Continuing Education, Performance, Composition, Movement and Dance.
>
> Our new songbook, *Songs of Praise and Thanksgiving,* is available now for purchase. Two evenings were devoted to a recording of the new songs in this collection, sung by all of us plus the Sunrise choir—a glorious sound! Guest presenters included Elaine Gagné on "Releasing Genius," Bob Hollis and Gary Brooks in the field of finance, Alan Hammond who explored the influence of tone in our worlds, Roger de Winton on the development of music since the early days of the ministry, and Hugh Malafry in the area of poetry or artistic creation. We viewed a video on "Cymatics" which shows the effect of sound waves in shaping matter, and explored the nature of sound: harmonic overtones, acoustics and listening. Gary Diggins demonstrated overtone chanting. The instrumentalists had opportunity to play together, and on one occasion presented the embryonic sketch of a new symphonic work by Ralph Kessler.
>
> On Friday morning we had the privilege of spending time with Martin Exeter, who commented on the variety of musical forms, and human addiction to them. "If one is a person in the midst of all this, who sees things for what they are, one can easily utilize forms that may have value in freeing up other people so that they may experience the drawing power of love. Many people can play instruments, some well and some badly, but it doesn't make much difference until there is a true person present, utilizing the facility available now to sound the Tone."

On Saturday, the concluding day, Grace recounted the event of the Easter pageant in 1947 with Uranda, and we all took a walk up the Rimrock to view the site of that drama. It was a time to honor what was, what is and what is to come. Looking over Eden Valley, we extended a blessing to the beautiful setting of Sunrise Ranch. When we returned to the Dome, Lillian offered some concluding thoughts, and emphasized the simple things of life. "We have created very simply this week, I trust true to the Tone. Thank you, each one, for participating in this very special creative cycle." It was unanimous that all were experiencing a new depth of love and appreciation, a more vivid sense of purpose for the use of music.

In a service on August 3, "The Tone Sustained," Martin expanded on the meaning of the coined word *pneumaplasm*. It has a variety of consistencies. In view of the fact that the heaven is the habitation of antispirit as well as of spirit, the quality of pneumaplasm will reflect the character of either one. If I use an analogy now, don't get stuck with it. Lloyd was mentioning cymatics and the fact that there is a membrane upon which the physical substance rests, and the vibration is transmitted by reason of the membrane to the physical substance. There might well be a vibration present and the physical substance, but if there wasn't a membrane it would have no effect on the physical substance. In this analogy the membrane would represent the pneumaplasm which is required to vibrate according to the invisible vibration brought to bear. And when it does so, it in turn transmits that vibration to the physical substance, which stands up in a variety of forms according to the nature of the vibration.

The dissolution of clumps in the pneumaplasmic glue begins to break up the crystallized forms. Ultimately life won't be prevented from moving. If it can't appear through this gelled form, it will appear through another. But substance needs to be broken up in the one that is fixed and glued together, and we see this in progress now, in all the world. As this happens, a new creation can begin to put in an appearance: and the creation isn't a dying structure but a living form. We can testify to the fact of this living form. Some may define it in terms of EDL. It doesn't really matter how you define it; it's what it is that counts. There is what we call a body and to the extent that there is the fine substance generated it is capable of accommodating the spirit of truth and therefore the spirit of life, and the design begins to emerge.

There has been a sustained vibratory tone sounded over the last fifty or so years. Various ways have been introduced that make possible the sustaining of the tone with respect to the field of the creative process. There has been the release, week after week, year after year, of the live expression of the tone, and that has been complemented by the printed word, more recently by audio and video reproduction of the word. Now it begins to emerge in a more direct way from the body itself.

In his morning service on August 10, "Receive the Kingdom," Martin spoke of this beautiful Dome building, which has a natural dignity and order. What about us? Is there an atmosphere of dignity and order in our hearts and minds?

There tends to be so much clutter, much of it deemed to be good clutter; most people have good intentions. The human mind has no idea of the ultimate repercussions of doing anything. So many things seem to be so good to start with, but further down the line they turn out to be destructive. Many people who are very anxious to fix up the environment are not so anxious to experience the state of genuineness in themselves. Until that is done there is no way by which the environment can be fixed up, by which the body of mankind can be organized to be peaceful and achieve some great creative purpose, which has been waiting at the doors—implied by the word *kingdom.*

Martin continued, in the evening service, to speak of the Dome,

which provides a stable and consistent atmosphere into which anyone may come. Of course the atmosphere originates with people. Those who were responsible for building the Dome did so according to their highest understanding, giving freely of themselves and their love in an attitude of delight in the emerging form. If we see this building as representing in symbol our flesh bodies, and the spiritual atmosphere generated in heart and mind, when we come into it *we* are symbols of something. We are the Dome then into which the Lord is invited to come.

This building was designed in a particular way and emerged in the form of an elliptical dome. We discovered there aren't any other elliptical domes around. There was no book of rules and regulations with respect to the construction of an elliptical dome; we were first on the scene, and the regulations emerged out of this Dome. John Summerbell had the focus of it and he had to do some pioneering work to get the required dimensional elements worked out. This came out of a computer in Boulder, giving the lengths of the members. As you have no doubt observed, the Dome is built up of triangles, each one individual. They are not repetitions of each other, which is significant.

The orbit of the earth around the sun is an ellipse, so we have a connection with the planet as a whole, as part of the solar system, placed strategically where it is. All this didn't happen by chance. There is a design. The kingdom has always been at hand, in other words to be accepted and received when there was substance to accommodate it. There has been the necessity, over the millennia, for those who would play a part consistently in the generation of the required spiritual substance. There has been such substance available for many, many years in fact. This Dome would not have been built if it hadn't been so. Obviously there has not been adequate substance to permit the ultimate restoration of man. Nevertheless there has been a continuing generation of substance by those participating in this which allowed it to be included beyond themselves, available for further generation of substance and greater accommodation of the kingdom, and therefore of the King. It is a progressive process which, obviously, depends upon people.

On August 26 in a service on Sunrise Ranch, "The Transcendent Significance of the Mailings," Martin shared with the Unit some of the considerations of the recent Central Council with regard to the significance insofar as the mailings are concerned. In addition to the words and the spirit in which they are spoken, and one's ability to read them and understand, he said there is another element which has tended to be overlooked, and used the analogy of an electromagnet. There is a visible aspect to the magnet: the core, and the coils. There is an invisible aspect, the magnetic field within the magnet and the current which is flowing through the coils. Both the visible and invisible aspects are essential.

Our bodies, minds and hearts are the visible facility by which whatever is required may occur, and the flow through the coils around the magnet relates to what is happening in the core. We are participating in that core. The mailings have provided this flow in which all could participate in a focused way and keep it moving through the coils, the focus for the current which rightly is moving in the moment through the coil which is one's own mind and heart, to get the job done.

In *Newslight* there was an article, accompanied by a photograph, of a startling addition to the scene that greeted the increasingly heavy traffic moving constantly through 100 Mile House:

This red, white and blue B.C. Railway caboose was bought for one dollar (and fixed up for quite a bit more!) to become the centerpiece of a western theme park across the highway from the Red Coach Inn. The caboose is now a Western souvenir store—Peter Castonguay's idea. The project is part of Cariboo Cowboy Adventures, which features dude rides for tourists and riding and roping demonstrations. Jim Pattison, chairman of Expo, spoke at a tourist promotion event in the park on his first trip away from the world exposition since it opened.

On September 3rd Martin, Lillian and I departed from Sunrise Ranch for an overseas trip. In England we stayed at Kingcombe for over a week. Michael and Nancy arrived at about the same time and also were accommodated there, with frequent trips to the 500-year-old halls of Eton College where their son Anthony had begun his school term.

The second week we moved to Mickleton where Martin spoke to the group on the 7th:

> It has been several years since I was here on a Sunday morning. We are aware of our responsibility for maintaining the spirit brought to focus by Jesus when he was on earth, one aspect of which has developed here at Mickleton. There are many other places in England where it might have happened; in fact several other places were considered; but it happened here, a focus of its special nature within the overall body, in the process of developing and growing, changing.

> You could say that in the older countries, England for instance, or Europe, there are all kinds of barriers. People have been going down the old convoluted routes for so long that, like the lanes in Devonshire, they are deep; you can't even see out. I'm sure we've all found that those ruts are in our very genes. But we need not be subject to that human-nature control. Now something else is being put together, a body to go in the way of life, with a different experience for each of those who compose it.

> On the North American continent originally there were no ruts. Many of those who went there brought their ruts with them. But by and large they are not so deep that most people cannot look out over the edge of them. This is why the development of this body was initiated in North America. It couldn't have been done here. I know that well enough; I had to go off to Canada! And it is only recently that an inroad has been made into this country and Europe in a more direct way. There has been some discussion with respect to what the physical development here should be in the days to come. We don't have to figure it out. The various parts of the body at their locations have their particular significance. Some of us may have studied a bit of anatomy, so we know where the various organs ought to be in our own bodies, but the body gets along quite all right even if we don't know.

A record number packed the Garden Room and the lean-to marquee for Martin's evening service, with 162 in attendance and shared at 100 Mile House via telephone. It was a most fulfilling time in which the purpose of that beautiful provision in the Cotswolds was reviewed and profound appreciation expressed for all that had been generated to bring it to that point.

The next stop was La Sauge, France, an hour's drive from the major city of Lyon and two hours from Geneva, Switzerland. It is in an excellent position in the geographical center of western Europe: within 500 miles are southern Spain, southern Italy, Holland, Belgium, West Germany, East Germany, Czechoslovakia, Hungary and England. Peter and Marina joined us there for the European Gathering.

In *Newslight*, under the heading "A Magnet in France—the European Core Is in Place" the event was described:

> In the spectacular foothills of the French Alps, in an unusual ivy-garlanded home once used as a barn for breeding silkworms, a pivotal event occurred. Fifty-three people from eight countries of western Europe attended the most purposeful coming together of Emissaries yet seen on the continental mainland. It was Martin's first visit to the Continent in 49 years. The five-day gathering concluded on the 54th birthday of the Emissary movement—and on the eve of the joint acquisition by Serge and Betsy Nicolet, and Marco and Sarah Jane Menato, of this beautiful place in the village of Velanne La Sauge (meaning "sage") to be a central, permanent Emissary home in Europe. It will shortly be the home of Serge and Betsy Nicolet, through whose family it came to us; Marco and Sarah Jane Menato, who have filled a focal position on the Continent; Antonio Marulli from Rome; and Jim Heaslip from Toronto, Canada and Padua, Italy. The Nicolets will move from their home of many years outside Grenoble, France; the Menatos from Padua.

The way had been paved for this event by smaller European gatherings in the two previous years. This year Spain was represented for the first time, by Doug Schreder and Rhonda Radcliff, presently in Barcelona. And for the Sunday services there were additional 15 guests, many from Italy and Germany. Robert Marcus of Munich observed:

> In many ways this was a time of beginning, of newness, and the spirit of victory predominated at the core of our experience, with an almost tangible vitality. At last, after all these centuries of stuckness in the ruts of the encrusted human state, the Old World received the New, and a door was opened, with great gusto and vigor, in the heaven of Europe.

Ingrid Rose from Belgium commented:

> The accents present were as many as the people, but the spirit clearly one. Our creative conversations in the group were as intimate as if they had been

between two people. What may have seemed to some to have been a disadvantage—that our new language has been emerging in English—produced much laughter, penetration and discussion.

As the new language had taken years to develop and be understood, Martin noted, it was no wonder that translating it into other tongues was a delicate business. Robert Marcus felt that

> the barriers of language, national boundaries and cultures which have for so long maintained the false state of European separation, vanished amidst the fusing power of the atmosphere of loving friendship that prevailed throughout. Old ruts and expected rights crumbled as the pressure of the controlled fire of love broke surface once more on the continent of Europe.

It was typical of Martin that, observing the need for some definite changes in the room which would accommodate the Sunday services and could seat about 75, his fertile mind quickly saw the answer in objects right at hand. For several hours he, and his delighted helpers, worked and put together an ingeniously improvised lectern and podium, which worked perfectly. In his service the next morning, the 14th, after he noted that on that date, and the two following days, the initiation of this ministry took place in 1932, and recalled Uranda's experience and that of Jesus two millennia before, he said: So the veil was rent, and I am sure we have all had some experience to confirm that fact because it has begun to be rent in our own consciousness, the beginning awareness of something that has not been known before.

> It is emerging into the consciousness of mankind. It is emerging here because of people, not because of the place. When the place becomes filled with the radiant substance of the people, then it begins to carry increasing significance. This occurs because of what may be called a creative field. It is similar to a magnetic field. There must be a magnet if there is to be a magnetic field. And what is attracted into that field (illustrated by iron filings or something of the sort) will reveal what the design of the magnetic field is. The heaven is there first, the magnetic field, and then what relates to that will fall along the lines of force. This is the way our physical forms were created; of course there are distortions in the world the way it is. There is a design which transcends the earthly heredity design and is available for the substance of body, mind and heart to reform along the lines of force. The awakening is to this.

> Now this magnet emerges through many people in many locations. It is not a haphazard business. There is something specific happening, a vast change occurring throughout the body of mankind, but that change comes because

there is the focus provided in the magnet. If the magnet isn't there things swirl back and forth until there is nothing. What a privilege it is to participate in allowing an expansion to occur of this basic magnet, which is happening here. We see a central point in western Europe, which is up against eastern Europe, and the Soviet Union is part of eastern Europe, and that goes all the way through to the Orient. "The earth is the Lord's, and the fulness thereof." It belongs in the univeral whole, and we have a part to play in that. Man is essential to that operation as it relates to this earth, which is fortunate or he would not exist anymore. But let him come back, let *me* come back. Letting it happen for oneself, the magnet is present, there are others who are letting it happen, the lines of force are there, and the job is done.

In the evening service Martin said:

> We find, as angels, that we belong together—not always nudging up against each other. We may be anywhere on the face of the earth but still know we belong together. We are aware that there is an easy and natural movement occurring by reason of this forming body through which the angelic expression appears, the creative lines of force are set up, and the whole process is in action. Nobody can make it work; it *is* working. Let that working be accommodated in our own living and, behold, all things are made new. And no one can stop it; it is absolute.

The question arose as to a name for the place and after extensive discussion there was agreement with a suggestion from Martin: La Vigne. It means "the vine," and upon entering the grounds one's eye is caught by a magnificent vine that covers the main building. The symbolism of the word was fitting, with the firm spirit established there spreading throughout that great continent, tendrils matured into strong branches and bearing the leaves for the healing of the nations.

All the participants except Martin, Lillian and me, Michael and Nancy, Rupert and Tessa, and Serena Newby (Rupert's sister) were housed in hotels and homes nearby. Building was begun shortly afterward, providing more accommodation and improvement in myriad ways. The weather was sunny, and meals were enjoyed outdoors in the shade of four majestic lime trees. There were wonderful walks in the countryside, swimming in a local lake, and some of us spent a fascinating day at the famous lakeside resort of Annecy.

On the 16th, after four wonderful days in La Sauge the three of us, and Peter and Marina, Michael and Nancy sped off to Paris on the 170-mph TGV train—first-class experience, dinner and all! It was a different reception that greeted us there, with the city full of armed policemen because of a bomb that had just been hurled into a store. However, thanks to the chauffeurs of two Mercedes limousines, we had the opportunity to go for a short sightseeing tour in the middle of traffic jams and police sirens!

The schedule was tight because of the next flight. Martin took Lillian on a trip to Sweden, one she had long hoped might materialize. They were accompanied by Marina and Peter, and Serena. Lillian related her experience:

> It was a moonlit flight and below us twinkled lights of Europe and Scandinavia, especially Amsterdam, Copenhagen, and finally Stockholm and Arlanda, the airport city. My Swedish grandfather, who loved Uranda, was born and raised in Uppsala, Sweden. We were reminded, by flowers in our rooms at the Lady Hamilton Hotel in Old Town, that the Larsens of Oslo and other Emissaries were delighted that we were in Scandinavia. The weather was warm and autumnal as we drove north to Uppsala to visit the Cathedral and the Old Palace and walk through some of the university grounds and city.
>
> The morning of the 19th we flew to London, where Rupert's car awaited us, so Peter with Marina's expert road-navigating drove us to Stamford and into the Park at Burghley House. Approaching, we saw the flag of the Marquess flying above, raised only when he is in residence. The butler greeted us at the door. [Michael and Nancy had gone directly to England from Paris, where they participated in activities, including visits to Anthony at Eton, and so were present at the gathering at Burghley.] At Lord Exeter's invitation two generations of the Cecil family came to a special luncheon on Sunday. The halls and rooms of Burghley were filled with joy and laughter and genuine pleasure to be together. Fun events were a tour of the House with Lady Victoria Leatham, niece of Lord Exeter and present resident, and a slide show of 100 Mile House family and area by Peter Castonguay.
>
> On Monday we returned to Bank House in London, where we immediately welcomed Enos Mabusa and his wife Esther; Mr. Mabusa is the Chief Minister of Kangwani. We had lunch together before Michael and Nancy left for the airport. Meanwhile Rupert arrived from Rome, then Grace and Tessa.

In the meantime, when Martin and his party left for Sweden I had remained in Paris with Rupert and Tessa for two more days, where we were entertained for a dinner in the apartment of Jean-Michel Corbet, Danielle Soleillant and Jocelyne Jean-Wisslin. The Eiffel Tower offered a new experience, also the fine cuisine proudly presented in that city's restaurants and many cafes. The Louvre was closed because of the bomb incident, but a visit to one of Europe's magnificent cathedrals compensates for a great deal.

From Paris we flew to Italy where we visited Lida Radziwill in her palatial resi-

dence in Rome (shared with her daughter Marie Louise and husband Tony Moncada).
In Rupert's words:

> Four nights in Italy rolled by in grand style, in Lida's stately home base
> (Palazzo Taverna) in the old quarter of Rome, no more than a few hundred
> yards from the banks of the Tiber and within easy walking distance of St.
> Peter's and the Vatican, which we visited, among other landmarks. We saw
> mile upon mile of antique marble statuary, thousands upon thousands of
> square metres of heavily decorated ceiling and wall. A memorable dinner was
> given for us by Lida and Marie Louise, accompanied by Tony Moncada and
> Antonio Marulli on the Hassler Hotel roof verandah. A 24-hour visit to Tuscany
> (accompanied by Lida) allowed us a flavor of Florence where we spent a relax-
> ing time in a beautiful resort. [The drive through Tuscany had a special charm
> for me, with visits to the old fortress-like towns perched on the very tops of
> the hills.] On our return journey to Rome a stop in Sienna on a brilliantly
> sunny morning was extraordinarily vivid.

Back in London we joined Martin and Lillian and their party at Bank House. We all
attended a reception at Hornton Court, meeting Emissaries and others invited by resident Des Dornan. There was a time for a bit of shopping and a visit to Anthony Cecil at
Oxford, then home via another flight on the Concorde. Martin, Lillian and I spent two
weeks on Sunrise Ranch where we enjoyed an evening sharing our trip with the Unit,
which evoked a light-hearted and humorous spirit of fellowship, the perfect culmination to an event of vast import that opened doors long closed.

On September 28 in his service, "Belief Transcended," Martin referred to his latest
book, published under the title *Beyond Belief*, and pointed out that

> human function in the human state has never gone beyond belief: not only in
> religion but scientific, cultural, political, all kinds of beliefs and systems of
> belief. Then there are systems of belief within each person. People are words-
> oriented, belief-oriented. Those who hear the Word and are not hung up on
> the words find they come into position to *be* the Word, so that what takes
> form in words or thoughts or action will reveal the Word to those who are
> open to receive it.

His evening service, "The Creative Process Made Known," included this gem:

> When consideration is given to the state of man before the fall it usually
> evokes a picture of a naked couple gamboling in a beautiful, natural setting,
> in a state of friendship with the animals and the birds and the plants, and
> even the insects. For the most part I do not think this would be attractive

enough for people to relinquish their hold on their TVs and on their bank accounts! Of course this is foolish imagination, because the true state was never anything like that. It would have been a purposeless state, and there is a purpose, not only for this planet and what has existed on its surface but for man himself. He has a very key part to play in this scenario—whatever that is, and we can't imagine what it is.

The world the way it is is well on the way to passing out of the picture. Then the question arises as to what the alternative is. There is no way of portraying that, because it doesn't exist yet within the consciousness of human beings. We realize there is a creative process in which we may participate, and certain effects put in an appearance; and we begin to be assured that those effects are what they should be. We don't know what they are going to be next week, necessarily, or next year, or in ten years' time or a hundred years' time, but we *do* know something of the experience of participating in the creative process by which whatever should take form, will.

Martin, Lillian and I were at Glen Ivy October 7 through 21, where we shared an account and slides of our recent travels and Martin gave services on the two Sunday mornings, which many attended from surrounding areas. "By the Fire of Love" entitled the one on October 19, in which he said:

One stands in the place, rightly, from which this fire emanates, the blue of the flame, where it is cool. Slip out of the blue into the yellow, the red, and it's uncomfortable. In the blue it is cool; beyond that is hellfire. There is no separate place: heaven over here and hell over there, or heaven up above and hell down below. It's all one space, and the experience for oneself determines where one is.

I think it is a tremendous thing that we live in these times when the consummation is at hand. It is difficult to remain completely unaware. One can try to bury oneself in the joys of human existence, I suppose, whatever they are: eating, drinking, marrying and giving in marriage, satisfying the appetite in whatever way. But there are those who cannot do that anymore. They have assumed responsibility for letting the motivation of whatever finds expression in thought or word or deed spring out of this intensity of love, the fire of love which operates under control according to an already established living design. You don't have to make it; it is already present.

From Glen Ivy we went to the Bay area in San Francisco and visited the new Emissary Center, a beautiful 8,000-square-foot house built in 1904 by lumber baron R. A. Vance. The fine wood is balanced by many windows, including stained glass; tapestry and fine cloth wall coverings. Its strength withstood the earthquake of 1906. Extensive remodeling and redecorating had been done, with a chapel/meeting room for fifty. Resident were Rod Shorter, Sharon Baxter, Steve Short, Steve Orsary, Carole Hershey, Mary Ann Stewart, Nan Gravelle and Joyce Forgang.

A stop at the Portland airport was memorable. The entire area group came to share some time with us, and presented Martin with an exquisite vase carved by Kim Lewis, which has a home in the foyer of the Dome Chapel on Sunrise Ranch.

At 100 Mile House on October 26 in a service, "Restoration to Wholeness," Martin said:

> This burgeoning whole has been defined in many minds as the Emissary ministry. Some will disagree and say there are other programs in the world and fine people everywhere doing their thing; what's so important about the Emissary ministry? It has no importance if seen with cultic eyes, but the name may be used to indicate the unfoldment of the creative process. It relates to what is working out through the whole body of mankind, but it is appearing consciously through relatively few. Even within the range of those directly associated with the Emissary ministry there are still very few consciously aware of what is really happening.

Conrad O'Brien-ffrench passed away at his home on Sunrise Ranch on October 23 at the age of ninety-three. On November 7 there was a "Service of Thanksgiving" for Conrad in which Roger de Winton paid beautiful tribute to this exceptional man. There was a telephone hookup with Glen Ivy and 100 Mile House, where Martin continued, repeating Roger's closing words from the 23rd Psalm:

> "Surely goodness and mercy shall follow me all the days of my life: and I will dwell in the house of the Lord for ever." I will dwell in the presence of life, what life brings, whether I am in these facilities or under other circumstances in life's eternity. Most people do not have any experience of dwelling in the house of the Lord during the course of their earthly existence, so it is generally considered to be applicable after that existence ceases. *Then* we may dwell in the house of the Lord forever. If the house of the Lord is forever it is available right now. The trouble is that most of us have occupied another house, one of human construction. I suppose it might even by called the house that Jack built—or was it Jerry? Everybody lives in this jerry-built house, oblivious of the fact that the house of the Lord is available for occupancy.
>
> Conrad was aware of this, and he was concerned to dwell in the house of the Lord while present in this jerry-built contraption, rather than waiting for some future time when one might somehow graduate to a more meaningful

experience. We have all shared in this burgeoning experience of the factual va-
lidity of the presence of the house of the Lord now. I thank God for the part
Conrad played in the creative process by which these things become increasingly apparent to those with open hearts and minds to receive the spirit of the
living God. We move together in that spirit, no more separate from Conrad or
any other who is not in form on earth at this time than when they were in form.

During Conrad's Memorial Service, several deer frolicked in the field just east of the
Dome at Sunrise Ranch—a fitting tribute to this dynamic man and lover of nature.

In a service at 100 Mile House on November 9, "Heaven From the Heavenly Perspective," Martin commented on the failure of the First Sacred School and movement into
the Second, after which we have the Third:

> And while there had been failure previously, both after Moses and after
> Jesus, if anything was to be salvaged out of all this there had to be some sort of
> success or victory from the standpoint of the Third Sacred School. Thus far it
> has been proving itself out. Something remained in clear polarity after Uranda.
> I necessarily had something to do with that, but there were others who held
> the point with me, so that there might not be a failure *this* time.

On November 16 Martin spoke of "Responsibility for a Consistent Radiation":

> We have talked about Emissaries of Divine Light. Some who heard the
> words and touched the body in some way had no faintest notion what the
> words meant. One of the reasons for reaction is fear of the unknown. It has
> been difficult for people to put their finger on what was represented by an
> Emissary of Divine Light, an indication of its genuineness. They cannot grasp
> it, get hold of it, bend it to their own wills....
>
> Our sole concern is to let the radiation be present. Then there is no
> need for judgment, no need for self-judgment, no need to imagine there is
> going to be failure anywhere. We see changes going on all over the place.
> Those concerned with trying to make changes do not realize what it is that
> is happening. But surely we do. There are those who take credit for some of
> the changes, just as there have been those who are downcast because of some
> of the changes. Why be either one? What is happening is happening. We
> know why. Or *do* we? Is it just a theory? We prove whether it is a theory to us
> or not by our behavior, by what happens when changes come. There are still
> some pretty fancy concepts about what should happen by reason of the im-
> pact of the Emissary ministry. Everybody is going to fall into line! I doubt
> that very much. We learn to take it as it comes, but we learn to be true to our

own awareness of responsibility in the creative process. Judge not.

We are willing to let it happen. We respect this body, we love this body, through which the radiation occurs. We leave the radiation in the hands of the One whose radiation it is. We trust Him and we trust the radiation, and hold it steady and let it intensify because we are not jerked hither and yon by the changes that occur round about. Our imagination of what a "good" change will be is just as ridiculous as our imagination of what a "bad" change is. The process takes care of itself, provided that we take care of our own responsibility in the matter. That's the only thing in question. Are we on hand? Is the radiation steady? Is the light shining, regardless of what effects put in an appearance? Let us be sure that this stability is there, this manhood and womanhood is there, giving glory to Father God and Mother God.

On November 30 Martin addressed a gathering in a large hall of the Vancouver Music Academy, where there were telephone connections with Sunrise Ranch; Seattle and Walla Walla, Washington; Still Meadow Farm and Medford, Oregon; Redding, San Francisco, Santa Barbara and Glen Ivy in California; Phoenix, Arizona; and 100 Mile House.

38

CHEESTAYE NYEBA

December 1986 ~ May 1987

*I*n his morning service, "Cosmic Identity #1," at 100 Mile House on December 28, Martin noted that it was the last Sunday in the year and welcomed those who were connected via telephone at the Hohenort in Cape Town and in the Dome Chapel on Sunrise Ranch.

The solstice is past, Christmas Day is past, New Year's Day is at hand. Here are three events: one cosmic, the other two man-made.

The planet upon which we dwell is included in the cosmic rhythms and purposes. Its existence as a planet is absolutely dependent upon the fact that it is a part of the solar system. The solar system's existence, as a fact, is consequent upon its inclusion in the galaxy; likewise with the galaxy by reason of its inclusion in the larger universe. Here are the natural cosmic rhythms and purposes, beyond the comprehension of human minds. The planet has a cosmic identity because it is a part of the cosmic whole. Likewise with mankind on the surface of this planet, there is also a cosmic identity, which has been long lost to human awareness both individually and collectively. Substituted for this is a human identity, which human beings constantly attempt to validate.

We assemble today in these three configurations in the recognition that there is really only one, all together with one accord in one heavenly place. There seem to be three earthly places, but the distances between vanish to the extent that there is the experience of being together at the heavenly level, which could also be called the cosmic level. There is one universe, one whole, inclusive within the scope of which is a tremendous variety, from what are deemed to be the very large to what are deemed to be the very small. Appearances of distance and vast space do not deny the fact of oneness. There is no separation; however, in human identity, separation brings alienation and conflict, the daily fare of human experience, all consequent upon the fact of the invalid human identity. The only valid one, the cosmic, has been lost to human experience. We assemble today in these various locations but in one heavenly place, to let that seeming state of separateness recede in our consciousness.

The evening service, "Cosmic Identity #2," was shared by telephone with those gathered at Hillier Park in Australia.

The unwillingness of human beings generally to relinquish their determinations has prevented the already existent clear focused orientation point from coming into form on this planet. It is present, awaiting the facility for manifestation in human form on earth. Our whole concern over many years has been to let this be known for ourselves. There has been some awakening to the possibility at least, the potential, of cosmic identity, in other words an ongoing identity. I doubt if the cosmos is going to fold tomorrow! As human beings we are already capable of sharing that identity. We refer to ourselves as "I am." The true identity allows for that focus point of orientation, clear and true, to be experienced. And when that is known in the expression of life the light shines and a tone is sounded within the hearing of the body of mankind.

Catch Fire With Me was the title of a one-woman show created and performed by Ann Foorman. Her first public audience was in the Dome Chapel on January 16, 1987, which followed an initial presentation for the Sunrise family a few weeks earlier. The public performance comprised our annual offering to the Loveland community and was followed by a reception in the Pavilion. Ann gave another performance in Fort Collins at the Lincoln Center on February 12. Her program, which covered a wide range including a soliloquy of an actual experience of one of our African friends, did catch fire, and she took her show to delighted audiences in many places, one of which was Vancouver.

A Land Stewardship Conference was held on Sunrise Ranch February 5 through 7. David Lynch reported in *Eden Valley News:*

It is refreshing when those who come to participate in Emissary-sponsored public events bring with them a wealth of understanding and vision. It was fulfilling to sit in the Dome and listen to our newly found friends from Japan speak of "Johrei, very similar to your attunement." It is an integral part of the work of those who practice Nature Farming: a way of working with nature and the living soil. Our guests from the Malachite Small Farm School in southern Colorado, deeply moved by their time with us, referred to their educational and agricultural programs as a labor of love. Lynn Miller, editor of the *Small Farmers Journal,* a keynote presenter at our symposium, delighted everyone with his penetrating view of the farm crisis. His comments on true purpose and unselfish motivation in stewardship of the land paved the way for a meaningful event that soared far beyond methods and techniques so often over-emphasized.

John Kimmey, founder and director of the Talavaya Center, held everyone in rapt attention as he wove the story of his adventures with Hopi people, an Indian tribe of the Southwest who hold sacred their origins in Mother Earth. Ours is not a labor for mere survival but a ceremony of honor, demonstrated by the act of tilling, planting, nurturing and harvesting, a symbol of reverence and respect for the Great Spirit. Delmar Akerlund showed slides that demonstrated that natural, wholistic farming is more than a fancy but is indeed the only approach that upholds the integrity of the environment. After twenty years of organic farming, Akerlund Farms in Nebraska provides a model for farmers, conservationists and public officials the world around. Many others contributed to the spirit of the occasion. Mark Anderson and his comments on nutrition emphasized the correlation between land stewardship and our food source. Vance Martin, president of the World Wilderness Congress, and Darby Junkin, author and journalist, emphasized our true relationship with this living planet.

Michael Burghley touched on the various themes of the day, and we were thrilled to share two telephone connections with Lord Exeter at 100 Mile House at this momentous occasion. Here is a new avenue to reach into the world and make ourselves available to all who long to come Home.

Martin announced, on February 15 at 100 Mile House, that a telephone connection had been successfully made with Chandigarh, India. PenDell Pittman was instrumental in the accomplishment, with Rob Cass on the other end. Seventeen people were gathered and three of them (A. B. Singh, Bonny Sodhi and Janis Barker) spoke, with Rob, to a few of us in Martin's office, where he and Michael said a few words.

The Cariboo Ski Marathon of 1987 at 100 Mile House was a great success. Over a thousand from many parts of the country participated in the 30-km trek.

A very dear and greatly talented friend, Dr. John D. Waskom, passed away on February 20 in Natchitoches. His departure was sudden and unexpected, "leaving behind much creative work in process," wrote Ronnie Lim in *Newslight*.

His was a spirit of adventure, exploration and discovery, born of a deep, perceptive stillness which allowed him to see worlds of cosmic rhythm and design.

John's understanding of the earth as a living planet, with cycles and pulsations interrelated with the larger universe, evidenced itself in his work over the years as a geologist and geophysicist. Whether working for Humble Oil Company, teaching at Northwestern State University of Louisiana, doing research for NASA (National Aeronautics and Space Administration), or more currently private geological and geophysical consulting, his accurate observation and discernment of the earth earned him high regard. In 1960 he was named "Geophysicist of the Year" by Humble Oil Company and in 1983 was selected as professor emeritus following his retirement from NSU.

John was profoundly interested in education. [John and his wife Sara had five children, four boys and a girl. Sara commented, in her delightful southern accent, before Tina arrived, *"Nobody* needs five boys!" What a beautiful surprise!] John frequently said, "The solution to education today lies within the adults. When the conscious awareness of what is required in the educational process occurs in adults, the children will easily and gladly respond."

His contribution was profound, his love of life unquestionable.

He was a pioneer in the rare art of allowing a very keen mind to be directed by the impulse of the spirit. I was enthralled by his wisdom regarding spirals (his hallmark) and the "golden section." Many besides his bereaved wife and family were deeply touched by John's passing.

On that same day, February 20, Alan and Jean Hammond were in Houston, Texas, where 37 participated in a gathering, from Texas, Louisiana and Oklahoma. A dinner was held at The Houstonian Hotel, and the following day the doors were opened to include 50 additional people to hear a public EFI talk, "Exploring New Dimensions of Man and Woman," with Alan and Jean the speakers. A service was held the next day, Sunday, shared by Brian and Leslie Lanes, who focalized the area. Upon receiving word of John's passing, with a quick change in flight schedules the four proceeded the next day to Edgewater Acres to share in a memorial service for him and spend time with his family.

On February 22 Martin's service was entitled "Be Awake to the Potential in Each Role and Task." Edgewater Acres was connected by telephone, and Martin announced that there would be a memorial service for John Waskom the following Tuesday at Edgewater.

> The power of love draws this planet with its burden of life forms back into alignment with cosmic purpose. Because there has been this lack of alignment the world has been filled with tribulation, but the planet and all on its surface are in the process of being drawn back into alignment with the creative purpose.
>
> The reason for our presence on earth is that we might awaken to what is happening and participate in the process, letting it be drawn to focus. The focus has been absent. What human beings refer to as nature has been left on its own without the necessary direction, which was man's responsibility. It has been able to survive thus far in a very distorted state. So it is useless to look to nature, as in a "back to nature" movement, for human guidance. It is the restoration of man that is required. Without that focus there is no control out of heaven to set the dominion of the ordinances of heaven in the earth. "All things work together to perfection." This is one reason why we can very easily and naturally give thanks for the life and contribution of our friend John Waskom. All is well. There may be changes in the external sense, but there is something which does not change, that remains constant, and we are individually responsible for bringing that to focus—the expression of spirit in the cosmic creative process.

Upon Martin's invitation John's son, David, spoke from Edgewater:

> My vision expands greatly as I listen to you this morning, and I'm sure I speak for all gathered here when I say that the events of the last seventy-two hours have brought clearly to focus for us the knowing that there is no fooling around here. Although my emotions in this period have quaked a few times, my connection with you and with the Word has never once even shivered. Life moves on, and it has been a very maturing opportunity to participate with you in this creative cycle this morning.

That evening in his service, "Total Availability to the Creative Process," Martin relayed a telemail comment from Jim Miller that on a recent occasion in Calgary when Michael and Nancy spoke, 207 tickets had been sold, with a seating capacity of 200. Jim referred to some who came "out of the woodwork" on occasion, in this case requesting tickets, and he told them they were all sold but if they came to the door there might be some "no shows," which was the case.

Martin used the analogy of the parable about the wise and foolish virgins:

Some were locked out. There is a time when the door closes, for the job that we are aware of must be done. There have been, all along the way, many who have felt it was their right to associate or disassociate with this body, as they happened to choose. It tends to be the case when I go into the field, that there are some, as Jim indicated, who come out and momentarily we have a large gathering, and then back they scurry. The Children of Israel thought of themselves as the chosen ones, and we have had opportunity to awaken to what that means. It doesn't depend upon our earthly heredity in any way but on the control of spirit with respect to body, mind and heart.

How many have had the experience of being a quitter? Most people have, in one way or another. Of course they had very good reasons why. But whatever is undertaken is one's responsibility. Amongst all the people over the years there were maybe a couple of people, without spiritual understanding, who nevertheless were of a character that wouldn't quit. I blessed them and I do so in retrospect, because they made my task that much easier. They owned what they did. I owned what I did. So we were in agreement. The creative process works. Let us let it work. But it takes backbone, it takes guts. We can't stand back from it and say, "Well it's going to work, somehow or other." It is going to work somehow or other, but in its working it is going to carry a lot of people out. What about encompassing it, so that it has an opportunity to be brought to focus and reveal its nature because we are there with the authority and ability to do it?

Martin's words were followed by a potent period of silence, after which he left the Chapel.

Martin, Lillian and I arrived at Glen Ivy in late February for a season. Executive Council was in session March 2-11. In a service on the 1st, "Out of the Pit," Martin spoke of a gathering that had just been completed at Edenvale under the title "Stewardship in Design and Technology." The weekend event was under the leadership of Jim Leckie of Vancouver, with assistance from Gib Currie of Seattle and David Pelland of Edenvale. Don Hynes from Still Meadow in Oregon provided an overall perspective, which drew together 25 participants from western Canada and the United States.

After Jim Leckie spoke from Edenvale via the teleconnection, Martin spoke:

I am sure this was a useful time for those assembled. Technology occupies a prominent place in the world as we presently know it. We're all involved one way or another, at least in the effects of technology if nothing else. What is called technology is one way of trying to second-guess the creative process. It all seems to be so necessary, because the creative process has been overlooked and ignored. So it is assumed that human beings need to take care of the apparent lack. Seeing that this is a part of the world as we know it, it is capable of being used by certain people on hand in a way that does not violate the creative process. We have begun to awaken to the possibility of the factual nature of the creative process and have some experience of the way it works.

Our concern is to play our part in the demise of the human state. Such an approach is not popular in the world where everyone is so locked into it. Many people are aware, at least subconsciously, that there is a very great deal of disintegration going on and it seems as though collapse in various ways is imminent. We are looking at the process of rising up out of the pit, not by shoveling, not by great human effort, but by simply assuming a character which is not governed by those elements round about, some seemingly external, some internal, which make us comfortable or uncomfortable. Heaven is the place to be. One cannot lift oneself physically into some heaven, but that doesn't stop one from being in heaven, even though for the time being one may physically still be present in the pit. One may rise up into an identity which does not exist in the pit. It exists in heaven. It is already a comfortable state, but one cannot know that without being in heaven.

The event was reported by Grant Clarke of Edenvale in *Newslight*:

The objective of the gathering was to examine the nature of our experience and responsibility in the field of technology. We had engineers, designers, computer sales and systems people, and others who had a vital interest in the topic. We were concerned to distil the essences of what a creative and fitting approach would be in our handling of what is presently with us.

We examined representative samples of technological "disasters," such as the Chernobyl nuclear accident, the Bhopal, India, chemical tragedy and the Challenger space shuttle destruction. One could see clearly the bleak end of a road that had seemed to many to hold the great promise of the future: technological advancement. At the same time we were aware of the responsibility to utilize with appreciation what is present, but with a new vision, so that we are not subject to our contrivances or mesmerized by them. It was clear that a large part of the problem has been the tendency to develop and espouse more and more capable tools of manipulation in the hope of exerting some sort of control in a world where the natural controls and rhythms of life have been rejected and forgotten.

It was obvious that the real value of our gathering had to do not at all with the grinding out of solutions to an obviously insoluble problem, but with the regeneration of a sense of connection with the immediate design and control of life itself. It was the fuller development of that connection which characterized the majority of our time together, and the result was most remarkable. In a field characterized in terms of noisy thought and desperate feeling, there was a place of significant gentleness and stillness, an easy, cooperative agreement. Where there has been a feeling of powerlessness, there was an awareness of stable certainty, of the actual ease with which what needs to be done may be done as we remain reliably in place as representatives of life's grand creative process.

Martin's service on March 8 was entitled "From Complaint to Contentment." Preceding all of his services, in whatever location, there was exceptional music by choirs and/or artists, vocal and instrumental, with occasional dramatic contributions, dance or sometimes a chant. At Glen Ivy there were always telephone connections with the surrounding area, that morning with San Francisco, Phoenix and Houston. Martin said:

> A group of us have been in session during the last week. This is a name, Executive Council, given to a group of people. It is convenient to identify such groupings, but it isn't the name that has importance. If there is importance it is because of the people. There are incidentally thirteen in number, six men and seven women. Apart from the physical state of having to sit for considerable lengths of time, it has been easy and delightful for those concerned, in agreement in a cycle of adventure.
>
> Here is the provision of a clear focus point which could not be in place at all but for the whole body, which is necessary and also shares in what it is that this body is all about. There is a body; if it were not so, there could be no point of focus. The body may be small, it was but one individual human body to start with, but it has expanded. We have a collective state of affairs, with all of those participating beginning to do so contentedly. Only then does the body become healthily operational.

Following the cycle of Executive Council, 39 gathered, many of them area coordinators across North America, to participate in "Sessions With Martin." The Latin American Council convened for a few days after that.

The next exciting event was an example of the extent of expansion occurring in the ministry. Soviet delegates to the U.S.-U.S.S.R. Entertainment Summit held in California visited Glen Ivy, with their American hosts. Present were Elem Klimov, head of the U.S.S.R. delegation; Vladimir Posner, media spokesperson for the Soviet government; Derek Hart, Tolomush Okeyev and Jim Hickman. Barbara Coffman was one of the principals (project manager/Soviet liaison for the Summit) in bringing about the event, joined by translator Bruce Allyn who had been studying at Moscow University, and Peri Chickering from Sunrise Ranch. Afternoon workshops in the theater arts were followed by dinner with the three of us, the Burghleys and others. Our Soviet friends were moved by the magic of the hospitality received and thoroughly enjoyed a musical dance number, "The Rhythm of Life" performed by an ensemble of Glen Ivy players.

On March 22 at Glen Ivy Martin's service was entitled "Clear Sky," in which he referred to the Entertainment Summit and added that the word *summit* had tended to have political implications in the past and there was some objection on the part of some members of the Politburo to the use of the word.

> However, it is not a political event. It might be called a spiritual event and, further, is designated as an entertainment summit. The derivation of "entertainment" relates to the matter of coming together. The spirit in the creative process works everywhere through everyone; it is no respecter of persons. We have an increasing awareness of the internal working by which those with open hearts are moved. And there were those in this gathering who were certainly moved.

In his service on March 29, "The Opening Door of Memory," he said:

> Our Soviet delegation in this Summit have had experience of focalization and understand it. They moved very easily together because there was a point of focus. People then think it must be the party line, the KGB or some nefarious business. But it wasn't. Here was just a person, Elem Klimov. He commented (after interpretation; he spoke in Russian) that "there will never be harmony, because it is finite and life is not." It is being thought of in human experience as relating to human relationships, harmony between people. People have our different cultures and backgrounds and are trying to get together all the time but don't make it. The finite and the infinite never seem to be able to get together. The finite, rightly, is simply a reflection of the infinite when the connection is made, and man is the connection. The finite reflects the truth that is present in the infinite. Then there is harmony.

On April 12 in a service titled "Genuine Understanding" Martin spoke of understanding, which he said is both a conscious and a subconscious thing. In the human state the tendency is to imagine that it is merely conscious: "I understand because I can define it." Understanding requires the right use of all the facilities. You can't just have conscious understanding; you can't just have subconscious understanding. The human intellect cannot know what the truth is as long as it is trying to define it. Only when the mind comes again into position to let the creative process move consciously and subconsciously can there be genuine understanding.

Martin, Lillian and I arrived on Sunrise Ranch on April 14 to a valley full of spring blossoms after another wonderful flight in Citation. Martin gave the annual Easter Sunrise Service on April 19 on a mild, rather cloudy morning. After Frank Jeffries sounded seven notes on the ram's horn, Martin spoke:

> There has been a group of people assembling for a sunrise service on Sunrise Ranch for about forty years, one evidence of consistency. There has been a generation of spiritual substance that has permitted the formation of a body of agreement—all this in spite of manifold factors of human nature present in those concerned. Here is a miracle, that such a body could be drawn together and continue faithfully over the years. In spite of such resistance and rebellion as there may have been, the body is present and alive. We rejoice this morning to let the Incarnate One in His body speak and say, "I am present. I am the resurrection and the life."

At that point the clouds parted to reveal the sun in all its brilliance, and Frank Jeffries again sounded seven notes on the ram's horn, which was followed by some overtone chanting by the men's chant group.

In Martin's service later in the Dome Chapel, "Resurrection in Fact," he referred to the story of the resurrection of Jesus two thousand years ago and pointed out that this has been limited to a belief that it could apply only to one person, which kept the truth of it external to oneself.

> The resurrection is of the body of the Son of God. Let us see how it applies, what it means in present, practical experience; otherwise it is a waste of time to consider it.

> During the last fifty-five years a miracle has been occurring in the body of mankind. That miracle relates to many of us, and others who are not here present or at the end of the telephone line [Durango, Albuquerque and Shreveport]. There has been the emergence of a body of people, not on the basis of some belief—some have tried to make it be on that basis, which it isn't—but on the basis of the fact of the magnetic force which has drawn it into form. This is the resurrection of the body.

> This body belongs to the Most High. It doesn't belong to anyone who composes it. But those who compose it love it. I have loved this growing body for many years. I loved it just the way it was. But those who composed it didn't always agree with me. They had complaints. They wanted me to change something, so that they would be more comfortable, or so that whatever was happening would conform more with their view of what should happen. But no-

body knew what should happen. I was content to let it happen the way it would and I have delighted over the years in those who agreed with me on that point, so that they weren't always trying to stick their two bits' worth in to make things be the way they thought they ought to be. If human beings are so clever, why is the world the way it is now? They don't know, but are totally unwilling to admit it, so they go blindly on, destroying everything, including themselves. There is nothing new about that, except that it is coming to some point of climax.

Well if that self-destruction can come to a point of climax, so can the resurrection. I have been interested in that, and I have loved the body. I didn't know what the body was going to be. Let it be the way it is, with the creative process at work because the spirit was brought to focus, the Word spoken and the tone sounded. I trust that, and as this spoken Word and sounded tone amplifies, I trust *that*. It amplifies through those who accept absolutely this growing body and love it as I love it. I love the body because I love my King, and it is His body.

In Martin's evening service on that Easter Day he spoke of the "Sign of the Times" events that would take place the next weekend, and of one central and primary sign of the times which has not been recognized, let alone acknowledged, by the population in general. That is the sign of the Son of man in heaven.

People are aware of many things in the earth, but virtually nothing in the true heaven. That awareness shall come. The Son of man is the body of the Son of God, of which we have some immediate experience and is only known in heaven. The fact that it is present on earth is easily recognized, but the reality of it is in heaven. We only know the Son of man to the extent that we ourselves abide in heaven.

In *Eden Valley News* Nick Giglio outlined some of the occurrences in the Emissary community,

which has approximately 155 meeting locations in 23 countries. Seminars and classes are held throughout the year. Numerous public gatherings have been held around the world, with no need to join anything but to discover for oneself life's ability to bring integration. Life works—don't fix it! Just align with the way life works. A book called *The Rising Tide of Change* was compiled from a number of talks given at the gatherings of that name which were held at 19 locations in 9 countries and attended by approximately 4500 people. An "At Home" day was hosted in a hundred locations, where our video *Climate for the Garden* was aired nationally on many PBS stations.

In April of this year open gatherings called "The Signs of the Times," sponsored by Emissary Foundation International, were held in 73 locations in 23 countries. Included in overseas participants were Argentina, Australia, England, France, Germany, Ghana, India, Ireland, Israel, Italy, Japan, Korea, Mexico, Netherlands, New Zealand, Nigeria, Norway, South Africa, Switzerland and Zimbabwe. Approximately 4600 people were drawn, with about 2400 who had never attended an EFI event. A glimpse into the essence of these events is conveyed by the following: "The signs of disintegration are legion. But there are signs of integration as well: individuals who are recognizing the power of innocence, who are releasing self-centeredness in favor of a vision of wholeness, who are finding purpose in living that is in harmony with the rhythms and cycles of life itself. These are the signs of the times."

On Sunrise Ranch the event was honored on April 26. In his service entitled "The Sign of the Son of Man Appears in Heaven #1" Martin spoke to many in the Dome Chapel and those connected by telephone, "some on this continent, some in England, Europe, Israel, Africa and even, I trust, India (it seems a little difficult to make telephone connections with that country)." The Dome was a visual delight, with numerous objects representing many cultures and a colorful map of the world as a backdrop across the entire stage. Martin invited Rupert Maskell at Mickleton in England to speak, who reported that 65 were gathered in Kensington the previous day for three hours, and continued:

> Peter Russell, author of the book *The Global Brain,* said he caught a glimpse of your book *Beyond Belief* on the bookshelf during the break and was delighted; he said he nearly leapt out of his skin. After that we met in Mickleton with 70 people, hosted by John and Nicola Kurk. We used the theme "A Change of Heart" and concluded with a chant and a period of silence.

Rupert conveyed reports from Gary Gillespie and Jeffrey Newman.

> There was an all-day gathering at Cape Town in the Hohenort Hotel with about 130 people. Fifty stayed on for a special dinner of Muslim and Indian food specially prepared by Abdullah Aziz, the hotel bookkeeper. In Johannesburg approximately 65 gathered at Fourways, where Glenn Babb, recent ambassador from South Africa to Canada, made a valuable contribution. At Empumalanga about 20 people from Durban joined 80 from that area in KwaZulu to spend some focused time together, surrounding the rapidly rising EFI house being built there. Michael Boon was chief speaker—I imagine mostly in English translated into Zulu, although he has an increasing fluency in the Zulu language.

Jean Michel Corbet in Paris let us know of their event. David Lesser joined them from England. There were 19 present, the majority newcomers. There was also an event in Geneva yesterday, to which Marco and Sarah Jane Menato, Jim Heaslip and Serge Nicolet went from LaVigne. That was attended by 20 people and went well. Today Lindsay Rawlings is in Oslo, Serena Newby in Munich, Marjon den Haan in Amsterdam, Des Dornan in Dublin and Antonio Marulli in Rome. These are all concurrent with what we are doing now. It has been a very eventful time, marked by spontaneity and initiative, considerable numbers of people coming forth in their own expressions of victory and assurance, for which these events have provided a wonderful opportunity. It is a great joy to bring this to you, Martin.

Michael Burghley was invited to speak from King View in Ontario:

About 140 are gathered here. Yesterday an event in Ottawa took place at the Venture Inn with about a hundred participants, half of them from Quebec. Yesterday I was in Toronto where 265 met at the St. Lawrence Hall downtown, with about 30 presenters at the four-hour session. Among them were: Dr. Alastair Cunningham, an immunologist and cancer specialist, a courageous pioneer in the spiritual approach to working with cancer patients; Goody Mogadime, a beautiful Zulu lady, expert in crisis intervention, in the educational systems in Ontario and in South Africa, who commented that there really isn't much difference in what needs to be done in either place; Dr. Tom Verny, psychiatrist and author of *The Secret Life of the Unborn Child;* David Gouthro, an executive with Apple Computers of Canada, concerned with appropriate encompassment of personnel in business; Brian Bedard, a consultant on Third World animal health. It all fit together—the message of the day: It takes all of us to make up an effective whole.

Martin concluded the service:

I personally am aware of what has been happening in many places around the North American continent. However I do not propose to speak of them specifically. The events of yesterday were the events of yesterday. This is the event of today. What went before has led up to this present moment and what is available to be experienced now. It would seem that the theme of stillness and of assuming personal responsibility were threads that unified the many events. A recognition is emerging increasingly that it is not through human effort that what is needful to happen can happen. "Signs of the Times" was the title given to these events. There have always been signs of the times—

everything that happens on earth is a sign of the times. But in and of them-selves the happenings have virtually no meaning. They do give evidence, how-ever, that there is something invisible at work, resulting in the effects of the signs of the times in any given moment.

One may speak of this invisible element in terms of a creative process, which is not limited to this planet or the affairs of men but is operative through-out the whole universe. To contend with that, principally by ignoring it, would seem to be the height of stupidity. Is it to be supposed that human beings can prevent or divert the movement of that creative process which operates on such a vast and powerful scale? It is remarkable that human beings continue to exist on the face of the earth. There must be some built-in condition in the creative process which extends mercy, giving human beings time to repent of their foolishness and awaken once again to the fact of the creative process, so that they may accommodate it in their own living.

That creative process must operate with design and purpose, capable of extending control. The control is evident in the observable effects, particu-larly on the larger universal scale. However the effects, the signs of the times, with which human beings are involved give little evidence of coordinated de-sign and control. Rather, there is much evidence of something out of control, not characterized by any discernible design. All this is consequent upon the way human beings behave.

Human behaviour is essentially self-centered. It is assumed that one may do as one pleases if one can get away with it. Nobody ever really does; it catches up eventually. We can see that this has been happening everywhere on the face of the earth, and we may nod our heads in agreement that it is stupid, particularly when we speak of "they." But it isn't a matter of "they" or "we." It is a matter of "me." It can't be done en masse in the way human beings at-tempt to do it. *First* it must be done in my own experience.

I am most thankful we have had the opportunity of sharing this hour in many locations the world around. Incidentally, those whose time zones didn't permit participation this morning will be sharing with us this evening, so that the whole world will be encompassed in this way and the invitation provided, be-cause there are those on earth now who compose a coordinating body through which the creative process may work to draw man and God into union. How much of this present body of men and women may remain is a question, of course. But we needn't concern ourselves about that—simply do what we are here to do.

The evening service, "The Sign of the Son of Man Appears in Heaven #2," included telephone connections with a variety of locations including some across the Pacific. The overseas contacts in the morning service spanned the Atlantic. Martin emphasized the point that we continue to share the spirit of the living God with those who compose the resurrected body of the Son of God wherever they may be on the face of the earth.

The next day, the 27th, was Martin's birthday, which annually presented a unique opportunity for his family in whatever location he happened to be, to express their great joy in myriad ways of giving to this beloved leader. It was a special celebration that year, with a sumptuous meal enhanced by both hilarious and serious entertainment. Martin commented afterward:

> Those who dwell on Sunrise Ranch are in a very special location. It has changed over the years, but it has always been a location that could not be improved upon, ever since Uranda first set foot in this place. Out of his sowing has come the garden which we now inhabit both in the internal sense and the external sense. Here is a vivid example of the fact that as the heaven is accommodated and maintained, the earth reflects the fact—not that the job is complete yet, but we see that as representing what rightly occurs for the whole earth.

Honeymoon visitors from Nigeria were Emeka and Ana Maria Emeh. Emeka is a fine lawyer and his wife a medical doctor. In season they became parents of beautiful twin boys and continue to serve in the furtherance of the works of the Lord in their own land.

Ted Black has always been very active in the realm of translation of the Word into other than the English language. Examples of this were his work with Eric Crocker, then living in San Miguel de Tucuman, Argentina, which resulted in *Con alas de aguila (On Eagle's Wings)* introduced to Latin America. *Climate for the Garden* was released with Spanish spoken over the original video, as well as French, German and Korean. Portions of *On Eagle's Wings* were in print in Korean.

Jim Higerd gave an update on the situation regarding the reservoir in the Valley:

> Learning of the City of Loveland's desire to flood Sunrise Ranch with the construction of its raw-water storage reservoir, the Emissary family around the world sent over 1200 letters to the City Council requesting they consider other options. The City Council voted to undertake a $180,000 Water Supply Study to determine its course of action. The City is now into Phase II of its Study. Phase I concluded that Loveland could supply water to 114,000 people (current population 36,400) for normal use during a 1-in-100-year drought severity if it purchased additional water or increased its raw-water storage capacity. The projected increase, if placed in our valley,

would inundate a substantial portion of Sunrise Ranch.

In Phase II Loveland is studying the effects water conservation will have on its water demand during a drought, along with looking at the cost of purchasing additional water supplies and two reservoir sites—our valley and a valley located approximately two miles southwest of the Ranch... Included in Phase II is the formation of a citizen forum, which we have been invited to attend and offer comments and suggestions. While we carry the primary responsibility with respect to the sacredness of these grounds, we are not alone. Mark Collier, a Sierra Club representative, expressed that the Sierra Club is interested in helping us maintain what we have established in our valley. Likewise the local Audubon Society have expressed their desire to protect the wildlife balance that has been established in this valley and feel any increase in the present reservoir capacity would upset this balance. You can be aware that this study is in progress and we have a very keen interest in the outcome.

The various Sunrise departments were enjoying creative work in an atmosphere of delighted companionship. The office staff consisted of twenty-five, sometimes more, capable and willing friends ably and lovingly coordinated by Shareen Ewing. The Sunrise kitchen staff, under Keith Fairmont's direction, were blest by a visit from Max von Hartmann who focused some training sessions. Judy Morris did an admirable job heading the home staff, Ed Haimes the maintenance department, and David Lynch the farm and garden areas. As for the smallest Emissaries, Evelyn Swanson worked wonders with the preschool children, as well as focalizing the JTS program for the entire ministry. The publication *JTS World* was a blessing to many.

A "Visual Arts Forum" convened on Sunrise Ranch on May 3 in the Conference Room (previously the West Chapel), with 37 visual artists from Sunrise and the Rocky Mountain Region. In *Eden Valley News*, Bob Ewing, coordinator, reported:

The visual arts activities burgeoning on Sunrise Ranch are characterized by a wide range of group participation, from flower arranging in the Dome Chapel to landscaping. Graphic arts are coordinated by Pam Holloway, assisted by Georgene Higerd and Cher Skoubo—of inestimable value in *Eden Valley News*, *Northern Light*, magazines, designs for book covers and brochures. Jim Huckabay has also contributed his expertise from his business ("Focus Design" in Shreveport, Louisiana), with the cover of *Beyond Belief* and the "Rising Tide" and "Signs of the Times" brochures. Will Carpenter, Jim Paine and I have crafted new signs for the entrances to Sunrise Ranch, and David Gray and crew are landscaping around the Pavilion, plans for which include a pond with a sculpture designed by Martin and executed by Pam Holloway and Georgene Higerd.

New life is being breathed into RimRock House at the Gateway property, with a series of art shows [some held in the Pavilion] and classes over the past year, and also refurbishing. My own art studio is being reestablished there. Classes include watercolor painting by Michael Gress, graphic arts by Pam Holloway, calligraphy by Richard Heinberg, and acrylic/watercolor painting by me. Conrad was a leading force in his masterful expression in drawing and painting, and large canvases of his art adorn the walls of the Pavilion. Sunrise Ranch is a place of burgeoning beauty, with a visual quality of order that shines like a jewel in this rock-crowned valley—evidence that truly wholesome men and women care to live artistically in every way.

My comment at the Visual Arts Forum recalled some words in the first chapter of Genesis which referred to the fact that the seed was "in itself, upon the earth. The seed is present here, and in every moment is ready for whatever phase of coming forth." Martin spoke:

Sunrise Ranch is a focus for the emergence of the creative process. We are becoming adept at accommodating the process by which the veil dissolves and beauty is revealed. It is all a living process, whether it relates to what have heretofore been considered inanimate objects, or to the earth and the things growing out of it, the animate world. It is all animate world as far as we are concerned. Sunrise Ranch is a living focus of spirit, and spirit permeates everything.

Martin, Lillian and I left in the Citation on May 8 for the Midwest Servers Conference at Oakwood Farm, near Muncie, Indiana, and a brief tour of the Midwest before moving on to 100 Mile House. Martin entitled his service at Oakwood on May 10 "Clear Sky and Open Heaven," and mentioned the recent Entertainment Summit in California with the Soviet filmmakers and writers present:

I was going to give the blessing at the meal and wished to tread rather cautiously. I had talked previously with Bruce Allyn, interpreter, seeking to find a Russian phrase to conclude my blessing. He came up with something that, literally interpreted, meant "clear sky": "cheestaye nyeba" in Russian. So I duly pronounced those words at the close of my blessing, and it was the first time I've ever received a round of applause after I gave a blessing! Of course it means more than "clear sky"; it means "open heaven." And there truly was something moving in the spirit that evening which emphasized how willing and anxious people are to experience a clear heaven.

39

THE VIBRATIONAL ARK

June ~ September 1987

On June 2nd Helen Jerome, sister of Gladys Miller and member of the Berwick group, passed away. Then Helen Jones, she and her husband Ralph attended the first Class on Sunrise Ranch in 1952. Ralph died a few years later. In 1961, remarried, she again attended Class, with her husband Harry Jerome. They had a health food store and attunement service in Marion, Indiana, until Harry's death in 1969, after which Helen moved back to Berwick and was an active member of the group there.

At 100 Mile House, on the 8th, another dear friend, Bob Barbour, left us. Sixty-three years old, he was enjoying his favorite sport of golf when he died suddenly of a heart attack. In the mid-1950s Bob had connected with the Emissary ministry in Montreal, and he and his wife Alice were inspired to be servers in Edmonton, Alberta, and in Ancaster, London and Windsor, Ontario. They moved to 100 Mile House in 1975 and Alice passed away two years later. In 1979 Bob married Irene Polack and they shared a new cycle of service. Bob's daughters, Pauline Price of King View and Nancy Barbour of 100 Mile House, served in various places through the years. A service for Bob was held on June 12 in the Chapel with about 200 people in attendance, many of whom were friends from the Village.

Some unique and valuable events were occurring on Sunrise Ranch. In June, Peri Chickering brought the "Outward Bound International Exchange Program" participants and instructors (from the Soviet Union, Hungary and the United States) to Sunrise Ranch for a special time together. An equine gathering, "Mastery in Horsemanship," was held in February, with participants Elaine Gagné, Stephanie Wilson, Melanie Jones, David Lynch and Thomas Walsh of Sunrise Ranch; Peter Castonguay and Catherine Leckie from British Columbia; Barbara Lourgos from California; and Jack Carver from New Hampshire. An "Earth Stewardship" group included David Lynch, Nick Giglio, Chief Oren Lyons and Rashmi Mayur. Over twenty attended a gathering of Nurses being hosted on Sunrise Ranch; and a "Design and Technology" group numbered 28.

In Martin's service at 100 Mile House on June 14, "No More Sea," he noted the fact that, as described in the Book of Genesis, the earth was once covered with water.

> When man was present and available to the creative process, there were changes. There are other elements involved, but the oceans are the principal one for maintaining the balance of the gases in the atmosphere, so that existence as we know it may be sustained. We are concerned with the restoration of man and see that the substitutes are all temporary. Somewhere along the way they don't work anymore. They have provided time and opportunity for human beings to awaken. Because of the changes which have occurred on the face of the earth, which allowed for the establishment of substitute patterns of control in the absence of true man, existence has continued.

> The world the way we know it has been produced by human beings, not by God; and it is going down the drain, because the day of the substitutes is coming to a close. And unless man is on hand, there is nothing insofar as man's responsibility in this planet and in the whole solar system is concerned. It is not a little matter, but a vital part of the whole, and the whole is not complete without its parts. So there has always been the necessity that this aberration be brought, in whatever way found to be possible, back into the design and under the control of truth, powered again by love. We have offered ourselves to let this happen in our own physical forms, where there is a variety of physical substance representative of the substance in the earth as a whole, and where mental substance is available, both in the range of the subconscious and a little layer of the conscious. It is necessary for the spiritual substance to be cleaned up, the radiation penetrate, and restoration occur.

At 100 Mile House in his service on June 21, "When the Genuine Appears the Substitutes Pass Away," Martin observed that there are organizations everywhere.

There is a tendency to go along with the current of movement which has swept and is sweeping human beings everywhere into slavery. Clearly, because of bureaucratic controls in operation in the world in general it is necessary to render unto Caesar the things that are Caesar's. But we also have clearly in consciousness that we render unto God the things that are God's. And when it comes right down to it, all the things of Caesar belong to God.

As it has been put, we now live in a "global cottage," and whether it is farther afield or near at hand it all impacts in one way or another. This is the realm of bureaucratic control: the realm of effects, the realm of form. It is through the manipulation of form that the controls are established and maintained, so that there comes greater and greater rigidity, until eventually presumably nobody can move at all. That is rigor mortis! Manipulation of externals is bureaucracy, which becomes increasingly pervasive everywhere. As Hugh Malafry pointed out, bureaucracies are the same regardless of the political system, and the bureaucracies are the means of governing. This is a substitute for the creative process, the endeavor of man as he now is to defeat God.

In the evening service of the 21st, "The Anti-Force Rendered Impotent," Martin referred again to the state wherein people may think to find a degree of security by conforming,

a feeling that one can thread through this labyrinth successfully and perhaps even make a buck, or be rewarded in some fashion for being so good.

Over the millennia mankind has created what may be called an entity. The devil is supposed to lie in wait for his innocent victims, but the devil is a human creation. One may look for those ultimately evil people who are subjecting all of us to this terrible condition, and various people and groups of people are fingered from time to time as being the authors of the evils which assail us. The fact is that there has been created, over a lengthy period of intensifying bureaucracy, a very compulsive force in human experience. It compels toward judgment of good and evil.

There is what might be called an anti-force—it has been called the antichrist—which is very compelling insofar as human beings are concerned in their present state; it compels them to do what they do. It isn't a cosmic entity that roams around through the galaxies—but it is more than a comic-strip character! Its purpose is to bring human beings into absolute slavery to it. It is strange, because they have created this but are intent upon being enslaved by it, and have been since the fall. It has been building and building, and we see in this bureaucratic model how everybody is being brought into absolute slavery; and they are not kicking and squealing, for the most part, but happily giving themselves to it without any apparent awareness of what is happening.

Some people wake up to it, and they are going to really do something about it, so they organize. They create anti-anti-forces! There are all kinds of organizations against all kinds of things—of course they say they are "pro-" but actually are against. The best way to strengthen something is to fight against it. You may eliminate a form along the way by fighting, but you still have the anti-force after it's all done. We have heard the words, "Come out of her, my people"—stop contributing to this process, stop giving power to the anti-force. And how is that done? By accepting the one supreme power, that of love. No doubt there are those who particularly embody the anti-force in the human sense, profiting by the deal; but there is little awareness of the tree of life, the body of the Son of God, the power of love, the creative power of the universe. As there is the tree of life, as there is the body of the Son of God on earth, that power can move by reason of it. And as it moves freely there, it is withdrawn to that extent from the anti-force, which consequently perishes.

On the 19th, in a service, "Summer Is Nigh," Michael referred to a remark by Sir Laurens van der Post:

"It's not the atom bomb that's a threat to our existence, it's the destruction of nature, because nature can't take much more. Nature will survive but it will disown us... And nature's very near that point." Speaking about the upcoming World Wilderness Congress he said: "We all feel that conservation efforts need updating... We are going to try to make this model, a world model." Prime Minister Nakasone of Japan said in a speech: "Our generation is recklessly destroying the natural environment. This folly can only be called suicidal. If we are to preserve our irreplaceable Earth and ensure the survival of mankind I believe we must create a new global ethic and devise systems to support it."

The serious attention of many people is turning to this issue of the disintegration of the planetary environment, and inevitably the suggestion is that we will need to devise some overall plan to help nature. You and I can guess what such a plan will produce. I was touched by the passionate concern in these men for the planet, representative of many no doubt. But human schemes devised in isolation from the inherent design for this planet and ultimately for this universe, will only produce a fuller array of problems. Nowhere do I see stated in public the one central element that would make the difference. It is put precisely and perfectly in the 24th Psalm in the Bible; "The earth is the

Lord's, and the fulness thereof; the world, and they that dwell therein." Simple and to the point. It is a wonderful time on earth.

Martin spoke:

"The earth is the Lord's, and the fulness thereof; the world, and they that dwell therein." The earth refers to substance; all substance is the Lord's. It is natural for substance to belong to the Lord. It is presently held in humanly created structures—a large amount of it; perhaps not large if we are considering the total substance of the earth but large enough within the range of human operations. It is held firmly, in nuclear armaments for instance and in the armed forces. There are countless structures humanly created in concrete, and in the sense of the bank account—pieces of paper, plastic these days—very valuable!

There is all this substance, masses and masses of it. It all belongs to the Lord. It has a natural affinity with the One I Am and will naturally, if allowed to do so, flow easily, in whatever way, into the Lord's design. The only reason it doesn't flow is because of the human forms all over the earth that firmly maintain it in these structures. It takes quite an effort to keep it in the structure. As soon as anything is built it begins to decay, with the need for constant repair. And that is apparently true of human forms, the need for constant repair. But there is a natural process, a natural cycle which occurs in living form. The earth is the Lord's, all this substance at every level. And it is not only physical substance; there is mental and emotional substance. Once there is a means by which that invitation, "Come unto Me," may be extended, the substance is most willing to come home.

On August 2nd in his service on Sunrise Ranch, "The Focus of the Spirit of the Living God," Martin welcomed all into the Dome, which he said

was conceived in 1973. It was at the time of the Servers' Conference and all those present on the Ranch at the time stood together and joined hands in a circle on this site. Some words were spoken, and the creative process by which this Dome has put in an appearance was initiated—we could say out of heaven. The building itself was not completed until 1977, ten years ago. The first service was held in 1976, before it was completed.

Over the years many have played their parts in generating an atmosphere in this space. Here in a particular form and shape is a symbol of the focus of the spirit of the living God. It has become more than a symbol, and is a true symbol to the extent that those who participate in generating the atmosphere are, themselves, in their living, the evidence of a focus of the spirit of the living God.

Man was made in the image and likeness of God. There is some evidence
of this in view of the fact that he is the only creature on earth who can say "I
am," who has the conscious experience of identity. Because of that we are,
potentially at least, the means by which the living God can be revealed. But
there needs to be a focus. We did not come into the Dome particularly to relax
into the atmosphere that has been generated, but to allow that continuing
generation, and that is only possible as the focus of the spirit of the living God
is here present. It is here individually speaking—and each one can say this—
because I am present. We don't look around and say "because you are present."
It is because I am present. I take the responsibility for bringing to focus the
spirit of the living God in my expression of living. Nobody else can do it for
me. That is true of each one.

At 100 Mile House on August 6th shortly after takeoff, Dr. Jim Williamson, piloting his Cessna 180 float plane, and passenger Carol Skinner, were killed instantly when
the plane crashed and burst into flames. Carol had a coordinating role at the Edenvale
Unit for several years and for the past eight years was part of the 100 Mile Unit. Jim
was a dentist in the town of 100 Mile House and he and his wife Joy were closely
associated with the Unit. Jim was piloting Carol to visit her relatives at Savary Island.
Over 300 people attended a service of tribute for Carol and Jim conducted by Ross
Marks in the 100 Mile Emissary Chapel, in which the Edenvale Unit shared via telephone connection.

An impromptu event in the service was the appearance at the podium of Joy
Williamson. She spoke with great feeling of an aspect of her husband that "many of you
may not be familiar with—his love for God. It took the form of love for nature at first,
but his spirit of integrity and love for life was what attracted me to him and attracted you
to him." The expression of Joy's beautiful and brave spirit has continued through the
years to bless her many friends, in the Unit and elsewhere.

In his service at Sunrise Ranch on August 16, "The Vibrational Ark," Martin said:

There is a vibrational ark taking form, generated because there are those
who have been drawn together by spirit to participate in the process, which
involves changes in one's own human nature. As these occur vibrational substance is generated, and that accommodates the design in spirit. In the book
of Matthew there is a reference to the gathering of the elect from one end of
the heaven to the other. It doesn't say from one end of the earth to the other,
but of heaven—that is, in the field of this vibrational substance. Wherever
there is substance in people which resonates with the radiation of the focus of

the spirit of God on earth, they are drawn.

Martin, Lillian and I left for 100 Mile House, and on September 9 on Sunrise Ranch an incarnating angel and cherished friend, Gladys Miller, moved up "Jacob's ladder" after a brief illness. A Memorial Service was held in the Dome Chapel on the 18th, under the direction of Roger de Winton and Louis Rotola.

In *Eden Valley News*, Shareen Ewing paid tribute to that very special servant of the Lord:

> In the early days of the Emissary ministry Eddie and Gladys Miller estab-
> lished a strong point of agreement with Uranda by opening their home in Berwick,
> Pennsylvania, as a center for service and healing [one of the first to move from
> chiropractic practice to attunements]. They held annual Christmas sales, with
> homemade crafts and baking, and the proceeds were used to buy needed items
> for Sunrise Ranch: it could be stainless steel for the kitchen, machinery for the
> farm, dictionaries for the office, or candlesticks and decor for special parties. A
> Christmas gift was always sent each year to every child on the Ranch.
>
> Gladys had a profound love for the Bible and taught the "Story of Man"
> classes at Lake Rest and Green Pastures for over a decade. Eddie and Gladys
> joined the Sunrise Ranch family in 1981. Their depth of wisdom in the field of
> attunement and nutrition has blest the lives of many, here and throughout the
> world. While Gladys's physical presence will be missed, the substance of her love
> for the Lord remains very tangible, part of the fabric of this holy place.

Stan Grindstaff was busy writing a book, based on his impressions and experiences as a child growing up on Sunrise Ranch during the '40s and '50s. It is a beautiful poetic expression by a devoted and gifted man entitled *The Boy*. It incidentally gives some in-sight into the character of those who made up his environment, including Uranda—and I learned a few things about myself!

In September the 4th World Wilderness Congress was held in Colorado. Many from Sunrise Ranch and the surrounding area participated. Under the coordination of Nick Giglio of Sunrise and Carol Gillespie from Fort Collins, a task force hosted dignitaries and presenters from all over the world.

Craig Sarbeck reported the event in *Newslight*:

> Almost a thousand people from over fifty countries came to Denver and Estes
> Park to consider the critical state of the environment and see what could be done
> about it. Political luminaries such as James Baker, U.S. Secretary of the Treasury;
> Thomas McMillan, Canada's Minister of the Environment; and Gro Harlem
> Brundtland, Prime Minister of Norway and chairman of the World Commission
> on the Environment, all offered their perspectives. The Minister of Forestry from

the People's Republic of China and a Soviet delegate were present. David Rockefeller represented the growing interest of business to preserve our environment. Every major non-governmental environmental group in the United States was represented, as well as their counterparts from around the world.

Much time was given to efforts of scientists, politicians and economists to seek new ways to "manage" wilderness in such a way that what little we have left may be preserved for at least a few more years. But also present were those who recognized that the earth's state was not going to improve through human manipulation. "Our Mother Earth has had enough destruction and cannot possibly bear more," said Norma Kassi, an Inuit from the Old Crow Reservation in northern Canada. An Onandaga Indian chief, Oren Lyons, said that "the natural law is a spiritual law. Its powers are both light and dark. We are blessed and we prosper if we live by the law; it is dark and terrible if we transgress it. There is no discussion with the law, only understanding and compliance. Its tenets are simple: obey or perish."

Michael Burghley said: "The leaf emblem of the Wilderness Congress represents the wisdom just expressed. The idea for that emblem came from Magqubu Ntombela, the Zulu elder. The two smaller leaves represent man's relationship with man and his relationship with the earth. But the central frond, pointing upwards and much larger, represents man's relationship with God. It is interesting that thus far in the plenary sessions there has been very little mention about population. I enjoyed a session this afternoon on that topic; however, out of a total of 700 there were only about 40 people there. Yet the population explosion is the ultimate problem we are all facing. We talk about the need for education in the sexual aspect of our lives, the impact our actions are having on the planet as a whole, but the population problem epitomizes the feeling in the human race that we have the right to have the sexual aspect of our lives to ourselves."

Martin, Lillian and I left 100 Mile House for a tour of eastern Canada, from September 10 to 16. We were hosted by Ron and June Polack and family at King View Farm where the tour began. Jim Wellemeyer joined us there, and servers from eastern Canada arrived two days later for sessions, which culminated in a lively forum with the three of us. Martin's Sunday presentation at the Chimo Hotel in Toronto was attended by 330 people. The theme was repentance, which was echoed by the Toronto Film Festival's showing of the Soviet film *Repentance* that evening. The next stop was Ottawa where we visited the Parliament Buildings, with the House of Commons in session. Another guest in the Senate visitors' gallery was Anatoly Scharansky, a recently released Soviet dissident. Later at the Pfaffs' home we met with their group before flying to Montreal, Quebec. There Margaret Dobson hosted lunch in the garden of the Ritz Carlton Hotel. That evening fifty people joined us, with Margaret, Annick Gregoire and others of the group at the new center.

The following morning the Polacks returned to King View, and the Citation took our party to Green Pastures. A special reception was held in Cambridge, Massachusetts, near Harvard, where we met friends of Emissaries in the Boston area who were leaders in their fields. The next day a session convened at Green Pastures with 65 participants, all active in our program in the New England states. On Sunday the room overflowed with 295, drawn in the midst of a heavy downpour to share the magic of Martin's presence and hear his words of wisdom.

Some exciting events awaited us on our next stop. On September 21 en route in the Citation from Green Pastures to Long Island, our party, which included Jim Wellemeyer, Liddy Martin and Steve Frankel, stopped off at Mohonk Mountain House in upstate New York. This exquisitely beautiful century-old resort has long been a haven for naturalists, ecologists and lovers of quiet serenity. We were hosted to luncheon and a tour of the scenic surrounds by Keith and Ruth Smiley in a wonderful old horse-drawn carriage. The Smiley family has operated the hotel and 7500-acre nature preserve since its inception. It was a very special time with great new friends, and we continued on our way to Garden City in New York.

There, on Tuesday morning we visited "The City" (via Harlem, just to have a taste of everything!) and then, joined by Steve and Karen Frankel, and Peter and Tina Kafka, had an impressive tour of the massive Cathedral of St. John the Divine, the largest basilica structure in the world and under carved-stone construction since 1896. Our hosts were John Walsh, architect; Canon Lloyd Casson; and David Pelletier, verger, historian. A portion of the building was under construction and we were invited to take a ride in a rather precarious looking elevator on the outside of the building for a view from above. Martin, Jim and I accepted and, outfitted with hard hats, ascended; the view was worth it, as was the adventure!

Then back out to a Long Island tea party hosted by 15 of our children. The cookies were good, but the real flavor was in the shared time with these angels. That evening we had the opportunity to be with 130 close friends at a reception across the street from the Center, at the Unitarian Church. The group presented a great musical dance number (their own production), *Up on the Roof*, a portrayal of policemen, business people, joggers, village bums—all sorts of city types. That marked the end of our journey, then home to Sunrise Ranch in our beautiful ship in the sky.

40

"Let Your Light So Shine"

September 1987 ~ January 1988

On September 26 a 24-hectare lemon farm was purchased in Tucuman, Argentina, a district with a reputation for being one of the foremost lemon producers in the world. John Gray and Vince Bond were welcomed from Glen Ivy to Casa Paraguay, the Emissary Center in Tucaman, by Eric Crocker and the group there. John held four meetings during his stay which averaged 18 per meeting. *Con alas de aguila*, the Spanish translation of Martin's book *On Eagle's Wings* arrived with Vince, signal for an "On Eagle's Wings" study group initiated under the direction of Maria del Sol and Eric.

In *Northern Light* Andreé Vaillancourt reminisced on the history of the "108," her home for the previous four years:

> In the earlier days of the Cariboo the "108" was part of a large ranch owned by the Monical family. Some forty square miles of this prime land was purchased by Block Brothers Realty, who developed a recreational ranch with full resort facilities, golf course, horse arena, tennis courts, etc. The land surrounding the lakes was subdivided into spacious lots with majestic views. In the early '70s most of these were sold to Vancouverites and Albertans as vacation

sites. However, eventually much of the "recreational ranch" turned into residential property. Today some 650 families live there, which makes a population of about two thousand.

> A walk or ski through Walker Valley to the southwest is inspiring. It is easy to spot ducks, geese and eagles; foxes, coyotes and deer are not uncommon. The "108" and Sepa Lakes are surrounded by a belt of public land which hikers, mountainbikers, horseback riders and skiers love. During the summer the loons share their home with canoeists, swimmers and the occasional windsurfer. Gas motors are not allowed on these lakes, which gives space to fishermen. Ice fishing is also popular. To the east of the lakes are the golf course and the Resort. An evening at the restaurant offers the diner a spectacular view of the sun setting over the lake. During the winter months a lit ski trail encircles the golf course. I trust I shall never take any of it for granted.

Cathy Evans reported in that issue:

> Terry Young's position is to oversee both Red Coach Inn and the "108." Stephen Leckie is the capable manager of the restaurant, and I encompass a variety of jobs which encompass sales and public relations. Don Savjord charms the tourists with local yarns as he takes them on covered wagon rides. Don built new corrals this year, bringing our Western Cowboy experience right to the back doorstep. New on the scene is Sabrina French, a wonderful addition with her administration and catering experience from the Bayshore Inn in Vancouver. Also, borrowed part-time from Red Coach Inn are Linda Brown and Michael Donck. In our brochure we say, "Capture the spirit, share the magic at the 108 Golf & Country Inn."

At Glen Ivy on October 18 Mike McCann passed away. He and Dorothea, Pam Gray's parents, shared many fruitful years of service in their home there.

On October 25 Betty Romaner, of Miami, completed her cycle on earth. She and Al, treasured friends and servers, were parents of Janine and her brothers, Carl and Skip.

In *Eden Valley News* there was an article by Rich Clark which he entitled "Sunrise Bell":

> In November it was beginning to become obvious to Ron Kirby and me that our present telephone system was doomed, sentenced for execution about March of 1988, for a number of reasons. We and our next-door neighbors, the Eden Valley Institute, had used up all the Mountain Bell service available in the valley. And, more important, Mountain Bell was installing a brand-new switching system called the "ESS #2 Loveland Central Office," and were, by a series of events that were about to occur, going to cut off our means for accounting for the over

one hundred business calls made from Sunrise Ranch every business day...

We took all the party lines we had, all the private and business lines, mixed them all together, extracted what telephone service we could from all of them and attached them all to our PABX (Private Automated Branch Exchange). In addition, up to 256 telephones could be placed anywhere on the Ranch or within the valley, and Leopold (I named it!) would do the rest. He could call any of the phones on the system, or call to Loveland and connect someone to a vital service. He can hear you trying to call someone living here and connect you with them, all the time communicating and working harmoniously with that new ESS #2. And Leopold can keep track of who called where for how long, which makes Ron absolutely ecstatic.

Following comments after his service on Sunrise Ranch on November 6, "Calling Resonant Substance Home," Martin said:

Touching upon the matter of levity, there are those who have interpreted this as meaning that one should somehow levitate! I watched a TV program where a group of people were sitting in the lotus position and leaping up and down on their behinds, in an endeavor to levitate. Well I suppose they have the urge to rise up, and it's interpreted that way! It may seem to be funny to us; they were enjoying it apparently. But they weren't getting very far or very high.

We are concerned with levitation in the sense of rising up in lightness, so that the light is shining, which is experienced because we accept the identity of the One who is already up. But from the actual experience one stays where one is and discovers that living where one is is a light business. It is light in the sense of humorous, even; it's fun. That sense of lightness is natural to the creative process. This building is not hard work. It only happens because there is lightness, and that may have had something to do with the building of the pyramids. It was not slave labor—light work!

So it is delightful to share a little fun at times in the recognition that while what needs to happen is likely to be a very serious business to a lot of people, it needn't be so serious insofar as we are concerned. We know how it works, and it's easy and light. Many make hard work of it and destroy themselves in the effort. But the substance will come home if we're there with radiant light and love to draw it home, and along with the substance come human beings. We let it work the way it works—the only way it works!

Back at 100 Mile House, on November 8 Michael announced before the service that Martin would not be there that morning because he had a sore ankle and can't stand very well. The very fact that he isn't standing here this morning emphasizes to many of us the remarkable example in him of consistency of expression. I wonder how many times over the last number of decades Martin has not been present to speak at a Sunday morning service in whatever location he happened to be. One could count on the fingers of one hand the times when he was not present in person. This consistency of presence is representative of what is centrally needed in our world today. There seem to be so many distractions, so many reasons why a person's life expression cannot represent a clear quality of truth and love.

The next Sunday morning, November 15, Martin was there:

If you will excuse me for sitting this morning, I'll excuse you! [The never-failing ready humor of this man vividly colored the grace of his presence. It was never limited by his surroundings or personal feelings of any kind.] For many years in times past I customarily sat at service, and Uranda before me, but then when we graduated to more formal chapel settings the lectern put in an appearance; so I, and others, stood behind the lectern. It is perhaps a lot easier and more relaxing to sit.

These occasions in the Chapel give us opportunity in a particular way to be aware of what may well be referred to as the new heaven. We have shared Sunday services for thirty or forty years, opening a door in our own experience of another heaven of which we and most people have been largely unaware in the ordinary experiences of human existence. While there have been other purposes for such services, one of the principal ones was to become increasingly aware and accustomed to a new heaven in our own minds and emotions. What was referred to in Revelation as the first heaven must pass away for this to happen.

The first heaven refers to the usual state which is present in human minds and hearts and has been present generation after generation for millennia. There is a certain variety in the particular quality and nature of that heaven, but underneath it all there is the commonly shared attitude and approach which places human beings, oneself probably in particular, at the center of the universe, requiring everything round about to be, as far as possible, pleasing and comfortable to oneself. This of course multiplies into groups of people.

Various cultures have been developed so that people might feel somewhat at home in the earthly settings in which they found themselves. We ourselves have all been involved in this state but have had the opportunity of allowing it to recede somewhat during these times which we share in the Chapel, so that something new might be received. Then what was received repeatedly over all these years might increasingly permeate our consciousness and experience in between times, so that at last there might be a few human beings on the face of the earth who are willing, not only to accept on Sunday, but to abide in, a new heaven.

In his evening service, "The Garden Eastward," Martin commented:

There always has been the statement around: "Things are seldom what they seem." I think we could say things are *never* what they seem; hence the futility of judgment.

In his service on November 29, "To Be Genuinely Thankful," Martin said that circumstances have no power of themselves but are a reflection of what is present in people. The world reflects perfectly what is present in the minds and hearts of the inhabitants of this planet. He pointed to the futility and time wasted in trying to change circumstances to please the manipulator. He used the illustration of what occurs when looking into the mirror:

There is a reflection, which is quite accurate (reversed of course) of the person. If the reflection is a mess it's no use blaming the reflection or trying to change it, or to break the mirror. Let the changes come in the one who looks in the mirror and the reflection will change. The form of things, the circumstances in the environment round about, are the reflection in the mirror.

On November 29 Martin spoke of "The Supreme Gift" which all of us have had opportunity to receive, the spirit of our King, offered over many years in many ways.

The Word has been spoken, the tone sounded, the gift made freely available. To what extent has it been received? There have been many associated with this ministry over the years who appreciated the wrapping of the gift and its freshness, but it is the gift itself that is important. The gift is for an outpouring of radiation, and to the extent that we have participated in the expression of the spirit of the King we know this. It makes possible radiant vision, and we are no longer looking in the mirror. With radiant vision comes radiant perception through all the facilities, heretofore used to examine the reflection in the mirror.

The mind, which has been busy doing the interpreting of what comes in through the eye and through the other senses is rightly a window of heaven, not a mirror. It is a window through which the light may shine, Lucifer restored to heaven. Part of that radiant seeing is of the working of the creative process, which reveals what it is that is being brought forth in that process. The mirror mind is the satanic mind. There is so much reflection in the mirror that it has blocked the shining of the light. It creates separation. It has been creating a self for itself: a mental creation, coming up out of the subconscious mind and added to assiduously by the conscious mind; and the mind thereby gains a sense of self, of identity. It is all artificial. This has been done over many generations and is accepted as being so by each newborn person quite rapidly.

The window mind has no need to create an identity, because what shines through the window mind is the identity. It isn't a mind-made identity; it isn't even a heaven-made identity. It is the one identity, namely the One I am. As the window mind puts in an appearance, because of the shining of the light, it illuminates the scene, which is not what it was deemed to be in the mirror. It is a radiant scene; and there is no separation in what puts in an appearance. The morning stars sing together, an easy and natural experience; and the sons of God shout for joy in the radiant outpouring of the spirit of the King. We may speak of these things; this is the wrapping of the gift. Receive the gift, now, and consequently forever.

On December 6 Martin gave a service, "The Radiant Focus of Spirit on Earth," in a spacious hall in Vancouver. There was a variety of individual musical offerings before he spoke, including a lusty rendition by the area choir. This introduction to Martin's talk calls vividly to my mind the incredible wealth of exceptional talent and training offered worldwide throughout the years of the ministry. It encompassed all aspects of vocal and instrumental expertise.

A few of those who provided a focus in that field at Sunrise Ranch and 100 Mile House through the years under Lillian's guidance were Diana de Winton, Betsy Hanson, Wesley Jones, Donna Bahan, Nancy Cecil, PenDell Pittman, Zoe Brunson, Peggy Gretsch, Marjorie Gilbert, George Hanson, Lloyd Meeker, Judy Smookler, Carolyn Rhodes, Gloria Brooks, Melanie Fairmont, Jean Hammond, Meridy Migchelbrink, Bob and Mary Lou Patton. Bill and Doreen Thompson, of Powell River, B.C., worked closely with Lillian in composition, and Doreen's beautiful voice enhanced many Emissary presentations. This was true of talent worldwide; there was never a dearth of treasured substance ready and waiting to be given expression, wherever we went in our travels.

The list of names that could be added to the foregoing is endless, as is true of the other aspects of the arts. Along with our primary artists were many others, whose masterpieces of creativity in photography, drawing, graphics and calligraphy were integral parts of our publications. Of special note is Bob Schmeer, who has offered much on Sunrise Ranch over the years in graphics, fine art, special cards and signs for all occasions, as well as beautiful blackboard artwork for special events through the years.

Ann Foorman provided focus for the world of drama; and, again, many contributed in related areas: Stan Grindstaff, Nancy Barbour, Linda Aldrich, Rodney Conway, Paul Batten, Linda Grindstaff—and the list goes on and on.

The field of dance was beautifully represented by many: Linda Grindstaff, Nancy Cecil, Lotus McElfish, Janine Romaner, Sanford Baran, Christina Lockie, Robin Bryant.

The finest of writers—Craig Sarbeck, Chris Foster, Ted Black, Hugh Malafry, Cliff Penwell, Tom Cooper, Bob Moore—for scripts, stories or whatever the need, were always available to complete the portrayal of Art in the kingdom.

Martin spoke, following the musical rendition on December 6:

That was very beautiful. I had a particular opportunity to hear the choir! [He had been seated on the stage, in very close proximity to the choir.] It's wonderful to see so many of you, and we are joined by others via the telephone gathered in various locations: Green Pastures, Glen Ivy, Still Meadow and 100 Mile House. About a thousand are sharing this hour with us. Why is this so? Was an advertising program put on? No. The requirement is that there should be an attractive force, a point of spiritual radiation, so that the substance of the quality of character in people may begin to resonate therewith. This radiation has been present in a specific way for many years. The substance has been resonating and been drawn, and has brought with it all these people.

It is a matter of coming home, to a place where we all belong. We have managed, with a great deal of effort, sweat of the brow, to stay away from that place, together with most of the human population, but it takes much effort and much grief. It is a matter of yielding to a compulsion, which relates to a focus of spiritual radiation. I know how it works, because it had to work for me, just as it is available to work for anyone, anywhere, at any time. The spiritual point of radiation insofar as I was concerned was the one many of us knew as Uranda. Yes, he had a name like the rest of us—Lloyd Arthur Meeker—but he offered himself on the basis of this name Uranda so as to indicate something which was not merely of human nature.

I met him here in Vancouver in person in 1940. I had been in touch with him before and arranged for him to speak in a room in the medical-dental building opposite the Vancouver Hotel. He spoke seven times there, where a handful of people thought it worthwhile to come and listen. I had a rented house on Blenheim Street almost at Marine Drive, and it was there that I, and Michael who was about five years old, first met Uranda. There was something about him that was very familiar. I attended all the lectures; and at the time I felt rather desolate because I could hear what was being said, and it seemed like an impossible task was being undertaken. I am sure we have all had that sensing at times as there has been an initial movement with this creative focus of spirit. Uranda provided this for me.

It took a while for me to realize that I had a responsibility in the matter and so proceed to assume some of it. Then, along the way, it all fell into my lap, because Uranda was no longer here and I was specifically compelled to accept responsibility. That is what one needs to recognize for oneself in whatever field one may be: that what is required in your individual world will not be available unless you provide it. It is very specific. The essential element that has been entirely lacking, as far as history goes back, is this focus point of spiritual radiation on earth. It comes because there is somebody present, oneself, who is actually doing it, not merely telling someone else to do it.

At 100 Mile House on December 13 Martin spoke eloquently of "EDL: The Door," after acknowledging the telephone connection with Mickleton in England.

A door has indeed been opened in heaven. EDL is a door. There are many fancy doors to great buildings. We saw massive doors opening into the Cathedral of St. John the Divine in New York. They are brass, and we were told it took twelve men to open them. Doors may appear to be very impressive. One may be in awe of the door; one may also examine such doors critically.

If we turn to EDL and recognize that here is a door, then indeed there may be something impressive about the door, or there may be those things to which observers take exception. A door is useful because it can be opened. It is most useful when it is scarcely visible. One can then move easily in and out through the doorway, which was previously blocked by the door. Would it be helpful if Emissaries of Divine Light changed its name to "The East Gate," for instance? If a person really begins to recognize that EDL is a name given to a form which composes a door capable of being opened, there might be less concern about the design of the door, if one accepted the fact that its value was in being opened. When open it is scarcely visible; it is only visible and therefore subject to human judgment when it is closed to the person who judges.

However, the first door to be opened relates to oneself. The design on the door of EDL will give some clues as to how one's own door may be opened. That, after all, has been the suggestion all along, hasn't it? When one is willing to let oneself be opened, behold, EDL is open and no longer a subject for judgment. EDL is the name of the form which needs to be opened in order to discover what the true identity is. The opening of the door lets the light shine. EDL is an accurate name because the identity is in the light.

Unless the light shines one cannot experience one's own true identity, which is found in heaven. It isn't discoverable on earth by examining the earth, by looking into our psychological character, for instance, or by examining our physical forms. They are a door, which must be opened by the shining of the light. The physical form as it is now known in this human state is dense, one might say. There is something much more to be known than is presently conceivable to the human mind.

The human mind is the means by which the light may shine. We have spoken of Lucifer, the light-bearer. The transparent mind allows the already existing angelic light to shine through. The mind is not an entity of itself, as it tries to be in the human state, which then becomes satan; it lands up in darkness. This state of separation between the heaven and the earth of the individual has taken place because satan, the darkened mind, has usurped the position of the true identity, which isn't Lucifer but is revealed by the fact of Lucifer's presence, which makes possible the experience of the true identity.

What a very practical suggestion: "Let your light so shine before men, that they may see your good works, and glorify your Father, which is in heaven." (This verse is the source of our name). That simply means, allow Lucifer to be restored so that the light of true being may shine forth. Then we are identifiable by the light which is shining. Is this not the way that Emissaries of Divine Light are aware of each other? We discover that we have friends all over the face of the earth. We may never have met them before, but when we do, we know, simply because there is some measure of light shining. Lucifer begins to come again into place; and the darkened satan consciousness, while one may be aware of the fact of it, carries little or no weight.

What is deemed to be spiritual light has its counterpart in the earth, which could be said to be literal light. The evidence, the truth of man, is in the light. This physical form, which can be something of a burden, has enabled the continued existence of potential Man on earth and is useful because of this. But to become the form of Man it must be filled with light. "If thine eye be single, thy whole body shall be full of light"—literal light. Light weighs very little, and if the composition of human expression in living is light, the body becomes light. Here is something of a transmutation to occur.

However, Man is more than one person, composed of a body made up of individuals. The light shines through the form of EDL to the extent that it is shining through the forms of those who compose its form. EDL doesn't exist except for those individual forms that are drawn together to compose it. The sum of the light—in this instance light shining through these individuals—is not the total light shining through the form of EDL. The composition of the body of EDL provides a facility which can radiate far more light than the sum of all the light of the individuals who compose it, and because of that it enhances the individual expression of light. We begin to find something happening exponentially here, but it only comes because responsibility is being taken individually for letting the light shine, to the extent that it may now do so.

There are variations in the shining of the light. We may take what is occurring now as an example. My responsibility is of a particular nature which will permit an intensification of the light to shine by reason of my expression. This is different to what may occur in conversation, for instance, during the day. In other words, as Uranda put it once in a Class, the sun rises, and there is day; there is a bright intensity of radiation for whatever period of time is necessary, and then the sun sets. But the morning star is still there. Lucifer is always on hand, but he is the light-bearer. He doesn't bear a flaming torch which is always the same intensity. He bears whatever light is necessary in the particular circumstance of the moment. And there is a variation in the intensity of that light, but it is always the same light. There are pulsations in the creative process, and it shines with the intensity that is necessary in the moment, unless we block it.

The only way that there may be participation in creation is when the facility for the shining of the light is available to that shining; and the facility is the human mind, which includes the unconscious mind. We are familiar with the process: radiation, response, attraction, union, unified radiation.

It is not only what may be deemed to be spiritual light, but literal light also. When the light shines, the flesh is revealing of it and is transformed by it. But it is not possible for it to occur individually without it at the same time occurring collectively. The collective shining of the light is what clarifies and restores the flesh to the point where the light may be intensified so that the transformation occurs. However, the flesh is the last along the line. The light only comes to the flesh because there is a transparent mind, and it is the transparent collective mind that permits the intensity of radiant light to be of such power that the very flesh may be transformed. Moving together in the assumption of individual responsibility for the light, the fulfilment comes.

That evening, December 13, 1987, we heard the Angel we knew as Martin speak for the last time in a service, saw the beloved form before us, and knew the experience of sharing the glorious light of his being. It is obvious, in these most recent services, that light was increasingly dominant in his consciousness, the physical form almost a separate entity.

A few of Martin's words:

> It's good to see your smiling faces. All is well! Let your light so shine. I am the light of the world... As there is the clear shining of the light through a unified body, the prince of darkness is cast into the earth. There is no heaven for him anymore, and all power is given to this new heaven present on earth by which the creation occurs. Magic! to the human view. It's been happening all along in a way, but when Lucifer is in place and the light is borne, behold I come quickly!

> Let the light shine exactly where you are. That's why you are where you are. And when the light shines, creation occurs. The light is stable, always present. There is always that point of orientation. It is obviously there when the sun shines but it is also there when the morning star is present; it provides a point of orientation.

> The yoke is easy and the burden is light. The burden of the physical form of Man is light. That is the nature and quality of the form of Man. The light is the creative power; by Him all things were made that are made. So, in every circumstance, in every moment of your living, let your light so shine.

A few days later Martin was very ill with what were interpreted as flu symptoms but proved to be otherwise. After about a week of extreme pain he lost the ability to speak, though conscious, and was taken to the hospital in Kamloops where he went into a coma. During the three weeks he was there, members of his family and a few friends were constantly with him. What a strange Christmas that was. On the 12th day of January, 1988, Martin's physical form released the magnificent light body so unspeakably dear to those of us who truly knew him.

"A Thanksgiving Service for Martin Exeter" on January 15 was held in the 100 Mile Chapel, focalized by Michael who would then assume the place of leadership for the Emissary body. The service was shared via telephone hookup with several thousand people at 121 locations throughout the world. There were expressions from a number in their various places, including Ross Marks, 100 Mile House; Roger de Winton, Sunrise Ranch; Jim Wellemeyer, Green Pastures; and Rupert Maskell, Cape Town. In the weeks that followed letters poured in from every part of the body that had loved and been loved by this great man. Depths of thanksgiving and profound appreciation for the gift of life he had given them found every conceivable avenue of expression.

Some time later on Sunrise Ranch the beautiful water fountain in the pond by the Pavilion, designed and built by Pam Holloway and Georgene Higerd in agreement with Martin, with its exquisite five lilies and their leaves, was completed. It was dedicated to the memory of Martin, and beside it is a plaque with his poem inscribed on it:

Thus It Is

From age to age
Love's word rings forth,
"The truth is true and all is well,
Unconquerable life prevails."

Oh, man, whose strident dreams
 Lead gravewards,
Return to calm and noble
Character of life.
Blaze forth pure virtue;
Depart false ambition's restless schemes.

Busy thought and troubled feeling
Trespass not in virtue's wise serenity
Where firm control and awful power
Eternally abide.

Here earth's pains are healed
And cruel chaos of mind's spawning
Is called again to order and to beauty.

The magnificent building which was achieved by Martin, initiated by Uranda before him and with him, was a wonder to behold: structures the forms of which were excitingly new, and groups of people drawn together in countries all around the globe. These are symbols of the true creation of two faithful servants of our King, described by Jesus when He said:

Lay not up for yourselves treasures upon earth, where moth and rust doth corrupt, and where thieves break through and steal:

But lay up for yourselves treasures in heaven, where neither moth nor rust doth corrupt, and where thieves do not break through nor steal:

For where your treasure is, there will your heart be also.

The treasure is established in the hearts and minds of those who allowed love and truth to work wonders of change and renewal. The treasure abides, safe from all efforts to "corrupt" or to "steal" that which cannot be touched by the self-destructive actions of human beings. The achievement of these two great men is of cosmic proportions. It is a finished creation, and we who heard and understood their words agree that the new heaven is laid up in our hearts. Thereby the new earth is an assured reality, fulfilment after many dark ages: "Eye hath not seen, nor ear heard, neither have entered into the heart of man, the things which God hath prepared for them that love him."

I still know the feeling today, which I expressed many years ago in a poem as I walked in this exquisite spot of God's glorious earth:

Golden days in this beautiful place,
Heaven on earth below,
What could I hope for that is not here?
What, that I do not know?

Sweet air is sheer delight as it fills
My lungs, to overflow
In the exquisite love of living,
One with all things that grow.

Beholding a sky of flawless blue,
Basking in sun's clear heat,
I revel in joys of paradise,
Eternal and complete.

Yes, this beautiful valley still radiates the essence of its name bestowed many years ago by its founder. An old song, once sung with great gusto that caused the air to vibrate with the power of God's spirit, describes it well: "Beautiful Valley of Eden, home of the pure and blest; How often amidst the wild billows I think of thy rest, sweet rest. Beautiful Valley of Eden"—and the land and sky, earth and heaven, resounded with the wonder of men and women revelling in the image and likeness of almighty God in which they were created.

Only as there are those, here and everywhere on this great planet, who live in this spirit of the Creator and imbue it with the climate of the Garden can all that has been built, by Emissaries of our King since the dawn of history, not be in vain. All the heavens are waiting to hear it resound again from this part of the cosmos—the morning stars singing together and the sons and daughters of God shouting for joy.

———————

In his book *As of a Trumpet* Martin said:

"Advanced civilizations" have vanished from the face of the earth several times in the past, leaving virtually no record other than in legend. Violent upheavals of the earth's crust were involved. On each occasion opportunity had been extended to the inhabitants of the earth to accept and experience the true Self, and consequently to recreate the divine world. The present world state obviously indicates that those opportunities were neglected or rejected. Because the chance has never yet been taken does not mean either that it does not exist or that it cannot be taken.

The self-destruction of the unreal world of the false self is again at hand. Once more the opportunity to regain the consciousness of divine being is offered to the children of men. These words are one such reminder.

The inevitable passing of the unreal world need not be ultimate disaster for mankind, although vastly greater tribulation will surely occur. If there are those on earth who have accepted and experienced the divine Self then the divine world shall take form as surely as the unreal world disintegrates.

Nothing that is real or true can ever be lost. These words are spoken to you. Should you have ears to hear them and a heart to understand, then the future is in your hands.

EPILOGUE

I wrote the following on April 27, 1988:

I awoke this morning to a silent world. It was as though all activity in the Valley was suspended; not a sound was heard. Then I realized it was Martin's birthday, the first since his departure four months before. Suddenly I was struck with the stark contrast between this atmosphere and the one that always filled Sunrise Ranch on his "day," every corner and person throbbing with the joyous activity of preparations for celebration: food, drama, dressing up—all the fun and laughter imbued with love for him. A surge of feeling engulfed my being, and I sobbed deeply in an abyss of longing and loneliness in a world without him in person. Then I realized that he did not have a marker in our cemetery on Sunrise Ranch.

With no one around, I felt I was alone in the universe, and was compelled to go to the cemetery and place there a memorial to him, something to give form to my feeling that Martin's presence was in every part of this Valley, beyond the amazing buildings which were testimonials to his incredible vision and imagination.

I wrote a few words of tribute to Martin and encased them in a tiny plastic envelope. Then I walked, alone, to the little cemetery at the foot of the rim-rock and looked about for a place to put my offering, but the ground was hard and dry everywhere, impervious to my ineffectual digging. Then I noticed three wondrous juniper trees that stand there in a line next to the fence at the north end of the little garden. I chose a spot in the fragrant expanse under one of them. I placed my tribute in a little hole I dug next to the trunk, with all the reverence of the ages, and covered it with the soil he loved so well. There it is, close to the markers which commemorate the lives of Uranda and of many loved ones who have given themselves to our Lord and His work.

Before I left that place, as I stood there, feeling him very close, my gaze was drawn upward, and I saw an eagle that had come up behind me over the rimrock. It flew to the southernmost point of the Valley, then straight up the center (with no other visible thing moving in earth or sky) to the northernmost point of the Valley. I knew it was his Spirit up there, as I watched, transfixed, the freedom of that magnificent flight. At the northern extremity it turned east and followed the rimrock. With the whole Valley spread out below, it chose the spot directly above me to turn and fly straight across the Valley westward to Green Ridge, where it disappeared momentarily below the horizon. Then it came again into view and flew straight to where I stood. When it was directly overhead it slowly dipped its beautiful wings several times, and I waved as it vanished over the eastern horizon.

The entire length and breadth of this Valley was encompassed in the soaring sweep of eagle's wings, and I knew it included all the earth in that magnificent gesture. This, in itself, was a fitting tribute to two great men, Uranda and Martin, and all that they built, nothing of which has been, or ever can be, lost. They continue to work with their Lord and King, and with members of His body on earth, wherever they may be, the true Vine of which Jesus spoke two thousand years ago.

Grace Van Duzen